DESCENT INTO CHAOS

ALSO BY AHMED RASHID

◆ ◆ ◆

THE RESURGENCE OF CENTRAL ASIA

Islam or Nationalism?

TALIBAN

Militant Islam, Oil and Fundamentalism in Central Asia

JIHAD

The Rise of Militant Islam in Central Asia

AHMED RASHID

DESCENT INTO CHAOS

How the war against Islamic extremism
is being lost in Pakistan, Afghanistan
and Central Asia

ALLEN LANE
an imprint of
PENGUIN BOOKS

ALLEN LANE

Published by the Penguin Group
Penguin Books Ltd, 80 Strand, London WC2R ORL, England
Penguin Group (USA) Inc., 375 Hudson Street, New York, New York 10014, USA
Penguin Group (Canada), 90 Eglinton Avenue East, Suite 700, Toronto, Ontario, Canada M4P 2Y3
(a division of Pearson Penguin Canada Inc.)
Penguin Ireland, 25 St Stephen's Green, Dublin 2, Ireland (a division of Penguin Books Ltd)
Penguin Group (Australia), 250 Camberwell Road, Camberwell, Victoria 3124, Australia
(a division of Pearson Australia Group Pty Ltd)
Penguin Books India Pvt Ltd, 11 Community Centre, Panchsheel Park, New Delhi – 110 017, India
Penguin Group (NZ), 67 Apollo Drive, Rosedale, North Shore 0632, New Zealand
(a division of Pearson New Zealand Ltd)
Penguin Books (South Africa) (Pty) Ltd, 24 Sturdee Avenue, Rosebank, Johannesburg 2196, South Africa

Penguin Books Ltd, Registered Offices: 80 Strand, London WC2R ORL, England

www.penguin.com

First published in the United States of America by Viking Penguin, a member of Penguin Group (USA) Inc. 2008
First published in Great Britain by Allen Lane 2008

2

Copyright © Ahmed Rashid, 2008

The moral right of the author has been asserted

Maps by Jeffrey L. Ward

Printed in Great Britain by Clays Ltd, St Ives plc

A CIP catalogue record for this book is available from the British Library

HARDBACK
978-0-713-99843-6

TRADE PAPERBACK
978-1-846-14175-1

www.greenpenguin.co.uk

Penguin Books is committed to a sustainable future
for our business, our readers and our planet.
The book in your hands is made from paper
certified by the Forest Stewardship Council.

This book is dedicated to my children

Rafael and Saara

and to their friends Mohammed, Ameera, Emile, Sasha, Mehvish, Graham, Naveen, Arooj, Taimur, Mamdot, Rachel, Louise, Shabaz, Charley, Zoha, Sarah, Amar, Jamal, Dona, and many more.

May you build nations.

◆ ◆ ◆

And in loving memory of Begum Qamar F. R. Khan.

If the Central Asian Society exists and is meeting in fifty or a hundred years hence, Afghanistan will be as vital and important a question as it is now.

—Lord Curzon, speaking at the annual dinner of the
Royal Asiatic Society, London, 1908

Go massive—sweep it all up, things related and not.

—U.S. secretary of defense Donald Rumsfeld,
speaking to his aides on September 11, 2001, after the Pentagon was attacked

CONTENTS

MAPS

Countries and Cities of Central Asia   XVI–XVII
Ethnic Distribution Within Pakistan and Afghanistan   XVIII
Afghan Provinces and Federally Administered Tribal Areas   XIX
NATO Deployment and Provincial Reconstruction Team Locations
    in Afghanistan, 2007   XX
Opium Poppy Cultivation in Afghanistan, 2007   XXI
Military Offensives Launched by the Taliban in Pakistan
    and Afghanistan, 2007–2008   XXII

Glossary   XXIII
Acronyms   XXXV

INTRODUCTION   XXXVII
Imperial Overreach and Nation Building

PART ONE

9/11 AND WAR

1 A MAN WITH A MISSION   3
The Unending Conflict in Afghanistan

2 "THE U.S. WILL ACT LIKE A WOUNDED BEAR"   24
Pakistan's Long Search for Its Soul

3 THE CHIEF EXECUTIVE'S SCHIZOPHRENIA   44
Pakistan, the United Nations, and the United States Before 9/11

4 ATTACK!   61
Retaliation and Invasion

5 THE SEARCH FOR A SETTLEMENT   84
Afghanistan and Pakistan at Odds

PART TWO

THE POLITICS OF THE POST–9/11 WORLD

6 A NUCLEAR STATE OF MIND   109
   India, Pakistan, and the War of Permanent Instability

7 THE ONE-BILLION-DOLLAR WARLORDS   125
   The War Within Afghanistan

8 MUSHARRAF'S LOST MOMENT   145
   Political Expediency and Authoritarian Rule

PART THREE

THE FAILURE OF NATION BUILDING

9 AFGHANISTAN I   171
   Economic Reconstruction

10 AFGHANISTAN II   196
   Rebuilding Security

11 DOUBLE-DEALING WITH ISLAMIC EXTREMISM   219
   Al Qaeda and the Taliban in Pakistan

12 TALIBAN RESURGENT   240
   The Taliban Return Home

PART FOUR

DESCENT INTO CHAOS

13 AL QAEDA'S BOLT-HOLE 265
   Pakistan's Tribal Areas

14 AMERICA SHOWS THE WAY 293
   The Disappeared and the Rendered

15 DRUGS AND THUGS 317
   Opium Fuels the Insurgency

16 WHO LOST UZBEKISTAN? 338
   Tyranny in Central Asia

17 THE TALIBAN OFFENSIVE 349
   Battling for Control of Afghanistan, 2006–2007

18 CONCLUSION 374
   The Death of an Icon and a Fragile Future

Acknowledgments 405

Notes 407

Suggested Reading 457

Index 463

Perm

Yekaterinburg

Nizhny Novgorod   Kazan   Chelyabinsk
                         Ufa

R U S S I A

                  Samara

Saratov

                              K A Z A K H S T A N
Volgograd

UKRAINE

                    Atyrau

                                          Aral Sea   Syr Darya River

Black Sea

        GEORGIA   Caspian   U Z B E K I S T A N
              Tbilisi   Sea
                                                                    Amu Darya River
        ARMENIA   AZERBAIJAN
          Yerevan   Baku   T U R K M E N I S T A N

  T U R K E Y   Ashgabat

                        Tabriz   Mashhad

          SYRIA   Mosul   Tehran   Herat
CYPRUS
                  Kirkuk
LEBANON
  Beirut   Damascus   Esfahan
ISRAEL   Baghdad   I R A N
Jerusalem   Amman   I R A Q   Zaranj
      JORDAN
                                                              Shiraz
              KUWAIT
                    Kuwait
        SAUDI ARABIA   Persian
                              Manama   Gulf
                    Mecca   BAHRAIN   QATAR
      Jiddah   Doha
EGYPT   Riyadh   Abu Dhabi   Chabahar
                                                    Muscat
            Red   UNITED ARAB
            Sea   EMIRATES
                                          O M A N
SUDAN

© 2008 Jeffrey L. Ward

✦ COUNTRIES AND CITIES OF CENTRAL ASIA ✦

Krasnoyarsk

Novosibirsk

Omsk

Barnaul

Astana

MONGOLIA

Qaraghandy
(Karaganda)

Lake Balkhash

Urumqi

Almaty

Bishkek

Tashkent KYRGYZSTAN

Andijan

Ferghana Valley

Kashi

Dushanbe TAJIKISTAN

CHINA

Mazar-e-Sharif

Kabul

Peshawar

AFGHANISTAN Islamabad

Kandahar

laram

Lahore

Quetta

0 Miles   200   400

0 Kilometers   400

PAKISTAN

New Delhi

Indus River

NEPAL

Kathmandu

Lucknow

BHUTAN

Jaipur

Kanpur

Karachi

INDIA

BANGLADESH

Ahmadabad

Arabian Sea

Nagpur

Bay of
Bengal

Mumbai (Bombay) Pune

ETHNIC DISTRIBUTION WITHIN PAKISTAN AND AFGHANISTAN

0 Miles 100 200

0 Kilometers 200

Mazar-e-Sharif

Panjsher Valley

NWFP

Herat

Kabul • Jalalabad

Peshawar • Islamabad

Khost • Rawalpindi

Farah

FATA

AFGHANISTAN

PUNJAB

Kandahar

Lahore •

Quetta

PAKISTAN

BALOCHISTAN

SINDH

Karachi •

PERCENTAGE OF TOTAL POPULATION

AFGHANISTAN

Pashtun 42%
Tajik 27%
Hazara 9%
Uzbek 8%
Other 14%

PAKISTAN

Punjabi 44%
Pashtun 15%
Sindhi 14%
Baloch 4%
Other 23%

ETHNOLINGUISTIC GROUPS

Pashtun — Pamiri

Tajik — Kyrgyz — Baloch/Sindhi

Hazara — Turkmen — Sindhi

Uzbek — Nuristani — Punjabi

Aimak — Baloch — Mixed/other

© 2008 Jeffrey L. Ward

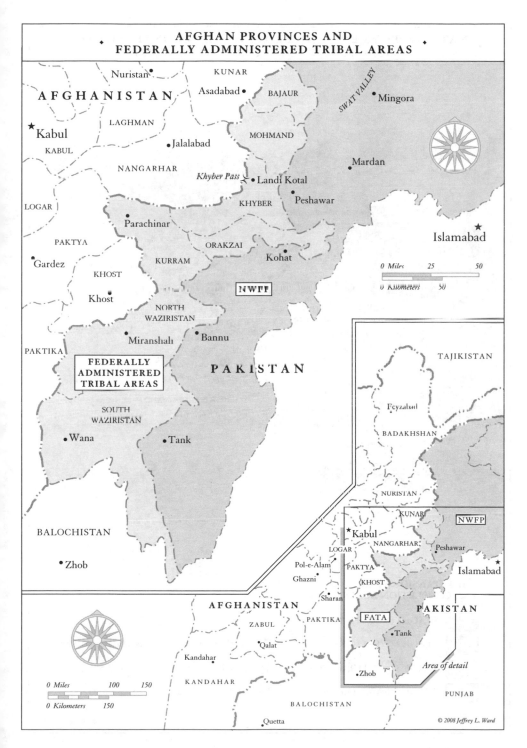

AFGHAN PROVINCES AND
FEDERALLY ADMINISTERED TRIBAL AREAS

Nuristan
KUNAR
AFGHANISTAN
Asadabad
BAJAUR
SWAT VALLEY
Mingora
LAGHMAN
MOHMAND
★ Kabul
KABUL
Jalalabad
Mardan
NANGARHAR
Khyber Pass
Landi Kotal
Peshawar
LOGAR
KHYBER
★ Islamabad
Parachinar
ORAKZAI
PAKTYA
KURRAM
Kohat
Gardez
KHOST
NWFP
Khost
NORTH
WAZIRISTAN
PAKTIKA
Miranshah
Bannu
FEDERALLY
ADMINISTERED
TRIBAL AREAS
PAKISTAN
SOUTH
WAZIRISTAN
Wana
Tank

0 Miles 25 50
0 Kilometers 50

TAJIKISTAN

Feyzabad

BADAKHSHAN

NURISTAN

KUNAR
NWFP
★ Kabul
LOGAR
NANGARHAR
Peshawar
PAKTYA
Islamabad
Pol-e-Alam
KHOST
Ghazni
FATA
PAKISTAN
Sharan
BALOCHISTAN
PAKTIKA
Tank

AFGHANISTAN
ZABUL
Zhob
Qalat
Area of detail
Kandahar
KANDAHAR
PUNJAB

0 Miles 100 150
0 Kilometers 150
BALOCHISTAN
Quetta
© 2008 Jeffrey L. Ward

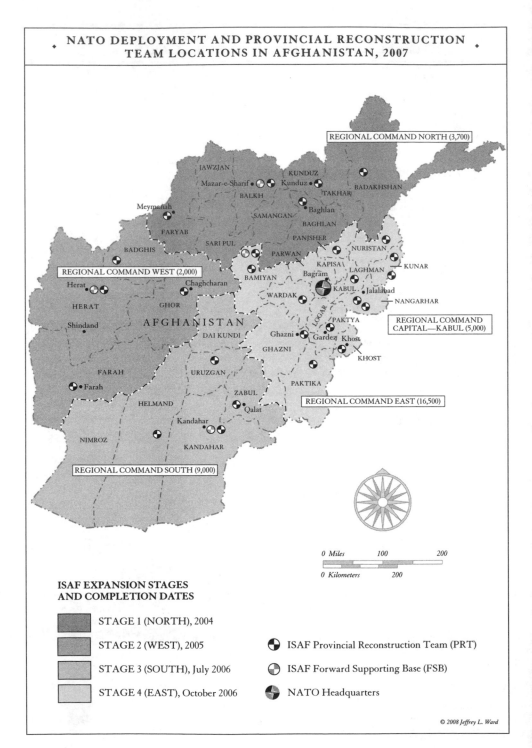

NATO DEPLOYMENT AND PROVINCIAL RECONSTRUCTION TEAM LOCATIONS IN AFGHANISTAN, 2007

REGIONAL COMMAND NORTH (3,700)

REGIONAL COMMAND WEST (2,000)

REGIONAL COMMAND CAPITAL—KABUL (5,000)

REGIONAL COMMAND EAST (16,500)

REGIONAL COMMAND SOUTH (9,000)

JAWZJAN
KUNDUZ
Mazar-e-Sharif
Kunduz
BADAKHSHAN
BALKH
TAKHAR
Meymanah
Baghlan
SAMANGAN
FARYAB
BAGHLAN
SARI PUL
PANJSHER
BADGHIS
PARWAN
NURISTAN
KAPISA
LAGHMAN
KUNAR
Herat
Bagram
Chaghcharan
BAMIYAN
KABUL
Jalalabad
WARDAK
NANGARHAR
HERAT
GHOR
AFGHANISTAN
LOGAR
PAKTYA
Shindand
DAI KUNDI
Ghazni
Gardez
Khost
GHAZNI
KHOST
FARAH
URUZGAN
PAKTIKA
Farah
ZABUL
HELMAND
Qalat
Kandahar
NIMROZ
KANDAHAR

0 Miles   100   200
0 Kilometers   200

ISAF EXPANSION STAGES AND COMPLETION DATES

STAGE 1 (NORTH), 2004

STAGE 2 (WEST), 2005

STAGE 3 (SOUTH), July 2006

STAGE 4 (EAST), October 2006

ISAF Provincial Reconstruction Team (PRT)

ISAF Forward Supporting Base (FSB)

NATO Headquarters

© 2008 Jeffrey L. Ward

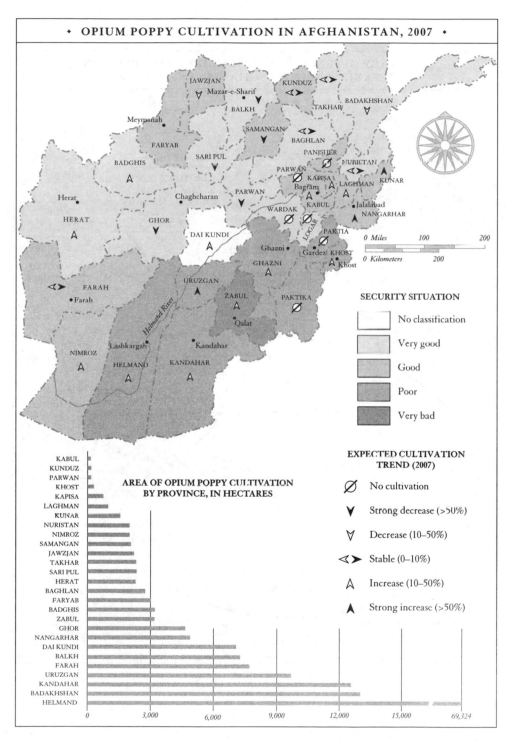

• OPIUM POPPY CULTIVATION IN AFGHANISTAN, 2007 •

SECURITY SITUATION

No classification
Very good
Good
Poor
Very bad

AREA OF OPIUM POPPY CULTIVATION BY PROVINCE, IN HECTARES

EXPECTED CULTIVATION TREND (2007)

∅   No cultivation

∀   Strong decrease (>50%)

∀   Decrease (10–50%)

◁▷   Stable (0–10%)

△   Increase (10–50%)

▲   Strong increase (>50%)

MILITARY OFFENSIVES LAUNCHED BY THE TALIBAN IN PAKISTAN AND AFGHANISTAN, 2007–2008

UZBEKISTAN

TAJIKISTAN

TURKMENISTAN

NORTHERN FRONT
Hizb-i-Islami Gulbuddin (HIG)
Hizb-i-Islami Khalis (HIK)
Pakistani Taliban
al Qaeda

CENTRAL FRONT
Haqqani Network
Pakistani Taliban
International Islamic Front
al Qaeda

NURISTAN

NORTH-WEST
FRONTIER
PROVINCE

KAPISA

KUNAR

LAGHMAN

SOUTHERN FRONT
Taliban
al Qaeda

Kābul ★
KABUL

NANGARHAR

Peshawar

LOGAR

FATA

Islamabad ★

GHAZNI

PAKTYA

KHOST

FARAH

URUZGAN

ZABUL

PAKTIKA

• Miranshah

HELMAND

NIMROZ

KANDAHAR

PUNJAB

• Quetta

PAKISTAN

AFGHANISTAN

BALOCHISTAN

0 Miles   100   200   300

0 Kilometers   300

SINDH

INDIA

© 2008 Jeffrey L. Ward

GLOSSARY

Abdali, Ahmad Shah — King and founder of modern Afghanistan in 1747.

Abu Ghraib Prison in Iraq where U.S. soldiers carried out torture and abuses.

Afghan Militia Force (AMF) — Tribal mercenaries hired by the CIA and U.S. forces to help guard the border with Pakistan.

Ahmad, Mehmood — General and director-general of ISI from 1999 until October 2001.

Akayev, Askar — President of Kyrgyzstan, 1991–2006.

Albright, Madeleine — U.S. secretary of state, 1997–2001.

Al Qaeda — Islamic terrorist group led by Osama bin Laden.

Amin, Hafizullah — Second president of Afghanistan from the Khalq Party, killed by Soviet invaders in December 1979.

Andijan — Town in the Ferghana Valley, in Uzbekistan, where 800 to 1,200 people were killed in May 2005.

Awami National Party — Moderate and secular Pashtun nationalist party in the North-West Frontier Province, which did well in the 2008 elections.

Azhar, Maulana Masud — Leader of Jaish-e-Mohammed, a Pakistani extremist group allied to al Qaeda and backed by the ISI; set up in 2000.

Babar, Naseerullah — Lieutenant-general and Pakistan's interior minister who helped launch the Taliban in 1994.

Bagram — Large U.S. military base outside Kabul where Afghan prisoners are also held.

Bakiyev, Kurmanbek — President of Kyrgyzstan, 2006– .

Balochistan— Province of Pakistan.

Barno, David— Lieutenant-general, commander of U.S. forces in Afghanistan, 2003–2005.

Berdymukhamedow, Gurbanguly— President of Turkmenistan, 2006– .

Bharatiya Janata Party (BJP)— Major political party in India.

Bhutto, Benazir— Leader of Pakistan Peoples Party and twice prime minister of Pakistan; assassinated in December 2007.

Bin al-Shibh, Ramzi— Planner of 9/11 and a leader of the Hamburg cell; captured in Karachi in 2002.

Bin Laden, Osama— Leader of al Qaeda.

Blair, Tony— British prime minister, 1997–2007.

Brigade 555— Brigade of Arabs and North Africans, led and funded by al Qaeda; used by bin Laden to strengthen Taliban front lines against Ahmad Shah Masud during the Afghanistan civil war.

Chemonics International— U.S. consulting firm based in Washington; contracted by USAID to help in counter-narcotics programs.

Dadullah, Mullah— Taliban commander and, after 2003, in charge of Taliban operations in southern Afghanistan until he was killed in 2007.

Daud, Mohammed— President of Afghanistan, 1973–1978; killed during the Afghan communist coup.

Daud, Sardar Mohammed— Governor of Helmand who replaced Sher Mohammed Akhunzada in 2006.

Dobbins, James— Former U.S. ambassador to the Afghan Northern Alliance.

Dostum, Rashid— General and the Uzbek anti-Taliban commander from northern Afghanistan.

Durand Line— Border dividing Pakistani and Afghan Pashtun tribes; demarcated by Sir Mortimer Durand in 1893 but which the Afghans do not recognize.

Durrani—One of the two major sections of the Pashtun tribes, the other being Ghilzai.

DynCorp International—U.S. contracting firm hired to train Afghan army and police.

Ecevit, Bülent—Former prime minister of Turkey.

Eikenberry, Karl W.—Lieutenant-general and commander of U.S.-led Coalition and NATO forces in Afghanistan, 2006; in 2002, head of the Office of Military Cooperation in the American embassy, Kabul.

Fahim, Mohammed—General and successor to Ahmad Shah Masud as leader of the Panjsheri Tajiks and the Northern Alliance; later defense minister in President Karzai's government.

Fallon, William—Became chief of U.S. Central Command (CENTCOM) in January 2007; resigned in March 2008 after differences with President Bush.

Farooqi, Amjad Hussain—A leader of Jaish-e-Mohammed who planned the two assassination attacks on Musharraf in December 2003.

Fazlullah, Maulana—Head of extremist militants in the Swat Valley; fought against government forces in 2007. Commander in the Taliban movement in Pakistan famous for his broadcasts on illegal FM radio.

Federally Administered Tribal Areas (FATA)—Comprises the seven semi-autonomous tribal agencies on the Pakistan-Afghanistan border.

Ferghana Valley—A valley bordering Uzbekistan, Tajikistan, and Kyrgyzstan, and a hotbed of Islamic radicalism in Central Asia.

Fischer, Joschka—Former German foreign minister and leader of the Green Party.

Franks, Tommy—General and head of CENTCOM during the U.S. invasions of Afghanistan and Iraq.

Frontier Corps—Eighty-thousand-strong Pakistani paramilitary force made up of Pashtun tribesmen.

Gailani, Pir Sayed Ahmad—Sufi Afghan leader who led a party that fought the Soviets in the 1980s; after 9/11 headed the Peshawar group of Pashtuns.

Ghilzai—One of the two major sections of the Pashtun tribes, the other being Durrani.

Goss, Porter—Chairman of the U.S. Congressional Intelligence Committee in 2001 and later head of the CIA.

Guantánamo Bay—Prison in Cuba where al Qaeda prisoners were interrogated by the United States.

Haass, Richard—Director, Policy Planning, State Department.

Haq, Abdul—Pashtun commander killed by the Taliban in October 2001.

Haq, Muhammad Zia ul-—President of Pakistan, 1977–1988.

Haqqani, Jalaluddin—Leader of Taliban front based in Miramshah, Pakistan; his son Sirajuddin Haqqani led his father's troops against U.S. forces in Afghanistan.

Harkat ul-Ansar—Pakistani extremist group fighting in Kashmir and allied to al Qaeda.

Harkat ul-Mujahedin—Movement of Holy Warriors, extremist group based in Pakistan fighting in Kashmir, Afghanistan, and Central Asia.

Hikmetyar, Gulbuddin—Leader of the Hizb-e-Islami Party, allied to the Taliban.

Hizb-e-Islami—Afghan party allied to the Taliban and led by Gulbuddin Hikmetyar.

Hizb ut-Tahrir (HT)—Islamic party very active in Central Asia.

Hussain, Altaf—Leader of the Muttahida Quami Movement of the Urdu-speaking Muhajirs, who migrated from India to Pakistan in 1947.

Inter-Services Intelligence Directorate (ISI)—Pakistan's military intelligence service.

Islamic Movement of Uzbekistan (IMU) — Islamic radicals in Central Asia who provided support to the Taliban and al Qaeda.

Jaish-e-Mohammed — Army of Mohammed, militant group that introduced suicide bombing in Kashmir; formed in 2000 by the ISI and Maulana Masud Azhar in the aftermath of the hijacking of an Air India plane to Kandahar.

Jalali, Ali Ahmad — Minister of interior in Karzai's cabinet, 2003–2005.

Jamiat Ulema-e-Islam — Main Islamic party in the Pashtun areas of Pakistan and key supporter of the Taliban; after the 2002 elections formed the government in the NWFP and Balochistan.

Jehangir, Asma — Head of the Human Rights Commission of Pakistan.

Jundullah — Army of God, terrorist group trained by al Qaeda and active in Karachi.

Kabulov, Zamir — Senior Russian diplomat representing Russia at major conferences on Afghanistan; later Russian ambassador to Kabul.

Kamal, Babrak — Installed as president of Afghanistan by the invading Soviet army in December 1979; belonging to the Parcham Party.

Kargil — Mountainous region of Indian Kashmir, briefly captured by Pakistani forces in 1999.

Karimov, Islam — President of Uzbekistan, 1991– .

Karshi-Khanabad, or K2 — U.S. base in Uzbekistan; used until 2006.

Karzai, Abdul Ahad — Father of Hamid Karzai; murdered by the Taliban, 1999.

Karzai, Ahmed Wali — Younger brother of Hamid Karzai.

Karzai, Hamid — President of Afghanistan, 2001– .

Kayani, Ashfaq — Former head of the ISI, he was appointed as the new chief of staff of the Pakistan army in November 2007.

Kazemi, Syed Mustafa — Afghanistan's commerce minister, killed by a suicide bomb attack in 2007.

Kellenberger, Jakob—President of the International Committee of the Red Cross.

Khalili, Karim—A leader of the Hazara resistance to the Taliban and later vice president under President Karzai.

Khalilzad, Zalmay—U.S. chief of mission to the United Nations; former U.S. ambassador to Afghanistan and Iraq.

Khalq—The Masses, one of the communist parties of Afghanistan.

Khan, Ismael—Anti-Taliban leader in western Afghanistan.

Khan, Jan Mohammed—Governor of Uruzgan province, former Taliban.

Khan, Mohammed Ayub—Military ruler of Pakistan, 1958–1969.

Khan, Yahya—Military ruler of Pakistan, 1969–1971.

Khatami, Mohammed—President of Iran, 1997–2005.

Lashkar-e-Jhangvi—The Army of Jhangvi, a militant Sunni group opposed to all Shias.

Loya Jirga (LJ)—Traditional meeting of Afghan tribal chiefs and elders.

McColl, Sir John—General and British commander of ISAF troops in Kabul in 2002.

McNeill, Dan—Lieutenant-general and commander of the U.S.-led Coalition forces in Afghanistan in 2002; reappointed to head NATO forces in Afghanistan in February 2007.

Manas—Air base used by NATO alliance in Kyrgyzstan, close to the capital, Bishkek.

Mansur, Saif ur-Rahman—The Taliban commander at the battle of Anaconda.

Marshall, George C.—President Harry Truman's secretary of state and the architect of the Marshall Plan for Europe in the 1950s.

Masud, Ahmad Shah—Leader of the anti-Taliban Northern Alliance; assassinated by al Qaeda two days before 9/11.

Mehsud, Baitullah— Head of the Taliban Movement of Pakistan, formed in 2007. Named by the Pakistan government as assassin of Benazir Bhutto. Fought against the Soviets in 1980s, alongside the Taliban in the 1990s, and against the U.S. and NATO forces after 2001. Member of the Mehsud tribe of North Waziristan, near the Afghan border.

Mohammed, Faqir— Based in Bajour agency, considered a key aide to al Qaeda's Ayman al Zawahiri. Primary recruiter for young men to fight in Afghanistan and to enlist as suicide bombers.

Mohaqiq, Mohammed— Hazara leader in northern Afghanistan.

Muhajirs— Urdu-speaking refugees from India settled in Pakistan after Partition.

Mujaddedi, Sibghatullah— One of the seven Mujahedin leaders based in Pakistan; headed the National Liberation Front of Afghanistan, to which Hamid Karzai belonged; also a spiritual leader and head of the Naqshbandiyah order of Sufism in Afghanistan; president of Afghanistan in 1992 and later headed the Peace and Reconciliation Commission dealing with the Taliban.

Murray, Craig— Former British ambassador to Uzbekistan.

Musharraf, Pervez— Military ruler of Pakistan, 1999– .

Muttahida Majlis-e-Amal (MMA)— Alliance of five Islamic parties that won many seats in the 2002 elections in Pakistan.

Muttawakil, Wakil Ahmad— Taliban foreign minister.

Myers, Richard— General and chairman of the U.S. Joint Chiefs of Staff.

Najibullah, Mohammed— Last communist president of Afghanistan, 1986–1992.

Namangani, Juma— Military commander of the Islamic Movement of Uzbekistan; killed by U.S. bombing in Afghanistan, October 2001.

Naqibullah, Mullah— Warlord from Kandahar and ally of Karzai.

National Directorate of Security (NDS), or Riasat Amniat-e-Meli ("Amniat" for short)—Afghan intelligence service, headed by Director-General Amrullah Saleh.

Natsios, Andrew—Head of U.S. Agency for International Development.

Nazarbayev, Nursultan—President of Kazakhstan, 1991– .

Negroponte, John—Deputy secretary of state. He moved from a position as director of national intelligence to become deputy secretary of state in January 2007.

Niyazov, Saparmurat—President of Turkmenistan, 1991–2006.

Noor, Sadiq—Powerful tribal leader in North Waziristan whose followers have fought both U.S. forces in Afghanistan and Pakistani forces in Pakistan; close ally of Afghan commander Jalaluddin Haqqani.

Northern Alliance—Anti-Taliban opposition centered on commander Ahmad Shah Masud, also called Shura-e-Nazar.

North-West Frontier Province (NWFP)—Province of Pakistan.

Omar, Mohammed—Mullah; leader of the Taliban movement, 1994– .

Orakzai, Ali Jan—Corps commander, Peshawar, from 2001 to 2004, before becoming governor of the NWFP. Responsible for many of the peace deals with the Pakistani Taliban, he was removed as governor by Musharraf in 2008.

Pakistan Muslim League—Quaid-e-Azam (PML-Q), the ruling party, loyal to the military regime.

Pakistan Peoples Party (PPP)—Led by the Bhutto family and often in opposition to military rule.

Panjsheri Tajiks—Tajiks from the Panjsher Valley, north of Kabul, and followers of Ahmad Shah Masud and later General Fahim.

Parcham—The Flag, one of the communist parties of Afghanistan.

Pearl, Daniel—American journalist murdered by al Qaeda in Karachi in 2002 after being kidnapped by Ahmed Omar Sheikh.

Popalzai—Pashtun tribe in southern Afghanistan headed by Hamid Karzai.

Provincial Reconstruction Team (PRT)—Group of 100 to 150 Western soldiers and civilian advisers based in a province to help improve security and governance.

Punjab—Province of Pakistan.

Pushtu—The language of the Pashtun tribesmen.

Qanuni, Younus—Leader of the Northern Alliance, former minister, and currently speaker of the Afghan parliament.

Rabbani, Burhanuddin—Tajik leader who was president of Afghanistan from 1992 to 1996 and a leader of the Northern Alliance.

Rehman, Abdul—King known as the Iron Amir, 1880–1901.

Rice, Condoleezza—National security advisor, 2001–2005; U.S. secretary of state, 2005–.

Richards, David—Lieutenant-general and commander of NATO forces in Afghanistan, 2006.

Rocca, Christina—Assistant secretary of state for South Asia at the State Department, 2001–2005.

Rome group—Group of Afghan exiles around the former king Zahir Shah.

Sayyaf, Abdul Rasul—Pashtun warlord, member of the Northern Alliance, and Wahhabi leader close to Saudi Arabia.

Scheffer, Jaap de Hoop—Former Dutch foreign minister who took over as NATO secretary-general in January 2004.

Schröder, Gerhard—Chancellor of Germany, 1998–2005.

Shah, Zahir—King of Afghanistan, 1933–1973.

Sharia—Islamic law.

Sharif, Shabaz—Younger brother of Nawaz Sharif.

Sheikh, Ahmed Omar—Kidnapper of U.S. journalist Daniel Pearl.

Sherzai, Gul Agha—Warlord who captured Kandahar and became governor of the province.

Sindh—Province of Pakistan.

Singh, Jaswant—Indian foreign minister.

Sipah-e-Pasadran—Army of God, Iran's Revolutionary Guard paramilitary force.

Sipah-e-Sahaba—Soldiers of the Companions of the Prophet, a militant Sunni group opposed to all Shias.

Talbott, Strobe—Deputy secretary of state in the Clinton administration.

Taliban—Pashtun extremist group that ruled Afghanistan before 9/11.

Taraki, Nur Mohammed—First communist president of Afghanistan, in April 1978, from the Khalq Party; murdered by his successor, Hafizullah Amin, in September 1979.

Tehreek-e-Nafaz-e-Shariat-e-Mohammadi (TNSM)—Movement for the Enforcement of Islamic Law, led by Maulana Sufi Mohammed; founded in 1989 and fought for the Taliban in Afghanistan; tried to take over the Swat Valley in Pakistan in 2007 under his son-in-law Maulana Fazlullah.

Tenet, George—Director of the CIA during the September 11 crisis.

Termez, Uzbekistan—NATO military base close to the border with Afghanistan that was run by the Germans.

Tora Bora—In the Koh-e-Sufaid, or White Mountain range, which spans Nangarhar province, where Osama bin Laden fought his last major battle in 2001.

Uighurs—Chinese Muslims mainly from Xinjiang province.

Ulema—Islamic religious leaders and scholars.

Uruzgan—Province in southern Afghanistan.

Vajpayee, Atal Bihari—Prime minister of India, May–June 1996; second term, 1998–2004.

Wahhabism—A deeply conservative sect in Sunni Islam practiced in Saudi Arabia.

Wali, Abdul—General and son-in-law to former king Zahir Shah and influential leader of the Rome group.

Wardak, Rahim—General and defense minister of Afghanistan, 2004–.

Yuldashev, Tahir—Leader and ideologue of the Islamic Movement of Uzbekistan; sought shelter in Pakistan after 9/11.

Zawahiri, Ayman al-—Egyptain doctor and second to bin Laden in al Qaeda; still at large.

Ziauddin, Khwaja—Lieutenant-general and former head of ISI; deposed by Musharraf coup.

Zubaydah, Abu—Head of al Qaeda's overseas operations; captured in Faislabad in March 2002.

ACRONYMS

ADB—Asian Development Bank

AMF—Afghan Militia Force

ANA—Afghan National Army

ANP—Afghan National Police

CENTCOM— U.S. military's Central Command

CIDA—Canadian International Development Agency

CND—Counter Narcotics Directorate of Afghanistan

DART—Disaster Assistance Response Team (part of USAID)

DFID—Britain's Department for International Development

DOD—U.S. Department of Defense

ETIM—East Turkistan Islamic Movement

EU—European Union

FATA—Federally Administered Tribal Areas

GAO—U.S. Government Accountability Office

G-8—Group of countries with the strongest economies

HT—Hizb ut-Tahir

ICRC—International Committee of the Red Cross

IMU—Islamic Movement of Uzbekistan

IOM—International Office for Migration

ISAF—International Security Assistance Force

ISI—Inter-Services Intelligence Directorate

JCMB—Joint Coordination and Monitoring Board (for the Afghanistan
    Compact)

JI—Jamiat-e-Islami

LJ—Loya Jirga

LOC—Line of Control (between Indian and Pakistani Kashmir)

LT—Lashkar-e-Tayyaba

MI5—British secret service (domestic)

MMA—Muttahida Majlis-e-Amal

NA—Northern Alliance

NATO—North Atlantic Treaty Organization

NDS—National Directorate of Security (Riasat Amniat-e-Meli)

NGO—Nongovernmental organization

NWFP—North-West Frontier Province

PRT—Provincial Reconstruction Team

PUC—Person Under Control (category of prisoner)

UN—United Nations

UNAMA—United Nations Assistance Mission for Afghanistan

UNODC—United Nations Office on Drugs and Crime

UNSC—United Nations Security Council

USAID—U.S. Agency for International Development

U.S. SOF—U.S. Special Operations Forces

+ + +

Imperial Overreach and Nation Building

Everyone, everywhere, will always remember the moment when he saw or heard about the airliners striking the Twin Towers on September 11, 2001. It is a historical event that will be embedded in our emotional psyche for all time and will mark our era as much as the dropping of the nuclear bomb on Japan or the Vietnam War marked earlier times. Later, as terrorist bombs exploded around the world, we all momentarily thought of what it could mean to become a terrorist's target. We have had to get used to the idea of living with the possibility of sudden death and a new world of bloody violence, unprecedented if not in its scale then in its randomness. While suicide bombings in Afghanistan, Pakistan, or Iraq were entirely predictable, the suicide attacks in London, Madrid, Istanbul, and Bali were not.

Initially it seemed that 9/11 would ensure that the world addressed the social stagnation and state failure in South and Central Asia—what in this book I call "the region." Afghanistan had to be rescued from itself. Autocratic regimes in Pakistan and Central Asia had to change their repressive ways and listen to their alienated and poverty-stricken citizens. Iran had to be made part of the international community. The West had to wake up to the realities and responsibilities of injustice, poverty, lack of education, and unresolved conflicts such as those in Kashmir and Afghanistan, which it had ignored for too long and which could no longer be allowed to fester. The West and democratic-minded Muslims had to help each other counter this new and deadly form of Islamic extremism.

The attacks of 9/11 created enormous trepidation in the region as America unsheathed its sword for a land invasion of Afghanistan, but they also created enormous expectations of change and hope for a more sustained Western commitment to the region that would lift it out of poverty and underdevelopment. Surely the three thousand American dead lying in the rubble on the Hudson, as well as in Pennsylvania and Washington, had not died in vain? Surely we would remember them not for the revenge that the United States was about to take on al Qaeda but for the hope that their deaths had brought to a neglected corner of the globe?

Instead, seven years on, the U.S.-led war on terrorism has left in its wake a far more unstable world than existed on that momentous day in 2001. Rather than diminishing, the threat from al Qaeda and its affiliates has grown, engulfing new regions of Africa, Asia, and Europe and creating fear among peoples and governments from Australia to Zanzibar. The U.S. invasions of two Muslim countries, billions of dollars, armies of security guards, and new technology have so far failed to contain either the original organization or the threat that now comes from its copycats— unemployed young Muslim men in urban slums in British or French cities who have been mobilized through the Internet. The al Qaeda leader, Osama bin Laden—now a global inspirational figure—is still at large, despite the largest manhunt in history.

In the region that spawned al Qaeda and which the United States had promised to transform after 9/11, the crisis is even more dangerous. Afghanistan is once again staring down the abyss of state collapse, despite billions of dollars in aid, forty-five thousand Western troops, and the deaths of thousands of people. The Taliban have made a dramatic comeback, enlisting the help of al Qaeda and Islamic extremists in Pakistan, and getting a boost from the explosion in heroin production that has helped fund their movement. The UN representative Lakhdar Brahimi had promised what he termed "a light footprint" for the UN presence in Afghanistan, while some U.S. officials eventually promised that they would carry out "nation-building lite." In fact, barely enough was done by any organization in the first few years when 90 percent of the Afghan population continued to welcome foreign troops and aid workers with open arms. The international community had an extended window of opportunity for several years to help the Afghan people—they failed to take advantage of it.

Pakistan's military regime, led by President Pervez Musharraf, has undergone a slower but equally bloody meltdown. The military has refused to allow a genuinely representative government to take root. In 2007 Musharraf, after massive public demonstrations, suspended the constitution, sacked the senior judiciary, imprisoned more than twelve thousand lawyers and members of civil society, and muzzled the media in an attempt to stay in power and ensure that any elections favored him rather than the opposition. The country is beset by a major political crisis and the spread of Islamic extremism that now sees its chance to topple the state. Musharraf's plunge from hero to villain was compounded by the assassination of the country's larger-than-life opposition leader, Benazir Bhutto, in December 2007, followed by a wave of suicide bombings and mayhem.

Across the five independent states of Central Asia—Kazakhstan, Kyrgyzstan, Tajikistan, Turkmenistan, and Uzbekistan—dictatorships have ruled continuously since the breakup of the Soviet Union in 1991. The lack of basic political freedoms, grinding poverty, huge economic disparities, and an Islamic extremist political underground are set to plunge Central Asia, despite its oil and gas reserves, into ever greater turmoil.

The consequences of state failure in any single country are unimaginable. At stake in Afghanistan is not just the future of President Hamid Karzai and the Afghan people yearning for stability, development, and education but also the entire global alliance that is trying to keep Afghanistan together. At stake are the futures of the United Nations, the North Atlantic Treaty Organization (NATO), the European Union, and of course America's own power and prestige. It is difficult to imagine how NATO could survive as the West's leading military alliance if the Taliban are not defeated in Afghanistan or if bin Laden remains at large indefinitely. Yet the international community's lukewarm commitment to Afghanistan after 9/11 has been matched only by its incompetence, incoherence, and conflicting strategies—all led by the United States.

What is at stake in Pakistan is even greater. A nuclear-armed military and an intelligence service that have sponsored Islamic extremism as an intrinsic part of their foreign policy for nearly four decades have found it extremely difficult to give up their self-destructive and double-dealing policies after 9/11, even under the watchful eye of the CIA. The recent blowback from these policies is now threatening the state, undermining the army, decapitating the political elite, and drowning the country in a sea of blood. In 2007 there were 56 suicide bombings in Pakistan that killed 640 people, compared to just 6 bombings in the previous year.

President Bush's embrace of Musharraf and the military, rather than of

the Pakistani people and the development of state institutions and a democratic process, has created immense hatred for the U.S. Army and America,
hatred that penetrates all classes of society. Ninety percent of the $10 bil-
lion in aid that the United States has provided Pakistan with since 9/11
has gone to the military rather than to development. Moreover, anti-
Americanism has hit Pakistani society's core values, undermining people's
understanding of democracy, secular education, modernization, and civil
society—because all these facets of society are deemed to be American.
When the Bush administration continued to back Musharraf in late 2007,
despite the general's rampage against the judiciary and civil society, Pakistan's middle class was overtaken by feelings of anti-Americanism, making
it impossible to persuade Pakistanis to resist the extremists. Neither was it
possible to convince people that the struggle against extremism was not
just America's war but equally Pakistan's.

With a population of 175 million, Pakistan is the fifth largest country
in the world. Its society is riddled with deep ethnic, social, and economic
fissures. Quite apart from the Islamists, there are grave dangers of secular
separatist movements in the provinces of Balochistan and Sindh that could
divide the nation, just as ethnic nationalism did in 1971, when East Pakistan became an independent Bangladesh. With such threats, is it surprising
that foreign experts are worried about Pakistan's nuclear arsenal?

My three books before 9/11 dealt with the problems of failed states, the
rise of al Qaeda and the Taliban, and the failure of U.S. policy in the region, topics I have covered as a reporter and analyst since the late 1970s.
What I term "the region"—Pakistan, Afghanistan, and the five Central
Asian Republics—is even more vital to global stability now than when I
first wrote about it. When I wrote about the Taliban and called for greater
international commitment to help the Afghans, I did not expect any response. Today nobody can plead ignorance about what is at stake, the
worsening state of affairs, or the risks involved in once again letting this
region stagnate.

As with my other books, this one is a mixture of reportage, analysis, and
the accumulation of decades of knowledge and experience traveling in the
region and to Western capitals. For many of these major events I was on
the ground personally, and almost all the interviews with key political actors were conducted as events and crises were unfolding, rather than afterward. This book is an attempt to define history in the making rather than
a scholarly reappraisal years after the event.

My previous books were based on reporting about people, movements, and events that surrounded the rise of Islamic extremism and that few people seemed particularly interested in at the time. It proved immensely difficult even to get these books published. Now there is a vast literature on 9/11 and its consequences in the region. I have absorbed all this literature, but that has not distracted from the fact that I was intimately involved as a reporter or an adviser or an onlooker to most of the events in this book.

I have also resisted the temptation to delve too deeply into the past. This book is not about the causes of 9/11 or the story of al Qaeda or the history of specific individuals and countries in the region. There are other, better books for such information. This book will not tell you where bin Laden is hiding. Nor is this book about Iraq—although the war in Iraq serves as a vital backdrop to everything. This book shows how the United States ignored consolidating South and Central Asia—the homeland of global terrorism—in favor of invading Iraq. American resources and military manpower that Afghanistan should have received went to Iraq. "Iraq was more than just a major distraction to Afghanistan," says Kofi Annan in retrospect. "Huge resources were devoted to Iraq, which focused away from nation building in Afghanistan. The billions spent in Iraq were the billions that were not spent in Afghanistan."[1] Moreover, the U.S. attack on Iraq was critical to convincing Musharraf that the United States was not serious about stabilizing the region, and that it was safer for Pakistan to preserve its own national interest by clandestinely giving the Taliban refuge.

What makes the war in Iraq, and the enormous human losses there, even more tragic is that all the mistakes made by the Bush administration in Iraq had already been made in Afghanistan—yet nothing was learned. First in Afghanistan and then in Iraq, not enough U.S. troops were deployed, nor were enough planning and resources devoted to the immediate postwar resuscitation of people's lives. There was no coherence to U.S. tactics and strategy, which led to vitally wrong decisions being taken at critical moments—whether it was reviving the warlords in Afghanistan or dismantling the army and bureaucracy in Iraq.

The bitter divisions that surfaced within the administration as the neoconservatives clashed over power and prerogative effectively paralyzed decision making as both wars were being fought. The cabinet system of the U.S. government virtually collapsed, ruinous laws were enacted that flouted the U.S. Constitution, and torture became the norm for U.S.

security agencies. Foreign policy became the prerogative of the Department of Defense, which was unaccountable to the U.S. Congress or the public, rather than the domain of the State Department. Insufficient regional alliances were forged to neutralize Afghanistan's neighbors before, during, and after the invasions. An invasion force that does not first politically neutralize all potential sources of trouble in its rear does not understand either military strategy or diplomacy. Above all, arrogance and ignorance were in abundant supply as the Bush administration invaded two countries in the Muslim world without any attempt to understand the history, culture, society, or traditions of those countries.

Today some retired American generals and historians call the U.S. invasion of Iraq the greatest strategic military disaster in American history, a massive squandering of lives and resources that will affect the Middle East and reduce the power of the United States for years to come. Yet compared with what is at stake in Afghanistan and Pakistan, Iraq may well turn out to be a mere sideshow, a historical folly that diverted global attention for some years but had little impact in changing the real nature of power and politics in the Middle East. The U.S. failure to secure this region may well lead to global terrorism, nuclear proliferation, and a drug epidemic on a scale that we have not yet experienced and I can only hope we never will.

This book is about American failure to secure the region after 9/11, to carry out nation building on a scale that could have reversed the appeal of terrorism and Islamic extremism and averted state collapse on a more calamitous scale than could ever have happened before 9/11. The World Bank estimates that there are now twenty-six failing states in the world that could breed terrorism, as opposed to seventeen such states in 2003. Clearly we have gotten a great deal wrong about the post–9/11 world.[2] This book is an attempt to frame events and their consequences across the largest landmass in the world, and to show what went wrong on the ground and why, while describing how such poor decisions were made in Washington. It tries to answer the question of why the world is less secure seven years after 9/11.

The quick American victory in Afghanistan in 2001 created the feeling that a new era was now inevitable. Despite their cowboy president, the Americans were momentarily humbled by their own vulnerability and felt guilty about having ignored Afghanistan for the past decade. U.S. TV networks suddenly began to cover the Muslim world, and the Koran became a bestseller in U.S. bookshops. The rest of the world rallied around America as international organizations such as the UN sanctioned the U.S. invasion of Afghanistan.

At the time of the invasion, I broke with many of my colleagues by arguing that the war in Afghanistan was a just war and not an imperialist intervention, because only external intervention could save the Afghan people from the Taliban and al Qaeda and prevent the spread of al Qaeda ideology. My book *Taliban,* which had been published in 2000, criticized the United States for abandoning Afghanistan for too long and argued for just such an intervention. At the time my conclusions were strongly criticized by Islamic fundamentalists, the liberal left, and the Pakistani military, who considered my critique of their interventions in Afghanistan as traitorous.

I had seen the accumulating dangers posed by al Qaeda's expansion in Afghanistan and Pakistan early on, due to my intense involvement with the Afghan saga. I had seen firsthand Afghans' fortitude during a quarter century of war.[3] Afghanistan had become an incubator for al Qaeda, but so had my own country, Pakistan, because of the nexus between Islamic extremists and the army, both of which tolerated an al Qaeda presence before 9/11. The army backed the Taliban and encouraged thousands of Pakistani youngsters to fight and die for the Taliban, just as it mobilized thousands of Pakistanis to fight in the Kashmiri insurgency against India. I warned that armed with nuclear weapons and fueled by jihadism, a military regime led by the rash and impetuous General Musharraf was capable of creating a perfect storm of circumstances and events that could plunge the region into even greater danger and chaos and undermine Pakistan's very existence. That is what we are seeing today.

To the north of Afghanistan, in Central Asia, five states newly independent from the Soviet Union remained largely isolated from world events. Economic misery in four of these states was now far worse than it was during the Soviet era. These four were ruled by dictators, holdovers from the Soviet era, but the region was ripe for reform and democratic change. The increased birth rate of the 1980s had produced an alienated, angry, and jobless mass of young people under age twenty-five who were looking for change. The longer such change was delayed, the greater the chances that underground Islamic extremist movements linked to al Qaeda could exploit the coming crisis.

The major center of any turmoil would be Uzbekistan, the most populated state, where the twin forces of severe state repression and Islamic fundamentalism were in conflict. Ignored by the world and in turmoil, Uzbekistan could destabilize an immense zone lying between the vast landmasses of Russia and China; al Qaeda could exploit the situation readily.

After the overthrow of the Taliban regime, optimists like me expected that the U.S.-led international community would commit to rebuild Afghanistan and help undertake reforms and nation building in Pakistan and throughout Central Asia. The region had to be seen as a single entity because it was beset by many of the same problems. Rebuilding Afghanistan alone would only push its problems into neighboring states. Ending the "failing states syndrome" in the region and integrating those states into the world economy would require massive aid, internal economic reforms, democratization, and literacy. This would need nothing less than a Western-led Marshall Plan for the region and a commitment that would have to be measured in not months or years but decades. The leaders in the region would be persuaded to change their autocratic ways only if they saw an unfaltering Western military and aid presence on their doorstep.

It was equally important to wean Muslims away from the message of al Qaeda and its perversion of Islam. As I saw al Qaeda evolve in Afghanistan in the 1990s, I considered it nothing more than a blatant power grab by men whose naked political aims were cloaked in the garb of Islamic ideology. Yet to a handful of Muslims, al Qaeda posed a civilizational solution—albeit an extreme one—to the issue of justice denied to Muslims in Palestine, Kashmir, and elsewhere. Now Muslims had to be in the forefront of changing their own environment and governments, and taking responsibility for creating the mechanisms in which the rule of law and civil society could grow and flourish.

The American response to events in the region was not encouraging. The Republicans had won the 2000 U.S. elections on the basis of not more but less involvement in the world and a shortsighted "go it alone" philosophy that ignored existing alliances and treaties. Condoleezza Rice wrote in a January 2000 article for *Foreign Affairs* that a Bush presidency would focus on the national interest instead of international humanitarian actions, as Clinton had done. Muslim leaders in the region read this as a lack of U.S. interest. Bush said he would avoid "open-ended deployments and unclear military missions," adding, "I don't think our troops ought to be used for what's called nation-building—I think our troops ought to be used to fight and win wars."4 These words were to haunt Bush after 9/11.

Bush became president with no knowledge of or interest in the outside world—reflective of the attitude of most Americans at the time. He had barely traveled outside the United States, did not read about other countries, and knew no foreign leaders, frequently mixing up their names and designations. During his election campaign in 2000, he committed two grand faux pas—the first when he did not know the name of General Pervez Musharraf, who was then president of Pakistan, and the second when he thought the Taliban were an all-girls pop group. His ignorance toward the region was on full display every time these jokes were told.5

The ease with which Bush's lack of interest in foreign policy was accepted by the American political elite was unfortunately also a reflection of the attitude of President Bill Clinton to global problems. During his eight years in office, Clinton had cherry-picked his way through a whole raft of foreign policy issues, determining that intervention was a good idea when the polls told him that Americans supported intervention and doing nothing when the polls indicated the contrary. Thus, intervening in the former Yugoslavia was a good idea once the U.S. media had built up traction for the case, while the Rwanda genocide was ignored.

Clinton blew hot and cold when it came to Afghanistan and chasing al Qaeda. There were long periods of inaction; whimsical plans, such as the CIA hiring hit squads from Pakistan and Uzbekistan to capture bin Laden; and a sudden decision to use cruise missiles to hit al Qaeda camps after the bombing of the U.S. embassies in Africa. But there was no clear American determination to get rid of al Qaeda or the Taliban, and there was even less of a policy toward Pakistan, especially one that addressed the military's support to the Taliban. In the second Clinton term, U.S. government departments seemed to have different agendas for the region. For the State Department the main issue was easing India-Pakistan tensions, deterring nuclear proliferation, and persuading both countries to sign the Comprehensive Nuclear Test Ban Treaty after they had both tested nuclear weapons. The CIA focus was on bin Laden and the threat of the Pakistani military supporting causes that were deemed to be terrorist by the outside world. Yet the CIA refused to support the anti-Taliban Northern Alliance and mistrusted its leader, Ahmad Shah Masud. The Pentagon declined to get involved either way and did not even bother to draw up contingency plans for any possible military action in Afghanistan.

Nevertheless, Clinton was affable, a brilliant speaker, and a firm believer in sharing decision making with his European allies. In contrast, Bush was seen around the world as brash, cocky, profoundly unreflective, and unresponsive when it came to sharing decision making on global issues. There was a total absence of debate with European partners. Within the first few months of taking office in 2001, Bush was conducting a unilateralist foreign policy that aimed to force allies to accept a U.S. agenda. A senior Bush official called it "the doctrine of integration," which was aimed at integrating "other countries and organizations into arrangements that will sustain a world consistent with U.S. interests and values, and thereby promote peace, prosperity and justice, as widely as possible."[6] Bush's message to the rest of the world was "it's either my way or the highway."

Bush immediately broke with the international community on several issues. In December 2000 Clinton had signed the treaty that created the International Criminal Court, the world's first war crimes tribunal. Bush's first act was to refuse to send the treaty to the Senate for ratification. After 9/11 Washington threatened those countries that signed up to the Court with the loss of U.S. military aid. The Bush administration said it was opposed to the Comprehensive Nuclear Test Ban Treaty, which 150 countries had signed and which was the bedrock of nuclear nonproliferation. In March 2001 the United States refused to support ratification of the Kyoto Protocol, which would reduce global warming, and in June the United States withdrew from the Anti-Ballistic Missile Treaty. Europe was shell-shocked. Allies were unable to understand how to structure their relationship with the Bush White House and with the neoconservatives, or "neocons," who dominated policymaking.

The neocons carried complex political baggage. Dick Cheney, Paul Wolfowitz, Donald Rumsfeld, and others were archconservatives who considered themselves as radicals with a messianic vision of using American military power to reshape the world according to their own interests. Many of them had military backgrounds—G. W. Bush's first administration had appointed sixty-three retired military officers into senior government positions. To some outsiders the neocons were classic imperialists who were influenced by neofascist writings from the 1930s about the use of state power. For others their intellectual roots lay in Trotskyism or America's past, making them "a complex amalgam of the military imperialism of Theodore Roosevelt and the idealistic imperialism of Woodrow Wilson."[7] They claimed that in the post–cold war era, the United States was now running an empire and needed to project the kind of power that went with being the sole global imperial force.

The anger, grief, and rage felt by many Americans after 9/11, and the determination to hit back under any circumstances, was the perfect playing field for the neocons, who were to exploit retaliation for 9/11 into a much broader foreign and domestic agenda. They saw the war on terrorism as a means to fulfill a long-desired venture to remodel the Middle East, starting with destroying Saddam Hussein's regime in Iraq, securing more of the region's oil fields for American companies, and propping up the state of Israel. At home they saw the war as a means of carving out greater presidential power by ignoring legal constraints and the checks and balances of the U.S. political system.[8] The neocons were to use 9/11 as justification for making themselves exempt from American or international law.

The neocons deliberately manipulated the worldwide sympathy for the United States after 9/11 as an endorsement of their ideas. Overnight the U.S.-led war on terrorism could become, according to Zbigniew Brzezinski, "the central organizing principle of the West's global security policy."[9] It was a chronic mistake, as all other global issues were subsumed in a monolithic view of fighting terrorism. The vast majority of Europeans and Muslims could not connect with the militarized, self-obsessed policies of the neocons, who cared nothing for the rest of the world or its problems. When others wanted to discuss development or global warming, Bush wanted to discuss terrorism.

Naming the adversary as "terrorism" enabled the neocons to broaden the specific struggle against a bunch of murderous criminals (al Qaeda) into a global conflict with Islam. The neocons identified "state sponsors" of terrorism such as Iraq and Iran, who suddenly became part of the al Qaeda network, even as they overturned international law in the process. All this tapped into the fear and anger of a largely ignorant and accepting American public still in shock over how easily a small group of terrorists had destroyed so many lives on American soil.

Even the phrase "war on terrorism" was a misnomer, a rhetorical device, an emotive manipulation of the public's horror after 9/11. It had no more legal or practical meaning than would a war on cancer, drugs, or poverty.[10] *Terrorism* cannot be party to a conflict, so there can be no war against it. Moreover, there was no internationally accepted definition of what constituted terrorism, given the cliché that one man's terrorist is another man's freedom fighter. And the *war,* which is fought by soldiers, ignored all other policies needed to fight Islamic extremism—political, economic, and social reforms. Al Qaeda had a political strategy wrapped in the flag of Islam, so defeating al Qaeda required an equally broad political strategy, one that would win hearts and minds in the Muslim world.

Instead, the phraseology of the neocons became more and more disturbing as it aimed to terrify the American public. Paul Wolfowitz, then U.S. deputy secretary of defense, warned about ending states. "It's not just simply a matter of capturing people and holding them accountable but removing the sanctuaries, removing the support systems, ending states who sponsor terrorism," he said as the war in Afghanistan got under way.[11] Not surprisingly such comments were hated and ridiculed by Muslims everywhere, and helped convince many Muslims that the United States was out to target all Muslim civilization.[12]

In the heady days after 9/11 the neocons sold Bush a predetermined foreign policy based not on reality, good intelligence, and analysis but on an ideology. "We're an empire now and when we act, we create our own reality," a Bush adviser told Ron Suskind—a quote that historians will doubtlessly use as a defining one for the Bush era.[13] "And while you're studying that reality—judiciously, as you will—we'll act again, creating other new realities, which you can study too, and that's how things will sort out. We're history's actors . . . and you, all of you, will be left to just study what we do." The neocons truly believed that 9/11 was a God-given opportunity to make up history as they went along, and so changing the target from bin Laden to Saddam Hussein, from Afghanistan to Iraq, was their prerogative to rearrange their own reality.

For all their intellectualism, the neocons seemed to have no knowledge of what history had taught us about empires. The great empire builders quickly learned that when it came to ruling newly conquered lands, they had to put back in almost as much as they took out. If the conquerer was to extract the raw materials, taxes, and manpower he needed from the colony, he had to establish a system of security and law and order over the conquered and help his subjects maintain their economic livelihoods. Most significantly, empire builders from Alexander the Great to Queen Victoria had to learn about their subjects if they were to rule over them with any authority. At the very least they had to be curious about them. In the nineteenth century the British epitomized a colonialism that exploited with responsibility, used force judiciously, and yet learned about its subject peoples.

In comparison, the first thought of the Bush administration after the Afghan war ended was how to declare victory, get out, and move on to Iraq. The administration wanted no responsibility for reconstructing the now-occupied nation of Afghanistan and was unwilling to learn about the people or the country. In their haste to move on, security in Afghanistan was handed over to warlords and drug barons, who were supported lavishly by the CIA and the Pentagon with a one-billion-dollar budget, because Washington wanted to focus on the upcoming war in Iraq.

In 2003 the misinformation the Bush administration fed to the American people through a pliant and mostly willing media confirmed Saddam Hussein's possession of nuclear weapons and his links to al Qaeda. "You can't distinguish between al Qaeda and Saddam when you talk about the war on terror," said a confident Bush in 2002.[14] A completely false justification for going to war in Iraq and abandoning Afghanistan had just been created. It was only after the U.S. invasion that al Qaeda truly arrived in Iraq, luring in extremists from all over the world to act as suicide bombers.

It was an Orwellian experience to visit Washington during Bush's first term. Outsiders like me found it remarkable that a U.S. president could live in such an unreal world, where the entire military and intelligence establishments were so gullible, the media so complacent, Congress so unquestioning—all of them involved in feeding half truths to the American public. "Official intelligence analysis was not relied on in making even the most significant national security decisions," wrote Paul Pillar, a former senior CIA official.[15] I feared the worst kind of criticism when I made these points to young American students during a lecture tour of U.S. university campuses just before the Iraq war began. However, my ideas were well received and applauded. It became apparent to me that most Americans had the right instincts, but they were so poorly educated about world history, geography, and politics that they could not make political decisions for themselves about the world outside and left such choices to their leaders. The neocons counted on just this ignorance and compliance to conduct their foreign policy.

Compared to the pre–9/11 isolationism, the neocon ideology now focused on keeping the American public in a constant state of fear, with looming exaggerated threats and potential war. The administration was helped by the fact that it had arrived on the political stage when the United States had unquestioned military prowess around the globe. In the decade after the collapse of the Soviet Union, the Department of Defense or the Pentagon had been steadily displacing and obscuring the State Department in the formulation and conduct of U.S. foreign policy in the third world. "The military simply filled a vacuum left by an indecisive White House, an atrophied State Department, and a distracted Congress," wrote journalist Dana Priest.[16] Well before 9/11, military treaties with foreign armies eclipsed political agreements between the State Department and foreign ministries.

Under Secretary of Defense Donald Rumsfeld, the Pentagon's influence in the U.S. decision-making process was to become overwhelming, as the State Department, led weakly by Secretary of State Colin Powell, was steadily bypassed. The wars after 9/11 gave the Pentagon even more power and money. In 2001 the U.S. defense budget was $293 billion—still more than the aggregate budget of the next fifteen ranked countries in the world, including all the European powers and China. In 2003 the defense budget reached $360 billion, and in 2006 it topped $427 billion, growing by a phenomenal 40 percent in the five years since 9/11. In 2008 it reached $647 billion, by which time the wars in Iraq and Afghanistan were expected to have cost more than $1 trillion.[17] By now the U.S. defense budget was equivalent to what the entire rest of the world spent on defense.

Meanwhile, the State Department's budget was a mere fraction of the defense budget. In 2003 State received $26 billion, or just 6 percent of the defense budget. "We are conducting diplomacy on a shoestring in an era when . . . we depend on diplomats to build alliances," berated Richard Lugar, chairman of the Senate Foreign Relations Committee.[18] By 2008 State's total budget, including its loan and aid programs, amounted to $42 billion, or 6.5 percent of the defense budget. Even the foreign aid traditionally distributed by the State Department was being undercut by the Pentagon. Between 2001 and 2007, a virtually unknown Pentagon department called the Defense Security Cooperation Agency had secured 20 percent of Washington's $15 billion in foreign aid, while also managing some $12 billion in foreign arms sales.[19]

The might of the U.S. military should not be underestimated. The 1.37-million-strong U.S. armed forces divided up the world into regional commands that have more assets and facilities than similar divisions in the State Department or the CIA. The combined U.S. military has joint command operations stretched right around the world, including CENTCOM, or Central Command, in the Middle East, which fought the wars in Afghanistan and Iraq; PACOM, in the Pacific; EUCOM, in Europe; and SOUTH-COM, in Latin America. Each of these joint command headquarters has a staff of more than a thousand officers, far larger than the staffs of most U.S. embassies. The U.S. Navy has thirteen aircraft carrier battle groups, whereas no navy in the world has even one such carrier group. Before 9/11 the U.S. military deployed more than a quarter of a million men at 725 bases in 38 foreign countries, and during the war in Afghanistan it acquired 14 more bases, in Pakistan and Central Asia. CENTCOM had the widest theater of operations, covering 25 countries stretching from Kenya through the Middle East to China's western borders.

After the war in Afghanistan, the forty-seven-thousand-strong Special Operations Forces (SOF), involving soldiers from all three armed services, led the worldwide attack on Islamic extremists. The SOF budget of $3.0 billion in 2001 more than doubled, to $6.5 billion in 2004, and then doubled again four years later. Even before 9/11, SOF were operating in 140 countries, acting as virtual ambassadors to allied armies, offering specialized training and other support.[20] In sharp contrast, the one group of American soldiers considered essential for nation building—army civil affairs units, which rebuild bombed villages, bridges, power lines, and water supplies—were downgraded by Rumsfeld. When the terrorists struck the Twin Towers, most civil affairs units had been relegated to the U.S. Army Reserves and few were mobilized when the United States invaded Afghanistan. It was not until 2007, after the massive failure in Iraq, that the Pentagon decided to increase civil affairs officers by 33 percent, to 3,500 men.

Rumsfeld was involved not just in fighting the wars in Afghanistan and Iraq but in expanding his powers even further. He tried to undermine the FBI by secretly encouraging the Pentagon to carry out large-scale domestic intelligence gathering and he undercut the CIA by creating a new spy agency within the Pentagon, although the agency was later dissolved. In the immortal words of Maureen Dowd, "First he [Rumsfeld] and his brainy advisers, Paul Wolfowitz and Richard Perle, set up their own State Department within the Defense Department . . . then they set up their own Defense Department within the Defense Department staging a civilian coup. . . . And now they have set up their own C.I.A. within the Defense Department."[21]

To outsiders it appeared that when Rumsfeld wanted to do something he just went ahead and did it, disregarding everyone else in the U.S. government. That message was not lost on authoritarian regimes in the

Muslim world, who preferred to deal with the all-powerful but accommodating Rumsfeld and his generals rather than U.S. diplomats who might raise issues of human rights and democracy. A visiting CENTCOM chief, who arrived in his own plane with twenty staff officers, was given a guard of honor as though he were a head of state. How could the local U.S. ambassador compete with such a demonstration of power before autocratic rulers in the region?

When General Musharraf carried out his coup in 1999, he did not bother to get in touch with the U.S. ambassador in Islamabad, but instead telephoned Gen. Anthony Zinni, the CENTCOM chief at the time.[22] In Uzbekistan, after massacring hundreds of his own citizens in Andijan in 2005, President Islam Karimov continued a dialogue with the Pentagon, which was trying to keep the State Department's criticism of his actions to a minimum. Rumsfeld constantly used his generals to deliver strong political messages of support to heads of state in the region, undermining what the State Department or the White House was telling them.

Historically when the United States has intervened in the third world— largely in Latin America and Southeast Asia—it has never been much concerned with nation building or rebuilding shattered societies. Regime change during the cold war was all about replacing one pro-American corrupt dictator with another, while societies trundled on in their misery. As I've said, some observers hoped that after regime change in Afghanistan, the Americans would do more simply because the U.S. homeland had suffered such terrible consequences. The neocons, obsessed with the mechanics of regime change and instant gratification, never linked successful regime change with nation building. As a direct result, Afghanistan and Iraq both witnessed renewed insurgencies *after* the quick victories by U.S. forces precisely because of the failure first to plan and then to pursue nation-building policies the moment the war was won. A military doctrine of "shock and awe" could not substitute for boots on the ground and an inclusive strategy that would win hearts and minds.

Moreover, Pakistan, the base area, recruiting ground, and logistics center for both al Qaeda and the Taliban, needed major help in both state and nation building if it was to overcome past legacies. By state building, I mean the opportunity for countries to rebuild their infrastructure such as the army, police, civil service, and judiciary, which would provide security and services to its citizens. However, state building is prolonged, expensive, and requires a long-term commitment from international donors as well as a democratic culture prevailing at home—something the Pakistan army was to deny its citizens. Defined in the broadest possible way, nation building involves aid and support to civil society to rebuild the shattered economy, provide livelihoods, create social and political structures, and introduce democracy. The process of democratization is about not just holding elections but creating institutions and a culture of tolerance and shared responsibility among rulers and citizens alike.

Since the end of the cold war, the United States has been wary of getting involved in nation-building exercises. Washington has been involved in six such operations—Cambodia, East Timor, Haiti, Somalia, and the states of the former Yugoslavia. None of them was initiated by the United States, except for Somalia, which failed. The United States never took part in UN peacekeeping operations, although it has funded and supported many of them. Out of fifteen such UN peacekeeping operations worldwide in 2007, which involved more than one hundred thousand troops wearing UN blue helmets, just ten American soldiers were involved. Ironically, Pakistan is the largest provider of peacekeeping troops, contributing more than ten thousand in 2007.[23]

Its unwillingness to take part in nation-building exercises, and the lack of importance it gave the issue, fed into the Bush administration's growing conviction that it could fight and win the war on terrorism on its own. The United States refused the offers of help and shared responsibility made by multinational bodies such as NATO. Bush's formula was to create "a coalition of the willing." Only those countries willing to surrender decision making to the U.S. command could join.

After 9/11 the United States ignored the UN until after the bombing campaign against the Taliban had begun. Only when it realized that somebody had to pick up the pieces and put together a new Afghan government did Washington approach Secretary-General Kofi Annan. Four days after the bombing campaign began, a reluctant Bush admitted that "it would be a useful function for the United Nations to take over the 'nation building.' I would call it the stabilization of a future government after our military mission is completed."[24] Afghanistan later became a multinational effort, but the United States refused to take its partners seriously and continued to make all major military and aid decisions on its own.

Under difficult conditions, working against a deadline that was brought even closer by the unexpected collapse of the Taliban, the UN effort was remarkable for its creativity. The UN had been set up to prevent wars between states, not to mediate civil wars or set up postinvasion governments. Today the UN is having to do far more than it was ever mandated for. Today's global threats include civil wars, ethnic cleansing, terrorism, proliferation of weapons of mass destruction, organized crime, disease, poverty, and mass starvation. Many of these issues are interconnected, making the role of a multinational organization such as the UN indispensable, yet the organization was essentially ignored by the neocons.

In the giddy days after the Afghan victory, outsiders could not believe that the U.S. administration would undermine its own war in Afghanistan by failing to carry out nation building. After the success of my book *Taliban,* European foreign ministers, aid organizations, the media, and think tanks invited me to meetings and conferences. I visited Washington several times, hoping that the administration would want to do good in Afghanistan and convinced it just needed the right ideas as to how to proceed. I spent much time in the office of the U.S. Agency for International Development, whose boss Andrew Natsios was enthusiastic about helping the Afghans and needed ideas as to where to start. However, USAID was to be swiftly superseded by the CIA and the Pentagon.

Everywhere I went after 9/11, I urged governments and experts to devote resources for nation building in Afghanistan so that the country could emerge as a bastion of development and democracy to counter the growing trends of extremism and state repression in the Islamic world. The United States and the West had the opportunity to show Muslims and the world that they may be bombing a country to free it from Taliban tyranny, but they also had the willingness and patience to help rebuild it. I strongly countered the myths being circulated in the Western media at the time that the Afghans would oppose the presence of Western troops. Instead, after being battered by twenty-five years of war, most Afghans saw the presence of Western forces as a way forward to stability and development.

I urged audiences that warlords should not be empowered, that disarming the militias was a priority task for U.S. forces, that international peacekeepers should be deployed outside Kabul, that Pakistan must not give refuge to the retreating Taliban, and that developing Afghan agriculture to ward off a revival of poppy cultivation should be a priority. I also advocated a regional view of development and reconstruction that looked at the problems of development in Pakistan and Central Asia. Much of what I spoke about was commonsense stuff and should have been obvious to Western governments—or so I thought.

Most experts reckoned that Afghanistan, a country the size of Texas, needed about $4 to 5 billion every year for the next ten years to put it on its feet—a small amount in geopolitical donor terms and a pittance compared to what was later spent in Iraq. Such an act of sustained commitment by the international community would also help undermine support for extremism in the neighboring states and encourage them to pursue reforms.

Every item on my checklist was studiously ignored by Washington.

Within a few months of 9/11, Bush had added to his counterterrorism agenda the "axis of evil" (Iran, Iraq, North Korea) and the ideas of "pre-emption" and "regime change" in which the United States could presume a nation's guilt and attack it before it had carried out any hostile act. Never before had the United States presented the world with such an aggressive global strategy that reeked of overt imperialism, alienated Europeans and Muslims alike, and made the job of winning hearts and minds around the globe virtually impossible. Bush was now truly the global cowboy. "The problem is that President Bush has reframed his initial question. Instead of simply asking others to oppose al Qaeda, he now asks them to oppose al Qaeda, support the invasion of an Arab country, and endorse the doctrine of preemption—all as part of a single package," said former secretary of state Madeleine Albright.[25]

At home Bush presented his global agenda as a result of sudden world-wide anti-Americanism rather than a result of past American policy failures. "Why do they hate us? . . . They hate our freedoms—our freedom of religion, our freedom of speech, our freedom to vote and assemble and disagree with each other," Bush told Congress on September 20, 2001.[26] Such words ignored past failures and created a culture of fear and hysteria among many Americans, even as it created disdain and ridicule abroad. The unspoken implication of such rhetoric was that if *they* hated *us,* then Americans should hate Muslims back and retaliate not just against the terrorists but against Islam in general. By generating such fears it was virtually impossible to gain American public attention and support for long-term nation building.

The Bush doctrine was also doggedly to sweep under the carpet any discussion or understanding of the "root causes" of terrorism—the growing poverty, repression, and sense of injustice that many Muslims felt at the hands of their U.S.-backed governments, which in turn boosted anti-Americanism and Islamic extremism. The Bush administration was determined to prevent any alternative views on U.S. foreign policy from emerging, and the Washington-based media was cowed from asking awkward questions until the failures in Iraq and Afghanistan became too obvious. It took four years before anyone in the Bush administration admitted that the United States had failed to carry out nation building. "We didn't have the right skills, the right capacity to deal with a reconstruction effort of this kind," said Condoleezza Rice, speaking of both Iraq and Afghanistan in 2005.[27]

Bush did more to keep Americans blind to world affairs than any American leader in recent history.[28] In 2004 a strategic think tank supported by the Pentagon issued a damning report saying that America's strategic communications with the world had broken down and a total reorganization of public diplomacy was needed. The Department of Defense Science Board said the United States was losing the war of ideas in the Muslim world: "Muslims do not 'hate our freedom,' but rather they hate our policies. . . . The critical problem in American public diplomacy directed towards the Muslim world is not one of 'dissemination of information' or even one of crafting and delivering the 'right' message. Rather it is a fundamental problem of credibility. Simply there is none—the United States today is without a working channel of communication to the world of Muslims and of Islam."[29]

In Europe there was a vastly different approach to dealing with the terrorist threat. The continent was deeply divided over supporting the invasion of Iraq, but those divisions led to intense debate, saturation media coverage, and protest movements, which led to public mobilization and deep introspection about the wars in Iraq and Afghanistan. The European public was far better educated about the wars than the American public ever was. Whereas draconian laws were swiftly introduced in America after 9/11, as thousands of American Muslims were rounded up and many were deported for visa infringements, there was a far more careful attitude in Europe. Even the 2004 and 2005 bombings in Madrid and London, respectively, never generated the governmental hysteria regarding the fundamental rights of their citizens that 9/11 did in the United States. There were calls to improve the integration of Muslim citizens into Spanish and British societies rather than isolate them. European governments treaded slowly before they introduced new anti-terrorism laws. An enormous respect was shown to civil liberties and human rights for all their citizens—Muslims included.

In the early months of 2002, no outsider, least of all myself, had any idea that Iraq rather than Afghanistan was the real focus of the Bush administration's attention and that the "war on terrorism" would be fought in Baghdad rather than Kabul or Islamabad. The reluctance of the Pentagon to commit more American troops to Afghanistan should have alerted us that either the U.S. military was very stupid or it had preoccupations other than Afghanistan. Yet at the time few people I spoke to, including U.S. officials, could believe that the neocons would willfully give up tracking down al Qaeda leaders and would move on to Iraq. We now know that the chase was given up in March 2002—just three months after the fall of Kandahar—when the Arabic- and Persian-speaking U.S. SOF teams were moved out of Afghanistan to train for Iraq and surveillance satellites were pulled from the skies over Afghanistan and redirected to Iraq.

The American failure to rebuild Afghanistan and Iraq or to move Pakistan and Central Asia toward reform and democracy made it almost impossible for Muslim moderates to support the West's struggle against Islamic extremism or to bring about change in their own countries. The U.S. campaign to eliminate al Qaeda had turned into a much larger American intervention across the Islamic world that had nothing to do with al Qaeda and that Muslims could not support or tolerate. The treatment of prisoners by the U.S. military at Guantánamo Bay and Abu Ghraib were symptoms of an ever-expanding war that alienated the entire globe. By 2007 a decisive shift had taken place in key countries such as Pakistan, where hatred for Musharraf and the Americans took precedence over hatred for al Qaeda, even as Pakistanis died in large numbers from al Qaeda–sponsored suicide bombings. This made fighting the extremists much more difficult.

As the Bush era nears its end in 2008, American power lies shattered. The U.S. Army is overstretched and broken, the American people are disillusioned and rudderless, U.S. credibility lies in ruins, and the world is a far more dangerous place. The Iraq war has bankrupted the United States, consuming up to $11 billion a month.[30] Ultimately the strategies of the Bush administration have created a far bigger crisis in South and Central Asia than existed before 9/11. There are now full-blown Taliban insurgencies in Afghanistan and Pakistan, and the next locus could be Uzbekistan. The safety of Pakistan's nuclear weapons is uppermost in the minds of Western governments. There are more failing states in the Muslim world, while al Qaeda has expanded around the world.

The American people have understood the tragedy associated with Bush's imperial overreach, and as the 2008 U.S. elections will doubtless show, they are no longer as naïve, ignorant, or scared as they were after 9/11. However, it has taken the American people time to learn such lessons, and in the meantime American power has been squandered, and hatred for Americans has become a global phenomenon. Bush's historical legacy will be one of failure. This book is an attempt to explain how that came about in Washington and on the ground in Afghanistan, Pakistan, and Central Asia.

DESCENT INTO CHAOS

PART ONE

9/11 AND WAR

CHAPTER ONE

A Man with a Mission

The Unending Conflict in Afghanistan

Six weeks before 9/11, an old Afghan friend of mine came to spend the day with me at my home in Lahore. We had lunch and then began an intense discussion that went on until the evening, without reaching a conclusion. He had come to discuss a specific problem he faced. At issue was his future, his safety, and the fate of his country, which was inextricably linked to my life as a journalist for the past twenty-three years and to the fate of my own country, Pakistan.

My friend was Hamid Karzai, chief of the Popalzai tribe centered near Kandahar. He had just been delivered an ultimatum by the Inter-Services Intelligence Directorate, better known in Pakistan as ISI, the military's all-powerful and much-feared intelligence agency, which for two decades had run Pakistan's covert wars in Afghanistan and Kashmir, had harassed dissidents at home, and was now the principal supporter of the Taliban regime. The ISI told Karzai that he could no longer stay in Pakistan, his visa would not be renewed, and he must leave the country with his family by September 30. Karzai had resided in Pakistan since 1983, save for a brief stint in Kabul in the early 1990s. We both knew who had really ordered his expulsion: Mullah Mohammed Omar, the leader of the Taliban in Kandahar. The ISI was merely obliging the Taliban, who could no longer tolerate Karzai's anti-Taliban politicking from his home in Quetta, in Balochistan province, just 150 miles from Kandahar. We both knew that the expulsion order was as much a death threat as it was a warning, and it could not be taken lightly.

Karzai's father, Abdul Ahad Karzai, had been murdered by the Taliban in 1999—an assassination that Karzai believes also implicated the ISI. The elder Karzai had been chief of the Popalzai tribe, a former deputy speaker of parliament, and immensely respected for his honesty and wisdom by all the southern Pashtun tribes. The Pashtuns were the largest ethnic group in Afghanistan and had ruled and dominated the country for 250 years. Mullah Omar, an itinerant preacher, could not claim the pedigree of the Karzais, and the fact that they hailed from Kandahar, as did much of the Taliban leadership, only incensed him further. After murdering the elder Karzai, the Taliban and their agents murdered more than a dozen prominent Afghans living in Pakistan who opposed the Taliban regime. The Pakistani police never caught any of the assassins because they were well protected by the ISI. As the Taliban regime became more internationally isolated and condemned because of its crimes against the Afghan people and the hosting of Osama bin Laden, it became more desperate to wipe out all opposition to it.[1]

I, too, had earned the wrath of the ISI by criticizing the Taliban in my articles and exposing the considerable Pakistani support that kept them afloat. My book *Taliban,* published in 2000, led to threats by the ISI and their extremist supporters. The book was swiftly translated into Dari and widely distributed in Afghanistan, particularly by Karzai and Ahmad Shah Masud's tribal network. Moreover, a speech I gave in Lahore demanding that Pakistan reconsider its Afghan policy and drop support for the Taliban had been widely circulated in Afghanistan after being broadcast by the Dari and Pushtu services of the BBC.[2]

That day in Lahore, Karzai and I had a long discussion and determined that he had only two choices. He could leave for Europe to become just another émigré Afghan politician out of touch with his people and hovering around the entourage of the former Afghan king, Zahir Shah, now in Rome, where a new political effort was under way to oppose the Taliban. Or he could deposit his family abroad and then take his life in his hands and enter Afghanistan to rally the Pashtun tribes and foment rebellion against the Taliban. In fact, for the past three years Karzai had quietly been preparing for such a day, meeting in Quetta with dissident tribal leaders who came out of Afghanistan, collecting arms and money, and secretly distributing them to his supporters inside the country. Uppermost in the minds of his tribal supporters was whether Karzai could ever muster the international support crucial to his efforts.

Unfortunately, Washington and London considered Karzai a political lightweight, and any success at fomenting rebellion in the Pashtun heart-land of the Taliban was considered unlikely. Karzai had been a Mujahedin, a member of the Afghan opposition to the Soviet invaders, since the early 1980s, but he had never fought directly against the Soviets and he had no experience as a military commander. Karzai spoke six languages (Pushtu, Dari, Urdu, English, French, and Hindi), read voraciously, and was a snazzy dresser. Western diplomats considered him an intellectual but not a leader who could topple the Taliban. Moreover, the United States was not particularly interested in the future of Afghanistan or the Taliban regime. All they wanted was someone to deliver Osama bin Laden.

"Our people are not yet ready for guerrilla war against the Taliban, and the Taliban are still very strong and ruthless, and they will carry out reprisals against the civilian population," Karzai told me that day. "But how can I leave all my people and the anti-Taliban network I have created over these years and go abroad—I cannot betray or abandon them now." He asked for my advice, and I bluntly told him that I could not imagine him joining the bickering émigré leaders in Rome trying to exert influence over Zahir Shah, who was now more than seventy-five years old. Whereas other Afghan leaders had settled abroad, including many of his brothers, Karzai had spent the last decade close to his people. The chronic lack of real leadership among the contentious Pashtuns had been a major factor in the Taliban's rise to power in the 1990s. I was convinced that if he decided to do so, Karzai could fill the leadership gap among the Pashtuns.

Hamid Karzai was born in Kandahar in 1957, the fourth of eight children born to Abdul Ahad Karzai and his wife, Durko. Subsequently all the children except two, Hamid and his younger brother, Ahmed Wali, were to emigrate and settle in the United States. It was a typically tragic tale of the Afghan diaspora after the Soviet invasion. The eldest brother, Abdul Ahmad, became an engineer in Maryland. Qayum and Mahmood set up a chain of Afghan restaurants in the United States. Shawali became a businessman in the Arabian Gulf city of Dubai. The youngest son, Abdul Wali, became a biochemist on Long Island, while a married sister, Faozia, settled in Maryland.

Hamid Karzai went to primary school in his native city of Kandahar and then attended high school in Kabul. It was an unremarkable childhood for a member of the Pashtun tribal elite: a constant stream of visitors for his father arriving at their Kandahar home, long summer holidays in the hot city, picnics beside lakes and at mountain resorts outside Kabul.

Hamid's father supported King Zahir Shah, who attempted to set up a constitutional monarchy in the late 1960s but refused to yield power to a partially elected parliament. Finally the king was overthrown by his own cousin, Mohammed Daud, in 1973. Just before the Soviet Union invaded Afghanistan in 1979, Karzai gained admission to Himachal Pradesh University, in northern India, to study political science. As millions of terrified Afghans became refugees into Pakistan and Iran, and an anti-Soviet resistance began, he wished to join the guerrillas. His father urged him to finish his studies first.

Karzai's life was now to intertwine with the wars that had raged for more than two decades in his country, the forced migration of one quarter of the Afghan population, and the deaths of an estimated one million people. With such chronic breakdown and collapse, an international terrorist group found it easy to take over the country.

Situated on the crossroads between Iran and India, Central Asia and South Asia, and Central Asia and the Middle East, Afghanistan has been a gateway for invaders since the earliest Aryan invasions from Central Asia into the Indian subcontinent six thousand years ago. Easy to pass through, the country has nonetheless been impossible to conquer. Several of the world's largest mountain ranges and deserts make life difficult for the resident population and invaders alike. Modern Afghanistan is divided by the massive Hindu Kush mountain range, which stretches across the middle of the country. To the south live the Pushtu-speaking Pashtun tribes, intermingled with Persian-speaking ethnic groups; to the north live the Persian- and Turkic-speaking peoples: the Tajiks, Uzbeks, Hazaras, Turkmen, and others. In the northeast corner the towering peaks of the Pamir Mountains, called the "roof of the world" by Marco Polo, continue into Central Asia, Pakistan, and China. In eastern Afghanistan, the Suleman, the Spin Ghar, and other jagged ranges straddle the border with Pakistan—and, after 9/11, provided impenetrable hiding places for al Qaeda's leadership.

Where there are no mountains there are deserts and steppe. To the north of the Hindu Kush, the immense Central Asian Steppe begins its long sweep all the way to Siberia, while in the southwest stretches the Iranian Plateau, a land of harsh desert and scrub with sparse population centers. Even though agriculture is the mainstay for 80 percent of the population, only 10 to 12 percent of the terrain is cultivable. Before the Soviet invasion, nomadism and the grazing of goats and sheep, carried out by Kuchi nomads, ensured a livelihood for several million people.

Despite its harsh geography, Afghanistan was one of the major cross-roads of the ancient world, an important part of the old Silk Route used by pilgrims and traders, who along its length and breadth carried new religions, inventions, and ideas. Nearly all of the world's ancient religions found a home in Afghanistan, including Zoroastrianism, Manichaeanism, and Buddhism, with Islam the last arrival, in AD 654, when Arab armies invaded India and Afghanistan after the death of the Prophet Mohammed. Ancient invaders, such as the Persians, Greeks, and the Turkic tribes of Central Asians, Arabs, the Mongols under Genghis Khan in AD 1219, and the Moghals, either swept though Afghanistan on their way to India and Persia, or occupied it. Each invasion left behind social, cultural, or ethnic legacies that were to add to the mosaic of modern-day Afghanistan. Thus the Mongols, amid the destruction they wrought, left behind the Hazaras, who today inhabit the Hindu Kush mountains.

In 1504 Babur, a prince from the Ferghana Valley in modern-day Uzbekistan, conquered Kabul and then India, establishing the Moghul dynasty that was to last until 1857. The Afghan state recognizable today arose from the Pashtun tribes at a historical juncture when the Moghuls in India, the Safavids in Iran, and the Uzbek kingdom in Central Asia were all in decline due to political turmoil and civil war. At that time, the words *Afghan* and *Pashtun* were interchangeable, and the Pashtuns were seen as the only true Afghans. (Pashtuns today consider themselves a Semitic race whose ancestors were companions to the Prophet Mohammed.) They were divided into two major sections, the Ghilzai and Abdali (later called Durrani). A Ghilzai Pashtun revolt against the Safavids in 1701 led to a tribal confederation among the Abdalis. In 1747, all the tribes held a nine-day Loya Jirga, or grand meeting, in Kandahar, ultimately choosing a general, Ahmad Shah Abdali, to become their king. The tribal chiefs wrapped a turban around his head and placed blades of grass in the turban's folds, signifying their loyalty.

(The Loya Jirga was to become the source of all legal authority—a tradition that continues to this day and which legitimized Hamid Karzai as Afghanistan's president in 2002.) Ahmad Shah, who changed his last name and that of his dynasty to Durrani, became the father of the nation, and Afghans still flock to pray at his tomb in Kandahar. The Durranis moved the capital from Kandahar to Kabul in 1772 and conquered northern Afghanistan, incorporating other ethnic groups into the Afghan nation. *Afghan* means a people now, and not just the Pashtuns. Disputes and rivalries between the Ghilzais and the Durranis and between Pashtuns and non-Pashtuns were to continue for the next two centuries, but the country was governable and sustainable, despite its extreme poverty.

The threat from European empires was never far away. The British in India tried to conquer Afghanistan three times but were unable to occupy the country. Instead they paid off the Afghan amirs (kings) and tribal chiefs, turning Afghanistan into a client state rather than imperial domain. Tsarist Russia conquered Central Asia and encroached into northern Afghanistan, buying support in a bid to undermine the British. Both empires vied for influence in Kabul, sparking a clandestine war of wits, bribery, and secret agents dubbed "the Great Game."

At the end of the nineteenth century the two empires agreed to demarcate Afghanistan's borders—in the north with Russia, in the east with India, and in the west with Persia—thus dividing tribes and ethnic groups among several states but also defining Afghanistan as a nation-state for the first time. King Abdul Rehman (1880–1901), named the Iron Amir, used British subsidies to establish the first standing army and bureaucracy. Using brutal methods that were later closely copied by the Taliban, he suppressed forty revolts by the Uzbeks, Hazaras, and Tajiks, thus ending their autonomy and bringing them under the control of Kabul. He enticed Pashtun farmers from the south to settle in regions in the north, hoping to dilute their ethnicity and weaken their opposition to a central power. However, neither Amir Rehman nor any subsequent Afghan ruler accepted the Durand Line—named after Sir Mortimer Durand—which divides Afghanistan from the Pashtun tribes in Pakistan.

The two-hundred-year-old Durrani dynasty came to an end in 1973, when King Zahir Shah, who had ruled since 1933, was overthrown by his cousin and brother-in-law, Sardar Mohammed Daud, supported by the nascent communist parties inside the country, and Afghanistan was declared a republic under a presidential form of government. Afghanistan had initially tried to avoid getting involved in the cold war and received aid from both the United States and the Soviet Union, although Moscow was by far the largest aid provider, especially for Afghan officers trained in Russia. Between 1956 and 1978, Afghanistan received some $533.0 million in economic aid from the United States and $2.5 billion from the Soviets in both economic and military aid. It was still a client state, dependent on foreign aid for up to 40 percent of its budget. Even today it cannot raise sufficient revenue to pay for the necessary elements of a modern state.

Afghanistan had always tried to balance regional powers, taking money from the Soviets and the United States and balancing the demands of both Iran and Pakistan. However, Mohammed Daud overrode Afghanistan's balancing act and tilted decisively toward the Soviets, thereby increasing the influence of the two rival communist parties Khalq (the Masses) and Parcham (the Flag). Daud's tilt led to a crackdown on the country's nascent Islamic fundamentalist movement, which in order to avoid arrest fled across the border to Pakistan in 1975. The Afghan Islamists were linked to the "Muslim Brotherhood" and Pakistan's Jamiat-e-Islami, who gave them sanctuary. However, Pakistan's intelligence services, infuriated by Daud's support to Pakistani Pashtun and Baluch Marxists, decided to retaliate by enlisting the Afghan Islamists. They were trained by Lt.-Gen. Naseerullah Babar, the head of the paramilitary Frontier Corps, and sent back into Afghanistan to launch a guerrilla movement against Daud, which was quickly crushed. The Islamists included Gulbuddin Hikmetyar, Burhanuddin Rabbani, and Ahmad Shah Masud, who were to become more prominent in the subsequent war against the Soviet Union. Ironically it was Babar, interior minister in the government of Prime Minister Benazir Bhutto in 1994, who would be instrumental in launching the Taliban.

Daud's authoritarianism and communism's growing appeal in the army led to a coup in April 1978, carried out by Marxist army officers. They overthrew Daud, killed his family and the presidential guard, and then attempted to impose a purist Soviet-style Marxist state in Afghanistan. They were bound to fail. The two parties, Khalq and Parcham, began a bloody internecine conflict, even as they attempted to carry out unrealistic land and educational reforms in a conservative and tribal-based Muslim society. The first Khalqi president, Nur Mohammed Taraki, was murdered by his successor, Hafizullah Amin, who outlawed the Parchamis. The Soviets became increasingly perturbed at the civil war between the two parties and the growing strength of the Mujahedin insurgency and invaded Afghanistan on Christmas Eve 1979. They murdered Amin and installed the Parchami leader Babrak Karmal.

Afghanistan was catapulted into the center of the cold war as U.S. president Ronald Regan pledged to roll back communism. Afghan mullahs and political leaders declared a jihad against the Soviet Union as five million people fled east to Pakistan and west to Iran. In the next decade, the United States and its European and Arab allies poured billions of dollars' worth of arms to the Mujahedin, money that was routed through Pakistan and the military regime of General Zia ul-Haq. Zia did not allow the CIA or any other foreign intelligence agency to aid the Mujahedin directly, enter Afghanistan, or plan the Mujahedin's battles and strategy. That became the prerogative of the ISI, which with its newfound wealth and American patronage had become a state within a state, employing thousands of officers in order to run what was now also Pakistan's Afghan war.

The Karzai family fled to Pakistan and settled in Quetta in order to be close to Kandahar. Hamid Karzai completed his degree in India and arrived in Peshawar in 1983 determined to help the Mujahedin. Zia allowed only seven Afghan exiled political parties to operate from Peshawar and receive aid from the CIA. All seven were religion based, as Zia forbade Afghan nationalist, democratic, or secular left-wing parties to operate from Pakistan. He insisted that the parties speak of the war as a jihad and not as a national liberation movement. The ISI used the CIA cash and arms as bribes to keep the Mujahedin's parties in line even as it channeled the greatest proportion of the aid to the most extreme groups, such as Gulbuddin Hikmetyar's Hizb-e-Islami party.

Rather than throw in his lot with the fundamentalist parties in Zia's favor, Karzai joined the National Liberation Front of Afghanistan, led by the spiritual leader Sibghatullah Mujaddedi. The Mujaddedis were leaders of the Naqshbandiyah order of Sufism—the spiritual and mystical side of Islam that is widely popular in Afghanistan. The Mujaddedi family was so politically influential in Kabul that they were dubbed the "king makers." The communist Afghan president Nur Mohammed Taraki had murdered seventy-nine members of the family, leaving Sibghatullah the eldest survivor. A moderate man, he drew his support from tribal leaders who were Afghan nationalists rather than mullahs and militants, and became a fierce critic of the radical leaders who were favored by the ISI.

Hamid Karzai's urbane charm, easygoing manner, command of languages, and ability to seek compromise rather than confrontation with his Mujahedin partners won him many friends in Peshawar. He became the spokesman and then foreign policy adviser for Sibghatullah Mujaddedi. I had been covering the war in Afghanistan for the *Far Eastern Economic Review,* a weekly Asian magazine, and was the only Pakistani and one of the few foreign journalists who was able to visit Soviet-controlled Kabul as well as be welcomed by the Mujahedin leaders in Pakistan. The Soviets invariably refused visas to journalists who cultivated the Mujahedin but I had developed a reputation of giving evenhanded coverage to both sides. We became good friends, especially as I sympathized with many of his views, including his critique of the Afghan extremists such as Hikmetyar, who was to later put a price on my head for criticizing him.

Meanwhile, the Soviet occupation of Afghanistan was faltering, and with severe political setbacks at home, the Soviets were forced to withdraw their troops in 1989. Two years later the Soviet Union itself collapsed. President Mohammed Najibullah, the last remaining communist strongman, hung on to power after Soviet troops left, defying the bickering Mujahedin, until finally a revolt erupted from within his own ranks in the spring of 1992, forcing him to step down. A UN plan to transfer power failed, Najibullah was arrested, and there was a race for Kabul between the Pashtun forces of Hikmetyar and the Tajiks of Burhanuddin Rabbani and his military commander, Ahmad Shah Masud. The Tajik forces won, and the capital fell into the hands of non-Pashtuns for the first time in three hundred years.³ As part of a complex agreement between the Mujahedin in which they agreed to a rotating presidency, Mujaddedi became the president for the first four months of what was now the Islamic Republic of Afghanistan, and Karzai became deputy foreign minister.

The Soviet withdrawal from Afghanistan was followed by another withdrawal—that of the United States from the entire region under George H. W. Bush. Having won the cold war, Washington had no further interest in Afghanistan or the region. This left a critical power vacuum for which the United States would pay an enormously high price a decade later.

The Arabs, the Islamic extremists in Pakistan and Afghanistan, and other jihadis were left to their own devices, but even worse, the Afghan people were abandoned—something they have found very difficult to forgive. There was no funding for international efforts to revive Afghanistan, little help for the five million refugees eager to return, no diplomatic pressure to force the Mujahedin to come to a political compromise. The CIA handed over charge of its Afghan policy to its allies in the region, Pakistan and Saudi Arabia. To Afghan eyes, these two states, which had backed the extremists among the Mujahedin and had sabotaged any hope of an Afghan national government's emerging, were now being rewarded by the Americans. Some Pakistani officials looked upon Afghanistan as Pakistan's fifth province, while Saudi princes sought out the country as new hunting grounds for bustards, or plains turkeys.

The various Mujahedin parties, never united before, now broke up into warring factions. Of these, the most bloodthirsty and obstinate was that of Hikmetyar, who refused to accept any kind of compromise that did not make him president and who was openly supported by the ISI. His bitterest rival was the Tajik commander Ahmad Shah Masud, now the defense minister in Kabul under Rabbani, who had become president after Mujaddedi. Ethnic rivalries between Pashtun and non-Pashtun that had lain dormant during the war against the Soviets now erupted. A civil war broke out that was to be one of the most brutal phases in the history of the country. In January 1993 the forces of Hikmetyar and his allies began shelling Kabul, and hand-to-hand fighting broke out as Masud's forces defended the city. In the next few years, Kabul was destroyed, and tens of thousands of civilians were killed by Hikmetyar's rockets and shells and by Masud's defensive actions.

Karzai was an early victim. As a Pashtun in a largely Tajik-controlled government, he was arrested on the orders of the interior minister, Gen. Mohammed Fahim, and Mohammed Arif, the head of Masud's intelligence service, the National Directorate for Security. While Karzai was being interrogated, the directorate building was unexpectedly shelled and in the ensuing chaos, he escaped, fleeing to Peshawar by bus. Rabbani has always claimed he knew nothing about the arrest, and he later telephoned Karzai in Pakistan to apologize, but Karzai did not trust Rabbani or Masud again until 2001. In the way that all the Afghan warlords have been constantly reincarnated, Fahim was to become Karzai's defense minister and Aref his intelligence chief in the interim government set up after 9/11. When I asked Karzai if he subsequently raised the subject of his arrest with Fahim or Aref, he smiled and said, "Not at all—that is all in the past and forgiven."[4]

By 1994 the country was fast disintegrating. Warlord fiefdoms ruled vast swathes of countryside. President Rabbani, who had refused to relinquish the presidency, governed only Kabul and the northeast of the country, while the west, centered on Herat, was under the control of warlord Ismael Khan. Six provinces in the north were ruled by the Uzbek general Rashid Dostum, and central Afghanistan was in the hands of the Hazaras. In the Pashtun south and east there was even greater fragmentation, with one large fiefdom based in Jalalabad, which ruled three provinces bordering Pakistan; a small area adjacent to Kabul controlled by Hikmetyar; while in the south, multiple commanders ruled. Warlords seized people's homes and farms for no reason, raped their daughters, abused and robbed the population, and taxed travelers at will. Instead of refugees returning to Afghanistan, more began to leave the south for Pakistan.

The Taliban emerged as a direct consequence of these appalling conditions. Frustrated young men who had fought against the Soviets and then returned to madrassas in Pakistan to resume their religious studies or to their villages in Afghanistan gathered around their elders demanding action. "We would sit for a long time to discuss how to change the terrible situation. We had only vague ideas what to do, but we believed we were working with Allah as his pupils," Mullah Mohammed Ghaus, the one-eyed former Taliban foreign minister, told me.[5] These young men named themselves Talibs, which means religious students who seek justice and knowledge. They chalked out a minimum agenda: to restore peace, disarm the population, enforce Sharia, or Islamic law, and defend Islam in Afghanistan. Pledging to cleanse society of its ills, they chose as their leader the man they considered the most pious and least ambitious among them, Mohammed Omar, a thirty-nine-year-old itinerant mullah born in a poor village outside Kandahar with no social status or tribal pedigree. During the Soviet occupation, he had been wounded four times, once in the right eye, which was permanently blinded.

Just before he disappeared into Afghanistan in October 2001, Hamid Karzai described to me his first association with the Taliban:

> Like so many Mujahedin I believed in the Taliban when they first appeared in 1994 and promised to end warlordism, establish law and order, and then call a Loya Jirga to decide who should rule Afghanistan. The first Taliban I met told me that the jihad had become a disgrace and the civil war was destroying the country. After the Taliban captured Kandahar, I gave them fifty thousand dollars to help them out, and then handed them a cache of weapons I had hidden near Kandahar. I met Mullah Omar several times and he offered to appoint me as their envoy to the UN. They were good people initially, but the tragedy was that very soon after they were taken over by the ISI and became a proxy. When the Taliban captured Ghazni, I began to receive reports about foreigners in their ranks who were encouraging them to shut down girls' schools.
>
> I realized what was happening when I was called into the Pakistan Foreign Office to discuss the modalities for my becoming the Taliban envoy at the UN. Can you imagine? Pakistan was setting up the Taliban's

diplomatic corps. I refused and walked out. Later the Taliban were to come under the influence of al Qaeda. That is when I began to organize against them. In 1998, I warned the Americans and the British many, many times that Osama bin Laden was now playing a leadership role within the Taliban, but who was listening? Nobody.

The Taliban soon consolidated their power into a successful military force, seizing Kandahar in the winter of 1994 and then rapidly spreading north and west, capturing Herat in 1995 and Kabul in 1996. Pashtun warlords threw down their arms rather than confront the Taliban, who appeared to be invulnerable. With its ties to the Taliban leaders, Pakistan persuaded Saudi Arabia and the United Arab Emirates to give support, cash, and recognition to the movement, money that was channeled through the ISI. The Taliban's first defeat, in May 1997, when they were driven out of the northern city of Mazar-e-Sharif with huge losses, convinced many Afghans that the group was just one more warlord faction. By now the Taliban had dispensed with the idea of calling a Loya Jirga and determined that they alone would rule the country and enforce Sharia. Their definition of Sharia—influenced by extremist Islamic teachings in Pakistan and a perversion of Pashtunwali, or the Pashtun code of behavior—and its harsh enforcement across the country were utterly alien to Afghan culture and tradition.

The Taliban leaders' intellectual shortcomings were later to allow them to come under the influence of al Qaeda's global jihad philosophy. Al Qaeda's conscription of thousands of young men to fight their wars created widespread public resentment, especially among the Pashtun tribes. The Afghan civil war had again become an openly ethnic conflict between the Pashtun Taliban and the non-Pashtuns of Masud's Northern Alliance (NA), also called the United Front. Masud commanded his own Tajik troops, drawn largely from the Panjsher Valley and called Panjsheri Tajiks, but he also had the allegiance of other commanders, such as Herat's Ismael Khan, the Hazara commanders in central Afghanistan, and Gen. Rashid Dostum, the commander of Uzbek forces in northern Afghanistan.

In 1998 the Taliban captured Mazar and northern Afghanistan, squeezing the forces of the Northern Alliance into a sliver of territory in northeastern Afghanistan and another front outside Kabul. Masud gallantly resisted the onslaught, but his allies in other parts of the country crumbled. Ismael Khan was defeated and fled to Iran, where the Hazara leaders had also taken refuge. Dostum fled to Turkey. The Taliban's success, helped by Pakistan and Saudi Arabia's ability to lavish massive support to the movement, was due largely to Washington's silence.

During this period the Clinton administration simply stood by, allowing Pakistan and Saudi Arabia to pursue their own protégés in Afghanistan. Instead of putting forward peace plans to end the civil war, the U.S. State Department openly backed the American oil company Unocal in its plans to build an oil and gas pipeline from Turkmenistan across Taliban-controlled southern Afghanistan to Pakistan. Unocal began to provide humanitarian aid to the Taliban, while inviting Taliban delegations to the United States. The Americans believed, rather naïvely, that a pipeline would bring peace between the warring factions.[6] U.S. policy regarding the Taliban shifted only in 1996, after the capture of Kabul, when the U.S. media focused on the Taliban's brutal policies toward women, and Osama bin Laden arrived in the country.

The Clinton administration stopped well short of creating a strategic policy toward the region even when Taliban leader Mullah Omar invited bin Laden to live with him in Kandahar in the autumn of 1996. The CIA already considered bin Laden a threat, but he was left alone to ingratiate himself with Mullah Omar by providing money, fighters, and ideological advice to the Taliban. Bin Laden gathered the Arabs left behind in Afghanistan and Pakistan from the war against the Soviets, enlisted more militants from Arab countries, and established a new global terrorist infrastructure called al Qaeda.

The Taliban handed over to al Qaeda the running of the training camps in eastern Afghanistan that the ISI and Pakistani extremists had earlier run for Kashmiri insurgents. Bin Laden now gained control over all extremist groups who wanted or needed to train in Afghanistan. In return, he began to fund some of Mullah Omar's pet projects, such as building a grand mosque in Kandahar and constructing key roads. Until then, the Taliban had not considered America an enemy and showed little understanding of world affairs. But now Taliban leaders began to imbibe the ideas of global jihad.

In his strategic alliance with the Taliban, bin Laden received an entire country as a base of operations. He was able to gather around him thousands of Islamic extremists and extend his operations around the world. His main logistical support came from Pakistani extremist groups, who could provide the kinds of supplies and means of communication with the outside world not available in Afghanistan. This support base in Pakistan was to prove critical to al Qaeda's survival after 9/11. Between 1996 and 2001, al Qaeda trained an estimated thirty thousand militants from around the world.

From their separate perches, Masud and Karzai were the first to see the inherent dangers for the world in allowing al Qaeda control of Afghanistan, and both men repeatedly warned Western governments of this, especially the Americans. But nobody was listening. Less than two years after moving to Kandahar, bin Laden launched his first major attack on U.S. targets: the bombings of the U.S. embassies in Kenya and Tanzania, on August 7, 1998, which killed 224 people and wounded nearly 5,000. Each terrorist attack was to spur the Taliban on to greater conquests. A day after the bombings, the Taliban captured Mazar-e-Sharif and much of northern Afghanistan, massacring more than four thousand Hazaras, Tajiks, and Uzbeks. A few days later, when President Clinton retaliated by launching seventy-five cruise missiles on training camps in eastern Afghanistan, al Qaeda members had already fled. Some twenty-one people, mostly Pakistani militants and several ISI trainers, were killed.

The near-useless U.S. retaliation was only to further embolden al Qaeda and convince an already paranoid Mullah Omar that the Americans were scared of the Taliban. Washington now stepped up diplomatic pressure on the Taliban to hand over bin Laden. In their meetings with the Taliban, U.S. officials tried to drive a wedge between the Taliban and al Qaeda and to persuade Pakistan to do the same—but nothing seemed to work. The Taliban were promised everything, including at times formal U.S. recognition, if they handed over bin Laden. Meanwhile, Karzai, Masud, and other Afghans were openly critical of an American policy that offered no support to the anti-Taliban resistance, left the Taliban in place, and put no real pressure on the Taliban's main sponsors, Pakistan and Saudi Arabia.

Karzai joined his father around 1994 in Quetta, where both men ruefully watched as their country was taken over by al Qaeda. They understood that the key to saving Afghanistan was to undermine the Taliban's grip in the Pashtun belt. At clandestine meetings in Quetta, the younger Karzai began to build an underground opposition among his own tribe and elders from other tribes. The Taliban swiftly reacted. In 1999, assassins shot dead Abdul Ahad Karzai in broad daylight as he came out of a Quetta mosque—a move that created revulsion among the Popalzai and other Pashtun tribes. Hamid Karzai was both shattered and energized by his father's assassination. He took a daring step. Assembling a three-hundred-vehicle convoy of family members, mourners, and tribal chiefs in exile, he defied Pakistani and Taliban authorities and drove with his father's body from Quetta to the family graveyard outside Kandahar. The Taliban scowled but dared not intervene, fearing that an all-out civil war could erupt.

This single act of defiance redefined Hamid Karzai as a brave leader, equal to any in Afghanistan. The Popalzai tribal council chose him as their tribe's new chief, even though he had several older brothers living in the United States. Mullah Omar, however, was furious with Karzai and began to plot his assassination.

In 2000 the clear indications that the Taliban and al Qaeda were partners in creating an international army for terrorism based in Afghanistan were still receiving little attention abroad. I wrote about this alliance in *Foreign Affairs* magazine and spoke about it in forums in Washington, but there was no visible change in U.S. policy.[7] Al Qaeda now organized Arab and North African fighters into a special unit called Brigade 555, which backed the Taliban army in some of its bloodiest offensives against the Northern Alliance. Al Qaeda enlisted other extremist groups to fight on its behalf, such as the Islamic Movement of Uzbekistan (IMU), Chechen fighters from the breakaway republic of Chechnya, and Uighur Muslims from China's eastern province of Xinjiang. Meanwhile, al Qaeda training camps were churning out thousands of terrorists from around the world, many of whom remained behind in Afghanistan.

Foreign fighters made a huge difference on the battlefield. In September 2000, when the Taliban finally captured Masud's stronghold of Taloqan, in northern Afghanistan—after thirty-three days of heavy fighting and a siege in which some seven hundred of Masud's men were killed and thirteen hundred wounded—more than one third of the fifteen-thousand-strong Taliban force besieging Taloqan was made up of non-Afghans. These included three thousand Pakistanis, one thousand fighters from the IMU, and hundreds of Arabs, Kashmiris, Chechens, Filipinos, and Chinese Muslims. The ISI provided more than one hundred Pakistanis from the Frontier Corps to manage artillery and communications. Pakistani officers were directing the Taliban campaign in league with al Qaeda and the Taliban, and for the first time people in the United States and Europe began to take notice.[8]

Al Qaeda struck again on October 12, 2000, attempting to sink the

American destroyer USS *Cole* while it was taking on fuel in Aden's harbor. A tiny skiff packed with explosives piloted by three suicide bombers rammed into the *Cole,* killing seventeen U.S. sailors and wounding thirty-nine others. The Clinton administration never blamed bin Laden directly for the attack, although officials in Washington later told me they had determined that al Qaeda was responsible. The simple fact was that Washington had few viable options for retaliation after the firing of cruise missiles on training camps had proved to be such a dismal failure.[9]

Instead, the United States tried to mobilize the international community through a series of UN resolutions, although these meant little to the Taliban. In October 1999, the UN Security Council passed Resolution 1267, demanding that the Taliban hand over Osama bin Laden and stop providing sanctuary to terrorists. The Taliban ignored the request. In December 2000, UN Resolution 1333 imposed a complete arms ban on the Taliban and closing of training camps, as well as a seizure of Taliban assets outside Afghanistan. The resolution was aimed at stopping Pakistan's arms support to the Taliban. The Taliban reacted angrily, while Pakistan's ISI put together the "Afghan Defense Council," made up of forty Pakistani Islamic political parties, designed to resist UN pressure and register support for the Taliban. On July 30, 2001, as Islamabad continued to supply arms to the Taliban, the Security Council passed Resolution 1363, which authorized monitors on Afghanistan's borders to ensure that the UN arms embargo was enforced. The Taliban and their Pakistani supporters said they would kill any UN monitors who arrived.

Increasingly isolated and reviled by the international community, the Taliban became more confrontational. At the encouragement of bin Laden, Mullah Omar ordered his troops to destroy the two giant eighteen-hundred-year-old-statues of Buddha that dominated the Bamiyan Valley, homeland to the Shia Hazaras. Despite international condemnation and demonstrations by Buddhists around the world, on March 10, 2001, the statues were blown up. The Taliban also escalated tensions with the UN and aid agencies, passing new laws that made it virtually impossible for such agencies to continue providing relief to the Afghan population. The Taliban shut down Western-run hospitals, refused to cooperate with a UN-led polio immunization campaign for children, and imposed even more restrictions on female aid workers, such as preventing them from driving cars. The Taliban arrested eight Westerners and sixteen Afghans belonging to a German aid agency and accused them of trying to promote Christianity, a charge punishable by death.

Osama bin Laden had a clear strategy in mind: to isolate the Taliban from the outside world so that it would become even more dependent on al Qaeda. The Taliban leadership would then have no choice but to defend al Qaeda when greater U.S. pressure was exerted once the attacks on American soil had taken place. Bin Laden wanted the Taliban to take over the country and so offered to assassinate Masud, which was certain to lead to the defeat of the weakened Northern Alliance.

By now Afghanistan was not just a security threat; it was the world's worst humanitarian disaster zone. A countrywide drought had entered its fourth year, destroying 70 percent of the country's livestock and making 50 percent of the land uncultivable. The drought forced millions of people into the cities, where aid agencies were overwhelmed. In June 2001, the UN warned of mass starvation in Afghanistan. There were now 3.6 million Afghan refugees outside the country, constituting the largest refugee population in the world, while another 800,000 Afghans were internally displaced. The economic crisis was aggravated by the Taliban's single success: the elimination of the poppy crop, from which opium and heroin is derived. Mullah Omar had banned poppy cultivation in July 2000, a ban that was rigorously enforced the following year, depriving farmers of their livelihoods. Meanwhile, UN agencies were too slow in providing funding for alternative crops or livelihoods.

Throughout 2001, Hamid Karzai held a series of meetings with other Afghan opposition leaders willing to join a revolt against the Taliban. He met with Abdul Haq, a prominent Pashtun commander from the Jalalabad region in eastern Afghanistan whose wife and daughter had been murdered by the Taliban in Peshawar. (Abdul Haq was to be killed by the Taliban when he entered Afghanistan after 9/11.) Karzai also met with Gulbuddin Hikmetyar at his base in Meshad, Iran, simply because Hikmetyar claimed to be opposed to the Taliban. His most significant meeting, however, was with Masud in Dushanbe, the capital of Tajikistan. Masud offered Karzai the choice of either joining him and the NA in the north or accepting weapons and ammunition if Karzai planned to take independent action in the south.

As international pressure against the Taliban mounted, other exiled Afghan leaders decided to return home and take up arms against the

Taliban. General Dostum, Ismael Khan, and the Hazara leaders all returned to Afghanistan and resumed fighting. All of them nominally joined the Northern Alliance and accepted Masud as their leader. Iran, Russia, and India, which had traditionally funded and armed the Northern Alliance, stepped up their military support, although Masud still had to buy most arms with the cash he earned from the gems and drug trade. Tajikistan had allowed Masud to use air bases in the country for his helicopters, while India opened a frontline emergency hospital for his wounded NA fighters in southern Tajikistan.

Compared to a year earlier, the Northern Alliance dramatically improved its situation in 2001, with several new fronts opened against the Taliban and renewed supplies of weapons. It also came to an agreement with Zahir Shah to forge a common front against the Taliban. The former king's efforts were now being supported by all Afghans opposed to the Taliban. There was agreement on convening an emergency Loya Jirga, or traditional tribal gathering, to elect a new government for Afghanistan.

Yet while neighboring countries were prepared to back their proxies to return to Afghanistan and take up arms against the Taliban, U.S. support for the Northern Alliance was still only lukewarm. As we see in later chapters, although several advocates within the Clinton and Bush administrations wanted U.S. arms to flow to the Northern Alliance, the State Department disliked Masud intensely because of his association with Iran and Russia. U.S. officials also feared U.S. involvement in an arms race in Afghanistan, as this would put Washington at odds with Islamabad's and Riyadh's support for the Taliban. In August 2001, Hamid Karzai, along with two other prominent Pashtun émigrés, Abdul Haq and Gen. Rahim Wardak (who was to become Afghan defense minister in 2004), went to London to meet with British officials. Karzai's message was simple: Osama bin Laden was making key decisions for the Taliban, and al Qaeda was fully embedded in the Taliban government. MI6, British intelligence, was keen to foment unrest in the Pashtun belt, but it remained skeptical of the capacity of these three visitors to do so.

Karzai had made several trips to Washington and was angered by the simpleminded and one-directional questions of American officials and lawmakers, who asked if he could capture bin Laden. Karzai, for his part, wanted to discuss the overthrow of the Taliban. Meanwhile, Masud, in the summer of 2001, made his first trip to Europe to address the European

Parliament, and there were plans to invite him to speak at the opening of the UN General Assembly in New York that September.

In my last meeting with Masud a few months before he was killed, he had visibly aged. He was dressed in slacks, his much-used battle jacket, a beret, and army boots—even though we were seated in a house in downtown Dushanbe. His beard was now gray, and he was much slower in his actions than before. His intellectual inquisitiveness, however, had not dimmed. He was deeply angry with Pakistan—asking me repeatedly why Pervez Musharraf was pursuing what Masud described as "a suicidal policy of supporting the terrorists"—and even angrier with the United States and the international community for not stopping Pakistan's support to the Taliban.[10] He described to me how CIA agents had visited him in his Panjsher Valley stronghold and asked for his help in getting bin Laden, but he scoffed at them when they told him they were unable to offer him support or arms.[11]

It was clear to me that Masud was making a momentous transition from being a parochial local leader, often intolerant and sometimes ruthless, to becoming the most important national leader in the country. He had patched up things with the Uzbek and Hazara leaders, had met with Pashtun leaders whom he had distrusted in the past, and had compromised with Zahir Shah, whom he had disliked all of his adult life. He had also dropped his Muslim Brotherhood sympathies and become an Afghan nationalist, ready to embrace anyone who opposed the Taliban. He had, in short, developed a vision for a future Afghanistan at peace.

He was never to see that vision. At noon on Sunday, September 9, Masud was at his base in Khoja Bahauddin, in northern Afghanistan, when he granted an interview to two Tunisian television journalists carrying Belgian passports who had been pursuing him along the battlefront for several weeks. Masud's oldest friend, Masud Khalili, the NA ambassador to India, was with him and advised him not to give the interview. Masud insisted, and the two men were shown in. They set up a camera on a tripod close to Masud. When it was switched on, the bomb inside it, and possibly a second device around the cameraman's waist, exploded. Masud took the brunt of the blast and was fatally wounded. Khalili was badly wounded but survived. Asim Suhail, a young member of Masud's team, was also killed, along with the cameraman, whose body was split in two from the waist. The second Tunisian walked out calmly past the guards but was caught in the street, arrested, and then escaped again before being shot by pursuing guards on the banks of the Panj River.

Masud was dead, but the fiction that he was still alive was maintained for several days so that NA morale would not collapse in the face of what was now feared—a massive Taliban and al Qaeda offensive. "The days after Masud's death were the closest we ever came to a total debacle and defeat because morale had just plummeted and we were leaderless—everyone knew that Masud had died," Dr. Abdullah Abdullah, Afghanistan's first foreign minister after 9/11, told me in Kabul in December 2001 as he sat on Masud's chair and wept throughout our long late-night conversation.

A week later, Masud was buried near his village of Jangalak, in the Panjsher Valley, on a hilltop with a magnificent view. His twelve-year-old son, Ahmad, and his successor, Gen. Mohammed Fahim, officiated. Some twenty-five thousand people—family, friends, soldiers, diplomats, and journalists—were mourning as one. At Masud's new home, which he had designed and moved into only three weeks earlier, his wife, Parigul, and their five daughters, aged three to ten, grieved, surrounded by the women of the valley. It was the largest and most heartrending outpouring of grief for a commander that Afghanistan had witnessed in its twenty-five years of war.[12]

The murder plot had been meticulously planned by al Qaeda. The two assassins had been able to carry a bomb from Pakistan to Kabul and then across Afghanistan to explode in Masud's face. If the attack had taken place a few weeks earlier, as planned, and the Northern Alliance had been destroyed by the Taliban offensive, the Americans would have had no allies on the ground after 9/11 took place. For the first time in more than a decade, the trajectory of Afghanistan's sad, desperate history was to cross paths with a major international event, and Masud was not alive to take advantage of it. If he had lived, there is little doubt that many of the early difficulties faced by the Afghan interim government and the international community would have been mitigated.

Karzai was grief-stricken at Masud's death, but he now knew he had to defy the ISI request that he leave Pakistan for Europe and instead enter Afghanistan to foment a revolt among the Pashtuns.

Karzai was in Islamabad walking on the Margalla Hills on the evening of September 11, when the first plane crashed into the World Trade Center. His younger brother Ahmed Wali Karzai called him from Quetta and told him to return to the guesthouse to watch TV. I spoke to Karzai several times that evening. We both knew that the attack had been the work of al Qaeda, and I joked to Karzai that I did not think Musharraf would be able to throw him out now.

Over the next few days, Karzai met with diplomats from all the major Western embassies, hinting strongly that he was preparing to go into Afghanistan. He was offered little immediate support—except from the British, in the form of a satellite phone, which he declined to accept. When he returned to Quetta, his house was crowded with tribal elders wanting to know his plans. The ISI sent around two officers also to try to discover his intentions. The latter were politely asked to leave without being offered even a cup of tea—a sure insult. Karzai told only a handful of people of his plans, his wife, Zeenat, and his brother Ahmed Wali among them.[13] A few days later he asked Ahmed Wali to get a hold of some money because he had no funds. Then, packing an old satellite phone, whose number he gave to the Americans and British, he got onto a motorbike and, with a few friends, headed into Afghanistan.

• • •

CHAPTER TWO

"The U.S. Will Act Like
a Wounded Bear"

Pakistan's Long Search for Its Soul

On the morning of September 11, 2001, Gen. Mehmood Ahmad, director-general of Pakistan's clandestine military intelligence service, the Inter-Services Intelligence Directorate (ISI), was on Capitol Hill meeting with Porter Goss, chairman of the Senate Intelligence Committee, and other lawmakers, explaining all that Pakistan was doing to persuade the Taliban to hand over Osama bin Laden to the Americans. With his handlebar moustache, piercing eyes, and ramrod-straight figure, the general seemed to be a throwback to a whiskey-drinking officer from the British Raj. As one of the three generals who had played a critical role in the 1999 coup that toppled Nawaz Sharif and put Pervez Musharraf in control, Mehmood was both powerful and influential in the Pakistani army. As head of the ISI, he was now virtually running the country's foreign policy. Since the coup, Mehmood had also experienced an epiphany that had turned him into a born-again Islamic fundamentalist. Within the military junta, he was now one of the most vociferous supporters of the Taliban and the Islamic militant groups fighting in Kashmir.

In Washington, Mehmood was a guest of CIA director George Tenet, who had secretly visited Islamabad that summer to urge Mehmood to put more pressure on the Taliban to hand over bin Laden. Now Mehmood was doing the rounds in Washington, trying to convince the State and Defense departments and U.S. lawmakers of the sincerity of Pakistan's efforts on the bin Laden front. The Pakistanis were well aware that the Bush administration was conducting a major policy review on al Qaeda and Afghanistan. They also knew that the most difficult question under review for the

Bush administration, as it had been for President Clinton, was how the United States would deal with Pakistan. The current regime—with its unabashed military and financial support for the Taliban, its links to a network of Islamic extremist groups and madrassas (religious schools), which were churning out fighters for Kashmir and Afghanistan, and its public support for jihad as a legitimate foreign policy—was viewed with enormous suspicion by the international community. In January 2001, the UN Security Council had imposed sanctions on the Taliban regime that were directly aimed at stopping Pakistan's weapons supplies to the Taliban.

The Pakistani military considered its support to the Taliban as part of the country's strategic national interest. Since the Soviet withdrawal from Afghanistan in 1989, the ISI had tried to bring its various Afghan proxies to power in Kabul in the search for a friendly Afghan government that would keep rival India out of Afghanistan. The Taliban had provided just such a government, even if their extremism was now an embarrassment. Pakistan also felt the need to support the Afghan Pashtuns because of the large Pashtun population in Pakistan and because the non-Pashtuns had sought support from Pakistan's rivals—India, Iran, and Russia. The Pakistani military also determined that a friendly government in Afghanistan would provide Pakistan with "strategic depth" in any future conflict with India—a theory that had been convincingly dismissed by Pakistani civilian strategic thinkers but which the military continued to espouse—refusing to acknowledge the destabilizing fallout from the Taliban inside Pakistan: the growth of extremism and sectarianism.

Moreover, in its support of the Taliban, Pakistan was indirectly strengthening al Qaeda in Afghanistan. Pakistani militants were providing manpower for both the Taliban and al Qaeda and running a vast logistics, communication, and transit network in Pakistan on behalf of al Qaeda. Most of the thirty thousand foreign militants trained at al Qaeda camps had traveled to Afghanistan and returned home with the help of this network. No U.S. plan to capture bin Laden could work without Pakistani cooperation and a reversal of Islamabad's foreign policy. However, Mehmood was telling Goss—who in 2004 would head the CIA for a disastrously short spell—that any CIA-ISI cooperation would depend on a more positive U.S. attitude toward Pakistan.

Mehmood had been in Washington before, as had other ISI officers who continued to insist that the Americans misunderstood the Taliban.[1] He knew that his American interlocutors remained deeply skeptical of what they had heard so far, and his visit was critical to ensuring that the Bush policy review on al Qaeda and Afghanistan not blame Pakistan. The Pakistanis were hopeful. The State Department had signaled that it wanted to engage with Pakistan rather than isolate it. While the Clinton administration had taken a tough, uncompromising line with Islamabad, and slapped more sanctions on the military regime while befriending rival India, the Bush administration seemed much more encouraging.

Mehmood had little new to offer. The ISI's bottom line was that unless the United States lifted the multiple sanctions on Pakistan and improved relations, Pakistan would neither turn on the Taliban nor provide the intelligence or military support needed to snatch bin Laden. "If you need our help you need to address our problems and lift U.S. sanctions," Mehmood said.[2]

Mehmood's analysis only further obscured the reality on the ground. The Taliban's response to greater international isolation was to become more extreme and threatening. Such extremist policies were openly encouraged by al Qaeda, who wished to make the Taliban leadership more dependent on them. Meanwhile, the ISI continued to pump money, arms, and advisers into Afghanistan to help the Taliban achieve victory over the Northern Alliance, even though the ISI's influence over the Taliban leadership was waning. The ISI had proved powerless in persuading Mullah Omar to stop the destruction of the Bamiyan Buddhas or save the UN agencies on the ground in Afghanistan from humiliation.[3] It was absurd for Mehmood to insist now that the Americans engage with the Taliban when Islamabad's own influence over them was declining and al Qaeda's was increasing.

As the breakfast meeting between Goss and Mehmood wore on, Zamir Akram, an accompanying Pakistani diplomat, left the room for a break. Outside in the hallway, a group of congressional aides were gathered around a TV set. As Akram walked up to them, he saw the second plane scream into the World Trade Center. He ran back to the meeting even as a congressional aide bounded in to tell those assembled that Capitol Hill was being evacuated. "There is a plane heading this way," the aide said.

General Mehmood, Ambassador Maleeha Lodhi, and Zamir Akram left the building as the town was overtaken by sirens, rushing people, panic, and smoke rising from the Pentagon across the Potomac. Accompanied by a CIA escort car, their vehicle took three hours to travel the handful of blocks back to the Pakistan embassy in the gridlocked Washington traffic. Mehmood and the ambassador assumed the worst—that al Qaeda had perpetrated the attacks—and now they concentrated on the implications of this for Pakistan. Along with everyone else around the world, they spent the rest of the day watching television. Lodhi had served before in Washington, as the ambassador in the early 1990s. A polished, highly educated former newspaper editor who was close to the military, she had been reappointed to Washington by Musharraf after the 1999 coup to improve relations with the United States, a task she had found difficult as the bin Laden issue loomed over every attempt she made to better relations. For some months now, she and other liberal Pakistani ambassadors had been arguing with the military for a change of policy on the Taliban. Now she knew that everything would change.

The next morning, September 12, Deputy Secretary of State Richard Armitage summoned Mehmood and Lodhi to his office. Armitage was direct but polite, saying he had just come from a cabinet meeting with President Bush, who was about to make a TV address. In that address he would deliver a blunt message to the world, saying, "Either you are with us or you are with the terrorists." Armitage then asked, "Where would Pakistan stand?" Mehmood replied without hesitation that "we have always been with you," but it was the United States that had always let Pakistan down. Armitage cut him short: "The past is the past. Let's discuss the future." The deputy secretary of state said he would soon have a list of what the United States wanted from Pakistan. Mehmood made an unequivocal commitment that Pakistan would stand by the United States.[4]

Musharraf heard about the attack on the Twin Towers while attending a military briefing in Karachi. He immediately ordered a meeting of his generals and a few key civilian cabinet ministers when he returned to Islamabad the next evening, on September 12. The meeting took place in a secure bunker—the Operations Room of the Pakistani Joint Chiefs of Staff headquarters in Chaklala, a suburb of Rawalpindi, where the army's general headquarters (GHQ) were located. The bunker's walls were covered with maps of the region. The map of Afghanistan showed the areas under Taliban control. Musharraf's first words were ominous: "The U.S. will react like a wounded bear and it will attack Afghanistan," he said. He told those assembled that Pakistan could not oppose American demands and could no longer support the Taliban, but it would not take part in any U.S. attack on Afghanistan. Bush had already said that the United States would punish not just the perpetrators of the attack but also any states that harbored terrorists.

Musharraf asked for other views, but there was no disagreement. "We agreed that we would unequivocally accept all U.S. demands, but then later we would express our private reservations to the U.S. and we would not necessarily agree with all the details," said Abdul Sattar, who as foreign minister attended the meeting.[5] That night the policy that Pakistan would adopt toward Washington was summed up in the phrase "First say yes and later say but . . ." It was a policy Musharraf was to follow consistently for the next few years.

On September 13, Armitage handed Mehmood a one-page list of seven U.S. demands. Pakistan was asked to agree to blanket overflights of its territory and landing rights for all U.S. aircraft; give the United States access to naval bases, airports, and borders for operations against al Qaeda; provide immediate intelligence sharing and cooperation; stop al Qaeda operatives on the Pakistan-Afghanistan border and intercept all arms shipments through Pakistan while ending all logistical support for bin Laden; cut all shipments of fuel to the Taliban and stop Pakistani fighters from joining the Taliban; publicly condemn the terrorist acts; and end support for the Taliban, breaking diplomatic relations with them.[6] Armitage said the demands were nonnegotiable. Mehmood promptly replied that Pakistan would do whatever the Americans asked of it. Secretary of State Colin Powell spoke to Musharraf by telephone, telling him that although the United States did not have a war plan yet, he expected an early reply on the U.S. demands. That same day, a cabinet meeting in Washington concluded that if Pakistan did not help the United States, "it would be at risk of attack."[7]

The next day Musharraf summoned his nine corps commanders based around the country and a dozen staff officers to discuss the U.S. ultimatum. The corps commanders were the real kitchen cabinet of the army and the regime. Each general commanded around sixty thousand troops, and Musharraf could not be assured of the army's support without first winning over these men. Musharraf told them Pakistan had no choice but to accept the demands or face being declared a terrorist state by the United States. Several generals protested. Many Pakistanis considered Musharraf a prisoner of three hard-line generals who had carried out the 1999 coup. These were Mehmood Ahmad, who at the time of the coup was the corps commander of the Rawalpindi garrison and was now ISI chief; Lt.-Gen.

Mohammed Aziz, a former director of the ISI who had been chief of general staff during the coup—an invaluable position for getting commanders around the country to support the takeover—and was now the Lahore corps commander; and Lt.-Gen. Muzaffar Usmani, who had been corps commander in Karachi at the time of the coup and was now deputy chief of army staff.

All three men were considered ardent supporters of the Islamic fundamentalist parties, the Taliban, and Kashmiri militants. Aziz, born a Kashmiri, was immensely popular among Islamist officers in the army and the leaders of the Islamic parties. As director of covert operations in the ISI in the late 1990s, he had been the principal organizer behind the Taliban's spate of victories against the Northern Alliance and had run the covert Kashmir insurgency programs. Even though he was now corps commander in Lahore, he continued to travel frequently to Peshawar to monitor ISI's covert support to the Taliban, which was run out of the Peshawar corps headquarters. The three generals raised serious objections to the U.S. demands, pointing out that Pakistan was getting nothing in return, and that there would be a dangerous domestic fallout from their dumping the Taliban, an act that would send a negative message to the Kashmiris.[8] They thought saying yes to the Americans on all counts would not allow Pakistan any future leverage over the United States. The officers knew they were discussing the most historic policy decisions Pakistan had ever had to face.

The meeting lasted an excruciating seven hours—the longest Musharraf had ever convened with his generals. He finally clinched their acceptance by playing a vital card, one he knew they could not oppose. If Pakistan only partially accepted U.S. demands, Musharraf told his generals, India would immediately step into the vacuum and offer bases and support to the United States. India had spent the past five years trying to persuade the Americans to declare Pakistan a state sponsor of terrorism because of its support to Kashmiri militants. Pakistan could be faced with a hostile India allied to the U.S. military, while hostile U.S. forces in Afghanistan could target Pakistan's nuclear weapons under the guise of preventing them from falling into the hands of Islamic extremists.

Musharraf used words similar to those he later used publicly: "We were on the borderline of being or not being declared a terrorist state—in that situation, what would have happened to the Kashmir cause?"[9] Pakistan would lose on all fronts, and its very existence would be threatened. The three generals were silenced. "Musharraf came out of that meeting exhausted and angry, convinced that he would have to replace the three generals who had raised the objections," a senior military adviser to Musharraf later recalled. Late that night Musharraf summoned Wendy Chamberlain, the U.S. ambassador to Pakistan, and told her he accepted all the U.S. demands. He then telephoned Colin Powell and warned him that the domestic fallout from his decision could be unpredictable, and he expected the United States to be patient and understanding. Chamberlain cabled Washington that "to counterbalance" acceptance of the U.S. demands, Musharraf "needed to show that Pakistan was benefiting from his decision"—a strong hint that Pakistan needed immediate economic relief and an end to sanctions.[10]

Powell later recalled the sequence of events: "Three days later [after 9/11] I called President Musharraf after we had suggested to him it was time to make a strategic decision to move away from that and we gave him some things we hoped he would do. . . . And he reversed the direction in which Pakistan was moving."[11] Getting Pakistan on board so swiftly was an enormous success for Powell and Armitage. Bush later said it was the most important thing Powell did after 9/11. "He single-handedly got Musharraf on board."[12]

Mehmood, stranded in Washington because of the shutdown of all air traffic over the United States, spent the next few days at CIA headquarters, in Langley, Virginia, discussing the details. He persuaded Tenet not to insist on Pakistan's breaking diplomatic relations with the Taliban until the ISI could have one last chance at persuading them to hand over bin Laden, and he pleaded that the CIA not depend solely on the Northern Alliance for its war plans, which would alienate the Pashtun population in the south. He also asked that U.S. forces not use Indian military bases. "The ISI was keen to help shape the U.S. war plan, so that the fallout on Pakistan itself would be minimum and not provoke a domestic crisis," said a Pakistani diplomat then based in Washington.

The 9/11 attacks had shocked most Pakistanis, although there was satisfaction among some Islamists that the Americans had gotten what they deserved. People were glued to their TV sets for days, and as the American pressure became apparent, the country became deeply polarized. Islamic parties and their supporters among the elite denounced the United States for blaming al Qaeda without any evidence and insisted that there was an "Israeli-U.S.-Indian" plot to defame Pakistan and the Taliban. Unwilling to accept that Muslims could have been responsible for such carnage, they railed against President Bush for launching a campaign against Islam. The more outrageous the stories and rumors in the Urdu-language media— such as the claims that no Jews had been killed in the Twin Towers or that four thousand Jews did not go to work that day because Israel had warned them not to—the more certain many people became of American perfidy.[13]

The majority of the urban and educated population, however, hoped for a kind of salvation, convinced that the military regime now had an opportunity to crack down on the Taliban, Islamic extremists, and the gangs carrying out Sunni-Shia sectarian killings inside Pakistan. The country could end its pariah status and reenter the international market, which would lead to foreign investment, jobs, and economic revival. When the terrorists struck, Pakistan was facing its fourth year of a severe recession— in 2000 the growth rate was just 2.6 percent, down substantially from the average 6.0 percent growth it had experienced in the 1980s and '90s. Momentarily, 9/11 had led to a crash in business confidence. Pakistan's three stock exchanges were shut down for five successive days, after hemorrhaging massive losses in the first three days after the 9/11 attacks. The Karachi stock exchange, the largest in the country, lost 9.5 percent of its total value.

Musharraf now asked the United States for urgent economic support. As a result of its nuclear program and the military coup, Pakistan faced three layers of U.S. sanctions dating back to 1990. All of them had to be removed by the U.S. Congress before aid could flow.[14] The Pakistani government put in a request to Washington for the removal of all U.S. sanctions, forgiveness of its $3 billion debt to the United States—just a fraction of Pakistan's $32 billion total foreign debt—the resumption of military supplies, and quick disbursement of loans from the United States and the World Bank. Bush responded swiftly, lifting all U.S. sanctions and allowing aid to flow.

When Musharraf addressed the nation on television on September 19, he said the decision to side with the United States was in line with the wishes of the international community and the Islamic world, but also in defense of Pakistan's national interests. "Pakistan comes first, and everything else is secondary," he said. "Where national interests are at stake, the decision should be taken with wisdom and sagacity . . . it was not a question of cowardice or bravery." A wrong decision could spell disaster for the country's existence, he said, jeopardize the Kashmir cause, and endanger Pakistan's nuclear installations. If Pakistan had refused the U.S. demands, India would "want to enter into an alliance with the U.S. and get Pakistan declared a terrorist state."[15]

He said he now had leverage with the Americans and would try to persuade Mullah Omar to hand over bin Laden "without any damage to Afghanistan and the Taliban." At no point in his speech did Musharraf condemn the Taliban or al Qaeda or blame them for the 9/11 attacks—a clear refusal to accede to one of Washington's demands. And by claiming to have saved Pakistan's Kashmir policy from U.S. interference, he signaled to the fundamentalists that the insurgency in Kashmir would continue. The military had wrongly surmised that the "global war on terrorism" would not include U.S. pressure to clamp down on militants in Kashmir. The army's faulty conclusions would have profound implications for Pakistan in the months ahead. The next day (September 20), Bush addressed the U.S. Congress and sent an uncompromising message: "Every nation, in every region, now has a decision to make. Either you are with us, or you are with the terrorists. From this day forward, any nation that continues to harbor or support terrorism will be regarded by the United States as a hostile regime."[16]

From Washington's perspective, Pakistan had over the years become intractable and unstable, settling into a permanent state of political crisis—a nation on the verge of becoming a failed state. Its long-running conflict with India was destabilizing the region, and since both countries had become nuclear powers in 1998, the problems Pakistan posed had only been magnified. Since 1999, when Musharraf as army chief had ordered Pakistani troops into Indian Kashmir, nearly provoking a nuclear conflict, he was viewed in the West as rash, unpredictable, and easily manipulated by extremist generals. The army's support for the Taliban had turned Pakistan into an international pariah.

The Americans distrusted the ISI, which was known to be riddled with Islamic extremists who supported the Taliban and had shown a tolerance toward al Qaeda. The CIA was apprehensive about placing so much of the intelligence-gathering burden for the upcoming war on such an unreliable agency. But there was little choice, as Pakistan had the longest border with Afghanistan and was the only country that could provide intelligence about the Taliban's military preparedness and targets for U.S. bombing. The ISI hoped that by initially complying with U.S. demands, it could create sufficient room to maneuver in order to circumvent those very demands. The ISI had no intention of dumping the Kashmiri militants and their struggle against India.

Many skeptical Pakistanis opposed to military rule were experiencing déjà vu. In 1977, when Gen. Muhammed Zia ul-Haq seized power, Pakistan became a pariah state. Yet in 1979, after the Soviets entered Afghanistan, Zia became a major U.S. ally by agreeing to confront Soviet expansionism. His military regime was to survive for eleven long years. Once again, it appeared that Afghanistan had come to the rescue of another beleaguered military regime. Yet most Pakistanis still hoped that 9/11 would provide the opportunity for the military to cut its ties with Islamic fundamentalism and set the country on the path toward democracy.

For the first twenty-four years of Pakistan's existence, its military, bureaucratic, and political elite carried out ruinous policies at home, alienating both the ethnic and religious minorities and the ethnic majority, sparking the 1971 uprising in East Pakistan, defeat at the hands of India, and the secession of half the country. The creation of Bangladesh was the most traumatic event in the country's history. For the next thirty-five years, that same elite, now dominated by the military and often in alliance with the United States, nurtured Islamic extremists, which helped prepare the ground for 9/11. At the height of the cold war, the United States poured billions of dollars into arming anyone who would oppose the Soviets, including Islamic extremists in Afghanistan, Pakistan, and Central Asia.

Since its birth in August 1947, when India was partitioned and Muslim-majority provinces were joined by a hastily retreating British empire to create a new country, Pakistan has grappled with an acute sense of insecurity in the midst of a continuing identity crisis. As a result, it has developed into a national security state in which the army has monopolized power and defined the national interest as keeping archenemy India at bay, developing nuclear weapons, and trying to create a friendly government in Afghanistan. The development of political institutions, a constitution, democracy, and a prospering economy—the true indicators of national security—have been considered secondary. Two relationships have dominated the politics of the country: that between military power and civil society and the one between Islam and the state.

Pakistan's insecurity is partly a legacy of two centuries of British rule in India. The region that makes up Pakistan today was conquered by the

British in the mid-nineteenth century, at least one hundred years after the British conquests of Bengal and central India. Sindh was conquered in 1843 and Punjab six years later. The British conquest of northwest India was aimed solely at providing security from marauding Afghan, Baloch, and Pashtun tribes and later by the fear of tsarist Russia expanding into Central Asia and interfering in India through Afghanistan. After two wars in Afghanistan (1839–1842 and 1878–1881), the British needed secure lines of communications and so turned northwest India into a garrison colony ruled from Lahore, the capital of Punjab province. More than half the British army garrison in India was to be based along the Balochistan–North-West Frontier Province (NWFP) border with Afghanistan.[17]

In Punjab, the British used both patronage and repression, allying themselves with a landowning feudal class, for whom it built a lavish canal irrigation system, and recruiting large numbers of the Punjabi peasantry for the army. Pakistan inherited this security state, which has been variously described by scholars as "the viceregal tradition" or "a permanent state of martial law."[18]

Pakistan's identity crisis is rooted in the fears, insecurity, and contradictions inherent in Muslims living during the Raj, Muslims who had once ruled India and now lived in a Westernized colonial state after they had been heavily defeated—most recently in the 1857 uprising. Modern Muslim reformists and elitist landlords saw a majority Hindu population favored by the British and so began to consider themselves as a separate "nation" from Hindu India. This "two-nation theory," which was to form the basis for the Pakistan movement, disregarded ethnic and linguistic differences and considered a separate religious identity sufficient to create a nation. Yet adherents had no support from the ulema, or religious leaders, who saw Indian Muslims as inextricably linked to the ummah, or the global community of Muslim believers, whose leadership still lay with the defunct Ottoman Empire. The ulema did not consider a new nation-state for Muslims as being valid, although they were to change their minds after Partition. This identity crisis became even more complicated when the Muslim League, founded in 1906 and led by Pakistan's founder, Mohammed Ali Jinnah, drew its main support from Muslims in central and eastern India rather than the western regions that were to become the future Pakistan.

The League made its demand for an independent Muslim state in Lahore on March 23, 1940, at its annual general meeting, when it passed the Pakistan Resolution. Seven years later Britain handed over a truncated Pakistan, with Sindh, Balochistan, Punjab, and the North-West Frontier Province forming West Pakistan, while the eastern province of Bengal was divided between India and Pakistan to create the geographically distinct East Pakistan. Kashmir's status was left undecided by the British, leading to immediate conflict between India and Pakistan. The speed and nature of Partition satisfied nobody. Millions of Hindus and Sikhs living in Pakistan crossed over into India, while Indian Muslims migrated to East and West Pakistan. A staggering twelve million people moved home and between five hundred thousand and one million were killed in the ensuing sectarian violence. Pakistan emerged from a bloodbath of religious and ethnic hatred even as millions of Muslims chose to remain in a secular India. It was a tragic beginning for a new nation-state.[19]

Immediately the question of Pakistan's identity arose: Was it to be a pluralistic, democratic country for Muslims and other religious minorities or a theocratic Islamic state? Founder Mohammed Ali Jinnah was perfectly clear that Pakistan had to be a secular, democratic state. In his most famous speech, in 1947, Jinnah was emphatic: "You may belong to any religion or caste or creed—that has nothing to do with the business of the State," he said.[20]

Jinnah died early, in 1948, and since then many Pakistanis, but particularly the military, have ignored his wishes and the democratic founding creed of the country. Today no state-funded school's textbooks teach children Jinnah's words because they would infuriate the mullahs.[21] Today the military and the mullahs stress the Islamic nature of the state and pervert Jinnah and history by claiming that Pakistan was created as a result of a religious movement. "It is an established fact that Mr. Jinnah did not struggle for a secular Pakistan as it is against the basic creed and faith of a Muslim to sacrifice his life for such a secular cause. The driving force behind their tireless efforts was . . . setting up a country where people could practice Islam as their state ideology," said Qazi Hussain Ahmed, the leader of the Jamiat-e-Islami, the most influential Islamic party in the country.[22] The army trains its men to defend Islam rather than the nation and protect Pakistan's territorial and "ideological" (Islamic) frontiers. The army's deeply rooted Islamic orientation would profoundly affect Musharraf's inability to deliver on his promises to the United States after 9/11.

For half of the sixty years of the country's existence, Pakistanis have lived under four military regimes. Each one has reinvented the wheel by debating whether democracy is possible in an Islamic state and whether a parliamentary or presidential system best suits the country's "Islamic identity." The 1973 constitution, which established a parliamentary system of democratic government and is still in force today, has been amended so many times by politicians and generals alike that it is barely recognizable. Attempts by secular politicians to live by the rule of law and the constitution have failed. The first free and fair elections took place only in 1970—twenty-three years after Partition.

Pakistan's inability to forge a national identity has led to an intensification of ethnic, linguistic, and regional nationalism, which has splintered and fragmented the country. The largest province, with 65 percent of the population and providing the bulk of the army and bureaucracy, Punjab never accepted Pakistan as a multi-ethnic state necessitating equal political rights, greater autonomy for the smaller provinces, and a more equitable distribution of funds. A rebellion of these smaller provinces against so-called Punjabi domination led to the rise of Bengali nationalism in East Pakistan, war, and, in 1971, the creation of Bangladesh.[23]

Ethnic nationalism has continued to tear Pakistan apart. Four insurgencies by Baloch nationalists seeking greater autonomy (1948, 1958–1959, 1962–1963, 1973–1977) have been put down with brute force by the army. A fifth insurgency has been under way in Balochistan since 2002. In the NWFP, a secular Pashtun nationalist movement was suppressed in the 1970s. In Sindh province since the 1980s, there have been severe tensions and rivalry between local Sindhis and Muhajirs, Urdu-speaking migrants from India settled in major cities such as Karachi.

The failure of a political culture to take root encouraged the army to seize power as early as 1958. Desperately weak and with few resources, the army sought U.S. support, agreeing to become an anti-Soviet prop in the cold war in exchange for military aid. In 1954, Washington agreed to provide a military and economic aid program to Pakistan worth $105 million a year, but also decided to covertly equip four infantry divisions for the army, six fighter squadrons for the air force, and twelve navy ships. By 1957 the covert U.S. military commitment to Pakistan had grown to an astonishing $500 million a year. Pakistan became a frontline bastion for the United States in the cold war, joining several U.S.-led regional pacts, allowing a large CIA office to be established in Karachi, and letting American high-altitude U2 spy planes fly over the Soviet Union from an air base near Peshawar.

Pakistani leaders assiduously courted Washington in the hope of gaining security guarantees against India.[24] Their main aim in accumulating U.S. weaponry was to confront India, against whom Pakistan went to war in 1965 and again in 1971, when it lost East Pakistan. After this debacle, Zulfiqar Ali Bhutto became president. A charismatic, brilliant, flamboyant but deeply flawed politician from rural Sindh, Bhutto initiated the first sustained period of democratic rule by a civilian politician. He had founded the Pakistan Peoples Party (PPP) and started out as a populist with policies rooted in the deep public thirst for social and economic justice and democracy, and its dislike for military rule. He was to end his rule in 1978 as an intensely disliked autocratic ruler whose ruthlessness and hunger for absolute power led to his downfall after he rigged national elections.

One of Bhutto's major successes, in August 1973, was achieving a political consensus for the constitution, which has become the bedrock of the state's legality, even though it has been amended many times. He also removed Pakistan from the milieu of South Asia to play a larger role in the Arab world, as he sought money from the newly rich oil states to revive Pakistan's economy. In 1972 he initiated Pakistan's nuclear weapons program, which was stepped up after India tested a nuclear device in May 1974.

Ironically for an aristocrat, Bhutto's other major legacy was introducing the Pakistani public to populist politics. The PPP inspired millions of people as it espoused secularism and democracy and mobilized supporters who were anti-mullah and anti-military. By contrast, the Pakistan Muslim League, once the party of Jinnah, was to become the party of the military. With no clear ideology or political roots and an opportunistic membership, the Pakistan Muslim League was dubbed the "King's Party," catering as it did to a succession of military rulers. Generals Ayub, Yahya, Zia, and Musharraf all were to refashion it to suit their own political needs, to perpetuate their rule, or to provide themselves with a civilian façade when it suited them.

General Zia's eleven-year rule was to have the most long-lasting and damaging effect on Pakistani society, one still prevalent today. Zia, who seized power from Bhutto in a coup in 1977, dealt with Pakistan's identity crisis by imposing an ideological Islamic state upon the population. Many of today's problems—the militancy of the religious parties, the mushrooming of madrassas and extremist groups, the spread of drug and Kalashnikov culture, and the increase in sectarian violence took place during the Zia era.

Although self-effacing and pious, Zia was also ruthless and vindictive, with a sharp sense of political timing, which he used to undermine his opponents. He frequently invoked a "divine mission": "I have a mission, given by God, to bring Islamic order to Pakistan," he said in 1978.[25] Zia banned politics and censored the media, while his new Islamic laws victimized non-Muslim minorities and women. In Islamizing the legal system, he ordered public floggings and the use of torture. His supporters were drawn from the religious right and the army, where he inculcated the conviction that only soldiers were capable of ruling Pakistan. The epithet that "all countries have armies, but in Pakistan the army has a country" came true under Zia.[26]

Zia's longevity as a ruler was made possible by the unstinting support he received from President Ronald Reagan and the U.S. administration after the Soviet Union invaded Afghanistan in December 1979. Zia offered the ISI to act as a conduit for the arms and funds the CIA wanted to supply to the Afghan Mujahedin. In the next few years the Americans built up the ISI into a formidable intelligence agency that managed to run the Afghan war and the political process inside Pakistan. Widespread corruption within the ISI through its involvement in the Afghan heroin trade and the CIA arms pipeline enriched many ISI generals and also provided covert funds for Pakistan's nuclear program and the promotion of new ISI-backed Islamic insurgencies in Kashmir and Central Asia. Musharraf was to have the same strategy after 9/11, using U.S. funds provided for combating al Qaeda to strengthen the army against India, modernize the ISI, and undermine his political opponents.[27]

Zia bargained hard for maximum U.S. support. In January 1980 he dismissed President Jimmy Carter's offer of a $400 million aid package as "peanuts." A year later, he accepted an alliance with Reagan, agreeing to a five-year (1981–1986) military and economic aid package worth $3.2 billion, which included the sale of forty F-16 fighter aircraft to Pakistan. This was followed by a six-year (1987–1993) $4.02 billion aid package that was never completed. Between 1982 and 1990 the CIA, working with the ISI and Saudi Arabia's intelligence service, funded the training, arrival, and arming of some thirty-five thousand Islamic militants from forty-three Muslim countries in Pakistani madrassas to fight the Soviets in Afghanistan. This global jihad launched by Zia and Reagan was to sow the seeds of al Qaeda and turn Pakistan into the world center of jihadism for the next two decades.[28]

Zia's quid pro quo with the Americans was that they were not to question his domestic politics or his grip on power—exactly what Musharraf negotiated with Washington after 9/11. As long as Zia backed the Afghan Mujahedin, Reagan turned a blind eye to Pakistan's lack of democracy, the floggings and torture, the drug trafficking by the army, and even the country's clandestine nuclear weapons program. Similarly, two decades later, as long as Musharraf pursued al Qaeda, President George W. Bush declined to question his domestic policies or insist upon democracy.

Reagan was to severely compromise the U.S. stance on nuclear proliferation by declining to question Islamabad's development of nuclear weapons—as long as Zia did not embarrass Washington by testing them.[29] It is widely believed that with the help of China, Pakistan developed a nuclear weapon by the late 1980s. The U.S. Congress did monitor Zia's nuclear program and imposed the Pressler Amendment, in which the U.S. president had to verify every year that Pakistan did not possess a nuclear device. The inability of President George H. W. Bush to make such a verification in 1990 led to U.S. sanctions on Islamabad. Pakistani generals became bitter, accusing the Americans of a grand betrayal, as the sanctions came just a few months after the Soviet withdrawal from Afghanistan, when Pakistan was of far less value to the Americans.

The aims of Pakistan and the United States in relation to Afghanistan now diverged considerably. Zia wanted to secure a pro-Pakistan fundamentalist government in Kabul, led by Gulbuddin Hikmetyar, whom the ISI favored.[30] Washington wanted a more moderate Mujahedin government, but at the same time was rapidly losing interest in the region. Neither aim was to be met as Afghanistan slipped into a brutal civil war.

When Zia was killed in a plane crash in 1988, public anger against the army forced the new army chief, Gen. Mirza Aslam Beg, to hold elections. Benazir Bhutto, the daughter of Zulfiqar Ali Bhutto, had returned to Pakistan from exile in 1986 to a rapturous reception by the public but had been sidelined by Zia. Now under the watchful eye of a nervous military, Bhutto mobilized public support for a PPP victory at the polls. To prevent a PPP landslide, the ISI cobbled together a right-wing alliance of nine Islamic parties and the Muslim League, called the Islamic Democratic Alliance (IDA).[31] No party secured a clear majority in the election, although the PPP won the largest number of seats in the National Assembly.[32]

The army refused to let Bhutto govern as prime minister until Washington brokered a deal in which she had to agree to allow the army to run foreign policy and the nuclear program, and not to reduce the military's budget. General Beg was to encroach even more upon Bhutto's decision-making prerogatives. Bhutto was not allowed to ask about the military's budget for the nuclear program, backing the Kashmir insurgency, or the Afghan Mujahedin. She was further hobbled in the provinces as her main political rival and the army's protégé, Nawaz Sharif, became chief minister of Punjab, which led to a state of open confrontation between the two leaders. Sharif, a businessman from Lahore whose family had prospered enormously under the Zia regime, was a dour, unintelligent politician who had been promoted and patronized by the military.

After widespread corruption allegations against Bhutto's husband, Asif Ali Zardari, became known, President Ghulam Ishaq Khan, backed by the army, dismissed Bhutto's government on August 6, 1990, and ordered general elections. They were to be won by Nawaz Sharif and the Pakistan Muslim League. For the next decade Pakistan was on a political and constitutional roller coaster. A ruling "troika" emerged, consisting of the president, the army chief, and the prime minister. The state of tension and jockeying for power among the three never allowed an elected government to consolidate itself. The army played divide-and-rule among the political parties, stunting their development as genuine vehicles for democracy. Both Bhutto and Sharif were twice elected prime minister and both formed governments, only to be twice dismissed by the president at the urging of the army.[33] Although the president had the legal power to dismiss the government, it was the constant undermining of the democratic process by the army and the ISI that failed to allow democracy to take root. No elected government ever completed its tenure, and the public was never given the opportunity to dismiss a government through the ballot box.

Sharif and Bhutto carried on a bitter personal vendetta against each other that stymied issue-related politics and the opportunity to carry out desperately needed economic reforms. The army and the Islamic fundamentalist parties fueled this rivalry and continued to undermine elected governments even as they dominated foreign policy. The uprising in Kashmir against Indian rule through the 1990s allowed the military to sponsor new Islamic militant groups, which in turn trained thousands of Pakistani fighters for both Kashmir and Afghanistan. Pakistan's foreign policy became associated with jihad against India and support to the Taliban. Relations with the United States deteriorated further, and in 1993 President Clinton placed Pakistan on a watch list of state sponsors of terrorism because of the ISI's open involvement in training Kashmiri insurgents. The army was forced to remove the ISI chief and relocate its training camps to Taliban-controlled Afghanistan.

Nawaz Sharif was elected for a second time in February 1997, after general elections that saw the lowest voter turnout in Pakistan's history—only 32 percent of voters took part—a clear indication of public frustration at the stagnant political process.[34] India and Pakistan became locked in a new rivalry in the spring of 1998, after India carried out nuclear tests. Pakistan responded by testing five nuclear devices on May 27, 1998. However, the government failed to prepare for global sanctions imposed on both countries. Pakistan went bust as its economy and exchange rate went into freefall. Although Pakistan had become a nuclear power, it had neither a stable economy nor a political system to match such responsibilities.

Sharif tried to improve relations with India but was undermined by Gen. Pervez Musharraf, whom he had recently appointed as the new army chief. In the spring of 1999, Musharraf and a handful of generals secretly deployed troops into Indian Kashmir to occupy mountaintops in the Kargil sector. It was the first time since 1971 that Pakistani troops had violated the sanctity of the Line of Control, or LOC, dividing the two Kashmirs between India and Pakistan.[35] Meeting no Indian forces, the Pakistanis advanced until they looked down on a major road to the important town of Leh. The Indians were taken by surprise as the Pakistanis started shelling the road and the town of Kargil. On May 22, Indian forces began to move dozens of heavy guns to Kargil to shell the mountaintops. A conventional but localized war ensued, although there were serious fears that it could escalate into a conventional or even a nuclear conflict.

Musharraf had calculated that India would never escalate the conflict for fear it could lead to an unsheathing of nuclear weapons. He expected the United States to step in and mediate a cease-fire, after which Pakistan could demand talks on Kashmir. The Pakistanis believed that their nuclear capability would deter any Indian escalation of the conflict. The world was stunned at Musharraf's audacious threat of using nuclear weapons as a form of blackmail to settle an international dispute. Moreover, Pakistan was creating a deliberate air of unpredictability about when and how it would use such weapons. Pakistani officials told journalists they had indirectly conveyed to New Delhi that if Indian armored columns were to cross the international border and penetrate deep into Pakistani territory, the army was ready to use battlefield nuclear weapons against them—inside Pakistani territory and despite the possibility of massive Pakistani civilian casualties.

Musharraf had been easily influenced by a few madcap generals and had not even informed his own high command or the navy or air force of his plan.[36] The world swiftly turned against Pakistan, and President Clinton forced Sharif to carry out a humiliating climbdown during the Pakistani prime minister's visit to Washington on July 4. Pakistan was forced to withdraw its forces and abandon Kargil after suffering some one thousand casualties. According to Bruce Riedel, then a senior director at the National Security Council, Clinton's swift intervention was necessary because there was "disturbing evidence that the Pakistanis were preparing their nuclear arsenal for possible deployment." Musharraf subsequently denied that Pakistan planned to use nuclear weapons.[37]

Pakistan lost on all counts. Rather than highlighting the Kashmir dispute, Musharraf's adventurism had ensured that Kashmir was further eclipsed and that India would win the propaganda war. "Its folly [in the war in Kargil] lay in the fact that it committed Pakistan to a battle which it could not, under any circumstances, win. . . . Kargil has done more to obscure the Kashmir issue and damage the cause of the Kashmiri people than anything else in recent memory," wrote Pakistani columnist Ayaz Amir.[38] Kashmiri leaders felt humiliated and betrayed. Pakistan's actions had undermined their own credibility. However, Musharraf refused to accept failure and promoted all the generals involved in the Kargil debacle.[39] Nobody was held accountable. Musharraf claimed that a great victory would have been possible had Sharif not chickened out.[40]

Musharraf was now branded by friends and foes alike as a brash, adventurous hardliner mesmerized by the idea of military success against India yet unaware of strategy, diplomacy, or the economic chaos that even a minor war could bring upon Pakistan. The Clinton administration had no doubt that Musharraf was responsible for the incident. "Musharraf . . . bears . . . the lion's share of the responsibility for Kargil," said U.S. deputy secretary of state Strobe Talbott.[41] Islamabad was soon rocked by a blame game as Sharif pointed the finger at Musharraf, while Musharraf insisted that Sharif had been "on board" with all the key decisions regarding Kargil. The ISI began to mobilize the Islamic parties to hold rallies against Sharif.

At the end of September, Sharif sent his brother Shabaz Sharif and the ISI chief Lt.-Gen. Mohammed Ziauddin, a Sharif loyalist, to Washington, where they told U.S. officials that Musharraf was preparing a coup. The two promised to try to help capture bin Laden if the United States supported Nawaz Sharif, although the CIA knew that Ziauddin did not fully control the ISI.[42] Nevertheless, on September 20, the State Department issued a terse statement warning the army not to carry out any unconstitutional act. Musharraf was furious and prepared to launch a countercoup if he was sacked by Sharif. The 111th Brigade of the Tenth Corps, based close to Islamabad—the traditional coup-making unit—was put on fifteen-minutes-readiness notice. Ultimately it was Sharif who moved first.

On the evening of October 12, 1999, while Musharraf was in the air returning from a trip to Sri Lanka, Sharif dismissed him and appointed Ziauddin as the new army chief. Musharraf's plane, which was supposed to land in Karachi, was diverted to Nawabshah airport in Sindh province, where the police were waiting to arrest him. The army, however, moved swiftly to defend its chief and preserve its unity, taking control of the country and arresting Sharif, Ziauddin, and some two hundred politicians.[43] Musharraf's plane landed safely at Karachi, from where, in the early hours of the morning, he told the nation on television that Sharif had tried to divide the army.[44]

For a decade the army had taken a backseat in political affairs but had pulled the strings without taking responsibility for its actions. Now it was back in the driver's seat. Some Pakistanis were happy to see the end of the Sharif government, which had become increasingly repressive, while others resigned themselves to another long period of military rule. In the West, the coup was viewed with enormous concern. An unstable, nuclear-equipped nation that only six months earlier had almost gone to war with India was now led by a general considered reckless and unpredictable. With the army in control, there was even less chance that Pakistan would go after Osama bin Laden or end its support to the Taliban regime.

CHAPTER THREE

♦ ♦ ♦

The Chief Executive's Schizophrenia

Pakistan, the United Nations, and the United States Before 9/11

When Musharraf was asked just after the 1999 coup why he had decided to call himself chief executive—an odd title for a military dictator—he gave a surprising reply: "For your [the media's] consumption—might I say it's a very palatable name instead of chief martial law administrator, which is draconian in concept and name. I want to give it a civilian façade."[1] Blunt, frank, always in a hurry, sometimes outrageous, but ever defensive of the military's role, Musharraf was obsessed with his image when he seized power. He wanted to be palatable to everyone, from Islamic fundamentalists to liberals but most of all to the international community. He thought that a title that sounded as though he were the head of a multinational company would hide the reality of his military rule. Whatever he called himself, though, abroad he was treated as an unreliable pariah and a dictator who had nearly plunged the world into nuclear war.

Musharraf was born in New Delhi in August 1943, the second of three sons. His family moved to Pakistan after Partition in 1947—the trauma of which he describes movingly in his otherwise unreliable autobiography.[2] Both his parents were well educated and liberal, a working couple long before such things became the norm. His father joined Pakistan's foreign service and in 1949 was posted to Turkey, where his mother worked for the United Nations and the entire family learned to speak Turkish. The young Musharraf's hero was Mustafa Kemal Atatürk (1881–1938), the secular founding father of the Turkish republic, and for a time after the coup, Musharraf tried to emulate him.

He was educated in Christian missionary schools in Karachi and Lahore, where he made lasting friends—some of whom were later to become his advisers. His friends nicknamed him "Gola," which means "round" or "ball," because of his pudgy physique. According to his contemporaries, the young Musharraf was not particularly bright—a poor student who never read books—but he loved sports, dancing, dressing up, seeing girls, and riding around on his motorbike.

At a loss with what to do with himself, he entered the Pakistan Military Academy at Kakul in 1961 and was commissioned in the field artillery three years later. "I joined the army because of the glamour," he said.[3] A happy-go-lucky junior officer who partied a lot, he was frequently hauled in for disciplinary charges. He fought in the 1965 war with India and then joined the Special Service Group (SSG), the commando force of the Pakistan army. In the 1971 war, he commanded an SSG unit that went behind Indian lines, and he later became the head of the SSG. He often alluded to his commando training and, after the coup, always met the press in the camouflage uniform and beret of a commando. "He has brilliant tactics but no strategy, and that is what you learn as a commando," a retired army chief told me. Musharraf later described how he had launched the coup. "I took a fast decision. I keep to Napoleon's view that two thirds of the decision making process is based on analysis and information and one third is always a leap in the dark."[4]

Musharraf trained at Fort Bragg in the United States and led the SSG in joint exercises with U.S. Special Forces. He later attended a military course in Britain. When Prime Minister Nawaz Sharif appointed him army chief in October 1998, he considered Musharraf a safe bet because as a Muhajir—an Urdu-speaking refugee from India—he did not have the breadth of support in the officer corps, which was dominated by Punjabis and Pashtuns, to become too powerful. Sharif thought Musharraf would do as he was told. Yet within the next twelve months, the impetuous Musharraf was to launch a war in Kargil and mount a coup.

After the coup, Musharraf held three posts, chief executive of Pakistan, chief of army staff, and chairman of the Joint Chiefs of Staff Committee. In his first press conference he showed both strength and vulnerability, which initially made him very appealing to the domestic media. "My work and appointments I have made are transparent, my judgments may be wrong but not my intentions. This is not martial law. We will be honest and dynamic so give us a chance," he appealed to the press.[5] He appeared to be personable, charming, and a great talker, as he rarely spoke in public with a text. George Polk, a European technology entrepreneur who sat down to breakfast with Musharraf in 2006, later described him as "a tightly coiled spring" whose chest any moment "would begin to swell, like the Hulk."[6]

Musharraf had had a liberal upbringing, but while training young officers, the army inculcates in them a powerful bias that includes hatred for India, distrust of the United States, contempt for all civilian politicians, and a heightened religiosity and respect for Islamic militants fighting the army's foreign wars in Kashmir and Afghanistan. Musharraf and his generals were personally liberal, but their worldview and politics remained extremely reactionary. Thus Musharraf could dance at parties and rarely enter a mosque but, at the same time, strongly defend jihad, the Taliban worldview, and the right for militants to cross into Indian Kashmir. After the coup, he stepped up support for Kashmiri militants and the Taliban to show that he was not soft on India. After 9/11, his gregarious nature and bluntness appealed to Western leaders, but they soon realized that he spoke too much, made more commitments than he could realize, and was arrogant.[7]

Despite Musharraf's allegiance to the Taliban and the Kashmiri militants, the mullahs considered Musharraf too secular as an army chief and quite different from Zia ul-Haq. They were appalled when he compared himself to Atatürk, who, in the 1920s, drowned hundreds of Turkish mullahs in the Bosporus Sea. "Musharraf's knowledge on Islam and madrassas is zero, he has no idea even of what a madrassa looks like or any idea about Islamic education," Maulana Fazlur Rehman, of the political party Jamiat Ulema-e-Islam, told me after the coup.[8] Added Amir ul-Azim, of the Jamiat-e-Islami, "Musharraf has no roots in the traditions of this country or of Islam."[9] Even though Musharraf personally disliked the extremism of the mullahs, he had no compunction about using militants as an extension of the state's foreign policy. Before 9/11 he was a vociferous defender of jihad who tried to convince skeptical Western audiences. "There is no question that terrorism and jihad are absolutely different. You in the West are allergic to the term *jihad,* but jihad is a tolerant concept," Musharraf said in 2000.[10]

After seizing power, Musharraf declared an emergency but did not impose martial law. He suspended the constitution and legislatures, sacked the heads of all political institutions, and restricted the courts from passing any judgments on his actions. He later forced judges of the Supreme Court to swear a new oath of loyalty to the regime. He gave no timetable for the army's remaining in power. He announced a seven-point agenda to rebuild Pakistan by reviving the economy, improving law and order, and going after loan defaulters and the corrupt.[11] The ISI vetted a civilian cabinet that included several well-known businessmen, bankers, and liberal politicians. Shaukat Aziz, favorite nominee of the ISI who had dealt with him extensively in the past, was given the daunting task of reviving a virtually bankrupt exchequer.[12]

Liberal figures who joined the cabinet did so believing that this time around the army would rebuild public faith in civil society and carry out long-needed reforms of the bureaucracy, the police, and the judiciary. They expected the army to sow the seeds of genuine democracy and nation building, but they were to be severely disappointed. Military rule at the tail end of the twentieth century was an outdated model for rebuilding a deeply polarized and fractured society. The army could never carry out a reform agenda as long as it continued to support jihadis and extremist religious groups who carried out the army's policies toward India and Afghanistan. These same jihadis would become the biggest obstacle to reform and nation building at home.

In January 2000 the army put Nawaz Sharif and six others on trial, charging them with treason and hijacking an aircraft—charges that carried the death sentence. Sharif looked weak and wan but unrepentant as I chatted with him in a Karachi courtroom full of intelligence officers, lawyers, and family members. He accused Musharraf of "preparing a blueprint for the overthrow of my government."[13] The trial could hardly be considered free and impartial.[14] On April 6, 2000, Sharif was found guilty and given two life sentences, but after a year in jail he was sprung by the Saudi royal family, who took him into exile, promising Musharraf that Sharif would not take part in politics for ten years. The country's three major political leaders were all now in exile: Sharif, Bhutto, and the muhajir leader Altaf Hussain.

The international community's main demands from the military regime were to cease support to the Taliban, help deliver bin Laden, and stop aiding Kashmiri militants fighting in Indian Kashmir. There was already deep suspicion running among U.S. congressmen and the media that the regime was a state sponsor of terrorism, suspicion fueled by an effective Indian media campaign that blamed the uprising in Kashmir as entirely a result of Pakistani interference. Thus, in 1999, terrorism was already on the agenda for Musharraf.

The hijacking of an Indian aircraft in December 1999 appeared to confirm the world's worst fears. ISI agents appeared to be involved when Harkat ul-Ansar, a Pakistan-based and ISI-backed Kashmiri extremist group, hijacked an Indian Airlines aircraft and flew it to Kandahar. After days of tense negotiation on the tarmac of Kandahar's decrepit airport, between UN officials and the Taliban, India was forced to release three Kashmiri militants in exchange for the 160 passengers held hostage. U.S. officials privately said that the hijacking had been backed, if not carried out, by the ISI, while India blamed the ISI publicly. The United States and Britain demanded that Pakistan ban Harkat and other extremist groups. Britain's chief of the Defence staff, Gen. Charles Guthrie, delivered the first of several tough messages to Musharraf in January 2000. "Everything is now up to General Musharraf to convince us that he is taking steps in the right direction," Guthrie told me.[15]

The first official U.S. delegation to visit Islamabad since the coup also arrived in January. The U.S. assistant secretary of state Karl Inderfurth delivered a blunt message urging Pakistan to ban terrorist groups and hand over al Qaeda members known to be operating inside the country.[16] The ISI had never bothered to rein in al Qaeda's extensive logistics network in Pakistan because the terrorist group helped train Kashmiri militants willing to fight India. Al Qaeda was now also helping the Taliban, another ally of the military regime. Moreover, the same extremist Pakistani groups the ISI funded and sponsored helped al Qaeda find safe houses and deliver young men for training.

U.S. intelligence had discovered that Abu Zubaydah, a senior al Qaeda recruiter, was operating openly from a house in Peshawar and vetting foreign recruits before sending them on to training camps in Afghanistan. Inderfurth asked Musharraf to hand him over. "The Pakistanis told us they could not find him, even though everyone knew where he was," William Milam, the U.S. ambassador to Pakistan, told me. "The ISI just turned a blind eye to his activities," Milam added.[17] In fact, Zubaydah played a role in vetting Kashmiri militants on behalf of the ISI before sending them to Afghanistan for training.

Within the U.S. administration there were serious differences of opinion as to how to pressure Musharraf. The Pentagon feared losing its long-standing relationship with the Pakistan military and wanted no punishments, while the State Department called for sanctions and further isolation. State itself was divided as to what to emphasize, with Michael

Sheehan, the coordinator of the Office for Counterterrorism, wanting to make terrorism the most important issue with Pakistan. Others, such as Inderfurth and Strobe Talbott, wanted to stress nonproliferation and improving relations with India. The only leverage Washington had was to halt loans from international financial institutions, but it balked at taking such a step because it would only have destabilized Pakistan further. "The only thing we could have done that we didn't do was cut off their access to IMF loans, which would have collapsed Pakistan," said National Security Advisor Samuel Berger.[18]

However, the Clinton administration still had no coherent strategy for undermining the Taliban regime, and as long as it delayed shaping one, there was confusion as to what exactly it could demand from Pakistan. Washington's only clear position for the Taliban and Pakistan was to help deliver bin Laden to the U.S. justice system. There were no hard-and-fast U.S. demands regarding the Taliban or Pakistan's continued support to the regime.

The U.S. lack of trust regarding Pakistan was self-evident when President Clinton arrived in Islamabad for a five-hour visit on March 25, 2000, after spending five days in India. A marked business jet first landed as a decoy, followed by a second, unmarked jet carrying Clinton. Six bulletproof limos lined up in front of the plane to form a barrier as U.S.-manned helicopters flew overhead. No armed Pakistani security officers were allowed near the U.S. president. It was the first time a foreign airport had been taken over by the U.S. Secret Service for a presidential visit. Clinton made it clear that the visit did not imply an endorsement of Pakistan's military regime, and he was never photographed shaking hands with Musharraf. The visit should have been a humiliating experience, but Musharraf did not seem to mind. Clinton made a fourteen-minute national television address to the Pakistani people. It was a powerful speech in which he issued a blunt warning that Pakistan had to face a reality in which jihad was not an option.

"This era does not reward people who struggle in vain to redraw borders with blood." Clinton said. "It belongs to those with the vision to look beyond borders, for partners in commerce and trade. . . . Democracy cannot develop if it is constantly uprooted before it has a chance to firmly take hold. There is a danger that Pakistan may grow even more isolated, draining even more resources away from the needs of the people, moving even closer to a conflict no one can win."[19]

The speech made a deep impact on many Pakistanis, but Musharraf ignored Clinton's words, saying he had given no assurances to Clinton on stopping the jihad in Kashmir or support to the Taliban, but he was ready to hold talks with India and would go to Kandahar to discuss with Mullah Omar the Osama bin Laden issue. In private, Clinton had told Musharraf that Pakistan had to deescalate tensions over Kashmir. "You have to decide do you want Kashmir or do you want to save Pakistan. You cannot do both at the same time," Clinton had bluntly told Musharraf, according to a U.S. official who briefed me. Nevertheless, Clinton's visit did ensure that the relationship between the two countries not break down completely. "If Clinton had not come to Pakistan, our relationship with the United States would have gone into freefall," said interior minister Moeenuddin Haider lamely.[20]

Musharraf continued to make even plainer his differences with the United States on the issue of terrorism. "I just want to say that there is a difference of understanding on who is a terrorist. The perceptions are different in the United States and in Pakistan, in the West and what we understand is terrorism," Musharraf insisted in May.[21] The United States responded by chastising Pakistan for doing nothing to bring bin Laden to justice, given its relationship with the Taliban.

The war of words with the United States continued as Musharraf then publicly stated that Pakistan's strategic interests lay with supporting the Afghan Pashtuns, whom he associated solely with the Taliban. His comments were widely presumed to be prompted by hard-line generals such as Mohammed Aziz and Mehmood Ahmad. "Afghanistan's majority ethnic Pashtuns have to be on our side," Musharraf said. "This is our national interest . . . the Taliban cannot be alienated by Pakistan. We have a national security interest there," he added. His comments outraged many Afghans, including all the anti-Taliban factions. The usually withdrawn former king Zahir Shah termed the comments "interference and aggravation of the national unity of Afghanistan."[22] Hamid Karzai remarked to me that the comments made him "feel sick in the stomach." Such remarks were to make Musharraf a hated figure for most Afghans, something he could not live down even after 9/11.

Musharraf's aides made it clear that they would oppose all U.S. efforts to undermine the Taliban regime. "We are trying to stop the U.S. from undermining the Taliban regime. They cannot do it without Pakistan's help, because they have no assets there, but we will not allow it to happen," said Maj.-Gen. Ghulam Ahmad Khan, principal staff officer to Musharraf.[23]

Musharraf's promised reform agenda was blocked by the same kitchen cabinet of hard-line generals who wished to maintain the army's close relationship with the Islamic fundamentalist parties and who did not want to antagonize them by introducing liberal reforms at home. After Musharraf reneged on his promise to reform the unjust blasphemy law, liberal civilians who had joined his cabinet began to resign.[24] "The lack of reforms, the control of policy and decision making by the ISI and a few generals, the army's pandering to the fundamentalists, the refusal to change direction in foreign policy—all this has disillusioned me," one cabinet minister told me after his resignation. On October 15, information minister Javed Jabbar, a close personal friend of Musharraf, resigned, signaling a decisive shift in the public politics of the regime.[25]

Musharraf became known as "double-talk Musharraf," speaking with one breath about how he would turn Pakistan into a moderate Islamic state, and then just as vehemently with another supporting jihad and militancy. He began to invoke divine will as a justification for military rule. "God has chosen me to lead the nation and he will protect me," he said on television at the end of 2000.[26] Disillusionment with Musharraf increased rapidly across the country. Qualified people voted with their feet and began to leave the country in droves. A Gallup poll conducted in November stated that 38 percent of the entire adult work force wanted to emigrate, while 62 percent said they wanted to work abroad. Such impulses were not difficult to understand. There were no jobs, the Pakistani education system remained in a state of dilapidation, and the army had failed to improve law and order. In their reports for 2000, Amnesty International and the Human Rights Commission of Pakistan said violence against women, torture and deaths in police custody, and intolerance toward non-Muslims were all on the increase, despite the army's commitment to reform.

In 2000 the army began a political experiment to create a pliant political superstructure that would owe its first loyalty to Musharraf. Heavily rigged local council elections were held, followed by attempts to create a "king's party" that would do the army's bidding once general elections were held. Every previous military regime had gone down the same path, revamping the Pakistan Muslim League and cutting deals with small-time politicians who would remain loyal to the army. The ISI was used extensively to twist the arms of feudal politicians, young technocrats, and opposition politicians to join the Muslim League. The ISI's investigative arm, the National Accountability Bureau (NAB), ostensibly exposed corruption among politicians and bureaucrats, but also provided these files to the ISI. NAB compiled dossiers on the income, property holdings, taxes paid or unpaid, bank loans, telephone bills, and even children's school fees of every politician in the country, enabling the ISI to pressure them.[27]

In a speech on August 14, 2000, Musharraf promised that general elections would be held in October 2002 and that he would amend the constitution to validate army rule. Opposition parties formed the Alliance for Restoration of Democracy (ARD) and tried to hold protest rallies to oppose the military's plans, but thousands of their supporters were arrested. Meanwhile, Musharraf abused Bhutto, Sharif, and other politicians. "Those who are useless politicians should stay at home," he said in April 2001. "They have played their innings and they have played useless innings and have been getting out on zero."[28] From her exile in London, Bhutto gave a rapid-fire response: "The Pakistan army is infected by the extremists," she claimed. "By aiming to disqualify the mainstream leaders, the army plans a vacuum which can be filled by extremists linked to the Taliban."[29]

In June 2001, Musharraf simply declared himself president, saying that it was in the "supreme national interest."[30] It was a familiar path struck by former military rulers. "Military rulers in Pakistan traverse a familiar and well-trodden route, sooner or later assuming the title and office of president," wrote the newspaper *Dawn*. "It took General Ayub Khan three weeks to arrive at this stage, General Yahya Khan a few days, General Ziaul Haq about a year and it has taken General Pervaiz Musharraf a little over 18 months to cover the same journey."[31]

With the September 11 attacks just three months away, Musharraf faced growing criticism for the army's support of the Taliban. At a conference of Pakistani ambassadors in January 2001, Musharraf heard one envoy after another demand an end to such support because it was making his job untenable in foreign capitals. For the usually timid diplomats, this was a landmark event and demonstrated their desperation. There was also growing opposition from within the army. In April, Lt.-Gen. Imtiaz Shaheen, the corps commander in Peshawar who was responsible for providing logistics to the Taliban, was removed by Musharraf after he demanded a change in Afghan policy.[32] A senior civilian adviser to Musharraf told me that any ideas of policy change "were systematically blocked by Generals Aziz and Mehmood."[33]

In April 2001, the ISI funded the Jamiat Ulema-e-Islam, headed by Maulana Fazlur Rehman, to hold a three-day International Deoband Conference near Peshawar. (The Deobandi are a sect of Sunni Islam, among whose adherents are the Taliban and Pakistani extremists who believe in active jihad.) Hundreds of thousands of people attended the meeting, which pledged support to the Taliban. A message from Osama bin Laden was read out in support of Mullah Omar. Western embassies in Islamabad were appalled at the rally, as it was in total defiance of UN sanctions against the Taliban. In late April, the ISI allowed Lashkar-e-Tayyaba, one of the largest extremist groups fighting in Kashmir, to hold a similar rally near Lahore, in which it denounced the British government for placing it on a list of terrorist groups.[34] By staging such rallies, when all political rallies were banned by the regime, the ISI was sending an unambiguous message to the Americans and the UN: that Pakistan continued to support the Taliban even as the UN attempted to seek an end to the civil war in Afghanistan.

Since the United Nations had brokered the 1988 Geneva Accords, which ended the Soviet occupation of Afghanistan, a "Special Representative of the Secretary-General to Afghanistan" was charged with trying to end the civil war between the Taliban and the Northern Alliance. By July 1997, when Kofi Annan appointed the experienced Algerian diplomat Lakhdar Brahimi to this post, any UN role in ending the conflict was considered near hopeless. Without significant U.S. and European involvement or pressure on the neighboring states who continued to arm their proxies, there was little the UN could do. Brahimi told Annan he would make a one-shot attempt at brokering a deal. His main interlocutor on the Taliban side was Mullah Omar's deputy, Mullah Mohammad Rabbani, who was to die of cancer before 9/11, but the key would be Pakistan's attitude.

"I told Mullah Rabbani," said Brahimi, "the conflict is not about territory. It is about the Afghans finding a peaceful solution that is acceptable to them. An offensive may bring more territory under your control, it may even bring all of the territory under your control. And then what? You know well there will be more Afghans willing to fight against you."[35]

In a bid to end the interference in Afghanistan by neighboring states, the UN had created the six-plus-two group of countries: Afghanistan's six neighbors plus the United States and Russia. Brahimi banked on their holding a productive meeting in Tashkent in July 1999, just before the Taliban launched a major offensive against the Northern Alliance. If the meeting could persuade the Taliban to halt their offensive, then talks on a cease-fire could begin. The Tashkent meeting ended with a Pakistani pledge to bring about a cease-fire as their diplomats promised to persuade the Taliban. Instead, just ten days after the Tashkent meeting, the ISI encouraged the Taliban to launch their offensive. The UN was insulted; Brahimi was incensed and resigned, publicly blaming the Pakistanis. "A lot of Pakistanis lied to me through their teeth . . . my temptation to slam the door and tell everyone to go to hell when the offensive started was very strong," he told me. Meanwhile, the ISI had stories planted in the Pakistani media that Brahimi was working for the Indians. Coming on top of Islamabad's flagrant refusal to comply with UN sanctions on the Taliban, Brahimi's resignation was to increase the mistrust between Pakistan and the international community.

Brahimi had brought the few scholars and experts on Afghanistan into a working group to advise him about seeking ways to end the civil war. The core group consisted of Barnett Rubin, the best and at one time the only American scholar on Afghanistan, who had written several books on the country and ran conflict-prevention programs at the Council on Foreign Relations, and later at New York University; Oliver Roy, the French scholar who had written several books on Afghanistan and Islamic fundamentalism and was an adviser to the French government; William Maley, an Australian scholar who had edited the first book on the Taliban and advised the Australian government while teaching diplomacy in Canberra;[36] Ashraf Ghani, an Afghan anthropologist and economist at the World Bank; and me, the only non-scholar in the group. Other experts were called in when needed.

We brainstormed with Brahimi and other UN officials several times a year—at the UN headquarters in New York, in Berlin, and in Oslo in 1999, where we met with Terje Roed-Larsen and his Norwegian team, who had concluded the Oslo peace process in the Middle East, to see if its methodology could be applied to Afghanistan. (We failed; nothing, it seemed, could be applied to the Taliban.) All of us in the group had been good friends for a long time. Afghanistan had drawn us together for many years, and we admired one another's work. And we all had enormous respect for Brahimi, to whom we gave very frank advice as to what was and was not possible.

After Brahimi's departure in October 1999, the task of UN mediation was considered even more hopeless. Nevertheless, the challenge was taken up by Francesc Vendrell, an experienced Spanish-born UN diplomat who had brokered peace processes in Nicaragua, El Salvador, Guatemala, and most recently East Timor.[37] Vendrell, who took up the job in January 2000, knew he was not going to make much progress with the Taliban. Instead, from his base in Islamabad, he prepared the diplomatic ground for when and if the geopolitical situation changed in favor of negotiations. He continued meetings with our experts group and set up a second track of negotiations between retired senior diplomats and generals from the United States, Russia, Iran, and Pakistan.[38]

Another group Vendrell set up in December 2000 came to be known as the Geneva Initiative. It consisted of representatives from the United States, Iran, Germany, and Italy. Its purpose was to bring together the three non-fighting Afghan groups based in Europe. These consisted of the Rome group, comprising Zahir Shah's supporters; a splinter of that movement, called the Bonn group; and the Cyprus group, made up of Pashtuns and Hazaras who detested the king and were backed by Iran. These meetings were the only venue where U.S. and Iranian officials met face-to-face, and they became even more important after 9/11. Iran sent some of its top diplomats to the venue. "There were essentially two sets of conversations going on between the Americans and the Iranians, one in public and the other in private, where they discussed how to undermine the Taliban," said Vendrell.[39] During the spring of 2001, Vendrell and his aides prepared a concept paper that aimed to achieve minimal agreement among those in the international community on what pressures it would be prepared to put on the Taliban. The paper called for the rearming of the Northern Alliance in order to deny the Taliban total victory.[40]

Along with Vendrell's initiative, the experts group began to promote a new thesis. Led by Barnett Rubin, we wrote a joint paper that was circulated widely to international organizations and Western governments.[41] We proposed using economic aid related to the reconstruction of Afghanistan as a tool to isolate the Taliban and create an alternative political infrastructure that could also become a lobby for peace inside the country. Similar thoughts were being advocated by other U.S. and European officials. In his last report to the UN Security Council before 9/11, Kofi Annan urged a new "comprehensive approach" to try to bring peace to Afghanistan, terming past attempts "fruitless endeavors." He outlined the need for a plan to reconstruct the country.[42] UN sanctions on the Taliban had failed, as they provided no incentives for ending the civil war, made no provisions for reconstruction, and demanded only that the Taliban hand over Osama bin Laden. Most significantly, there was insufficient pressure from the Clinton administration to mobilize an international effort to end the conflict in Afghanistan.

When the Bush administration took office at the beginning of 2001, it was unclear what its policy would be—continuing to demand the extradition of bin Laden, or brokering an end to the Afghan civil war, or pressuring Musharraf to end support to the Taliban. In the nine months it was in power before 9/11, the administration took none of these issues seriously enough, although there was no shortage of warnings about the dangers of letting the problem fester. When Bush visited the White House on December 16, 2000, for the first time, Clinton had briefed him on "the biggest security problems" he would face. Of the six major threats Clinton listed, three involved al Qaeda and Pakistan. These were al Qaeda itself, nuclear tensions between India and Pakistan and nonproliferation, and "the ties of the Pakistanis to the Taliban and al Qaeda."[43]

Clinton's terrorism tsar, Richard Clarke, gave a thirteen-page document to incoming national security advisor Condoleezza Rice outlining the al Qaeda threat. Clarke recommended arming the Northern Alliance, developing Uzbekistan's capacity to attack al Qaeda, destroying terrorist camps, and sending in U.S. Special Operations Forces (U.S. SOF) to collect intelligence on bin Laden.[44] CIA director George Tenet later said that it was the CIA that prepared the first paper presented to the Bush team. However, the CIA station chief in Islamabad refused to endorse arming the Northern Alliance because it would have infuriated the ISI.[45]

The Bush administration arrived in office pledging to challenge Clinton's foreign policy, including his steps against al Qaeda that had been so ineffective. Rice ordered a policy review of al Qaeda, Afghanistan, and Pakistan but set no timetable for its completion. The administration appeared to be least interested in Afghanistan. State Department officials told me that the new secretary of state, Colin Powell, was aloof from the entire policy review, showing little interest. Christina Rocca, the new assistant aecretary of state for South Asian Affairs, was far too timid and wary of the neoconservatives to offer her opinion. It had taken the administration four months to nominate her to the post, and she was confirmed only in June, five months after the administration took office. South Asia was clearly not a priority on Powell's or Rice's to-do list.

Rocca had spent fifteen years at the CIA (1982–1997) and then worked as foreign policy adviser to Senator Sam Brownback, a Republican from Kansas.[46] "She is a faithful implementer of what her bosses decide," a senior U.S. diplomat told me at the time. The Pakistanis liked dealing with Rocca because they considered her so ineffective. "She had no ability to take decisions and she was not a risk-taker, so that suited us," said a senior Pakistani diplomat. Early on she got rid of Alan Eastham, her deputy in the South Asia Department and the most knowledgeable person about the region.

Musharraf had written an effusive congratulatory letter to Bush upon his taking office, pointedly criticizing the Clinton administration and asking for a better relationship with him. In his reply in February 2001, Bush urged Musharraf to work with the United States to "address Afghanistan's many problems—the most pressing of these is terrorism and it inhibits progress on all other issues."[47] The letter made little impact in Islamabad, and it was not until June that the Bush administration held its first substantive talks with Pakistan, when Foreign Minister Abdul Sattar visited Washington as well as London and Ottawa. In all three capitals, Sattar heard similar dire warnings that Pakistan's failure to cease its support to the Taliban, and by extension to al Qaeda, would affect its relations with the West. However, nobody was threatening Islamabad with anything specific.

In Washington, on his own insistence, Sattar was accompanied by the ISI's Maj.-Gen. Faiz Jilani, who explained Pakistan's Afghan policy because U.S. officials knew that the Foreign Ministry had no say in Afghan policy. "Nobody from the Foreign Office ever went to Afghanistan. We were trying to influence the ISI, but we had no knowledge of what was going on or what Pakistan was giving to the Taliban," Sattar told me.[48] As Sattar arrived in Washington on June 1, twenty thousand Taliban troops, including thousands of Pakistani militants, launched another major offensive against the Northern Alliance. Condoleezza Rice gave Sattar an earful. "She told us that the Taliban were dead in the water and we should drop them. It was a very rough meeting," said a Pakistani diplomat. Rice later admitted that "I delivered a very tough message, which was met with a rote, expressionless response."[49] However, there were still no specific threats or incentives for Pakistan to change policy. If the U.S. administration had decided to arm the Northern Alliance and informed Islamabad of that fact, it may well have made a difference in the military's thinking, but so far there was no U.S. policy decision to speak off.

Instead, the Bush administration chose to improve relations with Islamabad. The new deputy secretary of state, Richard Armitage, encouraged the military regime. "I don't want to see Pakistan only through the lens or the prism of Osama bin Laden," he said. "We want to look at Pakistan and see what Pakistan thinks about Pakistan's future."[50] Other U.S. officials echoed this sentiment. "It is in no one's interest for declaring Pakistan as a failed state," said Harry Thomas, the director for South Asia at the National Security Agency. "We don't want Pakistan becoming another Afghanistan," he said just three weeks before September 11.[51]

Musharraf welcomed Washington's conciliatory stance and hoped that unlike with Clinton, the Bush administration would put the issues of terrorism, nonproliferation, and restoration of democracy on the back burner. There was now even less incentive for Musharraf to change his policies toward the Taliban and there was no extraordinary U.S. pressure to go after al Qaeda. Dealing with Bush was going to be much easier than dealing with Clinton. Whereas Clinton resisted the wool being pulled over his eyes, the Bush administration simply closed their eyes themselves. Three years later Rice was to admit her failure:

> America's al Qaeda policy wasn't working because our Afghanistan policy wasn't working. And our Afghanistan policy wasn't working because our Pakistan policy wasn't working. We recognized that America's counter-terrorism policy had to be connected to our regional strategies and to our overall foreign policy. . . . Al Qaeda was both a client of and a patron to the Taliban, which in turn was supported by Pakistan. Those relationships provided al Qaeda with a powerful umbrella of protection, and we had to sever that.[52]

In fact the Bush administration made no attempt to sever these relationships because the policy review kept getting delayed. Moreover, it seemed to lack all seriousness, according to U.S. diplomats at the Islamabad embassy, who were never consulted on it. In January, William Milam, the U.S. ambassador to Pakistan, prepared two cables in order to brief the incoming Bush team about Pakistan and the threat from the Taliban and al Qaeda. His first cable reviewed current policy, while the second proposed options for a policy change. There was no response from Washington and no demand for further information—even though Milam was the U.S. point man for meetings with the Taliban leadership and had warned the Taliban that Washington would hold them responsible for any al Qaeda attack on a U.S. target. In May, Milam met with Armitage in Washington, but nobody asked Milam for his views or mentioned the policy review. The Islamabad embassy was not consulted once about the review—which indicates how low a priority it was for the State Department.

"Al Qaeda was not on the radar screen in Washington," said a senior U.S. diplomat at the time. "Nobody thought there was any urgency to the policy review. Papers were circulated, dates were made to meet, and were broken—it was the usual bureaucratic approach."

Through the summer there was still no sense of urgency about the policy review, even though there were more than enough warnings about an al Qaeda threat. The FBI issued 216 internal threat warnings about the possibility of an attack by al Qaeda between January and September 2001, while the National Security Agency reported 33 intercepts indicating possible al Qaeda attacks.[53] U.S. forces in the Arabian Gulf were placed on the highest state of alert on June 22—Threat Condition Delta. Richard Clarke wrote to Rice on June 28 saying that warnings of an imminent attack "had reached a crescendo."[54] On July 10, the CIA prepared a briefing paper for Bush that was emphatic: "We believe that [bin Laden] will launch a significant terrorist attack against US and/or Israeli interests in the coming weeks . . . attack preparations have been made . . . and will occur with little or no warning," the paper said.[55]

The first formal meeting of deputy heads of departments in the U.S. government to consider the policy review had taken place only on April 30.[56] The meeting bogged down over a technicality: whether the Pentagon or the CIA was to pay for and run the program for the covert Predator drone that would fly over Afghanistan. The $3 million Predator, which was being tested, was now more lethal, as it had been armed with a Hellfire missile.[57] It would take another five months for the Principals Committee to meet.

On August 6, the CIA's daily brief to the president was headlined, "Bin Laden Determined to Strike in U.S." The State Department's Bureau of Intelligence and Research had tried to motivate Condi Rice and Colin Powell by sending them papers on the history of the fruitless attempts to persuade the Taliban and Pakistan to hand over bin Laden and, prophetically, a paper urging the overthrow of the Taliban regime—but there was silence from above. Other officials were angry and frustrated at Pakistan's attitude. "The ISI is totally inflexible," the Afghan-born Zalmay Khalilzad, then working at the National Security Council, told me when I visited Washington in the first week of July. "We wanted a joint project with them to change the Taliban leadership, but the ISI backed out. We don't want to confront Pakistan, but we may have to."[58]

At the UN, Russia and France presented intelligence dossiers to the UN Security Council showing that Pakistan continued to flout UN sanctions by providing fuel and other supplies to the Taliban. Up to thirty ISI trucks a day were still crossing into Afghanistan. Musharraf brazenly condemned UN sanctions, saying, "The Taliban are the dominant reality in Afghanistan. . . . The unilateral arms embargo on the Taliban government is unjustified, discriminatory and will further escalate the war."[59] U.S. officials continued to warn Pakistani diplomats of the possible consequences for both the Taliban and Pakistan of an al Qaeda attack anywhere.

I witnessed one such exchange at a conference organized by the British Foreign Office in July, at Weston Park, a mansion deep in the English countryside. A senior U.S. diplomat rounded on his Pakistani counterpart, telling him that "the Taliban and al Qaeda are one enterprise and we see Pakistan as backing that enterprise." He went on: "Bush is very serious and could declare the Taliban a terrorist group in which case Pakistan would be directly held responsible for backing terrorism." The American then counted off on his fingers the nine senior ISI officers directing military policy for the Taliban inside Afghanistan.

Finally, on September 4, nine months after Bush became president and a week before the 9/11 attacks, the long-awaited interagency cabinet meeting of the principals took place in Washington. Those assembled agreed to provide the CIA with $125 million to arm Masud and the Northern Alliance. There was still disagreement over which agency would handle the Predator. The all-important issue of how to deal with Pakistan, especially once U.S. arms started to flow to Masud, was left unresolved. Powell argued for putting more pressure on Pakistan, but he outlined no strategy. The meeting ended with White House lawyers being tasked to finalize a "National Security Presidential Directive" that would call for the elimination of al Qaeda. Rice said any new strategy to topple the Taliban regime would take three years to work.[60] A few days later, Mohammed Atta and his accomplices were saying their last prayers as they prepared to attack the American homeland.

CHAPTER FOUR

◆ ◆ ◆

Attack!

Retaliation and Invasion

The Bush administration was staggered by the attacks of September 11, and was initially at a loss as to what to do. The easy option of launching a blitz of cruise missiles, as Clinton had done in 1998, was ruled out, as al Qaeda personnel had abandoned their camps. In a prearranged plan, bin Laden had quickly sent many of his top managers out of Afghanistan. He himself left his home in Kandahar and disappeared. Al Qaeda was virtually dismantled, except for the fighters belonging to Brigade 555, some of whom remained on the front lines outside Kabul, while others retreated east into the mountains to await the U.S. attack.

There was enormous reluctance on the part of the U.S. military to invade Afghanistan, given the fate of the British and Soviet land armies in that country during the past two centuries. The U.S. Central Command, or CENTCOM, which had responsibility for the Middle East region, had no ready-made plan to invade Afghanistan, and it would take weeks before it could prepare one. And how would U.S. troops arrive in the landlocked country? Iran and Pakistan, the two most critical neighbors of Afghanistan, were hostile to the United States, while the Central Asian neighbors were tied to Russia and did not have the necessary facilities or access to the Taliban-controlled south. "CENTCOM had not developed a plan for conventional ground operations in Afghanistan. Nor had diplomatic arrangements for basing, staging, overflight and access been made with Afghanistan's neighbors," admitted CENTCOM chief Gen. Tommy Franks.[1]

The ease with which the nineteen suicide bombers arrived in the United States undetected was a massive intelligence failure that was swiftly laid at the feet of CIA director George Tenet. With his agency demoralized, Tenet realized that he had better make himself indispensable in the run-up to the war in Afghanistan. If the Pentagon had no plans for an invasion, he would preempt Secretary of Defense Rumsfeld. CIA planners quickly came up with an audacious plan, putting together a package that would see NA troops on the ground linking up with teams of CIA and U.S. Special Operations Forces, who would combine NA ground operations with U.S. air power using sophisticated technology. The aim was to avoid a major deployment of American troops, although the CIA was taking an enormous risk by presuming that the Taliban could thus be defeated.

On September 15, Tenet and his aides presented the hypothesis at a meeting at Camp David. With no other options on the table and the Pentagon having no plans to mount a full-scale invasion, his idea was accepted. The CIA now liaised with the Pentagon to send joint teams into Afghanistan. On September 17, Bush signed an order giving enormous powers to the CIA, allowing it to conduct the war in Afghanistan and make foreign policy decisions using the help of foreign intelligence agencies, in order to capture or kill members of al Qaeda. Up to $900 million and perhaps more than $1 billion was allocated to the CIA for covert operations.[2]

Tenet insists in his autobiography that the CIA was ready for this moment because it had been preparing such a plan for years.[3] The facts would suggest otherwise. For over a decade, CIA officers had made only five trips to the Panjsher Valley to meet with Masud, but Masud was now dead and the CIA had only a sketchy relationship with his successor, Gen. Mohammed Fahim. The CIA had provided only pocket money to Masud and had had nothing to do with the recent return of exiled warlords Rashid Dostum, Ismael Khan, and Karim Khalili, a leader of the Hazara ethnic group who had opened new fronts against the Taliban after reconciling their differences with Masud. They had returned with the help of Turkey, Russia, Uzbekistan, and Iran—countries that before 9/11 were far more worried about a Taliban victory than the United States ever was.

Moreover, the CIA had shown no sense of urgency in supporting the Northern Alliance when many feared that the Taliban offensives in the summer of 2001 could wipe out Masud's forces. Washington's decision to arm Masud's forces was made only one week before 9/11. Most critically, despite what Tenet and journalist Bob Woodward present in their books, the CIA had very few contacts with the Pashtun tribes in the south and had to go through the ISI every time they needed Pashtuns to monitor bin Laden.[4] When the time came for the CIA to unleash anti-Taliban Pashtuns in October, the agency found it had none and fell back on Britain's MI6 and the ISI to provide them. When Dick Cheney, frustrated by the CIA's slowness in opening a southern front against the Taliban, visited the CIA, he found it had few contacts among the Pashtun.

MI6 reverted to what its forefathers had done a century earlier during the British Raj—passing out large sums of money to Pashtun exiles living in Pakistan with the aim of persuading them to move into Afghanistan. Much of this initial funding ended up in the purchase of fancy cars and new houses in Peshawar. Few Pashtun leaders in Peshawar believed that the Taliban could be defeated on its home turf in the south.

Apart from a handful of CIA officers, no U.S. officials had been inside Afghanistan for a decade. Few CIA officers spoke Persian or its Afghan dialect, Dari, and nobody spoke Pushtu, the language of the Pashtuns. CIA and Special Operations Forces personnel who entered Afghanistan spoke either Russian or Arabic. This lack of language skills in every department of the U.S. government was exposed as being a critical problem. I was flooded with e-mail appeals from American companies hired by the U.S. government to find U.S. citizens who could speak "Farsi, Pushtu, Dari, Turkmen, Urdu or Uzbek."[5]

The Dari-speaking CIA veteran Gary Schroen, fifty-nine, was pulled out of retirement to head the first ten-man Afghanistan Liaison Team, code-named Jawbreaker, that flew to Tashkent and landed in the Panjsher Valley just two weeks after 9/11. They brought with them $3 million, which was immediately dished out to NA leaders—Fahim received $1 million as goodwill money. Another $10 million was quickly flown in so that the CIA could pay off other warlords, such as Abdul Rasul Sayyaf and Rashid Dostum.[6] When Gen. Tommy Franks met with Fahim on October 30 in the back of his giant C-17 cargo aircraft parked at Dushanbe Airport, there was some haggling before Franks handed him $5 million for the NA's military operation to take the north but to promise to stop short of Kabul.[7]

It was the cheapest war America was ever to fight. Yet on the back of its easy success and the laxity given to the CIA by Bush, for the next two years the agency was to run Afghanistan not by democratization or nation building but by paying off warlords to keep the peace, determining what was to be rebuilt and at what pace, running the Karzai administration, and slowing down everything else with the excuse that it was pursuing bin Laden. The attaché cases full of dollar bills they received would allow the warlords to build huge houses in Kabul and the Panjsher Valley after the war, set themselves up in business as suppliers of goods and local manpower to U.S. bases, ply the drug trade, and play the region's currency markets. General Fahim would become one of the richest men in Afghanistan, buying up property and an entire gold market in Kabul, while Abdul Rasul Sayyaf would buy up most of Paghman. When the CIA money ran out, the same warlords would turn back to the drug trade.

Even as Cheney and Rumsfeld were preparing to fight the war in Afghanistan, they were already thinking of fighting the next war in Iraq. The distraction of Iraq, which materialized just hours after the 9/11 attacks and continued indefinitely, was first to undermine and then defeat both U.S. policy in Afghanistan and the struggle to capture al Qaeda leaders. From insider accounts, we now know that even as the Pentagon building was still burning on the morning of September 11, the neocons were trying to blame Iraq's Saddam Hussein for the attacks. Donald Rumsfeld told his aide Stephen Cambone to look for evidence of Iraqi involvement: "Hard to get good case. Need to move swiftly. Near term target needs—go massive—sweep it all up, things related and not," Cambone's notes read.[8]

Richard Clarke attended meetings on Iraq on September 12. He later wrote, "At first I was incredulous that we were talking about something other than getting al Qaeda. Then I realized with almost a sharp physical pain that Rumsfeld and Wolfowitz were going to try to take advantage of this national tragedy to promote their agenda about Iraq."[9] I visited Washington several times in early 2002, sincerely believing that now the United States would do the right thing by Afghanistan and rebuild the country. I came up with suggestions for the State Department and the U.S. Agency for International Development as to how they could speed up nation building. By the early summer of 2002, when it became clear that the United States had no intentions of rebuilding Afghanistan, disillusionment set in as I saw that Iraq was the real target.

Despite the total absence of evidence, the neocons wanted to believe that bin Laden had pulled off 9/11 with help from Iraq. On September 15, at Camp David, Deputy Secretary of Defense Paul Wolfowitz argued for a simultaneous attack on Iraq and Afghanistan.[10] On November 21, the day before Thanksgiving and just as the Northern Alliance was trying to negotiate the Taliban surrender of Kunduz and Kandahar, Bush asked

Rumsfeld to draw up new plans for attacking Iraq. "What kind of a war plan do you have for Iraq?" Bush asked him.[11] Rumsfeld then ordered an incredulous Franks to draw up the plans. "Son of a bitch," Franks muttered under his breath.[12]

For decades the neocons had pushed for promoting big ideas on how to get Saddam Hussein, secure Iraq's oil supplies, and secure Israel.[13] Their idea for Iraq could immediately be translated into a military strategy, but there were no such plans for Afghanistan, even though bin Laden had been living there since 1996 and had directly attacked American power several times. The neocons had assiduously avoided any serious discussion of the real threat from Afghanistan.

The first U.S. failure was to snub potential allies. Two days after the 9/11 attacks, NATO invoked Article 5 of its constitution, declaring that the attack on the United States had been an attack on NATO, which was now obliged to respond. NATO and Russia issued an unprecedented joint statement of support. European countries primed their militaries, expecting to be called upon by the United States on the lines of the grand alliance the elder Bush had created for the first Gulf War, in 1991. They were totally unprepared for the policy of unilateralism Washington now followed. The message to NATO from Rumsfeld was essentially, "Thank you, but no thank you—we don't need you." When NATO secretary-general George Robertson arrived in Washington, he was first abused and then badly snubbed by an arrogant Wolfowitz. Senior German, French, and Scandinavian diplomats complained to me bitterly about the attitude of Rumsfeld and Wolfowitz. The bitterness it created was to linger until the United States asked for European help for the war in Iraq.

Only British prime minister Tony Blair seemed oblivious to the damage being done to the Atlantic alliance as he accepted America's unilateralism without question. Blair became obsessed with his role as an interlocutor between the international community and Bush, who in fact wanted no international help. Blair was convinced that as the world's great charmer and persuader, he could get people to do things by the sheer weight of his personality.[14] European pique at Blair was somewhat tempered by the hope that British input into planning the war would be beneficial, since the Americans were so ignorant about Afghanistan. After Blair and his aides read my Taliban book, I was invited to meet the prime minister when he came to Islamabad. I was impressed by his knowledge and charmed by the interest he showed in Afghanistan and the perceptive questions he asked me. But even in his asking them there was an element of showmanship, as one question followed another without his waiting for an answer—as though he wanted to perform rather than learn.

Blair was the only European leader whom Colin Powell asked for help in bringing Afghanistan's neighbors on board. Pakistan was on board within the first forty-eight hours of 9/11. The sensitive task of wooing Iran was handled by British foreign secretary Jack Straw. The Iranian leader, President Mohammed Khatami, was amenable to a war that would see Iran's hated enemy, the Taliban, destroyed, and he sent Bush a message to that effect through the Canadian government. On September 20, U.S. officials met with Iranian diplomats as part of the Geneva Group, after which Straw visited Tehran. Iran promised to provide search-and-rescue help if U.S. pilots were shot down, and deployed its military to seal its 560-mile-long border with Afghanistan. Turkey, which had opened a secret supply route to General Dostum through Uzbekistan even before 9/11, was asked for further help. On September 22, Prime Minister Bülent Ecevit declared that Turkey would join with Russia and Iran and step up aid to the Northern Alliance.

Muslim nations urged the United States to go to the UN Security Council for a clear mandate for war. On September 28, the Security Council adopted Resolution 1373, authorizing the use of force against terrorists. The resolution demanded that all 189 member states of the UN shut down financing, support, and safe havens for terrorists. President Bush ordered a freeze on all assets in the United States held by twenty-seven terrorist entities and asked all countries and banks to follow suit or risk jeopardizing their relations with Washington.

The next challenge was the complex task of wooing Central Asia. Although the five states—Uzbekistan, Kazakhstan, Kyrgyzstan, Tajikistan, and Turkmenistan—were ruled by dictators who could say yes or no to U.S. demands, they all had a supreme adviser in the shape of Russia. Ten years after achieving independence, it was still inconceivable that the five states would take a major foreign policy decision without Moscow's go-ahead, and President Vladimir Putin was determined to extract the maximum concessions from Washington. Both the United States and Russia had had a complex relationship with Central Asia in the past decade.

In 2001, Washington's relations with Central Asia were at a low ebb. After showing some initial concern for the welfare of these states in the early 1990s, largely dictated by the possibility of oil and gas contracts in three of the states, Washington all but lost interest. However, in 1994 and 1995, the United States helped Kazakhstan dismantle 104 SS-18 ballistic missiles and the 104 nuclear warheads were transferred to Russia under agreement. Kazakhstan was declared free of nuclear weapons.[15] In 1994 all the Central Asian states except Tajikistan joined NATO's Partnership for Peace alliance, and their forces participated in joint exercises with NATO. There was a renewed flirtation with Central Asia by the Clinton administration in 1997, when Strobe Talbott, a Russia specialist and deputy secretary of state, outlined a "Silk Road Strategy" for supporting democracy in Central Asia, but it never caught the imagination of Congress or the American public. Most important of all, the infrequent U.S. appeals for democratic and economic reform in the region increasingly fell on deaf ears among its authoritarian leaders because the United States never backed such appeals with either serious aid or serious recriminations.

Russia had gone through similar swings in its policy toward Central Asia. In the early 1990s, it pulled back from Central Asia as its own economy and armed services went into decline. Moscow could not project power when it did not have the instruments of power, and there was no public support for sustaining a relationship in a region that many Russians considered a backwater. Under Putin, Russia—now considerably richer and stronger on the back of Siberian and Central Asian oil and gas exports to Europe—began to insist that Central Asia was its backyard and that no major power should try to gain influence there without first going through Moscow.

Central Asian leaders also had to consider China's reaction. In 1996, Russia, China, Kazakhstan, Kyrgyzstan, and Tajikistan had joined the Shanghai Cooperation Organization, with China pledging to demilitarize their common borders. A year later China pulled its troops from 4,300 miles of its borders with Central Asia. China's major security thrust was to deter the Central Asian states from providing any support to the ethnic Uighur Muslims in Xinjiang province. The Uighurs were China's only Muslims, living mainly along the borders of Central Asia. Many had gone into exile in Central Asia to escape repression during the Maoist revolution. Now China considered any political expression of Uighur sentiment as a sign of separatism and Islamic extremism. China was extremely reluctant to see U.S. troops based just a few hundred miles from its borders.

Yet all the Central Asian regimes were predisposed to helping the Americans, because by doing so they could distance themselves from both

Russia and China, demonstrate their independence to their own people, and gain from the political legitimacy that an alliance with the United States would offer—legitimacy that would allow them to rule more ruthlessly at home. Moreover, they all felt threatened by the Taliban. Afghanistan borders three of the Central Asian states—Tajikistan, Uzbekistan, and Turkmenistan. Tajikistan had long supported Masud and the Northern Alliance, allowing Russia, Iran, and India to provide military supplies to Masud through Dushanbe. Uzbekistan had supported the Uzbek faction of the Northern Alliance, led by Dostum, providing him arms and funds as well as a sanctuary when his forces were routed by the Taliban. Only Turkmenistan had reached an understanding with the Taliban regime, providing it electricity and other commodities. All the Central Asian states had become saturated with the heroin emanating out of Afghanistan and they were anxious to stem the flow of drugs.

The post-communist regimes in Central Asia were all deeply secular and fearful of Islamic extremism spreading within their territories. They were eager to defeat the Taliban for another reason. Before 9/11, incursions by the Islamic Movement of Uzbekistan (IMU) had terrified governments in the region. Made up of Uzbek and Tajik militants from the Ferghana Valley and led by commander Juma Namangani and ideologue Tahir Yuldashev, the IMU had undergone several political metamorphoses. It had first emerged as an Islamic party opposed to Uzbek president Islam Karimov, before he drove them underground. The IMU reemerged to fight in Tajikistan's bloody five-year civil war (1992–1997), on the side of the Islamists. After the war, they settled uneasily in the Pamir Mountains, in central Tajikistan, where I tried to track them down to write the first book about the IMU.[16] They continued to build underground cells in Uzbekistan and the Ferghana Valley, with help from the ISI and the Saudi intelligence service, which had funded them for some time. At one point Yuldashev spent several years as a guest of the ISI in Peshawar. The IMU aimed to create an Islamic state in Uzbekistan and then in the rest of Central Asia, but their ideology was confused and contradictory.

In February 1999, explosions in Tashkent close to President Karimov's office, which claimed two dozen lives and wounded several hundred people, were assumed to have been carried out by the IMU. Karimov used the bombings to arrest hundreds of political dissidents and Islamic activists, leading to speculation that the government itself may have carried out the bombings. The IMU then led guerrilla incursions into southern Kyrgyzstan and eastern Uzbekistan in the summer of 1999, and again in 2000, creating mayhem and fear. In the winter of 2000, the IMU retreated into Afghanistan and into the arms of Osama bin Laden, who immediately adopted them, seeing them as a ready-made instrument for introducing al Qaeda into Central Asia. The Taliban also were anxious to enlist the IMU fighters, as a source of additional manpower in their battle with the Northern Alliance.

By now Namangani was a cult figure among Islamists in the entire region—all the more so because, like Mullah Omar, he remained mysterious, never giving interviews or allowing himself to be photographed. In September 2000, the United States designated the IMU a terrorist group, thus providing Karimov with a major political boost, as now his enemies were also America's enemies. After 9/11, Mullah Omar appointed Namangani head of all Taliban and foreign forces in the north. He had proved to be fearless and brave, if not rash, while his IMU fighters were known for their ferocity and barbarity on the battlefield.

The roots of radicalization in Central Asia among young people lay in the appalling policies of leaders such as Karimov, who waged war against all political dissent and anything remotely Islamic. In Uzbekistan there was a total ban on all political parties, trade and student unions, and political gatherings. More than ten thousand political prisoners filled Uzbek jails, where torture and death under interrogation were common. Anyone appearing too Islamic or even saying his prayers five times a day could be arrested and tortured. As long as such regimes considered secular democratic parties a threat, it was natural that a violent Islamic underground would flourish.

Yet Uzbekistan was the potential springboard for any U.S. invasion of northern Afghanistan. The largest country in the region, with a population of twenty-nine million, Uzbekistan also had the largest air bases, inherited from the Soviet era, and the only trained army in the region. It was from these bases that the Soviet Union had launched its disastrous invasion of Afghanistan in 1979. Moreover, the CIA and the Pentagon had been closely collaborating with the Uzbek army and secret services since 1997, providing training, equipment, and mentoring in the hope of using Uzbek Special Forces to snatch Osama bin Laden from Afghanistan, a fact I uncovered on a trip to Washington in 2000.[17] Now the CIA wanted to inject its own teams into northern Afghanistan using Uzbekistan's air bases.

Anticipating this, Russia first tried to block any U.S. deployment in

Central Asia. Two days after 9/11, Russian intelligence officials held a meeting in Dushanbe with the Northern Alliance and their counterparts from Iran, India, and Uzbekistan, promising to step up military assistance to the Northern Alliance—in a bid to outbid the CIA. Russia also persuaded Tajikistan's president, Emomali Rakhmonov, to say that his country would not to allow its air space to be used by U.S. aircraft. The seven-thousand-strong Russian division guarding the Tajikistan-Afghanistan border was placed on a heightened state of alert, as Russian officials insisted that Central Asia would not offer the United States military bases.

Behind the scenes the mood was entirely different, as Karimov and other leaders were all anxious to entice the Americans. After Washington offered to increase U.S. aid, Tashkent privately told the American embassy that it would offer the United States bases. The Uzbek assurance was hastened by news from Kabul that the Taliban had appointed Juma Namangani commander of northern Afghanistan. Putin now realized that once Karimov had broken with Russian guidance, other Central Asian leaders would do the same, so it was better for Moscow to make a collective offer to the United States.

Almost overnight Moscow began to play the role of conciliator and ally to the United States. On September 17, Putin hosted a meeting of all Central Asian leaders in Moscow to hammer out a joint stand on the bases issue. A formal deal was finally struck between Moscow and Washington on September 22, after Bush spoke with Putin on the telephone. Putin insisted that any U.S. bases in Central Asia should be temporary. In return, Bush promised to desist from criticizing Russia's controversial war in Chechnya and to consult with Moscow before taking any steps in Central Asia, while promising to help accelerate Russia's integration into Western economic institutions. By then, the CIA was already flying its teams into the massive Karshi-Khanabad, or K2, air base in southern Uzbekistan, where U.S. army engineers were repairing the runway. Now Tajikistan said that it, too, would offer the United States bases on its soil.

The United States had arrived in Central Asia—the first Western army to penetrate the region since the Greek armies of Alexander the Great. Uzbekistan provided a base for multiple types of U.S. operations out of K2 and later allowed Germany to set up a resupply base at Termez, close to the border with Afghanistan. Tajikistan hosted French Mirage fighter bombers at Dushanbe Airport, which did not pull out until November

2005. Later, Kyrgyzstan was to provide bases for U.S. and Coalition forces and aircraft at Manas Air Base, outside Bishkek. After the war, Manas became a major hub for supplies to Western forces in Afghanistan. Kazakhstan and Turkmenistan provided overflight facilities for U.S. aircraft. Turkmenistan balked at any other support except for facilitating humanitarian aid to Afghanistan. In Moscow, U.S. Army generals were given extensive briefings from Soviet-era commanders who had fought in Afghanistan.

When Rumsfeld arrived in Tashkent on October 5, to acknowledge the deal formally, Karimov still wanted to camouflage it. He was bargaining for the maximum from the United States: immediate membership in NATO, $50 million in loans, and a defense treaty. He played hard to get, insisting that no attacks on Afghanistan would be carried out from Uzbek soil—even as U.S. fighter jets arrived at the K2 air base. He was still fearful of a reaction from the Taliban and the IMU, who had mustered some ten thousand troops to defend Mazar-e-Sharif and had threatened to retaliate against Uzbekistan if it dared joined the U.S.-led Coalition.

Rumsfeld was opaque, saying only that "the two countries have met; the two countries have talked; the two countries . . . have worked out a series of arrangements that make sense from both our standpoints."[18] Finally, on October 12, both countries signed the formal agreement on the use of K2. It included a vague U.S. security guarantee for Uzbekistan, speaking of "the need to consult on an urgent basis about appropriate steps to address the situation in the event of a direct threat to the security or territorial integrity of Uzbekistan." Karimov had fought hard to get the clause in so that he could show his people and Russia that he had not sold himself cheaply.[19]

The United States paid Uzbekistan an initial $15 million, but by the end of 2002, Uzbekistan would receive $120 million in military equipment and training to the army, $55 million in credits, and another $82 million for the intelligence services—the same agencies that were to help the CIA render al Qaeda prisoners and torture Uzbek civilians.[20] By mid-October, more than two thousand troops from the U.S. Army's Tenth Mountain Division were at K2, ready to invade Afghanistan.

The United States successfully forged an alliance of neighboring countries. It was much less successful in forging an anti-Taliban alliance among the Pashtuns inside Afghanistan. Pashtun attention was focused on Rome and the group of bickering exiles surrounding former king Zahir Shah, now eighty-five years old. To millions of Afghans, his name evoked memories of a golden past in the 1960s and 1970s, when Afghanistan was at peace—although the golden hues of that era were more myth than reality because the country had also been desperately poor. The exiles in Rome were consummate intriguers, incapable of uniting, and few had set foot in Afghanistan since the 1970s. Many of them thought the king was being manipulated by his son-in-law Gen. Abdul Wali and by his influential cousin Mahmood Ghazi.[21]

Before 9/11, and after some prodding by the Clinton administration and the UN, Masud and the Northern Alliance had reached out to the Rome group. Both agreed to set up a joint council that would prepare to hold a Loya Jirga presided over by the former king. After 9/11, the United States tried to get the Rome group and the Northern Alliance to move toward greater coordination, and Richard Haass, heading the State Department's Policy Planning Division, visited Rome to anoint the king's new role.

Whatever happened in Rome, the key to defeating the Taliban would be raising the standard of rebellion in the Pashtun belt. The ISI played all sides of the Pashtun equation, wooing prominent members of the Rome group, who detested working with the Northern Alliance, secretly contacting Pashtuns who were in the NA, while also trying to create an alternative Pashtun group in Peshawar that was anti-Taliban. This Peshawar Group was led by Pir Sayed Ahmad Gailani, a Sufi leader of some prominence whose party had fought the Soviets in the 1980s. Gailani hosted a conference with some seven hundred exiled Pashtuns living in Peshawar. Each participant received money and free meals (4000 rupees, or 65 dollars), leading to accusations that the ISI had manipulated the meeting. None of the participants volunteered to start fighting the Taliban.

The CIA wanted to see the Peshawar group merge with moderate Taliban defectors—if the ISI could produce them—to form a new anti-Taliban Pashtun alliance. The most elusive chimera that the CIA pursued, with the encouragement of the ISI, was that "moderate" Taliban Pashtuns would rise to denounce Mullah Omar, hand over bin Laden to the Americans, and join a new coalition government in Kabul. Since 2000, the ISI's Gen. Mehmood Ahmad had been holding out to the CIA the promise of a "Taliban lite," but doing absolutely nothing to produce one. The idea took on a new life after 9/11, but there seemed to be no Taliban takers. In fact, the reality was that the ISI had no intention of splitting the Taliban, even if it had the power to do so. There were moderates among the Taliban earlier on, but the ISI had betrayed them to Mullah Omar long ago. Where the ISI succeeded was in manipulating the U.S. media, especially *The New York Times* and *The Washington Post,* convincing them that it was earnestly trying to create moderates among the Taliban.[22]

The earlier Taliban moderates who were fed up with Mullah Omar's unnatural alliance with bin Laden had been grouped around Mullah Rabbani, the head of the government in Kabul, who died of cancer in a Karachi hospital in April 2001. The moderates were now leaderless, and those from Rabbani's group who had secretly talked to the UN or Western diplomats in Islamabad and who had complained about Mullah Omar were now too scared of the ISI to do so again. In reality, General Mehmood was not promoting moderates but trying to ferret them out so they could be exposed and betrayed to Mullah Omar once again. The threat of death hung over any Taliban leaders if they betrayed Mullah Omar or the ISI. It was a masterful double game that the ISI was to play with even greater dexterity after 9/11.

Musharraf himself played the game adroitly, pretending several times that Pakistan was on the verge of producing moderates. "Extremism is not in every Taliban," he said in the presence of Colin Powell just before the bombing campaign began. "I would not like to get into the details of who are moderates, but one knows for sure there are many moderate elements."[23] Powell appeared to buy Musharraf's words, replying that "if you got rid of the regime there would still be those . . . willing to participate in the development of a new Afghanistan." At the end of October, when Taliban foreign minister Mullah Wakil Ahmad Muttawakil arrived in Islamabad for secret talks with the ISI—again talks deliberately leaked to the U.S. media—Musharraf asked the Americans for a bombing pause because "there are some people who may be waiting to change sides."[24] The entire exercise was shadow-boxing by the ISI.

Inside Afghanistan, the Northern Alliance was also deeply divided and buffeted by the conflicting claims of its newfound American advisers and its old supporters Iran, Russia, and India. General Fahim, the successor to Masud, was infuriated that the CIA had provided cash and weapons to each warlord individually rather than through him. The other warlords did not trust Fahim. He also proved incapable of keeping the Panjsheri Tajiks united. Burhanuddin Rabbani, the Panjsheri political leader who had been president of Afghanistan from 1992 to 1996, now expected to return to Kabul as president, but many Panjsheris detested both him and Fahim. However, there was progress in Rome, where on October 1, the Rome group and the Northern Alliance established a Supreme Council of 120 members who planned to set up an interim government after the Taliban. The Taliban responded by arresting hundreds of Zahir Shah supporters inside Afghanistan.

On September 21, Rumsfeld received from General Franks the first draft of a battle plan, Operation Enduring Freedom. On October 2, Bush approved the four-phase plan that would lead to the defeat of the Taliban regime. There was no commitment to reconstruct Afghanistan.[25] The United States would deploy four aircraft carrier battle groups comprising thirty-two naval vessels, forty thousand soldiers, and four hundred aircraft, although few soldiers would ever see Afghanistan. Britain would deploy some eighteen battleships, fifty aircraft, and twenty thousand troops. But the real work woud be done by the one hundred and fifteen CIA officers and three hundred U.S. Special Operations Forces personnel inside Afghanistan, working with NA leaders. After the liaison team Jawbreaker arrived in Panjsher, other joint CIA–Special Forces teams arrived at the side of Generals Dostum and Mohammed Atta (not the 9/11 hijacker of that name) in the north, Ismael Khan in the west, Karim Khalili in the Hazarajat (central Afghanistan), and eventually Hamid Karzai in the south.

It was already becoming clear to some U.S. officials that a military victory alone would not be enough and that America's allies in the region would be more helpful if they knew the United States was committed to rebuilding Afghanistan. Bush had all along rejected nation building. "We are not into nation building, we are focused on justice," he said as late as September 26.[26] Some State Department officials, however, urged Powell to defend nation building. "We are looking at a defining moment, if only we will grasp the opportunity to shape a post-Taliban Afghanistan," a senior official told me at the time.[27] Tony Blair also told Bush that the United States could not ignore the issue of political transition and how the next Afghan government would be formed.

Powell ordered Richard Haass to organize a meeting with experts on post-Taliban Afghanistan. Those who gathered on September 24 included Tom Gouttierre, who ran the Center for Afghanistan Studies at Nebraska University; Arnold Schifferdecker, a U.S. diplomat who had been assigned to the UN Afghanistan mission; David Champagne, a former trainer of U.S. Special Operations personnel in Afghanistan's culture and society;

Barnett Rubin; Ashraf Ghani; and Daud Yakub, a young, dynamic Afghan who had worked with U.S. congressmen on Afghan initiatives and now ran the king's office in Rome.

The meeting ended with an overwhelming conclusion that the United States had to get involved in forming the next government but that the process should be carried out by the UN. "We owe it to the Afghans to stick around after the defeat of the Taliban," said one participant. Another explained how the United States should help in "basic stabilization rather than bringing about a full democratic set-up." Haass commented: "You mean nation building lite." The epithet, related more to beer than to nation building, stuck. Haass recommended to Powell that the political transition be undertaken by the UN while the United States and its allies pursued an agenda of "nation building lite."

The meeting focused attention on the problem of the successor government in Kabul. On October 3, Kofi Annan reappointed Lakhdar Brahimi as his special representative to Afghanistan, and Vendrell as Brahimi's deputy. Bush appointed James Dobbins, a veteran U.S. diplomat experienced in dealing with failed states such as Haiti and Yugoslavia, as the U.S. ambassador to the Afghan opposition. Dobbins and Brahimi knew each other well, having worked together in Haiti. John Negroponte took over as U.S. ambassador to the United Nations. A week later Bush told the press that "it would be a useful function for the United Nations to take over the so-called 'nation building'—I would call it the stabilization of a future government—after our military mission is complete."[28]

The neoconservatives gritted their teeth as just two weeks after Bush rejected nation building, he was now endorsing it. Powell tried to dampen enthusiasm, saying, "It isn't a huge Marshall Plan kind of investment."[29] The key issue was what kind of armed force should occupy Kabul after the Taliban were driven out. Annan and Brahimi were strongly against a UN blue-helmet force, which would take months to set up. The United States preferred a force provided by "willing nations," possibly led by Turkey. Brahimi and the French were initially in favor of an Afghan peacekeeping force drawn from all ethnic groups.

Brahimi now summoned his group of "experts"—the same one he had formed in 1998 and which Francesc Vendrell had continued to work with. Over dinner at his favorite Chinese restaurant in Manhattan, Brahimi discussed what to do next. Those present included Barnett Rubin; Ashraf Ghani; Iqbal Reza, the chief of staff to Kofi Annan; Fatemeh Zia, an

Iranian-American UN diplomat who would become Brahimi's special assistant; and me. Brahimi asked Rubin and Ghani to start writing a draft document outlining how a political transition, security, and a peacekeeping force could be set up and managed. Rubin, Ghani, and a handful of UN officials became known as the UN Strategy Group for Afghanistan, and the document they prepared eventually became the basis for the UN Security Council resolution that empowered the UN to oversee the political transition in Kabul.

Before leaving for the region to speak to Afghans in Pakistan and Iran, Brahimi went to Washington to see what ideas the Americans might have. Haass told him that "when Americans say 'we' have come to consult with you, it usually means we have already taken our decision and we have just come to inform you what it is." But this time, Haass said, "I can assure you we have no idea of what to do or what needs to be done." The White House was in a hurry to get the UN to come up with a workable strategy. Powell met Brahimi and told him, "Speed, speed, speed." Brahimi replied, "Slowly, slowly, slowly," emphasizing that negotiations to form a new government with the Afghans could not be rushed.[30] When British foreign secretary Jack Straw also urged Brahimi to hurry up, Brahimi reminded Straw that to try, after two decades of war, to form a new government in Kabul overnight was "a totally crazy objective."

Inside Afghanistan millions of Afghans scared of U.S. bombs began a mass exodus from the cities to the countryside. Thousands of Afghans arrived on the borders of Pakistan and Iran desperate to be let in as refugees. UN agencies prepared for an expected outflow of 1.5 million Afghan refugees once the U.S. offensive began. The UN's World Food Programme, which was already feeding some three million Afghans inside the country before 9/11, said it had only two to three weeks of food stocks left and no hope of sending more food into Afghanistan, as the Taliban had closed the border and UN staff had been withdrawn. "There are pre-famine conditions in some areas, people are eating grass and animal fodder," WFP country director Khaled Mansur told me.

At his heavily guarded home in Quetta, Hamid Karzai was meeting with dozens of tribal and clan leaders a day. Taliban officials would arrive secretly from southern Afghanistan to pledge their loyalty to him and the king. "Hundreds of Taliban are sending their families to Pakistan and are ready to defect the moment the king gives the call for a national uprising,"

Karzai told me. The mayor of Kandahar and some judges had crossed over into Pakistan and contacted him as well.

Pakistan had asked the Americans to delay any attack so they could talk to Mullah Omar. Two days of secret talks between Omar and an ISI delegation headed by General Ahmad in Kandahar failed to deliver any concession, save for Omar's agreeing to call a meeting of Afghan ulema to decide the fate of bin Laden. It was a delaying tactic. Omar met with two more delegations from Pakistan. On September 28, Ahmad traveled to Kandahar for the last time, leading a delegation of hard-line ulema from the Deobandi sect, including Maulana Nizamuddin Shamzai, an extremist Karachi-based cleric who had been a mentor to Omar and bin Laden.

Subsequently there were leaks to the CIA that General Ahmad had encouraged Omar to resist an American attack rather than give up bin Laden. Shamzai also told Omar to hold firm. The CIA, convinced now that Ahmad was playing a double game, informed Musharraf of what had happened. Meanwhile, the agency had opened up its own channel to the Taliban. In great secrecy, it had sent Robert Grenier, the Pakistan station chief, to Quetta to meet with Mullah Akhtar Mohammed Usmani, the Taliban's senior military commander. Grenier urged Usmani to persuade Omar to give up bin Laden, but there was no response. In a second meeting, on October 2, Grenier asked Usmani to desert Omar and help deliver the Saudi terrorist. However, Usmani remained loyal to Omar.

The ISI was playing an even larger double game. An ISI report sent to Musharraf predicted that the Taliban resistance would continue into the spring of 2002, that the United States' reluctance to commit ground troops would deny itself a quick victory, and that Taliban fighters, now bolstered by thousands of al Qaeda and Pakistani militants, would hold firm for some time. When the Taliban eventually lost the cities, they would conduct a guerrilla war from the mountains. Musharraf, a firm believer in the ISI's predictive capabilities, used the report to justify the ISI's continued supplies of arms, ammunition, and fuel to the Taliban, in direct defiance of the UN resolution to cease all supplies to the Taliban and of his own promise to the Americans.

ISI fuel tankers and trucks, covered in heavy tarpaulins, daily rumbled across the Khyber Pass and other border crossings into Afghanistan. At Chaman, in Balochistan, from where ISI trucks traveled to Kandahar, the crossing point was sealed off as customs officials waved the trucks through without checks. The trucks belonged to the National Logistics Cell, an army-owned trucking company that had ironically been set up with CIA funds in the 1980s to deliver arms to the Afghan Mujahedin fighting the Soviets. Thus, even as some ISI officers were helping U.S. officers locate Taliban targets for U.S. bombers, other ISI officers were pumping in fresh armaments to the Taliban. On the Afghan side of the border, NA intelligence operatives compiled lists of the arriving ISI trucks and handed them to the CIA.

Musharraf had promised the Americans that all ISI operatives inside Afghanistan would be withdrawn before the U.S. bombing campaign began. However, dozens of operatives and soldiers from the Frontier Corps stayed inside, helping the Taliban prepare their defenses. "I assumed from the beginning of the conflict that ISI advisers were supporting the Taliban with expertise and material and, no doubt, sending a steady stream of intelligence back to Islamabad," said CIA officer Gary Berntsen.[31] Moreover, Ahmad allowed more ISI officers to go inside, including five senior officers who met with Mullah Omar at the end of September.[32] "The ISI is an institution full of intelligence, but devoid of wisdom," M. P. Bhandara, a seasoned Pakistani politician and businessman, told me at the time.

The ISI justified its actions as stemming from fear of an Indian-controlled NA government in Kabul after the overthrow of the Taliban. It also did not want to totally abandon the Taliban, its only proxy in Afghanistan. At the same time, the army wanted to keep the Americans engaged, fearing that once Kabul had fallen, they would once again desert the region. With one hand Musharraf played at helping the war against terrorism, while with the other he continued to deal with the Taliban.

There was now enormous U.S. pressure on Musharraf to replace Gen. Mehmood Ahmad. India had attempted to defame Ahmad by linking him to the 9/11 hijackers, although there was never any evidence of that.[33] However, the upsurge in violence in Indian Kashmir, which threatened to undermine the U.S. attack on Afghanistan, was placed at his door. On October 1, militants had exploded a car bomb outside the parliament building in Srinagar, killing twenty-nine people. Meanwhile, the Afghans feared that the Bush administration's tolerance of ISI machinations could lead to a replay of the nineties, when the United States handed over policy jurisdiction on Afghanistan to Pakistan and Saudi Arabia, which led to the rise of the Taliban. Ashraf Ghani warned the Americans about "outsourcing the management of Afghanistan to Pakistan."[34]

A few hours before U.S. air strikes began, Musharraf made a move to reassert his authority in the army and reassure the international community about his intentions: he sacked his three senior-most generals, who had helped him carry out the coup in 1999 and were known for their hard-line Islamist views. All three had opposed his rapid acceptance of U.S. demands after 9/11. The ISI chief was forced to resign from the army and was replaced by Lt.-Gen. Ehsan ul-Haq, a close confidant of Musharraf, who had previously headed up Pakistan's Military Intelligence (MI), a smaller military intelligence service. Lt.-General Aziz, the former ISI officer who had run the Taliban in the 1990s and was now corps commander, Lahore, was kicked upstairs to a largely ceremonial job.[35] The deputy chief of army staff, Gen. Muzaffar Usmani, resigned after he was replaced. Musharraf extended his own term as army chief, as his original three-year term had expired on October 7.

U.S. and other Western embassies in Islamabad were ecstatic at the move, which showed that Musharraf was still very much in charge. The replacement of Ahmad allowed the new ISI chief to remove dozens of mid-level ISI officers who had been involved with the pro-Taliban policy. However, an organization that had trained and motivated hundreds of its officers to support extremist Islamic factions in Afghanistan and Kashmir for two decades could not be expected to change its views overnight. Some of these officers, deeply religious and vociferously anti-American, considered themselves more Taliban than the Taliban.

Musharraf knew that as long as the Americans did not trust the ISI, they would not listen to his advice about the conduct of the war. Now he demanded that he be consulted on any future U.S. policymaking regarding Afghanistan. He wrote a four-page letter to Bush saying Pakistan would not accept an NA government in Kabul and that Pashtuns must be fully represented. The Saudi foreign minister, Prince Saud al-Faisal, signed on to it and agreed to carry it to Bush, accompanied by the new ISI chief. After flying on a plane lent by Prince Bandar, the influential Saudi ambassador to Washington, General Haq and Saud first handed the paper to Tony Blair in London, and then to Bush and George Tenet in Washington. However, the United States was going to make its own decisions regarding the conduct of the war and would consult with neither its NATO allies nor Musharraf.

This became clear on the evening of October 7, on the Shomali Plain north of Kabul, which had been fought over for a decade. The CIA team there told Afghan commanders to ground their helicopters by sunset. The commanders in turn alerted some 250 foreign journalists camped out with the NA forces, who pointed their TV cameras toward Kabul, some thirty miles away as the sun set. Around the world people watched in anticipation. It was the best-advertised beginning of a war in recent memory— reassurance that nothing is secret in Afghanistan for very long. The first U.S. attack on the Taliban delivered fifty cruise missiles and dozens of laser-guided bombs on thirty-one military targets, hitting airports, anti-aircraft defenses, and radar installations around all the major cities. The Taliban Defense Ministry, in the center of Kabul, received a direct hit that killed twenty Afghans.

That night, the U.S. Air Force also dropped 37,500 humanitarian food packages to help refugees and to impress upon the population that the United States was not conducting a war against them. The U.S. military later said it exhausted its list of fixed Taliban targets in the first two nights of bombing, in which more than one hundred Afghans were reported killed.

That same night, Osama bin Laden delivered a chilling message to the American people through a pre-recorded video aired on Qatar's Al Jazeera television, promising more terrorist attacks on America. "Neither America nor the people who live in it will dream of security before we live it in Palestine and not before all the infidel armies leave the land of Mohammed," said bin Laden, shaking a finger at the camera.[36] The next day, violent protests erupted in many Pakistani cities, although the Islamic students and mullahs involved were not joined by the general public. In Quetta, some fifteen thousand militants burned down cinemas, a shopping plaza, and UN offices. Musharraf told his countrymen that Bush and Blair had promised him that a government "friendly" to Pakistan would emerge in Afghanistan and the military campaign would be swift.

The Taliban had massed an estimated sixty thousand troops on the battlefields stretching from the northeastern province of Takhar to Kabul, Herat province in the west, and Kandahar in the south. Every day, Taliban numbers were supplemented by foreign fighters arriving from Pakistan. Three thousand Arab fighters from at least thirteen Arab countries who had taken an oath of loyalty to bin Laden were on the Kabul front and in the north. More than nine thousand Pakistani militants, poorly armed and destined to be cannon fodder for the Taliban, had arrived from the tribal areas of Pakistan. The Islamic Movement of Uzbekistan had some twenty-five hundred Central Asian fighters defending three cities in northern Afghanistan. They were joined by hundreds of Chechens and Uighurs.[37]

The most obvious plan for the Coalition and its NA allies was first to concentrate on the north, where the Taliban were most vulnerable, the population hostile, and U.S. supply routes to Uzbekistan close by. However, Mazar-e-Sharif was surrounded by the forces of three NA commanders who were bitter rivals—the Uzbek general Rashid Dostum, the Tajik general Mohammed Atta, loyal to Fahim, and the Hazara leader Mohammed Mohaqiq. They refused to cooperate with one another until the CIA placed separate teams alongside each general.

From his base at Jabal ul-Saraj, on the Shomali Plain, Fahim's twenty thousand largely Tajik infantry were now better armed, clothed, and fed thanks to the CIA. Fahim wanted to hold them back from attacking the Taliban until American bombing had softened up Taliban positions. However, Fahim's commanders were impatient, insisting upon a ground attack, fearful that there was a conspiracy between the United States and Pakistan to deprive the Northern Alliance of taking Kabul. U.S. bombers were avoiding flattening Taliban positions outside Kabul, fearing a premature collapse of the Taliban while there was still no UN-sponsored alternative government in place. On October 17, Fahim held an NA commanders meeting in the Panjsher Valley, where he persuaded the Northern Alliance to hold off any attack on Kabul for a month.

Although Western diplomats in Rome were urging Zahir Shah to move speedily to create an interim government when the Taliban fell, the bickering between the Afghans continued, and it became clear that only the UN could establish a new government. The key problem was that there were still no Pashtun leaders inside Afghanistan resisting the Taliban. While Pakistan and Saudi Arabia wanted a Pashtun-dominated future government, Russia, Iran, and the Central Asian states were adamantly opposed to any compromise with the Taliban. After meeting with NA leaders in Dushanbe on October 22, Vladimir Putin said he would never agree to any future role for moderate Taliban.

Four weeks of bombing had weakened the Taliban and made them unable to resist a determined ground assault. The first breakthrough came in the north, where the CIA teams had finally united Dostum and Atta and coordinated a single battle plan that involved a two-pronged pincer attack on Mazar-e-Sharif. Dostum's cavalry advanced on the left flank as CIA air traffic controllers guided U.S. aircraft to rain down bombs on Taliban positions. The Uzbeks, the bravest but among the cruelest fighters in Central Asia, were mounted on horses and led cavalry charges against fixed Taliban positions and tanks in a dramatic replay of eighteenth-century warfare. On the evening of November 9, some eight thousand Taliban troops were routed outside Mazar-e-Sharif. As they fled in their four-by-four pickups, U.S. bombers targeted them from the air. The entire north became a shooting gallery, and over the next few days several thousand Taliban were killed. The remainder fled to Kunduz, which they turned into the last redoubt.

The capture of Mazar-e-Sharif held enormous strategic significance. It was just forty miles from the border with Uzbekistan, where two thousand U.S. troops were now based. Its large airport, six miles from the city, became a bridgehead for U.S. supplies and aircraft. UN relief agencies, which had stockpiled large quantities of food at Termez, on the Uzbekistan side of the border, could now set up the first refugee camps inside Afghanistan. Moreover, Mazar was the backbone of the country's economy. Sixty percent of Afghanistan's agricultural production and 80 percent of its former industrial, mineral, and gas wealth were concentrated in the north. One of the earliest casualties of the bombing was the IMU's Juma Namangani. Critically injured at Cheshmai Shefa, near Mazar, on November 26, when his convoy was hit by U.S. aircraft, he was taken to Kabul, where he died—only thirty-two.

With the death of Namangani, Uzbek president Karimov's gamble of siding with the United States at the risk of annoying Russia seemed to have paid off. Yet he refused to open up the Friendship Bridge—a road and rail link across the Amu Darya River to Afghanistan that would have allowed supplies to flow easily. For several months Tashkent refused to budge, citing the fear of the Taliban or IMU retreating into Uzbekistan. There was tremendous resentment against Karimov among U.S. commanders and aid workers until Colin Powell visited Tashkent in early December and persuaded Karimov to open up the bridge.

Just three days after the fall of Mazar-e-Sharif, the Northern Alliance captured the whole of northern, western, and central Afghanistan. While the NA captured the north, Ismael Khan's forces pounced on Taliban troops trying to flee down the western side of Afghanistan. On November 13, Khan captured Herat after its six-thousand-strong Taliban garrison fled. In central Afghanistan, or the Hazarajat, Hazara fighters persuaded thousands of Taliban fighters to defect, and then captured Bamiyan, where the two ancient Buddha statues had been destroyed by the Taliban in April. The Taliban now held just a small pocket in the northeast, around the city of Kunduz, where there was a large Pashtun population.

The issue of what kind of administration would supplant the Taliban now became paramount. Zahir Shah had appealed in vain to Dostum and northern commanders to set up a civilian administration loyal to the council the Rome group had set up. Instead, each warlord took control of what he had conquered. Mazar-e-Sharif was divided into two zones by the bitter rivals Generals Dostum and Atta. At the UN, where the General Assembly had just started, diplomats were pleased at the unexpected victories but aghast at the slow-moving plans to create a new government.

Russia still insisted upon a major say in the makeup of the future Afghan government. Putin arrived in Dushanbe on October 22 to sign a pact with Tajikistan's president Rakhmonov and the former Afghan president Burhanuddin Rabbani, recognizing Rabbani as the president of Afghanistan. Russian defense officials then began discussions with Rabbani as to what military aid he needed, in a bid to create a Russian-backed proxy. It was a blatant attempt to undermine the UN effort and create divisions between the Tajiks and the Uzbek warlords, who no longer recognized Rabbani as president.

The Americans countered Putin by sending Secretary of Defense Rumsfeld to Dushanbe a week later. He offered aid to Tajikistan, which agreed to allow U.S. forces to use three small air bases—Kulyab, Kurgun Tube, and Khujand, near the Afghan border. Rumsfeld made it clear that Rabbani was unacceptable as the new president. He delivered the same message in Tashkent the following day. In order to prevent further deterioration in their relations, Bush invited Putin to his ranch in Crawford, Texas, on November 14, to discuss the future of Afghanistan. The same day, the UN Security Council approved Resolution 1378 endorsing Lakhdar Brahimi's efforts to bring the Afghan factions together and form a new government in Kabul.

CHAPTER FIVE

◆ ◆ ◆

The Search for a Settlement

Afghanistan and Pakistan at Odds

On top of a cupboard in his bedroom in Kabul's presidential palace, Hamid Karzai still keeps an old satellite phone. The phone is old-fashioned and bulky, shaped like a laptop computer. Its cover lifts to become the antenna. On the evening of October 7, 2001, the day after the U.S. bombing campaign began, Karzai packed this phone into a small bag, mounted a motorbike driven by a friend, and rode around the border town of Caman, Balochistan, to cross into Afghanistan. Other close friends followed. For the next few weeks, Karzai's satellite phone was to be his only contact with the outside world. The American and British embassies in Islamabad knew he was going in, but he had made sure that Pakistan's ISI would have no knowledge of his journey.

He spent the first night near Kandahar, and two days later arrived in a small village close to Tarin Kot, the dusty, dirty, and isolated capital of Uruzghan province perched in the midst of formidable dry mountains. Uruzghan was the home province of Mullah Omar and a major recruitment center for the Taliban's army, but Karzai also had friends here who had helped him smuggle in weapons months earlier. He stayed in the village for eleven days, until the Taliban got wind of his presence and sent up a strong force from Kandahar to capture and kill him. Before he fled into the mountains with sixty men, he met secretly with tribal elders from Tarin Kot, who told him that they were powerless to help him unless he had the support of the Americans. Only then would they be prepared to rise up. "It was then that I realized that the whole nation was ready for change, but people felt helpless," Karzai told me.

On the march escaping the Taliban and with his satellite phone battery running low, he called the American embassy in Islamabad asking for help. U.S. officials there moved swiftly, asking him to light fires on the hills around his position for two consecutive nights. On the second night they called to say they had found him, and the next morning U.S. aircraft dropped canisters with weapons and food. The BBC's Lyse Doucet, from London, and I, from Lahore, would alternately speak with Karzai by phone. "The Americans are finally taking me seriously because for the moment there is nobody else resisting among the Pashtuns," he shouted into his satellite phone after the airdrop. After the fall of Mazar-e-Sharif, Karzai reported that "there is a tremendous weakening of morale amongst the Taliban, who are loosing their repressive grip on the countryside." On November 8, Karzai and his men were surrounded by Taliban forces, who had been trailing them through Uruzghan province. Later, Karzai recalled, "The first Taliban unit surrounded us before dawn and we broke up into several groups to escape. Then a second Taliban unit, consisting of Arabs and Pakistanis, arrived and we fought them until ten thirty that night. Our units lost touch with each other because we had no walkie talkies. We were walking for eighteen hours a day for three days to escape the encirclement."[1]

Later I heard that Mullah Omar was apoplectic with rage at Karzai's escape. He issued a special decree ordering Karzai to be killed. Fearful that Karzai would be trapped, the CIA asked him to leave the region for a few days. Some U.S. officials insist that he was flown out to Quetta, although Pakistani officials and Karzai deny this. Karzai himself says he was flown to a deserted runway in southern Helmand. The flight took four hours, following a circuitous route, as it could not go over Taliban-controlled areas. Karzai spent four nights at the Helmand runway guarded by his men and U.S. Special Operations Forces. On the second night a shepherd appeared telling Karzai that Tarin Kot had fallen to his supporters. Karzai sent a motorbike rider to confirm this and waited for his return.

The next day, twenty Toyota pickup trucks loaded with Karzai's men returned to the runway, waving flags, whooping, and shooting into the air as they saw their leader. Tarin Kot had indeed fallen, and the elders there were calling Karzai back. When he returned, on November 14, he was accompanied by a six-man CIA team, a twelve-man SOF team, and a three-man Joint Special Operations Command unit, code-named 574 and led by

Capt. Jason Amerine. The Americans had decided to give an unprecedented commitment to Karzai as the only Pashtun fighting the Taliban and a potential leader of the country. A senior U.S. intelligence official now retired described to me how Karzai finally became acceptable to the Americans: "Karzai had it in his head that he could rally the Pashtuns. Nobody really believed him before 9/11. The U.S. embassy in Islamabad ignored him, and their reports back to D.C. were negative about him. Even after 9/11 he was not seen as the real guy, until he went inside without any support from us. It was only after we pulled him out from that first battle that we took him seriously. He was the only Pashtun fighting the Taliban and staying alive. After the CIA met up with him and reported back, George Tenet made a very quick decision that this is the guy we back—this is the guy who will lead a free Afghanistan."[2]

By now the Pakistanis were deeply concerned that the Pashtun insurrection in the south was not under their control. Musharraf arrived at the UN in New York for his first-ever meeting with Bush, telling him to dissuade the Northern Alliance from taking Kabul and to let the ISI run the Pashtun insurrection. Musharraf showed abject contempt for the NA leaders, describing them to U.S. officials as "a bunch of thugs." At their meeting, which took place a day after the fall of Mazar-e-Sharif, Bush pledged $1 billion in aid to Pakistan. Musharraf said this was not enough and instead asked for F-16 fighter aircraft for his air force. He said that only the delivery of F-16s would show that the United States was seriously committed to Pakistan. "It would be the most visible sign of your support, to blunt domestic criticism," he reportedly told Bush. "We are not ready to talk about F-16s now, but this is a long friendship," Bush replied. Musharraf asked, "How do we know the United States won't abandon us again." Bush replied, "You tell your people that the president looked you in the eye and told you that he would stick with you."[3] Musharraf asked Bush not to pressure him about democratization, or criticize what he would do politically. He received carte blanche from the Americans.

The fate of Kabul was also of major concern to Musharraf. After meeting with Bush, the two leaders stood in the ballroom of the Waldorf-Astoria hotel before reporters. "We will encourage our friends to head south, across the Shumali Plains, but not into the city of Kabul," Bush said. He knew then that it was too late to stop the advance of the Northern Alliance. On the night of November 12, 2001, the Taliban began to loot Kabul, and by the next day they had abandoned the city, stealing more than eight hundred cars and taxis to escape south. One Taliban group had hit the city's money exchange and another the state bank, emptying both. Now there was nothing to stop the victorious NA troops and hundreds of foreign reporters from walking into Kabul unhindered. The city celebrated with noise, music, dancing, and, for the men, the shaving off of beards.

Pakistan's worst fears were realized when NA general Mohammed Fahim immediately moved six thousand soldiers into the city, ensuring total control. Musharraf put on a brave face, but Pakistani commentators were stunned, especially after Bush's assurances. Pakistani newspapers called it "a strategic debacle" for the army and quoted ISI officials as saying "Pakistan's worst nightmare has come true" with NA control of Kabul.[4] The ISI told the Pakistani media that Bush had double-crossed them, that Fahim and other NA leaders were Indian agents, and that India now controlled Kabul.

However, the military victory was quickly giving way to chaos from region to region, as NA forces could not move south or east due to their lack of support in the Pashtun areas. Warlords and former Taliban commanders took control of the eastern provinces. Three separate militias claimed to be in control of Nangarhar, the key eastern province, where Osama bin Laden had fled.[5] Between Kabul and Kandahar was a vast, chaotic no-man's-land ruled by commanders, criminals, and former Taliban. The vacuum in the east might never have been created, however, if the Americans had earlier backed another Pashtun leader who had entered Afghanistan to fight the Taliban: Abdul Haq.

Charismatic, charming, and lionized by his followers, Abdul Haq was a legendary commander from the Afghan war against the Soviet Union with powerful tribal connections.[6] He had been wounded sixteen times, including losing his right foot after stepping on a mine. We had been good friends since 1982, when to our mutual amusement I spent hours in his Peshawar office watching Western intelligence agents offer him plans and explosives to carry out another bombing of Soviet facilities in Kabul. The ISI labeled Haq a playboy because he refused to do their bidding.

In 1999 the Taliban had killed Haq's wife and daughter in Peshawar, and he had moved to Dubai. Now he was back in Peshawar to persuade tribal elders to join him in a rebellion against the Taliban. Haq's aim was to avoid the bloodshed that was sure to follow an American invasion. "I am meeting secretly with Taliban commanders and elders, telling them the only way to minimize the bloodshed is to join in a national resistance led by the king against the Taliban," he told me in Peshawar. "Some Taliban are good people who can stay on in any future setup," he added. Haq received no help from the ISI or the CIA, who considered him unruly and unwilling to be directed. He had requested a meeting with Musharraf, who had declined, even though Haq was trying to mobilize the moderate Taliban whom Musharraf claimed to support. The CIA station chief in Islamabad refused to help Haq for fear it would annoy the ISI.[7] Colin Powell insisted that the CIA do nothing without consulting the ISI, in case Pakistan's support flagged.[8]

Instead, Haq was supported by an American millionaire options trader from Chicago named Joseph J. Ritchie and his brother, James, who before 9/11 had lobbied the Bush administration to listen to Haq's plans for an anti-Taliban revolt.[9] Now they were in Peshawar supporting Haq's venture. I warned Haq several times not to rush into Afghanistan, but he was convinced the Taliban were cracking. Ignoring all advice, an unarmed Haq, now age forty-three, entered Afghanistan on a white horse on October 21, 2001. Four days later, he and his group of nineteen men were surrounded in Logar province by Taliban forces.

Ritchie desperately contacted CENTCOM, which belatedly sent a Predator drone to fire a missile on the Taliban. But it was too little too late. Haq was captured and taken to Kabul, where he was tortured and then hanged, along with two companions, in the rubble of a house where earlier twenty-two Pakistani militants had been killed by a U.S. cruise missile.[10] Haq's murder was revenge for the killing of the Pakistanis. I heard the news of Haq's death while giving a TV interview, and I burst into tears. I was inconsolable, feeling both extreme grief and enormous anger at the Taliban, who had killed a peacemaker. His death was the saddest of moments, and all over Afghanistan people were in mourning.

I attended Haq's funeral in Peshawar. "I can cope with my son being killed—I have other sons who can take his place—but my brother was a national leader who was known across the country and he can never be replaced," said Din Mohammed, Haq's elder brother, whose twenty-two-year-old son, Izzatullah, was hanged alongside Haq. Many mourners openly blamed the ISI for Haq's death, saying the ISI had betrayed his location to the Taliban. Pakistani officials denied the allegations. With the murder of Masud and now Haq, the Taliban were killing off every Afghan leader with a national standing. People feared that Hamid Karzai was next.

It slowly dawned on Washington that the ISI had no intention of splitting the Taliban, creating a moderate Taliban, or supporting Karzai. The ISI kept telling U.S. officials that Karzai had no support in the Pashtun belt. The CIA had relied too much on the ISI's promises, but now that it had a potential Afghan leader in place it needed the ISI far less. To the Americans, the ISI appeared to be drifting, rejecting all options suggested by others but incapable of coming up with a strategy or options of its own.

Nevertheless, there was a massive Western diplomatic effort to keep Musharraf on side. One after another Western head of state and foreign minister visited Islamabad to bolster Musharraf and offer him debt write-offs and aid. Almost all European leaders, followed by Asian heads of state and a string of top U.S. officials—Rumsfeld, Wolfowitz, Powell, and Armitage—came through Islamabad in October and November. Tony Blair advised allies to appoint special envoys to Afghanistan to coordinate aid and diplomatic initiatives and keep Pakistan under pressure. Aid flowed to Pakistan from all quarters, especially from the United States. On September 23, 2001, Bush had waived all sanctions against Pakistan and asked Congress to reschedule repayment of $379 million in earlier loans and give a fresh loan of $597 million and a cash grant of $50 million. Similarly, Japan and the countries of the European Union rescheduled debt repayments and offered fresh loans and grants.

In return, Pakistan had granted the U.S.-led Coalition forces enormous facilities. Unknown to Pakistanis at the time, 1,100 U.S. forces were based in Pakistan for the duration of the war, including Combat Search and Rescue Units, U.S. Special Ops and CIA paramilitary teams, Red Horse squadrons (engineering teams that repaired airfields in the midst of war), and aircraft from the 101st Airborne Division. Pakistan agreed to a list of seventy-four basing and staging activities, such as overflight facilities, medical evacuation, refueling, and the setting up of communication relay sites for U.S. forces inside Afghanistan. Each agreement was premised with a note that the U.S. campaign would not involve the Indian military.[11]

CENTCOM planes flew 57,800 sorties out of Pakistani air bases. Karachi's seaport and airport were handed over to the Coalition, while U.S. naval operations at Pasni, off the Makran coast, were described as "the largest amphibious operations in size, duration and depth that the US Marine Corps has conducted since the Korean war."[12] Thus, despite the lack of cooperation from the ISI, the quick collapse of the Taliban would have been impossible without the massive cooperation extended by the Pakistan army to the Coalition, which is why Powell resisted any criticism of Musharraf or the ISI.

Moreover, Musharraf had weathered the protests by Islamic groups, which petered out after Mazar fell. The mullahs failed to spread the protests to the largest province of Punjab or to the metropolitan business capital of Karachi. Instead, several government-sponsored rallies supporting Musharraf drew sizeable turnouts. The military had closed the border with Afghanistan, but it turned a blind eye to anyone wanting to fight for the Taliban. The army was unwilling to confront fired-up Pashtun tribesmen and it also wanted to show Washington the risks Musharraf was taking on behalf of the United States. Thousands of Pakistani tribesmen were killed or captured after Mazar fell. The main culprit in mobilizing tribesmen was the Tehreek-e-Nafaz-e-Shariat-e-Mohammadi (TNSM), or the Movement for the Enforcement of Islamic Law, led by a charismatic, fiery orator, Maulana Sufi Mohammed, from the Malakand region of the North-West Frontier Province.[13]

The Taliban were now cornered at two extreme ends of the country: in Kandahar, where Mullah Omar held out, and in the northeast corner in Kunduz, where the Taliban were joined by surviving Arab, Central Asian, and Pakistani fighters—some eight thousand in all. The Arabs insisted on fighting to the death. The Taliban wanted to surrender to U.S. forces rather than to the NA commanders, who had surrounded them on all sides. Dostum and his Uzbeks were to the west of the city, and Tajik generals Atta and Daud to the south. There was intense rivalry between these two factions, as they both wanted to capture any al Qaeda leader for whom the CIA had promised large cash rewards. Dostum held secret negotiations with Mullah Dadullah, a senior Taliban commander, and offered to give the Taliban free passage to Kandahar—as long as Dadullah handed over the Arabs.

The Taliban feared they would be killed if they surrendered to the Northern Alliance. Speaking to anyone they could on their wireless, the Taliban commanders offered to surrender to U.S. forces, the UN, or the International Committee of the Red Cross (ICRC). They even offered to surrender to Karzai—anyone but the Northern Alliance. Jakob Kellenberger, the president of the ICRC, who was visiting Islamabad, was pressed by Musharraf to save the surrounded Taliban, but in Kabul, Kellenberger was unable to get any guarantees for their safety. He went to

Washington to talk to Colin Powell and Condoleezza Rice.[14] CENTCOM declined to accept the Taliban members' surrender, while the UN and other international organizations said they had no capacity to accept such large surrenders. The Pentagon wanted it both ways: declining any responsibility for surrendered Taliban but wanting to interrogate any high-level al Qaeda prisoners.[15]

Gen. Tommy Franks could easily have put the U.S. troops waiting in Uzbekistan on the ground in Kunduz to accept an orderly Taliban surrender. The absence of U.S. troops, I believe, led to the deaths of thousands of Taliban prisoners at the hands of the Northern Alliance and the escape of top Taliban and al Qaeda leaders—an escape that was to be repeated in Tora Bora a few weeks later, when Franks again refused to deploy U.S. troops. Until the end of November, when some U.S. troops were deployed to help capture Kandahar, Franks did not deploy any American soldiers. It was a major strategic mistake, and it had awful consequences: it had resulted in the leaders of the Taliban and al Qaeda escaping.

For Pakistan, the stalemate in Kunduz was turning into a disaster as hundreds of ISI officers and soldiers from the Frontier Corps aiding the Taliban were trapped there. They had been ordered to quit Afghanistan after 9/11 and had two months to escape, but instead they had stayed on to fight alongside the Taliban. Musharraf telephoned Bush and asked for a huge favor—a U.S. bombing pause and the opening of an air corridor so that Pakistani aircraft could ferry his officers out of Kunduz. Bush and Vice President Cheney agreed, but the operation was top secret, with most cabinet members kept in the dark.

On November 15, 2001, NA commanders outside Kunduz reported that Pakistani aircraft were flying into the city at night to airlift the Pakistanis. "Last night two planes, perhaps Pakistani, landed at Kunduz airport and we think they evacuated Pakistanis and Arabs from there," said NA spokesman Mohammed Habeel. By November 23 *The New York Times* was reporting that as many as five Pakistani air force planes had landed in Kunduz.[16] The Pakistanis certainly hinted strongly that something was on. Maj.-Gen. Rashid Qureshi, the army's chief spokesman, said that Islamabad was engaged "in negotiations" with the U.S. Coalition for the safe evacuation of Pakistanis from Kunduz.[17] The Pentagon denied that any such flights were being allowed. Gen. Richard Myers, chairman of the Joint Chiefs of Staff, said that "the [Kunduz] runway is not usable, I mean there are segments of it that are unusable."[18] Rumsfeld reiterated on December 2 that "neither Pakistan nor any other country flew any planes into Afghanistan to evacuate anybody."[19]

In fact, neither man was telling the truth. A former U.S. intelligence analyst, another senior U.S. official, and two ambassadors in the region confirmed to me that the airlift had taken place. ICRC and UN officials who were on the ground in the north also confirmed the airlift. The American investigative reporter Seymour Hersh, who wrote about the airlift, reported that "the Pakistanis were indeed flown to safety, in a series of nighttime airlifts that were approved by the Bush administration."[20] Hersh said that Taliban and al Qaeda leaders also escaped with them. Hamid Karzai told me that the airlift took place but that he never asked the Americans who escaped because "even the Americans did not know who got away." One senior U.S. intelligence analyst told me, "The request was made by Musharraf to Bush, but Cheney took charge—a token of who was handling Musharraf at the time. The approval was not shared with anyone at State, including Colin Powell, until well after the event. Musharraf said Pakistan needed to save its dignity and its valued people. Two planes were involved, which made several sorties a night over several nights. They took off from air bases in Chitral and Gilgit in Pakistan's northern areas, and landed in Kunduz, where the evacuees were waiting on the tarmac. Certainly hundreds and perhaps as many as one thousand people escaped. Hundreds of ISI officers, Taliban commanders, and foot soldiers belonging to the IMU and al Qaeda personnel boarded the planes. What was sold as a minor extraction turned into a major air bridge. The frustrated U.S. SOF who watched it from the surrounding high ground dubbed it "Operation Evil Airlift."

Another senior U.S. diplomat told me afterward, "Musharraf fooled us because after we gave approval, the ISI may have run a much bigger operation and got out more people. We just don't know. At the time nobody wanted to hurt Musharraf, and his prestige with the army was at stake. The real question is why Musharraf did not get his men out before. Clearly the ISI was running its own war against the Americans and did not want to leave Afghanistan until the last moment."[21]

In fact the CIA could have insisted that it monitor all those who got off the planes in Pakistan, but it made no such demand. When the Kunduz garrison finally surrendered to the Northern Alliance on November 24, large numbers of people were missing. Only 3,300 Taliban came out, compared to the 5,000 to 7,000 believed to be there, implying that a large number had been airlifted out or had escaped the city by bribing top commanders of the Northern Alliance.

The "Great Escape," as one Pakistani retired army officer dubbed it, would have enormous implications on the subsequent U.S.-led war on terrorism. It is believed that more foreign terrorists escaped from Kunduz than made their escape later from Tora Bora. In both cases, the foreign terrorists were allowed to stay in South and North Waziristan, the wildest of Pakistan's tribal areas. In both cases CENTCOM could easily have placed U.S. troops on the ground on the Afghan side of the border, but it refused to do so. The ISI was now confident that it could play a double game with the Bush administration, as the Bush team was amenable to taking on board Pakistani desires and concerns. After helping the ISI escape from Kunduz, Cheney took charge of all future dealings with Musharraf and the Pakistani army.

More mistakes were to follow. The Taliban who surrendered at Kunduz were taken to Qala Jangi, the Fort of War, Dostum's massive fortress of mud-baked walls outside Mazar, which looked like the set for a Hollywood film on the French Foreign Legion. There they were interrogated by a handful of CIA personnel, who had them sit down in long rows in the huge courtyard. On November 26, Arabs who had not been disarmed properly staged a revolt. They killed their Uzbek guards and a CIA officer, Johnny "Mike" Spann, who became the first U.S. casualty of the war. ICRC officials working inside the compound clambered over the walls to escape. Dostum sent in 700 of his crack soldiers to quell the rebellion while U.S. aircraft dropped bombs into the courtyard. It took six days to subdue the rebellion in which 230 prisoners and 100 of Dostum's best fighters were killed. One of the survivors of the uprising was John Walker Lindh, the so-called American Taliban, who had held out in the basement of the fort.

The several thousand surviving Taliban prisoners were packed into container lorries—stuffed in like sardines, 250 or more to a container—so that the prisoners' knees were against their chests and there was no air to breathe save for holes punched through by machine-gun bullets. The prisoners were driven to a jail in Dostum's home town of Shiberghan. Only a handful of people in each of the thirty containers survived the journey—in one container only 6 out of 220 survived, according to UN officials. The dead were taken out to the Dasht-e-Leili desert and buried in huge pits dug by a bulldozer. Dostum's spokesmen insisted that only a handful of prisoners suffering from war wounds died. Despite the presence of U.S.

SOF in the region, what occurred was the most outrageous and brutal human rights violation of the entire war.

Physicians for Human Rights later uncovered the extent of the atrocities by investigating the mass graves where the asphyxiated prisoners were buried, but the UN and the Afghan government declined to carry out any investigation against Dostum because the issue was too sensitive. Dostum was to be promoted to higher posts within the Karzai administration and was even allowed to stand for president in 2004. Uzbek eyewitnesses who had given testimony, such as the lorry drivers, mysteriously disappeared. Eyewitness accounts and video footage showed that U.S. Special Operations Forces were present in Kunduz, and the Pentagon was repeatedly asked why these U.S. soldiers did not try to stop the loading of the prisoners into the containers.[22]

CENTCOM refused to answer any questions. Physicians for Human Rights sent a copy of their report to Donald Rumsfeld and General Franks in February 2002, but they received no reply. It was not until the U.S. magazine *Newsweek* wrote a cover story about the atrocities in August 2002 that Karzai, Brahimi, and Franks expressed support for an investigation into the mass graves.[23] Ironically the same A team 595, led by Capt. Mark Nutsch, which had led cavalry charges against the Taliban, was also at Kunduz. Nutsch's name became public when he was later honored by the Kansas state legislature. CENTCOM said it found no evidence of U.S. SOF complicity in the prisoners' deaths.

When Brahimi was questioned about the mass graves he said his responsibility lay with the living and not the dead, and he had neither the police nor the judicial system to pursue the investigation further.[24] Brahimi subsequently told me that he did not regret those words, given the paucity of UN power. "I said what I said for those who wanted me to hang Dostum on the first pole. If we started doing that, where would we end up? My business was to talk to all the wrong people, the murderers and rapists and killers."[25]

The massacres of the Taliban and civilian Pashtuns in the north during the war led to ugly pogroms against them in the months ahead by the victorious Tajik and Uzbek warlords. Within a few weeks Pashtun farmers were being forced to flee their villages by Dostum's troops. Human Rights Watch reported that Uzbek and Tajik troops were raping women, kidnapping civilians, looting, and seizing the farms and houses of Pashtuns. More than half of the one million Pashtuns in the north fled south. When I visited a refugee camp for Pashtuns set up by the UN near Kandahar in March 2002, the horror stories the refugees told me were appalling. Meanwhile 3,600 Taliban and Pakistani prisoners were to stay incarcerated in Shiberghan until May 2004, living in terrible conditions. Many Pashtuns died of starvation, cold, and disease while in prison. The atrocities committed against the Pashtuns by the NA commanders, while the Americans remained silent, were to fuel Pashtun anger in the south and help revive the Taliban movement.

Kandahar was now left as the last Taliban redoubt. The ISI and the CIA recruited several former warlords from Quetta to invade Kandahar province from Pakistan. The main warlord was Gul Agha Sherzai, whose father had been prominent during the anti-Soviet jihad. Gul Agha was ousted by the Taliban in 1994 and since then had lived in Quetta under ISI protection. A huge, powerful man whose embrace sucks the breath out of your body, Sherzai is both jovial and cruel, with a penchant for a good fight. The CIA regularly loaded him with dollar bills, which he carried in the back of his jeep.

On November 25 the first U.S. Marines landed in Afghanistan, deployed from U.S. battleships off the coast of Pakistan. They established forward operating base Camp Rhino, sixty miles southwest of Kandahar, in order to trap fleeing Taliban. On December 5, Sherzai's men, accompanied by a U.S. SOF A team, captured Kandahar airport, where al Qaeda had a major training center.

Karzai was still in Tarin Kot, from where he negotiated with Mullah Omar to abandon Kandahar. The Taliban made one last attempt to kill him. On November 18, one thousand Taliban in one hundred pickup trucks drove up the rough mountainous road from Kandahar toward Tarin Kot. On the last ridge before the town with a glorious view of the road snaking up away before them, they were hit by precision bombs from U.S. aircraft guided by U.S. SOF spotters. At least thirty vehicles were destroyed. The rest fled back to Kandahar. "We broke the back of the Taliban that day," said Capt. Jason Amerine, who led the SOF group.[26] The Taliban prolonged negotiations on the surrender of Kandahar so that Mullah Omar and the majority of fighters could escape. Omar drove out on a motorbike at night with a handful of bodyguards.

On November 27, at Bonn, all the Afghan factions gathered for the opening of the UN conference that would choose an interim government and a leader, who was now certain to be Karzai. In a tiny room with mud-baked walls in Tarin Kot, the CIA rigged communications equipment so that Karzai could address the opening of the Bonn conference, thereby cementing his nomination as leader. A few days later, on December 5, he was nearly killed when a U.S. SOF target spotter misread his global positioning device and gave coordinates to a B-52 to drop a two-thousand-pound bomb on the exact position where Karzai was standing. Three U.S. soldiers were killed, along with seven Afghans, and many people were wounded. Karzai's face took the blast, but he suffered no major injuries; Captain Amerine was wounded. A moment later the BBC's Lyse Doucet telephoned Karzai from Bonn to say that he had been chosen as the interim president of Afghanistan. Half an hour later the Taliban arrived to surrender Kandahar. Karzai was forty-three years old. His first feeling was not elation, but stress, over the tremendous responsibility on his shoulders. He said he thought of his father.

Karzai had promised the governorship of Kandahar to Mullah Naqibullah, a warlord with considerable political clout, but Sherzai, backed by the ISI and the CIA, also wanted the post.[27] Kandahar deteriorated into a chaos of looting and disorder as Sherzai occupied the governor's house and refused to accept the Naqibullah nomination, despite Karzai's orders that he do so. Karzai's indecisiveness was to now emerge for the first time for all to see. He had waited too long for the Taliban to surrender Kandahar, the seizure of which proved worthless because all the Taliban had escaped to Pakistan. Then he waited two more days, until December 9, before entering the city, and was forced to appoint Sherzai as governor. It was the first of many showdowns with the warlords that all too often ended in a humiliating compromise or a climbdown for Karzai.

The Taliban regime had been routed and driven from power, but it was still not possible to say it had been fully defeated. Between eight thousand and twelve thousand Taliban, or 20 percent of their total force, had been killed, with twice that number wounded and seven thousand taken prisoner. Those remaining fled to their home villages or to Pakistan. Only one American and several NA soldiers had died. The use of new technology, tactics, and weaponry appeared to have empowered the United States at the very moment it launched its global war on terrorism. After the horror of 9/11, the easy victory seemed to trigger a deep emotional and intellectual catharsis for the American public and media. The media ran stories of future wars being fought in a similar way: cheap in dollar and manpower terms and driven by technology. The new laser-guided bombs, drones armed with Hellfire missiles, and the seventeen A teams on the ground were considered to be the wave of the future. The fact that there had been no major deployment of U.S. troops was trumpeted by Rumsfeld as a success, whereas in the months ahead it became clear that this decision would lead to major disasters.

The innovations in warfare that emerged from Afghanistan were major factors in convincing Cheney, Rumsfeld, and Wolfowitz that the same methodology could be used in Iraq—the use of SOF, the deployment of fewer U.S. troops, overwhelming air power, and the arming of local militias on the ground. Moreover, such wars were cheap. By January 2002, the Afghan war had cost just $3.8 billion—peanuts compared with the staggering sums to be spent later in Iraq.[28] For the neocons, the most important political factor was the overturning of the Powell doctrine—concentrate the maximum number of troops and firepower before attacking the enemy—which for more than a decade, since the first Gulf War, had held sway. The doctrine involved such a massive commitment of U.S. troops that it had acted as a deterrent to the United States' going to war. Now everything was different. "In the Pentagon there was no appetite for troops on the ground and they wanted it done with minimal cost—it was a complete reversal of the Powell doctrine," said Ryan Crocker, the first U.S. diplomat in Kabul after the war.[29]

However, the conditions in Afghanistan were unique—and were not to be found in Iraq. Without an active anti-Taliban resistance, the war could never have been won so quickly, and the Northern Alliance had opened new fronts against the Taliban just before 9/11 without American help. The real undermining of the Taliban was caused by dollars not bombs. Guided by Britain's MI6, the CIA had bought every NA commander in sight and had then gone on to buy off the Taliban commanders. Pashtun leaders living in Pakistan took American money but never set foot in Afghanistan. Richard Clarke estimated that the CIA spent around $70 million in bribes to win the war, although the figure may have been as high as $100 million.[30] The CIA's open-ended budget of $1 billion plus is actually what won the war.

Despite the easy victory, there were victims: Afghan civilians. Between three thousand and eight thousand Afghan noncombatants were killed or injured by U.S. bombing. Professor Marc Herold, of the University of New Hampshire and Human Rights Watch, put the number of Afghan civilian casualties at around four thousand between September and December

2001. This figure was four times higher than civilian deaths in the 1999 war in the former Yugoslavia. The United States dropped 1,228 cluster bombs, which released a quarter of a million bomblets that continued to kill or maim civilians years later.[31] The bombing caused massive dislocation as thousands fled their homes, the distribution of food aid to drought-stricken areas was halted, and there were widespread revenge killings. Up to twenty thousand Afghans may have died indirectly as a result of drought, hunger, and displacement.[32] In the months to come, U.S. aircraft were to cause hundreds more civilian casualties by targeting the wrong villages.

Many of the al Qaeda and some Taliban fighters retreated to the stark, inaccessible heights of Tora Bora, in the Koh-e-Sufaid ("Spin Ghar," in Pushtu), or White Mountain range, which spans Nangarhar and backs on to the Khyber and Kurram tribal agencies in Pakistan. Tora Bora was just twenty-five miles southwest of Jalalabad. The Mujahedin had developed extensive cave systems in these mountains during the war with the Soviets, while al Qaeda had made their own preparations before 9/11 in order to sustain a long siege. There was food and water, and the sights of heavy machine guns and mortars had been fixed at predetermined ranges so that attackers could be eliminated as they climbed the heights.

At the end of November, General Franks sent in three Afghan commanders and their militias, who were not backed by American troops. They were Hazrat Ali, a brutal minor NA commander who belonged to the Pashai minority ethnic group; Haji Zaman, an adventurer who had arrived from exile in France; and the young Haji Zahir, the inexperienced twenty-seven-year-old son of Haji Abdul Qadir, the elder brother of the murdered Abdul Haq. It was bitterly cold, snow covered the ground, and the attackers had to contend with the hunger pangs of Ramadan, the day-long fast.[33] The three commanders were to spend as much time fighting one another as they were the Arabs. The only thing that united them was the wads of dollar bills the CIA paid them.

Some thirty U.S. SOF arrived three days after the battle started—and, in reality, was already lost—while B-52s carried out heavy bombing of the mountains. The main force of Arabs had escaped with the help of Afghan commanders who had been bribed. Between six hundred and eight hundred Arabs were escorted out of Tora Bora by Pashtun guides from the Pakistani side of the border, at an average cost of $1,200 each. It was the cheapest getaway in modern history. The short battle had been staged by the Arabs to allow bin Laden and the main force of foreigners to escape.

Bin Laden and a few bodyguards escaped on horseback into Parachinar, the administrative headquarters of the Kurram tribal agency in Pakistan. Kurram is one of seven tribal agencies that make up the semiautonomous Federally Administered Tribal Areas (FATA), where the writ of Pakistan's central government has historically been limited. Having entered Pakistan and made sure that the news leaked out, bin Laden then doubled back into Afghanistan, to Khost, before once again reentering Pakistan. For some weeks he took refuge with Jalaluddin Haqqani, in a safe house between Khost and the Pakistani town of Miranshah, in North Waziristan. Pakistan had deployed troops in the Kurram and Khyber tribal agencies, but they were not on the mountaintops or deployed in the South and North Waziristan agencies through which the Arabs had escaped.

Gary Berntsen, a CIA officer, wrote that on December 10 his Arabic-speaking operative Bilal heard bin Laden's voice on a satellite telephone urging his men in Tora Bora to keep fighting—although by then bin Laden was speaking from the safety of Pakistan. Berntsen was one of several officers who had requested that General Franks deploy eight hundred U.S. Rangers along the border with Pakistan to prevent bin Laden's escape, but Franks refused to do so. Berntsen described his frustration: "Day and night I kept thinking, we need U.S. soldiers on the ground! We need them to do the fighting. We need them to block a possible al Qaeda escape into Pakistan . . . Franks was either badly misinformed by his own people or blinded by the fog of war."[34]

A few days after his escape, bin Laden appeared on the world's TV screens dressed in camouflage and holding a gun, and taunted the Americans who had let him escape. "We say that the end of the U.S. is imminent, whether Osama or his followers are alive or dead, for the awakening of the Muslim Ummah has occurred."[35] Franks had failed to deploy U.S. troops even though thousands of them were waiting offshore and one thousand British marines were at Bagram desperate to be deployed. By December there were only thirteen hundred U.S. troops spread out in seventeen different locations in Afghanistan.

During the U.S. presidential election campaign of 2004, Franks, now retired, vehemently denied Democrat contender John Kerry's claim that he had let bin Laden escape. He accused Kerry of "distortions of history," saying that "bin Laden was never within our grasp."[36] Bush and Cheney cited Franks repeatedly during the election campaign. It was rare for an American general to become so partisan. Besides, it was Franks who had distorted history, to the dismay of U.S. officers at Bagram, who admitted to me that bin Laden had been at Tora Bora.

Subsequently, the U.S. Army was to learn more about bin Laden's presence in Tora Bora as several captured Arab prisoners in Guantánamo were interrogated. One of bin Laden's bodyguards and a Yemeni doctor told U.S. interrogators that bin Laden had been present at Tora Bora.[37] The evidence clearly showed Franks to be disingenuous. Even he had admitted earlier to bin Laden's presence in Tora Bora: In an interview he gave at MacDill Air Force Base, in Florida, on January 7, 2002, Franks said that while searching the caves after the battle, U.S. troops provided evidence that bin Laden had been in the area "at one point or another."[38]

In February 2002, Taliban and al Qaeda members gathered again, in the high valley of Shahi Kot, in the mountains near Gardez. This time the Americans launched a better-prepared attack, called Operation Anaconda, using some two thousand U.S. troops and Afghan militia.[39] However, too many things went wrong. The enemy was thought to number two hundred when they actually numbered one thousand. The battle started badly when a U.S. officer leading Afghan militia was mistakenly killed by U.S. jets and the Navy SEAL commandos dropped onto the snow-covered mountain-tops were quickly surrounded by al Qaeda. U.S. forces had inadequate air support and no artillery. The battle raged for two weeks. Eight Americans were killed and eighty-two wounded. The Americans claimed that up to eight hundred militants were killed, but Afghans disparaged that number. The Taliban commander Saif ur-Rahman Mansur escaped.

As the battle of Tora Bora raged, I returned to Kabul for the first time in two years, the longest period I had been away, having visited the city regularly since 1978 and seen it in its brightest and darkest colors. No regime had ever banned my entry, until the Taliban refused me a visa after my book *Taliban* was published in March 2000. None of the Taliban had read the book. Now everywhere I went I was warmly greeted by NA commanders whom I knew well and by ordinary people who had heard me interviewed on the BBC. Returning to Kabul was as much a liberation for me as it was for Kabul's citizens.

Under the Taliban, Kabul's lights had gone out and a deafening silence descended upon the streets as people literally tiptoed their way to work. Kabulis described their city then as a living graveyard. Now Kabul's narrow dusty streets were filled with rubble—the result of ten years of civil war and Taliban neglect—but that did not stop thousands of women from laughing, chatting, and pouring out of their homes to walk in the bazaars. For the first time in years, the proud, beautiful women of Kabul negotiated the muddiest of sidewalks in the highest of heels. Everyone wanted to see and be seen. Boys flew kites, girls gawked at the shops, which poured out music and noise. All these simple pleasures had been illegal under the Taliban. However, Kabul was still an island of hope in a sea of instability. Roads into the capital remained dangerous as the remnants of the Taliban, now turned into gangs of bandits, held the countryside hostage. At Maidan Shahr, just twenty miles south of the capital, twelve hundred Taliban held out for several weeks before surrendering their heavy weapons to the Northern Alliance in exchange for two hundred thousand dollars.

I had come to Kabul in the tense days before the Bonn talks began to get a sense of how the NA leaders would compromise. They were taking charge of the city as if they were already the government. Many Afghans feared that if Bonn were delayed, the Northern Alliance would never relinquish control of Kabul. However, the NA was not a monolith. I spent an emotional evening with Abdullah Abdullah as he cried, describing to me Masud's last moments and his own sense of loss. Abdullah, who was appointed foreign minister at Bonn, spoke about how the Northern Alliance was now torn between the former warlords, whose only aim was to regain their status, and a younger generation of Panjsheri Tajik politicians with a broader vision, who wanted to unite with Pashtuns to form a national government that would have credibility and legitimacy.

These latter NA figures included Abdullah, Younus Qanuni, the two younger brothers of Masud (Ahmad Zia Masud and Ahmad Wali Masud), and young members of the intelligence service Masud had established. None of them accepted the idea of Burhanuddin Rabbani, nominally the head of the Northern Alliance and still regarded as the president of Afghanistan, continuing as president. At Bonn there was agreement on choosing Karzai as president, but Rabbani would have to agree to step down voluntarily, as there was no other mechanism for removing him. Yet even the younger NA leaders wanted majority control over any new government because they felt they had sacrificed in resisting the Taliban and had won the war. Abdullah said Bonn should be only the first step in forming a government:

> We are fully aware that we are not the government and we don't want to
> be considered the government until all Afghans have a say, but at the same

time there is the problem of ensuring security in Kabul. The international community must be sensitive to our dilemma. We hope the Bonn meeting will result in a set of principles which will help us form the transitional government at the next meeting, which must be held in Kabul. If the international community wants to support the moderate wing of the Northern Alliance, then it must recognize that Rabbani has to be outflanked in his bid to become president, as Iran and Russia want Rabbani.[40]

During the next few days the NA leaders met around the clock, trying to work out a plan of action. The UN deputy envoy Francesc Vendrell arrived in Kabul and told NA leaders bluntly that "territorial control or further conquest would not legitimize any faction's right or claim to rule over Afghanistan," something that he had earlier told the Taliban.[41] As the Bonn talks were being held, I went to see Rabbani, who was holding court in a guesthouse of the presidential palace. Since we were old friends, I asked him why he did not retire and give the new generation a chance. He would have none of it. However, after several hours of talk and a lavish lunch, he told me on the record that he would consider stepping down. "As far as my future role is concerned," he said, "the people will determine the role of every concerned personality. I will accept the decision of the Bonn meeting and let me make it clear that I have no personal ambitions."[42] This is exactly what those at the Bonn meeting wanted to hear. As the global media picked up my story, Rabbani swiftly issued a retraction. It was a game he was to play over the next few days.

By November 13, 2001, Brahimi had outlined a plan to the UN Security Council that called for a meeting of the Afghan factions to agree upon a two-year provisional government and the deployment of a multinational force to Kabul to guarantee security. The German government offered to host the meeting, and invitations went out to the four major Afghan groups: the Northern Alliance and the Rome, Cyprus, and Peshawar groups. The UN insisted that women be included in each delegation. The Taliban were not asked to participate.

The conference began on November 27, in the luxurious Petersburg Hotel, perched on a Rhineland hill above Bonn, where the kitchens were told to prepare meals according to Muslim rules and, as for the timing of the serving of food, to make sure the rules of Ramadan were observed. Interpreters were flown in from the BBC to help the hotel staff. Except during mealtimes, the Afghan delegations and the foreign diplomats lodged in the hotel were kept separate. All the powerful states had a high-level diplomatic presence in the hotel during the conference. Washington sent two ambassadors, James Dobbins and Zalmay Khalilzad. Several Western intelligence agencies had reportedly wired the hotel so they could listen in on the rooms. Serious conversations took place in the corridors.

A total of twenty-five delegates would take part.[43] The Rome group produced the most irreverent list of delegates, none of whom had been to Afghanistan in the past two decades, and they ignored Karzai, their most famous member. The NA team was led by Younus Qanuni and made up largely of Panjsheri Tajiks, with few delegates from the other ethnic groups the Northern Alliance claimed to represent. Dostum's Uzbeks, Ismael Khan's Heratis, and the Hazara Shias were barely represented, which led to profound resentment among these groups. The Peshawar delegation was made up almost entirely of the family of Pir Gailani. There were no Pashtun delegates from the south or from Kandahar, raising fears among Pashtuns that Bonn would endorse a Tajik-dominated government.

Joschka Fischer, the German foreign minister, opened the conference: "I urge you all to forge a truly historic compromise that holds out a better future for your torn country and its people." Brahimi reminded them of past failures and warned them that failure was not an option now.[44] He was aided by a large UN team as well as Ashraf Ghani and Barnett Rubin, who had been given temporary diplomatic status by the UN.

Brahimi had no plan before arriving at Bonn. "He was going to wait and see how fast or how slowly he could go," said Fatemeh Zia, his special assistant. "And there was even talk of having second-stage discussions in Kabul."[45] Qanuni said a new government should be composed of a leadership council of one hundred personalities and a prime minister, a post he coveted for himself. Qanuni was playing many different games. He wanted to undermine Rabbani, but he had to pretend he did not have the authority to sign an agreement. He also wanted the maximum number of cabinet seats for the Northern Alliance. From Kabul, Rabbani was trying to undermine Qanuni, receiving backing from Russia and Iran and, in his most audacious move, secretly meeting in Dubai with ISI chief Gen. Ehsan ul-Haq to gain Pakistan's support. This move infuriated Qanuni and the NA delegates, and there was a breakdown within the Northern Alliance, stalling the Bonn talks. Qanuni asked for a ten-day break so he could confer in Kabul. Brahimi declined and now insisted that a government be formed as soon as possible.

Over the next two days there was a blitz of phone calls to Rabbani by European leaders asking him to stand down as president and accept the decisions of Bonn. The Iranians helped the Americans, via James Dobbins, to put pressure on Rabbani and were the first to insist "that the agreement include a commitment to hold democratic elections," said Dobbins. U.S. and Iranian diplomats met continuously night and day in the hotel.[46] Finally Khalilzad telephoned Rabbani and reminded him what the Americans had done to the Taliban. The next day a rocket "accidentally" fired by a U.S. plane landed close to Rabbani's home. Rabbani caved and said he would not insist on being president.

After an all-night session, agreement was finally reached as dawn broke on December 6. "Nobody slept that night. Even at the eleventh hour it looked like everything may come crashing down," said Fatemeh Zia. That morning the Bonn Agreement was signed in the presence of German chancellor Gerhard Schröder. It was a personal triumph for Brahimi and the UN, but Brahimi knew that without the participation of the Taliban, its implementation would be difficult. The Taliban had not accepted defeat, and so Bonn was never a peace agreement between victor and vanquished. The agreement made no provision for a cease-fire or the demobilization of forces. Brahimi later said, "The Taliban should have been at Bonn. This was our original sin. If we had had time and spoken to some of them and asked them to come, because they still represented something, maybe they would have come to Bonn. Even if none came, at least we would have tried."[47]

Others such as Kofi Annan held a different view: "What would have been the dynamics of Bonn if the Taliban had been there, how would the other parties have reacted, including the neighboring countries? The Taliban were never an all-inclusive organization, and I doubt if any Taliban would have been amenable to taking part."[48]

The Bonn Agreement called for "a broad-based, gender-sensitive, multiethnic and fully representative government" and the creation of a central bank, a supreme court, an independent human rights commission, and an independent commission for the convening of an emergency Loya Jirga by June 2002, which would decide on a new transitional government.[49] This would be followed by presidential and then parliamentary elections. A constitutional Loya Jirga would be established to adopt a new constitution by 2003, and in the meantime the 1964 constitution would be restored. Zahir Shah was to be given the title of father of the nation.

Bonn was a victory for the Northern Alliance, which had demanded twenty seats in the cabinet until the Iranians persuaded them to drop the demand to seventeen. However, they would hold the crucial posts of ministers of defense, interior, intelligence, and foreign affairs. The Northern Alliance also received three of the five deputy president slots. The Rome group was given nine cabinet seats, the Peshawar group four, while the Cyprus group refused all posts. The ethnic division among the ministries consisted of eleven Pashtun, eight Tajik, five Hazara, and three Uzbeks. There were no Pashtuns from the south except for Karzai himself.

The Bonn Agreement sketched out a road map for the UN and the Afghan government until the end of 2005, a period that would, it was hoped, allow for the establishment of all the structures of a modern democratic state such as a bureaucracy, an army, and a legal system. Bonn was also a compact between the international community and the Afghans in which both had to deliver certain results. Initially much would depend on whether the international community, led by the United States, would provide the money, troops, and international attention Afghanistan now needed. The critical issue of disarming the warlord militias was left vague, although the agreement called for the demilitarization of Kabul and the withdrawal of all heavy weapons from the city—something the Northern Alliance would comply with only two years later.

On December 13, Hamid Karzai boarded a U.S. military plane in Kandahar for his journey to Kabul to take the reins of power. Musharraf had asked Karzai to travel via Islamabad, so the two could meet, offering to send a plane for him. Karzai thought about it and then declined. "I consulted with the elders and they said no," he told me. "They did not want their new leader to go to Kabul 'via Islamabad,' as if I needed the stamp of 'Made in Pakistan.' There had been enough outside interference from Pakistan already."

Karzai arrived in Kabul in the evening. General Fahim, who was now defense minister, other NA leaders, and one hundred heavily armed men were on the tarmac to receive him. It was a defining moment as Karzai, the raw, inexperienced president, was received by the battle-hardened NA leaders. Karzai got off the plane with just four unarmed companions. As he and Fahim shook hands, Fahim looked bewildered. "Where are your men?" he asked, expecting a large band of Pashtun tribesmen to be protecting Karzai. In his most disarming manner, Karzai replied, "Why, General, you are my men, all of you. All of you who are Afghans are my men.

We are united now—surely that is why we fought the war and signed the Bonn Agreement." Fahim was stumped. Afghanistan's past dictated by the barrel of a gun was meeting its future dictated by a new logic of rationality and unity, which had not been heard of in the past quarter century.

Karzai was sworn in on December 22 in a solemn ceremony attended by some two thousand tribal chiefs, warlords, General Franks, and the world's diplomats. The new president gave an enormously moving speech that brought tears to the eyes of many grizzled warriors. "Our country is nothing but a ruined land. Oh God! The journey is long and I am a novice. I need your help," Karzai said. The event was mired in deep anguish for Karzai when U.S. jets attacked a convoy of fifteen vehicles in Paktia province en route to the inauguration. More than sixty people were killed, including some of Karzai's close friends. Such mistakes—this one a result of incorrect intelligence provided to U.S. forces by Afghan warlords working out local rivalries—were already becoming widespread.

On December 1, U.S. planes had attacked several villages near Tora Bora, killing fifty-five civilians after warlords had given the wrong village names to U.S. intelligence. Later, on December 29, fifty-two people were killed near Gardez after the United States was wrongly informed about a Taliban ammunition dump. More than two hundred Afghans were killed by U.S. bombing in December alone, but for the moment most Afghans were too relieved to be free of the Taliban to condemn the United States. However, the killing of innocent civilians was to worsen in the years to come and prove a convenient propaganda tool for the Taliban.

PART TWO

THE POLITICS OF THE POST–9/11 WORLD

CHAPTER SIX

A Nuclear State of Mind

India, Pakistan, and the War of Permanent Instability

After 9/11 the wars and rivalry between India and Pakistan that had already lasted a half century were to show no signs of abating, despite the fact that the two countries were now allied with the United States in its global war on terrorism. Both governments badly misinterpreted the consequences of 9/11, believing that the war in Afghanistan would allow them to carry on an even deadlier rivalry over Kashmir. This led to near-war between the nuclear-armed nations in 2002, while impeding Pakistan's attempts to deal with al Qaeda along its borders.

Since 1947, no U.S. administration has recognized how crucial the India-Pakistan dispute over Kashmir is to stability in the region. Periodic wars and breakdowns in diplomatic relations between the two countries, unwarranted expenditure on their armies, and a nuclear arms race, despite poverty and underdevelopment, have fueled new generations of Indians and Pakistanis growing up in the midst of mutual hate and a widening divide. Successive American administrations simply calculated that there were no major U.S. strategic interests at stake in the region, and the most Washington could do was to keep the temperature down by brokering temporary cessations of hostilities, rather than intervening in the core area of the Kashmir dispute. "American interests in South Asia tend to drop dramatically between periods of crisis," wrote Shirin Tahir-Kheli, a Bush administration official. "The US attention span has been notably short-lived, triggered by crisis conditions and lasting mostly for the duration of a crisis."[1]

With the end of the cold war, South Asia had slipped off Washington's radar, even though Indian Kashmir was suffering from its worst bout of insurgency, which was to run from 1989 to 2004. Moreover, U.S. intelligence was well aware that al Qaeda and the Taliban had taken over the training of Kashmiri militants in Afghanistan after 1997 and were promoting the jihad in Kashmir as part of its global jihad. Yet South Asia was so far from the CIA's attention that when India tested nuclear bombs in 1998, President Clinton learned about it only from watching CNN. Thus the Bush administration was naïve in the extreme to expect that in the post–9/11 world both countries would de-escalate their rivalries in the interest of establishing a common front against al Qaeda.

The Kashmir dispute continued to be a key factor in the intense rivalries that erupted between India and Pakistan after 9/11. Islamabad viewed its Afghan policy through the prism of denying India any advantage in Kabul. For nearly a decade, Pakistan had successfully blocked an Indian presence in Kabul through the Indian-hating Taliban. Now the ISI saw the Northern Alliance, supported by the Americans and all of Pakistan's regional rivals—India, Iran, and Russia—as claiming victory in Kabul. For Pakistan's military regime, this was a strategic disaster and prompted the ISI to give refuge to the escaping Taliban, while denying full support to Hamid Karzai. It was precisely because of such calculations that Musharraf had used the Americans to rescue his beleaguered assets from Kunduz in November 2001. Meanwhile, India immediately seized the advantage that came with the defeat of the Taliban. India supported Karzai, established a lavish diplomatic presence in Kabul, funded aid programs, and according to Pakistani intelligence, sent Indian agents to train Baloch and Sindhi dissidents in Pakistan. Kabul had suddenly become the new Kashmir—the new battleground for the India-Pakistan rivalry. The Americans, obsessed with the hunt for bin Laden, could not understand the larger strategic picture that was changing before their eyes.

The dispute over Kashmir is one of the bitterest legacies of the 1947 Partition, when the British left India in such haste that they did not finalize the status and loyalties of the 550 princely states existing in undivided India. The Muslim-majority population of the Kashmir Valley was ruled by a Hindu, Maharaja Hari Singh. While many Kashmiri Muslims wanted Kashmir to join Pakistan, the Hindu majority in Jammu and the Buddhist majority in Ladakh—both parts of the Kashmir princely state—were as keen to opt for India.[2] Many other Kashmiris, however, wanted total independence for their state. As the maharaja vacillated on accession, some Muslim Kashmiris rose in revolt in September 1947 and were swiftly aided by Pakistan. A panicked maharaja asked New Delhi for military assistance and signed the accession document to India as Indian troops drove back the insurgents. A cease-fire was declared on January 1, 1949.

Both sides held on to the parts of Kashmir they had acquired, with India holding two thirds of the former state. Both countries claimed the whole of Kashmir—with India basing its claim on the accession documents and Pakistan on UN Security Council resolutions drawn up in 1948, which called for a plebiscite to allow the Kashmiris to decide whether they wanted to join India or Pakistan.[3] India and Pakistan fought another war over Kashmir in 1965, while the war in 1971, which led to the humiliating defeat of the Pakistan army and the loss of East Pakistan, fueled a desire for revenge by Islamabad. Thus when an insurgency by Kashmiris against Indian rule broke out in 1989 it was quickly backed by Pakistan.

Seizing the opportunity to weaken India, the ISI encouraged young Kashmiris to come to Pakistan for training. The ISI first trained secular and nationalist Kashmiri groups but quickly switched its support to Kashmiri Islamic groups, who were linked to Pakistan's own Islamic parties. These Kashmiris drew their inspiration from the Muslim Brotherhood and described their struggle as an Islamic war of national liberation, but not as a jihad. However, in 1995–1996, fearing that the insurgency was petering out, the ISI shifted its support again—this time to Pakistani and Kashmiri extremist groups belonging to the Deobandi sect of Sunni Islam, which believed in a jihad to defeat India and "Islamize" Kashmir. It was precisely at this juncture that the ISI also switched its support in Afghanistan from Gulbuddin Hikmetyar to the Deobandi-inspired Taliban. This decision had less to do with religion than with the fact that in both Kashmir and Afghanistan such groups were more extreme in their hatred for India and more willing to do the ISI's bidding. The ISI soon shifted many of the Kashmiri training camps to Taliban-controlled Afghanistan.

The ISI's shift to supporting Deobandi and Wahhabi extremist groups increased funding and support for these groups from Saudi Arabia and the Arabian Gulf states and later drew in al Qaeda. By the late 1990s the Pakistani military justified jihad in Kashmir as a legitimate part of its foreign policy, even as it played a game of divide and rule in order to prevent any single Kashmiri group from gaining ascendancy. In 1993, in Indian Kashmir, several Kashmiri groups and parties formed an umbrella alliance—the All Parties Hurriyat Conference (APHC)—which, despite splits and desertions, emerged as the strongest voice of the Kashmiri people.[4] Aside from the insurgency, the Kashmiri population conducted continuous public strikes and protests in response to the harsh punitive policies and bloody military tactics adopted by the Indians, which included the killing of civilians in reprisal attacks, extrajudicial killings, torture of prisoners, and the systematic use of rape as a weapon of terror by Indian soldiers.[5]

For the Pakistan army, the insurgency was a successful strategic ploy to tie down hundreds of thousands of Indian troops who would otherwise have been deployed on the border and possibly threatened Pakistan. The army carefully calibrated the kinds of weapons and level of funds it provided the Kashmiri militants, and at times reined in the ISI so as not to provoke Indian military retaliation against Pakistan. The level of support was kept just below what India might use to justify an attack on Pakistan. This "strategic restraint" by the army also prevented Western governments from coming down too hard on Pakistan. However, General Musharraf, rash and impetuous, was to undermine this carefully calibrated restraint by launching the Kargil War in 1999. That conflict underscored the severe differences between Musharraf and Prime Minister Nawaz Sharif and led to the coup that brought Musharraf to power. Thus the Kashmir issue was now also a determining factor in the domestic politics of Pakistan.

The Musharraf regime continued to pursue an aggressive line with India, especially in the aftermath of the December 1999 hijacking of an Indian Airlines plane bound for New Delhi. The plane, with 160 passengers on board, was hijacked on its way from Katmandu, the capital of Nepal. After several landings, the five hijackers finally put the plane down in Taliban-controlled Kandahar on Christmas Day. A war of words between India and Pakistan began immediately. The world was already on a high state of alert due to the threat of al Qaeda attacks during celebrations for the millennium on December 31.[6] All the hijackers were subsequently discovered to be Pakistanis, members of Harkat ul-Ansar, a group closely linked to al Qaeda and the Taliban. They initially demanded $200 million and the release of thirty-five Kashmiri militants from Indian jails, including Harkat leader Maulana Masud Azhar and Ahmed Omar Sheikh.[7]

Harkat ul-Ansar had been set up by with ISI support in the mid-1990s as a fringe militant group primed to carry out spectacular acts of terrorism.

After several kidnappings and killings of Westerners in Indian Kashmir, the United States declared it a terrorist group in 1998, after which it changed its name to Harkat ul-Mujahedin. By then Harkat was a key ally of the Taliban and al Qaeda, helping run training camps in Afghanistan for Kashmiri militants. It was Harkat camps that U.S. missiles destroyed in 1998 after President Clinton retaliated for the al Qaeda attacks on two U.S. embassies in Africa. Ten Harkat militants and at least five ISI instructors were killed.[8] America continued its war against Harkat after 9/11, when on October 23, 2001, U.S. warplanes bombed a Harkat office in Kabul, killing twenty-two Pakistani members of Harkat.

Masud Azhar had been in jail in India since 1994 and was considered one of Pakistan's most important international jihadists, having fought in Afghanistan and set up Harkat affiliates in Chechnya, Somalia, and Central Asia. After President Clinton deployed troops to Somalia in 1993, Azhar was credited with teaching Somalian warlords how to trim the fins of their rocket-propelled grenades so that they would explode in midair and bring down U.S. helicopters. (The Somalis later shot down several U.S. Black Hawk helicopters, an incident that was recounted in the bestselling book and movie *Black Hawk Down*.)[9] Bin Laden had wanted Azhar freed and, according to several authoritative sources, had ordered al Qaeda to plan the Indian Airlines hijacking with Harkat.[10] Ahmed Omar Sheikh, twenty-nine, a highly educated Pakistani-born British citizen, had been in an Indian jail since 1994 after trying to kidnap British and Canadian tourists in New Delhi. A member of Harkat with close ISI ties, Sheikh gained ultimate notoriety after 9/11 for organizing the kidnapping and execution of the American journalist Daniel Pearl.

The hijacking standoff in Kandahar continued for a week, until New Year's Eve, when a humiliated Indian government freed Azhar, Sheikh, and another Kashmiri militant. Indian foreign minister Jaswant Singh delivered the three men to the hijackers on the tarmac of Kandahar airport. The three men and the five hijackers were released by the Taliban and returned to Pakistan, where they were never apprehended. The Indians accused the ISI of planning the hijacking and were furious with the Clinton administration for refusing to condemn Pakistan, but U.S. diplomats did not want to escalate the already high state of tension between Islamabad and New Delhi by seeming to take sides.[11]

Azhar was a charismatic leader and organizer whose stint in an Indian jail had greatly enhanced his reputation. A short, heavily built man with a flowing beard, he spoke in a booming voice, preaching at Friday prayers at army mosques around the country, where his message was the need for jihad. He continued to preach even after 9/11, when the militant Islamic group he later founded had been officially banned. I heard his sermons frequently and met with him—once at the army-run mosque in a Lahore cantonment in 2003, even though Musharraf had declared him a terrorist. In 2004 some Jaish militants working closely with Al Qaeda tried to assassinate Musharraf.

At home, Azhar was lionized, and encouraged by the ISI to set up the new group for jihad in Kashmir called Jaish-e-Mohammed (the Army of the Prophet Mohammed). With ISI officers by his side, Azhar toured the country giving rousing speeches. "Marry for jihad, give birth for jihad and earn money only for jihad till the cruelty of American and India ends," he told crowds at a rally in Karachi.[12] Indian leaders were apoplectic, and once again Prime Minister Atal Bihari Vajpayee called on the international community to declare Pakistan a terrorist state. Jaish later introduced the first suicide bombings in Indian Kashmir.

The Indian Airlines hijacking was a spectacular success for al Qaeda and all extremists in the region, a daring act in that it took place when the entire world was on a high terrorist alert and extraordinary because the hijackers crisscrossed five countries with impunity—Nepal, India, Pakistan, the United Arab Emirates, and Afghanistan. The hijacking made India even more determined to punish Pakistan, but the country failed to garner American support for this. Pakistan's military considered the lack of direct condemnation from abroad as a victory and surmised that the world was still willing to give it the benefit of the doubt when it came to Kashmir. I was constantly told by army officers that the more unpredictable Pakistani actions were, the more notice the Kashmir cause would receive abroad. It was this cocksure attitude of Musharraf and his generals that led them to take major risks after 9/11 in order to highlight the Kashmir cause.

The hijacking caused relations between India and Pakistan to plummet to dangerously low levels, as a war of words erupted. On April 20, 2000, Jaish-e-Mohammed carried out the first suicide bombing in Kashmir when a guerrilla exploded a bomb in an Indian army barracks, killing five Indian soldiers and himself. Other Kashmiri militant groups swiftly copied the example of Jaish.

India welcomed the 2000 Republican victory at the U.S. polls, hoping for a shift in policy from the neocons. In fact, the incoming Bush admin-istration was keen to befriend India, but more in order to enlist it as a part-ner in the strategic containment of China than to punish Pakistan. In February the CIA's annual report concluded that the risk of war between India and Pakistan "was unacceptably high."[13]

Then, in May 2001, in a surprise move aimed at winning even greater U.S. support, Prime Minister Vajpayee invited Musharraf for talks. In a gross misinterpretation, Musharraf saw Vajpayee's offer as coming from a position of weakness, in resonse to the stepped-up attacks by the militants. Vajpayee, too, underestimated Musharraf. As a result, the three-day sum-mit in Agra in mid-July between the two leaders ended in failure. In an orgy of bloodletting, eighty-six militants, soldiers, and civilians in Kashmir were killed during the summit.

After 9/11, India was stunned at how easily and quickly the United States embraced Pakistan as a strategic ally. But both countries were to misinterpret world reaction to their dispute. The Pakistani army never understood what was obvious to liberal Pakistanis—that after 9/11 the international community would have zero tolerance for Islamic extremism and that the ISI's backing of militant groups would have to cease, not just in Afghanistan but also in Kashmir. Logic also dictated that at home, Pakistan would have to take control of the madrassas that were turning out militants in the thousands, fight extremism, and prevent al Qaeda from using Pakistan as a base. There was genuine hope that the army would have no choice but to break its nexus with the extremists.

The military and the ISI thought otherwise, believing instead that help-ing the United States overthrow the Taliban regime would absolve it of reining in the Kashmiri militants. Now that Pakistan was allied to the United States, and the United States was dependent on Pakistan for con-ducting the war in Afghanistan, the military believed it could force India to the negotiating table by stepping up attacks. It was the same logic that had prompted the 1999 war in Kargil. When, after 9/11, Musharraf de-clared that by siding with the United States he had "saved" the Kashmir issue, he was signaling to the militants that nothing would change.

India, on the other hand, viewed 9/11 as a major opportunity to per-suade the United States to declare Pakistan a state sponsor of terrorism. Surely the U.S. alliance with Pakistan would last only until U.S. forces were victorious in Afghanistan, at which point the Bush administration would see the light about Pakistan. In fact, New Delhi underestimated U.S.

dependency on Pakistan for continuing to hunt down al Qaeda and supplying its forces in Afghanistan. India also thought that Bush's new policy of preemption would give it the right to take unilateral military action against Pakistan. After Kargil, the Indian military had been planning to launch short, hot pursuit strikes against militants in Pakistani Kashmir, but the Americans had to warn the Indians several times that preemption did not apply to India over Pakistan.

For its part, the Bush administration failed to understand the degree to which it had annoyed the Indians by taking on Pakistan's help in Afghanistan, while failing to denounce terrorist attacks in Kashmir more vehemently. Colin Powell and the State Department took for granted Indian acquiescence to the new alignments in the region, and as U.S. officials poured into Islamabad and lionized Musharraf for his statesmanship, no official deigned to visit New Delhi. Washington was, therefore, taken entirely by surprise when tensions between India and Pakistan suddenly escalated. The opaque position of the United States, and continuing covert ISI support, encouraged the Pakistan-based Kashmiri groups to gamble on stepping up the insurgency. On October 1, 2001, a massive car bomb exploded outside the Kashmir parliament building in Srinagar, killing twenty-nine people. Indian leaders responded in an uproar of condemnation, blaming Pakistan for the attack. Attacks multiplied until, on December 13, five militants shot their way into the Indian parliament in New Delhi, killing fourteen people, before being shot dead themselves. India called it an attack on democracy, while Indians demanded retaliation.

India immediately began large-scale troop movements to the Pakistan border, and within days war fever built up on both sides of the frontier. "Our anxieties are mounting not only by the day, but by the hour as we receive information about the movement of Indian forces on the border," said Pakistan's foreign minister, Abdul Sattar, on December 30. "Pakistan does not want war, local or general, conventional or nuclear. The decision lies with India," he said.[14] Colin Powell was on the telephone to Musharraf almost every day, urging him to take steps to rein in the jihadis. On December 30, Bush got involved, telling Musharraf "to take additional strong and decisive measures to eliminate the extremists who seek to harm India."[15]

On January 1, 2002, India announced it had begun the largest war games in the past fifteen years on the Pakistan border. Pakistan retaliated with its own war games and began to move troops from the Afghan border to the eastern front, abandoning the hunt for Osama bin Laden.[16] U.S. commanders in Kabul were furious but could do nothing. In dense winter fog, I watched as massive Pakistan army convoys stretching for twenty-five miles lumbered across Punjab province, returning sixty thousand troops from the Afghan border to the Indian border. Fighter aircraft and missiles were moved to small secret air bases around the country. India began to rip up the electrified fence along the border so that its tanks would not be impeded. A Pakistani general told me that 80 percent of India's one-million-strong army had been mobilized in an offensive posture. The United States became concerned about its own bases in Pakistan. If there was a war, all U.S. forces would have to be evacuated from the country.[17]

What came as a shock to the generals was that there was little Pakistani public support for war with India. During the Kargil crisis, most Pakistanis had reacted negatively to what they saw as the military's adventurism, and they regarded this buildup the same way.

Realizing that the Indians would not budge, Bush made it plain to Musharraf what he expected if Pakistan was to remain a U.S. ally, delivering an ultimatum in the same blunt words that had been used by Richard Armitage after September 11: "I think it's very important for President Musharraf to make a clear statement to the world that he intends to crack down on terror." Bush said. "And I believe if he does that . . . it'll provide relief . . . on a situation that's still serious."[18] The world watched with bated breath as the government announced that Musharraf would address the nation on television on January 12. U.S. diplomats in Islamabad told me that Washington had provided Musharraf with a wish list to include in his speech. Musharraf had no option but to offer a significant climbdown. His January 12 speech was dubbed a U-turn as significant as the one he had made after 9/11. Musharraf told his countrymen that "Pakistan rejects and condemns terrorism in all its forms and manifestations. Pakistan will not allow its territory to be used for any terrorist activity anywhere in the world. . . . No organization will be allowed to indulge in terrorism in the name of Kashmir."

However, he said that Pakistan would never surrender its claim to Kashmir. "Kashmir runs in our blood," he insisted. For the first time he spoke out against jihad, saying it should be waged only against poverty and hunger. "We are not the custodians of taking jihad all over the world," he said after announcing a ban on five extremist groups. The reaction from the jihadi groups was hostile as hundreds of militants were rounded up. The Jamiat-e-Islami did not hesitate to take a blatant dig at the ISI. "Will Musharraf care to explain who has been patronizing jihad for all those 25 years in Afghanistan and 12 years in Kashmir," said Jamiat leader Munawar Hussain.

Yet public and media cynicism was widespread. Ayaz Amir, the renowned columnist, wrote, "By joining America's war effort we thought that we had neutralized the threat from India and indeed left India out in the cold. Now it turns out that it is we who were caught in a bind. Helpless then, helpless now but justifying every turnaround by reference to that mystical entity, the national interest."[19]

Colin Powell visited India and Pakistan to ask both countries to deescalate tensions, but the Vajpayee government faced a political crisis and rising unpopularity at home, and India prepared for war again in May.[20]

Stock markets in both countries crashed, and foreigners started to pack up and leave. Musharraf had once again badly miscalculated by refusing to shut down the militant attacks. "By March it was clear to us that Musharraf was not going to implement his promises of January 12. All the arrested militants were freed, and the military had no intention of imposing any curbs on their activities," a U.S. diplomat in Islamabad told me. In Washington there were differences of approach between the State and Defense departments. Powell's deputy, Richard Armitage, handled South Asia. Powell liked Musharraf enormously and had developed a close relationship with him—he telephoned the Pakistani leader eleven times in eight weeks—but that did not stop Armitage from getting tough with Musharraf when it was needed.

Donald Rumsfeld, however, was less willing to put pressure on Pakistan, fearing that Musharraf would cut off assistance to U.S. forces in Afghanistan and stop cooperating in the hunt for al Qaeda. Throughout the crisis, Rumsfeld did not criticize Musharraf once, and General Franks made no bones about how much he trusted Musharraf as one soldier to another. Referring to a visit to Islamabad back in January 2001, Franks wrote, "As we spoke, it struck me that it was appropriate we both wore uniforms." The United States had for years "hectored soldier-politicians such as Pervez Musharraf about human rights and representative government. Of course I believed in these issues with equal conviction, but at this point in history we needed to establish priorities. Stopping al Qaeda was such a priority."[21]

Again the United States issued an ultimatum. On May 25, Bush warned

Musharraf to stop infiltration into Indian Kashmir and to live up to the commitments he had made on January 12. "It's very important for President Musharraf to do what he said he was going to do and that is stop the incursions across the border," Bush said.[22] Musharraf continued to deny support for the militants. Bush reiterated his demands on May 29. For an administration that preferred conducting its foreign policy in the shadows rather than in public, Bush's interventions were highly unusual and demonstrated how serious the confrontation between India and Pakistan had become.

After receiving messages from Islamabad that it was prepared to rein in the militants if India de-escalated on the border, Washington began to use coercive diplomacy against India for the first time. On June 1, in an unprecedented coordinated move, the United States, Britain, and Germany advised all their nationals to leave India on a voluntary basis because of the danger of war. With sixty thousand American and twenty thousand British citizens in India—many of them business executives—the warning came as a rude shock. New Delhi had not contemplated the fallout of a war on its booming economy. A senior U.S. official later told me that "it was a calculated move carried out by Armitage to shock India into seeing the consequences of even a limited incursion across the [Line of Control]."[23] U.S. intelligence had learned that India planned for a brigade-level commando raid across the LOC to attack militants' training camps, which would certainly have resulted in all-out war.

Now Armitage met with a positive response when he arrived in Islamabad. Musharraf promised that the infiltration of militants would cease, and Armitage conveyed the message to a still-skeptical Indian leadership.[24] U.S. intelligence knew that Musharraf and senior ISI officers had met with Kashmiri extremists to tell them that their entry into Indian Kashmir was now forbidden. By late June, Indian officials were admitting that infiltration was much reduced, while artillery guns on both sides of the LOC had fallen silent.

India still delayed withdrawing its forces from the border, largely because the government had no idea how to explain such a climbdown to its own people. By July, attacks in Indian Kashmir had resumed. India now demanded that Pakistan dismantle all terrorist training camps and that the United States monitor the process. The United States weighed in once again with a visit to the region at the end of July by Powell, who admitted that "we still do not have evidence whether infiltration has been stopped on a permanent basis or not."[25] In September, elections for the state assembly in Indian Kashmir turned into a bloodbath, with militants gunning down twenty-three political activists and two candidates in the space of two weeks. Over the two-month campaign period, more than eight hundred soldiers and civilians were killed.[26] However, India termed the elections a triumph, as the international community endorsed them as free and fair. That claim of success gave India the excuse to move its troops back from the border.

The possibility of the Indian-Pakistan conflict quickly escalating into all-out conventional war and then turning into a nuclear exchange was a persistent worry for the White House, but of even greater concern was the potential of an al Qaeda attack using weapons of mass destruction (WMD). In the first months after 9/11, the CIA was deeply fearful of a follow-up nuclear or biological weapons attack on the American mainland by al Qaeda. In 1998, bin Laden had said that obtaining nuclear weapons was "a religious duty," and he spoke frequently about creating an American Hiroshima.[27] The discovery at al Qaeda safe houses in Afghanistan of computer disks, laboratories, and even a crude diagram of a nuclear bomb, showing that al Qaeda was experimenting with biological and nuclear warfare, only confirmed the worst about al Qaeda's intentions.

Another intelligence failure by the CIA would have been catastrophic, and now to err on the side of a heightened threat perception was preferable to ignoring the danger. As al Qaeda fighters were captured, there was an urgent demand from Washington for "instant actionable intelligence," about what prisoners could reveal about possible WMD attacks. Right after the war ended, several U.S. officials told me that the fear of a WMD attack and the lack of intelligence about how well prepared al Qaeda was to launch one haunted the CIA and the Pentagon. "The kind of warnings and threat perceptions that passed across my desk every morning would not let me to sleep at night," one U.S. intelligence official told me. "It was without doubt the scariest time of our lives—there was a real fear that al Qaeda had a follow-up plan to 9/11 which involved WMD," said a State Department official."[28]

Due to the penetration of Pakistan's nuclear establishment by Britain's MI6, the CIA learned astonishing information about contact between Pakistani nuclear scientists and al Qaeda. Sultan Bashiruddin Mahmood and Abdul Majid, two retired nuclear scientists from the stable run by Dr.

Abdul Qadeer Khan, the founder of Pakistan's nuclear weapons program, met with Osama bin Laden and Ayman al-Zawahiri several times—the last time just a few weeks before 9/11. According to journalist Ron Suskind, at first the CIA was uncertain of the extent to which it could trust the ISI with this information. The uncertainty prompted Dick Cheney to lay out a guiding principle for the administration that was later to justify many of the half-truths stated as the reasons for invading Iraq. Cheney said, "If there's a one percent chance that Pakistani scientists are helping al Qaeda build or develop a nuclear weapons, we have to treat it as a certainty in terms of our response. It's not about our analysis or finding a preponderance of evidence. It's about our response."[29]

One reason for the stepped-up fear was that neither MI6 nor the CIA had a complete picture of the extent of contacts between Pakistani scientists and al Qaeda on WMD. Before 9/11 several retired ISI officers had boasted that one of the key reasons for Pakistan's support to the Taliban regime was to gain access to vast former Soviet underground storage bunkers built at major airfields such as Bagram. Here Pakistan could stash away conventional and nuclear-tipped missiles in order to enhance its second-strike capability against India in case of war. After U.S. forces searched these Soviet-era airfields it became clear that no such bunkers existed.

With so many scary stories floating around, the U.S. administration imagined the worst when it heard about the two scientists' possible ties to al Qaeda. In fact, Mahmood was a bit of a crackpot. He had been part of the nuclear program since 1974, and had helped A. Q. Khan set up his global clandestine network to purchase nuclear parts. Later, though, he had written a book called *Cosmology and Human Destiny,* in which he tried to connect major historical events to sunspots, while suggesting that the power of "jinns"—mythical beings who are a cross between humans and angels—could be harnessed to generate energy. After retiring, he had established Ummah Tameer-e-Nau (Rebuilding the Ummah), an Islamic aid agency that attracted Islamic fundamentalist technocrats and former ISI officers and ostensibly provided medical care in Afghanistan.

At the CIA's behest, the ISI arrested Mahmood, Majid, and four others. Mahmood later admitted to meeting bin Laden. "I met Mullah Omar, members of his council of ministers as well as Osama bin Laden only to seek their cooperation in pursuing the goals of my organization," he said.[30] The CIA was not satisfied and George Tenet secretly visited Islamabad on

December 1 to insist that Musharraf allow the CIA to interrogate the scientists. Tenet also asked Musharraf to carry out a more extensive purge of officers from the ISI whom the CIA considered closet extremists.[31]

Musharraf was already in the dock concerning nuclear proliferation. A few months before 9/11, suspicions that Dr. Khan had sold nuclear technology to North Korea and Iran had led the United States and Britain to force Musharraf to remove Khan as head of Khan Research Laboratories, one of the key atomic weapons centers in the country. However, Khan was considered a true local hero, especially by the army, and Musharraf made him his special adviser, a perfunctory post with no powers. At a dinner in Khan's honor held on March 27, 2001, in Islamabad, Musharraf described him as "a giant of a man," "our national hero," "imbued with supreme patriotism and a sense of destiny." Yet Musharraf failed to root out the criminal actions in the sale of nuclear technology that Khan had begun, which would lead to a far bigger scandal in 2005, when Khan was caught red-handed selling nuclear plans to Libya.[32]

After the scare of 2002, India refused to hold talks with Pakistan, although the Bush administration tried to convince New Delhi that in order for India to play a larger role in the region it needed to put the Pakistan problem behind it. "It is simply a fact of life that India will not realize its immense potential on the global stage until its relationship with Pakistan is normalized," Richard Haass told an Indian audience in Hyderabad in January 2003.[33] Such appeals to India's sense of self-importance seemed to work, as in April 2003 Prime Minister Vajpayee offered to talk to Pakistan.

A back channel for secret talks had already been opened by both sides. Tariq Aziz, a national security adviser to Musharraf, and Brajesh Mishra, Aziz's Indian counterpart, began a series of meetings in London, Dubai, and Singapore. Relations began to normalize as diplomats returned to take up their posts and both sides took small steps to rebuild mutual confidence. The ISI made greater efforts to stop militants from crossing into Indian Kashmir. A full year later the back-channel dialogue led to the two leaders' meeting on January 5, 2004, in Islamabad, at a regional summit. This time there was no rush to judgment as there had been during the Agra summit. This summit had been well prepared and nothing was left to chance, especially as in the previous month there had been two attempts on Musharraf's life in Islamabad.

Vajpayee, now seventy-nine and ailing, arrived saying this was his last attempt to make peace. Musharraf echoed similar sentiments.[34] In the negotiations, Pakistan wanted India to announce a date for the start of a structured dialogue on the Kashmir issue, while India wanted stronger commitments from Pakistan on controlling "cross-border terrorism." In the end, both sides got something of what they wanted. Pakistan assured India that it would not allow its territory to be used for terrorism—exactly what Musharraf had promised but never implemented earlier, in his January 12, 2002, speech. Vajpayee promised to negotiate on settling the Kashmir dispute.[35] It had taken nearly three years since 9/11 for relations between the two countries to normalize.

India held general elections in May 2004, and the results jolted Pakistan as the Bharatiya Janata Party lost to the Congress Party and its allies. Congress had not been in power for twelve years, and it would now move very cautiously in its relations with Pakistan. Instead of substantial dialogue on Kashmir the Congress government launched a blitz of small confidence-building measures with Pakistan, which deeply frustrated the Pakistanis. When Musharraf met with Congress Party prime minister Manmohan Singh for the first time at the UN General Assembly in September 2004, Singh told him that India would not accept any redrawing of its borders. India remained wary of any new arrangements in Kashmir.[36]

Talks between the two countries limped along for the next three years. The militants continued to launch periodic attacks in Indian Kashmir, but New Delhi acknowledged that infiltration was down. India's counter-insurgency efforts were also proving to be more effective. Musharraf became increasingly frustrated with the slow pace of progress in the talks. He told his aides that he wanted a major breakthrough in 2006, so that the following year he could get elected as president for the second time on the back of having "resolved" the Kashmir dispute. Yet the Indians told interlocutors that they would never dream of obliging a military dictator in such a way, even if a solution were possible.

Pakistan had also lost the war of influence in Washington, as the United States built a new and long-lasting relationship with India, which had become the main U.S. ally in the region. In the summer of 2007, an Indo-U.S. deal that legitimized India's civilian nuclear program removed a fundamental roadblock between the two countries and was to promote even closer cooperation in all fields. India had become Washington's major geostrategic ally in combating the rising power of China, and was considered a responsible nuclear power, while Pakistan was still considered a pariah.

It was Musharraf who had gone to war in Kargil and had upped the ante after 9/11, and he now found himself reaping the bitter harvest he himself had sown. Since Kargil, Musharraf had followed a continuous policy of brinkmanship by using extremists, in the belief that they could force India to the negotiating table. His policies were opportunistic and dangerous, and ultimately damaged his political credibility at home and abroad. Musharraf got away with so much for so long simply because the Bush administration did not want to jeopardize Pakistan's cooperation in chasing al Qaeda leaders.

The years of conflict had also given enormous powers to the intelligence agencies of both countries, which waged a nonstop proxy war, funding and arming dissidents in each other's territory. "The intelligence agencies of India and Pakistan have fed paranoia about each other and have engaged in cross-border interference. Theirs is a dangerous game," warned Bush administration official Shirin Tahir-Kheli.[37] In 2005 and 2006, Afghanistan became a new battleground for their rivalries as Musharraf accused Karzai of giving Indian agents access to Pakistan's western borders. The ISI accused India's Research and Analysis Wing, or RAW, of funding the insurgency by Baloch tribes in Balochistan, while RAW accused the ISI of funding Maoists and other dissidents in northeast India.

For five decades Pakistan's army had used the threat from India as the principal reason for building a national security state in Pakistan and to justify long bouts of military rule and large expenditures on the army. Every attempt by elected civilian leaders to make peace with India had been deliberately undermined by the army. Now Musharraf used making peace with India as a rationale for consolidating his power, insisting that only the army could sustain peace and hoping the international community would look favorably upon his continuing in power now that he led an army whose ostemsible goal was peace with India.

CHAPTER SEVEN

✦ ✦ ✦

The One-Billion-Dollar Warlords

The War Within Afghanistan

In the spring of 2002, some forty American U.S. Special Operations Forces and CIA agents were ensconced in a huge, white-domed marble palace perched on a hill overlooking the city of Herat, in western Afghanistan. The palace had been lent to them by the warlord Ismael Khan. At the bottom of the hill was the Iranian consulate, and farther along were the offices of the paramilitary Sipah-e-Pasadran, or Army of God, extremists who were loyal to Iran's fundamentalist supreme leader, Ayatollah Khamenei, and who tended to ignore the moderate government of President Mohammad Khatami. The Americans considered Herat the front line in the war against the newly coined "axis of evil," which Bush had delineated in his January State of the Union address as comprising Iran, Iraq, and North Korea. From being a good and helpful interlocutor during the Bonn talks, Iran had suddenly been demonized by the U.S. president. The team on the hill was concerned that al Qaeda leaders were escaping to Iran through Herat.

In a typical Afghan ploy, the wily Ismael Khan made sure that the Iranians and the Americans spent most of the time watching each other rather than him, as he fed them tidbits of misinformation and gossip that kept their daggers drawn. In a country where all the institutions of state and civil society had been destroyed by war, the resulting vacuum was filled with heavily armed militias and warlords. Ismael Khan was a genuine warlord in that he was both ruthless and popular, a provider of essential services to the people and a perpetrator of terror. He commanded territory—five western provinces—and an army of some twenty thousand men, who lived off the land. Khan was the epitome of the warlord who learns the art of survival by being extremely flexible. "Iran has been supporting us militarily for many years against the Taliban but it is not supporting us now," he told me. "And I am a friend of the U.S. because it supported us in the war against the Taliban."[1]

As the Iranians clandestinely provided spare parts and ammunition for Khan's Soviet-era tanks and built roads for him, the Americans tried to reciprocate with canal-cleaning projects and ego-building gestures. On his first trip to visit a warlord outside Kabul, Donald Rumsfeld described Khan as "a very interesting, deep man."[2]

Now age fifty-six, with a bushy snow-white beard that covered his chest, Khan had been a young Afghan army captain when he led a revolt against the Soviet garrison in Herat in 1979, killing some fifty Soviet officers and their wives while they slept. In retaliation, the Soviets bombed half the city, killing more than fifty thousand Heratis. I visited the city a few months later, and the rubble still smelled of dead bodies. Khan had liberated Herat twice, once in 1992, after the fall of the communist regime, and then again after the fall of the Taliban. In the meantime he had spent two years in a Taliban jail.

I had known Khan for nearly two decades and we had got on well. In the 1990s he ran the best warlord fiefdom in Afghanistan, which educated girls and set up industry. His authoritarian rule had turned Herat into the most peaceful and cleanest city but also the most repressed, where 75 percent of children went to school but nobody could utter a word in support of President Karzai or Zahir Shah. The time Khan spent in a Taliban jail had turned him into an insomniac and changed him from a religious conservative into a fanatic. Now he insisted that all women wear the burqa, and human rights advocates allege that he tortured his opponents. A Persian-speaking Herati, he persecuted the Pashtuns living in his territory.

On my first trip to Herat after its liberation I was ushered into Khan's presence in the governor's palace well past midnight, bypassing the hordes of petitioners waiting to see him. Like many insomniacs, Khan preferred doing business at night. I had come to interview him but also to ask for a favor. With some of the earnings from my book *Taliban,* I had started a small NGO to provide start-up funds for new print media in Afghanistan. The Taliban had destroyed journalism in Afghanistan, shutting down presses and exiling most journalists. Now the Open Media Fund for Afghanistan offered any credible Afghan group a cash grant to start a publication. In Herat, an extraordinary group of men and women, all with university degrees, had formed the Shura, or Council of Professionals, to help nation-building efforts. They were led by Mohammed Rafiq Shahir, who brought out a monthly magazine called *Takhassos (Experts),* which offered professional and technical advice on reconstruction projects.[3] It was the only magazine of its kind in Afghanistan, and Khan had just banned it. He saw the Shura as a political threat and Shahir as a potential rival. I asked Khan if he would allow the magazine to be published, as it was non-political, and leave Shahir alone. He promised to do so as a favor to an old friend. The magazine came out, but Shahir was arrested twice in the next few months and severely tortured—once just before the Loya Jirga to which he had been elected as a delegate. It took direct intervention from the U.S. military, the American embassy in Kabul, the UN, and Karzai before Khan deigned to free him.

Khan's source of income made him especially important. He earned between three and five million dollars every month in customs revenue from the crossing point at Islam Qila, on the Iran-Afghanistan border. Here every day hundreds of trucks arrived loaded with Japanese tires, Iranian fuel, secondhand European cars, cooking gas cylinders from Turkmenistan, and consumer goods from the Arabian Gulf. Khan refused to share any of this income, let alone hand it over to the central government. The most powerful and richest warlords commanded border posts with Pakistan, Iran, or Central Asia, where they could gather customs duties, but none earned as much as Ismael Khan.

Warlords such as Khan had emerged as result of the civil war in the 1990s, when they divided up the country into fiefdoms, until being swept out of power by the advancing Taliban. Now they had defeated the Taliban, and felt stronger than ever. Empowered by, but not necessarily loyal to, the Americans and Karzai, they dominated the political landscape. Often rapacious, corrupt, and ruthless, they hired large militias that terrorized the population but also kept a kind of peace. Their income came from road tolls, the drug trade, or the patronage they received from their foreign backers. Afghans hated them most because, invariably, they were the cat's paw for neighboring countries. In fact, the Taliban's initial popularity with the Afghan people had come from the group's hatred of the warlords.

Just before he died, Ahmad Shah Masud, the leader of the Northern Alliance, was trying to create a new disciplined political structure out of the loose alliance of warlords in his group. A few months before 9/11, the most important warlords, Rashid Dostum, Ismael Khan, and Karim Khalili, who had been defeated and driven out by the Taliban, returned to Afghanistan and took up arms under Masud's leadership.

The routing of the Taliban by the Americans had left the warlords in place and immeasurably strengthened. They were now considered U.S. allies and were all on the CIA's extensive payroll, but they were a motley bunch. In the north, the Uzbek chief, Gen. Rashid Dostum, protected former Taliban commanders for a price even as his soldiers carried out widespread pillaging and looting against the minority Pashtun population, making it impossible for UN agencies to start humanitarian relief operations there. By February 2002, a few weeks later, fifty thousand Pashtun farmers fled the north. Turkey and Russia were supporting Dostum, but exercising little pressure on him to cooperate with Karzai.[4] Dostum's main rival was the Tajik general Mohammed Atta, who was loyal to Fahim and also armed by the Americans. Another Tajik warlord, General Daud, held sway over Kunduz and three northeastern provinces.

In the east, Abdul Qadir, the governor of Nangarhar province and the brother of slain commander Abdul Haq, had received lavish CIA funding during the war to mobilize thousands of Pashtun fighters against the Taliban. Yet he failed even to clear the strategic road between Jalalabad and Kabul of bandits. Convoys of relief supplies and foreign aid workers were frequently ambushed as they traveled from Peshawar to Kabul, and three Western journalists were killed on this road. Qadir's control of four eastern provinces—Nangarhar, Laghman, Nuristan, and Kunar—was fiercely contested by Hazrat Ali, thirty-eight, a small-time tribal leader directly recruited by the CIA and now elevated to warlord.[5] Hazrat Ali belonged to the Pashai ethnic minority, whom the Pashtuns considered an underclass, so inadvertently he became the symbol of Pashai assertion. Barely able to write his own name, he was given so much money by the CIA that he quickly created an eighteen-thousand-strong militia. At Tora Bora his men had allowed bin Laden to escape.

In the southeast, former Taliban commanders were being paid by the CIA to keep the peace. The four critical provinces in the south were ruled by the governor of Kandahar province, Gul Agha Sherzai. The complex amalgam of Pashtun tribes that had supported the Taliban in the south needed special attention, but above all, fair-minded leadership. Instead, Sherzai empowered his own Barakzai tribe at the expense of the others.

The Barakzai had a long historical rivalry with the Popalzai, Karzai's tribe. (Ahmad Shah Abdali Durrani, the founder of modern Afghanistan, was a Popalzai, while his main rival, Jamal Khan, was a Barakzai.) Sherzai's tribal rivals exposed him for trafficking in drugs, maintaining close contact with the Taliban, and allegedly remaining on the payroll of the ISI even as he earned money from the CIA.[6]

In the west there was Ismael Khan, and in the center of the country, in the Hazarajat, the Hazara warlords Karim Khalili, Syed Akbari, and Mohammed Mohaqiq held sway. As they were alienated by Mohammad Fahim and his Tajiks, the Hazaras began to receive extensive aid from Iran. Fahim was by far the most powerful warlord in the country. Although defense minister, he had a narrow parochial interest in keeping the other warlord militias on the government payroll because that made them dependent on his support. He had little interest in building a national army. Fahim and the Tajik Panjsheris in the cabinet controlled all the key security ministries—Defense, Intelligence, Foreign Affairs, and Interior—which made Fahim, as their leader, the most powerful warlord in the cabinet.

In the aftermath of the war, the Americans institutionalized these divisions, making Karzai and the central government weak and irrelevant. Washington was distracted by preparations for the war in Iraq, unwilling to put U.S. troops on the ground in Afghanistan to maintain the peace or spend the money needed to reinforce the government's authority. As a result, the warlords were seen as a cheap and beneficial way to retain U.S. allies in the field who might even provide information about al Qaeda.

The wealth of the warlords contrasted sharply with the interim government's immediate poverty. Karzai had no state income, and for the first four months, no cash from donors to pay the salaries of civil servants and police officers. His presidential palace had been bombed out and the gaping holes in many of the rooms brought in snow flurries and chilling draughts. Some ministers moved into their offices to find no windows, desks, chairs, or even pens, while others did not even have a building to call their own. The UN organized the delivery of office supplies to every minister, which included the kind of basic items one gives to a child before he or she starts school. Meanwhile, the warlords were rolling in millions of dollars.

The new transitional government faced far more daunting tasks than finding furniture for ministers after the war ended. Afghanistan boasted some of the worst living conditions and statistics ever recorded. Its first

Human Development Report, compiled in 2004, showed the extent of public suffering.[7] The country ranked 172nd out of the 178 countries on the UN Development Programme's Human Development Index, effectively tying for last place with several African countries. Easily preventable epidemics such as measles, flu, and even diarrhea were killing thousands of people every month, while fifteen thousand women died every year from pregnancy-related illnesses. The country had the highest rate of infant mortality in the world, with 165 infants out of 1,000 dying at birth, while 250, or a quarter, died before they reached the age of five. Life expectancy for women was just forty-four years, one year less than for men. As a result, Afghanistan had the youngest population in the world, with 57 percent under age eighteen. Multiple generations of adults had not had any education and had known only war.

Despite such appalling conditions there was a powerful feeling of optimism on Kabul's streets in those early months of 2002. Public confidence in the new government and in Karzai grew as officials and teachers were called back to their jobs, refugees from Iran and Pakistan returned home, and educated Afghans arrived from the West to see their families, bringing with them money to invest. Clean-shaven young men in trousers and shirts appeared in the corridors of the ministries. Shops refitted and painted their premises. A dozen embassies quickly opened, and rental prices soared as diplomats and Western aid agencies sought housing in the destroyed capital. The U.S. embassy reopened in December, under Ryan Crocker, the Dari-speaking diplomat who had led the Geneva talks with the Iranians. The first U.S. diplomat in Kabul for more than a decade, Crocker became the U.S. chargé d'affaires. The embassy building, situated in a vast compound off the main road to the city's airport, was in total disrepair, and living conditions were tough. Crocker described them: "There were ninety marines and thirty staff, and we were all living and working together. The staff slept in a bunker next to the main building, and there was one room for men and one for women, with bunk beds in very cramped conditions. There were only two wash toilets for one hundred and twenty people, no running water, and it was very, very cold."[8]

In March 2002, Robert Finn was appointed the first U.S. ambassador to Afghanistan since 1992. Finn had spent the past ten years in war zones and spoke fifteen languages, including all the Central Asian tongues. He belonged to the school of diplomacy where expertise, knowledge, and intellectual interest in the countries where you worked were considered vital, as compared to the neoconservatives, who considered the CIA and intelligence gathering the epitome of success in nation building. Even living conditions in Kabul reflected the differences. While senior U.S. diplomats lived in camping trailers, the CIA vetted new recruits and enjoyed far better living conditions in a former Kabul hotel once used by al Qaeda. After the war, dozens of CIA agents were pulled out of retirement from the CIA's Clandestine Service reserve and rushed to the region. They expanded their premises constantly, taking over adjacent buildings with the help of Fahim and his cronies. The hotel also housed the headquarters for joint CIA-SOF operations, whose goal was to nab al Qaeda leaders, and included space for the young CIA techies who were trawling through captured al Qaeda computers looking for intelligence.

The CIA's operations in Afghanistan were vast, complicated, and expensive. They were also inefficient, ineffective, and self-defeating. By funding warlords, who in turn recruited thousands of militiamen who acted as ground forces, bodyguards, and spies for the Americans, the CIA only created further mayhem in the countryside. When CIA–U.S. SOF teams set up bases along the Pakistan border to gather intelligence about al Qaeda, they hired Pashtun tribesmen, paying them up to two hundred dollars a month, plus bonuses to their commanders, when a top monthly wage in Kabul was only fifty dollars. These mercenaries—called the Afghan Militia Force, or AMF—were still being hired as late as 2006. SOF officers had the authority to employ up to one hundred AMF to guard their camps and act as drivers and interpreters. The AMF's Afghan commanders received cash, weapons, uniforms, communications equipment, and their pick of unearthed Taliban weapons caches, which they then sold on the black market—and which were invariably bought by the Taliban. These commanders became an enormously destabilizing factor in the country, as they considered themselves as unaccountable as their American commanders. The irony was not lost on the Afghan people. Although the Americans had liberated them from the evil of the Taliban, they had brought back another evil: the warlords.

Meanwhile, the warlords created even greater tensions as they fought one another over control of tolls, drugs, and weapons caches that had been hidden by the Taliban and were being uncovered. In the spring of 2002, when warlord armies were fighting one another in the north and east of the country, the Americans refused to intervene. Dr. Abdur Rehman, forty-nine, the jovial minister for tourism and civil aviation, had been stabbed to death on the tarmac of Kabul international airport by rival war-lords in February. In his first nationwide radio address on January 10, 2002, Hamid Karzai spoke of the need to disarm the warlords. In reply, the war-lords spurned him by saying that if the Americans had armed them, who was Karzai to tell them to disarm?

Fahim and the warlords were deeply suspicious when the first British officers arrived in Kabul to head the UN-mandated International Security Assistance Force (ISAF), which would take over security of the capital from Fahim's forces. Fifteen hundred British troops formed the core of ISAF, with twenty-one more countries pledging to provide another five thousand. They were led by the tough, no-nonsense officer Gen. Sir John McColl, who commanded the British army's Sixteenth Air Assault Bri-gade. Fahim set about defying McColl's mandate and delaying the deploy-ment of ISAF, refusing to demilitarize Kabul or remove his troops from the city, as the Bonn Agreement had stipulated. While visiting Tajik units in the city I discovered that Fahim had told his commanders that the for-eign forces would soon leave and they should prepare to take control of Kabul again.

In March, under pressure from ISAF to show more cooperation, Fahim called all the warlords for a conference and a dressing-down in Kabul. It was a remarkable sight to see all the perpetrators of some of the worst crimes in Afghanistan's history gathered in one room, pledging allegiance to Karzai and ISAF. Their hyperbole was even more extraordinary: "I have no desire for power. I only want to serve my country," boomed Dos-tum, the former plumber and recent mass murderer. Ismael Khan stated that a modern army was not needed: "What this country needs are Muja-hedin and not an army—marching up and down is a waste of time." At the end of the conference the warlords promised to behave, but they all knew that as long as Fahim did not demobilize his own militia or rein in his forces, none of the other warlords would feel the need to do so either.

McColl was a tough and brilliant soldier, with a patient, dogged nego-tiating style that stunned even the Afghans. He now argued for the need to expand ISAF outside Kabul so that international troops could replace the warlords in keeping the peace. Washington refused to allow any ISAF expansion, however, claiming it would interfere with the hunt for al Qaeda leaders. Rumsfeld quickly cut McColl out of all decision making and refused to meet with him. The biggest obstacle to peacekeeping was now not just warlords such as Fahim but also those in Washington such as Wolfowitz and Rumsfeld.

As the war wound down, the Bush administration was faced with two policy choices. It was clear by the summer of 2002 that the warlords were becoming stronger while the Karzai regime lacked the resources to compete. The unstated U.S. strategy was to leave Karzai ineffectual in the capital, protected by foreign forces, while relying on the warlords to keep Pax Americana in the countryside and the U.S. SOF forces to hunt down al Qaeda. It was a minimalist, military intelligence–driven strategy that ignored nation building, creating state institutions, or rebuilding the country's shattered infrastructure. By following such a strategy, the United States left everything in place from the Taliban era except for the fact of regime change.

An alternative strategy for the United States would have been to adopt a more complex but productive policy of using its power, money, and recently won influence and goodwill to supplement Karzai's scant power. The United States could have started rebuilding the economy and the army to reduce the influence of the warlords. Yet Washington followed the first option as the way to minimize U.S. exposure in Afghanistan as it prepared for war in Iraq. Thus for the first eighteen months, until late 2003, the Americans employed a "warlord strategy" in order to be relieved of Afghanistan's security and political and human rights responsibilities.[9] This same strategy was to be recast in Iraq in 2003, when the United States disbanded the Iraqi army and then preferred allowing Shia warlords to mobilize militias rather than to rebuild state structures. Rumsfeld refused to comprehend that keeping the peace and rebuilding nations often needed more troops and resources than winning wars.

Moreover, even attempts to achieve the first objective of the United States—hunting down al Qaeda—were to fail miserably as the upcoming war in Iraq sucked out the best U.S. resources from Afghanistan. General Franks began moving his best intelligence assets out of Afghanistan and to the Iraq theater. The specially constituted Task Force Five, made up of some 150 SOF who were hunting for bin Laden, was moved in its entirety to Iraq, while another 150 SOF troops in Afghanistan had their numbers cut to 30.[10] In February, Franks cut by half the CENTCOM naval force deployed in the Arabian Gulf, even though al Qaeda was known to be escaping by sea to the Middle East. He also sent home the B-1 bombers based in Oman whose smoke trails across the Afghan skyline had signaled the omnipresence of U.S. power. The CIA closed its forward bases in Herat, Mazar-e-Sharif, and Kandahar in March and postponed an $80 million refit of the Afghan intelligence service.

With the huge demand on CIA officers in Iraq, tours of duty in Afghanistan were just six to eight weeks long. In April, satellite surveillance over Afghanistan and the use of drones and other technological spying facilities were first reduced and then withdrawn. When I met with skeptical junior U.S. officers at Bagram in March, they told me that Franks believed the job in Afghanistan had been done. The war in Afghanistan had cost $17 billion between October 2001 and May 2002, and with an invasion of Iraq on the horizon, Franks had no interest in increasing costs in Afghanistan.[11]

Before the plan to invade Iraq became widely known, the State Department argued for an expansion of ISAF outside Kabul. In February 2002, Powell had proposed to the White House that American troops join the ISAF peacekeeping force in Kabul and then help ISAF expand beyond the capital. Rumsfeld immediately shot down the idea. That spring, American and European diplomats in Kabul told me that if there was U.S. support for an ISAF expansion, a force of thirty thousand European peacekeepers could be assembled quite quickly. If that had happened early on, the history of stabilizing Afghanistan and the battle with Islamic extremists worldwide might have turned out completely different.

Ryan Crocker, the first U.S. ambassador in Kabul later said, "We [the State Department] were asking how can central authority be established? Who was going to set up the police, army, carry out nation building and disarm the militias? The Pentagon's view was our job is done and let's get out of here. We got rid of the evil and we should not get stuck."[12]

Some U.S. legislators realized the great dangers posed by Rumsfeld's shortchanged policy. In May, Senator Joseph Biden warned, "America has replaced the Taliban with the warlords. Warlords are still on the US payroll but that hasn't bought a cessation of violence. Not only is the US failing to rein in the warlords, we are actually making them the centerpiece of our strategy. Why does the Administration steadfastly resist any expansion of ISAF when everyone has called for an expansion of ISAF."[13]

Rumsfeld, for his part, infuriated Biden and other senators, and the Afghans, by saying that the warlords should share power with the government: "How ought security to evolve in that country depends on really two things; one is what the interim government decides they think ought to happen, [the other is] what the warlord forces in the country decide they think ought to happen, and the interaction between those two."[14]

Even U.S. women's groups and humanitarian agencies pleaded with the administration: "How can we win the war and lose the keeping of the peace—not having more security forces is a disaster," said Eleanor Smeal, the head of the Feminist Majority Foundation.[15] The media weighed in against Rumsfeld: "Increasingly US support for the warlords is serving to undermine the efforts of the Afghanistan government to establish its political authority," said *The Washington Post*.[16] Almost all the major U.S. newspapers and think tanks called for more troops to expand ISAF beyond the capital. Rumsfeld ignored them.[17]

Rumsfeld's determination to legalize warlord authority against the wishes of the Afghan government and people was the most fatal mistake he was to make. It gave the Taliban just the propaganda excuse they needed to reorganize themselves. Karzai considered Rumsfeld's statement an insult to all Afghans, and from that time on, he saw the secretary of defense as being completely out of touch with reality. Karzai spent the spring of 2002 touring world capitals appealing for more peacekeeping troops and money, but it was a hopeless task as long as the Americans refused to support the idea. Brahimi and Kofi Annan traveled separately to Washington in February to talk to the Bush administration. "It's very difficult to have a major peace operation in Afghanistan without the Americans involved," a sarcastic Brahimi said in Washington on February 10.[18]

The debate was all the more acrimonious and relevant because ISAF was proving to be a huge success, creating immense goodwill in Kabul as Western soldiers carried out foot patrols, helped local communities, and befriended citizens in a way unheard of by the Kabul police. When British soldiers patrolled the streets of Kabul, there would be an instant traffic jam. Hordes of well-wishers, including burqa-clad women and laughing children, crowded around them. Sadly, contrary to what many people thought, an ISAF expansion outside the capital did not need tens of thousands of troops. A blueprint drawn up by William Durch of the Henry L. Stimson Center, in Washington, argued for a modest expansion of 4,500 more troops to be based in six key cities, 6,500 troops to patrol the roads between those cities, and some combat engineer units to help repair roads between the cities and manage the demobilization of Afghan militias.[19]

In March 2002, disgruntled aid officials at the American embassy in Kabul told me that the CIA's $1 billion budget was being used to pay off warlords and their militias, carry out quick-impact development projects, find al Qaeda leaders, and conduct classified operations against extremists. The State Department and the United States Agency for International Development (USAID) had been completely cut out of policymaking. Even the British tried to complain about this monopolization of policymaking by the CIA and the Defense Department. Tony Blair was dismayed to hear that "the CIA was given $1 billion of extra funding to identify local groups and provide them with the cash and weapons to do America's work."[20] By the early summer, forty-five thousand Afghan mercenaries were being paid by the CIA.

Moreover, in many areas, USAID humanitarian food deliveries and development projects were being taken over by the joint CIA-SOF teams. Credible Afghan tribal leaders who had been identified by the Afghan government or the UN as "positive agents of change," capable of fostering stability at the community level, were bypassed in favor of the commanders and warlords preferred by the CIA. Afghan civil society was being strangled even as it emerged, and the Afghan government was made to look incompetent and powerless. Afghan policy was now in the hands of covert CIA-SOF operatives, who had vast sums at their disposal but no mandate to rebuild the country.

The warlords were becoming even richer by receiving lucrative U.S. contracts for the supply of food and fuel to U.S. bases. Kandahar's governor, Gul Agha Sherzai, endeared himself to U.S. commanders in the city by giving them everything they needed. He was soon earning an estimated $1.5 million a month for providing building materials, fuel, and other items. Gravel needed to repair the Kandahar runway costing eight dollars a truckload was sold to the base for one hundred dollars—and some three hundred truckloads a day were being delivered. Sherzai provided one thousand guards, laborers, and cleaners to the U.S. base in Kandahar, raking in a commission from both the base and the workers' salaries.[21] Paul Wolfowitz, the architect of the warlord policy, was in a state of denial about the U.S. role in supporting the warlords. "I don't think in most parts of the country that the power of the warlords is a function of any support they get from us," he said. "The real strength of the warlords comes from their local roots."[22] With a new warlord state being established under the patronage of the U.S. military, Karzai and his government could not compete.

Bush's lack of control over the Pentagon and the extent to which Rumsfeld was making his own rules in Afghanistan became clearer in April. Until April 2002, Bush was firmly committed to "no nation building" in Afghanistan.[23] Then, on April 17, in a speech given at the Virginia Military Institute, where Gen. George Marshall once trained, Bush surprised everyone by calling for a "Marshall Plan" for Afghanistan, referring to the plan the United States provided Europe after World War II. Bush promised to rebuild the government and the army and provide health and education services.[24] He called Marshall's work "a beacon to light the path that we, too, must follow." This sudden U-turn, a result of the State Department and Colin Powell trying to regain a grip on policy, caused immense excitement in Kabul. Karzai telephoned me to say that his and my skepticism about the Americans had been misplaced and that Bush had finally come around. Then, nothing happened. The orders never went down. The National Security Council, under Condoleezza Rice, never presented any plan. The resources were never allocated.

Rumsfeld had blocked the idea even before it got off the ground. He said that U.S. troops would never be involved in nation building and he claimed that European countries were not prepared to expand ISAF— a lie. They had never been asked. In fact, Richard Haass had taken informal soundings from the Europeans for more troops, and the response had been very positive.[25] "The last thing you're going to hear from this podium is someone thinking they know how Afghanistan ought to organize itself," Rumsfeld said in response. Wolfowitz said that Afghanistan was "notoriously hostile to foreigners and notoriously difficult to govern," so the United States should not even try. He said that the CIA-SOF teams would continue working with the warlords, or "regional leaders," as he now liked to call them. To do more, Wolfowitz added, would be to ignore an Afghan culture of "regional power with a great deal of autonomy," while to intervene too actively on behalf of the central government would create a risk.[26] Bush said nothing more, and no U.S. official ever again mentioned a "Marshall Plan" for Afghanistan.

Instead, the Defense Department now virtually took over reconstruction in Afghanistan from the State Department. Dov Zakheim, the Pentagon's undersecretary of defense and comptroller, became its reconstruction coordinator in Afghanistan. Defense rather than State Department officials began to mobilize money from donor countries, which shocked their governments. Zakheim ordered army officers to go on fund-raising trips to Europe, Japan, and the Arabian Gulf. Later, Swedish diplomats told me they were appalled when a U.S. brigadier general arrived asking for more money for Afghanistan.

The warlords presented the biggest obstacle to the UN in 2002 as it implemented the first stage of the political agenda set out in the Bonn Agreement—the holding of a representative Loya Jirga (LJ), or grand tribal council. The LJ would choose an interim president until presidential elections were held, decide on the shape of the government, and choose a commission, which would then draw up a new constitution the following year. The holding of LJs to elect kings and decide upon weighty matters such as going to war were a long tradition and an accepted form of decision making by the Afghans. Traditionally the LJ had no rules of procedure or agenda, as each was specific to the time and the need. Chiefs and elders of the tribes were automatically all members. The first Loya Jirga, held in 1747, founded the modern Afghan state and established the Durrani monarchy. The last genuinely representative LJ was held in 1964. After the monarchy was overthrown in 1973, strongmen rulers, including the communists, held Loya Jirgas, but none was considered representative or legitimate. Taliban leader Mullah Omar considered the Loya Jirga anti-Islamic and refused to hold one.

This new Loya Jirga for Afghanistan would elect members through an indirect process that would be supervised by the UN and the twenty-one-man Loya Jirga Commission, appointed by Karzai. Ismael Qasimyar, a constitutional law expert, was appointed chairman of the Loya Jirga Commission. He had taken part in every LJ since 1964 and now promised to bring together a far more complete mix of representatives, including women, than ever before so that nobody could question the LJ's legitimacy. "The only disqualification is that members cannot belong to terrorist groups or the Taliban," said Qasimyar.[27]

The key issue for the commission was to limit the control of the warlords, who would try to determine who was elected from their region. In a process of indirect elections, people would vote for 1,050 delegates from across the country. The commission would select another 500 delegates to represent women, technocrats, refugees in Pakistan and Iran, nomads, and Afghans in exile in the West. At least 150, or 10 percent of the 1,501 representatives, would be women.[28] Across the country women were to assert themselves for the first time in decades. Female teachers and midwives were the most active, and they mobilized illiterate peasant women.

There were no Western peacekeeping forces outside Kabul to maintain the impartiality of the voting process, while local security forces were thin on the ground or controlled by warlords, yet the elections passed remarkably peacefully. The warlords did try to influence the process in every corner of the country. Delegates were threatened, harassed, or even kidnapped to make sure they represented the warlord's views or supported the warlord's candidate in the next round of voting. Yet when the LJ was held, more than one third of the delegates declared themselves to be independent.

There was an enormous amount of politicking before the LJ started. Zahir Shah had returned to Kabul from Rome on April 18, 2002. He was eighty-seven years old and frail, but all the warlords and thousands of people arrived to pay him homage. I met him a few days later. The excitement of coming home after twenty-eight years seemed to have reversed the aging process by a decade. He spoke with an energy and lucidity I had not seen in him before. Then the problems started. The Rome group and other Pashtun notables who had felt left out at Bonn urged the former king to stand against Karzai for president, although he was not well enough to do so. Karzai, the Northern Alliance, and the international community wanted him to accept a symbolic title, such as father of the nation.

For the UN, a key aim of the elections was to make sure that the Pashtuns felt fully enfranchised. So it was difficult for the UN to openly oppose the machinations of Zahir Shah's supporters, although no one wanted to see a weak old man as head of state. The UN was also concerned that unless the United States exerted pressure, the most powerful warlords could totally ignore the democratization process. Zalmay Khalilzad, now President Bush's special representative for Afghanistan, took it upon himself to pull the rug out from under the king's supporters and end the uncertainty. After persuading Zahir Shah to renounce all aspirations toward the presidency, Khalilzad held a press conference on June 10 in the garden of the king's house. In front of a bemused press, he sat with the king, Karzai, and Foreign Minister Abdullah Abdullah. The king's spokesman, Nasir Zia, read out a statement from the king: "I have no intention of restoring the monarchy and I am not a candidate for any position." Khalilzad said the confusion about the king's role had been due to a misunderstanding.

The Panjsheri leaders warned that they would walk out of the LJ if the king were nominated president.[29] Behind the scenes Khalilzad convinced the three powerful Panjsheri Tajiks, who held the ministries of Defense,

Foreign Affairs, and Interior, that they would have to relinquish one post as a gesture to the Pashtuns. Subsequently during the LJ, Younus Qanuni stepped down as interior minister after a dramatic speech and was replaced by a Pashtun, although Qanuni returned to the cabinet as education minister.[30] The opening of the LJ was postponed by twenty-four hours so that everyone could digest what had happened. Some Pashtun delegates denounced Khalilzad for acting like a British viceroy. Others criticized American activism in keeping out the king in sharp contrast to the American accommodation of the warlords. However, there is little doubt that if the king had been given any political role, the LJ would have ended in chaos.

There was no building in good repair to house such a large meeting, so Germany provided a huge tent, normally used for beer garden festivals along the Rhine, as the venue for the LJ. Delegates arrived by UN aircraft from the farthest corners of the country, others by jeep and even by tractor and on horseback. Some wealthy delegates arrived in processions that included dozens of heavily armed gunmen, dancing camels, drummers, and long-haired tribal dancers who swayed through the streets in celebration. Kabul's traffic was gridlocked, and clouds of exhaust fumes hovered over the city. For the first time in nearly three decades the country was enjoying a national political event. Men and women delegates all ate together in an enormous communal dining hall. A massive security operation was undertaken by ISAF, which set up three security perimeters around the LJ complex. "This process has been much less than perfect," said Brahimi. "But after nearly thirty years of conflict, the process is truly representative and much, much better than we could have hoped for."

Many delegates were dismayed when at the last moment the UN invited all the warlords and the governors of the provinces to sit in the front row of the LJ, although according to the rules of LJ Commission they had not been elected and there was no reason for their presence. An exclusion clause in the rules did not allow anyone who had committed human rights abuses to be elected, although the commission did not exclude anyone on those grounds. European ambassadors were also angry, saying the warlords had been brought in at the behest of the Americans. "Giving the warlords a front seat was a blow to the Afghans and a negative symbol of U.S. influence," said one ambassador.[31] However, the Americans, with their pro-warlord policy, were anxious to show that the warlords supported the political process.

When Zahir Shah, helped by aides, finally climbed up onto the stage to open the LJ, he received a five-minute standing ovation and many delegates wept. Below him sat men in every conceivable kind of attire, from three-piece Armani suits to Uzbek capes to the long flowing shirts and baggy trousers of the Pashtuns to turbans of every tribal color and pattern. On one side sat two hundred women delegates—their heads covered but their faces bare; they had discarded the burqa, or full veil, enforced by the Taliban. The warlords sat up front, across from the world's diplomats. It was a breathtaking scene full of exhilaration and heartbreak as people rejoiced to see Zahir Shah back in Kabul and remembered the millions of Afghans who had lost their lives in the wars.

Day and night Afghans were glued to their radio sets, which broadcast the LJ sessions live. In his address Karzai appealed for peace: "Everywhere I go people don't ask for money or food or jobs but they ask for peace. The nation's wish is clear, the nation wants peace and to be free from the warlords. After that people want education."

The sessions quickly got bogged down in denunciations of the warlords, factionalism, and parliamentary minutiae. One session, which elected the speaker of the LJ and his deputies, ran all day and night for twenty hours. In a path-breaking step, a woman, Simar Samar, was elected as one of the three deputy speakers of the LJ.[32] Karzai's main challenger for interim president was Masuda Jalal, a forty two-year-old former medical professor at Kabul University who had lost her job under the Taliban. Even though General Fahim threatened her husband to stop her from running, she still garnered 171 votes. Mir Mohammed Mahfooz Nadai, a little known medical doctor, won eighty-nine votes. Karzai won the presidency with a resounding 1,295 votes.

The LJ had achieved its wider aim. It had mobilized the entire country in a national purpose. Afghans from every ethnic group, tribe, and community had gathered under one roof in an atmosphere of discussion rather than conflict. Afghan women had come out of the shadows for the first time. The LJ legitimized a political process that no warlord could now question and showed the warlords that they were held in public contempt. It gave Karzai, the government, and the international community a base from which to start rebuilding state institutions. The danger now was that Afghan expectations would be pitched too high. "All the Afghans were speaking as though the LJ would solve all their problems," Brahimi said later. "It was one step to empower people but it was crazy to think it could change the country overnight."[33]

Many Afghans later argued that neither Karzai nor the UN had tapped the true potential of the LJ. Karzai had failed to envisage a strategy for what he wanted out of the LJ, apart from his own election as president, and had failed to put together a team to exploit the positive public mood toward him and the international community. Most significant of all, the LJ had offered Karzai a chance to put the warlords in their place, but the United States, which depended on them, had vetoed any such idea. Karzai had succumbed to U.S. pressure and refused to do so. In forming the new cabinet of twenty-nine ministers, he endorsed the status quo. General Fahim remained defense minister and one of three vice presidents. The new Pashtun interior minister, Taj Mohammed Wardak, was eighty years old and could make no headway in reforming the police. The brilliant Pashtun technocrat Ashraf Ghani continued as finance minister, which offset Panjsheri power, as the Pashtun ministers now held the purse strings. From among the king's supporters Zalmay Rasul became the new national security adviser, with the British pledging to fund and train Afghans for a national security council based on the American model.

In the final tally, the Pashtuns had supported Karzai, even though many felt betrayed by Khalilzad and angry at the rising toll of civilian casualties due to U.S. bombing in the Pashtun south and east. In July, AC-130 gunships shot up four villages in Uruzghan province, killing fifty-four people while families were celebrating a wedding. That month, U.S. forces launched six raids into Uruzghan, but did not capture a single Taliban leader, although eighty civilians were killed. Global Exchange, a human rights organization run by Marla Ruzicka, a young, vivacious American who was later tragically killed in Iraq, listed 812 Afghan civilians killed by U.S. air strikes in June alone. Ruzicka said that most of the deaths were a result of faulty intelligence given to U.S. commanders and overreliance on air power due to the chronic shortage of U.S. troops on the ground.[34]

The LJ also did little to end the conflicts between the warlords. During the summer months, there was severe fighting in the north between the militias of Dostum and Atta. In the west, Pashtun commander Amanullah Khan fought to oust Ismael Khan from Herat. There was also severe tension between Ismael Khan and Gul Agha Sherzai, the governor of Kandahar.

Senior U.S. officials and generals, however, persisted in treating the warlords like heads of state, inflating their egos even further. In September alone, the U.S. Treasury secretary, John Taylor, visited Ismael Khan in Herat, Dov Zakheim met with Dostum and Atta in Mazar, while Lt.-Gen. Dan K. McNeill, the commander of U.S.-led Coalition forces, met with them all. In retrospect, the new U.S. ambassador, Robert Finn, wondered if the United States could have done things differently: "None of these warlords were openly defying Karzai, but could the U.S. take the risk, without enough troops in the country to do something about them, that could prompt a civil war? However, we should have moved away from the warlords much earlier and we should have stopped visiting them. We should have supported the government more visibly. I stopped visiting Ismael Khan and Dostum, but Rumsfeld visited them several times."[35]

Unable to take a tough position against the warlords, Karzai spent much of his time trying to maintain a balance between them and hold on to his authority and that of the government while Afghan citizens demanding the warlords' removal. Karzai told me in December, "The warlords know that they cannot survive without the center, and they are not strong enough to challenge the center—there may be acts of defiance, but no challenge. We call the shots, they don't call the shots, but there is a huge disconnect between the central government authority and the lack of an administration—we need to fill that gap very quickly, and I need good, trained people, which I don't have."[36]

Senior European officials now told U.S. diplomats that warlord power had to be curtailed, a new Afghan army had to be swiftly built up, and the United States had to force Fahim to agree to reforming the warlord-controlled defense ministry. At a conference in Spain, the Europeans asked the Americans for "a strategy that deals with the warlords that includes incentives and disincentives."[37] U.S. protection of the warlords had become a major constraint to Afghanistan's ability to move forward and a growing bone of contention between Europe and the United States.

At a commemorative meeting in Bonn on December 3, 2002, to celebrate the first anniversary of the Bonn Agreement, Karzai signed a decree formally inaugurating the new Afghan National Army, banning all militias and formalizing a program to disarm them. The warlords were given one year to surrender all heavy weapons. It was the start of something new but it would be extremely slow and difficult to implement. Then, just as the government tried to shift gears with the warlords, the Taliban ignited a slow-burning fuse in the south, reemerging to attack soft targets. Karzai escaped a Taliban assassin's bullets by a hairsbreadth while driving through

Kandahar on September 5. That same day, bomb blasts in Kabul killed 15 civilians and injured another 150. It was not a good time for the country to start looking fragile, as the rift in the international community over the U.S. intention to invade Iraq had begun to drive a deep wedge in joint efforts to rebuild Afghanistan.

CHAPTER EIGHT

• • •

Musharraf's Lost Moment

Political Expediency and Authoritarian Rule

The war may have been fought and won in Afghanistan, but it left Pakistan confronting the fallout and the most dangerous political challenges. Musharraf faced near-war with India due to attacks by Kashmiri militants, anti-U.S. protests in Pakistan's streets, the escape of thousands of al Qaeda and Taliban into Pakistan, an economic slump, and suicide bombings by terrorist groups targeting Shia and Christian minorities. Pakistan had become without doubt *the* front line in Bush's global war on terrorism.

The ensuing chaos was also a time of enormous opportunity, and the future of Pakistan would depend on how President Musharraf reacted. In Western capitals, there was a strong desire to see the pariah military regime brought in from the cold to act like a cooperative, acquiescent regime against the terrorists. Pakistanis hoped that Musharraf, who had made the right decision after 9/11, would now follow that up by restoring representative government and curbing jihadism across the board. Both hopes were to remain unfulfilled.

The reality was that Musharraf lacked any political consensus from which to build democracy. The army's pro-extremist policies in Kashmir and Afghanistan strengthened its ties to Islamic fundamentalist parties at home, making any real curtailing of fundamentalism impossible. Some generals viewed 9/11 as an opportunity to carve out a permanent role for the army in the political system. They were not about to yield power to a bunch of squabbling civilian politicians. In the post–9/11 era, Washington's sole objective was to catch al Qaeda leaders, and it asked for the Pakistan army's cooperation. That suited Musharraf fine. He was not being asked simultaneously to rein in militants at home, democratize, or rebuild national institutions that would turn Pakistan away from the legacy of jihad the army had cultivated for three decades. As in Afghanistan, the Bush regime was demanding of Pakistan the very minimum—far short of the kind of nation building that was required.

For a brief moment Musharraf hinted that perhaps the army had seen the light and was cutting its umbilical cord with the Islamic extremists. "The writ of the government is being challenged," he said in what would become his famous speech of January 12, 2002. "Pakistan has been made a soft state where the supremacy of law is questioned. This situation cannot be tolerated any longer."[1] Minutes after he had spoken, an excited Wendy Chamberlain, the U.S. ambassador in Islamabad, telephoned Colin Powell and told him that Musharraf had delivered everything the Americans had on their wish list. Powell immediately welcomed Musharraf's "explicit statements against terrorism."[2] The army's promised crackdown on militancy delighted most Pakistanis, and marked the highest point of Musharraf's popularity. A poll by the U.S. State Department in February showed that 82 percent of Pakistanis supported the government's decision to side with the United States, up from 64 percent in a poll taken after September 11. Seventy-nine percent of people voiced a good opinion of Musharraf, up from 57 percent in September.[3]

After the January 12 speech, Pakistanis began to look at what they had gained from the present crisis. The army faced an unprecedented opportunity to reform the country—if it wanted to do so. The war in Afghanistan had been mercifully short, the threatened inundation by Afghan refugees had receded, the Islamic parties had failed to muster public support outside the Pashtun areas, and Pakistan's support to the United States was being rewarded with unprecedented aid and debt relief by the international community. The potential repercussions for Pakistan during the war could have been much more severe, but now the rewards were turning out to be life-saving.

Moreover, Pakistan's Islamic groups were in disarray. Thousands of Pakistanis had been killed or wounded fighting for the Taliban, several thousand taken prisoner by the NA warlords and not to return home for another three years, while those who did return home alive were demoralized and disillusioned by their leaders. Senior clerics, retired ISI officers, and right-wing pundits who had filled the media with their predictions that the Americans would meet their Armageddon in Afghanistan, as had the former Soviet Union, were proved embarrassingly wrong. The ISI had told Musharraf that the Taliban would hang on until the spring of 2002 and then conduct guerrilla war from the mountains, but the Taliban had collapsed in just six weeks.

The mullahs were bewildered and in a state of shock. None could explain to their followers why so many Islamists had died so uselessly in Afghanistan or how the hated Americans and the Northern Alliance had won so easily. Historically the jihadi groups had been committed to a regional strategy enforced by the ISI, which targeted India and supported the Taliban regime. Now the ISI's regional strategy was in tatters.[4] If Musharraf was serious about implementing even half the measures outlined in his January 12 speech, now was the moment to do so—but the chance passed. Instead, the army and the ISI, still obsessed with enemy India, were to resurrect the Islamists from defeat and demoralization. Taliban leaders were given refuge in Pakistan. Militant attacks in Indian Kashmir were encouraged in order to resuscitate morale among the jihadi groups and to show that the army had not abandoned them. By February 2002, the banned extremist groups were quietly encouraged by the ISI to reconstitute themselves with a change of name. Those militants arrested after January 12 were freed. The government abandoned its March 23 deadline for the madrassas to register themselves, and the promised disarming of the jihadi groups was put off indefinitely.

The army did set about implementing the minimalist strategy desired by the Americans—to catch escaping al Qaeda leaders. Working closely with the CIA and U.S. SOF teams now based in the North-West Frontier Province (NWFP), the military arrested hundreds of Arabs, but many were innocent civilians. The army carefully differentiated between Arabs and other foreigners, who were handed over to the United States, and the Afghan Taliban and Pakistani militants, who were left alone. Moreover, the CIA was offering large cash bonuses to any soldiers or police who handed over an Arab. Some four hundred alleged al Qaeda fighters were caught in the tribal agencies and the NWFP. There were several bloody incidents, such as on December 19, when fifteen people were killed after captured al Qaeda fighters overpowered their Pakistani guards while being transported from one town to another in the NWFP.

Pakistani forces had failed to cordon off all the seven tribal agencies that make up the Federally Administered Tribal Areas and the Afghan border. Troops were deployed in the Kurram agency but not farther south, in South and North Waziristan, from where bin Laden escaped into Pakistan. More al Qaeda escaped northward and crossed into Pakistan's Dir and Chitral regions, which were also unguarded. Taliban escaping from Kandahar were able to cross into Balochistan province unmolested by any Pakistan army presence. Thousands of Taliban escaped in this direction.

Several U.S. officers in Afghanistan later told me that they suspected that the army had deliberately left the Waziristan and Balochistan door open to allow fighters to escape. The CIA had intercepted communications between Pakistani officers not to harass any foreign fighters entering through Waziristan. Pakistani officials rejected these allegations, insisting that the tensions with India ruled out their having any spare troops to guard Waziristan. Whether the Waziristan door was left open deliberately or unintentionally, it would lead to major repercussions as Waziristan became not only a bolt-hole but a new base of operations for al Qaeda and the Taliban.

It was not until May 2002 that Pakistan moved regular army units into South Waziristan, basing eight thousand troops in the administrative headquarters of Wana, but deploying none on the mountainous border. By now thousands of al Qaeda–linked militants—Central Asians, Chechens, Arabs, Pakistanis, and Afghan Taliban, many with their families—had escaped Afghanistan and were living in South Waziristan under the protection of local tribesmen, who were paid handsomely for the sanctuary they offered. Other al Qaeda leaders were escorted by Pakistani jihadi groups to safe houses in large cities or taken to small ports on the coast, where they escaped by boat to the Arabian Gulf states. Soon, regrouped Arab fighters were crossing the unguarded border of South Waziristan to attack U.S. troops in Afghanistan. By August 2002, al Qaeda felt confident enough to set up small mobile training camps in South Waziristan, where Pakistani militants could come to learn bomb making and other skills.

In February 2002, when Musharraf visited Washington, he received another ringing endorsement from Bush and more aid. "President Musharraf is a leader with great courage and vision . . . I am proud to call him my friend," Bush told a beaming Musharraf.[5] The Pakistani leader certainly had reason to feel the glow of U.S. friendship. Since September 11 Pakistan had received $600 million in emergency aid and a moratorium on its debts to the United States. The military had received $500 million for its logistical support to U.S. forces, including the provision of fuel, food, and water. Finance minister Shaukat Aziz told the Americans that because of lost export orders after 9/11, Pakistan had suffered losses of $2 billion, rendering fifty thousand people jobless. Bush announced a further assistance package—canceling $1.0 billion of Pakistan's $2.8 billion debt to the United States, rescheduling the remainder, and offering $100 million for educational reform. Musharraf again insisted that the Americans sell Pakistan F-16 aircraft, but with Indo-Pakistan tensions so high, Washington wisely declined.

No one raised the issue of democracy with Musharraf. Officials at the State Department, the Pentagon, and the National Security Council told me that Musharraf was indispensable and that the United States had no desire to see the return of civilian politicians. If Musharraf was slow in disarming the militants or reforming the madrassas, that was acceptable to Washington for the time being. In fact, Musharraf's aides had adamantly told U.S. officials that any American criticism of Musharraf would undermine his position in the army and make it more difficult for him to help Washington.

The army's apparent willingness to go after al Qaeda yielded its first big catch at the end of March: Abu Zubaydah, the head of al Qaeda's overseas operations, was captured in the industrial city of Faislabad. He was to provide the CIA with its best information to date about al Qaeda membership and operations in Western countries. Then, on the first anniversary of 9/11, Ramzi bin al-Shibh, one of the leaders of the Hamburg cell that had planned the 9/11 attacks, was arrested in Karachi. (I deal with these arrests in a later chapter.) These successes only further convinced Bush and Cheney that Musharraf should not be criticized for lapses on other fronts. There would therefore be no substantial U.S. pressure placed on him to carry out the reforms he was promising.

Buoyed by the free hand Washington had given them, Musharraf and his generals chalked out their future political game plan. The army's nine corps commanders, who together with the army chief collectively made all strategic decisions, held lengthy discussions. They knew that at this moment Musharraf and the army had the political power, popularity, and moral authority at home, plus massive international support, to do whatever they wished. For years the army's alliance with the Islamic fundamentalist parties, dubbed the military-mullah alliance, which provided militants to fight the army's wars in Afghanistan and Kashmir, had prevailed. Now would have been the time to break with the mullahs, work out a political consensus with the opposition parties, and hold elections, thus moving the country toward greater democracy. Some of Musharraf's closest aides were later to admit that he should have implemented a power-sharing agreement with the exiled Benazir Bhutto and her PPP, still the most popular party in the country and one that was strongly anti-mullah.

Instead, Musharraf and his aides worked on an altogether different strategy—determining how to legitimize his role as president and army chief, and introducing a new political system that would ensure the permanent dominance of the military. Musharraf first consolidated his grip on the army by promoting twenty-seven officers to the rank of major-general, the largest number ever appointed in the army's history. In April 2002 he declared that he would hold a national referendum asking the people to give him five more years as president. "I am not power hungry but I don't believe in power sharing," he told the nation in a TV address on April 5. "I believe in unity of command because I am an army man. That's the way democracy in Pakistan will function."[6]

He lowered the voting age from twenty-one to eighteen in the belief that young people would vote for him. He set about putting together a new "king's party," persuading feudal and co-opted politicians to join the Pakistan Muslim League Party, which would support continued military rule. He promised that elections would be held in October. All the country's major political parties, as well as lawyers' groups, trade unions, and human rights organizations, condemned the referendum as unconstitutional, since, under law, only the national and four provincial assemblies could elect the president. Musharraf ignored the criticism and, convinced that millions of people would turn out to see him, began a barnstorming referendum campaign around the country, addressing political rallies organized by the ISI and the bureaucracy—even though there was no candidate standing against him.

He began his campaign from Lahore on April 9, where generals crowded a stage bedecked with balloons and colored paper streamers. Dressed in his commando uniform and wreathed in garlands of roses, Musharraf addressed the crowd, promising food for the hungry and jobs for the jobless. There was a pitifully low public turnout, with the first dozen rows filled with soldiers from the Lahore garrison wearing civilian clothes. Thousands of peasants had been forcibly bused in from outside the city.

The political parties all boycotted the referendum. There was total silence from the international community—only the European Union parliament spoke out, condemning the referendum and postponing ratification of a trade agreement with Pakistan.[7] On April 30, some eighty-seven thousand polling stations—double the normal number for an election—were set up in every corner of the country. There were no polling lists, however, no need for voters to show identity cards, and no independent monitors—making it easier for people to cast multiple votes. Sixty-two million voters were expected to go to the polls, but hardly anyone turned up. The government declared that 42.8 million people voted for Musharraf, while eight hundred thousand had voted against him—resulting in a massive 70 percent turnout. However, the Human Rights Commission of Pakistan, which had sent out thousands of monitors across the country, and other groups declared that the turnout was actually less than 10 percent. In Lahore, I toured empty polling stations that had registered only a handful of votes during the entire day and then shut down early. The five-hundred-thousand-strong army and three million government employees were ordered to vote for Musharraf—many times over.

The damage to Musharraf's credibility was catastrophic. "A much-liked general has emerged from this test a diminished man," said Shafqat Mehmood, who had served in Musharraf's first cabinet in 1999. "A sincere man who convinced almost everybody that he was above all this, has appeared as shallow and opportunistic as other politicians," said Najam Sethi, editor of *The Friday Times*.[8] Musharraf had severely miscalculated, and public resentment against him, and the Bush administration for its studied silence, skyrocketed.

Meanwhile, the world was gripped by the murder of an innocent American journalist. On January 23, 2002, Daniel Pearl, an American correspondent for *The Wall Street Journal*, disappeared in Karachi. Pearl, thirty-eight, was chasing a story about Richard Reid, who in December had been arrested while trying to detonate explosives in his shoes while flying from Paris to Miami. Reid had been inspired by a small Pakistani extremist group whom Pearl was now trying to track down. Instead, Pearl was lured into a trap by one of his contacts, who turned out to be the terrorist Ahmed Omar Sheikh, who had been rescued from an Indian jail after the 1999 Kandahar hijacking. Sheikh had cleverly befriended Pearl using an assumed name.

Four days after his disappearance, Pearl's pregnant wife, Mariane, and several newspaper offices received e-mail messages that showed photographs of Pearl crouching in chains with a gun to his head. An unknown group called the National Movement for the Restoration of Pakistani Sovereignty threatened to kill Pearl unless Pakistanis held at Guantánamo Bay prison were freed. They accused Pearl of working for the CIA and Mossad, Israel's intelligence service. *The Wall Street Journal,* the U.S. government, and Pearl's family strongly denied the accusations.

Musharraf appeared at a loss to condemn the kidnapping strongly enough. He first said the kidnappers were linked to Indian intelligence, an allegation that was quickly derided by the media. He then said that the kidnapping was a backlash by extremist groups. On February 12, while Musharraf was at the Davos World Economic Forum in New York, the Pakistani government announced the arrest of Omar Sheikh. Musharraf said he was "reasonably sure" that Pearl was still alive, and then insinuated that the kidnapped journalist had been too intrusive. "I wonder whether it was because of his overinvolvement that he landed himself into this kind of a problem," Musharraf told reporters.[9] The accusation that Pearl was "over-intrusive" was repeated by other Pakistani officials.[10] Musharraf's contradictory statements led the FBI and the Karachi police to believe that perhaps the Pakistani president was not being fully briefed by the ISI. In fact, Daniel Pearl was already dead.

Omar Sheikh had given himself up a week earlier, on February 5, to a former ISI officer, retired brigadier Ejaz Shah, who was now the home secretary of Punjab. The Karachi police were not even informed of Sheikh's surrender until he was handed over to them a week later. Sheikh told the police that he had been involved in the Daniel Pearl kidnapping and that Pearl was already dead. That missing week remains the darkest hole of the entire affair. It has never been explained, nor is it known, what transpired between Sheikh and the ISI.[11] Mariane Pearl later asked several pertinent questions, which many Pakistanis also asked, but which the government never answered satisfactorily: "Was there information they [the ISI] didn't want revealed? Were they making some kind of deal with him—'go to jail for a bit and we'll make sure you are set free'? Or are they just taking their time to erase any clues leading back to them?"[12]

As the American press exploded in a litany of accusations, Colin Powell was forced to go public and defend the ISI. "I cannot totally rule out anything, but there is no evidence to suggest that the ISI was involved or anybody in the Pakistan government was accomplice to this tragedy," he told CNN.[13] In late February a video was handed over to the U.S. consulate in Karachi showing Pearl's execution. The world was shocked—it was the first execution by al Qaeda to be recorded on video. In mid-May Pearl's body was recovered. It had been cut into nine pieces and his head severed. It is still unclear if Pearl was targeted because he was Jewish or a journalist or because he worked for a right-wing American newspaper that had unearthed a computer disk in Kabul on the inner workings of al Qaeda or because he had simply happened to be in the wrong place at the wrong time.

Some Pakistani journalists suspected that hard-line elements in one of the intelligence agencies may have encouraged militants to carry out the kidnapping of a Western journalist in order to disourage reporters from delving too deeply into extremist groups. After all, such tactics had been used in the past.[14] The government vehemently denied all such suspicions. What is certain is that extremist groups wished to embarrass the government and exert pressure on Musharraf to end his crackdown. In this they were successful, as after the kidnapping thousands of Pakistani militants were freed from jail. However, Daniel Pearl's death was a devastating blow to Musharraf and Pakistan's credibility.

Pakistan refused Washington's requests to extradite Omar Sheikh to the United States. From jail, Sheikh threatened the military regime with severe repercussions if he was extradited.[15] His videotaped trial was held in Hyderabad jail. On July 15, 2002, he and three others were convicted of kidnapping and killing Pearl. Sheikh received the death sentence. Investigators later revealed that he had directed the plot using separate cells of militants—some sixteen in all. While one cell carried out the abduction, another was used to negotiate with the authorities, while a third killed Pearl. Several of the sixteen militants involved were eventually arrested. The July trial involved only those in the first cell. Others who were caught belonging to other cells were never put on trial.[16]

The FBI later concluded that Daniel Pearl had not been executed by Omar Sheikh but by three Arabs, one of whom was Khalid Sheikh Mohammed, the principal organizer of the 9/11 attacks. Mohammed admitted killing Pearl in a March 2007 hearing in Guantánamo Bay, although the reliability of his confession was questioned, as there was little doubt that it came after he had been subjected to considerable torture by the CIA.[17]

Sheikh left a legacy of new tactics for extremists. For the kidnapping, he had recruited militants from several local terrorist groups, introduced them to al Qaeda, and forged operational unity through terrorist action. It was a model designed to maximize operational security and boost morale because it involved several groups. In the months ahead, jihadis from various extremist groups would contribute either manpower, expertise, or safe houses to conduct similar operations under al Qaeda's auspices. No single group would be responsible for an entire operation, thus making the police's task much more difficult. The militants came to hero-worship Omar Sheikh. Several subsequent terrorist acts were carried out by a cell calling itself Lashkar-e-Omar, or "the Army of Omar."

In the aftermath of Daniel Pearl's murder, a wave of deadly terrorist attacks swept Pakistan. On March 17, two suicide bombers threw grenades into Islamabad's Protestant International Church, close to the U.S. embassy, during the Sunday service, killing five people and wounding forty-one. Two of the dead were Americans—the wife and daughter of a diplomat—while many foreigners, including five Britons, were wounded. General Franks and the State Department's assistant secretary for South Asia, Christina Rocca, arrived as the American embassy was sending home all nonessential staff. On May 8 a car bomb blew up outside the Sheraton Hotel in Karachi, next to a bus full of French naval engineers. Eleven Frenchmen and three Pakistanis were killed. The bomb was so powerful that pieces of it landed on the roof of a ten-story hotel across the street. Now European embassies began to send all nonessential staff home.

On June 14 a car bomb blew up outside the U.S. consulate in Karachi, killing twelve Pakistanis and wounding forty-five. It was a daring attack against one of the most heavily guarded buildings in the country. The Karachi stock market fell by 3 percent the next day, and international airlines suspended all flights to Karachi as foreigners fled the city. When the police later arrested the perpetrators, they said that the same car bomb had been positioned in April to assassinate Musharraf but that the explosives provided by al Qaeda had failed to detonate.[18] Those arrested included military personnel—one was a naval soldier and another a paramilitary ranger—who had provided the terrorists with intelligence about the route Musharraf was taking. These arrests made it clear that the militants were recruiting from the armed forces in order to target Musharraf. The U.S. Secret Service stepped up training for Musharraf's security detail, which now numbered between two hundred and three hundred men.

In Karachi, sectarian Sunni jihadis began to kill Shia professionals, particularly doctors. Sunni extremists following the Deobandi and Wahhabism sects had long believed that Shias were not proper Muslims and should be eliminated. Al Qaeda had helped the Taliban carry out programs against Afghan Shias and now they helped Sunni militants do the same to Pakistani Shias. In the first four months of 2002 in Karachi, seventeen doctors, four lawyers, five journalists, four teachers, and sixteen government officials—all Shias—were gunned down. In mid-March, four Shia doctors were killed in five days. Doctors were furious with the government's inability to stop the mayhem and went on strike, shutting down the city's hospitals. The Karachi police, who faced the brunt of public anger, were infuriated at the lack of cooperation from the ISI in handing over lists of known militants.[19] Police officials in Karachi said they believed that the ISI had extensive information on the militants and their safe houses in the city but were refusing to help the police track them down.

The police were also angry that the government had failed to bring a single charge of terrorism against the three thousand militants arrested after Musharraf's January 12 speech. Pakistan's three hundred thousand policemen, with a basic average monthly salary of one hundred dollars, were notoriously underpaid, poorly equipped and trained, and had no fingerprinting or DNA-testing facilities. Not surprisingly, they were also notoriously corrupt. A senior police officer pointed out that the army received 25 percent of the national budget while the police received only 1 percent, and yet the police were the main victims of terrorist attacks.

The contradictions in Pakistan's counterterrorism strategy were becoming glaring. Even as the ISI helped the CIA run down al Qaeda leaders in Pakistan's cities, Pakistani Islamist militants, with quiet ISI approval, were attacking Indian troops in Kashmir or helping the Taliban regroup in Pakistan. Yet al Qaeda itself was involved in training and funding the Islamist militants ordered to kill Musharraf. The regime continued to differentiate between so-called good jihadis, who fought in Kashmir on behalf of the ISI, and bad terrorists, who were largely Arabs—but such differences had long ceased to exist. In a briefing, Musharraf divided the extremists into three groups—the al Qaeda–Taliban, the Pakistani sectarian groups, and the "freedom fighters of Kashmir."[20] The military was clearly signaling that it still considered some jihadis as acceptable and was maintaining links with them. "It is not possible to completely crack down on the fundamentalists, as they may be needed in any future conflict with India," one general told me.

Benazir Bhutto spoke of Musharraf's dilemma: "The regime is living day to day, surviving on the pats it gets from the world community. . . . Each external and internal crisis gets the rest of the world community dialing or visiting the general to hold his hand. Increasingly, the West's favorite dictator is viewed by his own people as nothing more than a foreign puppet. This creates the very environment that works to the advantage of the militants."[21]

The battle against extremism took second place to the military regime's fight to create a victory for the Pakistan Muslim League in the parliamentary elections, scheduled for October 10, 2002. The army wanted to push through twenty-nine amendments to the constitution that would legitimize the 1999 coup and make the president all-powerful. Benazir Bhutto and Nawaz Sharif would be banned from ever becoming prime minister again. The army also limited who was eligible to stand in the elections. Anyone without a university degree could not stand for election—a ridiculous supposition in a country with a 54 percent literacy rate. Meanwhile, graduation certificates issued by madrassas would be considered the equivalent of a university degree, thereby allowing thousands of mullahs to stand in the elections. Aitezaz Ahsan, a leading constitutional lawyer, called the decrees "the scorched earth policy of the military mind."[22] The amendments led to a storm of protests from the opposition parties, lawyers, and the media.

Maj.-Gen. Ihtesham Zamir, the head of ISI's political wing, prepared lists of candidates on a color-coded chart of black, white, and gray—signifying those who would support or oppose Musharraf and those who were in between. Through harassment, persuasion, and threats, dozens of politicians were forced to abandon the opposition parties. ISI officers would arrive at the homes of potential candidates with a dossier containing tax returns, property holdings, telephone bills, and estimates of income and use them to threaten them, citing corruption or living beyond their means. "The ISI colonel gave me a choice, either you are with us or against us," a politician told me. "It is like Bush's war on terrorism."

International monitors voiced deep skepticism about the intensive pre-rigging carried out by the military. A pre-poll report by a team of observers from the European Union described how "Pakistan appears to be the only country in the world where candidates can be disqualified for unpaid utility bills."[23] However, the United States looked away as officials visited Islamabad to boost Musharraf.[24] Christina Rocca made no mention of the pre-poll rigging when she addressed the American Congress. Several Democratic congressmen delivered withering rebuttals, accusing her of ignoring "the sham referendum" and describing the constitutional amendments as "an insult to democracy encouraging a dictatorship in Pakistan."[25]

On August 21 Musharraf issued a Legal Framework Order that made him president for the next five years and the proposed twenty-nine amendments part of the constitution that would increase his and the military's power. Waving the list of amendments in the air, he told reporters, "This is part of the Constitution. I am hereby making it part of the Constitution."[26] Legally, only parliament had the power to amend the constitution, with a two-thirds majority vote. The next day Bush quipped that Musharraf "is still tight with us in the war against terrorism. . . . He understands that we have got to keep al Qaeda on the run."[27] On September 28, just two weeks before the Pakistani elections, Washington authorized a $230 million package of military spare parts to Islamabad, signaling the strongest possible endorsement for Musharraf. Pakistanis joked that the key electoral alliance was not between the army and the Pakistan Muslim League but between Musharraf and Bush.

After such intensive pre-poll rigging, there was little public enthusiasm for the actual election campaign. The government had banned political rallies and processions, and a deep cynicism pervaded the streets. The only issue-based campaign came from the newly formed Muttahida Majlis-e-Amal (MMA), or United Council of Action, a six-party alliance of Islamic fundamentalist parties, who were able to put up large numbers of candidates due to the legalizing of madrassa certificates.[28] MMA candidates ran on a shrill anti-U.S. platform, demanding the withdrawal of U.S. bases from Pakistan and an end to American interference. Significantly, the MMA was the only group allowed by the military to hold political rallies because its members were described as religious and not political leaders.

The public understood that the elections were not about restoring democracy but about the military's attempt to legitimize a permanent political role for itself, weaken the secular parties, strengthen the Islamic parties, and create a hung parliament in which the military would become the main power broker. However, all the political parties participated in the polls, contesting 392 seats for the National Assembly and another 728 seats in the four provincial assemblies. Sixty women contested general seats—the highest number in the country's electoral history—while sixty seats were reserved for women in the assemblies. The increased participation of women decreed by Musharraf was the most progressive step he took before the elections.

When all the votes were in on October 10, the turnout was a poor 41.8 percent, reflecting the low level of public interest or credibility in the polls. Despite the effort to weaken Bhutto's PPP, that party secured sixty-three seats in the National Assembly, coming in second after the army's favored Pakistan Muslim League, which won seventy-seven seats. The MMA won a staggering forty-five seats, the largest number ever won by an Islamic alliance.[29] Voting patterns demonstrated how popular the opposition still was, despite the pre-poll rigging. The PPP received 25.9 percent of all votes cast, the largest number for any party in the country. The MMA won 11.5 percent of the votes cast, but it did extraordinarily well in the NWFP provincial elections, where it won half the seats and formed the new provincial government.[30] It also made substantial gains in Balochistan, where it set up a provincial government in alliance with other parties. The main winner within the MMA was the Jamiat Ulema-e-Islam—the party that supported the Taliban—gaining more seats than ever before.

Three hundred international observers monitored the polls, including a seventy-member team from the European Union. All of them said the polls were seriously flawed. The Commonwealth Observer Group described "many irregularities" and "chaotic scenes at many polling stations."[31] William Milam, the former U.S. ambassador to Pakistan, said that by rigging the elections, Musharraf had struck "a Faustian deal" with the MMA and destroyed the middle ground of Pakistan's political landscape.[32]

The staggering successes of the MMA shocked and dismayed many Pakistanis and even many in the army. In an internal assessment before the elections, the ISI had predicted that the MMA would win only twenty seats nationwide, compared to the forty-five it won. Several serving generals whom I spoke to after the polls were angry at the ISI, saying it had given its operatives in the NWFP the freedom to help MMA candidates get out the vote. Vali Nasir, a scholar on political Islam, explained the army's preference for the MMA: "The army's acquiescence to Islamization actually transcends its fear of it, by seeking opportunities in it to establish the military's hegemony and expand its control over society. The MMA is opposed to civil society and not to army rule, and periods of military rule have seen the expansion of Islamization."[33]

The elections resulted in a hung parliament. It took six weeks of intense horse-trading and arm-twisting by the ISI before a coalition government headed by the Pakistan Muslim League was formed with the slimmest of majorities. Zafarullah Khan Jamali, a Baloch politician and tribal chief, was elected prime minister. He was a safe bet who would insist on calling Musharraf "my boss" in public. Musharraf took the oath of president for a five-year term, but refused to submit himself to being elected by parliament, as was required. The opposition refused to accept Musharraf's unilateral measures, and their protests were to paralyze parliament in the months ahead.

For the U.S.-led Coalition and the Afghan government, the most worrying outcome of the elections was the creation of an MMA provincial government in the NWFP, with the JUI politician Akram Durrani becoming chief minister. Durrani said he would not allow U.S. agencies to operate in the province and promptly banned alcohol sales and gambling. He gave an extraordinary description of JUI plans for economic development, saying, "We believe that God prearranged food and clothing for every man or woman he created. If we give up the ways of God and devise our own solutions to perceived problems we may land in trouble."[34]

With these kinds of views and the NWFP provincial parliament now stuffed full of neo-Taliban mullahs belonging to the JUI, the Afghan government was extremely fearful of greater support for its own Taliban. "We are extremely concerned at the victory of friends of the Taliban in the NWFP," Zalmay Rasul, national security adviser to President Karzai, told me.[35] The JUI also helped form a coalition government in Balochistan. In both provinces the JUI was to use the state machinery now at its disposal and its own network of madrassas and mosques to help the Taliban regain Afghanistan. By rigging the elections, Musharraf had for the first time unleashed the Islamic extremist genie within the Pakistan state and handed it political power in two provinces.

The country had been on edge as a wave of terrorist attacks by al Qaeda and Pakistani extremists hit, this time aimed at Pakistani Christians. On August 4, 2002, six Pakistani Christians, including several children, had been killed in an attack on a convent school near Islamabad. Five days later four Christian nurses had been killed and twenty-three wounded in a grenade attack on a Christian hospital, also near Islamabad. On Christmas Day in Punjab province, three young Christian girls had been killed in a grenade attack during a church service. The four gunmen were later caught and admitted to belonging to Jaish-e-Mohammed. Yet the group's leader, Masud Azhar, now released from house arrest, was preaching in mosques across the country.

The rigged elections had only widened the political divide, further polarized society, and encouraged the extremists. Parliament was paralyzed by the opposition, who, for the next twelve months, denounced Musharraf at every session of the National Assembly by thumping their desks, shouting, and walking out. In March 2003 the opposition boycotted the elections for the chairman of the Senate—the upper house of parliament—after the ISI hosted a dinner for fifty-four senators to persuade them to vote for its favored candidate. The dinner made a mockery of the election, which was dubbed the "ISI selection."[36]

The MMA acted as cheerleader for the army while opposing its policy of alliance with the United States. It wanted to keep its public credibility intact by not being seen to be too close to the army's policies. In May 2003 in the NWFP, the MMA parliament adopted a Sharia, or Islamic law, bill that threatened to introduce Taliban-style Islamic measures in the province. Schools in the NWFP were ordered to replace boys' uniforms of shirts and trousers with traditional dress, and girls were told to cover their heads. Western aid agencies and the World Bank suspended their activities in the NWFP because of the restrictions placed on women there. Musharraf criticized the MMA actions, yet when he arrived at Camp David in June 2003, he assured Bush that "all the political restructuring that we have done is in line with ensuring sustainable democracy in Pakistan." Bush in turn continued to call Musharraf "a visionary and courageous leader."[37]

At their meeting, Bush announced a five-year aid package to Pakistan worth $3.2 billion, with half the money being allocated to the military. U.S. officials categorically said that the package was not linked to any specific demands on democratization. However, some mid-level U.S. diplomats feared that without tying down the aid package to specific political and social reforms, the Bush administration was creating long-term problems for itself. The White House's only concern was how to support Musharraf even as it turned a blind eye to the extremism the president and the military's allies were encouraging.

U.S. military aid to Pakistani forces on the Afghan border began to pour in. In January 2003, U.S. ambassador Nancy Powell had handed over to the military in the NWFP 400 military vehicles and 750 wireless sets worth $13 million. Two weeks later she had given a similar amount to the army in Balochistan province. Pakistan also had received 3 fixed-wing aircraft and 5 helicopter gunships, with more promised. Washington went to extraordinary lengths to satisfy the military. In the spring of 2004, the United States would promise Islamabad 26 Bell helicopters costing $250 million, to be used for a new airborne commando force. The U.S. Congress would take too long to allocate the funds, so Bush would approach Prince Bandar, the influential Saudi ambassador to Washington, who came up with funds to pay for 24 helicopters, which were immediately delivered.[38]

However, U.S. military aid could not shore up what was a weak political dispensation that was already showing signs of eroding. The fundamental institutions of government were failing. Parliament was discredited by the lack of importance given it by the army and the opposition protests. Newspapers dubbed the National Assembly the most ineffective in the country's history, as it passed so little legislation. The opposition parties and the MMA continued to demand that Musharraf give up his uniform as army chief and become a civilian president. Two assassination attempts against him in December 2003 created widespread shock and further political uncertainty. For many Pakistanis, Musharraf and his generals were devoid of a political vision or strategy and were merely following expediency to stay in power.

◆ ◆ ◆

The fallout from the war in Afghanistan did not affect only Pakistan but also the neighboring states of Central Asia, where political expediency also flourished. The Central Asian regimes had welcomed the arrival of U.S. forces and influence because they hoped that the United States would provide a balance to Russia's overweening power and influence. They also determined that the United States would provide international legitimacy to their repressive dictatorial regimes, which could use such legitimacy to end the years of international isolation and the lack of foreign investment they had endured since the breakup of the Soviet Union. The public response was also positive as people hoped for greater American influence and pressure on their respective regimes for democracy and economic reforms.

Central Asia was the only bloc in the Muslim world that had never experienced American power, interference, or largesse. Unlike in the rest of the Muslim world, in Central Asia the United States had an overwhelmingly favorable image—largely because nobody knew anything about America except that it was rich, powerful, and democratic. Washington started off with a major plus—neither the regimes nor the peoples disputed the U.S. presence.

The most important country for the United States was Uzbekistan.

With the largest armed forces in the region, numerous military bases, and a regime that had resisted Russian domination, President Islam Karimov was considered a significant ally. He had swiftly allowed U.S. SOF and the CIA to operate out of Uzbek bases even before the Uzbeks had granted formal permission for setting up a U.S. base. Karimov, sixty-three, had now governed for thirteen years, running a repressive and dictatorial state. After serving as first secretary-general of Uzbekistan's Communist Party, he had been elected president in 1990. In 1995 he had held a referendum to extend his mandate for five years, and in 2000 he had won another rigged election. Now he used the American presence to justify holding a referendum in January 2002 that would extend his term of office from five to seven years, keeping him in power until December 2007. As in Soviet times, the government claimed that 91 percent of the voters had polled in his favor. Karimov had scheduled the polls on January 27—the same day that American officials from the State Department and the Treasury arrived in Tashkent for a meeting of the newly formed U.S.-Uzbekistan Joint Security Cooperation. Karimov could boast that Washington fully supported the referendum.

In order to avoid any rivalry with Moscow, U.S. officials repeatedly clarified that they had no intention of maintaining a permanent military presence in Central Asia. "We do not anticipate a permanent presence in any of the countries in the region," General Franks said in Tashkent in January 2002.[39] Franks invited Russian officers to join CENTCOM to be briefed on the war's progress, and he asked retired Russian generals to brief his officers about Russia's war experiences in Afghanistan. At the May NATO summit in Italy, Presidents Bush and Putin signed a declaration that for the first time created a joint council for NATO that would allow Russia to join its decision-making process. "Two former foes are now joined as partners overcoming 50 years of division and a decade of uncertainty," said Bush at the NATO meeting.[40]

For Karimov, the real goal was to wangle a visit to Washington and use it to show Russia and his own people that he was now a world-class leader. His visit to the White House on March 12–14 aroused intense anger from human rights groups and some congressmen, but the Bush administration insisted it had succeeded in getting Karimov's commitment to carry out political reforms in the Strategic Partnership document that he and Karimov signed. The document committed Tashkent to "intensify the democratic transformation of its society politically and economically." The tightly controlled Uzbek media were never allowed to publish the document, due to the controversial commitments Karimov had made, while Washington knew those commitments were meaningless and that the United States would never hold Karimov to them. Bush pledged $155 million in aid to Uzbekistan for 2002—aimed largely at the military and security agencies. Total U.S. aid to Central Asia for 2002 was to more than double to $442 million from $200 million the previous year. Both the United States and Uzbekistan had begun a ritualized shadow dance that had little meaning for the long-suffering Uzbek people.

The United States had few intentions to help kick-start a reform process in Uzbekistan or any other Central Asian state. The Pentagon was looking for access to bases and it did not want other issues such as democracy or human rights fogging up its one-dimensional agenda. Colin Powell articulated the essence of the U.S. relationship with Central Asia at the NATO summit meeting in May: "We think it serves our interest to work with the nations of Central Asia, to have access agreements, to be able to go into their nations at their invitation, to train with them, and, perhaps if necessary, to help them in their own self-defense efforts."[41]

The U.S. presence encouraged international lending agencies to return to Central Asia with renewed optimism. In the past, both the World Bank and the International Monetary Fund had struggled in Uzbekistan. The IMF had closed its office in Tashkent in 2000, after Uzbekistan had refused to implement the terms of a memorandum it had signed committing itself to currency reform. The IMF now warily returned and made the same demands. World Bank president James Wolfensohn visited the countries of Central Asia for ten days in April 2002 and optimistically declared that "for the next two to three years Central Asia will be on everybody's agenda." He urged the regimes there to consider that "if they are going to take advantage of this opportunity for funding, for aid, for support then change will be needed."[42] It was a wake-up call to the Central Asian leadership and it offered people a glimpse of what they had hoped for from the new engagement with the West—reform.

However, economic cronyism—policies that benefited a few close relatives and associates of Karimov—continued unabated in Uzbekistan. In July the population was infuriated when the government suddenly imposed 90 percent duties on imported goods and packaged foodstuffs, which benefited a few Karimov cronies who held import licenses, but put tens of thousands of small stall holders and traders in the private markets out of business. There were unprecedented demonstrations by traders and shop-keepers in Tashkent and more unrest in the impoverished countryside as inflation surged and ordinary consumer goods became too costly to buy. In October, as unrest spread, the government reduced the duties to 70 percent, but it was not enough. Uzbekistan's countryside was deeply impoverished and becoming a breeding ground for extremism. The government set low prices for buying raw cotton from farmers—the major agricultural crop—while Karimov's cronies with special licenses were able to reap huge profits by selling the cheaply bought cotton at world prices abroad. Farmers became indebted and poorer. That same month an IMF mission to Tashkent announced that the government had again failed to fulfill any of its promises.

Karimov's strategy to retain his importance for the Americans was constantly to remind visitors that the Islamic Movement of Uzbekistan (IMU) remained a potent threat. To some extent this was true. The IMU still had an underground network in Central Asia. IMU fighters who had survived the U.S. invasion of Afghanistan retreated into Pakistan—some of them escaping in the Kunduz airlift organized by the ISI. Although the United States repeatedly said that IMU commander Juma Namangani was dead, Uzbek intelligence continued to plant stories in the Russian and Kazakh media that he was alive and waiting for the right moment to reappear. I was approached several times by Uzbek diplomats who knew my expertise at the IMU and tried to use me to plant stories that Namangani was alive.[43]

Tahir Yuldashev, the chief ideologue of the IMU, had settled in Wana in South Waziristan. I continued to hear stories about the popularity of Qari Tahir Jan, as he was called in Pakistan—his recitations of the Koran in chaste Arabic, his fierce demeanor, his skills reorganizing the IMU with al Qaeda support—and how numerous new recruits for the IMU were arriving from Central Asia. Washington feared that the IMU could still target U.S. troops in their Central Asian bases.

Karimov and other Central Asian leaders raised the specter of another Islamist threat from Hizb ut-Tahir (HT), a radical but nonviolent extremist group extending its influence in the region. Although HT was influential among some urban ethnic Uzbeks in Uzbekistan, Tajikistan, and Kyrgyzstan, it was hardly capable of toppling any regime.[44] HT was founded in 1952 by a Palestinian judge, who aimed for the group to mobilize public support to restore the Caliphate. HT was close to Wahhabism in many aspects of its extremist beliefs and developed a very secretive cell system to promote itself among young people, but it did not advocate violence. Between 1996 and 2001 the majority of political prisoners in jail in Uzbekistan were charged with belonging to HT. Several European countries were also affected by HT recruitment, especially among young Muslims studying at university. Despite HT's nonviolence claims, Germany banned the group in January 2003, citing that "it supports the use of violence as a means to realize political interests." Britain was under pressure from conservatives to do the same, but Tony Blair demurred.[45]

After 9/11, Karimov had launched another major crackdown on Islamists and anyone opposed to his regime. Hundreds of people were arrested and tortured. For the first time ever, antigovernment protests were staged by women whose male relatives had been arrested. In April 2002, wives and mothers had demonstrated in Tashkent and the Ferghana Valley for several days before being arrested and charged with belonging to HT. That month the ICRC had announced that it would withdraw its delegation from Uzbekistan because the government had failed to fulfill its obligations on torture or to respect an agreement the two sides had concluded in January 2001 giving the ICRC access to political prisoners.

The human rights situation in Uzbekistan had worsened considerably. Its jails held more than ten thousand political prisoners, who were tortured, abused, and beaten as a matter of course. Many were innocent citizens. The most embarrassing case had involved the deaths in August 2002 of Muzafar Avazov, thirty-four, and Khusniddin Alimov, thirty-five, who were held at the notorious Jaslyk jail. After the two were tortured to death, their bodies were returned to their families, who found that they had been forcibly drowned in boiling water. They had been punished for refusing to stop saying their prayers—guards at Jaslyk prevented prisoners from praying, fasting, or reading the Koran. Just after the two men died, Colin Powell reported to the U.S. Congress that Uzbekistan had made substantial progress in improving human rights, in order that Congress would release an additional $45 million in aid for Uzbekistan. Eleven prisoners died under torture in Uzbekistan the first fifteen months after 9/11, according to human rights groups.

Two further U.S. bases were established in Central Asia, in Kyrgyzstan and Tajikistan, in 2002. The United States rented thirty-seven acres outside the Kyrgyz capital, Bishkek, alongside the Manas International Airport, where it established the Ganci Air Base, named after a New York City firefighter who had died in the World Trade Center attack. Several European countries and Canada contributed to building the base. An enormous tent city had sprung up by the spring of 2002, capable of housing three thousand troops and some two dozen aircraft, including French Mirages and U.S. F-15 and F-18 fighter bombers. At the end of April, when Rumsfeld toured the base, only half of the two thousand troops there were American. Eleven nations were to contribute either planes or troops. Spain, Holland, and Denmark ran massive cargo planes to Europe, always taking off at night, while the U.S.-run KC-135 tanker aircraft provided in-flight refueling for bombers and surveillance flights over Afghanistan.[46] The United States agreed to provide Kyrgyzstan $92 million in aid for 2002, of which more than half went into building capacity in the country's poorly equipped twelve-thousand-man army.

The presence of the Ganci (or Manas) Air Base convinced the Russians that the Americans and NATO countries planned to stay on in Central Asia. Putin responded with his own base diplomacy, leaning on the Kyrgyz to provide Russia with an air base. In June 2002 the Kyrgyz were forced to oblige, giving the Russians an air base at Kant, ten miles from Bishkek and almost eyeball to eyeball with the Americans. The Kant base would deploy what Russia considered its answer to NATO, a rapid-deployment force aimed at countering IMU threats to Central Asia. In December 2002, when President Vladimir Putin arrived to sign the Bishkek Declaration with Kyrgyz president Askar Akayev, he said Russia would deploy twenty fighter bombers and some seven hundred troops to Kant. The Russian media lavished praise on Putin for reestablishing Russia's influence in its former colonies and not leaving the region to the Americans. Russia was now openly competing with the United States in Central Asia.

In January 2002, Tajikistan had signed an agreement with France for the use of Dushanbe Airport by French aircraft and air crews. France had agreed to help the Americans in Afghanistan with its own air power. For Tajik president Emomali Rakhmonov it was a risky venture. Russia maintained a large military force in southern Tajikistan, where eleven thousand Russian and Tajik troops guarded the porous border with Afghanistan. The Russian 201st Division also had a base in Dushanbe. However, Rakhmonov agreed to the presence of the base and joined NATO's Partnership for Peace program—the last Central Asian nation to do so apart from Turkmenistan. Tajikistan also received $125 million in American aid. At the end of the year, Rakhmonov was granted a visit to Washington, where he met with Bush and appealed for more help to deal with terrorism and the country's chronic economic crisis.

As a result of the civil war in the 1990s, Tajikistan was by far the poorest of the Central Asian states. Although GDP growth had jumped from 1.7 percent in 1997 to 10.0 percent in 2002, the economy was still less than half the size it was in 1991, when Tajikistan became independent. There was a huge unchecked population explosion, while some 50 percent of children were undernourished. The UN estimated that 80 percent of the population lived below the poverty level, while 60 percent of workers were unemployed. A staggering 1.0 to 1.5 million workers out of a total population of 6.5 million were forced to migrate to find work in Russia. Tajikistan was also vulnerable to crime, as it had hosted the IMU for several years in the late 1990s and had become a major exit point for Afghan heroin, which fueled corruption.

The real challenge to both the United States and Russia would now come from China, whose borders lay only two hundred miles from the Manas Air Base. China was angry and nervous about the U.S. military presence so close to its mainland. During the cold war the United States had tried to encircle China using proxies; now it was on China's doorstep. China's first response was to strengthen ties with all the Central Asian regimes and provide them military aid and training as a counter to U.S. influence. In January 2002, China called an urgent meeting of the Shanghai Cooperation Organization—the security association Beijing had forged with Central Asian states and Russia—to demand that U.S. forces stay in the region only as long as was necessary.

China held large-scale military exercises along its borders with Central Asia involving thousands of troops and also stepped up the resolution of border disputes with Kyrgyzstan, Kazakhstan, and Tajikistan. China's greatest fear was the penetration of its predominantly Muslim province of Xinjiang by Uighur extremists, who had found refuge in Afghanistan and Pakistan and might now slip back into Central Asia or even Xinjiang to escape the U.S. dragnet. At least a dozen Uighurs caught in Afghanistan were being held in Guantánamo Bay prison, while others were taking shelter in Pakistan tribal areas.

The U.S. bases in Central Asia were to prove a gold mine for those in power. Just as Gul Agha Sherzai had become rich by being the main provider for U.S. troops in Kandahar, so the sons and daughters of Central Asia's ruling elites made millions of dollars by maintaining a monopoly over who provided what to the U.S. bases. In Kyrgyzstan it was an open secret that President Akayev's own family had the contract to sell fuel to the Manas base—corruption allegations that became better known after Akayev was overthrown in 2005. For their part, the Americans did little to implement fair practices in issuing contracts for supplies. In fact they found that their access to the ruling families was considerably enhanced by encouraging these contracts. Far from pursuing democracy and encouraging reform, the American presence was to make already corrupt ruling elites even more powerful and corrupt, much to the anger of the people.

PART THREE

THE FAILURE OF NATION BUILDING

CHAPTER NINE

• • •

Afghanistan I

Economic Reconstruction

When the war against the Taliban began, my desk in Lahore was flooded with economic papers and plans. Governments, UN agencies, multinational lending institutions, universities, and NGOs were preparing concept papers on how to start reconstructing Afghanistan, but nobody had a clue about the country. None of the agencies had the capacity or the contacts to be able to consult Afghans about their basic needs or development priorities. Since 1978 no comprehensive census had been taken and no economic data gathered. Most of the plans were "guesstimates." Still, the aid agencies wanted to know how they could help.

Afghanistan had been more comprehensively destroyed after twenty-two years of continuous war than any country since World War II apart from Vietnam. Tragically, the Afghans had done more damage to their own country than had the Soviets. Whereas the Soviets had fought much of their war in the rural Pashtun belt, the Afghanistan civil war in the 1990s had destroyed the cities and infrastructure as warring factions bombarded Kabul and destroyed or looted the infrastructure—right down to selling off telegraph wire and road fences in Pakistan. Roads, power and telephone lines, water and sewer pipes, houses, shops, schools, and hospitals—everything looked like burned-out shells or upturned carcasses. When the Taliban arrived they had no interest in rebuilding the country nor the money to do so. Their only contribution was rebuilding some mosques and petrol pumps.

What little humanitarian aid did flow to Afghanistan in the last years of the Taliban regime became more and more problematic. The UN, Red

Cross, and a handful of NGO relief agencies kept millions of Afghans alive with food supplies and ran the few hospitals and schools that still functioned. Farmers had been crippled by a five-year drought and many had moved to the cities in anticipation of free food. Nearly one million Afghans were displaced inside the country, and a new flow of refugees was arriving in Pakistan and Iran. The Taliban had no concern for the public, nor any sense of responsibility toward them—rather, they created roadblocks for the UN, determined to make it as difficult as possible for international agencies to operate there. Osama bin Laden persuaded the Taliban to expel all Western aid agencies and impose such restrictive laws on Western aid workers that it became virtually impossible to work in Kabul. The Taliban imposed restrictions on providing health care, education, and food to women and then tried to force the UN to discriminate against women. This led to calls from within the UN system to stop all aid to Afghanistan. Just before the attacks of 9/11 the entire international aid program for keeping millions of Afghans alive was on the verge of collapse and a humanitarian and political crisis was clearly brewing.

After the war, Bush could not avoid the issues that confronted the Coalition and the enormous expectations of the Afghan public. The task of nation building also posed a major political dilemma for the United States. It was not that Washington lacked experience; since the end of the cold war the United States had helped nation-building operations in Somalia, Haiti, Cambodia, East Timor, and the former Yugoslavia. And the United States had been responsible for the most successful nation-building exercise the world had ever seen: the rebuilding of Germany and Japan after World War II under the Marshall Plan. In fact, *Marshall* became a byword for success. U.S. aid had helped rebuild the former Axis powers' army and police, revived the economy, rebuilt the infrastructure, and created a new political structure and constitution. "The cases of Germany and Japan set a standard for post conflict nation-building that has not since been matched," said James Dobbins, the most experienced American official engaged in nation building.[1] Scholars and diplomats now argued for a Marshall Plan for Afghanistan. The problem was that the Bush neocons had simply no interest before or after the war in doing anything like this.

Luckily it was not just up to the United States. The international community designated the UN as the main coordinator for peacekeeping and reconstruction in Afghanistan, although it had avoided deploying blue-helmeted troops on the ground. The UN had carried out forty peacekeeping operations since the end of the cold war and all had involved some aspects of nation building. In 2007 the UN had twenty such operations running worldwide, costing over $6 billion and deploying 100,000 soldiers and 15,000 civilians. While it cost $200,000 to deploy one NATO soldier in the former Yugoslavia, it cost only $45,000 to deploy a UN peacekeeper.[2] Kofi Annan described the link between peacekeeping and nation building: "UN peacekeeping operations are now increasingly complex and multi-dimensional, going beyond monitoring a cease-fire to actually bringing failed states back to life, often after decades of conflict. [They] . . . organize elections, enact police and judicial reform, promote and protect human rights, conduct mine-clearance, advance gender equality, achieve the voluntary disarmament of former combatants, and support the return of refugees and displaced people to their homes."[3]

A hesitant Bush blew hot and cold over nation building, while Rumsfeld refused to involve U.S. troops in any such task. He could not make the connection that the army's "full-spectrum dominance" on the battlefield could be achieved only if it also had the capacity to rebuild the countries it invaded.[4] The State Department was under pressure from its allies to show leadership in rebuilding Afghanistan, but no arm of government was dedicated to nation building, and Bush declined to elevate the task into a part of U.S. foreign policy.

In 1997 President Clinton had signed Presidential Decision Directive 56, which established an interagency planning and training process for handling "complex contingency operations" abroad—in other words, nation building. The order expired and was not renewed by Bush, leaving a legal vacuum in the U.S. foreign policy system. Meanwhile, before 9/11, Rumsfeld had shut down the army's Peacekeeping Institute in Carlisle, Pennsylvania—its only training institute for nation-building tasks. There was no institution in the U.S. arsenal to deploy for nation building. In a report after 9/11, the Council on Foreign Relations was blunt about the situation: "The stark reality is that the United States does not have the right structural capability to stabilize and rebuild nations. Responsibility is diffuse and authority is uncertain. The proper roles of the military and civilian agencies have not been articulated. And civilian players desperately need a 'unified command' structure to align policies, programs and resources."[5] The Pentagon's own Defense Science Board asked that "the Secretary of Defense should designate stabilization and reconstruction operations as core military tasks."[6] Rumsfeld ignored all such requests.

In the weeks after 9/11, I met with development officials from around the world, including Andrew Natsios, the head of USAID. Natsios was charming, and a heartfelt humanitarian. An expert on famine in North Korea, he had written a book about it and was now desperately keen to get USAID do the right thing for Afghanistan, but he had no idea where to start.

Moreover, USAID was not the organization I knew growing up as a child in Pakistan, when it had water engineers and agronomists in the field. Its total experience of Afghanistan in the past two decades was handing out large and generous checks to the UN's World Food Programme to buy wheat to feed Afghans. There was nobody in USAID who spoke the language or knew the country.

USAID had shrunk from thirteen thousand staff members during the Vietnam War to just twenty-three hundred in 2001. After 9/11 its budget was doubled, to $14 billion, but it hired only one hundred more people, barely enough for the huge rebuilding operations required in Afghanistan and later Iraq. In 2002 its Kabul office had just twelve staff members, a number that rose to thirty-nine the following year.[7] It hired Afghans who were not quite qualified but who could operate in the field. They were to suffer badly at the hands of the Taliban. More than one hundred Afghan staff members of USAID were killed between 2001 and 2006.[8] It was a sad epitaph for a once-vital organization, even though there had always been rumors that USAID was a CIA front. During the cold war, it planned and managed projects, deploying its own experts. Now it was just a glorified bureaucracy that wrote checks and implemented projects by hiring contractors—the notorious Beltway bandits, consulting companies with big offices inside the Beltway in Washington. After he retired, U.S. ambassador Robert Finn commented that "USAID is doing nothing itself now, it has become a contracting agency with layers of bureaucracy that did not exist in the past and too much of the money comes back to the US through consultancies."[9]

I knew none of this in those early weeks after the war was won and had high hopes. I urged Andrew Natsios and people at other agencies to invest in agriculture as a surefire way to win public support and get the economy moving. Although only 12 percent of the total land area was arable, and only 30 percent of that was irrigated, 80 percent of the population lived off agriculture. One good crop cycle would revive public morale in the countryside and convince people of the worthlessness of the Taliban. From this there would be other benefits. Millions of returning refugees would be encouraged to return to their villages rather than gravitate to the cities looking for work. Agriculture would provide jobs to the militiamen who would soon be demobilized and offer farmers alternatives to growing poppies for opium, a business that was certain to boom again. There was also an urgent need to rebuild key roads between the major cities and link them to neighboring countries so that aid could flow. Later Natsios told his senior staff that "our first task is to rebuild the agricultural system . . . reconstruction has to be done in such a way to get the economy moving."[10]

Natsios was quickly overruled by Rumsfeld at the Pentagon and Tenet at CIA, who were determined to ignore if not undermine USAID if such programs contradicted their own strategy. The CIA wanted every U.S. aid program to be used to help capture bin Laden and strengthen the warlords rather than to rebuild the country. The few USAID officials at the U.S. embassy in Kabul were seen as a mere nuisance. The U.S. military arbitrarily determined that all U.S. officials had to have a military escort when they ventured out, but because there were never enough soldiers to escort them, USAID officials rarely left the building. One official told me that the Pentagon did not want them to go outside and see how the warlords were being helped by the CIA. They complained that in the former Yugoslavia and other war zones, they were on the ground even during combat operations in order to direct aid. Only in Afghanistan were they forbidden to deploy by their own government.

One USAID official who eventually resigned told me:

> Volatile, security risk–prone areas never stopped USAID in the past, so what was so different about Afghanistan post 9/11? Nothing—except that DOD did not want us around to see how they were aiding the wrong guys. In Washington our leadership simply lacked the motivation to stand up to DOD. We were too tame, and DOD took advantage of that. We should have established a multiagency, multidisciplinary DART [Disaster Assistance Response Team] team out of the U.S. embassy to coordinate with the other NGOs and aid credible Afghan partners rather than just hand over everything to DOD and contractors. To simply contract out America's most important humanitarian response since the Marshall Plan was just too much for many of us.[11]

So USAID farmed out millions of dollars to contractors who often were not even present in Afghanistan. During the war, USAID officials based in Islamabad were ordered to pass money for quick-impact projects to the International Organization for Migration (IOM), a group that works closely with the UN, because IOM supposedly had staff inside Afghanistan. In fact, IOM, which is mandated to deal only with migration issues, had just two staff members in country. Several USAID officials were to resign disillusioned with their organization, disgusted at U.S. policy, and frustrated at their failure to be effective. USAID was eventually to get swept into the State Department and lose what little independence it once had. In keeping with prevailing views in the Republican Party, USAID became a source of funds for Christian fundamentalist NGOs active in the Muslim world—giving them $57 million between 2001 and 2005 out of a total of $390 million distributed to all NGOs. Natsios was later to resign, but even then he did not take a stand against the corruption of USAID's original purpose by the Bush team.[12]

The tragedy for Afghanistan was how feasible reconstruction actually could be when the entire Afghan population was supporting it. You did not need to be a rocket scientist to understand that a reconstruction program well coordinated with the UN-led political process would quickly help establish the credibility of the new government. Barnett Rubin and Ashraf Ghani, who were advising the UN and Karzai, were offering extremely sensible advice around the world, such as urging Western governments to set up a central deposit, or trust fund, to collect international donations, which the Afghan government could then draw on, rather than allowing individual donors to set up their own projects and programs, which would duplicate efforts while ignoring expensive infrastructure rebuilding such as roads. Such a trust fund could be run jointly by international organizations and the Afghan transitional government. Rubin, Ghani, and I urged donors to provide funds so that trained and qualified Afghans living in the West—many of whom we knew—could return to Afghanistan quickly and help develop the country.

A trust fund was set up in Tokyo, but few governments were keen on donating to it. Many countries had moribund aid bureaucracies, which took months to identify projects, more months to disburse the money, and then had nobody on the ground to monitor implementation. The United States was blighted with the same problems. At the end of the war it had the following agencies in Afghanistan carrying out quick-impact projects and humanitarian relief, all with their separate budgets and staff: the CIA, DOD, U.S. SOF, the State Department, and USAID. There was no central aid coordinator for the U.S. government's efforts and zero coordination with the UN, European allies, or the Afghan government. Quick-impact projects became a Washington favorite. These were swift and cheap, such as digging a well, rebuilding a small bridge, or repairing a broken-down school building, and were supposed to convince the population that reconstruction was moving ahead. Instead, such projects invariably helped only the local warlord or commander the CIA was supporting.

Reporter Stephen Kinzer wrote that the path chosen by the United States assured that "Afghanistan would remain in ruins; that warlords would continue to control much of the country; that remnants of the Taliban would re-emerge as a fighting force."[13]

All Western donors spoke the jargon of "building capacity" in the fledgling Afghan government. In a failed state such as Afghanistan, capacity would take years of patience and hard work to build. In the meantime, donors undermined their own efforts by funding programs that would benefit the population without consulting the relevant ministry. Thus as donors slowly built up capacity in the education ministry so that it could actually pay teachers around the country or devise a new curriculum, they also funded Western NGOs to build schools without ministry advice or guidance. It was tempting to do it yourself rather than spend years training Afghan officials. As a consequence, a parallel donor bureaucracy developed. Francis Fukuyama highlighted the dilemma: "The contradiction in donor policy is that outside donors want both to increase the local government's capacity to provide a particular service . . . *and* to actually provide those services to the end users. The latter objective almost always wins out because of the incentives facing the donors themselves."[14]

The Americans, too, wanted the best of both worlds, handing out multimillion-dollar contracts to consultancies in Washington for building capacity in the ministries, while at the same time hiring other consultants to carry out projects to win Afghan hearts and minds—projects that were not part of a broader plan connected to the ministry. Even five years later William Byrd, the architect for the World Bank program for Afghanistan, would lament that "the aid juggernaut is still outside the budget and outside government control—aid does not build government capacity which is what we need."

In 2002, after the war ended, the UN and Japan organized a major donors' conference for Afghanistan in Tokyo. The situation was dire. The Afghan government was barely functioning; the financial system was in total disarray with no banking system and three different currencies in circulation; millions of refugees were preparing to return home; while nearly one million people faced starvation. A preliminary "needs assessment" for the country, written jointly by the UN Development Program, the World Bank, and the Asian Development Bank, estimated that Afghanistan needed $1.7 billion in the first thirty months and $10.0 billion over the first five years. Experts scathingly called the figures "guesstimates." The European Union estimated the cost of rebuilding for the first five years at $9 to $12 billion, while planning minister Mohammed Mohaqiq insisted the country needed $22 billion in the first decade. In fact, nobody knew how much Afghanistan really required.

With sixty countries participating, Kofi Annan, Hamid Karzai, and Ashraf Ghani—who had left the UN to become de facto finance minister in Kabul—opened the Tokyo conference on January 21–22 with appeals for money.[15] Ghani now headed the government's Afghan Assistance Coordination Authority (AACA), which would coordinate all reconstruction projects. Karzai asked for $300 million in cash to pay salaries six months in arrears for 210,000 civil servants and 25,000 policemen. The government only had $9 million from a UN start-up fund.

At Tokyo, nations pledged $4.5 billion, of which $1.8 billion was earmarked for 2002—still short of what was required.[16] The donors concluded that it would take $12.2 billion over five years to "rebuild" Afghanistan. A trust fund was established, but donors did not give it any money. The Afghanistan Interim Authority Fund, to be managed by the Afghan government, UNDP, ADB, and the World Bank, remained an orphan of the aid effort.[17] However, the Tokyo meeting generated tremendous euphoria among Afghans, who believed everything was about to change for the better. It also focused international attention on the needs of nation building. What Tokyo failed to do was distinguish between money for humanitarian relief and money to rebuild the infrastructure.

In the next two years most of the funds pledged at Tokyo were to be spent on humanitarian relief rather than real reconstruction projects. No roads were built, no electricity or water was provided to the Afghans. Afghans complained bitterly that there had been no visible reconstruction, while donors would insist they had spent a lot of money. By April 2002, when even the smallest projects stalled for lack of funding, the UN called another meeting, where it was decided to carve up reconstruction responsibilities. The United States said it would take the lead in building the new army; Britain would take charge of counter-narcotics; Italy would rebuild the justice system; Japan would disarm the militias; while Germany would rebuild the police force.[18]

NGOs began to arrive in Kabul in large numbers. "There are billions of dollars in the pipeline and armies of expatriates are waiting like some tribal militia to get into Kabul when the weather turns warm," said a sarcastic Barnett Rubin. When NGOs and news organizations sought to rent the few private houses still standing in Kabul, rents jumped from $400 a month to $4000 and then to $20,000. Afghans would rent their house several times over, pocketing the cash and leaving the multiple tenants to sort out the mess. At the UN guesthouse, which had running water and electricity, senior UN and World Bank officials were sleeping four to a room.

International donors were helped considerably by the fact that they were dealing with Ashraf Ghani, fifty-eight, who was to play a critical role in the next few years. In exile, Ghani had been dreaming about reconstructing his country, and now he had the chance. He had left Afghanistan in the 1970s to study at Beirut University, where his contemporary was the fellow Afghan and future American diplomat Zalmay Khalilzad. After the Soviet invasion of his country, Ghani taught at American universities, before joining the World Bank in 1991 as its senior anthropologist. Ghani had arrived in Kabul as an adviser to Brahimi, but then left the UN to head the country's reconstruction effort. In June, the Loya Jirga would appoint him finance minister.

Ghani was one of the most brilliant Afghans of his generation and the most capable minister in the cabinet. He worked twenty hours a day in order to reorganize the Finance Ministry, introduce a new currency, and establish a new tax system. He encouraged educated Afghans to return home and help him, and persuaded wealthy Afghans abroad to provide investment. Ghani's office resembled a scene from the California gold rush, as it was always flooded with tribal elders, ministers, Western executives, delegations from foreign aid agencies, Afghan expatriates in sharp suits, and assorted gold diggers waiting to see him. He would give ten-minute appointments to all comers, while his son Tarek, an undergraduate at Stanford University, took notes and became his doorkeeper.

His energy was all the more remarkable considering his poor health. He had lost a large part of his stomach to cancer, and his immune system was destroyed. He could not eat a full meal, so every hour he could be seen nibbling tiny portions of food. He did not know how long he had to live and that gave him fierce urgency and determination and lent a kind of ruthlessness to everything he did. Arthur Helton, of the Council on Foreign Relations in New York, described Ghani as "a one man aid coordination agency . . . who has gained a reputation for ruffling feathers," while Robert Finn later said, "He is very smart, with a short temper, which is a dangerous combination—but he got things done and fought with Karzai to get them done."[19]

I had known Ghani for twenty years and he never allowed anyone to come too close, remaining aloof. Many of his contemporaries read this as arrogance. Unfortunately, his explosions of bad temper and displays of arrogance with fellow Afghans and Westerners were all too frequent and soon made him a loathed figure in the Afghan cabinet. Nobody wanted to work with him. He had few friends, and as other ministers asserted themselves, they turned on Ghani, accusing him of monopolizing all decision making. The complaints about him eventually forced Karzai to let him resign in December 2004. Brahimi, who had remained Ghani's supporter throughout, told him that he had resigned without a single minister willing to defend him.

What he achieved, though, was astounding. He built up the Finance Ministry from nothing. There had been no power or phone lines, no Internet, and no experienced staff. He hired the Chicago law firm Baker and McKenzie as consultants to help him run the AACA and asked Transparency International for help in creating mechanisms to prevent corruption. He hired the British firm Crown Agents to procure goods for the government so that donors would be satisfied that there was no corruption, and BearingPoint to provide a financial management system. Within a few months Ghani had fifty foreign advisers trying to reestablish the various departments of finance and trade while reorganizing other economic-related ministries and the central bank. Two advisers, Clare Lockhart, who had worked with Ghani at the World Bank, and an Australian economist, Michael Carnahan, who became his budget adviser, remained with him constantly.

Ghani was clear about what he wanted to do: "We want to build an efficient and transparent administration that is accountable and responsive to its citizens. We do not want the government as producer and manager of the economy, but rather as a regulator of the private sector and promoter of the entrepreneurial energies of our people."[20]

However, there was soon criticism by Afghans that Ghani was hiring too many foreign consultants at too high a price, with some of them charging up to fifteen hundred dollars a day. Ghani set about trying to raise taxes to demonstrate to the donors that the government was determined to become self-sufficient. He introduced an income tax for wealthy Afghans and a tax on rented accommodation and the import of luxury goods. Most Afghans had never paid taxes, and there was resistance. Lessons from other failed states trying to develop a taxation system were not encouraging. None had managed to collect tax revenues amounting to as little as 10 percent of national income.

Ghani riled Western donors by insisting that the government, rather than the donors, set priorities for development. "Government ownership is critical to the establishment of a prosperous, secure Afghanistan," he told a meeting of Western donors in Kabul on February 26, 2002. "We are fully committed to seeking partnership in this long-term process, but we must demand that it be a partnership of equals," he added. He also fought a losing battle with Western agencies to prevent educated Afghans from leaving the government. "Within six months of starting my job as finance minister, my best people had been stolen by international aid organizations who could offer them forty to a hundred times the salary we could," he said.[21] While civil servants earned an average of fifty dollars a month, Afghan drivers working for Western NGOs or the UN earned up to one thousand.

The lack of coordination meant that there was often an overlap in what the donors funded, as many of them wanted to fund the same high-profile projects. USAID, Britain's Department for International Development (DFID), the European Union, and the World Bank all hired separate contractors to modernize the collection of customs revenues on Afghanistan's borders. Donors duplicated efforts to revamp Karzai's office or fund women's and children's health projects and they spent far too much on foreign consultants.

In Geneva in July 2002, donors met for the first international assessment of aid to Afghanistan. The UN reported a shortfall of $397 million, which donors had pledged at Tokyo but failed to deliver. Humanitarian agencies reported such large shortfalls from donor countries that some were forced to close their programs. Nigel Fisher, the deputy head of the UN Assistance Mission in Afghanistan (UNAMA), described the situation as "fragile," adding that "failure to invest in Afghanistan at this critical juncture could help to fulfill our worst fears for the integrity, the economic development and the unity of Afghanistan." The UN said that money for reconstructing roads and power plants would be unavailable until the following year. Karzai's demands for urgent road building had met with no response. In these difficult conditions, Ghani prepared Afghanistan's first budget in a decade, which for 2002–2003 amounted to just $460 million. It had to be funded by donors, yet by July, three months into the budget, Ghani had received only one tenth of the money.

The government was as broke as it had been in January. At Karzai's urgent request Pakistan flew in $10 million in cash in suitcases to pay salaries. UN agencies were so lacking in funds that they could not provide for the 1.3 million refugees who had returned home in the first six months of 2002—three times more than had been expected. In November an assessment given to the UN General Assembly stated that out of $2.1 billion pledged for the current year, only $1.5 billion had been disbursed—a massive shortfall.[22] A year later, in November 2003, the Center on International Cooperation, in New York, estimated that only $110.0 million worth of reconstruction projects had actually been completed, out of a total aid disbursement of $2.9 billion. In the critical first year, when Afghan expectations were so high, the lack of leadership shown by the Bush administration was the crucial component in this shortfall, as it ignored Afghanistan and prepared for the invasion of Iraq.

It was self-evident that large investments by donors in the early years of a military intervention in a failed state pay off large dividends in the long term—something the United States and the international community had failed to foresee in Afghanistan. The United States think tank RAND calculated that a minimum investment of $100 per capita is needed to stabilize a country coming out of conflict. But, while Bosnia received $679 per capita, Kosovo $526, and East Timor $233, Afghanistan received only $57 per capita in the first two years after 2001.[23] "In manpower and money this was the least resourced American nation-building effort in our history," said James Dobbins, who had joined RAND.[24]

Nevertheless, the first year did yield some wildly successful programs. On March 23, 2002, millions of Afghan children attended school for the first time in many years as a result of a "Back-to-School" program organized by UNICEF and USAID, for an initial cost of just $50 million. Laura Bush, the American First Lady, took a keen interest in the program. Education in Afghanistan had been destroyed under the Taliban. In 1979, 54 percent of boys and only 2 percent of girls attended primary school. Under the Taliban regime, education had been decimated and girls were not allowed to study at all. So when 4,600 schools opened across the country and began classes, there was visible excitement among parents and children. I had seen girls pack their school bags three months earlier, in anticipation of going back to school. Tents were erected where there were no buildings, and ISAF provided troops and helicopters to deliver eight million textbooks to the remotest regions and supplies to fifty-two thousand teachers. "It is the largest educational program in UNICEF history and the first time that we have started nationwide primary education," said Eric Laroche from UNICEF.

Officials expected 1.8 million children to attend on the first day, but 3.0 million turned up. In Kabul's 160 schools, girls made up 45 percent of the enrollment, showing the commitment of Afghans toward educating their daughters. ISAF also helped rebuild schools in Kabul. On a blustery March day in a poverty-stricken slum in the southwest of Kabul, I watched hundreds of excited Hazara children milling around the six-foot-tall Edwin Fraser, a sergeant in the British army's Royal Engineers. The Irishman and his men had rebuilt the local school, cementing broken walls, putting in doors and windows, and painting the walls to ready the school for opening day. When registration began, 2,000 children signed up, a number that soon swelled to 6,500, and headmaster Muzaffar Khan was at his wits' end. "We will have to operate three shifts but we have only 118 teachers," he told me.[25] What was encouraging that spring as I traveled through the south, where the Taliban had once reigned, was that the Pashtuns were demanding schools for their sons and daughters.

By 2005, 5.2 million children were attending school in grades one through twelve. Enrollment in higher education had jumped to 31,000, from 4,000 students in 2001. School going became a symbol of the new Afghanistan that could be built if adequate resources were provided. The literacy program was the largest ever undertaken in any Muslim country. If the Bush administration had remained focused on this alone, it would have served as a remarkable beacon for Muslims worldwide, impressing people with American largesse and forcing Muslim governments to take education more seriously. An equally successful program in 2002, despite the lack of funds, was the return of more than two million refugees from Iran and Pakistan out of a total refugee population of five million. In the summer, fifty thousand refugees were returning every week, overwhelming the UN and the government. The tragedy was that due to the absence of investment in agriculture, most refugees returned to the cities rather than to their villages.

Another success story was the explosive expansion of the media after the Taliban had destroyed all vestiges of it. Within three years 350 publications were registered with the government, 42 radio stations operated around the country, and there were 8 private television channels. Tolo TV, the nation's favorite channel, ran everything from exposures on corruption and warlordism to Afghan versions of *Candid Camera* and *American Idol*. Tolo pushed the limits of what was acceptable and frequently ran into problems with the conservative Supreme Court or the government. Meanwhile, journalists and newspapers faced constant harassment from warlords, corrupt officials, and drug dealers—but they continued to publish. Several journalists were killed, but that did not restrain the enthusiasm and growth of the media or of its hungry audience.

The most significant economic achievement was the introduction of a new currency in October 2002, replacing the three different currencies still in circulation. The new currency was issued by Da Afghanistan Bank, or the central bank. Its governor, Anwar-ul-Haq Ahady, fifty, a former professor at an American college, and Noorullah Delawari, sixty-two, a banker from southern California, led the task force with help from the IMF, the UN, and the U.S. military. Some twenty-eight billion new Afghani notes were printed in Germany and Britain, at a cost of $16 million, and then distributed across the country, even though there was no banking system outside Kabul. The new exchange rate—50 new Afghanis to $1, compared to 48,000 Afghanis to $1 of the previous currency used in Kabul—was backed by $220 million in gold parked at the U.S. Federal Reserve Bank. Eight thousand workers helped in collecting eighteen thousand tons of old currency notes, which were airlifted to Kabul in U.S. Army helicopters, where they were burned and exchanged for new notes. Afghans once again showed that they were one nation acting together and not divided along ethnic lines.

A success story in 2003 was a national community-based development plan called the National Solidarity Program, set up by Hanif Atmar, the imaginative minister of rural rehabilitation and the World Bank. The program set up committees in 4,000 communities in all 364 districts of the country to decide upon development priorities in their area. They were then allocated small grants of between thirty thousand and sixty thousand dollars to carry out the projects they had voted for. The amount given to each village was based on a rough calculation of each family receiving two hundred dollars. NGOs helped villagers with the decision-making process and in building projects such as digging wells and reservoirs and building bridges and schools. It was the first serious attempt to get money into the countryside so that rural Afghans could see some improvement in their lives. The program was hugely successful, and within two years it had received $375 million in pledges from numerous countries. Parallel to this effort was the enormous improvement in the health system with the establishment of one hospital in every province and an enormous investment in women and children's health care.

Such successes were all the more remarkable considering that Afghanistan was on the back burner in Washington as the Bush administration planned for war in Iraq. It took a year before the State Department appointed a full-time coordinator for reconstruction in Afghanistan. The appointee, William Taylor, who arrived at the U.S. embassy in Kabul in October 2002, was a dedicated, charismatic diplomat who had learned his trade during the Balkans crisis. But he was to be constantly blindsided by the administration's concentration on the Iraq project.

On Afghanistan there was a lack of coordination and focus in Washington. Robert Finn described the complex process in Washington:

> Every morning there was an interagency meeting at the State Department on Afghanistan, chaired by Richard Haass [director of policy planning], which duplicated the meeting we would have in the U.S. embassy in Kabul. My role was to try and get all the various pieces of the government to work together, like a sheepherder managing his sheep. Khalilzad had his own team, the Pentagon was conducting its own foreign policy, while the State Department, USAID, the Pentagon, and the CIA were all trying to do reconstruction. To put it simply, you had a hundred and fifty cooks.[26]

The real hindrance was still the CIA, which even in 2003 was deciding what projects other agencies should undertake on the basis of how those projects would affect the war on terrorism. USAID officials complained bitterly about CIA interference, but Andrew Natsios refused to take a position to defend USAID's independence and work. Peter Tomsen, a former U.S. ambassador to Afghanistan, told Congress in October 2003 that CIA operations were the main hindrance to reconstruction and that the CIA had too much money and power.[27]

In one salient example, Karzai's pleas to Bush for money to rebuild the ring road encircling Afghanistan were initially turned down by the CIA. The road had been first built by the Americans and the Soviets in the 1960s but had been destroyed in the war. Road building made sense for Americans and Afghans alike, as it would spur internal trade and economic growth, allow for cheaper imports, and help bring the warlords under control by connecting them to Kabul. Robert Finn harassed the State Department and USAID, urging them to build the ring road, but USAID said it did not do road building, while the CIA declined to support the project.[28] Finally, in November 2002, Bush agreed to rebuild the highway connecting Kabul to Herat via Kandahar. The road would be built by the Louis Berger Company in thirty-six months, at a cost of $250 million, a financial burden to be shared equally among the United States, Saudi Arabia, and Japan.[29] So it took nearly a year after 9/11, and constant pleading by Karzai, to persuade the Bush administration to build its first road in Afghanistan.

A few months later Bush promised to have the Kabul-Kandahar section of the road finished by the end of 2003. Costs soared due to Washington's sudden urgency and as the Taliban attacked road crews. The Kabul-Kandahar section was completed on time but at the astronomical total cost of $190 million, or $1 million a mile. The entire cost was met by the United States because the Saudis refused to come up with their share, while the Kandahar-Herat section was delayed, as the Japanese who were building it refused to start until security had improved. The rebuilt road was a milestone, and soon the World Bank and the European Union began to build other parts of the ring road. Once road building started in earnest in 2003–2004, the shortage of electricity in the major cities became an embarrassing problem. No country was prepared to build new power houses or a national electricity grid. Ninety-five percent of Kabul citizens lived without power, and until 2005 the entire country generated just 260 megawatts of electricity—enough for a small American town of only a hundred thousand people.

Once road building started, Ashraf Ghani pushed for a tougher stance against rogue warlords who refused to surrender the vast sums they were collecting from customs revenue. Ghani's earlier efforts at this had failed because the warlords were supported by the CIA and used this relationship as an excuse to defy the central government. The annual revenue from customs was estimated at $500 million, more than the entire Afghan budget, but in 2002, only $80 million was collected. Washington's pro-warlord policy was hindering any kind of institution building within the government.

Ghani estimated that Ismael Khan in Herat earned $160,000 a day from the traffic arriving from Iran and Turkmenistan. Gul Agha Sherzai, the governor of Kandahar, controlled vast fees from the high volume of traffic from Quetta and from the movement of trucks from Herat to Kabul. In the north, at the Hairatan customs post with Uzbekistan, there was a brazen division of the spoils, with General Dostum receiving 37 percent of the take; his rival, Gen. Mohammed Atta, drawing 50 percent; the Hazaras, 12 percent; while 1 percent was used to cover costs and salaries. The warlords also controlled the country's natural resources: Coal and salt mines in Baghlan and Thakar provinces, cement and cotton factories, gas fields in Shebarghan that had once supplied Uzbekistan, and emerald mines continued to be controlled by them. They also controlled the import of petrol and diesel from Iran, Pakistan, and Uzbekistan. As long as this continued, Karzai's claim to rule the country was patently false.

In May 2003, at Ghani's urging, Karzai summoned twelve key provincial governors and warlords and threatened them with "serious action" if they failed to deliver customs revenues, and he also threatened to resign. "Day by day the people are becoming disappointed with the government," Karzai told them. "I will summon the Loya Jirga and say the government could not work."[30] The warlords signed on to a thirteen-point agreement in which they promised to remit money. A few days later Ghani flew to Herat to confront Ismael Khan. His preemptive boldness worked. On June 2 two heavily guarded Toyota Land Cruisers arrived in the courtyard of the Ministry of Finance in Kabul and unloaded sacksful of money—$20 million in all. In August, Karzai was to strip Ismael Khan of all military powers, but leave him as governor of Herat.

Some U.S. officials, particularly UN ambassador Khalilzad, were beginning to realize that the "path of least reconstruction" Washington had chosen was neither winning the war against al Qaeda nor winning over the Afghan people. Khalilzad discussed "a course correction" with Condoleezza Rice, the national security advisor, and the need for more resources. His direct access to senior figures because of his neocon connections made it easier for him to be heard—Robert Finn's long-standing pleas for more funds had fallen on deaf ears in Washington. Khalilzad's demands coincided with plans by Bush's senior adviser Karl Rove, who wanted to portray Afghanistan as a success story in the propaganda buildup to Bush's bid for a second term as president—elections were to be held in November 2004. At the same time, presidential elections were also due in Afghanistan, which the United States wanted Karzai to win and be a showcase for democracy. Khalilzad termed his plan "accelerated success" and was appointed ambassador in Kabul.

Just fifty-two, Khalilzad was now in his element. Tall and imposing, with a jutting jawline, he looked every bit the Afghan warrior, albeit one with a penchant for sharp Italian suits. Zal, as everyone called him, became the most powerful man in Afghanistan, and made no attempt to hide it. He was not in the least embarrassed when reporters described how Karzai did not make a move without first consulting him.[31] Khalilzad was a complicated personality: a Westernized scholar and neoconservative but an Afghan Muslim who had the taste for intrigue that is the hallmark of political culture in both Washington and Kabul. He was disliked by traditional diplomats but appreciated by the CIA and the U.S. military because of his can-do attitude.

Zalmay Khalilzad was born in Mazar-e-Sharif in 1951. His mother was twelve years old and illiterate when she married his father.[32] Khalilzad's family moved to Kabul, where his father was a civil servant. As a teenager, Zal was briefly an exchange student in California, and in 1970 he received a scholarship to study at the American University of Beirut. He did his doctorate at the University of Chicago, where he was influenced by the same teachers who influenced other neocons such as Paul Wolfowitz. Khalilzad became a professor at Columbia University and one of the founding members of a small group of neocon intellectuals there before joining a think tank, where he specialized in nuclear weapons and Iran. He made his mark in government in the mid-1980s, when, under Wolfowitz, who was then director of policy planning at the State Department, he wrote several papers on U.S. policy toward the Afghan Mujahedin.

During the first Gulf War, in 1991, Khalilzad served under Dick Cheney, who was then defense secretary, helping the neocons draw up the Defense Planning Guidance that outlined the themes that later came to be known as preemption. I got to know Khalilzad in the 1980s, and we would frequently spar at conferences on Afghanistan in Washington. It was a surprise to meet an Afghan who was so staunchly Republican, and at the time I found his knowledge of Afghanistan superficial because he had been away too long.[33] During the Clinton era he went back to the think tank RAND and became a consultant to the oil giant Unocal, which was trying to build a gas pipeline between Turkmenistan and Pakistan through Taliban-controlled Afghanistan. Khalilzad co-wrote a paper criticizing Clinton's policy in the region, saying the United States was underestimating its interests in Afghanistan.[34]

In May 2001, Khalilzad became senior director for the Gulf and Southwest Asia division of the National Security Council. Then, on September 11, his life changed completely. He was soon fielding calls from the NA warlords and every Afghan tribal leader. He helped run the war from his cell phone, urging warlords to cooperate with their rivals or to help the U.S. SOF teams. Even the CIA and the Pentagon had to go through Zal to cajole or motivate individual Afghan leaders. He was soon appointed special presidential envoy to President Bush on Afghanistan.

Nearly two years had passed by and there were few signs of U.S. efforts to reconstruct Afghanistan. Afghans were becoming restless with and critical of the lack of progress in developing their country, blaming both the government and the Americans. Several concerned U.S. officials at the State Department, including Khalilzad, urged greater focus on and aid for Afghanistan, especially in light of Bush's hope for reelection in November 2004. It took several months of persuasion before Condi Rice called an interdepartmental meeting of the National Security Council on June 20, 2003.

After almost two years of dismal waste, a meeting of the National Security Council chaired by Bush on June 20, 2003, took the secret decision to change direction in Afghanistan and step up aid. The new policy was never made public. Advertising it would have begged the question as to why the United States had provided so little aid until now and whether this change was a preelection stunt. Moreover, the war in Iraq had gone well and the White House could finally focus on Afghanistan. I was quick to notice the sudden change in U.S. attitudes. "We are seeking ways with the Afghan government on how to accelerate reconstruction in Afghanistan," Khalilzad told me in Kabul on July 15. "Improving security, reconstruction, political reform—all these are important areas which must be accelerated. Failure is not an option." A senior U.S. Army officer was more blunt: "We cannot spend seven times more in Bosnia and Kosovo than we do in Afghanistan and then pretend we are doing nation building," he said.

Certainly the plan offered great potential. With U.S. spending in Afghanistan doubling from $740.0 million in 2003 to $1.9 billion in 2004, Washington could now justifiably urge European donors to donate more money. There was stepped-up U.S. spending for building schools, clinics, and roads, and for training Afghans.[35] U.S. forces would expand from 10,000 to 18,000 troops, and the U.S. general in charge would move from Bagram to the capital so he could better coordinate with Khalilzad. The Pentagon would speed up training of the Afghan National Army (ANA) and take over the all-too-slow training of the police from the Germans. The Pentagon would embed 650 trainers with ANA units, and the ANA's Kabul Corps of 10,000 troops would be ready in time for the Afghan presidential elections in June 2004. In the first week of July 2003, a thousand ANA soldiers had gone into battle alongside U.S. forces in eastern Afghanistan for the first time, and they had performed very well. Afghanistan's intelligence service, the National Security Directorate, would be downsized from 35,000 agents to 12,000, who would be retrained by the CIA at a cost of $80 million.[36]

Robert Blackwell, the former U.S. ambassador to India, joined the National Security Council to handle the demands from Kabul in a newly formed Afghanistan Interagency Operations Group, which would include all U.S. government departments. Khalilzad arrived in Kabul with a team of nine retired business professionals who constituted the Afghanistan Reconstruction Group, based in the U.S. embassy. They helped restructure the ministries and organized a survey of Afghanistan's natural resources. However, once again there were too many cooks and tensions arose between the private-sector group, regular U.S. embassy staff, and USAID officials. At times it was unclear who was in charge. Khalilzad's efforts at centralization resembled L. Paul Bremer's plan for Iraq, which also tried to bypass the U.S. government. Bremer, the U.S. envoy to Iraq, reported directly to the White House just as Khalilzad did—a chain of command that sidelined the State Department.

The biggest failure of "accelerated success" was that it was implemented without any coordination with European countries, the UN, or even the Afghan government, as the Americans remained excessively secret about their plans and isolated from the rest of the world. Their plan floundered due to lack of coordination, overlapping projects, and a resulting waste of funds, which the American media were to highlight two years later. U.S. consultancies and construction firms, rather than local NGOs, won the contracts to implement the projects. Louis Berger alone won contracts to build ninety-six new clinics and schools in time for the Afghan elections, but a year later, at the end of 2005, only nine clinics and two schools had been completed.[37] Designs for school buildings drawn up in California did not take into account the excessive snowfall in Afghanistan, which buckled roofs. Some roofs were designed with so much steel that they could be put in place only with cranes, which were unavailable.[38] A report by the U.S. Government Accountability Office published in July 2005 stated that the projects were having little impact on reconstructing the country. The report stated that while the NGO CARE had built forty schools in 2004, costing between ten thousand and twenty thousand dollars, USAID contractors had built eight schools costing four times as much.[39]

By early 2004 there was visible frustration among Afghans about the lack of reconstruction as stories about corruption, incompetence, and overcharging by U.S. contractors, Western NGOs, and government ministers multiplied. Every Afghan in Kabul had a scandalous story to tell. Bearing-Point won a contract from USAID to revamp the Finance Ministry worth $98 million. According to Anwar-ul-Haq Ahady, who succeeded Ashraf Ghani as finance minister, the company appointed some fifty advisers who each cost five hundred thousand dollars a year if their expenses and security detail were taken into account. After a long battle with USAID, Ahady cut the number of advisers by half.[40] Such scandals became a major political issue. During the parliamentary elections prospective candidates gained instant popularity by lampooning this kind of waste. Ramazan Bashardost, a demagogic former minister who accused "a mafia" of foreigners and government officials of pocketing reconstruction funds, was elected to parliament with the third highest vote total in Kabul.

Ghani wanted the private sector to be a driver of growth, but with a cash economy there was neither a capital market nor the means to raise financing for industrial projects. The extraordinarily large population movements that had eaten up so much of the humanitarian aid earlier on now aggravated urban life as refugees poured into Kabul and other cities that lacked the infrastructure to cope with the deluge. Kabul had grown from 400,000 people in 1978 to 1.7 million in 2001 to an estimated 3.6 million in 2005. There was no electricity or water for the vast shantytowns that sprang up on the hillsides beyond the main city. Discontent and anger escalated as people believed the stories about the wasted aid. Experts stated that Afghanistan needed to generate a 9 percent annual growth rate in the next decade to raise annual per capita income from two hundred dollars to just five hundred, but that would be impossible if the country lacked an infrastructure that could in turn stimulate the economy.

Yet Afghanistan still averaged an annual growth rate of 15 percent during the 2002–2004 period, excluding the money generated by the drug trade. The country was so poor that anything—the expenditures of the foreign forces and organizations, the end of the drought, and the small capital sums returning refugees or expatriate Afghans brought back home—resulted in substantial growth. There were important models of successful businessmen, such as Habib Gulzar, a trader who had settled in Dubai in 1991 and returned home after 2001 to set up nine trading houses in Kabul and then invested $25 million in the country's first Coca-Cola bottling plant. While the Iraqi economy had collapsed after the U.S. invasion, Afghanistan flourished simply because of its previous dire poverty. The real concern was not how much development took place according to the conditions in 2001, but whether sufficient development occurred that would lift the country out of the cycle of civil war and violence.

For that, Karzai and Ghani promoted the idea of Afghanistan as a trading and energy hub. Afghanistan had played such a role during the Silk Road era. The years of war after 1979 created a vast vacuum in the heart of the natural trading routes linking Central Asia to the Middle East, Iran, and the Indian subcontinent via Afghanistan. If Afghanistan could rehabilitate its roads, its natural geographic location would allow it to become a major trading hub. Since the 1950s, the Karachi port had serviced trade for landlocked Afghanistan, but after 2001, the NA leaders, with their traditional antipathy to Islamabad, directed trade toward Iranian ports. A series of trade deals signed between Afghan commerce minister Syed Mustafa Kazemi and Iran, India, and the Central Asian states in the winter of 2002–2003 created new geopolitical possibilities.[41]

As a result of the deals, Iran drastically reduced transit rates and port charges to encourage the use of Iranian ports. India, barred from trading directly with Afghanistan across Pakistani territory because of tensions between the two rivals, supported the Iran entry point for Afghanistan. It funded new roads between the Iranian port of Chabahar and the Afghan border and to Dilaram, in southwest Afghanistan, via the border post of Zaranj. The new route through Zaranj would shorten the distance to Iranian ports and open up one of the poorest regions of Afghanistan. Existing road networks linking Dilaram to Turkmenistan via Herat and to Uzbekistan via Kabul were now being rebuilt, thereby giving Iran access to Central Asia. "We have no preferences, no favorites, as long as Afghanistan can benefit all round from multiple trade routes," Karzai told me.

Initially Pakistan reacted angrily, increasing its rail freight charges from Karachi to the Afghan border and refusing to sign a new transit agreement with Kabul. However, with the traditional strong links between the Pashtun populations on both sides of the border and the new business links brought home by returning Afghan refugees, Pakistan could not ignore for long the competition from the Iranian ports. Official trade between Pakistan and Afghanistan had leaped from $20 million in 2001 to $700 million in 2004, and Islamabad had to acknowledge that its own economic recovery was now heavily dependent on demand from Afghanistan. Businessmen from Lahore and Karachi were clamoring to sell their consumer goods in Kabul. The competition between Iranian or Pakistani ports proved positive, because eventually both ports were needed as volumes of trade increased.

There was competition between Pakistan and Iran to attract Central Asia's trade with the Arabian Gulf countries to their respective ports. Iran offered to dedicate the port of Bandar Abbas to Central Asian trade, while Pakistan developed Gwadar, a port on the Balochistan coast, with Chinese help.[42] This competition benefited Afghanistan because all routes passed through Kabul. If only Afghanistan could offer good roads, power, cold storage, and other facilities, trade and customs revenues for Kabul would increase dramatically.

New roads allowed neighboring countries to play a major role in providing adjacent Afghan regions with infrastructure support. Iran began to electrify Herat and western Afghanistan, while Turkmenistan pledged to supply natural gas to Herat city. In the north, General Daud, the military commander of Kunduz, opened up trade with Tajikistan, which agreed to provide electricity to the province. Additional bridges were built across the Amu Darya River, which runs along the border between Afghanistan and Central Asia. General Dostum tied up similar deals with Uzbekistan, increasing trade, reducing tariffs, and importing Uzbek electricity to Mazar-e-Sharif along a power line that would be extended to Kabul by the World Bank.

Khalilzad's "accelerated success" program was sufficient to see through Afghanistan's successful presidential and parliamentary elections in 2004 and 2005 and to help reelect Bush for a second term, but in the long term it was a failure There were insufficient resources to convince the alienated Pashtuns in the south or the jobless youth in Kabul that their lives had changed. The Taliban offensive escalated dramatically in 2005, heroin production increased, and riots were to grip Kabul. Moreover, once Bush was elected in 2004, U.S. funding dropped significantly and did not increase again until 2007, by which time the situation had again become dire. "Accelerated success" never addressed the structural deficiencies of U.S. policy. In June 2004, just nine months into "accelerated success," the U.S. Government Accountability Office issued a report that said the State Department lacked a full operational strategy for Afghanistan or "an annual consolidated budget" that would show all U.S. assistance to the country. "Expenditure data was not available and consequently, it is difficult to determine the extent to which U.S. assistance dollars are being used to achieve measurable results on the ground in Afghanistan," the report said.[43]

The U.S. embassy in Kabul became more isolated from the reality beyond its walls. One World Bank official described it as "so secure and cut off that it may as well be in Washington."[44] "Accelerated success" also failed to build the much-vaunted "capacity" in the Afghan ministries. Even in 2005 the government could spend only 44 percent of the money it received for development because it had no capacity to plan and monitor projects. The successful National Solidarity Program run by Hanif Atmar accounted for nearly half of the government's spending.

There was no panacea or quick fix for nation building. Nobody had a plan you could take off a shelf. Other attempts at nation building with far more resources than were ever given to Afghanistan also failed spectacularly. The former Yugoslavia was still struggling despite all the attention of the European Union. East Timor, which gained its independence in 1999 after a bloody struggle with Indonesia lasting twenty-five years, had garnered huge reconstruction funds, and the UN ruled the country for three years. However, violence erupted there in May 2006, and the capital, Dili, was nearly burned to the ground by rampaging mobs. If East Timor, with a population of just 1.1 million, could not be rebuilt, then the fate of much larger failed states were even more in doubt.

With all its wealth, resources, and expertise, the United States seemed to have a distinguished record of repeating the same mistakes again and again. The failure in Afghanistan would be spectacularly repeated in Iraq, which was conceived on a mammoth scale by Washington as compared with Afghanistan. Without adequate security and law and order, reconstruction was crippled from the start. Condi Rice admitted in 2005 that in Iraq "we didn't have the right skills, the right capacity to deal with a reconstruction effort of this kind."[45] Her confession came after the four years of U.S. government experience in Afghanistan and two in Iraq. In both countries the failure to reconstruct led to intensified insurgencies and the spread of al Qaeda. In 2006, with the Taliban on the offensive, Washington increased aid to Afghanistan to $3.2 billion—double the sum given in 2003 for "accelerated success." The following year, in 2007, aid was doubled once again as the insurgency got worse.[46]

In Iraq, the United States committed too much money for reconstruction when stability had not been established. In Afghanistan, the United States committed too little money for reconstruction. As a result, security worsened and the Taliban found an excuse to restart their insurgency. While the Pentagon expanded its personnel dealing with civil affairs, Condi Rice appeared determined to destroy USAID, which was merged into the State Department. USAID's total budget for 2008 was gutted, its program cut by 31 percent and its operations by 15 percent. More than one hundred senior USAID officers had resigned since 2005. The only arm of the U.S. government devoted to poverty alleviation would soon be no more.

The larger tragedy was the Bush administration's failure to convince the American public about the need for reconstruction. Bush and Cheney continued to treat nation building as something dirty that should be swept under the carpet, even as American soldiers died trying to improve sanitation in Baghdad or build schools in Afghanistan. There was no attempt to mobilize greater American public support for rebuilding the countries Washington had invaded. Cheney is not known ever to have made a statement supporting U.S. aid for poor countries. The United States remained at the bottom of the list of developed countries that gave aid to the developing world, and the American public remained largely ignorant of the humanitarian crises escalating everywhere.[47]

◆ ◆ ◆

CHAPTER TEN

Afghanistan II

Rebuilding Security

The United States and the international community could not hope to rebuild Afghanistan without more troops, a wider and deeper Western military presence that could offer greater security for the Afghan people against the Taliban and the warlords and allow for reconstruction to start. None of this was possible because the war in Iraq took precedence, and Afghanistan, the home of al Qaeda and the planning for 9/11, was considered a sideshow by a White House that had gotten its priorities seriously wrong.

The excuse the international community gave was that the Afghans would not tolerate a foreign military presence for long, just as they had not tolerated the British or Soviet occupations. Yet this was not an occupation, and the Afghan people were literally on their knees begging for a greater international presence so that their benighted country could be rebuilt. Afghans were savvy. They knew that more foreign troops meant greater security, and also a greater commitment to reconstructing the country. Moreover, the UN had pledged through the Bonn Agreement that a political process would put an elected Afghan government into the driver's seat. Yet the lack of a larger Western military presence meant that the warlords rather than the government remained empowered. Afghans understood well enough that without security there could be no economic development, and if the West was refusing to provide that security, and was instead depending on warlords, then it was also insincere about rebuilding the country.

Security in the era of failed states meant more than just issues of life and death. People had to be given a chance to hold jobs, go to school, and feed their families without warlords stopping them. Providing this "human security" was just as important as winning the war against terrorists. At the same time, failed states such as Afghanistan and Somalia lacked the institutions of modern states—for example, an army, police, a bureaucracy, and a judiciary. This process of state building, as opposed to nation building, would take much longer and demand an even greater commitment from the West. Afghanistan had always had a weak, decentralized state where the ruler governed through consensus over a confederation of tribes and ethnic groups. Now a modern state system had to be created on the ruins of a destroyed country.

When the first G8 meeting on security-sector reform in Afghanistan was held on the sidelines of the Tokyo conference in 2002, the U.S. delegation was instructed by Washington to say that it would not get involved in nation building or peacekeeping except to help build a new Afghan army. The United States wanted nothing to do with rebuilding Afghanistan's police or justice system. The European and Afghan leaders could not believe what they were hearing. Here was a superpower that had just conquered another country refusing to take responsibility for it. (The United States would do exactly the same in Iraq.) Even in building the army, the United States had to be constantly dragged to the table to speed up the process.

The most urgent issue in early 2002 was the need to deploy International Security Assistance Force troops outside Kabul. A crescendo of voices in Afghanistan and around the world, including the U.S. Congress, the British and European parliaments, and the UN, demanded an expansion of ISAF.[1] They said the Karzai government was faltering because security outside Kabul was deteriorating due to warlordism, crime, and drugs. Lt.-Gen. Dan McNeill, the head of U.S. forces in Afghanistan, grappled with the conundrum of how to extend a U.S. military presence outside Kabul without the need for too many troops or resources and, more important, without annoying Rumsfeld.

Tall, taciturn, difficult to fathom, and intellectually sharp, McNeill argued for a U.S. presence that would "produce the ISAF effect"—facilitate reconstruction and give people a sense of confidence, but without deploying thousands of soldiers.[2] Thoughtful and a good listener, he was a thinking man's general, fully aware of his own limited knowledge about Afghanistan. He held discussions with all the concerned foreign and local players, especially Brahimi. "We had nothing in any textbook that this is the way to do it—it's all new for us," McNeill told me in Bagram. It took months of discussion in Kabul and a prolonged debate within the Pentagon before his ideas won out.

As eight thousand U.S.-led Coalition soldiers began to celebrate the 2002 Christmas holiday season in their tented city at Bagram Air Base, an intense training exercise was under way that would see U.S. forces undertake their first redeployment since the end of the war. Their precooked Christmas lunch had been flown in from Germany, and the soldiers were entertained by movie stars, including comedian Robin Williams. In the giant tent holding McNeill's office and command center, dozens of U.S. officers sitting at wooden trestle tables stared at computer screens through which they kept in touch with every U.S. Army base, foot patrol, and plane in the sky. In another tent a group of seventy soldiers, civil affairs officers, engineers, medics, and a State Department official was being trained to form the first Joint Regional Team, which would be deployed to Gardez in eastern Afghanistan. These teams, later renamed Provincial Reconstruction Teams, or PRTs, were to provide "the ISAF effect" outside Kabul.

The military PRTs was an attempt to institutionalize the joint CIA-SOF A teams that had spread out across the country and linked up with warlords to hunt for Osama bin Laden. Once the war was over, U.S. Army civil affairs officers had joined these A teams to carry out small reconstruction projects to win hearts and minds. For a time these teams were the only source of information and intelligence regarding what was going on outside Kabul. By the summer of 2002, 450 U.S. Army civil affairs officers were operating around Afghanistan, but it was an informal arrangement. Made up of 100 or more soldiers and civilians, the PRTs would carry out small reconstruction projects, help train the local Afghan administration, and create sufficient local security for Western and Afghan NGOs to work in the area. They would also gather intelligence about al Qaeda.

Despite the existence of a document setting forth what were to be their goals, there was to be no nationwide strategy for setting up the PRTs, nor any means to assess their performance. Each PRT would set its own priorities and goals in consultation with the local authorities and warlords.[3] The success of the PRTs would depend on the Afghan government's providing well-trained Afghan administrators who could work alongside the PRTs and improve local governance. However, Karzai failed to plan for the training of competent Afghan administrators, while the U.S. military failed to push him sufficiently. As a consequence, the PRTs fell back on relying on local warlords for security and administration.

Once this happened it was clear that the PRTs could not provide security to the Afghan population. They would not carry out any peacekeeping or peacemaking role, unlike ISAF in Kabul. PRT commanders were not allowed to mediate in conflicts between Afghans, or "green on green" conflicts. Western aid agencies and NGOs objected, fearing that while the military's involvement in development activities blurred the principles of humanitarian relief, PRTs were offering no security to them or the population, and they did not want to be seen by the local people as helping the U.S. military, which would make them targets for the Taliban. The International Committee of the Red Cross, which according to its charter is forbidden to seek protection from the military, declined to work with the PRTs. Other international NGOs followed suit.

Despite these problems, by the summer of 2003 the PRTs expanded to six more locations—Bamiyan, in central Afghanistan; Mazar-e-Sharif and Kunduz, in the north; Herat, in the west; and Jalalabad and Kandahar, in the sensitive Pashtun belt. I visited several PRTs to see their worth. What they achieved in each location depended largely on how secure that region was and what kind of relationship the PRT commander had with the local warlord and the Afghan administration. In Bamiyan, the mountain stronghold of the Hazara people, the PRT had made a huge difference. It rebuilt schools, including Bamiyan University, which I had visited in the midst of the civil war in the 1990s, when it was housed in a couple of mud huts. The PRT was handed over to New Zealand soldiers in September 2003.

In the summer of 2003, British forces established a PRT in Mazar-e-Sharif that covered five provinces—an area the size of Scotland. The team mediated between Generals Atta and Dostum, trying to end their feuding, which had claimed two thousand Afghan lives since the end of the war. The British won the trust of many Afghans and showed the Americans that mediating "green on green" was not impossible, and was in fact essential if the PRTs were to be genuinely useful.

The U.S.-led PRTs in the Pashtun areas faced enormous local problems—envy, tribal feuds, land disputes, the drug trade, and competition among tribal elders to win the ear of the American officer. However, the U.S. commander had no mandate to help resolve local disputes, so he could do nothing except listen to the complaints. The Pentagon's funding for the PRTs was inadequate, allocating just $18 million a year in reconstruction funds for all U.S. PRTs deployed—a drop in the bucket compared with what was needed and with what was being spent in Iraq. A U.S. PRT that arrived in October 2004 in the Taliban- and drug-infested Helmand province spent just $9.5 million in two years. A U.S. officer in Helmand told me that it took him three months of paperwork to get even the smallest project passed by the Pentagon.

PRTs should have been staffed by the best and the brightest in the U.S. military. Instead they were manned almost entirely by U.S. Army Reservists whose short tours of duty—six months or less—kept them from getting to know their region before they were on their way home. There were so many different models of PRTs that any overall control became difficult. U.S. PRTs comprised 79 soldiers and 3 civilians, but only 16 out of those 79 soldiers were allowed "outside the wire" to strike up a relationship with the local administration and people. The European countries varied their PRTs enormously. The Germans, for example, deployed as many as 375 men in Kunduz. Despite this, the UN considered the German PRT the least effective because of its lack of contact with the local population and its refusal to patrol the region at night.

When General McNeill handed over his command in May 2003 to Gen. John Vines, Washington declared, despite all the evidence to the contrary, that PRTs were the only acceptable means to expand U.S. authority around the country. Rumsfeld waxed lyrical about PRTs, saying he would establish them in Iraq as well. In fact, PRTs became the symbol of stability, and no U.S. official talked about the need for more troops even as the Taliban began their resurgence. On May 1, 2003, just hours after Bush stood under the MISSION ACCOMPLISHED banner on a U.S. warship signifying that the Iraq war was over and won, Rumsfeld was in Kabul declaring victory in Afghanistan. "If one looks at Afghanistan and even Iraq today, it's very clear that we are and have been in a stabilization operation mode for some time," said Rumsfeld. "We clearly have moved from major combat activity to a period of stability and stabilization and reconstruction activities. The bulk of the country today is permissive, it's secure." He criticized those demanding an expansion of ISAF as people "mostly on editorial boards, columnists and at the UN."[4] In the next few weeks, Rumsfeld was to eat his words as the Taliban launched their attacks.

By early 2005 there were nineteen PRTs in Afghanistan—fourteen of them manned by U.S. forces and the rest by ISAF and NATO countries.

NATO assumed command of the ISAF force in Kabul in August 2003 and then took over from U.S. forces in the north, followed by the west, south, and east. In 2006, NATO promised to place a PRT in all of Afghanistan's thirty-four provinces. However, the establishment by every European government of "national caveats" stipulating what its PRT force could and could not do was to paralyze NATO's effectiveness in combating the Taliban.

The Pentagon had been stuck with the task of building a new Afghan army, but it seemed extremely reluctant to get on with the job. Rumsfeld was certainly not keen on the idea. He expected General Fahim to create an army, so why should the United States bother to invest in a new one?[5] Fahim continued to be fêted by the Pentagon, while the CIA continued to pay lavish salaries to warlords and their militias. There was little incentive from either side to change this cozy relationship and build a professional Afghan army. The officer who tasked himself with the job of persuading the Pentagon to take its responsibility seriously was Maj.-Gen. Karl W. Eikenberry, the head of the Office of Military Cooperation at the U.S. embassy in Kabul.[6]

As tall as a bean pole, Eikenberry tended to lean into you as he talked, as though a strong wind were blowing at his back. He had a surprisingly soft demeanor and abundant common sense, as a result of his expertise and time spent in China, about the problems of the developing world. At his urging in February 2002, Gen. Tommy Franks sent an assessment team from CENTCOM, led by his chief of staff, Maj.-Gen. Charles Campbell, to report on how a new Afghan army could be built. Campbell's report stated bluntly that the U.S. reliance on warlord militias was impractical and insufficient. Eikenberry helped persuade the Pentagon to train a brigade-size infantry unit of eighteen hundred Afghan soldiers to be ready for the June meeting of the Loya Jirga. One hundred American trainers arrived to start the training, while Fahim and the Ministry of Defense were tasked with selecting the recruits. Meanwhile, ISAF began separately to train a six-hundred-man battalion that would "act as a Presidential Guard, the central symbol of a new Afghanistan and its security structure," according to Gen. John McColl.[7]

The key to building a new army was making sure that no single ethnic group was overrepresented in it. General Fahim, the Tajik warlord, was tasked by the United States to provide recruits from all ethnic groups, but instead he sent in only his own Tajiks, and many of those failed to turn up.

On the first day of ISAF's training program, only 69 out of 630 recruits were present. Eikenberry knew that to rely on Fahim would prove to be a disaster and would create major ethnic tensions with the Pashtuns, who were being completely left out. Eikenberry persuaded both ISAF and the United States to recruit soldiers directly, with due regard for ethnic balance. Under new guidelines, 38 percent of all new recruits were to be Pashtun, 25 percent Tajik, 19 percent Hazara, 8 percent Uzbek, and 10 percent minority groups.[8] The slow work of training the battalions then began.

Fahim wanted an army of two hundred thousand men. Eikenberry politely informed him that nobody would pay for such a large army and that sixty thousand was more realistic. It took six months for the UN and Eikenberry to convince Fahim. In June 2002, at a conference in Geneva on security-sector reform, the international community agreed to a plan for an army of sixty thousand men, twelve thousand border guards, and an air force of eight thousand. The army would be divided into seven corps stationed around the country, with a quick-reaction corps based in Kabul. The Ministry of Defense would undergo restructuring to achieve professional and ethnic balance—in other words, dozens of Panjsheri officers would be removed.[9] The United States would be responsible for training the army, while the initial costs of $75 million, plus the cost of building new barracks ($80 million), would be met by a UN-run trust fund for security sector reform to which all nations were asked to contribute. The Germans took on the responsibility to train a new Afghan National Police (ANP), a force of sixty-two thousand men. Fahim grudgingly accepted these plans.

UNAMA now went ahead with the collection of heavy weapons from the warlords, such as tanks and artillery, and prepared for disarming some one hundred thousand militia. Fahim was one of the last to give up his tanks and heavy guns. Brahimi stressed that training the ANA had to run parallel to disarming the militias, but the Pentagon refused to help in this task. "We have to phase out the armed militias and ensure that we are not just creating another army in a country that has too many already," Brahimi said.[10] The United States, however, was still recruiting militiamen to protect its bases, thereby increasing militia numbers even as the UN was trying to disarm them. Yet U.S. officials insisted that there was "no contradiction" in its strategy.

Khalilzad's "accelerated success" program in 2003 pumped in more money and speedier training for the ANA. Finally Washington began to take seriously its responsibilities toward the new Afghan army, although it still refused to help the UN disarm the militias. U.S. expenditure on the ANA for 2004 was $797 million, the following year $788 million, and in 2005–2006 it rose to $830 million. Few other countries contributed, so the cost burden was almost wholly on the Americans.[11] The first units of the ANA deployed in 2003 and generated enormous pride among ordinary Afghans. U.S. trainers were embedded with the units, living and sleeping with their Afghan troops as the units were used to maintain law and order or fight the Taliban in the south.

By the spring of 2006, when NATO deployed in the south to counter a major Taliban offensive, the ANA numbered 37,000 men. With its 650 embedded U.S. officers, it was outperforming the police and gaining the confidence of the Afghan population. In the summer of 2006 the United States began to provide the ANA with $2 billion worth of heavy weapons, vehicles, and other equipment. Yet problems persisted. Between 20 to 40 percent of troops in a battalion were illiterate. The desertion rate was extremely high—around 25 percent in 2005 and 13 percent in 2006. Soldiers went absent without leave, partly because they were not used to serving so far from their villages and could not send their salaries home because there was no nationwide banking system. Soldiers now received basic pay of seventy dollars a month and a hardship allowance when on the front line.[12] Despite the initial reluctance of the Pentagon and interminable delays, the ANA has become the most successful U.S.-led nation-building exercise in Afghanistan.

Today the major issue is how to sustain the army, which at full strength will have a recurrent cost of $1 billion a year, or 4 percent of Afghanistan's gross domestic product. Afghanistan is not going to be able to pay for its own army for many years to come—perhaps never—so there will have to be long-term international funding for this, though it is still a bargain compared with the deployment of Western troops in the country, which cost ten times as much. (It cost the Pentagon $1 billion a month to maintain fifteen thousand U.S. troops in Afghanistan.)

Training a police force proved to be far more difficult. The UN has determined that rebuilding the police force in a failed state is even more important than rebuilding an army. The police are on the front line of public security, law and order, and extending the writ of the government. A police force is critical to helping build a democracy because it has the capacity to generate trust between the government and the people. However, the international community failed to grasp early on the centrality of law enforcement and justice-sector reform in helping stabilize Afghanistan. Law enforcement was left for last, was given the least funding, and commanded the least attention of Western donors. Unlike the ANA, the Afghan national police was not rebuilt from scratch. Instead the government constructed it piecemeal, using corrupt officers from the warlords.

During the civil war in the 1990s police stations were nothing more than an extension of the power of local commanders and warlords, and they continued to be so under Karzai. Justice was rarely meted out, and the police—lacking salaries or facilities—lived off the land by exploiting the public rather than serving it. They were heavily involved in the drug trade, land grabbing, kidnapping, and extortion. The Ministry of Interior, which ran the police after 9/11, became a center for drug trafficking, with police posts in opium-growing regions being auctioned to the highest bidder—sometimes for as much as a hundred thousand dollars for a job that had a salary of seventy dollars a month. Without police and judges, Afghans could hope for neither justice nor crime prevention.

In 2002 Germany had been given the task of training a new Afghan police force, but it was unwilling to provide sufficient funds and resources. Germany set up a police academy in Kabul to teach officers, but sent out only 41 trainers to train 3,500 Afghan officers over three years. There was no plan for the countrywide training of 62,000 policemen and almost no equipment handed out to police stations, which lacked radios, vehicles, and even weapons. Berlin spent a paltry $89 million between 2002 and 2006, a stinginess that angered the Americans, Afghans, and other European nations.[13] Germany's pathetic, next-to-useless performance in rebuilding the police and Italy's apathy in rebuilding the justice system became the two weakest points in the international community's efforts to rebuild state institutions in Afghanistan.

Washington decided to take over police training in 2003, but again there were interminable delays. The U.S. government had no organization through which it could help failed states develop police forces. USAID's Office of Public Safety, which was responsible for training police forces during the cold war, was abolished in 1974 and never replaced. Police training fell to the State Department's Bureau of International Narcotics and Law Enforcement Affairs, whose core job was to counter narcotics, not train police.[14] As the United States has no national police force—only state police forces—the State Department subcontracted police training in Afghanistan to DynCorp International, a private corporation that hired retired American police officers with no knowledge of Afghanistan to train Afghan police. (DynCorp had earlier been contracted to provide American bodyguards to protect President Karzai.)

The United States brought about a major change in the Interior Ministry by introducing Ali Ahmad Jalali into the government. In January 2003, Jalali, age sixty-two and a Pashtun, became the new interior minister and in effective control of police reform. An American-trained former Afghan army colonel who had settled in Washington, D.C., Jalali wrote military books and became head of the Afghan language section of the Voice of America radio service. He persuaded Karzai to sack several corrupt police chiefs and governors and joined up with other Pashtun reformers in the cabinet, such as Hanif Atmar and Ashraf Ghani, to put pressure on Karzai to sideline the warlords and drug traffickers. As a result, Jalali made many enemies, who eventually forced his ousting from office two years later.

The State Department had given DynCorp $24 million to set up seven regional training centers across Afghanistan. However, its three-week training courses were too short and they had no follow-up or mentoring, and there were no funds for equipment such as radios and vehicles. Between 2003 and 2005, the United States was to spend some $860 million in training forty thousand policemen, but the results were almost totally useless. DynCorp was training the police to fight an insurgency rather than win hearts and minds in their localities. The trained Afghan policemen returned home and continued acting in the same rapacious ways as before.[15]

"Having the police in the trenches fighting the Taliban is not a successful sign of counterinsurgency and means that army and police roles are being mixed up, which leaves the population bereft of law and order," said Chris Alexander, the deputy head of UNAMA in 2006.[16] The dynamic Alexander, the first Canadian ambassador to Kabul after 9/11, was seconded to the UN, where he became the most outspoken advocate of the need to train a police force. The failure of DynCorp in training an effective police force led to enormous criticism of U.S. policy objectives. "The US training program [for the police] under DynCorp is an appalling joke . . . a complete shambles," warned Richard Holbrooke, the former U.S. ambassador to the UN.[17] The Pentagon proposed embedding U.S. military trainers with the police, just as it had done with the ANA. This suggestion resulted in a turf war between the Pentagon and the State Department, which objected to military officers training the civilian police structure. The Pentagon won out in 2005, and U.S. trainers were slowly embedded with the police.

Early on, the UN was faced with how to reform the Defense Ministry and get it out of the clutches of General Fahim and the hundreds of Panjsheri Tajik officers he had installed there. A confidential UN report stated that thirty out of thirty-three directorates in the Ministry of Defense were run by Panjsheris, and the same was true in the Amanyat, or the intelligence service, run by Mohammed Arif (known as Engineer Arif).[18] Pashtun officials and governors in the south refused to trust Fahim or take orders from him. Pashtun warlords refused to disarm their militias as long as Fahim controlled the army.

At first the U.S. military was loath to pressure Fahim, even though his Panjsheri commanders had little love for the Americans or ISAF. Fahim was playing a double game, pledging loyalty to Karzai and the Americans, but at the same time telling his Panjsheri officers and men that the foreigners would soon be gone and they would be back in control. He kept his commanders sweet with cash, which he received in secret from Russia and Iran. In 2002 and 2003, Afghan and UN officials told me of their suspicions about money from Tehran and Moscow being carried into the country in diplomatic bags and handed over to Fahim. The Russians provided arms and spare parts for hundreds of tanks Fahim still held in the Panjsher Valley.

Russia, India, and Iran had been the long-term supporters of the Northern Alliance in its fight against the Taliban. These countries were convinced that U.S. forces would soon leave Afghanistan, and they were determined to maintain their influence with their former proxies. They saw Fahim as *their* player, someone who would confront Pakistani influence and any return of the Taliban. Russia and Uzbekistan supported the northern warlords, such as Generals Dostum, Atta, and Daud, while Iran supported Ismael Khan.

At a conference near London in the autumn of 2002, I goaded senior Russian officials about their support to Fahim. They reacted angrily, saying they were willing to provide Fahim's army—which they termed "the national army"—up to $100 million in arms and training.[19] Without blinking, they claimed Russia had a legal right to do this according to the defense treaties Moscow had signed with the Soviet-backed communist regime in the 1980s! The Russian assertion shocked the American participants from the State Department and Pentagon, and prompted high-level talks between Russia and the United States in the following months, as the Americans tried to persuade the Russians to back away from Fahim.

Moscow's diplomatic instrument was Zamir Kabulov, a tall good-looking man with floppy black hair whom I had known for twenty years. An Uzbek born in Tashkent, Kabulov spoke several Afghan languages, was fluent in English, and had served in the Soviet Foreign Ministry. We had first met in the mid-1980s during the Soviet occupation of Afghanistan, when Kabulov, then a junior diplomat, would brief foreign reporters every Wednesday at the vast Soviet embassy compound in Kabul. The press was never allowed to enter the embassy, so he did his briefing in a guard-room at the gate. Then, several evenings a week, he and other Russians, whom we presumed to be KGB officers, would visit the UN club, where the handful of foreign reporters gathered every evening to have a drink and dinner. After the breakup of the Soviet Union, Kabulov was one of a few non-Russian diplomats who did not return to their home country but opted to remain in Russia's Foreign Ministry. He represented Russia at all major events involving Afghanistan, and in the late 1990s, during the Taliban regime, he joined the UN mission to Afghanistan that was then based in Islamabad. He was the premier Russian expert on Afghanistan, so it was no surprise that he became ambassador to Kabul in 2005.

Brahimi and Karzai urged Fahim to carry out reforms in the Ministry of Defense, and to start by removing some Panjsheri officers. Fahim refused, and relations between him and Karzai became extremely tense. In July 2002, Vice President Abdul Qadir, forty-eight, the most prominent Pashtun in the Northern Alliance and brother to slain anti-Taliban leader Abdul Haq, was killed in a hail of bullets outside his office in Kabul. Qadir's bodyguards had failed to protect him, and U.S. officials urged Karzai to accept American bodyguards. In August, a forty-five-man squad of U.S. SOF took over Karzai's personal protection. Fahim took this as a snub, and relations between the two men worsened, especially as Fahim's car was now searched by the Americans whenever he entered the palace. Kabul was full of talk of a coup by Fahim when Zalmay Khalilzad arrived to cool down tempers. Karzai's American bodyguards were necessary, but they exposed both his dependency on the United States and a lack of trust for Afghans that went down badly with the population.[20]

Early on I bluntly asked Fahim whether he wanted to be the leader of an armed faction of one ethnic group or the head of a new national army and respected by all Afghans. I said he had the choice and on that choice would rest the well-being of the country. He looked at his aide in a moment of shock, then gathered his thoughts and gave a bland answer, saying he was not against "strengthening the central government, exercising greater control through demobilization and arms collections, and building the new ANA." I realized then that neither Afghans nor U.S. commanders had confronted him with reality. His conciliatory tone had convinced some U.S. commanders that he was reform-minded when, in fact, he would resist reform of the Defense Ministry and demobilizing his own troops for as long as possible, thereby delaying everything the UN was trying to do.[21]

Fahim was also at the center of acute jealousies and rivalries within the Panjsheri camp. A major bone of contention was the cash, bank accounts, and precious stones their dead leader Ahmad Shah Masud had held. Masud had personally handled the finances of the resistance, and had received donations from foreign countries and earnings from the sale of precious stones. He had even had control of emerald and lapis lazuli mines in NA areas. A close relation of Masud's would trade the stones in the Gulf and Europe, yielding Masud an income of up to $60 million in a good year. Fahim now reportedly controlled these mines. Millions of dollars were at stake, much of it secretly banked in Dubai and other Arab Gulf states. Some of the funds were held by Masud's family members; others by Fahim and Engineer Arif, his intelligence chief. The latter insisted that the Masud family hand over money they held because Fahim was now their leader. Professor Burhanuddin Rabbani, the former president, also insisted that he receive his share.

There were other sources of income. After Kabul fell, the Panjsheris who controlled the city got ahold of six containers of newly printed Afghani banknotes that by chance had just arrived from the printing press in Russia. When Karzai took office in December the government was bankrupt, but they refused to hand over any money. Since 1992, Afghani banknotes had been printed in Russia. Seven trillion Afghanis—the equivalent of $175 million—were printed between 1996 and 2001.[22] A dire situation ensued, in which a small group of warlords alone held more money than the entire Afghan government. This situation prompted the United States to ask the IMF to create a new currency as quickly as possible.

Another major source of funds for the NA warlords was the drug trade. NA commanders taxed all opium routed for export through Central Asia by traffickers. After the war ended, poppy production exploded in the northeastern province of Badakhshan—to the advantage of the NA warlords. With all the power, money, and other stakes Fahim held, it had become imperative for the UN to speed up reform of the Defense Ministry, but U.S. support was only halfhearted. The UN was demanding that the three thousand officers in the ministry be reduced to three hundred, while eighty of the top posts should be filled with non-Panjsheris. Brahimi blamed the slow pace of reform and disarmament on "insufficient cooperation from key partners," which meant the Americans and Karzai.[23] Only after Khalilzad arrived as U.S. ambassador to Kabul did the Americans fully support the reforms and put pressure on Fahim. On September 21, 2003, just one day before Karzai left for a trip to Washington, Fahim agreed to appoint twenty-two officers from all ethnic groups to senior posts in the Defense Ministry.

The UN was also determined to push ahead with disarming the warlord militias. The lack of security created by the militias had led to public despondency, further undermining the weak authority of Karzai. The UN program called Disarmament, Demobilization and Reintegration, or DDR, eventually disarmed sixty-two thousand men, but not before the UN battled a lack of support from the Americans, Karzai, and others. Among Afghans, it was the most popular move carried out by the UN, although thousands of armed men remained. DDR had become an essential part of peacemaking and nation building around the world. "Demobilizing combatants is the single most important factor determining the success of peace operations," said a UN report.[24] The report noted that DDR was always the most underfunded operation in building peace.

The United States put up major obstacles, refusing to fund or support DDR or allow U.S. troops to help the UN carry out disarmament, which was both dangerous and risky. The CIA refused to divulge which of the militias were still on its payroll. Brahimi told the Americans that it was just as important to create a new army as it was to demobilize old militias, but U.S. officials declined to see the linkage. With the invasion of Iraq around the corner, Washington's emphatic instructions to its commanders was not to get involved in "green on green" conflict. European governments were furious and frustrated at the American attitude, as were many junior U.S. officers in the field, who quietly helped the UN disarm the warlords.[25]

Washington's refusal to support DDR in Afghanistan was another factor, along with the much bigger issue of the unilateral invasion of Iraq, which created the gulf between the United States and Europe.

The DDR plan was finalized at the security conference in Tokyo in February 2003, when Japan pledged to meet half the $160 million cost.[26] Sultan Aziz, an Afghan-born development expert at the UN Development Program, led the team that drew up the DDR plan, which was called Afghanistan's New Beginnings Programme. Every disbanded militiaman who handed in his weapon would receive two hundred dollars in cash, a food package, and agricultural implements if he wanted to return to his village or a temporary job and retraining in a new skill. Fahim had drawn up a plan where nobody would actually be sacked but militiamen would simply be moved to the ANA. The UN and the reformist ministers in the Afghan cabinet, led by Ashraf Ghani, refused to accept the plan, which led to an intense debate with Fahim. Finally, the Japanese made it clear they would not provide funding for DDR until Fahim scrapped his plan. DDR finally began in October 2003—four months late—with a test run in Kunduz, where one thousand men were disarmed.[27] Simultaneously, the UN, with the help of ISAF, began to collect heavy weapons from the warlords and place them in central locations in preparation for the elections.

More than any other issue, DDR had divided the cabinet between reformists and the reactionary warlords who knew well enough that disarmament would spell the end of their military power. In May 2003 an anonymous paper written by a senior aide to Karzai circulated in the White House. (The author asked then and now that his name not be disclosed.)[28] The paper openly accused Fahim of subverting the Bonn Agreement and the government in order to retain power. It gave a detailed assessment of his sources of income, which amounted to nearly $1 billion a year. U.S. officials told me that the paper had shocked Rumsfeld and Wolfowitz, because the writer was too well known and liked by the Americans to ignore.

The reformist ministers now prevailed upon Karzai to take a stand against the warlords and Fahim. Karzai told Rumsfeld that he needed to sack Ismael Khan as governor of Herat, as Khan continued to refuse to hand over all customs revenues to the treasury. Rumsfeld replied that this was not the moment to make such a move, because of U.S. preoccupations with Iraq. The reformists in the cabinet told Karzai that if he got tough with the warlords, the Americans would have no choice but to respect his wishes and support him. If he asked their permission beforehand, the United States would never be willing to take any risks.

By the summer of 2004, the UN had succeeded in collecting all heavy weapons and completed the DDR of sixty-two thousand soldiers, but not before Fahim was removed from office, the warlords sacked from their military posts, and the Americans persuaded to stop financing them. DDR became one of the most decisive programs in the postwar period because it forced all the major players, from the Americans to the warlords, to come down on one side of the fence. For the UN it had been controversial and risky, but it had successfully forced the pace of reform. If the Americans had backed the UN program from the start, law and order would have improved much earlier and perhaps the Taliban resurgence could have been avoided. When the Taliban did reappear, their major slogan was that they would restore law and order. In June 2005 the UN launched the Disbandment of Illegal Armed Groups, or DIAG, which aimed to disband the hundreds of smaller groups of armed men who had not been affected by DDR.

The disputes over security were unsettled when the UN and the Afghan government embarked on the most ambitious part of the Bonn Agreement to date—framing a new constitution. In 2002, Vice President Nematullah Shahrani, an Uzbek from the north, had been appointed to head the nine-member commission that prepared an initial draft for a new constitution. The draft was then debated within the larger thirty-five-member Constitutional Commission that Karzai had appointed in April 2003.[29] The Constitutional Commission members toured the country to seek people's opinion on the draft. "On our tours people give the most importance to discussing how an Islamic system can be democratic," Shahrani told me. "The second important issue was whether Afghanistan should be a republic, a monarchy or a parliamentary democracy, and the third was the debate between federalism and centralism."[30]

Shahrani had been educated at Kabul University, Egypt's Al-Azhar Islamic University, and George Washington University in Washington, where he had studied corporate law. He epitomized what Afghanistan's Islam was like thirty years ago, conservative but not extremist, moderate but not overly modern. "Our constitution will be like a mirror," Shahrani assured me. "One side reflects the wishes of the Afghan people, the other side the world and the best laws of other countries. We want to relate Afghanistan to the world," he said. Three foreign experts—Guy Carcassonne, a French legal expert who had helped draft the 1964 Afghan constitution; Yash Pal Ghai, a Kenyan legal expert; and Barnett Rubin—helped the commission in the drafting process. The draft constitution was finally unveiled on November 3, 2003—two months later than the deadline—and the public was asked to comment again.

Indirect elections were held for a 500-member Constitutional Loya Jirga (CLJ), which would debate and approve the new constitution. The delegates, including 64 women—2 from each province—were elected by the 17,286 district representatives chosen during the 2002 Loya Jirga. Fifty of its members were appointed by Karzai. Ultimately there were 103 women in the CLJ, the highest percentage of women in any legislative chamber in the Muslim world.

This was to be Afghanistan's sixth constitution since the first constitution was promulgated by King Amanullah in 1923.[31] The new draft copied much from the 1964 constitution drawn up Zahir Shah, which envisaged a multiparty parliamentary system. "We took the very decent constitution of 1964 and just took out the king," is how Brahimi described it to me. The new draft constitution declared the country the Islamic Republic of Afghanistan and stated that no law repugnant to Islam would be adopted, although it steered well clear of imposing Sharia, or Islamic law. It envisaged a strong centralized state with a powerful president backed by a vice president. The president would be elected for a five-year term and would appoint the cabinet, judges, and senior military officers. The demands of NA leaders who wanted to have a powerful prime minister as well were rejected because of fears that two centers of power would be dangerous and unsettling, although this was to become a major issue during the CLJ.

The draft called for a two-house legislature—the lower Wolesi Jirga, or House of People, and the upper Meshrano Jirga, or House of Elders. Members of the lower house would be elected to a five-year term and would include at least one female delegate from each province. The president would have the power to appoint one third of the members of the upper house, of which 50 percent would have to be women. The Wolesi Jirga would have the power to impeach the president. The draft struck an important balance between the demands of the international community and Afghan tradition and religion. Thus the draft included the right of freedom of worship, stating there would be no discrimination on the basis of gender or ethnicity, and ratified all the major international human rights conventions.

Several groups opposed the draft, including monarchists wanting more powers for Zahir Shah, jihadi leaders who demanded Sharia law, and warlords who wanted a less centralized system, with greater authority given to the provinces. General Dostum's Junbish Party went as far as to suggest a new United Republic of Afghanistan, divided into multi-province states, each with its own government and budget. Dostum was particularly concerned about losing his autonomy in the north.

After being delayed for three months and then delayed three times in the second week of December, the CLJ finally opened on December 14, 2003, as the security situation worsened. Three security perimeters involving some eight thousand ISAF and ANA surrounded the enormous white tent housing the delegates in Kabul. In the past few weeks the Taliban had stepped up assassinations and kidnappings of foreign aid workers, contractors, and Coalition soldiers. Two Indian and three Turkish engineers were kidnapped by the Taliban in the week preceding the CLJ. On December 2, the U.S. military had launched Operation Avalanche, an offensive in seven southern and eastern provinces, in order to keep the Taliban under pressure. The worsening security situation had been highlighted by Kofi Annan as he spoke of "the risk of failure in Afghanistan" for the first time. He told the UN Security Council on December 8 that "unchecked criminality, outbreaks of factional fighting and activities surrounding the illegal narcotic trade have all had a negative impact. The international community must decide whether to increase its level of involvement in Afghanistan or risk failure."[32] A great deal was at stake as the CLJ delegates began to deliberate.

At the start of the CLJ meeting, four candidates stood in a hotly contested election to become its chairman. Karzai's candidate, Sibghatullah Mujaddedi, the first president of Afghanistan after the fall of the communist regime in 1992, won with 252 votes.[33] In his opening address, Karzai argued strongly for a presidential system and appealed for national unity. "The new constitution must bring order and good governance and organize the future of the country," he said. His opponents refuted him strongly. "Karzai wants a dictatorship which people will not accept," said Abdul Hafiz Mansur, an ideologue of the Northern Alliance.[34] Nearly half the delegates opposed the presidential system, and wanted a parliamentary system with power divided between a president and a prime minister and greater provincial autonomy.

All the non-Pashtun groups—Uzbeks, Tajiks, Turkmen, and Hazaras—temporarily buried their rivalries to oppose the presidential system. They were joined by Islamic fundamentalists and monarchists. There was a danger of an ethnic divide, as most Pashtuns supported Karzai and a presidential system. Just before the opening of the CLJ, Karzai had threatened to resign if the presidential system was not accepted. Over the next few weeks, Khalilzad, Brahimi, and Karzai's aides tried to persuade the opposition to vote for a presidential system in exchange for concessions on other articles of the constitution. There was much haggling on the floor of the tent. Washington considered the passage of the constitution, followed by presidential and parliamentary elections in 2004, as critical to persuading American voters that Afghanistan was a success story for Bush.

The delegates in the large tent were broken up into smaller groups to discuss each article of the draft constitution. There was intense lobbying as amendments to the constitution could be accepted only by the chairman and put to secret ballot if they were supported with the signatures of 151 delegates. (Ultimately 24 amendments were voted upon.) Faction leaders were in constant dialogue with UN and Western diplomats, in smaller hospitality tents outside. The atmosphere was both intense and jovial, intellectually challenging and lighthearted, as Afghans gossiped and cracked jokes. All the delegates knew that the life and death of the nation was at stake, which is why they fought so fiercely for their beliefs.

The jihadis, led by Abdul Rasul Sayyaf and Burhanuddin Rabbani, had a list of Islamic demands, including that Sharia become the supreme law of the land. Sayyaf was a notorious figure, a follower of the Wahhabi sect who had encouraged the first Arabs to join the anti-Soviet jihad in the early 1980s and a mentor to Osama bin Laden. The Filipino terrorist group Abu Sayyaf was named after him after its founder, Abdurajak Janjalani, received military training from Sayyaf. During the civil war in the 1990s Sayyaf's forces carried out massacres of Shia Hazaras in Kabul, which were documented by Human Rights Watch.[35] Sayyaf rejected the Taliban and joined the Northern Alliance, becoming the most important Pashtun within the largely non-Pashtun NA.

A tall, imposing man with a flowing snow-white beard, Sayyaf speaks fluent Arabic and English in a booming voice that he uses effectively to intimidate people. He lives in Paghman, outside Kabul, where his militia imposes a strict Islamic regime and regularly appears in the Western suburbs of Kabul to rob homes and rape women.[36] He was one of the first NA warlords on the CIA's payroll, according to CIA agent Gary Schroen, who gave Sayyaf one hundred thousand dollars after 9/11.[37] After the war ended Sayyaf ingratiated himself with Khalilzad, much to the chagrin of the reformist ministers. He continues to have enormous influence over the judiciary and the Supreme Court, which his nominees controlled until 2006.

In a plenary session of the CLJ held on December 17, Malalai Joya, a short, plucky young delegate from Farah province, took on Sayyaf and the warlords. She accused them of being criminals out to destroy the country. Before she could finish speaking, furious delegates led by Sayyaf accused her of being an atheist and communist, while others threatened to kill her. She was placed under ISAF protection for the rest of the CLJ. It was pure drama and it electrified the country, as the public watched the plenary sessions live on television. Joya's move did much to unite the women delegates and put the jihadis on notice not to browbeat them.

The most important outcome of the CLJ was that it led to the reemergence of the Pashtuns, who united under Karzai to insist upon a presidential system. Until then, despite Karzai's position as head of state, the Pashtun tribal leaders and elders felt disenfranchised, but now they came together as a cohesive political force ready to oppose the dominance of the Northern Alliance. They complained bitterly about the refusal of the Northern Alliance to carry out DDR and about the forced eviction of fifty thousand Pashtuns from northern Afghanistan by Generals Dostum and Atta; the refugees were still eking out a miserable existence in relief camps near Kandahar. Their grievances affected their reluctance to give official language status to Uzbek, a point that almost wrecked the CLJ. Meanwhile, the Pashtun delegates tried to get Pushtu declared as a national rather than just an official language, in order to reassert their dominance. Pashtun military officers were furious at Fahim, who had changed the names of ranks in the military from Pushtu to Dari.

This newfound Pashtun unity was confronted with acute divisions within the Tajik camp. Ever since 9/11, the Northern Alliance, led by the Tajik Panjsheris, had dominated the political scene. Now their power was being rapidly eclipsed. They were divided over which form of government to adopt, and over whether to support Karzai or not, and with Fahim discredited as he enriched himself and his minions, they were leaderless. His alleged corruption and business interests had lost him the support of his fellow Panjsheris.

With the Panjsheris in eclipse, the Uzbeks and Hazaras began to adopt their own leaders. The Uzbeks had gained a great deal, such as the declaration of Uzbek, and other minority languages, as official languages. The Shia Hazaras gained as the constitution recognized Shia jurisprudence for the first time, granting it equality with Sunni Hanafi jurisprudence. Nevertheless there were fears that the CLJ would exacerbate ethnic divisions in the country, as many of the amendments demanded by the minorities had a distinctly anti-Pashtun ethnic character. Ashraf Ghani and Ali Jalali, who led the reformist group opposed to the NA warlords and the Panjsheris, were accused of inflaming Pashtun ultranationalism.

The final agreement did not come easily. Toward the end, with still no agreement on the language issue, the role of Islam, or the question of dual nationality, an angry Mujaddedi walked out and did not return until Brahimi and Khalilzad privately met with him at his home. The CLJ's fate hung in the balance until the final compromises between the delegates were pulled off by Khalilzad, Brahimi, and his deputy, Jean Arnault.

The major concession won by the jihadis was that the Supreme Court was given the power to review constitutional legislation and presidential decrees. The Court was dominated by the conservative ulema and the eighty-year-old chief justice Fazl Hadi Shinwari, who was versed only in Sharia law and was controlled by Sayyaf. European ambassadors privately told me that Khalilzad had struck a deal with Sayyaf in which he would later have the power to nominate judges to the Supreme Court if he gave concessions now on other fronts. Sayyaf emerged more powerful from the CLJ. To the Americans, he was a fundamentalist, but he was "our fundamentalist."

After twenty-two days of intense debate, on January 4, 2004, the 502 CLJ delegates stood up to approve the new constitution. The closing day was full of high emotion and witnessed the most moving speeches to be made since the liberation of Afghanistan three years earlier. Everyone in the tent—men and women, Afghans and foreign diplomats—were weeping quietly or had pins and needles as Karzai and others made their final speeches.

Karzai told his opponents that those wanting a prime minister could revise the constitution down the road. Karzai said:

The other aim behind opting for a presidential system at present was the fear that under a parliamentary system, the country may be divided among political parties which are formed along ethnic lines, or split into small parties, which are disposed to forming alliances and coalitions along ethnic, sectarian or regional lines. . . . The constitution is not the Koran. If . . . we find that stability improves, proper political parties emerge, and we judge that a parliamentary system can function better, then a Loya Jirga can . . . be convened to adopt a different system of government.[38]

Lakhdar Brahimi, who was leaving his post after three years, was eulogized by Karzai. Brahimi urged the delegates to turn the constitution from just words on a page "into a living reality." Brahimi's last speech resonates even more strongly today: "There is the insecurity that we don't see much of in the press, the fear that is in the heart of practically every Afghan because there is no rule of law yet in this country. The people of Afghanistan are afraid of the guns that are held by the wrong people and used not to defend them and not to wage a jihad because the time for jihad is finished, but to frighten people, to terrorize people."[39]

The Afghan constitution is one of the most modern and democratic in the Muslim world. It stipulates equality between Sunni and Shia, men and women, Muslim and non-Muslim, and among all ethnic groups. Pushtu and Dari became official languages, but for the first time six other languages were recognized in the areas where they were spoken and fourteen ethnic groups were also recognized. Article 4 recognizes the full ethnic pluralism of Afghanistan: "The nation of Afghanistan is comprised of Pashtun, Tajik, Hazara, Uzbek, Turkmen, Baloch, Pashay, Nuristani, Aymaq, Arab, Kyrgyz, Qizilbash, Gujar, Brahui, and other ethnic groups. The word *Afghan* applies to every citizen of Afghanistan."

For some Afghans, in particular Pashtuns, the CLJ provided reconciliation and a healing process, but for others it was a divisive and bruising experience. For the first time ethnic divisions from the Taliban era, which had lain dormant after 2001, had reappeared. "The CLJ process exposed both the potential for bringing diverse interests and peoples together in order to rebuild the state, as well as the country's deep fractures which the CLJ served to deepen and even open new wounds," wrote Barnett Rubin.[40] Karzai emerged stronger than before, and there was widespread agreement that he now needed to seize the moment, reshuffle his cabinet, and establish a new political party that would project a national vision before presidential and parliamentary elections took place.

Now was the moment for Karzai to sweep out the warlords and drug traffickers in his government and carry out major reforms. Yet Karzai failed to assert himself and remained indecisive and hesitant as the crises around him multiplied, reconstruction halted, opium production boomed, and the Taliban reappeared. The new constitution was a landmark for the Afghan nation, but its implementation would be delayed as the country faced other mounting problems.

CHAPTER ELEVEN

Double-Dealing with Islamic Extremism

Al Qaeda and the Taliban in Pakistan

A year after 9/11 it was clear to many Pakistanis that Musharraf's support of the U.S.-led war in Afghanistan was not the promised strategic U-turn that would end the army's long-standing support to Islamic extremists but rather a short-term tactical move to appease the United States and offset India's hegemony. The near-war with India in 2002, the freedom given to the Kashmiri and Pakistani militant groups, and the refusal to grapple with homegrown terrorism created serious misgivings among liberal Pakistanis about Musharraf's ultimate intentions. The Bush administration did not question Musharraf as long as the Pakistani army cooperated with the principal U.S. objective to catch al Qaeda leaders. Many Pakistanis saw it as a continuation of U.S. policy since the 1950s, with Washington always preferring to deal with a single military dictator who made all the decisions and was unencumbered by parliaments, elections, or politicians.

Washington's limited aims suited the Pakistani army perfectly because they allowed for a new strategic alliance with the United States at minimum risk to the army's concept of national security, which rested on three pillars. These were resisting Indian hegemony in the region and promoting the Kashmir cause; protecting and developing the nuclear program; and promoting a pro-Pakistan government in Afghanistan. All three interests rested on unquestioned support from the Islamic fundamentalist parties and their extremist wings. Even though Islamabad had "lost" Afghanistan for the time being, the military was convinced that U.S. staying power in Afghanistan would be short-lived and that their opportunities to reshape the government in Kabul would return.

If the United States ever questioned the army's intentions, Musharraf could raise the stakes by pointing out the dangers of rising Islamic fundamentalism in Pakistan and how he was the only bulwark against it. Every Pakistani government since the 1970s had raised this bogey as a way to secure support from the Americans. U.S. administrations failed to ask the obvious question: If support for the army's national security interests rested on the Islamic parties, then how could the army claim to be putting down the very same Islamists?

Musharraf epitomized the new breed of senior army officers who were promoted as a result of the Zia era. His personal lifestyle was liberal, secular, and modern, and during his tenure he promoted corps commanders who embodied the same liberal values. He railed against extremism and terrorism, exhorting his countrymen to do the same, but when it came to decision making regarding Islamic fundamentalism, his policies reflected the army's institutional views, which were that the fundamentalists were the only patriotic allies who could help keep India at bay and liberal democrats in check. The personal views and lifestyle of Pakistani generals did not impinge on their institutional ability to support the Islamists. After 9/11, it was relatively easy for them to convince the international community that their personal views were also their political intentions. Musharraf insisted that only the army could control the fundamentalists.

The engineered success of the Muttahida Majlis-e-Amal (MMA), the alliance of five Islamic parties in the 2002 elections, their control of the two key provinces bordering Afghanistan, and the growing anti-Americanism in the country were all used to persuade the international community not to push the regime too hard on a return to civilian rule and democracy. At the time of 9/11 there were more than forty extremist groups in the country who all had links with the ISI and the mainstream Islamic parties. Some of these groups, such as Jaish-e-Mohammed, had been directly set up by the ISI. Before 9/11 these groups had also forged close links with al Qaeda, providing it with support, transport, and communication links. Al Qaeda in turn offered them an international agenda of global jihad, an alternative to being tied to the anti-India agenda dictated by the ISI. Many of these groups were to abandon the ISI because they saw their true calling as fighters for al Qaeda.[1] For them, Pakistan was a battlefield for global jihad and Musharraf a prime target. Yet until the assassination attempts on him in December 2003, the ISI ignored these changes within their own proxies.

The ISI gave refuge to the Taliban leadership after it fled Afghanistan and to its allies, such as Gulbuddin Hikmetyar, the leader of the Hizb-e-Islami Party, who arrived from exile in Iran and operated freely in the NWFP under ISI protection. Hikmetyar opened an office in the Shamshatoo Camp for Afghan refugees, near Peshawar, which was swiftly turned into a Hizb-e-Islami base. Jalaluddin Haqqani, whom the ISI had promoted as a possible "moderate" Taliban, was given sanctuary in North Waziristan, where he rebuilt his network on both sides of the border. The remnants of other foreign groups, such as the Islamic Movement of Uzbekistan (IMU), settled in South Waziristan.

The Pakistan army believed that Karzai's interim government was profoundly anti-Pakistan, as it was dominated by pro-Indian NA leaders at the expense of Pashtuns. Yet even as the two Loya Jirgas reestablished Pashtun preeminence and as Karzai brought more Pashtuns into the cabinet at the expense of the Northern Alliance, Islamabad considered his efforts as too little too late. To maintain its influence among the Taliban and Afghan Pashtuns, the ISI developed a two track policy of protecting the Taliban while handing over al Qaeda Arabs and other non-Afghans to the United States.

The CIA remained extremely suspicious of the ISI, maintaining the profiles of all ISI personnel and where they were stationed and requesting the removal of officers it did not trust. Musharraf purged ISI officers after 9/11 and ordered the ISI to open up its headquarters in Aabpara, in downtown Islamabad, to wider cooperation with the CIA. In turn, the CIA trained ISI personnel on new equipment and technology, which it provided. Frequent visits by CIA director George Tenet and heads of European intelligence agencies secured greater ISI cooperation.

Under the glare of Western agencies it was impossible for the ISI to both help the CIA and run the Taliban, whom the ISI had given sanctuary. Running a two-track policy was proving to be an institutional difficulty for the ISI, a difficulty that was resolved with the creation of a new clandestine organization that would operate outside the military and intelligence structure, in the civilian sphere. Former ISI trainers of the Taliban, retired Pashtun officers from the army and especially the Frontier Corps, were rehired on contract. They set up offices in private houses in Peshawar, Quetta, and other cities and maintained no links with the local ISI station chief or the army. Most of these agents held down regular jobs, working undercover as coordinators for Afghan refugees, bureaucrats, researchers at universities, teachers at colleges, and even aid workers. Others set up NGOs ostensibly to work with Afghan refugees.

Retired intelligence officials told me that this clandestine organization was modeled on the principle of an NGO, with a minimum of hierarchy and expense, casual working hours with frequent returns to civilian life, and an untraceable system of command and control. There were no records, and logistics and expenses came through not the ISI but the less scrutinized offices of the Frontier Corps. The close-knit bond and camaraderie between former ISI and army officers who had served clandestinely in Afghanistan over the past twenty years provided just the platform needed for such an organization. Meanwhile, senior retired ISI officers in the public eye, such as former ISI chief Lt.-Gen. Hameed Gul, played an equally important role in mobilizing public support for the Taliban in the media and for political platforms.

After Taliban attacks in Afghanistan intensified in 2003, the CIA and Britain's MI6 tried to unearth how the ISI was continuing to provide assistance to the Taliban—were these rogue operations conducted by a few ISI officers or did they have official clearance from the army and Musharraf? CIA and U.S. military officials in Islamabad first thought the attacks the work of a group of retired officers, perhaps headed by Hameed Gul. The CIA asked the ISI to place Gul under surveillance and drew up a list of retired officers friendly to him. Surveillance of Gul's group yielded little information. The CIA was unwilling to push too hard, fearing that the Pakistanis might end all intelligence cooperation. Likewise the ISI knew that the Americans were unwilling to draw any abrupt conclusions and put the blame on Musharraf. If Washington had determined that support to the Taliban came from the top rather than from a few rogues, the United States would have had to take Musharraf to task, and neither Bush nor Cheney was prepared to do that. The most U.S. and European intelligence officials in Islamabad would admit was that Pakistani support to the Taliban was being carried out by a few out-of-control ISI officers.

Over time evidence slowly collected by U.S. and NATO intelligence officers on the ground showed a systematic and pervasive system of ISI collusion. By 2004 they had confirmed reports of the ISI running training camps for Taliban recruits north of Quetta, funds and arms shipments arriving from the Gulf countries, and shopping sprees in Quetta and Karachi in which the Taliban bought hundreds of motorbikes, pickup trucks, and satellite phones. In 2003 and 2004, American soldiers at firebases along the border in eastern Afghanistan and U.S. drones in the skies watched as army trucks delivered Taliban fighters to the border at night to infiltrate Afghanistan and then recovered them on their return a few days later. Pakistani artillery gave covering fire to Taliban infiltrators crossing into Afghanistan, and medical facilities were set up close to the border by the army for wounded Taliban.

Most damning of all was the extensive monitoring at the U.S. base at Bagram of wireless communications between Taliban commanders and Pakistan army officers on the border. The Taliban would speak to officers at border checkpoints, asking for safe passage as they came out of Afghanistan. The ISI's activities emerged in the open when NATO troops deployed in southern Afghanistan in late 2005 and were faced with a full-blown Taliban offensive being run out of Quetta. Afghanistan's National Directorate of Security, which had been reorganized by the CIA and MI6, developed excellent sources in Quetta and Peshawar.[2]

When the first NATO troops deployed in the south in late 2005, they discovered that the Americans had not monitored Taliban activity in four southern provinces—Helmand, Kandahar, Uruzgan, and Nimroz—or across the border in Quetta. In 2006 a senior U.S. commander in Kabul admitted to me that the U.S. military's "biggest mistake for which NATO troops were now paying the price was the lack of a lookdown satellite capability" in the south and a shortage of intelligence manpower, because the Iraq war had drained away resources. Thus for four years, Mullah Omar and his commanders were able to operate freely in Balochistan and southern Afghanistan without being monitored by U.S. intelligence. In Balochistan, a pure Afghan Taliban movement was left undisturbed and allowed to take root. The ISI had made sure that American interest in Quetta would be minimal, as the Taliban did not have any Arabs coming or going or fighting for them. Until the spring of 2006 the Americans were to ignore the Balochistan base of the Taliban and focus solely on the northwest corner of the NWFP, where al Qaeda and its affiliates were settled.

After 9/11, hundreds of non-Afghan al Qaeda fighters and leaders came through the mountains along the border into Pakistan's tribal belt. Some were captured by the Pakistan army; those who evaded arrest or walked through the unguarded border into North and South Waziristan were to stay on unmolested for the next three years. Some mid-level al Qaeda officials made their way down to Karachi, from where they escaped to the Arab Gulf states by boat. The arrest in Karachi in July 2002 of Sheikh

Ahmed Saleem, a planner of the 1998 bombings in East Africa, provided information as to how members of al Qaeda were being smuggled out on boats from fishing villages along the Makran coast. The anti-Shia extremist group Lashkar-e-Jhangvi had provided Saleem with false passports, tickets, and money and had helped him smuggle al Qaeda gold out of the country. Naval forces from the U.S.-led Coalition that patrolled the Arabian Gulf had boarded 180 ships in the first ten months after 9/11 but did not apprehend any fugitives.[3]

Senior al Qaeda leaders gravitated to Punjab, where they felt safe and could reorganize the movement with the help of Pakistani militants from Jaish-e-Mohammed and other groups who looked after their safety. The first important al Qaeda leader to be arrested by the Pakistanis as he tried to escape from Afghanistan was Ibn al-Sheikh al-Libi, who ran the al Qaeda training camp at Khalden, in Afghanistan. He provided the first information about who was directly behind the 9/11 attacks.

Abu Zubaydah was caught during a raid of a house in the industrial city of Faislabad, near Lahore, on March 28, 2002. The intelligence breakthrough had come a week earlier, after the arrest in Peshawar of four Arab militants and their Pakistani driver from Faislabad. The Saudi-born Palestinian, age thirty-one, was asleep when one hundred security officials stormed the three-story house. He ran up to the roof and attempted to escape, but was shot in the groin. One of his companions was killed and another wounded in a shootout that also left three Pakistani police officers wounded. Over the next few days police arrested twenty-seven other foreign and Pakistani militants from nine houses in Lahore and Faislabad. Abu Zubaydah was treated by CIA doctors and then incarcerated in a secret CIA jail in Thailand—one of a number of "black sites" that were soon to be created around the world.

U.S. officials said that Zubaydah had planned major al Qaeda plots before 9/11.[4] He had been promoted as al Qaeda's head of military operations after Mohammed Atef was killed by a U.S. missile strike in Kabul in November 2001. He was planning new terrorist strikes in Pakistan and abroad when he was caught. Since 1997 he had lived openly in Peshawar, with the full knowledge of the ISI, running a guesthouse for al Qaeda called the House of Martyrs, where all foreign recruits were interviewed before being sent for training to Afghanistan. He knew the identities of thousands of recruits. The Clinton administration had repeatedly asked Musharraf to extradite him, but the ISI denied all knowledge of his whereabouts. In fact, before 9/11 Abu Zubaydah had worked with the ISI, vetting Kashmiri militants for training in al Qaeda camps. President Bush claimed in September 2006 that Zubaydah had revealed only "nominal" information until the CIA interrogated him more harshly, which resulted in intelligence that led to the capture of Khalid Sheikh Mohammed. However, according to lawyers and experts, that interrogation program amounted to torture.[5]

On April 30, 2002, Khalid al-Attash, a Yemeni wanted for the bombing of USS *Cole,* was arrested along with five Pakistani militants in a Karachi safe house. Fortuitously for the government, the next round of arrests occurred on the first anniversary of the 9/11 attacks, just as Musharraf was due to address the UN General Assembly in New York. Ramzi bin al Shibh, a leader of the Hamburg cell that carried out the 9/11 attacks, was arrested in Karachi when three apartments were raided.[6] Eight Arab men, an Arab woman, and children were arrested. In one of the apartments two suspects were killed, including a Pakistani militant who before he died inscribed "Allahu Akbar" (God Is Great) on the walls in his own blood. The police who dragged bin al-Shibh out of one house did not recognize him until FBI agents waiting in a car outside confirmed his identity.

For several days there was intense media speculation that Khalid Sheikh Mohammed, or KSM, as he was called, al Qaeda's third in line and a planner of 9/11, had also been killed in the raid. A few weeks earlier, bin al-Shibh and KSM had given an interview in Karachi to Yosri Fouda, a journalist for Al Jazeera TV network, claiming responsibility for 9/11.[7] KSM's wife and children had been arrested in the raid. A year after 9/11, the Bush administration said that twenty-seven hundred suspected members of al Qaeda had been arrested in sixty countries; nearly five hundred of them had been caught in Pakistan alone.

It took another six months to capture KSM. An informer walked into the CIA office in Islamabad with news of his whereabouts.[8] On March 1, 2003, twelve heavily armed ISI agents broke down the front door of a house in Westridge, in the military cantonment area of Rawalpindi, a few minutes' drive from the army's general headquarters. They found KSM, al Qaeda's chief operational planner, still groggy with sleep. Also captured was Mustafa Ahmed al-Hawsawi. A Saudi, he was al Qaeda's chief financial officer and fund-raiser, who had set up thirty-five bank accounts in the United States for the 9/11 hijackers. The raiders seized a computer, files, and computer disks. Within hours both men were on their way to a "black site" prison run by the CIA in Kabul and later to one in Poland. "It is hard to overstate how significant this is," said an elated Ari Fleischer, the White House press secretary. "[He is] the mastermind of the September 11 attacks."[9]

KSM had narrowly evaded capture several times.[10] A Pakistani Baloch who had grown up in Kuwait and studied mechanical engineering in North Carolina, in the 1980s he arrived in Peshawar to join the anti-Soviet war and became private secretary to the Wahhabi Mujahedin leader Abdul Rasul Sayyaf, now allied to Karzai. A master of disguises who held twenty different passports and spoke four languages, KSM had been the first to suggest the idea of the 9/11 plot to Osama bin Laden. He had built up extensive links with Pakistani extremists, who now provided al Qaeda with a support network. In July 2004, Pakistani extremists murdered Raja Saqlain, the police officer who arrested KSM in 2003.[11]

After 9/11 KSM had ordered his operatives to go after soft Western targets. A Jewish synagogue in Tunisia was bombed in April 2002. Twenty-one people, including fourteen German tourists, were killed. There were the lethal bombings on the island of Bali in October 2002, which killed 190 people. After his capture, the CIA raced to make him talk quickly, and within days there were red alerts in several countries, including one at Heathrow Airport, near London. His capture led to suspicions of his links within the Pakistan army because he had stayed in a secure military housing estate in Rawalpindi. His host there was Ahmed Abdul Qadoos, whose mother was an activist of the Jamiat-e-Islami and whose brother was a major serving in Kohat, close to the Afghan border; Qadoos was swiftly arrested.

The Jamiat connection with al Qaeda proved deeply contentious. The Jamiat is Pakistan's most ideological Islamic party, with close links to the army and the ISI. On behalf of the ISI it had spawned numerous extremist groups to fight in Kashmir and had twice helped the military undermine the government of Benazir Bhutto in the 1990s. Opposition politicians alleged that the Jamiat was protecting al Qaeda militants. Several alleged militants had been arrested from Jamiat members' homes in Karachi and Lahore, while the Jamiat leader, Qazi Hussain Ahmed, denied that al Qaeda even existed.

With its closest political ally under withering media criticism, on March 12 the ISI gave an unprecedented briefing to Pakistani newspaper editors, telling them that the Jamiat had no links with al Qaeda and that they should stop writing about such allegations. There was silence from Washington.

To this day none of the Islamic parties making up the MMA acknowledge the existence of al Qaeda and they maintain that 9/11 was carried out by the CIA and Israel. MMA leaders go unquestioned by Musharraf and the military when they insist that the "war on terrorism" is an American fiction created by Bush because he hates Muslims. Al Qaeda's attacks after 9/11 in Pakistan and abroad would have been impossible without the support network provided by Pakistani extremist groups and individual militants from mainstream Islamic parties such as the Jamiat-e-Islami. Even Musharraf acknowledges the links in his biography. "Al' Qaeda provided the money, weapons and equipment and the local organizations provided the manpower and motivation to actually execute the attacks," Musharraf writes.[12]

The Pakistani government also made no attempt to contain the inflammatory jihadi literature that flooded the country after 9/11. Some forty publications with a circulation of over one million were published by extremist groups. Lashkar-e-Tayyaba claimed that its weekly newspaper had a print run of more than one hundred thousand copies and it continued to publish gory accounts of suicide bombers killed in Kashmir.[13] Other publications by Sunni extremist groups spewed hatred against Shias, claiming they were apostates. The two main Sunni extremist groups, Sipah-e-Sahaba (Soldiers of the Companions of the Prophet) and its splinter Lashkar-e-Jhangvi (the Army of Jhangvi), launched a bloody sectarian war against the minority Shia population. These two Sunni groups who had fought for the Taliban and carried out massacres of Afghan Shias became a mainstay of al Qaeda planning in Pakistan.

Sipah-e-Sahaba was founded in 1985 with the aim of turning Pakistan into a Sunni state. Several splinter groups broke away from it, each more vicious than the one before. The last to do so was Lashkar-e-Jhangvi, which was set up in 1996 by Riaz Basra, who was based in Taliban-controlled Kabul. Although the military regime had declared war on all sectarian groups, the ISI still pursued a dual-track policy. In 2002 Sipah's leader, Maulana Azam Tariq, was freed from jail, where he had faced multiple murder charges, and allowed to contest the general elections on the condition that he would support the regime—which he did until he was assassinated two years later.[14]

The bloodiest sectarian attacks took place in Quetta, where Taliban leaders now lived and where Pakistani Shia Hazaras were recruited as interpreters by U.S. forces in Afghanistan. On June 8, 2003, eleven Hazara policemen were shot dead by gunmen believed to be from Lashkar-e-Jhangvi. The same group was responsible for the March 2, 2004, massacre of a procession for the Muslim holy day of Ashura in Quetta, which left 47 people dead and 150 wounded.[15] On the same day in Iraq, 180 Shias were killed by Sunni extremists in another Ashura procession. In May 2004 a massive bomb explosion in a Shia mosque in Karachi killed 16 worshippers. The blast followed the assassination of Mufti Nizamuddin Shamzai by suspected Shia militants in an escalating tit-for-tat war. Shamzai had headed the Deobandi madrassa in Binori Town, made famous by the Taliban leaders who had studied there, and was the notorious figure who had gone to Kandahar with the ISI chief after 9/11 and urged Mullah Omar to resist the U.S. invasion.[16]

The marginalization of mainstream political parties and the boost to religious parties given by military rule had fueled sectarianism in Pakistan.[17] Although the army had banned all sectarian groups after 9/11, Musharraf had legitimized Sunni extremism by endorsing Azam Tariq. Other Islamic groups banned by the government or named as terrorist organizations by the United States, Britain, and the UN continued to be granted special favors. In March 2003 the government allowed the banned Lashkar-e-Tayyaba to organize the Defense of the Ummah Conference in Islamabad, in which speakers called for jihad. The Lashkar-e-Tayyaba leader Hafiz Saeed condoned suicide bombings and urged fighters to go to Iraq—where at least seven Lashkar members were killed in 2003. Hafiz Saeed told his followers, "The powerful Western world is terrorizing the Muslims. We are being invaded, humiliated, manipulated and looted. How else can we respond but through jihad? . . . We must fight against the evil trio, America, Israel and India. Suicide missions are in accordance with Islam. In fact a suicide attack is the best form of jihad."[18]

Most Pakistanis were appalled at these double standards being carried out by the military. There was increasing cynicism among them when Musharraf toured world capitals and lectured Western leaders about the need for a moderate and enlightened Islam when just the opposite was happening at home. A senior official of the Interior Ministry complained to me in May 2003 that some five thousand militants were operating in FATA—Federally Administered Tribal Areas, adjacent to Afghanistan—

but the ISI had told the ministry to ignore them. A UN report to the UN Security Council described militants streaming into new training camps in Waziristan: "Particularly disturbing about this trend is the fact that new volunteers are making their way to these camps, increasing the number of would-be terrorists and the long-term capabilities of the network," said the report.[19]

By the summer of 2003, U.S. commanders in Afghanistan were becoming deeply frustrated. "Pakistani border troops have been given orders to allow extremists to cross into Afghanistan and then help them return home by giving them covering fire," a U.S. military officer told me in Bagram. Maj.-Gen. Franklin Hagenbeck, the deputy commander of U.S. forces in Afghanistan, warned, "Hot pursuit would probably be my last resort."[20] Karzai was frustrated with the Americans because no senior U.S. official was criticizing Islamabad for allowing the Taliban to operate out of Pakistan. On a visit to Islamabad in April 2003, Karzai gave Musharraf a list of Taliban commanders allegedly living openly in Quetta. Musharraf was furious and denied that there was such a list.

Meanwhile, Islamabad stepped up criticism of the Kabul regime for allowing Indian influence to grow in Afghanistan, asking why Kabul had allowed Indian consulates to be opened in Kandahar and Jalalabad, adjacent to the Pakistan border. New Delhi said it had reopened only the four consulates it had before 1979, including those in Herat and Mazar-e Sharif, just as Pakistan and Iran had reopened their consulates in the same cities. However, Musharraf was blunt in his accusations: "India's motivation in Afghanistan is very clear, nothing further than upsetting Pakistan. Why should they have consulates in Jalalabad and Kandahar, what is their interest? There is no interest other than disturbing Pakistan, doing something against Pakistan."[21]

Despite the army's attempts to deflect the real issues of terrorism taking root along Pakistan's border region, Musharraf faced low-key pressure from Washington to move troops into South Waziristan and combat al Qaeda. Occasionally the simmering tensions between the two countries erupted into the open. "I personally believe that President Musharraf is genuine when he assists us in the tribal areas . . . but I don't think that affection for working with us extends up and down the rank and file of the Pakistani security community," Richard Armitage admitted on October 1.[22] Islamabad retorted angrily, forcing Armitage to backtrack when he visited

Islamabad a few days later. He now said that Pakistan's security forces were "two hundred percent" behind Musharraf.[23] This American shadowboxing at the expense of Afghanistan made Karzai and the Afghans increasingly angry.

The Pakistan army continued to patronize extremist groups in the country even though such groups had been banned. After the U.S. embassy received threats from one group in November, U.S. ambassador Nancy Powell publicly warned the regime that these groups posed a serious threat. . . . "These banned groups are re-establishing themselves with new names." Musharraf promptly banned the same three extremist groups he had banned two years earlier but that had reappeared under new names.[24] Yet even as Musharraf remained soft on banning the extremists, they were planning deadly attacks against him. Al Qaeda leaders had issued unambiguous threats to kill him. In October 2002, bin Laden had called on "my Pakistani Muslim brothers . . . to get rid of the shameful Musharraf."[25] A year later Ayman al-Zawahiri called on Pakistanis to "unite and cooperate to topple this traitor and install a sincere leadership that would defend Islam and Muslims."[26] For months there was talk in extremist circles about plans to kill Musharraf.

On December 14, 2003, the day Saddam Hussein was captured by U.S. forces in Iraq, a massive bomb exploded under a bridge in Rawalpindi just thirty seconds after Musharraf's convoy had driven across it. The heavily guarded bridge was just a mile from the army's general headquarters and Musharraf's home, yet militants were able to spend several days undetected tying explosives to the bridge's pylons. Musharraf's life was saved only by a jamming device in his car provided by the FBI, which momentarily blocked off all telephone signals, thereby delaying the explosion.

A week later there was an even more determined attack. On Christmas Day two suicide bombers rammed their explosives-packed cars into Musharraf's convoy as he was returning home for lunch—just a few hundred yards from the first attack. Musharraf was hit by flying glass as his car windscreen shattered. Fifteen people were killed and fifty were wounded. Human body parts littered the highway. The face of one suicide bomber was lifted clean off his severed head and flattened against a nearby roof. The two suicide bombers were soon identified. One was Mohammed Jamil, twenty-three, a member of Jaish-e-Mohammed who had fought with the Taliban. On his return home in April 2002 he had been interrogated by the ISI, who had declared him "white," or safe. Found in the debris was the memory chip from Jamil's mobile phone, which showed that he had made one hundred calls before his death, including one to a policeman who told him about the timing of Musharraf's convoy.

The second suicide bomber was identified as Hazir Sultan, forty-two, who had also fought with the Taliban. Both men had received their explosives from an al Qaeda camp in South Waziristan. The very men whom the army had encouraged to fight for the Taliban were now returning to haunt them. The profiles of the two men were a clear example of how terrorist networks partially created by the ISI remained intimately linked and how little had been done by the regime to break them up. At one time or another these two men had been engaged with al Qaeda, the Afghan Taliban, Kashmiri militants, Pakistani extremist groups, and dissidents in the armed forces of Pakistan. The attacks shocked the world because they demonstrated the worst-case scenario: disaffected military personnel on the inside linked to terrorist groups on the outside. Only a handful of military officers knew the route and timing of Musharraf's travel plans or which of his several identical armored-plated cars he would be using.

After the attacks Musharraf carried out a widespread reshuffling in the army high command, including appointing Maj.-Gen. Nadeem Taj, a close confidant, as head of military intelligence, which now oversaw Musharraf's personal security. The extremist threat within the armed forces was growing. In August, after an FBI tip-off, five officers had been arrested for suspected links to al Qaeda. They included a lieutenant-colonel and a major serving on the Afghan border.[27] More than 150 police and security personnel were arrested and interrogated after the December attacks. Eventually six air force noncommissioned officers, several military personnel, and civilians were tried in a secret court-martial for the two assassination bids. It was alleged that the terrorists had been trying to kill Musharraf for the previous eighteen months. There was such secrecy around the trial that even the number of accused was never made public by the army, although twelve suspects were found guilty and given the death sentence in 2006.[28]

The air force personnel had been recruited by Amjad Hussain Farooqi, a leader of Jaish-e-Mohammed who had planned the two separate assassination attempts. Farooqi had fought in both Afghanistan and Kashmir since the age of nineteen and was well known to the ISI. Now twenty-seven, he and his deputy, Matiur Rehman, had been close associates of

Mullah Omar and bin Laden.[29] They had helped al Qaeda fighters escape to Pakistan and then helped reconstitute the terrorist network by compiling a Rolodex of jihadis whom they could call upon for special operations. A massive manhunt for Farooqi ensued, and he was finally killed by Pakistani police in Nawabshah, in Sindh province, on September 26, 2004. He had just gotten married for the second time and had been enjoying his honeymoon. Farooqi epitomized the new face of al Qaeda in Pakistan: local, in touch with many different groups and stratas of society, and capable of running several operations at the same time.

The attacks on Musharraf sent shudders through Washington and other Western capitals, as there was no clear line of political succession if Musharraf were to be eliminated and there were doubts as to whether a new Pakistani leader, even from the military, would continue as an ally of the United States. Just after the attacks, Indian prime minister Vajpayee arrived in Islamabad for his long-anticipated meeting with Musharraf in order to end the state of tensions between the two nations. In the past, Pakistani leaders may have promoted extremism in Kashmir, but now one was a victim of it. It was a point that the Indians did not hesitate to make.

The attacks on his life and the subsequent wave of public sympathy gave Musharraf another opportunity to cut the army's umbilical cord with the extremists. It was clear that the ISI no longer controlled the monster of extremism it had created, while the army's rank and file was becoming susceptible to extremist propaganda and recruitment, threatening the very institution that laid claim to be the guardian of the country. Yet even now Musharraf's reactions were minimal—a reshuffling of the army's high command, the roundup of suspects in the lower ranks, and the arrest of some civilians. None of the senior extremist leaders were arrested, nor were their parties forcibly disbanded. Washington, too, failed to use the moment to push Musharraf harder to curb terrorist violence. These seminal events— two assassination bids on a close ally of the White House—seemed to have had no impact on persuading Bush and Cheney that now was the moment to push Musharraf to do more.

Instead, the problem was seen as technical, the result of deficiencies in law enforcement. So the CIA provided more technology and equipment to the ISI. Hundreds of Pakistani law enforcement and intelligence officers, as well as bodyguards for Musharraf, were trained in the United States. The FBI provided money and training to the ISI to set up a counterterrorism Special Investigation Group made up of one hundred personnel. This squad was effective in gleaning evidence from suicide bomb sites to identify bombers, but there was no concerted drive to eliminate the sources of terrorism.

Musharraf still held the post of army chief and president, but there was mounting pressure by the Alliance for Restoration of Democracy (ARD), comprising all the nonreligious opposition parties, that he relinquish his job as army chief. He had promised time and again to do so but had failed to follow through, knowing full well that his power derived from that post. There was to be no pressure from Washington for him to relinquish the position. "You have a government which can't deliver everything we would like to see," Paul Wolfowitz told me in Washington in February 2004. "I think there is only so much change that can happen in Pakistan at any one time."[30] However, officials in the State Department were frustrated at the lack of U.S. pressure on Musharraf. "We refuse to question anything that Musharraf does at home," an official told me in Washington. "We fail to even admit that retaining his uniform is counterproductive, when we could have easily nuanced our disapproval. By turning a blind eye, we only give Musharraf enormous leverage over Washington."

Instead, in March 2004, the White House conferred the status of "a non-NATO ally" on Pakistan and announced a $700 million aid package for 2004 that earmarked $364 million for the military and a paltry $19 million for "improving democratic participation." The Pakistani military went on a spree, purchasing weapons worth $3.8 billion in 2003 and $6 billion in 2006. The support to Pakistan from around the world had dramatically improved the once-moribund Pakistani economy. By 2003 the servicing of Pakistan's $38 billion debt was reduced by half—to 36 percent of GDP, as compared with 66 percent in 2000. Exports grew dramatically as better trade deals were signed and Pakistanis working abroad sent more money home, fearing scrutiny of their foreign bank accounts.

Foreign exchange reserves grew to $9 billion in 2003, compared with just $1 billion in 2000. The Karachi Stock Exchange had surged by 112 percent in 2002, the highest percentage gain of any bourse in the world, and rose by another 65 percent in 2003. Before 9/11 the market capitalization of the Exchange was just $5 billion, but by 2004 it had reached $17 billion. As energy prices rose worldwide, a special oil facility from Saudi Arabia worth $1 billion per year allowed Pakistan to defer payments on expensive oil imports.

However, there was still inadequate funding for the social sector, especially health and education. State schools could challenge the madrassas only if they were plentiful and provided a better education, but that meant more money for the education budget. In 2002 the United States had given a $100 million grant spread over five years for educational reforms, but the funds were not matched with a similar commitment by the Pakistani government. Had Musharraf, on his first visit to Washington after 9/11, appealed for a major international aid effort to fund a countrywide literacy campaign rather than asking for F-16 fighter aircraft, there is little doubt that he would have been swamped with offers of government money. The regime appeared to have no strategy for turning around the chronic educational morass in the country, which was fueling ignorance and jihadism.

Sixty years after independence, Pakistan's literacy rate is an appalling 54 percent, with female literacy at less than 30 percent and, in some areas, such as Balochistan, less than 15 percent. The total number of illiterate people has more than doubled in the past half century. Public expenditure on education as a percentage of gross domestic product fell from 2.6 percent to 1.8 percent between 1990 and 2001, and remained at that level until 2003.[31] By one estimate, less than 25 percent of the work force is literate, making it impossible to train workers for anything other than menial jobs. Primary school enrollment grew only 1 percent between 1999 and 2002, the first years of the Musharraf regime, while the high-school dropout rate was one of the highest in Asia.[32] Next door, Afghanistan launched a major literacy drive that sent five million children back to school, but in Pakistan—a state far better equipped—there was no such endeavor. For those children who did attend school, educational standards had dropped drastically. A prominent educator commented that "most students have not learned how to think, they cannot speak or write any language well, rarely read newspapers and cannot formulate a coherent argument or manage any significant creative expression. This generation of Pakistanis is intellectually handicapped."[33]

School textbooks were developed by each regime as political manifestos to brainwash students into accepting a continuous state of tension with India or to justify military rule, hatred of non-Muslims, or symbols that promoted religious intolerance and jihadism.[34] The army was invariably glorified as the only patriotic institution in the country. Textbooks frequently portrayed Mohammed Ali Jinnah, who was a non-practicing Shia, as a pious man at prayer expounding reactionary religious beliefs rather than the democratic principles he had actually espoused. The ulema were portrayed as heroes of the Pakistan Movement, when in fact they had opposed the creation of Pakistan.

Higher education was in an even more deplorable state, with the country's universities producing just fifty Ph.D.s a year in 2001—a figure that rose to seven hundred with the help of U.S. Fulbright scholarships. However, the army had a limited agenda—to invest in higher education in the fields of science and technology so as to improve Pakistan's military-industrial complex, compete with India, and provide workers for its nuclear program. "This is an educational vision appropriate for a totalitarian state, not for one that aspires to be a free society," wrote Stephen Cohen, an American scholar of Pakistan.[35]

The most immediate problem was reforming the estimated 12,000 madrassas in the country. Once the seat of learning for Muslim priests and judges, madrassas had been taken over by Islamic parties and extremist groups in the 1980s and now taught a syllabus of jihad to recruit fighters for the wars in Afghanistan and Kashmir. In 1947 there were only 137 madrassas in Pakistan; but they doubled in number every ten years until the 1980s, when the military regime of President Zia ul-Haq approved state funding for a massive growth in madrassas.[36]

Many madrassas in the Pashtun belt in the NWFP and Balochistan, controlled by the Deobandi sect, promoted jihad to the detriment of all other Islamic teachings. Deobandi mullahs were also recruited in large numbers for the army. Even after 9/11 some madrassas continued to be funded by Wahhabi groups in the Arabian Gulf and large donations by Pakistanis. It was estimated that out of a total of $1.1 billion in donations by Pakistanis to charities, or the giving of *zakat*—the Islamic tax of 2.5 percent of income that is given to the poor—94 percent of the money went to religious institutions.[37]

In 2001 the government had approved a plan that would for the first time register madrassas, halt their funding from abroad, and modify their curricula to teach modern subjects such as math, history, and science.[38] The Islamic parties protested the new law, and the government promptly shelved it. Every year the state budget allocated one billion rupees for madrassa reforms, but the reforms were never implemented. The lack of international pressure on the regime to do so only encouraged further post-ponements. The U.S. State Department and USAID maintained the charade that Pakistan was actively carrying out reforms.

After a meeting at Camp David in June 2003, Bush praised Musharraf's commitment to reform: "He's taking on the issue in a way that is visionary and strong. He's dealing with the madrassas in a way that is productive and constructive," he said.[39] In fact, all reforms had stalled and hundreds of new madrassas were popping up all over the country. In Islamabad, with a population of just one million, there were 127 madrassas in 2006 and 42 new ones being created. One new madrassa was being opened every week in the capital.[40]

The Bush administration was forced to oblige Musharraf again in the spring of 2004 when scandal broke over Dr. A. Q. Khan, Pakistan's top nuclear scientist, who was caught proliferating nuclear technology to Iran, Libya, and North Korea. The world was shocked, even as the Bush administration went to extraordinary lengths to appear uncritical of any possible army involvement in the scandal. In February, Musharraf pardoned Khan after the scientist publicly took responsibility for the proliferation upon himself. In turn, Bush let Musharraf off the hook by accepting the steps Pakistan was taking to clean up its act. Keeping Musharraf onside was now vital to the White House as Bush went on the campaign trail for his reelection bid in the summer of 2004. With the insurgency in Iraq worsening, Karl Rove had scripted one stump speech for Bush in which he presented how the U.S. relationship with Pakistan was a stunning foreign policy success story. In July, Bush told an audience at Oak Ridge, Tennessee:

> Three years ago Pakistan was one of the few countries that recognized the Taliban regime. Al Qaeda was active and recruiting in Pakistan, and was not seriously opposed. Pakistan served as a transit point for al Qaeda terrorists leaving Afghanistan on missions of murder. Yet the United States was not on good terms with Pakistan's military and civilian leaders. . . . Today the governments of the United States and Pakistan are working closely in the fight against terror. . . . Pakistan is an ally in the war on terror and the American people are safer.[41]

The assassination attempts on Musharraf had allowed Bush to project him as the brave pro-American Muslim leader holding the front line to prevent terrorists reaching the shores of the U.S. homeland. At the time, nobody, including John Kerry and other Democratic candidates, questioned the assumption of how the United States could be safer if Musharraf himself was not safe.[42] Further attacks only belied Bush's claims. On June 9, 2004, in the midst of Karachi's morning rush hour, the convoy of the city's corps commander, Lt.-Gen. Ahsan Saleem Hayat, was ambushed. Gunmen raked the vehicles with machine-gun fire and exploded grenades. The general escaped, but his driver, seven soldiers, and three policemen were killed.

The terrorists involved belonged to a new group, called Jundullah, or the "Army of God," made up of educated middle-class professionals, including doctors and lawyers, who trained in South Waziristan with al Qaeda. Jundullah's leader, Attaur Rehman, had a master's degree in statistics from Karachi University. Rehman himself had fought with the Taliban and had helped al Qaeda set up an underground network in Karachi after 9/11. The wave of terror strikes the group carried out included attacks on the U.S. consulate, the office of a Christian group, and a peace concert. In all, seventeen people were killed in these attacks.[43] Jundullah demonstrated a disturbing new trend: well-educated individuals willing to create a terrorist group that had no past record or association with madrassas or extremists, thus making it next to impossible to identify its members. Police officials in Karachi estimated that some two dozen unknown terrorist groups like Jundullah were operating in Karachi alone. As al Qaeda's support base in Pakistan broadened, it was able to depend more and more on a class of well-educated Pakistanis.

In July 2004 the son of an executive of the national airline was arrested in Lahore. Naeem Noor Khan, twenty-five, who had studied in London, was the communications chief for al Qaeda in Pakistan, transferring e-mail messages on its behalf. His computer files contained surveillance photos of the World Bank and International Monetary Fund buildings in Washington, the New York Stock Exchange, and Heathrow Airport in London, and a long list of e-mail contacts. His interrogation by the ISI led to several terrorist alerts in Britain and the United States, while twelve foreigners and fifty-one Pakistanis were arrested in Pakistan. Those arrested included Ahmed Khalfan Gailani, a Tanzanian who had carried out the 1998 bombings of the U.S. embassies in Africa, and twelve suspected al Qaeda operatives in Britain, including Dhiren Barot, a Hindu convert to Islam. Barot admitted at his later trial to plotting to blow up the New York Stock Exchange building and limos in underground car parks in London.[44]

Pakistan had now caught 689 alleged al Qaeda members, of whom 369 were handed over to the Americans.

Reform-minded Pakistani politicians still hoped that the terrorist threats and the growing political criticism and isolation Musharraf faced at home would persuade him to strengthen the civilian government by empowering parliament and Prime Minister Jamali. On the contrary, Musharraf became more assertive in concentrating power in his own hands. He took to sitting in on cabinet meetings and overruling Jamali, which led to frustration and criticism from within the ruling Pakistan Muslim League–Q (Quaid-e-Azam) Party (PML-Q).

Musharraf's assertiveness led to a political crisis, which he tried to resolve by forcing Jamali to resign on June 26, 2004. He made it clear he would not appoint anyone as prime minister who did not support the centralization of power under the army. He chose Shaukat Aziz, the former Citicorp executive and present finance minister. In July a suicide bomber exploded himself next to Aziz's car, killing his driver. The attack had been planned by Amjad Farooqi and the same group of extremists who had targeted Musharraf.[45]

Aziz, an overly ambitious multimillionaire banker, had been appointed finance minister after the 1999 coup. He was strongly supported for the post by the ISI. After 9/11 he was instrumental in helping turn around the bankrupt economy and negotiate the debt write-offs given to Pakistan by Western nations. Aziz had been a private banker with Citicorp Inc. and had befriended both Prime Ministers Sharif and Bhutto in the 1990s, while currying favor with successive army chiefs. He was a smooth and glib talker who never showed emotion and who tailored his opinions to fit his audience. He had spent a lifetime trying to please anyone and everyone. According to one writer, Aziz had even tried to flirt with Condi Rice.[46] Now he was targeting Musharraf.

Aziz was a technocrat and no politician. Even though he had been a minister for five years he had declined to build up a political base for himself, insisting that he needed only the support of his "boss," General Musharraf. However, Aziz was also ruthless in his climb to power, making sure that he eliminated any civilian whom Musharraf might think highly of and demeaning any competent officials and technocrats who challenged him. He was to become the figurehead that Musharraf wanted, as Aziz left the politics of the PML-Q to the party's elder statesman, Chaudry Shujjat Hussain and government policies to Musharraf. However, in his desire to please as many people as possible he entered the record books by appointing the largest cabinet in Pakistan's history. A special room had to be found to accommodate meetings of the 126-member cabinet.

Jamali's replacement by a technocrat represented the failure of the artificial political system Musharraf had created. The co-opted politicians who supported the military in parliament knew that their political survival depended more than ever on the continuation of Musharraf's rule. After Aziz became prime minister, the PML-Q passed a bill in parliament that allowed Musharraf to stay on as both army chief and president until 2007. "The President to Hold Another Office Bill, 2004"—the strangest-named bill in the history of the country—rubber stamped Musharraf's prolonged tenure. The parliamentary opposition walked out. "Parliament has been stripped of all powers or legislative role and the president, who is supposed to be the symbol of unity for the federation, remains a divisive figure in both positions," said Pakistan Peoples Party parliamentarian Sherry Rehman.[47]

After the passage of the bill, Musharraf further strengthened his grip on the army. Lt.-Gen. Ahsan Saleem Hayat, who had been targeted in Karachi, became the new vice chief of army staff, and Lt.-Gen. Ashfaq Kayani, who had been Rawalpindi corps commander when the attacks on Musharraf's life took place, was appointed as head of the ISI.[48] Seven junior major-generals were appointed as lieutenant-generals, superseding thirty-seven of their colleagues. Musharraf's appointments ensured that those senior officers who had borne the burden of the war on terrorism alongside him were rewarded, while the new lieutenant-generals were so junior and owed everything to Musharraf that they would not offer any criticism of his policies. Musharraf may have felt secure, but the escalation of terrorist attacks in Afghanistan and Pakistan and a growing political crisis were to lead to severe repercussions for his rule.

◆ ◆ ◆

CHAPTER TWELVE

Taliban Resurgent

The Taliban Return Home

The Taliban did not just slip back across the border in the winter of 2001/2002; they arrived in droves, by bus, taxi, and tractor, on camels and horses, and on foot. As many as ten thousand fighters holed up in Kandahar with their weapons. For many, it was not an escape but a return home—back to the refugee camps in Balochistan where they had been brought up and where their families still lived; back to the madrassas where they had once studied; back to the hospitality of the mosques where they had once prayed. For those with no families to receive them, militants from Pakistani extremist groups and the Jamiat-e-Ulema in Pakistan—like benevolent charity workers—welcomed them at the border with blankets, fresh clothes, and envelopes full of money. ISI officials, standing with the Frontier Constabulary guards and customs officials at Chaman, the border crossing into Balochistan province, waved them in. Musharraf was not about to discourage or arrest these Taliban fighters who had been nurtured for two decades by the military. For Pakistan they still represented the future of Afghanistan, and they had to be hidden away until their time came.

Initially the arriving Taliban were a demoralized lot. In the previous three months thousands had been killed by American bombs or wounded and left to die in their burned-out pickup trucks. Some Pashtun villages in southern Afghanistan were now inhabited only by women, as all their menfolk had been killed in the bombings. The older Taliban blamed Mullah Omar for destroying their government for the sake of preserving Osama bin Laden. A few leading Taliban gave themselves up to U.S. forces in

Kandahar, either because they were compromised by the ISI or because they were so disgusted with Mullah Omar.[1] Two Taliban leaders surrendered to Gul Agha Sherzai, the governor of Kandahar, but he let them go. For the next five years not a single Taliban commander would be handed over to the Americans by the Pakistanis.[2]

The Pakistani military was stunned at the lackadaisical attitude of the Americans in mopping up al Qaeda. The U.S. failure to commit ground troops in the south and then at Tora Bora convinced army headquarters that the Americans were not serious, preferring that the NA militias do their fighting for them. Pakistani officers told me they were amazed that Rumsfeld would not put even one thousand U.S. soldiers into battle. The ISI sent memos to Musharraf stating that the Americans would not stay long in Afghanistan and that the Taliban should be kept alive. Afghan leaders feared the worst. Karzai had lived in Quetta for a decade and understood how the ISI thought and worked. In late January 2002 he sent Foreign Minister Abdullah Abdullah to Washington with a strong warning, asking the Americans to stop Pakistan from helping the Taliban regroup. Abdullah said, "I know that the Taliban leaders are in Pakistan. Pakistan should take this opportunity to clean its house because those elements who supported the Taliban for so long are still there in Pakistan, and they are strong, they are armed and they are well equipped."[3]

Abdullah told me that he was extremely blunt in Washington, but the Americans were interested only in the whereabouts of al Qaeda's leaders, and on that issue Islamabad was being helpful. "The CIA wanted Arabs, not Afghans," Abdullah said. Karzai went to see Musharraf in February, at which time he pledged "to forget the past" and urged Musharraf to do the same and rein in the Taliban. Musharraf gave Karzai $10 million in cash so he could pay Afghan civil servants. In April Musharraf visited Kabul, where he said the ISI was under his control. "Let me assure you that the ISI is doing or not doing whatever I tell them or don't tell them to do—they are behaving exactly as we want them to," he said.[4] Tensions between the two leaders did not ease, as nobody in Kabul believed Musharraf's words.

Mullah Omar, with a handful of bodyguards, had gone underground, moving between Helmand and Urzugan, where there was no permanent U.S. military presence and where he could easily avoid the infrequent U.S. military sweeps. In May 2002, he gave an interview: "The battle [in Afghanistan] has [just] started, its fire has been kindled and it will engulf the

White House, seat of injustice and tyranny." The future for the United States in Afghanistan, he said, was "fire, hell and total defeat."⁵

In the summer of 2002, Taliban commanders began to get back in touch with their fighters and told them to wait for the call. Many of the older fighters had had enough and joined the throng of Afghan refugees now packing up their homes in Pakistan and heading back to Afghanistan. The U.S. and British embassies in Islamabad reported that ISI officers were warning Taliban families not to return home; if they did, the ISI would hand them over to the Americans. The ISI told its American interlocutors that it was still trying to create an alternative Taliban leadership—not the much-disparaged moderate Taliban, but new figures who would accept President Karzai. During the summer several new Taliban groups emerged in Peshawar and Quetta, such as the Jaish-e-Muslimeen and the Jamiat-e-Khudamul Koran, but senior Taliban commanders refused to join up because they had pledged an oath of loyalty, or *beyat,* to Mullah Omar.

In the winter of 2002, Mullah Omar arrived in Quetta from Afghanistan. He was immediately accommodated by the ISI and stayed in safe houses run by the JUI Party, which now formed the provincial government in Quetta. Mullah Omar appointed four senior commanders to reorganize the fighters in the southern provinces of Uruzgan, Helmand, Kandahar, and Zabul. These were Mullah Barader Akhund, the former deputy defense minister; Mullah Akhtar Mohammed Usmani, former army chief; Mullah Dadullah, a famed one-legged corps commander; and the former interior minister Mullah Abdul Razzaq. All four men had close links to bin Laden and were known for their belief in global jihad. Mullah Omar appointed Usmani as his successor in case he was killed or captured. Razzaq, who was born in Chaman, became chief fund-raiser and recruiter in Balochistan, touring mosques and madrassas to motivate the Afghans there.

Dadullah, who had lost a leg in 1995 after stepping on a mine and received a prosthetic limb in a Karachi hospital, knew the Deobandi leaders of the Binori Town madrassa in Karachi, and spent many months in Karachi raising money from the large Pashtun population in the city. He was to become the most ruthless Taliban commander after 9/11. While leading Taliban forces in the Hazarajat in 1998, he ordered the massacre of several groups of Shia Hazaras, which brought him to the notice of bin Laden. The two men were instrumental in the decision to blow up the Buddha statues in Bamiyan. Dadullah had commanded the Taliban's last stand in

Kunduz and escaped its fall by paying off NA warlords, who allowed him to reach Pakistan.

These exiled Taliban leaders received important support after the 2002 elections when the JUI Party came to power in the North-West Frontier and Balochistan provinces. The JUI had helped launch the Taliban in 1994, and its madrassas in Pakistan had provided ideological training and refuge for scores of Taliban commanders.[6] Several JUI mullahs who had fought with the Taliban in the 1990s were now elected members of the provincial assemblies in the two provinces. The full state machinery and facilities of the provisional governments were now available to the Taliban, with the help of ministers such as Maulana Faizullah, the JUI minister of agriculture in Balochistan who had fought in Kandahar alongside Mullah Omar until the city was abandoned. Hafiz Hussain Sharodi, the minister of information for Balochistan, also became a spokesman in defense of the Taliban. Maulana Nur Mohammed, who ran the important Shaldara madrassa in Quetta, the first madrassa to send its students to fight for the Taliban in 1994, made it the major meeting place for Taliban commanders. The students were used to carry messages back and forth to Afghanistan for the Taliban. Maulana Abdul Qadir, the deputy of the madrassa told me, "We are proud that the Taliban are made and helped here and we do everything we can to facilitate them. The Afghan government and Karzai are the stooges and puppets of America, every Afghan knows this. Karzai cannot even go home to his village. Only the Taliban can constitute the real government in Afghanistan."[7]

In Afghanistan's eastern Pashtun provinces the Taliban's reorganization was headed by Saif ur-Rahman Mansur, the charismatic young commander from the Anaconda battle, Jalaluddin Haqqani, the former Taliban minister, and his son, Sirajuddin Haqqani. They operated out of Miranshah, in North Waziristan, one of the Federally Administered Tribal Areas. Haqqani, a tall strapping Pashtun and an old protégé of the ISI, was leader of the Zadran tribe based around Khost. In the 1980s he was a major recipient of CIA money and arms routed through the ISI. After 9/11 the ISI promoted Haqqani as a possible moderate Taliban, and he visited Islamabad under ISI protection to talk to the CIA, just before the war began. During the war, the ISI asked the Americans not to bomb Khost and Haqqani's home, saying that a deal with him was still possible, but Haqqani was a firm believer in al Qaeda. He now gathered around him fighters who had escaped, providing them with accommodation and money. In 2002 U.S. SOF made at least three attempts to kill him, including bombing a mosque near his home, an attempt that killed seventeen people—but he always seemed to be well tipped off before any U.S. attacks.

The Taliban received another boost when the Iranian government unexpectedly allowed Gulbuddin Hikmetyar to leave his exile in Meshed. After secret talks with the ISI in Dubai, he arrived in Peshawar and went underground. Hikmetyar had been Pakistan's most favored Mujahedin leader in the 1980s and was the ISI's nominee to take power in Kabul in 1992, but Ahmad Shah Masud had beaten him to it. Hikmetyar then unleashed the civil war by bombarding Kabul, until the Taliban routed his militia in 1996 and he fled to Iran. Washington accused the Iranians of backing Hikmetyar, and in order to curry favor with the Americans the Iranians had simply let him go. The ISI let Hikmetyar set up a base in the sprawling Shamshatoo refugee camp outside Peshawar, where many of his former fighters lived. He became an ally of the Taliban and al Qaeda yet never fully merged with either movement.

During late 2002 the Taliban began to move weapons, ammunition, and food supplies into Afghanistan, adding to those stockpiles that they had stored away during their retreat. U.S. and Afghan forces began increasingly to unearth caches of new weapons. In November alone they uncovered 475 large and small weapons caches. In one cache, 2,100 brand-new AK-47 rifles were discovered along with 70,000 mortar shells and 43,000 rockets.[8] Meanwhile, the Taliban were raising funds through Islamic networks in Pakistan and the Muslim world. Journalist Elizabeth Rubin described how "Karachi businessmen, Peshawar goldsmiths, Saudi oil men, Kuwaiti traders and jihadi sympathizers within the Pakistani military and intelligence ranks" helped raise money for the Taliban.[9] Hundreds of Arab and Central Asian fighters who were hiding out in FATA reenlisted with the Taliban.

Experienced Arab militants from al Qaeda set up training camps for the Pakistani and Kashmiri extremists who arrived from the cities to learn bomb making and other skills. Pakistan had withdrawn its troops from FATA to meet the threat from India, so al Qaeda and the Taliban were free to move around at will. Posters and pamphlets exhorting people to throw out U.S. forces began to appear regularly in Afghan villages. On September 5, 2002, Karzai was nearly assassinated in Kandahar, and a bomb exploded in Kabul city, killing fifteen people.

The Taliban began their military campaign in earnest in the spring of 2003 by launching guerrilla attacks in Helmand and Zabul provinces, where there was hardly any U.S. presence. The first major battle took place at the end of January 2003, when some eighty Taliban near Spin Baldak were surprised by a U.S. patrol. In the ensuing twelve-hour gun battle, in which B-1 bombers dropped twenty-one bombs, dozens of Taliban were killed. "It is without doubt the largest concentration of enemy forces that we've come across since Operation Anaconda," said a surprised U.S. officer.[10] In February there were rocket and mortar attacks on U.S. army fire bases in eastern Afghanistan and on the U.S. compound at Bagram. With the American invasion of Iraq imminent, the sudden escalation worried the Americans, and General Franks arrived in Islamabad to try to persuade the Pakistanis to do more to rein in the Taliban. The CIA arranged for Lt.-Gen. Ehsan ul-Haq, the head of the ISI, to meet with his Afghan counterpart, Engineer Arif, in Rome in mid-February to try to iron out their differences, but there was little progress and increasing distrust.

On the eve of the U.S. invasion of Iraq, bin Laden issued a taped message to his followers on what was expected of them in Iraq and Afghanistan. "We advise the importance of dragging the enemies' forces to a long, exhausting and continuous battle," he said. "The worst fear of the enemy is street and city fighting. . . . We stress the importance of martyrdom attacks against the enemy."[11] Hikmetyar also issued a message encouraging suicide bombings.[12] As the U.S. attack on Iraq began on March 20, U.S. forces launched an offensive in Kandahar province to keep the Taliban off-balance. The Taliban swiftly retaliated by killing four Westerners.

On March 27, a two-jeep convoy of the International Committee of the Red Cross with Ricardo Munguia, thirty-nine, a Salvadorian hydraulics engineer, on board was held up by Taliban gunmen in Uruzgan province. The Taliban commander checked with his superior, believed to be Mullah Dadullah, on a satellite phone. "We have three Afghans, one foreigner. Do you want four bodies or one?" he asked Dadullah, according to a survivor.[13] After receiving the reply, the Taliban executed Munguia and set fire to his body. Two days later two U.S. SOF soldiers inspecting a school near Gereskh, in Helmand province, were shot dead by Taliban gunmen mounted on motorbikes. On April 8 an Italian tourist was killed in Zabul province. The cold-blooded murder of the ICRC official had an enormous impact nationwide. Every Afghan knew that the ICRC had continued to provide medical care to Afghans during the Taliban regime when other Western NGOs had left. In killing an ICRC official the Taliban had delivered the uncompromising message that they had no compunctions about terrifying the local the population and Westerners.

Once again after the killings Zalmay Khalilzad traveled to Islamabad to try to encourage the Pakistanis to restrain the Taliban. "Success of Afghanistan's new stability is in America's interests and any effort that undermines that stability, that threatens it, is a challenge to America's interests," he warned. Pakistan rebuffed him and derided his comments as "totally ridiculous and baseless."[14] A few days later, on April 22, Karzai visited Islamabad to urge Musharraf to arrest Taliban leaders living in Quetta. He handed over a list of Taliban to Musharraf. When I met him, Karzai was very specific: "We have given the names of some top Taliban leaders for the Pakistani authorities to take action on," he told me that same day. "Pakistan has to address this issue of extremism—the actions of these extremists if they continue will have implications in Pakistan." The list included Taliban leader Mullah Omar and his senior commanders, Mullahs Dadullah, Usmani, and Barader—all believed to be living in Quetta. When I wrote up the story about the list, the military regime reacted strongly, denouncing Karzai and denying there was any such list. Washington declined to back Karzai publicly, even though the U.S. embassy in Kabul had helped draw up the list. The Americans were already deeply involved in Iraq and wanted no distractions such as a cat fight between the presidents of Afghanistan and Pakistan. Washington was unwilling to push the Pakistanis, and the Afghans were angry that the Americans had allowed Karzai's credibility to suffer. The Afghans did not consider it in the context of Iraq but saw it as yet another example of Washington being willing to push Islamabad on capturing al Qaeda leaders but unwilling to do the same regarding the Taliban.

With Iraq on his mind, Rumsfeld was tone-deaf to the regrouping of the Taliban and to rising Afghan-Pakistani tensions. Just a week after the debacle of the Islamabad meeting, he arrived in Kabul to declare "the end of combat operations" against the enemy, even as a new war in Iraq was under way. His own commanders offered a totally different assessment. General Franklin "Buster" Hagenbeck, the U.S. commander in Bagram, told me that al Qaeda and Hikmetyar were offering incentives of between five thousand and one hundred thousand dollars to kill or capture U.S. soldiers. "There are large numbers of Taliban coming back into southern

Afghanistan from the Quetta region," he said. "There are three groups of between twenty-five and one hundred Taliban operating in Helmand province facilitating the drugs trade."[15]

In June, Mullah Omar constituted a ten-man Taliban leadership council, creating four new committees dealing with military, political, cultural, and economic affairs.[16] The reorganization provided the impetus for more coordinated attacks on soft targets such as Afghan aid workers and officials. In the summer of 2003 one or two attacks by the Taliban occurred every other day. August proved to be the bloodiest month, with more than 220 Afghan soldiers and civilians killed. On a single day, August 13, 50 people were killed in multiple attacks in three provinces. The UN suspended travel for its officials in the south, and aid agencies fled Kandahar and Helmand. Whereas in April there were twenty two Western NGOs working in Kandahar, by August that number had dropped to just seven.

Zabul province—the main entry point for Taliban based in Balochistan—became a major battleground as the insurgents tried to secure a base area where they could assemble troops and supplies. Securing Zabul province was essential for pacifying the area along the Kabul-Kandahar highway, which passed through the province and was about to be rebuilt by the United States. In early September, U.S. forces launched Operation Mountain Viper to clear out some five hundred Taliban led by Dadullah. For the first time the Taliban stood and fought for nine days. Despite heavy air and artillery bombardment that killed more than one hundred of them, by the winter of 2003 the Taliban controlled 80 percent of Zabul and re mained popular; the pro-Taliban tribal and clerical network in the province had hardly been touched as a result of the war. Moreover, they were able to pour men, weapons, and money into the province from neighboring Balochistan.

The worsening security situation in the south delayed the political process set out at Bonn. The date for the Constitutional Loya Jirga, due to be held in October 2003, was pushed back to December, while the start of voter registration for the presidential elections was also delayed. Disarmament, Demobilization and Reintegration (DDR) was also delayed, with the warlords saying it was too dangerous to disarm their militias. Karzai's first attempt at offering the Taliban an amnesty to return home was derided by NA cabinet ministers, who said it would mean a surrender to the extremists.[17] Increasingly pessimistic reports by UNAMA failed to move the international community to greater action. Brahimi warned the UN

Security Council in December that "the international community must decide whether to increase its level of involvement in Afghanistan or risk failure."[18]

In those critical days in the autumn of 2003, a few thousand more U.S. troops on the ground, more money for reconstruction, and a speedier rebuilding of the Afghan army and police could easily have turned the tide against the Taliban and enhanced the support of the population for the government. It was a moment when even a little could have gone a long way, but Washington's preferred reaction to the Taliban resurgence was a blanket denial that anything was wrong. When Afghan leaders ruefully suggested that the war in Iraq might have diverted U.S. resources away from Afghanistan, Gen. Richard Myers, chairman of the Joint Chiefs of Staff, seemed to be one remove away from reality in his answer: "I don't think the war in Iraq has taken any of the resources away from the fight against international terrorism, especially al Qaeda. In fact I think the effort in Iraq has been very complementary. What we're doing here in Afghanistan and what we're doing in Iraq is in many cases the same thing."[19]

Tensions between Afghanistan and Pakistan intensified. Angry demonstrators broke into the Pakistan embassy in Kabul and ransacked it after reports of Pakistani troops intruding fifteen miles into Afghan territory along the border. Karzai quickly apologized and offered to pay for rebuilding the embassy, but Islamabad could now claim that it was being victimized by Kabul.[20] Meanwhile, India's successes in Afghanistan had stirred up a hornet's nest in Islamabad, which soon came to believe that India was "taking over Afghanistan." India had implemented a $500 million reconstruction strategy that was one of the best planned from any country. It was designed to win over every sector of Afghan society, give India a high profile with the Afghans, gain the maximum political advantage, and of course undercut Pakistani influence. Indian companies were directly favored and won major road-building contracts, including the contract for the road from Kandahar to the Pakistani border. When India reopened two consulates in Kandahar and Jalalabad that had been shuttered since 1979, Pakistan accused the Indians of using them to undermine Pakistan by funding Pashtun, Baloch, and Sindhi dissidents.

There was no doubt that the Indians were buoyant at their successes and aggressively trying to take advantage of Pakistan's lack of influence in Kabul. Excessive Indian arrogance provided the complaints that Musharraf used with Western leaders to explain away his reluctance to befriend Karzai. The ISI in turn generated enormous misinformation on India's role, such as briefing Musharraf that forty-two Indian agents were based at its consulate in Kandahar or telling Pakistani journalists that there were not two but six Indian consulates along the border. "If Pakistan is worried about the role of India, let me assure you, I have been very specific in telling the Indians that they cannot use Afghan soil for acts of aggression against another country," Karzai said.[21] Musharraf preferred to believe that Karzai was lying. Meanwhile, Pakistan evolved no coherent reconstruction strategy for Afghanistan. There were no high-profile Pakistani-funded projects that Afghans could see, although Pakistan's private sector traded massively with Kabul. Bilateral trade increased from $100.0 million in 2001 to $1.0 billion in 2004 and $1.6 billion in 2006.

In the summer of 2003, I made several trips through the border regions to see the extent of the Taliban resurgence through FATA, the NWFP, Balochistan, and southern Afghanistan. JUI leaders in both provinces made it clear that they openly supported the Taliban. Other religious figures openly supported al Qaeda. Javed Ibrahim Piracha, a member of parliament from Kohat, helped secure the release from jail of hundreds of al Qaeda and Taliban fighters who had been arrested by the Pakistan authorities. He hired lawyers to challenge their arrests in court and claimed to have returned 350 Arab fighters and their families to their countries of origin, paying all their travel expenses.[22] Piracha also set up the World Prisoners Relief Commission, which acted on behalf of extremists—all without any hindrance from the ISI or any questions about where his funds came from.

In Quetta the JUI virtually handed over Pashtunabad, a large sprawling suburb, to the Afghan Taliban. Thousands of long-haired, kohl-eyed, black-turbaned Taliban roamed the streets. They forced or bought out the local residents and soon owned every home, shop, tea stall, and hotel in Pashtunabad. New madrassas were built to house a new young generation, who banned television, the taking of photographs, and the flying of kites, replicating Kandahar in the early 1990s. Local people, including the police and journalists, were too frightened to enter the suburb.

In the villages along the eighty-mile drive from Quetta to Chaman were more than fifty JUI-run madrassas, part of a well-organized cycle in which young militants were brought in for several weeks of religious training before being sent to the front line by Taliban recruiters, who often arrived with ISI officers. In the summer months—the fighting season inside Afghanistan—the madrassas provided accommodation to a majority of Afghan Pashtuns, while in the winter, Pakistani Pashtun students returned. Every month all the heads of the JUI madrassas met in Quetta with a senior ISI officer to work out their rotation of young men and their expenses.

The Taliban leaders treated Quetta as their new capital. Taliban spokesmen pretending to be in Afghanistan briefed Pakistani journalists on local mobile phones and threatened them if their newspapers did not carry Taliban propaganda. Mullah Dadullah's extended family—some seventy people—lived openly in Kuchlak, a village just outside Quetta. In September 2003 he celebrated a family wedding in lavish style, inviting leading members of the Balochistan government, JUI leaders, and military officers. Quetta became the center for Taliban logistics. Vehicle dealers in Quetta told me that over the summer the Taliban had bought nine hundred motorbikes, which now became their favored mode of battle transport. For improved communication they imported hundreds of Thuraya satellite phones from the Arabian Gulf (Thurayas bought in Pakistan were monitored by the CIA) and long-range walkie-talkies. Arms and ammunition, bought locally or imported from the Gulf states, were trucked up to Quetta and dumped just inside the Afghan border.

In a dusty lane in Chaman, I met the family of a young Pakistani Pashtun who had been killed fighting with the Taliban. In early June a fierce battle had taken place near Spin Baldak in which forty Taliban and seven government troops were killed after Taliban were discovered to be lying in ambush along the main road. Twenty-two of the Taliban dead were Pakistani Pashtuns, including Nazar Mohammed, seventeen, and his cousin Fida Mohammed, fifteen, who had been recruited from a JUI madrassa in Chaman. When the Afghan authorities tried to hand over their bodies, Pakistani officials in Chaman refused to accept them—even though the boys' families were there to claim the corpses. The corpses lay on the border crossing for several days while hundreds of family members held demonstrations against the army. Qadir Malizai, the father of Nazar, told me that a military officer had come to his home and told him not to hold remembrance prayers for his son or mourn publicly and not to speak to the media. He was never able to bury his son and he blamed the military for allowing the Taliban to brainwash the boy.

I had made the same journey through Balochistan and southern Afghanistan in the winter of 1994, when the Taliban had first arrived in Kandahar. What I now witnessed was history repeating itself in a worse way than before. In Kandahar, Ahmed Wali Karzai, the brother of President Karzai, echoed my worst fears: "The Taliban are gathering in the same places from where they started; it's like the rerun of an old movie," he said sadly.[23] Governor Yousuf Pashtun listed the Taliban training camps in Balochistan: in Dalbadin, Chagai, Qila Saifullah, Kuchlak, Loralai, and two camps just a few miles from Quetta. "Do the Americans want to destabilize Afghanistan at the cost of keeping quiet about Pakistan's support to the Taliban?" he asked. Afghans in Kandahar believed that the Bush administration's silence on the role of the ISI was a larger conspiracy in which the United States would soon hand over Afghanistan's Pashtun belt to the Pakistanis. Such conspiracy theories were far-fetched, but they had a lot of traction among Afghans.

What struck me was how little the Taliban had learned from their previous mistakes. Surely the second time around the Taliban would offer a more politicized agenda, either by exploiting Pashtun nationalism or offering a program to attract the people. Instead they had nothing new on offer—no program, no vision, and no political agenda. What they did offer was to drive out the foreigners, but it took several more years of abject failure by the United States and the Afghan government to reconstruct the country before that appeal took hold. Moreover, commanders such as Dadullah followed al Qaeda's terror tactics and burned down schools and clinics, killing and mutilating aid workers. Never before had the Taliban terrorized their fellow Pashtuns in such a way.

In the summer of 2003 there was still no support for the Taliban among Afghan farmers and townspeople. The Pashtun tribes had reestablished their political identity in two Loya Jirgas, interethnic harmony had improved, Karzai was standing up to the non-Pashtun NA warlords, and a window of opportunity remained to rebuild the country. Yet systematically, as the insurgency took hold, and with insufficient funds for reconstruction and no international troops to provide security, the southern provinces were ignored.

After I published a cover story about the Taliban revival being directed from Pakistan, the military regime was furious and accused me of lying.[24] Two weeks later the government flew Islamabad-based Western ambassadors to Chaman, where army bulldozers were throwing up a huge sand ramp in the desert along the Afghan border to demonstrate that it was being sealed off. None of the ambassadors bought this hopeless and futile gesture.

With presidential elections due in the United States and Afghanistan by the end of 2004, Rumsfeld and his generals insisted there was no insurgency. Yet behind-the-scenes policy changes were being made and there was a massive stepped-up effort to capture bin Laden. In the summer of 2004, Lt.-Gen. David Barno, the new head of U.S. forces in Afghanistan, introduced new counterinsurgency tactics involving small groups of U.S. soldiers living in villages to win hearts and minds and collect better intelligence. Task Force 121, the top-secret military unit that had caught Saddam Hussein, was moved to Afghanistan. The Pentagon redeployed from Iraq its top-secret reconnaissance aircraft, the E-8 Joint STARS (Surveillance Target Attack Radar System), which could track targets on the ground in any type of weather, and the RC-135 Rivet Joint, a long-range, high-altitude reconnaissance aircraft. U2 spyplanes and satellites were already involved in the hunt. For two years now, from the spring of 2002 until the summer of 2004, the United States had ignored Afghanistan, depriving U.S. forces of the technical surveillance needed to catch bin Laden because everything had been shifted to Iraq. Those two years represented a huge gap in U.S. intelligence gathering and efforts to win the trust of the tribesmen along the border.

Al Qaeda put itself back on the world's agenda in the March 11, 2004, bombings at a railway station in Madrid that killed 192 people and wounded more than 1,600, the most devastating terrorist attack in Europe since World War II. Al Qaeda Web sites had urged Spain to withdraw its troops from Iraq and restore "al-Andalus" (southern Spain) to Muslim control. In the aftermath of the bombing, Spain's Socialist Party won an unexpected victory at the polls. It was a chilling moment because suddenly al Qaeda seemed to have the ability to change governments and dictate political goals in Europe.[25]

With the war in Iraq and terrorist attacks, Afghanistan remained off the international radar. Afghanistan's southern provinces were still unmapped and off the intelligence-gathering beat for U.S. forces, even though the Taliban had accelerated their attacks there. Nobody was looking for Mullah Omar. In June the Taliban assassinated two dozen Afghan officials and killed fourteen foreigners, including French doctors and Chinese construction workers. Twice the number of U.S. troops were killed in Afghanistan in the first six months of 2004 than had been killed throughout

2003.[26] Villagers reported how the Taliban were sleeping in mosques during the day and coming out at night to persuade, bribe, or terrorize farmers into helping them kill U.S. troops. Not only Zabul but also more than 50 percent of four southern provinces were deemed to be in Taliban hands.

After four U.S. SOF troops were killed in Zabul on May 29—the single biggest loss for U.S. forces since 9/11—American soldiers fought a large force of five hundred to eight hundred Taliban led by Mullah Dadullah. Once again the Taliban stood and fought, and then made good their escape back to Pakistan. The extent of the Taliban's reorganization was evident with the capture in July of a minor Taliban commander, Mullah Sakhi Dad Mujahid. He had with him a satellite phone, telephone numbers including that of Mullah Omar, and a notebook of expenses showing that he had distributed $1.8 million in June for salaries and the purchase of supplies. An attempt to call Omar failed, but the number was for a Pakistani mobile phone.[27]

As the Afghan elections approached, the UN tried to persuade the Pakistanis to restrain the Taliban. In April the French diplomat Jean Arnault, who had replaced Brahimi as head of UNAMA, shared with Pakistani officials a dossier of hundreds of Taliban commanders who were regularly crossing into Pakistan, but Islamabad denied everything. On a visit to Washington in mid-June, Karzai again complained to Bush about Musharraf's refusal to clamp down on the Taliban. However, the Americans were more concerned with the crisis generated by Dr. A. Q. Khan involving the sale of nuclear technology to several countries. The administration decided it could not pressure Islamabad on the Taliban issue while it was trying to extract information about Khan. There was slow realization in Washington of the double game Musharraf was playing with the Americans. Paul Wolfowitz told me, "One of the ways they [Pakistan] slice it is to cooperate regarding al Qaeda. . . . Some of them say that we have to hedge our bets with the Taliban because we don't know about the future of Afghanistan. We have a government [Pakistan] which can't deliver everything we would like to see and . . . we don't have the ability to simply say, If you don't do it, we'll cut off our whole relationship with you and let you go under."[28]

The United States remained complacent about the Taliban as long as Pakistan continued to appear to chase al Qaeda. "The Taliban were always considered a lower priority by the United States," said a senior CIA official.

"They had been defeated and only needed cleaning up, which was considered to be Pakistan's job. Al Qaeda was the main priority for the U.S."[29] The CIA said that 70 percent of the al Qaeda leadership had been captured or killed since 9/11, while ignoring the fact that al Qaeda replaced every captured individual with someone new. "To take the two-thirds number as a yardstick is a fantasy—to say that they have only one third of their leadership left is a misunderstanding," explained Michael Scheuer, former head of the CIA's Bin Laden Unit. Islamabad invariably declared every captured al Qaeda leader as the "number three" man in the movement, confusing the public even further. Over the years dozens of "number three" figures were captured or killed.[30]

In the midst of the Taliban summer offensive, the Afghan government also had to contend with fighting between warlords in the west and the north. Yet in August 2004 Wolfowitz asked Congress to authorize $500 million "for training and equipping local security forces—not just armies—to counter terrorism and insurgencies."[31] The Pentagon wanted to hire warlords in Yemen, Pakistan, and Somalia to combat al Qaeda because it considered that its warlord strategy had worked so well in Afghanistan. It was an insult to the Afghans who had suffered so much under the warlords. In 2006, Somali warlords supported by the CIA were defeated and driven out of Mogadishu by radical Islamists who then established a Taliban-like regime. It took another CIA-backed invasion—this time by Ethiopian troops—to dislodge the Islamists.

Afghanistan's first presidential elections were fast approaching. There was an intense debate in Kabul among the international community and the Afghan government about whether to hold the presidential and parliamentary elections together, as had been promised at Bonn, or separately. The Americans desperately wanted presidential elections to take place before the U.S. elections in November 2004 and were happy to see parliamentary elections delayed. European governments were divided, although several wanted to hold the elections together, to keep the momentum of the Bonn process going. Almost all NGOs and experts advised delaying both elections until the security situation improved, reforms were implemented, and DDR completed, so that Afghans could see tangible benefits. A report called "The Great Gamble," by a Western-Afghan think tank in Kabul, warned that premature elections "could do more to promote instability and conflict rather than lasting peace." One third of the country was unsafe for holding elections, and warlords posed a threat to free voting.[32]

The cost of the elections would be better spent on improving state capacity, while holding them early would divert the international community's attention from reconstruction.

The diametrically opposed intellectual perspective on the value of elections was the European and UN approach, which asserted that a post-conflict country should be readied for elections slowly. The Americans wanted elections in a hurry, so they could show that the job had been done and move out. "Elections should come at the end of the stabilization process and not at the beginning like the Americans want them," said Lakhdar Brahimi.[33] Karzai wanted both elections on time. "I do not want to be like Rabbani and hang on to power without legitimacy," he told me. In 1992, Birhanuddin Rabbani had hung on to his presidency for four years, when the presidency was supposed to rotate among the Mujahedin leaders every six months.[34] However, Karzai's office was slow and disorganized in issuing the decrees needed to hold both elections. UNAMA drew up an electoral law to allow for the existence of political parties, but it took eight months for Karzai to sign the decree. The government also failed to resolve disputed district and provincial boundaries in time. Despite all the Western funds spent on improving the president's office, Karzai was becoming more disorganized and unfocused.

Afghan leaders were deeply divided. Former "jihadi" leaders such as Birhanuddin Rabbani, Abdul Rasul Sayyaf, Fahim, and other warlords wanted both elections at the same time and were willing to support Karzai as the presidential candidate as long as they were returned to power in parliament and DDR was not forced upon them. In June, under pressure from Khalilzad, the jihadis agreed to support Karzai's candidacy without conditions.[35] When reports of the agreement became public, many Afghans were furious because once again the warlords were dictating terms. "The jihadis will never allow reconstruction to take place or the collection of weapons—we will keep on having instability and anarchy," said Masuda Jalal, the only woman candidate in the presidential elections.[36] Meanwhile, the "reformers" in the cabinet, led by Ashraf Ghani, urged Karzai to hold the presidential elections first so that he could carry out reforms quickly and sideline the warlords. The reformers looked to the international community for support.

Much depended on Karzai's attitude. In the two Loya Jirgas he had appeased the warlords—who had then held back reform. "In the end—some would argue—the President has served the consolidation of jihadi hegemony rather than reform," said a UNAMA discussion paper on the election issue.[37] The reformers feared that simultaneous parliamentary elections would result in a warlord-dominated parliament. There was also a deep ethnic divide. The Pashtun tribal leaders wanted a strong Pashtun president elected quickly. The non-Pashtuns wanted a strong parliament that could protect them against any return to Pashtun hegemony.

The burden of organizing the elections fell on UNAMA. In a country that had not held a census since 1979, there were only "guesstimates" as to the total population or number of voters. However, UNAMA estimated that it needed to register some 10.5 million voters over the age of eighteen out of a total population of 27.0 million. Registration would involve issuing photo identity cards to all men and women voters. The UN made an urgent appeal for the $78 million required for registration and $100 million for the elections, but the money was slow to come in.

UN-trained teams of Afghans prepared to start registration in eight cities on December 1, 2003. Members of the public responded enthusiastically and were pleased to receive the first personal document issued to them by the state in twenty-five years. The laminated plastic ID card had a Polaroid shot of the voter and personal information that was fed into a massive database by three hundred data-entry clerks based in Kabul. The cards became the talk of the entire country, and many people had multiple cards made. At registration stations there was palpable excitement as crowds of relatives arrived to witness the registration of a single adult. Yet the procedure was slow, and at the end of January 2004 UN adviser Reginald Austin said he was "operating at only 18 percent capacity registering only 50,000 people compared to the 500,000 we should have done."[38] Registration in the south was especially poor due to the lack of security, with only one registration station open in Kandahar. Another 4,200 registration stations would open in small towns in May.

Every week Afghans, foreign diplomats, and journalists watched the figures issued by Reginald Austin's office slowly climb upward. By the end of March, when a conference in Berlin on aid for Afghanistan took place, 1.57 million people had been registered. However, the numbers registering in the Pashtun belt were still far lower, raising fears that the Pashtuns would cry foul if insufficient numbers did not register. Meanwhile, only 28 percent of those registered were women. Full female participation was essential to showcase progress in Afghanistan. The Taliban attacked six voter registration teams and issued death threats to others. Yet by July half the voters, or around 5.6 million, had registered, 38 percent of them women, and Pashtuns were registering in increasing numbers. The Afghans were demonstrating that despite the risks, they wanted the chance to vote.

Meanwhile, Fahim and his warlord allies continued to refuse to carry out DDR. In July, with the elections just eight weeks away, only 30 percent of the heavy weapons had been collected and just 12 percent of soldiers had been decommissioned. The election commission had decided that presidential elections would be held on October 9, and parliamentary elections would follow later in 2005. The reformers in the cabinet insisted that now was the moment for Karzai to dump Fahim as his vice presidential running mate. Those supporting the move included fellow Panjsheris, including the two brothers of Ahmad Shah Masud—Ahmad Wali Masud and Ahmad Zia Masud—who told Karzai, "You are tired of your warlords and we are tired with our warlords—let's get together and get rid of them."

Karzai agonized for weeks about whether to dump Fahim. I watched the process from close up, as we would meet regularly at the end of his busy day and walk in his small garden in the palace. European ambassadors told Karzai their governments supported the move, but the Americans continued to procrastinate. European heads of state got involved, telephoning Karzai and urging him to fire Fahim. Lakhdar Brahimi, now at the UN in New York, invited the U.S. ambassador Khalilzad to Cairo along with Jean Arnault. "Now is the time," Brahimi told them. "It's all about timing. Ismael Khan was taken out at the right time; now it's Fahim's time." Khalilzad finally accepted the verdict and threw his weight behind getting rid of Fahim. In two long telephone conversations, Brahimi and Tony Blair persuaded Karzai. On July 26, the last date for presidential nominations, Kabul was on a knife-edge. ISAF troops patrolled the near-empty streets and Western diplomats went into lockdown in their embassies, fearing unrest. Nobody knew how Fahim would react.

In the late afternoon, Karzai declared that his vice presidential running mates would be Ahmad Zia Masud and Karim Khalili. Kabulis erupted with joy as Fahim went into a sulk, stunned by the reversal. It was a defining moment, signaling hope for the end of open warlordism. Ahmad Zia Masud was an unassuming figure who had been a businessman in India and helped supply his brother, Ahmad Shah Masud, with weapons from abroad. He was married to Rabbani's daughter, so his nomination precluded any opposition from the jihadis. Khalili, from the minority Shia

Hazara ethnic group, was chosen to win the support of other Afghan minorities. With Fahim gone, the Northern Alliance disintegrated. They could not agree on a common candidate to oppose Karzai in the presidential elections, and instead each ethnic group put up its own candidate.

The most serious contender was Younus Qanuni, who had broad support among Tajiks and other non-Pashtuns. Ultimately twenty-three candidates filed nomination papers, including Masuda Jalal. When voter registration finally closed on August 15, 10.3 million people had registered, 41 percent of them women. The candidates had just four weeks to campaign. Karzai did little campaigning owing to security threats. On his first trip to Gardez, on September 16, rockets were fired at the helicopter landing pad moments before he was due to arrive, and he returned to Kabul.

Karzai spelled out his agenda: "To move Afghanistan from two hundred dollars per capita to seven hundred dollars in the next seven to ten years; to make Afghanistan a trade and business land bridge between Central and South Asia and build on good relations with our neighbors; to carry out fundamental institutional reforms and to especially institutionalize democracy; to create respect for the rule of law, build an army and police force, and create a performance-orientated administration."[39]

However, Karzai's supporters were dismayed at his refusal to set up a political party. Many Afghans argued that without one he could not promote democracy and parliamentary politics, which depended on parties, not tribal alliances. While the Pashtuns would clearly vote for him, his support among the non-Pashtuns would remain scattered and disunited. Karzai insisted that political parties reminded Afghans of the past, when the Communist and Mujahedin parties wreaked havoc in the country. I constantly berated Karzai for his failure to understand the usefulness of political parties and that a parliament without parties was not democracy, and was ultimately dangerous—but he remained adamant. It was his biggest mistake, and ultimately he would suffer because of his failure to build a political organization.

U.S. officials predicted that the Taliban would mount large attacks to disrupt the elections. Khalilzad said he feared a "Tet-like offensive," referring to the watershed offensive of the Vietcong during the Vietnam War. Security services arrested one hundred militants in Kabul and found containers full of explosives, as a massive security ring was thrown around the country.[40] Some 19,000 U.S.-led Coalition troops, 9,000 NATO-ISAF forces, 14,000 ANA troops, 50,000 police and local militia hired by Pashtun elders would guard 22,000 polling stations where 115,000 Afghan election officials would be deployed.[41]

Kept secret until now, a major diplomatic incident erupted when ISI officers attempted to sow panic in the south just before the elections. On August 9, ISI officials in Kandahar told the UNAMA office that the Taliban were about to launch a major offensive and the ISI was ready to evacuate UN staff to Quetta. The ISI officers vividly described how the Taliban planned to enter Kandahar "clean-shaven and without weapons, which could be provided from the numerous weapons caches inside Afghanistan." UNAMA reported back to Kabul and New York that there was no sign of a Taliban offensive and that the ISI had wanted "to create panic and lead the UN to leave Afghanistan in order to disgrace the elections." Munir Akram, Pakistan's ambassador to the UN, wrote to Kofi Annan harshly criticizing UNAMA.[42] Major tensions developed between Pakistan and the UN.

In fact, the ISI was furious because it had retrieved copies of reports from Western embassies in Kabul describing how senior Pakistani officers were meeting with Taliban leaders in the army's Command and Staff College in Quetta and that Taliban training camps were being emptied of fighters. On August 18, Kofi Annan wrote to Musharraf insisting that Pakistan do more to secure the elections. "I would be grateful for future measures you could take during the coming weeks to assist the Afghan authorities and the international community in protecting the presidential election from extremist groups bent on disrupting it," Annan wrote.[43]

Khalilzad knew that the key to stopping Taliban infiltration was to put the heat on Musharraf directly. He enlisted President Bush to do so. On September 22, on the sidelines of the UN General Assembly in New York, Bush met with Musharraf and Karzai in the first three-way meeting the leaders had held since 9/11. Senior U.S. officials told me that Bush was uncharacteristically blunt with Musharraf about the presence of Taliban leaders in Pakistan. "Where are Mullah Omar, Mullah Usmani and Gulbuddin Hikmetyar?" Bush asked a flustered Musharraf. "It was the first time that Bush totally focused on the Taliban threat rather than al Qaeda with the Pakistanis," a senior U.S. diplomat admitted.[44] Bush told Musharraf that he needed a successful election in Afghanistan, and Musharraf complied. For the first time Pakistan deployed troops on the Balochistan border to prevent Taliban infiltration and closed all border-crossing points.[45]

The UN and ISAF forces initiated a massive logistics campaign using helicopters and cargo planes and camels and donkeys to carry the polling materials and voting boxes to each location. Five thousand satellite phones were distributed to remote polling stations. Nobody could predict what would happen on the day, whether Afghans would turn out to vote despite the Taliban's threats and warlords' pressure. The evening before the elections, Kabulis rushed home early and the streets were eerily deserted except for armored cars and soldiers patrolling them. There was a sense of expectation but also enormous foreboding.

Even before dawn broke on October 9, it was clear what would happen as tens of thousands of Afghans began to line up at polling stations around the country. Along with Lyse Doucet, the BBC anchor, we rushed from polling station to polling station in Kabul and nearby villages and were so amazed at the huge turnout, the orderly queues, the patience of the women holding little children, the good humor and joking as people waited, the stories they told of their loss and hardship, that we burst into tears. After twenty-five years of covering the bloodshed and chaos of Afghanistan's wars, it was the most moving and memorable day of my life. I felt as if a vast black blanket of despair that had covered the country and the people had suddenly been lifted and sunlight was pouring through. For most Afghans it was the first time they had ever seen a ballot box, and polling was extended by two hours in the evening to allow everyone to experience voting.[46]

The public enthusiasm was palpable. In north Kabul, ninety-three-year-old Abdul Hakim arrived at a polling station on crutches. "I have lived nearly a century but I have never voted for my leader," he told me with tears in his eyes. Women turned out in huge numbers even in the Pashtun south, defying all expectations. Stunned UN monitors sent back messages of how thousands of Pashtun women came to vote in the afternoon after their men had voted in the morning. A total of thirty-eight people were killed on the day, including twenty-five Taliban who had attacked a U.S. patrol in Uruzgan province. There were no major Taliban attacks on polling stations.

The polling was far from perfect. Officials were supposed to mark every voter's finger with indelible ink to prevent their voting twice, but in some places the ink washed off easily and people voted several times. Afghans with more than one identity card also voted several times at different polling stations. At midday, opposition candidates jumped on the issue and called for a boycott of the election and its result. In the afternoon, Western ambassadors led by Khalilzad and Arnault, with journalists trailing behind them, met with each opposition leader to calm him down. The issue rankled while the count got under way over the next few weeks, but a UN-led panel of experts there to investigate all allegations of fraud was met with approval by the opposition.

It took nearly a month to bring in all the ballot boxes and count the votes. On November 3, Karzai was declared the winner with 55.4 percent of the vote, thirty-nine points ahead of his nearest rival, Younus Qanuni, with 16.3 percent of the vote. Mohammed Mohaqiq, the Hazara leader, won 11.7 percent, and General Dostum 10.0 percent. Four weeks later in the United States there was much greater electoral controversy when President Bush was reelected by a small margin amid allegations of fraud.

On December 7, with Vice President Dick Cheney in attendance, Karzai took oath as Afghanistan's first legitimate leader for nearly three decades. Many grizzled old Afghan leaders broke down in tears. Three weeks later Karzai appointed a new cabinet, which pushed out the warlords and brought in many technocrats. General Fahim's replacement as defense minister was the American-trained Pashtun Gen. Rahim Wardak. The only warlord accommodated in the cabinet was Ismael Khan. In the most controversial move, Finance Minister Ashraf Ghani, a favorite of Western donors but disliked by fellow Afghans, was dropped. Two women were appointed, including Masuda Jalal. Five of the "power" ministries went to English-speaking Pashtuns with U.S. connections, signaling the end of NA domination. Of the Panjsheri Tajiks, only Abdullah Abdullah remained, as foreign minister.[47] All the "security" ministries were in the hands of the reformist camp.

Nine of the twenty-seven new ministers held doctorates, but those with dual nationality—several ministers held U.S. citizenship—had to give up their foreign passports to comply with the constitution. Karzai now had a year before parliamentary elections to implement a reform agenda and end the Taliban resurgence. His success or failure to do so would determine the future stability of Afghanistan and the entire region.

PART FOUR

DESCENT INTO CHAOS

✦ ✦ ✦

CHAPTER THIRTEEN

Al Qaeda's Bolt-Hole

Pakistan's Tribal Areas

When Osama bin Laden escaped into FATA in December 2001, the place was so inviting that over the next few years he never strayed far. The seven tribal agencies that make up the Federally Administered Tribal Areas adjoining the North-West Frontier Province became the new base area for al Qaeda. It was from there that the bomb plots in London, Madrid, Bali, Islamabad, and later Germany and Denmark were planned. While Mullah Omar's command structure in Quetta deliberately did not include Arabs or any non-Afghans, so they would not become a focus for U.S. forces chasing only al Qaeda, FATA became a multilayered terrorist cake. At its base were Pakistani Pashtun tribesmen, soon to become Taliban in their own right, who provided the hideouts and logistical support. Above them were the Afghan Taliban who settled there after 9/11, followed by militants from Central Asia, Chechnya, Africa, China, and Kashmir, and topped by Arabs who forged a protective ring around bin Laden. FATA became the world's "terrorism central."

FATA's seven tribal agencies—Khyber, Kurram, Orakzai, Mohmand, Bajaur, and North and South Waziristan—are populated by just over three million tribesmen, adding to the twenty-eight million Pashtuns who live in Pakistan and the fifteen million in Afghanistan. The tribes on both sides of the border intermarry, trade, feud, and celebrate with one another. They all adhere to *Pashtunwali,* the tribal code of honor and behavior, which includes *melmastia,* or hospitality, *nanawati,* the notion that hospitality can never be denied to a fugitive, and *badal,* the right of revenge. Pashtun honor is maintained by constant feuding revolving around *zar* (gold), *zan* (women), and *zamin* (land).[1]

What makes the FATA tribes more rigid and conservative is that they live under a uniquely oppressive administrative system inherited from the British Raj and still maintained by Pakistan. FATA is designated a federal area directly ruled by the Pakistani president, whose agent is the governor of the North-West Frontier Province, who in turn appoints senior bureaucrats, termed "political agents," to each agency. These political agents adhere to a rule book called the "Frontier Crimes Regulation" (FCR), part of a century-old legal system introduced by a British act of Parliament in 1901. In 1947 the Indian Independence Act abrogated any special treaties the British had signed with tribesmen, but the tribal elders of FATA agreed to continue the FCR in return for autonomy and the removal of all Pakistani troops from their territories.

In the early years of Pakistan, the FCR had an even broader sweep, governing much of the settled areas of the NWFP until 1963, and Balochistan until 1977. Until 1996, when the government of Benazir Bhutto granted universal adult suffrage, FATA tribal elders "selected" their own representatives to parliament with the advice of their political agents. Even after 1996, FATA remained a backwater, as under the FCR, Pakistani political parties were banned from operating in the area, thereby giving the mullahs and religious parties a monopoly of influence under the guise of religion. Development, literacy, and health facilities in FATA therefore remained at a minimum.

The FCR gave no constitutional, civic, or political rights to the FATA tribesmen, and they could not claim the protection of the Pakistani courts. FATA was off-limits to journalists, NGOs, human rights organizations, and political parties. The political agents traditionally had sweeping punitive powers, such as imposing collective punishments on an entire tribe, levying fines, and demolishing the homes of wrongdoers. Civil and criminal cases were judged by a Jirga of handpicked elders whom the political agent paid off from a secret government slush fund. The political agent was one of the most powerful civil servants in the world—a direct hangover from the colonial era.

FATA's anachronistic status was sustained by the Pakistan army, which could claim that the territory was not accountable to international law. Thus FATA provided the space and leverage to maintain the army's influence among the Pashtun tribes in neighboring Afghanistan. FATA acted as a buffer against predatory Afghan influence while allowing the military to interfere freely in Afghanistan. This became critical in the 1980s when the CIA-ISI arms pipeline to the Afghan Mujahedin went through FATA while the Pakistani government denied all knowledge of it. In the 1990s, when Islamabad came under severe U.S. and Indian pressure to shut down militant training camps in Pakistani Kashmir, the ISI simply moved the camps to FATA and later to Taliban-controlled Afghanistan. Subsequently, FATA became a conduit for ISI's support for the Taliban regime. Successive Afghan governments, especially the communist regime in Kabul, played similar games, using money and weapons as bribes to persuade FATA tribesmen to create problems for Pakistan.

This unstable cross-border competition was enhanced by the fact that Afghanistan and Pakistan do not have a recognized frontier between them. In 1879, at the end of the second Afghan war, the Afghan monarch Amir Yaqub Khan was forced to sign the Treaty of Gandamak, in which he ceded parts of western Balochistan, Quetta, and much of FATA to Britain. In 1893 Sir Mortimer Durand drew up Afghanistan's present borders in order to create a stable buffer between tsarist Russia and British India. The Durand Line defined the modern Afghan state but definitively divided the Pashtun tribes. After the Partition of India, a Loya Jirga in Kabul refused to affirm the Durand Line, declaring that as Pakistan was a new state, Afghanistan's borders had to be redefined. Afghanistan refused to recognize Pakistan's accession to the United Nations and laid claim over FATA. In the 1960s and 1970s, diehard Afghan Pashtun nationalists, including Afghan president Mohammed Daud, claimed that Afghanistan's borders extended up to the Indus River, well south of Peshawar—a claim that, if acknowledged, would have cut Pakistan in half.

After 9/11, many Pakistanis maintained that if President Karzai only recognized the Durand Line, he would appease Islamabad sufficiently to halt the Pakistani military's support to the Taliban. Yet the military never insisted that the Taliban regime recognize the Durand Line and refrained from insisting that Afghanistan sign the Durand Line agreement, despite several opportunities to do so. Pakistan could have extracted recognition of the Line as part of the 1988 agreement that ended the Soviet occupation of Afghanistan, but it never raised the issue, despite considerable prodding by the UN. Neither the Afghan Mujahedin government in 1992 nor the subsequent Taliban regime—which depended on Islamabad's support— was asked to recognize the Line.

Some senior Pakistani officials, including Sahibzada Yakub Khan, who was foreign minister in the 1980s, admit that the military deliberately never asked for Afghan recognition of the Line. At the time, President Zia ul-Haq passionately worked toward creating a pro-Pakistan Islamic government in Kabul, to be followed by the Islamization of Central Asia. In military parlance, this was Pakistan's strategy to secure "strategic depth" in relation to India. Zia's vision of a Pakistani-influenced region extending into Central Asia depended on an undefined border with Afghanistan, so that the army could justify any future interference in that country and beyond. A defined border would have entailed recognizing international law and obligations and the sovereignty of Afghanistan. As long as there was no recognized border, there was also no international law to break if Pakistani forces were to support surrogate Afghan regimes such as the Taliban.

After 9/11, FATA became the escape hatch for al Qaeda and the Taliban, as we see in chapter 6. "Safe passage was provided to al Qaeda by not deploying Pakistani forces on the border in South and North Waziristan, although troops were deployed in Khyber and Kurram agencies," says Afrasiab Khattak, a veteran Pashtun nationalist politician.[2] "Thousands of al Qaeda and Taliban were allowed to settle in Waziristan, create bases, and restart military operations." Jalaluddin Haqqani, the former Taliban minister, became the key organizer by hiring FATA tribesmen to provide sanctuary or safe passage out of the region. Young Wazir and Mahsud tribesmen who had guided al Qaeda out of Tora Bora became rich as they provided logistical services for a price. Within a few years these guides had become commanders of the armed groups that emerged as the "Pakistani Taliban."

Al Qaeda's first sanctuary was the South Waziristan agency. With its high mountains, steep slopes, deep ravines littered with broken rock and shale, and its thick forests, it was an ideal hideout. Many of its valleys were virtually inaccessible, except along steep winding paths that required the agility of mountain climbers, and were easy to defend. In June 2002, U.S. military officers in Bagram told me there were up to 3,500 foreign militants hiding out in South Waziristan, and they could not understand why the ISI was turning a blind eye to them. At the time, Musharraf was deflecting U.S. pressure to send in troops on account of Pakistan's standoff with India.

Angur Adda, in South Waziristan, became the first headquarters of al Qaeda's reorganization. From here in 2002, fighters regularly attacked U.S.

firebases at Shikin and Lawara, just inside Afghanistan, and then retreated into Waziristan.[3] U.S. military officers complained that paramilitary soldiers from the Frontier Corps (FC) were helping al Qaeda fighters cross the border or were providing covering fire to distract U.S. forces. At times al Qaeda fighters on Pakistani soil brazenly launched rockets on U.S. positions. American officers on the ground were at first confused, then frustrated, and finally very angry, and they pressured the U.S. commander, Lt.-Gen. Dan McNeill, to allow them to chase al Qaeda fighters into South Waziristan. McNeill did not have permission from the Pentagon to do so, but finally even his patience ran out. In January 2003, he threatened to cross the border into Pakistan. "U.S. forces acknowledge the internationally recognized boundaries of Afghanistan, but may pursue attackers who attempted to escape into Pakistan to evade capture or retaliation," read a U.S. Army statement.[4] There was now mounting U.S. pressure on Musharraf to act or face unilateral attacks inside FATA.

The Pakistani army's corps commander in Peshawar, Lt.-Gen. Ali Jan Orakzai, a close friend of Musharraf, was in charge of Pakistan's complex policy of minimally satisfying American demands, not interfering with the resettlement of the militants in Waziristan, all the while assuring the JUI-led provincial government in Peshawar that the army would not stop their pro-Taliban policies. Pakistan's army conducted a massive public information campaign, denying there were any terrorist camps in FATA—even though the Pakistani media were reporting their presence. Quite separately, the ISI maintained a high-profile presence in FATA. Wazirs who fled the agency reported how ISI officers in civilian clothes met frequently with Taliban leaders such as Jalaluddin Haqqani, Tahir Yuldashev, the leader of the Islamic Movement of Uzbekistan (IMU), and the new crop of young local commanders. Confident of their safety, the Taliban and al Qaeda began to run their own fiefdom in South Waziristan, killing tribal elders considered to be spying on them for the Afghans or the Americans and forcing others to flee with their families.[5]

Pashtun bureaucrats in Islamabad and Peshawar told me of the ISI's internal debates, whose subjects included some officers' intentions to create a broad "Talibanized belt" in FATA that would keep the pressure on Karzai to bend to Pakistani wishes, keep U.S. forces under threat while maintaining their dependence on Pakistani goodwill, and create a buffer zone between Afghan and Pakistani Pashtuns. According to this view, a Talibanized Pashtun population along the border would pose a threat to

Karzai and the Americans but no threat to Pakistan, which would be in control of them. Whether such a strategy was ever formally adopted is doubtful, but Pakistan's policies certainly created the same effect. For two long years, from January 2002 until the spring of 2004, the military did nothing to stop the extremists from consolidating their bases in South Waziristan. Yet the idea that such bases would not affect Pakistan was overturned when it became clear to the ISI that the twin assassination attempts on Musharraf in 2003 had been planned from South Waziristan.

In the spring of 2003 severe clashes broke out between Afghan and Pakistani border guards on the Durand Line. As tensions between Kabul and Islamabad escalated, Al Jazeera released a videotape on the second anniversary of the 9/11 attacks showing bin Laden and Ayman al-Zawahiri strolling in a landscape very similar to that of South Waziristan. The image of the world's most wanted men roaming freely deeply embarrassed Washington, which again pressured Pakistan to move troops into South Waziristan. On the eve of a visit to Islamabad by Richard Armitage in early October, Pakistani forces attacked an extremist camp in South Waziristan, killing eight fighters.[6] Buying time by carrying out an attack just before the visit of a senior U.S. official became a pattern for Islamabad.

Ayman al-Zawahiri's fatwa calling for the death of Musharraf and the attacks on his life that followed in December 2003 finally convinced the Pakistani military of the need for action. The military determined that the suicide attackers had been trained in a joint Jaish-e-Mohammed–al Qaeda training camp. Two days before a visit by Colin Powell to Islamabad in mid-March 2004, Musharraf told tribesmen in Peshawar, "We have confirmed that 500 to 600 foreign suspects have been sheltered in South Waziristan."[7] It was his first admission that there was a problem. Powell gave Musharraf an ultimatum: either the Pakistan army would attack the al Qaeda camps in South Waziristan, or the U.S. Army would do it for them.

In the early hours of March 16, 2004, hundreds of Pakistani Frontier Corps forces surrounded a mud-walled compound in Kalosha village, a few miles west of Wana, looking for al Qaeda militants. Instead, the soldiers found they had walked into a trap, as IMU and al Qaeda fighters opened fire upon them. Tahir Yuldashev escaped the army cordon as the Uzbeks killed many soldiers and took one dozen hostage. The FC fled in disarray, while others hid in mosques and people's houses. Eight thousand regular troops were rushed in, and for the next two weeks the Pakistan army used helicopter gunships, fighter bombers, and heavy artillery to subdue the rebels. More than fifty thousand people from Wana and surrounding villages fled after the fighting destroyed their homes and shops.

The attack was a massive strategic blunder by Orakzai. He had committed the underarmed and poorly trained FC, with no air support and little intelligence, to a battle that he had avoided fighting for the past two years. The small FC force had faced some two thousand heavily armed militants. Well dug in along the valley floors and commanding the heights, the militants had sited their heavy weapons along the entrance routes in their stronghold. U.S. officers in Kabul and Islamabad who were closely monitoring the fighting later admitted to me that the attack was a disaster, a result of miserably poor planning and a total lack of coordination among the FC, the army, and the ISI. But there were deeper suspicions. The ISI had held meetings with the militants and possessed detailed information about the enemy's numbers and armaments, but this intelligence did not seem to have been conveyed to the FC. Western officers in Kabul and Islamabad wondered if the failed attack was due to a lack of coordination or was deliberate.

There was no internal inquiry and the reasons for the debacle were never made clear, but the hundreds of casualties created severe demoralization in the ranks. Dozens of FC soldiers deserted their units rather than killing their fellow Pashtuns; others feared retribution from the militants. Several pilots flying helicopter gunships refused to fire upon civilian targets and were disciplined. Six army officers arrested earlier for alleged links to al Qaeda were already undergoing courts-martial.[8] The debacle was made worse by Musharraf, who boasted to CNN on March 18 that a "high-value target" had been surrounded, and suggested that the target was Ayman al-Zawahiri. The government said that 46 soldiers lost their lives, while 63 militants were killed and another 166 captured. In fact, army officers privately admitted that nearly 200 soldiers had been killed.

The Wazir militants emerged as heroes. Their leader, Nek Mohammed, twenty-seven, became an icon. Over six feet tall, with long locks flowing out of his turban, he looked more like a Romantic poet than a guerrilla leader. He had fought with the Taliban in Afghanistan and then made his mark by helping al Qaeda leaders escape from Tora Bora. By 2004 he had accumulated a fleet of forty-four pickup trucks, which he used to supply the militants' training camps. In the Kalosha battle, he had driven Yulda-shev to safety by hurling his Toyota pickup through the ranks of terrified FC soldiers. A few weeks later he provided an escort for Mullah Dadullah, who arrived from Quetta to reorganize the Taliban fighters in South Waziristan.

Despite their losses, al Qaeda, the Taliban, and their allies emerged as victors, which Pakistan's army acknowledged when it signed an agreement with the militants at Shakai on April 24, 2004, pardoning their leaders and giving foreign militants a week to register with the authorities. The very idea that al Qaeda would "register" with the political agent was clearly ridiculous, and the agreement quickly broke down. The army went on the offensive again, blockading Wana and stopping all goods from entering South Waziristan. Nek Mohammed was killed by a U.S. missile strike on June 18, after a U.S. surveillance drone locked onto his satellite phone. Thousands of tribesmen turned out for his funeral.

I had traveled in FATA in 2002 and 2003 with my researcher, Abu Bakr Siddique, himself a Pashtun. After 9/11 the tribesmen were well aware that FATA's political status was redundant, and an intense political debate began about what options to pursue. Many tribesmen demanded that the government give them the choice of either joining the NWFP or creating a separate province out of the FATA agencies. If the military had held a referendum at the time, an overwhelming majority of tribesmen would have opted to become full citizens of Pakistan by choosing one or the other options. If such a political step had been taken and followed up with development funds and road building, it would almost certainly have changed the complexion of FATA and prevented it from becoming terrorism central. Instead, the army continued its old games, manipulating the tribesmen, using them to harass the Kabul regime, refusing to dig out al Qaeda, and allowing Talibanization to take root in the tribes. Failing to adopt a serious counterterrorism strategy, the army swung between using military means one day and signing peace agreements the next, confusing the population, Pakistani public, and the international community.

FATA desperately needed development. Annual per capita income there is just five hundred dollars, or half that of the rest of the country. The literacy rate is 17 percent, with just 3 percent female literacy, compared with a nationwide literacy rate of 56 percent.[9] In such a situation, the madrassas are the only means of an education and remain immensely popular. Since 9/11, new and even larger madrassas have been built with donations from al Qaeda and wealthy traders. There are few functioning hospitals and just 524 doctors for the entire population. Before 9/11, FATA received just $16.5 million in development funds from the federal government's budget. In 2002 the government promised $160 million, but the money was absorbed in military costs.

In 2006 the military regime sent Washington a 187-page FATA Sustainable Development Plan (2006–2015). The Americans, over the next five years, promised to spend $750 million in FATA, which would be matched by similar Pakistani funds.[10] It was a patently dishonest document, reminiscent of a British colonial policy paper, as it reasserted the myths about the region and the tribes that had allowed the army to exploit them for so long. The document contained blatant lies, such as "the strife that keeps FATA simmering has . . . its roots in the government's hands-off policy towards the tribal areas"—which couldn't be further from the truth. It also stated that the "failure to come up with a clear vision for integrated development in FATA as a sustainable solution to all the troubles in the region has kept the people marginalized and impoverished."

In reality what has kept the people marginalized has been the lack of political choices or freedoms. Meaningful development could only follow a change in the political status of FATA, more political freedom for its people, and FATA's entry into the Pakistani mainstream—all of which the army refused to contemplate. Instead, al Qaeda and the Taliban were carrying out political changes by renaming the region the "Islamic Emirate of Waziristan" and implementing their brutal code of behavior.

Yet the U.S. State Department bought the plan with barely a murmur. The State Department drew up its own plan, which echoed what Pakistan had already outlined, and said in March 2007 that the United States would give $750 million, or $150 million a year for five years, to the plan. The Bush administration had no expertise in FATA—no anthropologists, social scientists, or aid workers who spoke Pushtu and knew the tribes—and it did not bother to hire any. With FATA in the throes of an insurgency, any tribal elders and NGOs who could have implemented development were either dead or driven out, and with the army running scared from the Taliban, it was clear that the money would be utterly wasted or used by the military for its forces. "Without civilian implementing partners or elected political representation, the military and mullahs will stand to benefit the most from this plan," said Christine Fair, an American expert on Pakistan. "The money will only buttress the already Islamist leadership."[11] Yet the

State Department viewed political reform in FATA as anathema, fearing that it would undermine its relationship with Musharraf. In addition, the United States declared FATA to be a "reconstruction opportunity zone," so that goods manufactured there would have duty-free access to the United States—but nothing has ever been manufactured in FATA.

The growth of Taliban sympathies in FATA was also a direct result of gravely misguided policies by Rumsfeld and the Pentagon, which treated FATA as a war zone and never insisted that Musharraf offer real political solutions to its people. At the same time, Rumsfeld forced the U.S. military to become captive to Islamabad's whims and fancies. There was no U.S. political strategy for dealing with the army's support to the Taliban or with the real problems of FATA. Pakistan asked for weapons and helicopters, diverting the real issue of its lack of political will to a supposed lack of weapons capability. The United States obliged, providing new weapon systems while knowing full well that the army would divert some to fight the insurgency in Balochistan or to arm troops on the Indian border. Finally, when the United States became frustrated with the lack of Pakistani action, it launched episodic missile strikes against al Qaeda targets in FATA, which infuriated the tribesmen further.

After its 2004 defeat, the army sent eighty thousand troops and FC into South Waziristan. The militants promptly packed their bags and moved to North Waziristan, which was inhabited by the Mahsud tribe. New local leaders emerged, such as Abdullah Mahsud, thirty, a one-legged college graduate who rode a horse into battle to avoid walking on his prosthetic leg. In 2001 he had been captured by U.S. forces in Afghanistan and was transferred to Guantánamo jail, where he played dumb and convinced his U.S. interrogators that he was a simpleton. Released in 2004, he rejoined the Taliban in North Waziristan. Another leader was Baitullah Mahsud, thirty-two, who had fought with the Taliban in Afghanistan and become close to Mullah Omar.[12] These new young leaders led the various groups of Pakistani Taliban who were emerging as key allies of al Qaeda and the Afghan Taliban.

In early September 2004, heavy fighting erupted after the army killed some eighty people in an attack on a madrassa. Opposition parties across the country accused the government of carrying out a massacre as thousands of tribesmen and their families now fled North Waziristan. In retaliation, the militants ambushed army convoys, shelled army camps, and kidnapped two Chinese engineers. The army again capitulated, signing a peace deal in November in which it paid the militants over two hundred thousand dollars in compensation—in fact, a bribe.[13] By now the army had lost more than six hundred soldiers, and hundreds more were wounded.

The war against the militants went into a stalemate. The army cordoned off the whole of FATA, refusing to allow aid agencies or journalists to enter the region. Two local journalists were killed by unknown attackers in 2005, after which many journalists left the region out of fear of being targeted either by the military or the militants. In December 2005 a prominent local journalist, Hayatullah Khan, was kidnapped in North Waziristan and later killed. His family accused the ISI of carrying out his murder. When his body was discovered six months later, it was learned he had been restrained with military handcuffs, his body had torture marks, and he had been shot in the head. The government refused to initiate any inquiry into the deaths of the journalists. Meanwhile, Musharraf undermined the political agents, replacing them with army officers who did not know the tribes or their culture. Political agents were usually from the region and had spent years building up trust and faith among the tribesmen. The shift destroyed the entire management structure of FATA while forcing upon tribesmen new bosses whom they did not trust. In one fell swoop, Musharraf had cut off the only vehicle for a dialogue with the tribes. Bereft of any political strategy in FATA and with no ability to win over the people, the military was tasked with silencing local critics and ensuring that no negative news about the army got out of the region.

In both South and North Waziristan, the Pakistani Taliban tightened their grip on the population through intimidation and assassination. They imposed their own laws, banning television, music, and the Internet and making prayers and beards mandatory for all males, as they attempted to re-create the Taliban regime that existed in Afghanistan before 9/11. Sixty tribal and religious leaders were killed in 2005, accused of being American spies. Their beheaded bodies were hung up on lampposts and shown on Taliban-made DVDs, which circulated widely. In November 2005 Malik Khandan, an important Mahsud chief, was killed along with his son. Three months later the Taliban killed two more of his sons and a daughter, along with two nephews—thereby wiping out the entire family. The Taliban ritualized the killing of tribal elders to terrorize the population. To a tribal elder marked to be killed they sent a needle with a long thread and one thousand rupees ($16). The money was for him to buy his shroud and the needle to sew it with.

As Pakistani forces now rarely moved beyond their garrisons or checkpoints, increasingly U.S. forces carried out missile strikes in FATA, often without Pakistan's permission. On January 13, 2006, U.S. missiles targeted Ayman al-Zawahiri in the village of Damadola in Bajaur agency. Al-Zawahiri was reputed to have a Mohmand wife whom he visited on occasion. The missile attack killed five senior al Qaeda figures but generated enormous public anger as politicians accused Musharraf of allowing Washington to undermine Pakistan's sovereignty. Musharraf was forced to issue a sharp rejoinder to the United States that such strikes "must not be repeated."[14]

President Bush's visit to Islamabad in March 2006 prompted another short offensive by the army in North Waziristan. In retaliation, some 1,500 Taliban tried to overwhelm the military garrison in Miram Shah and capture the town. Bloody fighting lasted for three days and the army had to use heavy artillery to drive off the Taliban, destroying the town and killing more than 150 people. The crisis in FATA dominated the talks between Musharraf and Bush, who urged Pakistan's leader to do more. Further U.S. missile strikes against al Qaeda targets in FATA led to the first suicide attacks on the Pakistan army—a trend that had already escalated in Afghanistan. On November 8, after a U.S. missile strike against a madrassa in Bajaur agency that killed eighty people, a suicide bomber blew himself up at an army training camp in Dargai, in the NWFP, killing thirty-five soldiers and wounding forty. It was the single most devastating attack against the army and it shook public and military morale.[15]

Starting in South Waziristan in 2002, the Pakistani Taliban and al Qaeda had progressively occupied one agency after another, moving to North Waziristan, Bajaur, and Mohmand. Each army attack led them to find new territory to occupy and to spread their message. In each agency they introduced their harsh code, killing or driving out tribesmen who opposed them. In May 2006, Musharraf had appointed the now-retired lieutenant-general Orakzai as the new governor of the NWFP and tasked him with striking peace deals in FATA that would stop the militants from attacking the army. The government enlisted the help of Maulana Fazlur Rehman and other leaders of the JUI Party and covertly asked Afghan Taliban leaders Mullah Dadullah and Jalaluddin Haqqani to help persuade the Pakistani Taliban to agree.

General Orakzai was a slippery character for Musharraf to embrace so closely. As corps commander in Peshawar from 2001 to 2004, he had allowed al Qaeda and the Taliban to settle down in FATA undisturbed and was now advocating peace deals with them.[16] A tribesman from FATA who boasted of his inside knowledge of the tribal mind, in fact Orakzai appeared totally insensitive to tribal needs. Posing as an enlightened general, he was opposed to any democratic reforms in FATA and disliked the Americans and NATO intensely, while demonstrating a grudging sympathy, if not admiration, for the Taliban. He enlarged on the myth, advocated frequently by Musharraf and the ISI, that the Taliban were just Pashtun nationalists opposed to foreign occupying armies but with no connections to al Qaeda.

On September 5, 2006, Orakzai signed an agreement with seven Pakistani Taliban leaders in North Waziristan—although the government insisted that the agreement was signed with tribal elders and not the Taliban. The agreement, which was to become immensely controversial in Kabul and Washington, stipulated that all Taliban attacks on U.S. and Afghan forces in Afghanistan and on the Pakistan army would cease. In return the army would pull out its garrisons and checkpoints, release all prisoners, return captured equipment and vehicles, and compensate those tribesmen who had suffered losses. The army quickly fulfilled its side of the bargain, thereby legitimizing Taliban control of North Waziristan. The agreement turned into a capitulation by the army because there was no mechanism for its enforcement. The Pakistanis had no means to challenge or punish the Taliban if they continued their attacks across the border—which they did. Thus, while the Taliban stopped attacking Pakistani troops, they stepped up their attacks on U.S. forces in Afghanistan, which immediately aroused suspicions in Kabul that this was Islamabad's intention all along.

Two days later Orakzai accompanied Musharraf to the White House to convince Bush about the workability of the agreement. Bush naïvely supported the deal, saying it would not create safe havens for the Taliban and could even offer "alternatives to violence and terror." He reiterated his implacable trust in Musharraf, adding only one cautionary note: "You know we are watching this very carefully, obviously," he said.[17] Buoyed by Bush's approval of what was a dubious agreement, Musharraf now urged NATO forces in Afghanistan to strike similar deals with the Taliban.

Musharraf's most vocal critic was Karzai. In the United States for the UN General Assembly, both men fought a bruising battle, each heaping abuse on the other in media interviews. When Bush attempted to heal the rift between the two men by hosting a dinner for both of them at the White

House, they refused to shake each other's hand. The dinner failed as Karzai again insisted that Musharraf arrest Taliban leaders living in Pakistan and stop striking deals with terrorists, while Bush refused to take sides.

By November, Lieutenant-General Eikenberry, the head of U.S. forces in Afghanistan, was telling me that the number of Taliban attacks emanating out of North Waziristan had gone up three times since the September agreement was signed. Eikenberry was clear that Pakistan's aim was to stop attacks on its own soldiers while doing little to stop the Taliban from attacking U.S. forces.[18] By the end of December the State Department agreed with his analysis, saying the deal had failed. "The Taliban have been able to use these areas [FATA] for sanctuary and for command and control and for regrouping and supply," said the U.S. assistant secretary of state, Richard Boucher, on December 26.[19] With the population terrorized and under the influence of the Taliban, FATA was now out of the army's control. More than 120 tribal elders who opposed the Taliban were executed by them in 2006. Since 2004 the army had signed three agreements with the militants in FATA, and all three had failed.[20] Now Taliban influence was spreading to the settled areas of the NWFP, as all entertainment in small towns was shut down, and men were forced to grow beards and pray five times a day.[21]

FATA had become terrorism central, providing training and manpower for the insurgency in Afghanistan and pushing forward the Talibanization of the NWFP, while guarding the sanctuaries of al Qaeda where international terrorists were trained. Al Qaeda was so well protected that it set up a media production arm called As Sahab (The Clouds), which produced fifty-eight audio and videotapes in 2006, triple the number in 2005. Ayman al-Zawahiri described his concept of a post-9/11 base area in a letter to Abu Musab al-Zarqawi, the al Qaeda leader in Iraq: "Establish an Islamic authority or emirate, then develop it and support it until it achieves the level of a caliphate over as much territory as you can to spread its power such as in Iraq."[22]

Almost all latter-day al Qaeda terrorist plots around the world had a FATA connection. The four suicide bombers—three of them of Pakistani origin—who carried out the July 7, 2005, attacks on the London Underground that killed fifty-six people and injured seven hundred were connected to FATA. The ringleader, Mohammed Siddique Khan, visited FATA in 2003 and 2004, when he had "some contact with al Qaeda figures and some relevant training," according to a British government report.[23]

As Sahab released a video showing another one of the bombers making his martyrdom speech. Five of the twenty-four terrorists arrested in England in August 2006 for plotting to blow up nine aircraft flying out of Heathrow with liquid explosives had allegedly trained in FATA. Subsequent terrorist plots unearthed in Denmark and Germany in September 2007 also appeared to have links to FATA.

The 2005 London plot was investigated with the assistance of the ISI working closely with Britain's MI6, but Musharraf remained in denial about al Qaeda's presence in Pakistan and instead castigated Tony Blair for allowing radical mullahs to preach in Britain. Musharraf insisted: "Our . . . law enforcement agencies have completely shattered al Qaeda's vertical and horizontal links and smashed its communications and propaganda setup. . . . It no longer has any command, communication and program structure in Pakistan. Therefore it is absolutely baseless to say that al Qaeda has its headquarters in Pakistan and that terror attacks in other parts of the world in any way originate from our country."[24]

The British government was less sanguine. In October 2005 it banned fifteen Islamic extremist groups, half of which were based in Pakistan. Britain had seen a spate of al Qaeda plots, starting with Britain's first plot, uncovered in November 2000, and further plots in 2003 and 2004. In the latter, seven men, six of them British-born Pakistanis, were arrested with half a ton of chemicals ready to be turned into bombs. At their trial they testified that they had trained in Kashmir and in Kohat, in the NWFP.[25] In November 2006 Dame Eliza Manningham-Buller, the director-general of Britain's MI5, said that her organization was watching sixteen hundred people involved in thirty plots. The plotters, she said, "often have links back to al Qaeda in Pakistan and through those links al Qaeda gives guidance and training to its largely British foot soldiers here. . . ."[26] British Pakistanis, who were legally allowed to hold both Pakistani and British passports, were now the most closely watched group of people in the world.

By working closely with the British government on Britain's terrorism problems, the ISI gained sympathy from London for its efforts in FATA. Tony Blair declined to criticize Musharraf's policies or publicly pressure Pakistan about any clandestine support to the Taliban—even though British troops in Helmand province faced the brunt of Taliban attacks in 2006. Britain's attitude created severe differences with NATO and U.S. commanders in Afghanistan, who wanted to forge a common diplomatic front to force Pakistan to do more in curbing the Taliban. Instead, while on a visit to Islamabad in November 2006, Blair heaped praise on Musharraf's role in standing up to terrorism. However, by now Musharraf was being harshly criticized by the U.S. Congress and media for failing in FATA and in the hunt for bin Laden. The increasing estrangement in the U.S.-Pakistan relationship was sarcastically summed up by veteran columnist Jim Hoagland: "We've got Musharraf right where he wants us. Washington and Islamabad are condemned to such strategic ambivalence. Each is unable to do without the other, while wishing it could."[27]

Washington had lavishly aided Pakistan's military, and U.S. legislators now asked where were the results of that aid. Between 2002 and 2007, the Bush administration had provided Pakistan with $3.5 billion in aid, more than half of that for the military. Between 2002 and 2005 the military had received another $3.6 billion in payments for use of its facilities and services by the U.S. Defense Department, while the United States had forgiven Pakistani debt worth over $3.0 billion.[28] The CIA had paid large secret sums to the ISI in order to improve its performance and provide reward money for catching al Qaeda leaders. The army received another $30 to $40 million to improve border security. Washington provided for the computerization of all international passenger traffic at the country's airports, the creation of an air wing for the army to monitor FATA, the building of access roads in FATA, and police training in several fields, including crime scene analysis and a centralized fingerprint ID system. Officially, by 2007, the United States had provided $10 billion in aid to Islamabad, and unofficially the figure was much higher, yet FATA and indeed Pakistan were now greater threats than ever before. With terrorism on the increase, U.S. legislators were asking the Bush administration where the money had gone.

By the summer of 2005, Washington maintained that bin Laden was no longer hiding "along the Afghanistan-Pakistan border," but in FATA. Porter Goss, the director of the CIA, had made a tantalizing comment in June 2005 that rocked Pakistan. Asked about the whereabouts of bin Laden, he replied, "I have an excellent idea where he is . . . in the chain that you need to successfully wrap up the war on terror, we have some weak links."[29] Pakistanis took his comment to mean that bin Laden was in Pakistan, while the "weak link" was Islamabad. Bin Laden was said to be protected by several rings of security lookouts with radios to alert one another if helicopters approached. The United States had spent more than $57 million in payouts to informants along the Pakistan-Afghanistan border, but there were no leads on bin Laden.[30] Of the 37 senior al Qaeda leaders identified by the CIA in 2002, only 15 had been captured or killed, although some 3,000 suspects had been arrested in 90 countries, of which 650 were in U.S. custody. Two senior figures were killed in 2005 in North Waziristan, while another two were killed in April 2006, also in FATA.[31] However, al Qaeda had shown an uncanny ability to replace leadership figures so that its hierarchy of command and control was never too disturbed.

It was clear that after 2004 the army had stopped looking for bin Laden and acted only when U.S. intelligence provided information. On several occasions Musharraf said that he hoped bin Laden would be found and killed in Afghanistan rather than in Pakistan.

The United States was equally to blame for failing to provide sufficient resources and manpower to the hunt for bin Laden. American officials admitted in late 2006 that they had received no credible lead on his whereabouts for two years and that the trail had gone "stone cold."[32] None of the intelligence agencies seemed to be capable of carrying out the simplest of procedures, such as intercepting the couriers who delivered the dozens of video and audiotapes sent by al Qaeda to be aired on Al Jazeera. No courier was ever arrested.

The reorganization of the Taliban in FATA enabled al Qaeda to reestablish a base area and pursue its role in providing training and financing to its global affiliates. Pakistani groups such as Jaish-e-Mohammed and Lashkar-e-Tayyaba provided a constant flow of foreign recruits and would-be suicide bombers, among them British Pakistanis. The first port of call for foreign recruits was the countrywide network of madrassas controlled by extremist groups. These madrassas had undergone neither reform nor change, despite all the promises made by the regime. Before he left his command in Kabul in 2005, Lt.-Gen. David Barno had prophetically warned, "Al Qaeda clearly still wants to see the Taliban stage some kind of a comeback in Afghanistan. . . . They're still providing financing, with guidance, training, support and selected individuals that help lead and motivate the operations in Afghanistan. They clearly want to use the Taliban as they have in the past."[33]

The U.S.-led war in Iraq provided al Qaeda with an unexpected new battlefield and perhaps its greatest military successes, under Abu Musab al-Zarqawi, a Jordanian aged forty. Al-Zarqawi had fought against the Soviets in Afghanistan in 1989 and returned to Afghanistan in 2000, when he developed differences with bin Laden. After arriving in Iraq in 2002, he declared his loyalty to bin Laden and named his group "al Qaeda in Iraq." Zarqawi developed independent links with the Taliban, and by 2005 there was a steady traffic of extremists between Afghanistan-Pakistan and Iraq. The Taliban traveled to Iraq via Iran and Turkmenistan, often in the company of drug smugglers. Arab trainers, explosives experts, and financiers from Iraq traveled in the opposite direction. In Iraq the Taliban learned the latest military techniques in preparing mines, improvised explosive devices, and ambushes.[34] In November 2006, Gen. Michael Hayden, the director of the CIA, admitted that "the lessons learned in Iraq are being applied to Afghanistan" by al Qaeda.[35]

By 2006 potential suicide bombers traveling from Europe and North Africa to join al Qaeda operations in Iraq were increasingly being diverted to Afghanistan. French intelligence monitored a new route for militants from North Africa that ended up in Peshawar. "There is less need for them in Iraq," said Pierre de Bousquet de Florian, director of the DST, France's counterterrorism agency. "The Iraqi insurgency is now very well organized around Iraqis. In contrast in Afghanistan there are certainly many Pakistanis and people from Arab countries and some from North Africa."[36] Dozens of British Pakistanis and half a dozen Germans traveled to FATA. With the right Pakistani extremist contacts, it was now easier than ever for foreigners to get in touch with al Qaeda. Whereas before 9/11 it could take several months before a recruit could join an al Qaeda training camp in Afghanistan, now it took just a few weeks for a recruit to find himself in Waziristan.

The worsening situation in Iraq and Afghanistan, along with more al Qaeda plots for attacks being uncovered in Europe, prompted U.S. intelligence to reevaluate al Qaeda's potential. In January 2007, John Negroponte, the outgoing director of national intelligence, told Congress that "al Qaeda is the terrorist organization that poses the greatest threat," and pointed to Pakistan as its leadership base. "They are cultivating stronger operational connections and relationships that radiate outward from their leaders' secure hideout in Pakistan to affiliates throughout the Middle East, North Africa and Europe."[37] In mid-July a National Intelligence Estimate issued by the entire U.S. intelligence community stated that al Qaeda was based in FATA and that the United States would not hesitate to bomb or even invade any part of FATA if bin Laden was found to be hiding there.

In the past six years the Pakistan army had virtually ceded its writ in

FATA to the Taliban, in sharp contrast with how it reacted in another insurgency-hit region—Balochistan. The Baloch insurgency was to provide greater justification for the army to continue support to the Taliban and to castigate Karzai for allowing India to undermine Pakistan. The Baloch tribes, numbering just five million people, occupy the largest land area in Pakistan, much of it desert and arid mountains, agriculturally unproductive but rich in untapped mineral resources including oil, gas, and uranium. There are small Baloch minorities in eastern Iran and southern Afghanistan. Traditionally the tribes have been seminomadic, grazing sheep, goats, and camels within specified tribal boundaries, but hundreds of thousands have sought work in Karachi and Dubai. Sixty years after independence, 45 percent of the Baloch are estimated to live below the poverty level.

Unlike the Pashtuns, the Baloch are markedly secular, and mullahs have no standing in Baloch society, which has remained untouched by the waves of Islamization that have swept the region. Instead, Baloch leaders have joined up with secular Sindhi and Pashtun nationalists to oppose what they consider Punjabi hegemony. Since 1948, the Baloch have been demanding greater autonomy, more control over revenues from their gas fields, and greater funds for development. These demands have been ignored by the federal government and as a result Baloch nationalists have waged four insurgencies—in 1948, 1958–1959, 1962–1963, and 1973–1977—all of them brutally suppressed by the army. In 2003 a fifth rebellion got under way, led by the underground Balochistan Liberation Army, or BLA.

For centuries the Baloch have lived peacefully with other ethnic groups, especially the Pashtuns, who occupy a narrow band of territory along Balochistan's desert border with Afghanistan. However, Baloch tolerance was sorely tested in the 1980s when millions of Afghan refugees arrived, grabbing Baloch grazing lands and tilting the ethnic balance in favor of the Pashtuns. Baloch nationalists opposed the army's backing of the Afghan Mujahedin in the 1980s and of the Taliban in the 1990s because they saw the army strategy as one that favored Pashtun fundamentalism to the detriment of Baloch rights. Increasingly the Baloch have found themselves a minority in their own land.

Ever since he came to power, Musharraf had ignored Balochistan, treating it as a playground for the army's strategic aims in supporting the Taliban. In 2002 the army rigged the elections in favor of the Pashtun fundamentalist and pro-Taliban JUI Party, at the expense of Baloch nationalist parties. Quetta was turned into a Taliban town. The army's construction of new cantonments for troops and, with Chinese help, a naval and commercial port at Gawadar, on the Makran coast, was seen by the Baloch as a colonial incursion by an occupying military.[38] In Gawadar, local fishermen and farmers were deprived of their land, homes, and jobs to facilitate the building of the new port, and massive property speculation, much of it carried out by army officers, created widespread hatred for the military. The Baloch saw an unholy alliance of the ISI, JUI, and Taliban depriving them of their rights.

In 2003–2004 the BLA carried out hit-and-run raids against the military and the province's infrastructure, blowing up gas pipelines, electricity pylons, and telephone exchanges. In May 2004 this violence escalated dramatically when the BLA killed three Chinese engineers in Gawadar. The BLA had emerged out of the insurgency of the 1970s, which was led by two nationalist sardars, Khair Bux Marri and Ataullah Mengal, who led the Marris and Mengals, the two largest fighting tribes. At that time their opponent was a former colleague and chief of the Bugti tribe, Sardar Akbar Bugti, who was allied with the central government to crush the insurgency. A mercurial insomniac who could be both viciously cruel and intellectually engaging and charming, Bugti regretted his role in the 1970s and now tried to make amends in his old age by joining hands with the BLA, which was led by his grandson, Baramdagh Bugti, and Balach Marri, the son of Khair Bux. Ostensibly the BLA was demanding greater autonomy; in reality it was now fighting for an independent Balochistan.

The key to the conflict was the pittance of revenue that the Baloch and the Bugtis in particular received from the gas fields operated by a state-owned company at Sui, in the Bugti tribal area. The Sui gas fields provide some 45 percent of Pakistan's gas needs. Eighty wells in Sui produce between 720 and 750 million cubic feet of gas a day, which generates an estimated $1.4 billion in revenue for the central government In 2005, only $116.0 million was returned to Balochistan in the form of royalties. Tensions around Sui escalated dramatically in January of that year when a five-day battle ensued between the Bugti and the army. Pipelines were blown up and the supply of gas to the rest of the country came to a standstill. The army rushed 2,500 troops and tanks to defend Sui as Musharraf threw fuel on the fire by taunting the Baloch: "Don't push us. It isn't the 1970s when you can hit and run and hide in the mountains," he said. "This time you won't even know what hit you." Ataullah Mengal promised the Baloch would fight "till the last drop of our blood."[39]

Fighting continued around Sui as the Bugtis ambushed army convoys and the besieged military in Sui responded with artillery strikes. The rebels blew up pipelines, railway tracks, and electricity pylons across the province. Opposition politicians warned the army not to create "another Bangladesh"—referring to the 1971 civil war that divided the country. The civilian government tried to broker peace talks with Bugti, and a parliamentary committee tasked with compiling a report on Baloch grievances made considerable headway, offering the Baloch greater provincial autonomy, additional gas royalties, and jobs. However, the deal collapsed after Musharraf told the politicians to stand down.

On December 14, 2005, Musharraf was addressing a rally in the Marri area when the BLA fired eight rockets upon the gathering and on a helicopter carrying a general and his deputy, seriously wounding both men. A humiliated Musharraf ordered a major offensive against the BLA. Hundreds of guerrillas and civilians were killed as helicopter gunships, provided by Washington to fight the Taliban, were redeployed against the Baloch. Musharraf insisted that only three sardars were causing the trouble while the rest of the Baloch supported the government. In July, after his home in Dera Bugti was shelled, Akbar Bugti, seventy-nine, suffering from severe arthritis and unable to walk, mounted a camel and took to the mountains with hundreds of fighters. "I have had a good and full life—it is better to die quickly in the mountains than slowly in your bed," he ruminated. "If we are removed from the scene, I can guarantee the government will have a heck of a time from the younger generation because they are more extreme."[40]

As he had wished, his end came quickly and fiercely. On August 26, Bugti was killed, along with thirty-five followers, after a cave he was resting in was bombed. Some sixteen soldiers, including four officers, were killed in a fierce battle over possession of Bugti's dead body. The army had hoped also to kill Baramdagh Bugti and Balach Marri, but the two escaped. The entire province erupted in fury. Quetta and all major towns were shut down for a week as mobs rampaged through the streets, attacking and burning banks, vehicles, and government buildings. Protests intensified after the government refused to hand over Bugti's body to his family and buried him in a now-deserted Dera Bugti. In a later interview to an Indian television station, Musharraf acknowledged that Bugti had been deliberately targeted. "Anyone who maintains a military and tries to challenge Pakistan . . . there is no doubt in my mind . . . there is no duplicity in this—we will crush him," he said.[41] The media asked why, if the army could bomb Baloch rebels, it was unable to crush the Taliban. The ruling PML asked Musharraf to resume talks with the Baloch, but he refused.

The flight of BLA leaders to refuge in Afghanistan, harsh military action, and the mass arrests of thousands of civilians led to a temporary decline in guerrilla activity in Balochistan. There is no doubt that the BLA had escalated the conflict and underestimated the army's reaction. However, by killing Bugti, Musharraf had earned the permanent enmity of the Baloch people. The wave of anti-army feeling in Balochistan spread to Sindh and the NWFP. The government was further humiliated when it tried to hold a Jirga of all the Baloch sardars and they refused to attend. Instead, the Khan of Kalat, Mir Suleiman Daud, the titular head of the Baloch sardars, called a Loya Jirga in September, which was attended by eighty-five sardars and three hundred tribal elders. They condemned the army and decided to ask for justice from the International Criminal Court, in the Hague.[42]

The significance of the Baloch insurgency was that it provided the military regime with another excuse to accuse India and Afghanistan of supporting dissidents in Pakistan. Islamabad accused the Afghans of permitting the Indian consulates in Kandahar and Jalalabad to funnel arms and money to BLA insurgents. In February 2006, when Karzai presented Musharraf with yet another list of alleged Taliban leaders hiding out in Balochistan, Musharraf retaliated by giving Karzai reports of Indian involvement with the BLA via Kabul.[43] There was little doubt that India was supporting the Baloch insurgency, but the question was, from where? New Delhi had supported previous Baloch insurgencies, just as Islamabad had backed Kashmiri separatists. Each country had run dissident movements in the other's state, in a proxy war that had continued for half a century.

Western intelligence officials in Kabul said that India was not using Afghanistan—rather that Indian money was being funneled to the Baloch from Dubai, where many Baloch nationalists were living. Pakistan demanded that Dubai arrest another son of Khair Bux Marri, who was living there. Western officials also claimed that Iran was providing training camps to the Baloch. Other conspiracy theories swept through the Pakistani media. There were allegations that the United States and Britain were supporting the Baloch insurgents in order to counter the Chinese naval presence in Gawadar, that Dubai was doing the same because Gawadar would draw away sea-borne trade from Dubai port, and that Russia wanted to break up Pakistan. Although none of these theories appeared credible, the insurgency in Balochistan was now internationalized.

At the same time, international pressure on the military regime mounted as a result of the dramatic disclosure of Pakistan's extensive proliferation of nuclear technology to Iran, North Korea, and Libya. Since the late 1970s the army had directed Pakistan's nuclear weapons program, refusing to share control of it or even provide information or access to it to elected civilian leaders. In June 1989, when the United States warned Islamabad that it would face U.S. sanctions if it did not stop enriching uranium, American officials had to brief then prime minister Benazir Bhutto, as she had not been informed of what the army was up to. When the army refused to cease the process, Washington imposed sanctions—ending the decade-long U.S.-Pakistan cooperation in rolling back the Soviets from Afghanistan. Pakistan's generals accused Washington of abandoning Pakistan, but in fact President Ronald Reagan had looked the other way regarding Pakistan's nuclear weapons program for several years, so as to maintain Pakistan's cooperation in the war in Afghanistan. There was no civilian oversight of the nuclear program and no accountability ever demanded from the army.

To develop its nuclear and missile program, Pakistan secretly imported critical equipment from willing allies. In 1982 China gave Pakistan the complete design of a twenty-five-kiloton nuclear bomb and enough weapons-grade uranium for two bombs. In 1996 China supplied industrial furnaces for a nuclear reactor.[44] Similarly, since 1993 North Korea had sold missile technology to Pakistan. The Pakistani military had first deployed Chinese-made short-range M-11 missiles in 1991, and five years later, North Korean medium-range No-Dong missiles.[45] However, Pakistan's major acquisition of nuclear spare parts and materials came from an extensive global purchasing and manufacturing black market network, set up by Dr. A. Q. Khan, the revered godfather of the Pakistani bomb. Items were bought clandestinely in Europe and copied by Khan-run factories in Malaysia, Singapore, and Germany. Khan quickly realized that he could use the same network to sell equipment to other countries, as he believed in safety in numbers—the more third world countries that developed nuclear weapons, the less pressure there would be on Pakistan. His first customer, with the apparent approval of the army chief Gen. Mirza Aslam Beg, was Iran, which bought centrifuges to enrich uranium in 1987.[46]

Both India and Pakistan faced international economic sanctions after they tested nuclear devices in 1998. The sanctions crippled an already cash-strapped Pakistan. Thus when 9/11 occurred, Pakistan was under three layers of U.S. sanctions and had not received any U.S. aid for ten years.[47] A. Q. Khan's global network continued to function, but in 2001 Musharraf had been forced by a suspicious CIA to remove Khan as head of the Khan Research Laboratories.[48] After 9/11, U.S. intelligence began to monitor up to nine cargo flights a month to North Korea flown by the Pakistan air force. The planes delivered large crates and took on missiles.[49] Islamabad had speeded up research into miniaturizing nuclear bombs to fit North Korean missiles. When Pyongyang wished to restart its nuclear weapons program, after the breakdown of its earlier accord with the Clinton administration, it asked Pakistan for help. Nuclear experts concluded that a barter deal was struck whereby Khan provided uranium-enrichment technology to North Korea in exchange for missiles—"a perfect marriage of interests."[50] Pakistan denied any such barter deal, but when North Korea stunned the world by testing a nuclear device in October 2006, all eyes turned to Pakistan and Khan.

After 9/11, Washington was convinced that al Qaeda may have gotten its hands on some nuclear materials and could launch another attack on the United States. Nuclear proliferation went to the top of the list of concerns for the West. What has never been adequately answered was why the army allowed Khan to continue his marketing of nuclear parts after 9/11 when it was apparent that the West's greatest concern was that nuclear devices would get into the hands of terrorists. In 2002, when news reports of the Pakistani flights to North Korea emerged, Musharraf received a mild rap on the knuckles from Colin Powell, but by now Khan was under surveillance by several Western intelligence agencies.[51] He brazenly continued his activities, tying up a deal with Libya to deliver a full nuclear weapons program. On October 4, 2003, Khan's network was caught red-handed when a cargo ship, *BBC China,* was stopped and searched on its way to Tripoli from Malaysia. Inside were containers loaded with centrifuges. The CIA now bluntly told Musharraf to shut down Khan and provided evidence that he had sold nuclear technology to Libya, North Korea, Iran, and one other unnamed country.

Musharraf procrastinated, worried about the possible political fallout at home if he named Khan a traitor and about how to protect the army from being implicated. On December 19, 2003, after Libya declared it would give up its nuclear program, Musharraf was forced to act. Khan and twenty-five of his aides were interrogated by the ISI; he was then placed under house arrest and was persuaded to sign a twelve-page confession. In a carefully staged television appearance on February 4, 2004, Khan told Musharraf he accepted full responsibility for all proliferation activities, insisted that neither the government nor the army was involved, and asked the nation for forgiveness. "It pains me to realize this," said a strained-looking Khan, "that my entire lifetime achievement of providing foolproof national security to my nation could have been placed in serious jeopardy on account of my activities, which were based in good faith, but on errors of judgment related to unauthorized proliferation activities."[52]

Most experts accepted that Khan could not have carried out his business without the military's support. Pakistani journalists were discouraged from asking about his multiple bank accounts or where the money he earned had gone. Speculation was rife that although he had enriched himself, most of the profits had been ploughed back into Pakistan's nuclear program. Before any of these questions could be adequately answered, the United States provided Musharraf and the army with a clean bill of health. As in the Reagan era, once again U.S. officials said they believed Musharraf's assurances that the army was not involved in nuclear proliferation and had not supported Khan's endeavors. A few weeks later the Bush administration asked Congress to sanction the sale of F-16 fighter aircraft to Pakistan. It was clear that by declining to push Islamabad for full disclosure, the Bush administration wanted to preserve Musharraf's continued support in the war on terrorism. "This is the age-old problem with Pakistan and the U.S.," said nuclear expert David Albright. "Other priorities always trump the U.S. from coming down hard on Pakistan's nuclear proliferation."[53] Moreover, the Americans hoped they would now get more leverage over Islamabad in the hunt for al Qaeda. Paul Wolfowitz told me:

> In a funny way the A. Q. Khan piece . . . we feel it gives us more leverage, and it may give Musharraf a . . . stronger hand, that Pakistan has an act to clean up. The international community is prepared to accept Musharraf's

pardoning of Khan for all that he has done, but clearly it is a kind of IOU, and in return for that there has to really be a thorough accounting. Beyond that understanding, we expect an even higher level of cooperation on the al Qaeda front than we have had to date.[54]

Musharraf had become a master at playing off Americans' fears while protecting the army and Pakistan's national interest. It was perhaps his finest moment as he refused to budge and continued to provide only minimal satisfaction to the United States and the world. He declined to give the CIA access to Khan, and there was no stepped-up hunt for bin Laden. The CIA was allowed to interrogate Khan only through written questions passed to him by the Pakistani government. Even after North Korea exploded a nuclear device and Iran's nuclear weapons program went ahead, the Pakistanis refused to allow the CIA to interview Khan.[55] He was kept heavily guarded at his Islamabad home, with no access to the telephone or visitors. His friends said he had been made a scapegoat by the military.

Eventually Pakistan paid a high price, for the United States now looked to ratify India's nuclear and great power status. In March 2006, on a visit to New Delhi, President Bush offered Prime Minister Manmohan Singh an agreement that gave New Delhi virtual membership in the world's nuclear club, allowing India to buy nuclear fuel and reactors for its civilian nuclear program—while Pakistan was still denied any such right. When Bush arrived in Islamabad, he said Pakistan was not responsible enough to have the same benefits. "Pakistan and India are different countries with different needs and different histories," he said. "Our strategy will take in effect those well-known differences."[56] The military regime felt humiliated.

The years of praise by Bush and other world leaders, their unwillingness to impose tougher conditions on Pakistan's military regime, and Musharraf's ability to escape censure on all counts turned Musharraf's head. He became increasingly arrogant and distant, relying on an ever smaller coterie of advisers, listening less and less to anybody. He talked incessantly, giving a speech or interview almost every day, while critical questioners at his press conferences were bluntly put down. He considered himself an expert on everything from earthquake relief to education to solving the problems of Iraq and Palestine. The ruling PML and the cabinet were ignored to an even greater extent than before. Musharraf adroitly played on Western fears that a return to civilian rule would lessen Pakistan's role in the war on terrorism or that a free and fair election would bring the Islamic parties to power—although the likelihood of that was minimal.

As opposition to his rule grew, Musharraf diverted attention, insisting that there was nothing wrong with his policies but, rather, that Pakistan faced "an image problem" abroad. The government spent tens of millions of dollars hiring image consultants from London and Washington and staging fashion shows abroad to show Pakistan's "soft image." Musharraf's autobiography, *In the Line of Fire,* published in September 2006, was hailed as the book of the decade by the regime.[57] As long as Pakistan remained the center for Talibanization, terrorism, or nuclear proliferation, the world could not ignore the military regime or dispense with Musharraf. "It is essential for Musharraf that Pakistan be a 'dangerous place': he and his country . . . feed off the menace," wrote academic Fouad Ajami.[58] The West continued to view Musharraf as the only person capable of holding Pakistan together, even though some diplomats acknowledged that "Pakistan now negotiates with its allies and friends by pointing a gun to its own head."[59]

◆ ◆ ◆

Musharraf's most significant achievement in this period was to convince the army of the need for peace with India and a resolution of the Kashmir dispute. He realized that Pakistan could no longer compete with India or undermine it, as India's economic growth was turning it into a global power. The army also understood that if it wanted to continue ruling the country and to retain the largest share of the budget, then Pakistan had to concentrate on economic growth, which necessitated peace with India. Moreover, the international community would no longer tolerate Pakistani-backed insurgents entering Indian Kashmir. The ISI underwent a difficult balancing act with the Kashmiri extremist groups, secretly disarming and rehabilitating several thousand militants while still keeping a few in reserve in case the peace process floundered.

The devastating earthquake that hit northern Pakistan on October 8, 2005, did much to revive the militant groups and provide them with a new role. The earthquake, registering 7.6 on the Richter scale, killed 73,000 people and injured 75,000; half the victims were children, who were trapped in school buildings. Although the military took on the rescue effort and then dominated the rehabilitation and reconstruction of affected areas, it also allowed extremist groups to carry out relief work. They re-emerged as NGOs setting up hospitals and shelters and competing along-side a host of well-wishers, including NATO and U.S. troops, who also took part in the relief effort. Seventeen extremist groups that were either on the UN list of terrorist organizations or banned by the Pakistani gov-ernment were reactivated as Islamic NGOs. A year later Musharraf was preoccupied with how he was going to get himself elected as president for another five years while retaining his post as army chief. His hubris and overweening confidence and arrogance were ultimately to unleash the most severe political crisis in Pakistan's history.

◆ ◆ ◆

CHAPTER FOURTEEN

America Shows the Way

The Disappeared and the Rendered

If war has been mankind's most powerful negative urge, then the universal agreements that limit the horrors of war and protect civilians have been the hallmark of progress and have reflected man's deeper instincts for civilization. The Geneva Conventions may not have halted the Jewish holocaust, Rwandan genocide, or terrorism but they have given us a code of conduct by which we can judge the actions of our leaders in the desperate times of war. That is why the decision by President Bush on February 7, 2002, to deny captured al Qaeda, Taliban, and other terrorist suspects prisoner-of-war (POW) status or any access to justice was a step backward for the United States and for mankind—one that has haunted the United States, its allies, and the international legal system ever since. Whereas in the West it created a furious debate about civil liberties, in the Muslim world it further entrenched dictatorship and abuse of civilians.

For the greatest power on earth to wage its "war on terrorism" by rejecting the very rules of war it is a signatory to, denying justice at home, undermining the U.S. Constitution, and then pressuring its allies to do the same set in motion a devastating denial of civilized instincts. America's example had the most impact in Afghanistan, where no legal system existed; in Pakistan, ruled by a military regime; and in Central Asia, where the world's most repressive dictatorships flourished. By following America's lead in promoting or condoning disappearances, torture, and secret jails, these countries found their path to democracy and their struggle against Islamic extremism set back by decades. Western-led nation building had little credibility if it denied justice to the very people it was supposed to help. It could well be argued that over time Islamic extremists were emboldened rather than subdued by the travesty of justice the United States perpetrated. The people learned to hate America.

Today there are four Geneva Conventions (GC)—the first signed in 1864 and revised in 1949—and three additional Protocols. The first and second GC deal with the treatment of sick and wounded soldiers on the battlefield and at sea. The third—the most pertinent to the post–9/11 world—deals with the treatment of POWs, and the fourth with protecting civilians in war zones. The third Convention permits state armies to go to war, and if captured, soldiers are entitled to POW status and may be held until the end of active hostilities. The soldiers are considered lawful combatants who may not be prosecuted. POWs, however, may be tried for any war crime they may have committed. If their POW status is in doubt, the victor is obliged to set up a "competent tribunal" to determine if this status must be granted. The GC and the 1951 UN Convention against Torture, to which the United States is a signatory, prohibit torture, but the GC do not define *torture* or *terrorism,* giving states considerable latitude, as long as all prisoners are treated humanely. Detainees can be held until the end of a conflict if they are being prosecuted for war crimes. Thus the GC protect both the interests of states and humanitarian law. "Civil rights, human rights and the rule of law are not impediments to human security. They are, in fact, the ultimate repositories of it," says Gabor Rona, the international legal director of Human Rights First. "Humanitarian law is a bulwark of human security in times of conflict."[1]

The International Committee of the Red Cross, based in Geneva, which serves as the guardian of the GC, wrote to the Bush administration after 9/11 saying that the upcoming war was an "international armed conflict," and the United States was urged to treat humanely any combatant taken prisoner. The ICRC received no reply. Instead Bush decided to predetermine all al Qaeda and Taliban prisoners as "illegal enemy combatants" and deny them status as POWs under the GC or any legal rights under the U.S. Constitution. A legal black hole was willfully created in which all manner of abuse could be carried out. The holding of prisoners outside the jurisdiction of U.S. territory and law, in Kandahar, Bagram, Guantánamo Bay, and around the world in dozens of secret CIA jails called black sites, created a parallel system of justice that was to undermine the core values of the U.S. justice system.

What prompted the Bush administration's drastic measures? Initially it was believed that the sheer shock of the attacks on the U.S. homeland called for extreme measures. Bush's depiction of a war between good and evil and more talk of a war between civilizations conjured up strong feelings of revenge and retribution. There was little discussion in the media or Congress as to how this war would be carried out, as people wanted the administration to get tough with terrorism. There were fears of al Qaeda using nuclear weapons in a second strike, especially after Pakistani nuclear scientists were arrested for helping bin Laden. When the bombing campaign began in October 2001, phone intercepts hinted at something more to come. "We began to get serious indications that nuclear plans, material and know-how were being moved out of Pakistan [by al Qaeda]. . . . It was the vibrations coming out of everybody reviewing the evidence," Bush told Bob Woodward.[2]

However, it is now clear that the key impulse for the drastic measures was from the neoconservatives in the administration who wanted to exploit the crisis in order to gain more powers for the president and the executive branch. They reckoned that presidential authority could be increased enormously at the expense of Congress and the judiciary, who were never consulted about the new laws. The very checks and balances within the U.S. political system that should have restrained this cynical agenda were bypassed. Once Bush moved away from depicting the war as one against al Qaeda to one against terrorism in general, the neocons were able to move the goalposts of their agenda from Afghanistan to Iraq and later to Iran. Rejecting the GC also helped create fear and awe among the public by implying that the terrorist threat was greater than anything the United States had ever experienced before. Madeleine Albright wrote that Americans had had an overdose of fear. "We have been told to be afraid so that we might be less protective of our Constitution, less mindful of international law."[3]

Immediately after 9/11 a small group of political appointees in the Office of Legal Counsel at the Department of Justice and the White House Counsel's Office began to develop the new policy. Many of these lawyers belonged to the right-wing Federalist Society and shared a contempt for the Geneva Conventions. The White House Counsel, Alberto R. Gonzales, who became attorney general in the second Bush term, sent a now-infamous memo to Bush on January 25, 2001, stating, "The war against terrorism is a new kind of war. . . . In my judgment this new paradigm renders obsolete Geneva's strict limitations on questioning enemy prisoners and renders *quaint* [my italics] some of its provisions."[4] He argued that "Afghanistan was a failed state because the Taliban did not exercise full control over the territory and people . . . the Taliban and its forces were in fact, not a government, but a militant, terrorist-like group." Gonzales asserted that such a determination meant that the obligation to abide by the GC need not apply. Gonzales's entire analysis was false. The war on terrorism was not a new war, and the idea of failed states or what to do with them was not even covered by the GC. Moreover, the Taliban could hardly be considered terrorists when the Clinton administration had negotiated with them in the 1990s.

In a reply to the White House the next day, the State Department wrote that abrogating the GC would have a negative effect on the image of the United States abroad, the lives of captured American soldiers would be at risk, and U.S. leaders could be accused of war crimes. State argued that the United States was still obligated to determine the status of each prisoner by a military tribunal, and even if al Qaeda was to be refused POW status, the same could not be said for the Taliban. The Judge Advocate General's Corps, or JAG—the army's own lawyers—also protested. The army's Uniform Code of Military Justice made maltreatment of POWs a crime. JAG pointed out that with the U.S. military's global deployments, defiance of international law could create huge risks for U.S. soldiers. All this was to emerge in May 2004 when these memos were first published.[5]

Gonzales had the support of Bush and Cheney, and the debate was won. Bush stated on February 7 that al Qaeda and the Taliban would be collectively given the status of "illegal enemy combatants," and the United States would treat them "humanely and to the extent appropriate and consistent with military necessity, in a manner consistent with the principles of the GC." This clause allowed the administration to cherry-pick those parts of the GC it wanted. Coining the phrase "illegal enemy combatant" was masterful because it was outside the lexicon of humanitarian law and allowed the United States to term the whole world a potential battlefield. In the first few months after 9/11, more than ten thousand people were arrested by the United States and its allies in the war on terror. In the United States alone, the FBI arrested several thousand Muslims on suspicion of being involved in terrorism. These people were held without trial and many were freed without an apology or explanation.

At home, the U.S. administration built up public hysteria. "We are keeping them off the street and out of the airlines and out of nuclear power plants and out of ports across the country and across other countries," said Rumsfeld, as though he were an actor in a science-fiction movie. When he visited Guantánamo for the first time in February 2002, he said the United States was holding "the most dangerous, best-trained, vicious killers on the face of the earth."[6] Although most of the prisoners would turn out to be innocent of any crime, Rumsfeld had already determined their guilt. Even before the February 7 decision, the White House was considering a favorable prison site that "would be safe from attack and quiet enough for sustained interrogations," one U.S. official told me.[7] Prison ships parked in the ocean were considered, as was the island of Diego Garcia, a naval base in the Indian Ocean that the United States leases from Britain. However, the U.S. naval station at Guantánamo—the oldest overseas U.S. military base, dating back to 1903, when Washington leased forty-five square miles from Cuba for a refueling station at a cost of four thousand dollars a year— was both isolated and close to the U.S. mainland.

The ICRC only vaguely suspected that the United States was going to defy the GC. When U.S. officers gave the organization access to prisoners at the Kandahar detention center in December, they assured the ICRC that they would be applying the GC. Yet a few weeks later—on January 17, 2002—when the ICRC paid its first visit to Camp X-Ray, at Guantánamo, they saw sedated, hooded, and chained prisoners who had arrived by plane a week earlier. Once prisoners from places not connected to Afghanistan started to arrive in Guantánamo, it became clear to the ICRC that Washington had no intentions of adhering to the GC. Nobody in Washington had briefed the ICRC or given any indication of what U.S. plans were. Clearly the ICRC had been duped.

U.S. SOF and the CIA operating in northern Afghanistan also appeared to know that the rules of war were about to be changed, as they tolerated unprecedented abuse, torture, and death of Taliban prisoners at the hands of commanders such as General Dostum. "When we got to Shiberghan we could not believe the extent of the abuses and starvation carried out by the NA commanders and what U.S. SOF on the scene had tolerated there," a senior Western aid official told me. "It was because the Americans knew the rules of war were about to change."

For the most part Europeans refused to follow suit and did not dilute their obligations under GC, even after the devastating bombing of trains in Madrid in March 2004 that left 192 people dead. Britain was the only European country to follow the U.S. example, when Tony Blair removed

Britain from its obligations under the European Convention on Human Rights. Parliament passed an Anti-Terrorism, Crime and Security Act, extending the government's powers of arrest and detention.

The Americans introduced at least six different systems of holding prisoners and then encouraged their allies in the region to do the same. These systems included the main holding area at Guantánamo, jails at Bagram and Kandahar, a dozen secret sub-jails at U.S. firebases in the Afghan mountains where the SOF held their own prisoners, jails run by Afghan warlords and by General Fahim's intelligence service, jails run by the ISI, and, finally, the process of "rendition" by which the CIA transported prisoners to allied countries where they could be interrogated and tortured by local intelligence agencies. Each system had levels of secrecy, nontransparency, the lack of legal redress, and noncompliance with U.S. law, contradicting even what Bush had promised in February—that prisoners would be treated "humanely." What the United States imposed in those early months in Afghanistan would later be transported wholesale to Iraq. One Western official who knew all the prison systems well said it was "a descent into hell which the American legal system may never recover from."

The first prisoner abuses in Afghanistan took place in Kandahar's detention center, set up by U.S. Task Force 500, at the airport outside the city. Through the winter, prisoners from all over Afghanistan and Pakistan were flown there, including those captured outside the battlefields or those sold to the Americans by the warlords and Pakistani officials. Without documentation and only hearsay evidence that they were al Qaeda, the U.S. interrogators in Kandahar had to determine whether they should be sent onward to Guantánamo. Ultimately it was easier for the understaffed, undertrained, and all too few U.S. interrogators to send the prisoners to Guantánamo. In Pakistan the arrests were even more haphazard, due to the CIA paying bounties for any al Qaeda. As a result the army and police rounded up hundreds of innocent Arabs and Pashtuns.

The Afghanistan-Pakistan border region became an immense human bazaar where lives were traded with no limits or rules. Often the very old or the very young were sent to Kandahar. Three Afghan boys aged between thirteen and sixteen were held at Kandahar and then Guantánamo until March 2003. Another Afghan boy who had been a dishwasher at a restaurant where Taliban once ate was also held. Men over eighty years old, barely able to stand up straight, including one eighty-eight-year-old, also ended up in Guantánamo. Some Afghans just happened to be in the wrong place at the wrong time, such as Noor Habibullah, a landless Afghan farmer from a village near Jalalabad who had been conscripted by the Taliban at the end of the war. His story is typical of many:

> Immediately after the U.S. attack on the Taliban, I was forced to join Taliban ranks and was sent to the front lines in Bamiyan. The Taliban would have spared my conscription if I could have paid them six million Afghanis [some two hundred dollars]. On 5 November 2001, I was arrested by the NA and jailed in Bamiyan along with twenty seven others. We were never seriously interrogated beyond being asked a few questions about our identity. After six months in Bamiyan, foreign military people arrived and selected me and eleven others and we were flown in helicopters to Bagram. My hands and feet were tightly tied and my head was covered with a bag.
>
> Once in Bagram we were questioned by foreigners through translators. After one day I was flown to Kandahar where . . . I was forced to strip down in front of four or five people. We were forty-seven prisoners in one big room in different cages. I was mostly asked questions about why I was fighting for the Taliban. Which people I knew among the Taliban and al Qaeda. Did I know Osama bin Ladin? Although the interrogators were usually nice to us, those guarding our cages were very bad. One of the most disgusting things they did was to throw away the Koran, which angered many prisoners. One of the most difficult things in Kandahar was the lack of sleep. We were forced to sleep under strong lights and too much noise, so it was very difficult to sleep more than two hours at one time. After eight months in Kandahar, I was told that we were being taken somewhere else. In the plane I was tied to my seat and black goggles were tied around my eyes. Once in Guantánamo I was taken to a hospital, where again I was stripped naked. The prison guards there were very harsh, especially with Arabs or senior Taliban leaders.[8]

Habibullah was eventually freed from Guantánamo in September 2003 without any charges being filed. Western officials who visited Kandahar jail told me prisoners were detained in open-air cages where twenty men jostled for space in the freezing cold of winter or the blistering desert heat of the summer. They were strip-searched before every interrogation and their hands and feet were always shackled. Guards on raised platforms pointed guns at them and at night shone searchlights into their faces. There were dozens of American female guards—far too many for a conservative people such as the Afghans to get used to. Female guards began to use the tactics that would become infamous at Abu Ghraib—unbuttoning their blouses and displaying cleavage, taunting the prisoners by shouting obscenities at them or staring at them through the cages. The guards knew well enough how provocative this could be for conservative Muslims.

U.S. interrogators were operating under enormous constraints because of the catastrophic decline in intelligence and foreign language training within the CIA and the U.S. Army since the end of the cold war. Even though it had been combating al Qaeda since 1996, CENTCOM had failed to prepare for the task. U.S. SOF units could speak to their NA allies only in Arabic or Russian, as none was trained to speak Afghan or Pakistani languages. Interrogators were even worse off, depending entirely on interpreters. At the start of the war the U.S. Army had only 510 fully trained interrogators, including 108 who spoke Arabic—which is spoken by very few Afghans. Instead, the Americans had to depend on hastily trained Afghan translators—a surefire way to lose content, emphasis, and nuance in the interrogation process. After 9/11, U.S. recruiting agencies were used to hire Persian and Pushtu speakers in the United States. They recruited hundreds of Afghan Americans, including New York taxi drivers who had not lived in Afghanistan for years. Others, recruited from the Shia Hazara community in Quetta, Pakistan, had little connection with Afghanistan but spoke Persian. The exiled Taliban were to target these Hazaras, killing them in suicide bombings and worsening the Sunni-Shia conflict in Pakistan.

The few U.S. interrogators in Kandahar had completed only a sixteen-week military-intelligence training course at Fort Huachuca, in Arizona. Their knowledge of the region was close to zero. When Uighur prisoners—Muslims from western China—were delivered, there was no information in the CENTCOM database about who they were. The interrogators had to depend on the *Encyclopaedia Britannica* to learn more about them.[9]

Adding to the pressure of interrogators in Kandahar were Washington's demands for "immediate actionable intelligence" about any new attacks al Qaeda might be planning. Abuses, threats, and torture became the quickest way to try to glean intelligence from the prisoners—though most interrogators know that winning over the prisoner is far more profitable than beating him. Soon Kandahar's haphazard system of interrogation and prisoner abuse was to be transferred to other U.S. detention centers around the world.

The CIA fared no better in gaining reliable intelligence. Robert Baer, a former CIA officer, wrote that in the 1990s hardly anyone in the CIA spoke Pushtu or Persian. Case officers with knowledge of Afghanistan were too few.[10] CIA director Porter Goss was to admit in 2004 that it would take five years to rebuild CIA's HUMINT (for HUMan INTelligence) capability. "I can't emphasize enough that if you don't have case officers who can deal with the cultures and the language, you are not going to get much," he told a Senate hearing.[11] The CIA did not even have photographs of Taliban leaders. Afghan con men earned thousands of dollars from the CIA by selling them alleged photographs of Mullah Omar, although most were false. As a superpower engaged in a global war against Islamic extremism, having just invaded one Muslim country and preparing to invade an Arab country, the United States was in a pitiful state of readiness.

The Kandahar interrogation center was closed down in the summer of 2002 and prisoners were transferred to Bagram, where living conditions were equally abysmal. Bagram became the principal long-term detention area in Afghanistan, even though Kandahar jail was reopened in 2003 after the Taliban resurgence began. Known as the Bagram Collection Point, or BCP, the jail was in the middle of the large U.S. Army camp and air force base. Prisoners were housed in a dilapidated former Soviet machine workshop with corrugated iron roofs and cement floors that froze in winter and burned in summer. The building was refitted with five large wire pens for holding prisoners and several isolation cells constructed of plywood. Up to 250 Afghans were incarcerated there at a time. The ICRC complained consistently about the appalling conditions, but improvements were made only after the Abu Ghraib scandal in Iraq broke. Frequent reports by Carlotta Gall of *The New York Times* exposing cases of abuse and death of Afghan prisoners were ignored by U.S. commanders.[12]

Since 2002 at least eight Afghan prisoners have died in U.S. custody in Afghanistan, and for years the military did its utmost to restrict information about their cases. The first was Mohammed Sayari, who died while in the custody of U.S. SOF in August 2002, followed in November 2002 by the death of an unnamed detainee at a secret CIA interrogation center in Kabul called the Salt Pit. Dilawar, a taxi driver, and Mullah Noor Habibullah died at Bagram in December 2002. In January 2003, Wakil Mohammed, a woodcutter, was killed by the U.S. SOF near Gardez. Jamal Naseer, a recruit for the Afghan army, died at the hands of the same U.S. SOF unit in March 2003. Abdul Wali, who died at the Asadabad base in

June 2003, and Sher Mohammed Khan, who died at a base near Khost, were also in the hands of U.S. SOF.[13]

The military files regarding the deaths of Dilawar and Habibullah at Bagram were leaked to the press only after it became known that the military unit responsible for their deaths had also carried out abuses at Abu Ghraib jail in Iraq.[14] In the summer of 2002, Capt. Carolyn Wood, heading Company A of the 519th Military Intelligence Battalion, was assigned to Bagram. The unit sorely lacked experience, and only two of Wood's men had ever questioned prisoners before. Wood and her unit were to be redeployed to Iraq in March 2003 and later took charge at Abu Ghraib. Once the scandal there broke, it was clear that there had been considerable cross-fertilization in the pattern of abuses carried out by units who had served in both Afghanistan and Iraq.[15]

After a ponderously slow two-year-long military investigation, twenty-seven soldiers were implicated in the deaths of the two Afghans in Bagram. Fourteen soldiers were prosecuted nearly a year after the horrendous photos of prisoners at Abu Ghraib in Iraq were released.[16] The inquiry revealed that although the soldiers had little interrogation experience, they had received two days of training in peroneal strikes—disabling blows to the side of the leg just above the knee.[17] Mullah Noor Habibullah, a strong defiant man and the brother of a Taliban commander, and Dilawar, twenty-two, a meek man with no connection to terrorism, died within a week of each other in December 2002 after being viciously tortured. Dilawar was chained by his wrists to the ceiling for four days and received at least one hundred peroneal strikes. The guards hit him repeatedly to hear him shout, "Allah," which they seemed to find funny. Just before his death he could neither sit nor stand. His autopsy showed that his leg muscles were "crumbling and falling apart."[18] After he died he was declared innocent. Habibullah, who refused to be cowed and who spat at his interrogators, received even more strikes to the legs.

In court in the United States the defense for the soldiers lay in the ambiguous guidelines for torture the army was now operating under. The trials exposed the fact that with the GC no longer applicable, nobody knew where to draw the line. "The president of the United States doesn't know what the rules are," said Capt. Joseph Owens, a lawyer for one of the accused. "The secretary of defense doesn't know what the rules are. But the government expects this Pfc. to know what the rules are!" he added.[19] One soldier, Specialist Willie Brand, admitted to kneeing Dilawar more than thirty times because "I was fed up with him." Brand was convicted of maiming and assault and could have received sixteen years in prison. Instead, his only punishment was a reduction in rank to private. One U.S. soldier was sentenced to two months in jail, another to three months, a third was demoted, and a fourth had his pay reduced. The stiffest punishment any of the culprits received was five months in jail. There was enormous anger in Kabul at the leniency of the sentences and the failure of the U.S. justice system to punish those responsible. Ahmad Nader Nadery, of the Afghan Independent Human Rights Commission, said, "These punishments are a joke with the Afghan people."[20]

While all U.S. attention was focused on the abuse of prisoners in Iraqi jails such as Abu Ghraib, severe abuses continued in Afghanistan. Several Afghan prisoners died at U.S. SOF firebases, which the ICRC, the UN, and the Afghan government were barred from visiting. Conditions at these firebases were appalling and abuse was widespread. According to an investigation by the Crimes of War Project and the *Los Angeles Times,* an Afghan prisoner, Jamal Nasser, age eighteen and a recruit for the ANA, died under torture at a SOF firebase in Gardez in March 2003. Another, Wakil Mohammed, an unarmed father of two, was shot dead after he had surrendered. The cases were first reported as battlefield deaths, and an investigation by the U.S. Army was opened only two years later. The culprits belonged to the Alabama-based Twentieth Special Forces Group. Retired Afghan police colonel Syed Nabi Siddiqi, thirty-five, who was held by the same unit in 2003, was subjected to beating, kicking, sleep deprivation, taunts, and sexual abuse.[21] In early 2003 ICRC officials complained to staff officers of Gen. Dan McNeill about this unit and five other firebases, including Camp Salerno and Camp Chapman, near Khost, where abuses were being reported.[22] By 2005 the Afghan Independent Human Rights Commission had logged eight hundred cases of abuse against Afghan prisoners at some thirty U.S. firebases.

The CIA ran its own secret detention centers, which were off-limits even to the U.S. military. One was situated at the former Ariana Hotel in central Kabul, just a few minutes' drive from the U.S. embassy. The Salt Pit was at an old brick factory just outside Kabul. Here, in November 2002, Afghan guards employed by the CIA stripped naked a young Afghan detainee and chained him to the concrete floor in the middle of winter. He died the next day, ending up as a "ghost detainee," one of an unknown number of people who just disappeared from the face of the earth because nobody could ask the CIA any questions. By 2005, thirty-three military personnel were facing charges of prisoner abuse, but only one civilian, David Passaro, forty, a CIA contractor, faced such charges. He went on trial in August 2006 on assault charges in connection with the death of Abdul Wali, the prisoner who died in June 2003 at the U.S. firebase in Asadabad.[23] Passaro's trial in Raleigh, North Carolina, included testimony on how he repeatedly hit Wali, a twenty-eight-year-old farmer, who was chained to the floor of his cell and was in such pain he pleaded to be killed.[24] In February 2007, Passaro received an eight-year sentence, becoming the first U.S. civilian to be convicted of abuse in the wars in Iraq and Afghanistan.

One of the worst aspects of the military's lack of preparedness for the war in Afghanistan was the extent to which it had to rely on private contractors for simple tasks. Contractors carried out interrogations, ran jails, provided bodyguards, carried out drug eradication, trained the police and army, and built wells and schoolhouses—all tasks that used to be carried out by the U.S. Army, the State Department, or USAID. The contractors' role was even greater in Iraq. With the kind of button-down security in place in Afghanistan, these people were virtually unaccountable. Government auditors could not check on their work while they continued to be paid vast sums. The use of private contractors by the CIA expanded enormously after 2002 as more tasks needed to be done by the military and the Pentagon had to conserve its soldiers for the upcoming war in Iraq. Subsequently the extensive use of contractors became the norm. DynCorp had won a $52 million contract to protect President Karzai and other Afghan leaders in 2003. Contractors now carried out secret interrogations and guarded prisoners.

The possession of such extensive powers with little oversight was open to abuse, brutality, and scandal, as in the astonishing case of two self-described American contractors and a journalist who were caught running a private jail in Kabul. When he was caught, their leader, Jonathan Idema, claimed to be working for the CIA. At his Kabul home, three Afghans were found hanging from the ceiling and five others badly beaten. Idema was a bounty hunter, but he had easily posed as a U.S. intelligence officer. He and his accomplices were sentenced by an Afghan court to long periods in jail.[25]

Britain's MI6 worked with more discretion than the CIA but was equally untutored in the ways of Afghanistan. A UK government report in 2005 said that British agents had conducted more than two thousand interviews of suspects in Afghanistan, Guantánamo, and Iraq and that there were "fewer than 15 occasions when UK intelligence personnel" broke the law regarding interrogations. The report concluded that intelligence personnel "were not sufficiently well trained on the Geneva Conventions."[26] MI6 and CIA officers frequently conducted joint interrogations.

The most explosive policy adopted by the CIA was the process of rendition. Rendered prisoners were truly "ghost detainees," with no rights, no prospect of a trial, and a future of permanent detention by unsavory regimes. CIA snatch teams could pick up prisoners anywhere in the world and transport them anywhere they liked. In spring 2002, the ICRC demanded that it be given access to prisoners under rendition. Instead, CIA lawyers further twisted legal boundaries by establishing a new category of prisoner: Persons Under Control, or PUC. Anyone held as PUC was automatically denied access to the ICRC, and even his existence was denied.[27] The ICRC became extremely frustrated with U.S. obduracy. In January 2004, after meeting U.S. officials in Washington, ICRC president Jakob Kellenberger went public saying he was deeply concerned about "the fate of an unknown number of people captured as part of the so-called global war on terror and held in undisclosed locations."[28] By now the ICRC was maintaining its own files on some 100 rendered prisoners who had simply disappeared. U.S. human rights lawyer Scott Horton said up to 150 people had been rendered by the CIA between 2001 and 2005.[29]

At least a dozen countries were involved in providing the United States secret detention facilities for rendered prisoners, including Azerbaijan, Egypt, Jordan, Morocco, Pakistan, Poland, Qatar, Romania, Saudi Arabia, Syria, Thailand, and Uzbekistan. PUCs were flown around the world to different locations on private jets belonging to dummy companies owned by the CIA. Journalists tracked seventy-five trips around the world that one jet made between 2001 and 2005.[30] In the process of rendition, the guilty and the innocent disappeared for years. Maher Arar, thirty-five, a Canadian software engineer abducted by the CIA in New York in September 2002, was taken to Syria, where he was held for a year. He was never charged and was freed after protests by the Canadian government.

The worst abusers of human rights received the most prisoners. The CIA never explained why it was choosing as its partners dubious regimes that had been condemned by the State Department for human rights abuses. "All I want to say is that there was 'before 9/11' and 'after 9/11,'" said Cofer Black, the head of the CIA's Counterterrorism Center. "After 9/11 the gloves came off."³¹ For the Bush administration, that was enough of an explanation.

With the United States leading the way in the abuse of prisoners and flouting the GC and international law, it was natural that their allies, such as Pakistan, Uzbekistan, Saudi Arabia, and Afghanistan, would follow suit. These countries carried out their own renditions and disappearances of prisoners, undermining their own legal processes and opening the way for local rulers to deal with domestic political opponents in the same manner. The deterioration of human rights in each country became linked to that government's proximity to the CIA.

The international community had gone to great lengths to set up a credible government in Kabul, but the effort was totally undermined when the CIA used the fledgling government and the powerful warlords to run secret prison systems. Thus, captured Taliban were frequently transferred to the Riasat Amniat-e-Meli, or National Directorate of Security (NDS), which had been modeled on the KGB in the 1980s and was controlled by the Northern Alliance after 9/11. The NDS held dozens of Taliban and other rendered prisoners on behalf of the CIA, and was ordered not to disclose these prisoners to the ICRC.

Foreign diplomats in Kabul became aware that the NDS was holding such prisoners only in August 2002, when thirteen prisoners, including eleven Pakistanis, escaped from D-3, a secret NDS detention center in Kabul. Afghan soldiers who gave chase killed twelve of them. This incident, which has not been disclosed until now, was particularly embarrassing for the International Security Assistance Force because it occurred in a zone under its control. Human Rights Watch and other groups documented extensive use of torture and abuse by the NDS. The editor of a Kabul magazine whom I know well and who had published an offending cartoon of NA leaders was visited by NDS officials in his office and told bluntly, "Look, we have thirty bullets in our clip, we can shoot thirty bullets into your chest right now and there is no one who can stop us."

In 2004, Karzai appointed Amrullah Saleh as the director-general of the NDS. A former intelligence aide to Ahmad Shah Masud and his liaison with the CIA before 9/11, Saleh was a young Panjsheri Tajik, but he broke with his own group to support Karzai and started to reform and modernize the NDS with help from the CIA and MI6. Saleh purged hundreds of officers, improved pay scales, and modernized training, turning the NDS from a factional into a national organization. Intelligence gathering seemed to have improved, because when the Taliban began suicide bombings in Kabul, the NDS caught several Taliban groups before they could set off their bombs. However, under Saleh, the NDS continued to carry out renditions on behalf of the CIA, and there were continuing reports of the NDS's extensive use of torture even as late as 2008.

Until the summer of 2003, warlords and commanders on the U.S. payroll also maintained their own prisons, often holding them on behalf of the Americans. In Herat, the warlord Ismael Khan frequently used torture. Prisoners described how "beatings, hanging upside-down, whipping, and shocking with electrical wires attached to the toes and thumbs" were commonplace.[32] A close friend of mine and a prominent lawyer in Herat, Rafiq Shahir, was arrested by Ismael Khan, who wanted to stop him from contesting a seat for the Loya Jirga in 2002. His family asked me to save his life. I telephoned several prominent officials in Kabul, asking them to intervene, but by the time Shahir was freed he had been whipped, beaten, and threatened with death. The scars on his back and stomach still show.[33]

The fundamentalist warlord Abdul Rasul Sayyaf maintained several prisons just outside Kabul. Hazrat Ali, a key ally of U.S. forces in eastern Afghanistan, ran private jails, while his commanders indulged in robbery, kidnapping, and sexual violence against young boys, even as they served under the command of the U.S. SOF. The warlords terrorized civilians, knowing they would never be reprimanded by the Americans. U.S. forces were to establish the same systems of secret detention in Iraq, using Iraqi warlords and military units.[34] The abuse of prisoners by U.S. jailers at Abu Ghraib was only a follow-on to what had already happened in Afghanistan.

Pakistan's military regime learned American methods most quickly. Initially Musharraf did not want to hold al Qaeda prisoners, as he feared a domestic backlash, so captured foreign prisoners were flown to Kandahar. But as more foreigners were caught—many of them innocent—the ISI set up its own detention centers. Foreigners were held in Kohat jail, in the North-West Frontier Province, where joint teams from the ISI, CIA, and FBI interrogated them. Pakistanis were held at Haripur jail, close to Islamabad, where the Americans had only limited access. By the spring of 2002 two hundred foreigners were being held in Kohat and four hundred Pakistanis in Haripur jail. Later, the army set up another jail, in Alizai, in the tribal areas, for those caught in FATA. Musharraf established anti-terrorist courts, which allowed the government to detain prisoners for one year without being charged.

The ISI was anxious to keep certain captured Pakistani militants away from U.S. interrogators, especially those who had fought on behalf of the ISI in Kashmir or Afghanistan or who had trained at ISI-run training camps. The ISI was naturally nervous about these extremists divulging information to the CIA. After the assassination attempts against Musharraf in December 2003, hundreds of militants were arrested in Pakistan, but the Americans were not given access to them. Omar Sheikh, the abductor of American journalist Daniel Pearl, was barred from being interrogated by U.S. agencies, and Islamabad ignored a U.S. extradition request for him. Yet Islamabad provided major help to the United States in its rendition program, holding al Qaeda suspects on behalf of the Americans until they were moved to other locations.

The extent to which the ISI interrogated and tortured prisoners on behalf of the CIA was revealed after Marwan Jabour, a Palestinian, was freed in June 2006. He had been arrested in Lahore by the ISI on May 9, 2004, and moved to a safe house in Islamabad run jointly by the ISI and CIA. The safe house contained specially built jail cells, and Jabour saw as many as twenty other prisoners there—many of them Pakistanis. Human Rights Watch documented the cases of half a dozen more Arab and Pakistani prisoners being held in the same safe house. Jabour was beaten and abused by his Pakistani guards and chained nightly to a wall. Other abuses included tying a rubber band around his penis and burning his arms and legs with a red-hot iron. He had two heart attacks while in detention.

Jabour was interrogated by CIA officers who included two young American women. The Pakistanis never tortured him in the presence of the Americans—a clear indication of the rules under which the CIA operated: foreign intelligence agencies could not use torture in the presence of the CIA. Jabour was later moved to a CIA black site outside Kabul and then to Israel, where he was freed. He admitted to having trained at an al Qaeda camp in Afghanistan in 1998 and to helping Arabs escape from Afghanistan in 2003, but he was never a member of al Qaeda and had not fought against the United States.[35]

The secret prisons proved especially useful in 2004 after the Pakistan army launched military operations in Waziristan, where hundreds of tribesmen were arrested. In August 2004, the ICRC issued a démarche to

Islamabad, demanding access to all prisoners captured in Waziristan, but it was rejected by Islamabad, which claimed that the war in Waziristan was not an armed conflict but criminality. The military was angry with the ICRC for its alleged failure to free the six hundred Pakistani prisoners still being held by General Dostum in northern Afghanistan. These prisoners were eventually freed in 2004, but they were rearrested by the ISI when they arrived back home.

Musharraf used the same harsh antiterrorism laws to deal with his political opponents at home. Asma Jehangir, head of the Human Rights Commission of Pakistan (HRCP), drew up a list of more than four hundred missing persons—people abducted, detained, or simply "disappeared" between 2001 and 2006. The HRCP began to document each case and appealed to the courts to free these prisoners. "The government is using the war on terror as an excuse to pick up and disappear hundreds of its political opponents, including those who are just critical of certain policies," Jehangir told me. The disappeared include journalists, scientists, political workers, and nationalists, with the largest number being political activists from Sindh and the insurgency-hit province of Balochistan. Baloch nationalists claimed that more than seven hundred Baloch political workers disappeared in 2006. Using the courts to try to force the government to declare these people's whereabouts led to the disappeared being moved from the custody of one intelligence agency to another, so that the government could maintain deniability.

Housewife Amina Janjua's husband, Masud, disappeared in July 2005, and for the next two years Amina and her children struggled to discover his whereabouts. Amina began a very public campaign for his release, which soon snowballed into a nationwide campaign for the release of hundreds of the disappeared. She joined with other families of the disappeared to create the Defense of Human Rights group. In December 2006, dozens of women—wives, daughters, and sisters of missing men—held an unprecedented demonstration outside parliament in Islamabad, shouting, "Give us back our loved ones!" The police beat the protesters, including Janjua's seventeen-year-old son, whose pants were stripped off by the police.[36] Musharraf not only had copied U.S. policies on how to make prisoners disappear but had developed new ones in order to secure his own political future.

In January 2007 the usually pliant Supreme Court of Pakistan demanded that the intelligence agencies find forty-one people whose cases had been documented by human rights groups. The government suddenly declared that it had freed twenty-five people from the list, although they were too terrified to talk about their experiences. They had been held in safe houses around the country by either Military Intelligence (MI) or the ISI. As the Supreme Court took up more cases of the disappeared, and humiliated the ISI and MI in the process, Musharraf suspended Iftikhar Chaudhry, the chief justice of the Supreme Court, which led to a mass movement against the regime by lawyers. The army refused to tolerate an activist judiciary that for the first time was determined to implement the law.

Even before 9/11, Uzbekistan under President Islam Karimov was one of the worst human rights offenders in the world. There were ten thousand political prisoners in Uzbek jails, a result of a vicious crackdown in the 1990s against anyone who opposed the president. Uzbekistan was also the only Muslim country where a person could be jailed for being too Islamic, such as for saying his prayers five times a day at the mosque. There was no independent judiciary, and the courts were controlled by the government. During trials the accused was unable to defend himself or call upon witnesses.

It would seem that an alliance with the CIA could not possibly make the Uzbek secret service much worse, but it did. After Karimov allied with Washington, more Uzbeks were arrested and there were no limits to the extent that torture was used. Two prisoners, Muzafar Avazov and Khuzniddin Alimov, who were accused of belonging to an Islamic extremist group, died on August 8, 2002, after being boiled to death in hot water. In measures unheard of even in communist times, prisoners were forbidden to fast during the fasting month of Ramadan, and the Koran was banned from cells.

Uzbekistan became the main jailer for the CIA for rendition suspects caught in Afghanistan and Pakistan. The extraordinary details of the alliance between the CIA, MI6, and the Uzbek secret service came to light thanks to Craig Murray, the former British ambassador to Tashkent who was so appalled by what he witnessed in Uzbekistan that first privately and then publicly he tried to change British government policy. In a 2003 speech made in Tashkent that eventually lost him his job, he said, "Uzbekistan is not a functioning democracy, nor does it appear to be moving in the direction of democracy ... there are between 7,000 to 10,000 people being held as political or religious prisoners. Many have been falsely convicted. Let's not make the war on terrorism an excuse to persecute people with a deep commitment to the Islamic religion."[37]

Later Murray was to testify to the European Parliament that "under the UK-US intelligence sharing agreement the US and UK have taken a policy decision that they will get testimonies obtained under torture in third countries—I say that with regret and certainty."[38] Murray described photographs of Muzafar Avazov, who had been boiled alive: "His face was bruised, his torso and limbs livid purple. . . . [A pathology report] said that the man's fingernails had been pulled out, that he had been beaten and that the line around his torso showed he had been immersed in hot liquid. He had been boiled alive."[39] President Karimov was invited to the White House in March 2002, and the CIA provided aid to modernize his intelligence services. The massacre in Andijan of an estimated eight hundred people protesting against the regime on May 13, 2005, led to outrage around the world and finally forced the United States and Europe to roll back their cozy relationship with Uzbekistan. The Americans lost their military base in Uzbekistan in 2006, but the joint U.S.-Uzbek Counterterrorism Center in Tashkent continued to operate.

In order to enlist other countries in the war on terrorism, the United States was prepared to reject human rights concerns and often accepted the lies told by regimes. Thus Washington's desire to enlist China to fight terrorism gave Beijing the freedom to pursue a harsh campaign against its political adversaries in the province of Xinjiang. Underground nationalist groups among the largely Muslim Uighur population had been demanding greater autonomy and even independence from China for several decades. Although there was minimal Islamic extremism among the Uighurs, China executed twenty-five Uighurs for political activity in 2001 and accused the exiled East Turkestan Islamic Movement (ETIM) of being linked to al Qaeda. China claimed, without offering sufficient evidence, that the several dozen Uighurs who had fought with the Taliban all belonged to ETIM.

Despite the lack of evidence, in August 2002 the United States declared the ETIM a terrorist organization. Washington had carried out the move to enlist Chinese support at the UN Security Council for its invasion of Iraq. However, the Chinese were to use the U.S. declaration as justification for a stepped-up crackdown on the practice of Islam in western China.[40] A total of twelve Uighurs captured by U.S. forces in Afghanistan were held at Guantánamo. Five were eventually considered innocent, and the United

States tried to persuade a third country to give them political asylum, fearing that if they were returned to China they would be executed. They were released in 2006 to a UN-run compound in Albania. American lawyers defending seven other Uighurs filed suit, demanding that these prisoners also be freed, as they were innocent.[41]

Yet none of these extraordinary systems of detention, interrogation, and torture could prepare the world for the monstrosity that the Americans created in Guantánamo. "When the prisoners arrived in Camp X-Ray, they were put in open-air cages like animals in a zoo," said a Western official who knows the prison well. "It was very hot, they did not know where they were, they did not know their legal status or what would happen to them, and there was no privacy, even when going to the toilet," the official added. For months at a time prisoners were not even allowed to speak to one another. "If you want a definition of this place, you don't have the right to have rights," Nizar Sassi, a French prisoner, wrote to his family in August 2002.[42] Eventually Guantánamo was to hold more than six hundred prisoners of forty nationalities speaking eighteen different languages.

Guantánamo undermined several clauses of the U.S. Constitution—the rule of law and due legal process, the commitment to international humanitarian law, the non-use of torture, and the limits placed upon presidential power. Guantánamo was not just a detention center but a permanent intelligence-gathering and interrogation laboratory where its American jailers could experiment in new ways to increase psychological pressure, abuse, and isolation of the prisoners.

After the ICRC began to visit Guantánamo in January 2002, it wrote a series of confidential reports to the U.S. government demanding improvements in living conditions and methods of interrogation and that prisoners be informed where they were and offered a legal process. In May 2004, after a series of leaks of confidential ICRC reports to the U.S. government, the ICRC publicly stated its main concern: "We're dealing here with a broader pattern and a system, as opposed to individual acts."[43] By the summer of 2002, fifty-three inmates were receiving mental health counseling, and in the next twelve months there were thirty-two suicide attempts by twenty-one captives. Abdul Razzaq, a Pakistani in an acute stage of depression, tried to kill himself four times.

In 2003 conditions worsened at Guantánamo. There was a new camp commandant, Gen. Geoffrey Miller, who was later to become notorious in Iraq when he was sent to take command of the Abu Ghraib prison. Miller made the guards part of the interrogation process, with the task of softening up the prisoners before they were questioned. After the new methods were put into force, depression and suicide bids among the prisoners increased.

Ultimately a handful of dedicated lawyers were responsible for pushing the Guantánamo cases to the U.S. Supreme Court. The story of British lawyer Clive Stafford Smith, who headed the small New Orleans–based Justice in Exile, is a saga of persistence, determination, and belief in the rule of law. After losing several cases in the lower courts in Washington, lawyers formed a coalition to take their writs to the Supreme Court. A major shift in public and judicial concern occurred in April 2004 after American TV showed the first pictures of the abuse of prisoners by guards at Abu Ghraib.[44]

Conditions at Guantánamo continued to worsen. In July 2005, fifty-two prisoners went on a hunger strike, refusing all food. By September the number rose to two hundred, and U.S. guards began to force-feed the prisoners. In June 2006, three prisoners—two Saudis and a Yemeni—committed suicide by hanging themselves with their bedsheets. Their deaths sparked outrage in the Muslim world and among European governments, who called for the closure of Guantánamo. In October 2005 an amendment passed by the Senate demanded that the U.S. military and the CIA conform to standards for interrogation that adhered to the GC. The senator and later presidential candidate John McCain gave a blunt warning to the American people on the implications of continuing to torture prisoners: "The abuse of prisoners harms, not helps our war effort. In my experience the abuse of prisoners often produces bad intelligence because under torture a person will say anything he thinks his captors want to hear—whether it is true or false. . . . This is a war of ideas. . . . Prisoner abuses exact a terrible toll on us in this war of ideas."[45]

However, diehard Republicans waged a fierce rearguard action, criticizing the UN and the ICRC. A Senate Republican committee demanded that the United States reconsider its funding for the organization, saying the ICRC had "lost its way" and was willfully undermining the U.S. war on terrorism.[46] Cherif Bassiouni, an Egyptian appointed as a UN monitor for human rights in Afghanistan, issued a report in April 2005 accusing U.S. forces and contractors of "abusive practices, including torture." Under pressure from Washington, the UN first sacked Bassiouni and then declared his job redundant. Reports of abuse and torture by U.S. forces had visibly increased anti-Americanism in the Muslim world and Europe. In the summer of 2005, reports that guards at Guantánamo had flushed copies of the Koran down the toilets led to widespread demonstrations across the Muslim world, including in Afghanistan, where seventeen lives were lost in riots.

Under enormous pressure, the U.S. Supreme Court finally reacted, ruling on June 28, 2006, that fourteen Guantánamo detainees could file writs in U.S. courts and thereby challenge their indefinite detention. It was a landmark decision, although it had taken nearly two and a half years for the Court to pass the judgment. "A state of war is not a blank check for the President," said the Court ruling.[47] In September, Bush admitted the existence of the CIA's black sites and renditions and said that fourteen prisoners, including Khalid Sheikh Mohammed, had been transferred to Guantánamo and would face trial. Nine of the fourteen had been picked up in Pakistan. However, the fate of at least thirty-eight prisoners and possibly as many as sixty was still unknown, and it was presumed they remained in secret detention.[48]

The U.S. military now admitted for the first time that twenty-seven prisoners had died in detention in Iraq and Afghanistan, out of an estimated fifty thousand detainees held in both countries since 9/11. The Pentagon admitted to the deaths of seven prisoners in Afghanistan, although human rights groups put the number at eight. No senior U.S. officer was ever held accountable for any of the deaths.[49] In the meantime, hundreds of prisoners from Guantánamo who had been falsely accused were freed.

The Bush administration now attempted to undermine the Supreme Court judgment by pushing through Congress a new bill to legalize the military tribunals the Court had found unconstitutional. Another polarizing debate took place in Congress. Former secretary of state Colin Powell weighed in for the first time: "If you just look at how we are perceived in the world and the kind of criticism we have taken over Guantánamo, Abu Ghraib and renditions, whether we believe it or not, people are now starting to question whether we are following our own high standards," he said in his first criticism of the administration he had once served.[50]

Congress passed the new law just a few weeks before the critical November 2006 congressional elections, in which the Republicans were heavily defeated. The new law allowed the prosecution of terrorist suspects for war crimes by special military commissions but would limit suspects' rights in the trials, including restricting their ability to examine the evidence against them. (No decent legal system would deny an individual the right to see the evidence against him.) The law also granted legal protection to CIA interrogators.

By now there was a worldwide backlash against renditions and the ease with which the CIA was able to overturn state laws and kidnap anyone, anywhere. In late 2005 an Italian judge filed a case accusing twenty-six CIA officers of kidnapping Hassan Mustafa Osama Nasr, an Egyptian cleric who had disappeared in Milan in February 2003. In Sweden a parliamentary ombudsman criticized Swedish security services for collaborating with the CIA in handing over two Egyptian suspects in 2001. In Germany a judge questioned the kidnapping of Khaled al-Masri, a Lebanese-born German citizen, by the CIA in Macedonia in 2003.[51] In February 2007, Canada's Supreme Court struck down the indefinite detention of terrorist suspects.

European opposition parties accused their governments of helping the CIA render prisoners. In a report prepared for the Council of Europe in June 2006, fourteen European nations were named as facilitating the CIA in carrying out renditions. Air traffic control logs showed that the CIA had secret transfer points for renditions in Szymany, Poland, and Timisoara, Romania, while other countries had provided logistics, backup, and refueling stops for CIA aircraft. Human Rights Watch accused Poland's secret services of being at the heart of the CIA's European rendition operations.[52] The most damning report was issued by a special committee of the European Parliament in January 2007, which alleged that several European governments were aware of more than 1,245 secret CIA flights in and out of European airports between 2001 and 2005. The report marked a turning point in Europe as more governments were forced to rein in the activities of the CIA and their own intelligence services. However, the Bush administration refused to see these disclosures and protests from its allies as a reason to change policy and instead carried on as before.

In January 2007, hundreds of prisoners marked their five-year stay at Guantánamo—in the same legal limbo as when they arrived—without a single high-level suspect brought to trial. Ghulam Ruhani, a twenty-three-year-old Afghan shopkeeper seized near Gardez, was the prison's third inmate and was still there in 2007. Of the 773 prisoners who had spent time in the prison, 380, from twenty-nine countries, had been returned home.

Of the detainees remaining in 2007, Afghans made up the largest number, followed by Saudis and Yemenis. As the number of prisoners in Guantánamo was reduced to 275 by January 2008, the United States doubled the number of prisoners it was holding at Bagram air base, near Kabul. In January 2008, there were 630 prisoners being held at Bagram, including some who had been there for five years and whom the ICRC had still not been given access to. Across the world, Guantánamo had become the most negative image of the United States in its war on terrorism. The example of Guantánamo had encouraged Muslim governments allied to the United States to subvert their own laws and constitutions, bring their governments into disrepute, and alienate their own people. The result was a series of political crises that were to hit Pakistan, Afghanistan, and Central Asia.

CHAPTER FIFTEEN

Drugs and Thugs

Opium Fuels the Insurgency

In the summer of 1997, Abdul Rashid, the head of the Taliban's so-called counter-narcotics force in Kandahar, patiently explained to me his unique job— banning farmers from growing hashish while allowing them to grow and produce opium, even though the Koran forbids Muslims to take any intoxicants. Rashid explained the dichotomy succinctly: "Opium is permissible because it is consumed by *kafirs* [unbelievers] in the West and not by Afghans, but hashish is consumed by Afghans and Muslims," he said with a self-satisfied smile. According to his inescapable logic, what Afghans were addicted to was banned. Yet there was a more practical reason why opium was cultivated. "There would be an uprising against the Taliban if we forced farmers to stop poppy cultivation."[1] A few years later the Taliban's falsification of Islamic teachings, combined with their need to fund their insurgency against U.S. and NATO forces and generate a support base for their movement by protecting opium-growing farmers, would lead to the largest production of drugs the world had ever seen. The Taliban resurgence, al Qaeda's reorganization, and the restarting of its training camps for international terrorist groups after the U.S. invasion would have been impossible without the explosion in heroin production.

In turn, the attempts of the Afghan government and the international community to rebuild state institutions, curb warlordism, and create a viable legal economy were heavily imperiled by the illicit cash generated by drug traffickers. Despite spending large sums in aid programs, the international community failed to agree on how to eradicate opium, interdict shipments, catch drug traffickers, or provide farmers with alternative live-lihoods. The flood of money to tribesmen on both sides of the border led to the spread of Talibanization. In short, one of the major reasons for the failure of nation building in Afghanistan and Pakistan was the failure to deal with the issue of drugs.

After 9/11, growing opium was a matter of prudent judgment for farm-ers. Jalaluddin Khan, a farmer in Helmand province, cultivated poppy so he could feed his extended family of thirty, including four brothers and their families. In 2003 he planted poppies on his eighteen-acre farm— something he had done six times in the past ten years to make ends meet. Before winter set in, Khan would meticulously hoe his soil to uproot weeds, sprinkle fertilizer, and repair irrigation channels before sowing poppy seeds saved from the previous year's crop. A few weeks later thin shoots appeared and grew into cabbagelike plants, which soon sprouted bright red flowers. The flowers bloomed like a sea of red until their petals fell away to reveal a hardened capsule, which was lanced with thin homemade blades. Khan squeezed each capsule with his fingers until a milky white viscous sub-stance oozed out. The liquid solidified into a brown gum, which was scraped off with a trowel. This operation would be repeated every few days until the plant stopped yielding gum. The crop had taken just four months to mature and needed no excessive water or care.

The raw opium would be slapped into a cake and kept wet in plastic bags until the local drug dealer arrived. It would then be sent to makeshift laboratories in the mountains where, with the help of a few readily avail-able precursor chemicals, the dark brown paste would be turned into a fine white powder—heroin. Ten kilograms of opium paste produces one kilo-gram of heroin. For Khan it was the cheapest and fastest cash crop to grow, giving a good return, and could be stored for several years if prices dropped. The crop provided a support system for farmers that the state could not match. Since the early 1990s, farmers could mortgage their crop to dealers for a cash loan while dealers provided protection, agricultural extension services, technical assistance in the shape of better seeds, and even the skilled labor needed when harvesting began. To eradicate opium, the state would have to improve agricultural services. "We know that planting poppy is bad, but our country is destroyed and we have received little as-sistance, so we have no real alternative to poppy," said Khan. More than two million Afghan farmers like Khan were growing poppy as their pri-mary cash crop by 2005.[2]

Three decades of war had led to Afghanistan's dubious status as the world's heroin provider. By the late 1980s, as the CIA-sponsored Afghan Mujahedin bled the Soviet occupation forces, the region comprising Pakistan, Iran, and Afghanistan earned the title of the Golden Crescent, replacing the Golden Triangle of Laos, Myanmar, and Thailand as the lead producer of opium. Extensive opium production had first begun in Pakistan, which in 1986 produced more than eight hundred tons of opium a year, or 70 percent of the world's heroin supply. Afghan commanders transplanted the crop into southern Afghanistan, and opium paste was then carried back into Pakistan and used by the Mujahedin to fund the war, while the CIA-ISI turned a blind eye. Several high-ranking Pakistani army, air force, and ISI officials were caught trafficking heroin—in 1983 the entire ISI staff in Quetta had to be removed for dealing in opium. As I describe in my earlier book, the ISI used money from the drug trade to fund some of its covert operations.[3]

The CIA played a dubious role just as it had done earlier in Vietnam, condemning the trade but allowing it to flourish. In the 1980s the U.S. Drug Enforcement Administration (DEA) identified forty major heroin syndicates, including some headed by Pakistani government officials, yet not a single one was broken up, as the CIA wanted no embarrassing links among the "heroic" Mujahedin leaders, Pakistani officials, and drug traffickers. At least one DEA official resigned in protest and others left Pakistan in despair at the CIA's refusal to deal with the problem.[4] After the Soviet withdrawal from Afghanistan, the United States poured more than $100 million into Pakistan to eradicate poppy cultivation there. Production dropped to twenty-four tons of opium in 1997 and again to a mere two tons in 1999. Pakistan became virtually drug-free, as opium production shifted back to Afghanistan, now under the Taliban regime.

Opium fueled the Afghan civil war in the 1990s, when the warlords used drug money to pay soldiers' salaries and buy weapons and food, as the war had destroyed food production. Only 12 percent of Afghanistan's land was arable, but that was reduced a further 40 percent during the civil war. Once self-sufficient in food production, Afghanistan was now dependent on imported wheat from Pakistan, paid for in money earned from opium. As the Taliban expanded north and west so did their control over the illicit opium trade, and production rose from 1,570 tons in 1990 to 2,800 tons in 1997.

In the 1990s the Taliban collected *usher* from farmers, an Islamic agricultural tax ranging from 10 to 20 percent of production, and also charged traffickers a *zakat* tax on their shipments of heroin. Traditionally a charitable Islamic tax distributed to the poor, *zakat* should be no more than 2.5 percent of an individual's disposable income. Ironically, by taxing both opium production and trafficking, the Taliban became the first Afghan government to tax agriculture, which no previous regime had had the capacity to do. The Taliban expanded export routes, funneling drugs through Pakistan, Iran, Central Asia, and the Arabian Gulf. By 1998 the Taliban and drug traffickers were flying heroin out of Kandahar to the ports of Dubai, Abu Dhabi, and Sharjah—using al Qaeda contacts to sell drugs directly to the Gulf mafia and earn greater profits.

The Taliban were repeatedly told by the United States and the UN that if they banned poppy cultivation, it would win them international sympathy and perhaps even political recognition. After three consecutive bumper crops, the Taliban suddenly banned poppy cultivation in 2001. Harshly imposed on farmers, the ban was highly effective—opium production that year slumped to just 185 tons—and was termed "the most effective drug control action of modern times."[5] However, the Taliban did not prohibit trafficking in existing stocks, and it later became clear that the ban had been the result of overproduction and a slump in opium prices, which had collapsed from $600 to just $30 a kilogram. The ban promptly pushed the price up to $650 a kilogram. Nevertheless it had devastated many farmers, who were left with large unpaid loans to drug dealers and no source of income. The ban led to anger against the Taliban on the eve of 9/11 and increased opposition to the regime. The collapse of the Taliban regime coincided with the poppy planting season, and farmers immediately planted poppy to pay off their debts.[6]

Before the war, drug dealers had disposed of their stocks fearing that the United States would target them. "Dealers are preparing for the worst by selling their stocks, but they are also expecting farmers to grow poppy once the war is over," said Bernard Frahi, the UN Office on Drugs and Crime regional chief in Islamabad.[7] As a result of the great sell-off, the price of opium plummeted to $150 a kilogram. The Pentagon had a list of twenty-five or more drug labs and warehouses in Afghanistan but refused to bomb them because some belonged to the CIA's new NA allies. The United States told its British allies that the war on terrorism had nothing to do with counter-narcotics. Instead, drug lords were fêted by the CIA and asked if they had any information about Osama bin Laden. Thus, the

United States sent the first and clearest message to the drug lords: that they would not be targeted.

Britain became the lead nation in developing a counter-narcotics strategy. It had a vested interest because 98 percent of heroin sold on London's streets came from Afghanistan. Its intelligence service MI6 suggested buying the entire 2002 opium harvest from farmers. The Foreign Office objected and the plan was dropped in favor of compensating farmers for destroying their crop—a plan that was disastrous when implemented. Farmers were paid cash for eradicating their crop at the rate of $1,250 to $1,500 per hectare. MI6 and British commandos handed over cash to governors and police chiefs in the provinces to pay off the farmers.

The program, which cost more than $80 million, was mired in massive corruption, as Afghan officials distributed the money to their tribes or clans, who took the cash but failed to eradicate the crop. Other farmers used the money to increase cultivation, while thousands of others who did eradicate their crop received nothing. A huge piece of the money ended up in the war chests of the warlords. The opium harvest for 2002 had leaped to 3,400 tons, from 185 tons the previous year. Farmers earned an estimated $13,000 from a hectare of land under poppy versus $400 from a hectare under wheat.[8]

The center of the country's drug trade was Helmand, a province the size of Wales, with a population of one million. Helmand had once been the epitome of progress. The Helmand River flowed through the province, and in the 1960s Morrison-Knudsen, the company that built the Hoover Dam in the United States, was hired by USAID to build a dam and 300 miles of irrigation canals that would irrigate the Helmand Valley. The project was highly successful, creating 250,000 acres of arable land out of the desert, which quickly became the fruit and bread basket for Afghanistan and led to the training of an entire generation of Afghan engineers and agricultural extension workers. Hundreds of American families lived in Lashkargah, the capital, and a former American community center still boasts the remains of a dance floor, cinema, bar, and library. Historian Arnold Toynbee wrote in 1960 that the Americans were creating "an America-in-Asia."[9]

The irrigation system collapsed after the Soviet invasion, but the land was arable and farmers turned to cultivating poppy, encouraged by the Akhunzadas, a powerful family who headed the Alizai tribe that dominated the province. The Akhunzadas fought the Soviets and traded in opium. In the autumn of 2003, when I visited Lashkargah, there were no paved roads, electricity, or running water. Dust storms swept through the bare landscape, caking everything in a fine white powder. The American-built paved roads with street lighting were now sandy tracks. Amanullah, the chief of police, told me that his men had not received their salaries for a year, while teachers at a local girls' college had not been paid for six months. Kabul and the international community seemed to have abandoned Helmand province.

Yet at a massive car mall in the middle of this dust bowl town at least eight thousand brand-new vehicles were parked bumper to bumper, where buyers could pick up the latest four-wheel-drive Toyotas or Mercedeses. The customers were bearded Pashtun drug dealers and farmers, some of whom owned a dozen vehicles and dropped wads of cash to buy new ones. Helmand was the country's center for opium, and its traffickers began to spread their expertise and skills to other parts of the country, enticing farmers to grow poppy so they could buy their crops, too.

Farmers from northern Afghanistan visited Helmand to buy poppy seeds and hire skilled laborers. Ali Ahmad Jalali, the minister of the interior, told me he was tracking drug dealers from Pakistan and Helmand who were renting large tracts of land in northern provinces and setting up old-style plantations to grow poppy. According to British officials, the governor of Helmand, Sher Mohammed Akhunzada—who had accompanied Karzai into Afghanistan on a motorbike in 2001 and remained a close friend of the president—was generally believed to profit from drug involvement. He was accused of favoring his cronies with prime real estate parcels and commanded hundreds of well-paid gunmen, while the police force was undermanned and unpaid and mullahs, aid workers, teachers, and women activists who opposed poppy cultivation were being gunned down. Most Western NGOs had fled by 2003, fearing Akhunzada's gunmen or the Taliban.

Akhunzada strongly denied the accusations of corruption and involvement in drug trafficking and blamed the West for the lack of aid. "In the past two years no significant reconstruction has been done in Helmand, even though it is most strategic for the country's stability," he told me. "When the Taliban are paying their fighters thousands of dollars, I just have promises to offer people rather than aid projects."[10] Amazingly, the only U.S. military presence in Helmand comprised just the 120 U.S. SOF who made up a provincial reconstruction team. Their officers felt abandoned and they had only minuscule funds for reconstruction projects.

In 2004, USAID hired Chemonics International, a consulting firm from Washington, to implement a $130 million project to revitalize agriculture in Helmand, but the project could not be implemented because there were no U.S. troops to guard the technicians. The following year a canal-cleaning project funded by USAID, which provided employment to thousands of Afghans, was stopped after the Taliban killed five workers. Britain and the United States had committed $119 million for alternative livelihoods for farmers, but in 2005 the program had spent only $4 million—all of that for salaries. There was no coordination among the Western allies or among the Afghan government, the U.S. military, aid agencies, and the UN. Nobody, it seemed, was prepared to take the burgeoning crisis in Helmand seriously.

Some foreigners continued to stick it out in Helmand. Steve Shaulis, a stocky American from Maryland, had established a for-profit aid agency in Helmand to help farmers grow cash crops and fruit. "We can't stop farmers growing poppy, we can only take their arguments for growing poppy away one by one by offering real alternatives," Shaulis said.[11] He encouraged farmers to grow cotton, which was processed in local ginning factories, but it was a drop in the ocean in a sea of poppy. Sarah Chayes, a former American journalist with National Public Radio, settled in Kandahar and helped the Karzai family set up an NGO. Later she left them to work on income-generating schemes among Kandahar's women. Hardly any other foreign NGOs were prepared to work in the south.

The drug epidemic led to high volumes of crime and inter-clan feuds, further undermining security and giving the Taliban the opportunity to adjudicate between tribes. Corruption was rampant within the local administration. "Eighty percent of the crimes are being committed by local militias, commanders, and the police rather than criminals, so the Taliban are not to blame for everything," Yousuf Pashtun, the governor of Kandahar province, told me. "It's a vicious circle—if there is no peace there can be no reconstruction and if there is no reconstruction then peace is impossible to attain."[12]

Helmand soon became the major conduit for opium sales from other provinces, even the far northern provinces of Mazar and Badakhshan. The UN estimated that the entire opium crop from the provinces of Ghor, Bamiyan, and Uruzgan traveled through Helmand to be sold in Pakistan and Iran.[13] Opium arrived from as far north as Badakhshan province. Heavily armed convoys of four-wheeled vehicles crossed the desert to reach

Zaranj, in Nimroz province, which shared a three-hundred-mile deserted border with Pakistan and Iran. Up to twenty pickups or Toyota Land Cruisers armed with missiles and rockets that could bring down helicopter gunships would travel at 150 miles per hour across the sands. It was the favorite route for the traffickers, and there were no U.S. satellites monitoring them or U.S. SOF patrols to stop them.

The barely existent justice system compounded the problem. Honest police officers could not gather evidence against drug dealers because they did not have the training or technology to do so. Security forces had neither the training, arms, nor vehicles to catch them, while judges could not prosecute traffickers because the courts did not know the procedures. At least in Kabul attempts were made to create an antidrug infrastructure. With the support of UNODC, a Counter Narcotics Directorate (CND) was set up in 2003 to coordinate the fight against drugs. That year Britain helped establish the Counter-Narcotics Police Force within the Interior Ministry. In December 2004, UNODC set up the counter-narcotics Criminal Justice Task Force, consisting of thirty-five investigators, fifteen judges, and thirty-five prosecutors who were to receive special training, while British commandos trained an elite Afghan counter-narcotics force. Yet the impact on the ground remained minimal.

Ashraf Ghani, the finance minister, was one of the first to warn the world of the danger of Afghanistan developing into a "narco-state," and he urged Western donors to fund alternative jobs, crops, and livelihoods for the farmers. "Poppy farmers will accept the loss of their crops, their land, and their livelihoods only if they believe in an alternative future," Ghani said. The World Bank made equally dire predictions. "The linkages between drugs, warlords, and insecurity add up to a vicious circle of mutually reinforcing problems. . . . Afghanistan's opium economy presents a grave danger to the country's entire state-building and reconstruction agenda," said a World Bank report.[14]

There was no consensus or strategy within the international community on what to do. Initially the United States even refused to acknowledge that drugs were a problem. Rumsfeld and the military ignored the issue, claiming that it was an unimportant social issue unconnected to fighting terrorism. When Rumsfeld was pointedly asked in 2003 what the United States was doing about drugs in Helmand, he put the questioner down, saying, "You ask what we're going to do and the answer is, I don't really know."[15]

Rumsfeld refused Colin Powell's request that U.S. forces at least interdict the convoys of the drug traffickers. The Pentagon said it would not authorize interdiction in case it led to "mission creep," where the army ran the risk of getting involved in more missions than its limited numbers of troops could handle, as well as possibly antagonizing local warlords who might also be involved in drug trafficking. A frustrated U.S. SOF colonel in charge of the PRT in Helmand told me how he watched convoys of opium traveling past his camp every morning but did not have orders to stop them. His rules of engagement stated that if he discovered drug shipments he *could* destroy them, but there was no order saying he *must* destroy them or that he *must* interdict drug convoys.[16]

The huge amount of poppies planted in 2003 provided a massive harvest in 2004. Even though drought and disease ravaged some of the crop, 4,200 tons of opium were harvested compared with 3,600 in the previous year. Farmland under poppy cultivation increased by 64 percent, and for the first time poppy was cultivated in all thirty-four provinces. UNODC estimated that 2.3 million Afghans, or 14 percent of the rural population, were now involved in cultivation. Farm laborers earned ten dollars a day collecting opium resin—five times the average daily wage. The opium economy was now worth $2.8 billion, equal to 60 percent of the country's legal economy, which was calculated at $4.5 billion.[17] Over 80 percent of Afghan opium was now refined into heroin inside the country, rather than being exported as raw opium paste.

The 2004 harvest embarrassed Washington and London sufficiently for them to begin a more serious debate as to what to do. The United States wanted aerial spraying to eradicate the crop as it was already doing in Colombia. Britain and the Afghan government were adamantly opposed, fearing it would damage other crops and livestock and drive angry farmers into the hands of the Taliban. They proposed ground eradication, which was slow and cumbersome but more discriminatory. Robert Charles, the U.S. assistant secretary of state for International Narcotics and Law Enforcement Affairs, or INL, insisted that spraying was the only answer. Charles upped the ante in Washington when he demanded that U.S. forces get involved in both interdiction and eradication, but Rumsfeld refused. "We could have destroyed all the [heroin] labs and warehouses in the three primary provinces—Helmand, Nangarhar, and Kandahar—in a week," Charles said later.

Robert Charles rightly predicted that failure in 2004 would worsen the insurgency and force the United States to send in more troops. He was the first senior U.S. official to admit publicly that drug profits were funding the Taliban. However, in January 2005, with the new secretary of state Condoleezza Rice offering no support and Karzai and Tony Blair opposed to his views, Charles resigned. The internal debate in Washington was irreparably weakened but continued for more than a year. The United States committed larger sums to counter narcotics, but there was no agreement on how to spend the money. Out of $780 million allocated by Washington in 2004, only $120 million was for alternative livelihoods—the most important ingredient in weaning farmers away from poppy cultivation.[18] The opium crop was grown in only about 3 percent of the total arable land, so clearly farmers were growing other crops, and there was enormous potential for their improving yields and the incomes from them if aid was directed there. However, developing alternative crops and livelihoods was never a serious part of U.S. policy, and the debate circled around aerial or ground eradication.

Some ground eradication did start but only made matters worse. Among the Pashtun tribes, any kind of eradication was considered unfair because the poor farmer would be hit first while the rich ones could bribe their way out of trouble. Ground eradication was used by powerful tribes and officials to weaken their rivals. Those tribes out of power were targeted first, and sought further protection from the Taliban. The danger with aerial eradication was that it would unite *all* the tribes against the government. Traffickers actually welcomed limited eradication because it would raise the price of opium, which had fallen from six hundred dollars to ninety dollars per kilo after three massive harvests. The United States refused to recognize that the problem was not drugs per se but drug money, which undermined state institutions, encouraged corruption, and helped fund the Taliban and al Qaeda. Farmers received only about 20 percent of the revenue from drugs, while traffickers received 80 percent. The export value of the opium crop rose from just under $1.0 billion in 2000 to $2.5 billion in 2002 and $3.1 billion in 2006.[19] Only by targeting the major traffickers could drug money be stopped from reaching the extremists.

Karzai and the Kabul government shared the blame for failing to tackle the major traffickers. The UN and all the major Western embassies gathered evidence that Karzai was tolerating suspected drug traffickers because they were either his political allies or close friends or because he could not afford their removal from power. There was enormous pressure on Karzai to remove Akhunzada as governor of Helmand, but Karzai refused to do so. Finally, in late 2005, just before British troops were due to be deployed in Helmand, Tony Blair gave Karzai an ultimatum: Britain would not deploy troops as long as Akhunzada remained in his post. Karzai succumbed but gave Akhunzada a seat in the Senate while keeping on his younger brother as deputy governor—a move that undermined the British deployment. In 2006, during the Taliban offensive, Karzai turned to Akhunzada again, putting him in charge of an auxiliary police force in the province, despite strong British objections.

Another close friend of the Karzai family was Arif Nurzai, the minister for tribal affairs, whose sister was married to Karzai's younger brother Ahmed Wali Karzai. Western embassies accused Nurzai of protecting traffickers, which he vehemently denied. Western pressure forced Karzai to remove him from the cabinet, but he was then elected to parliament and became deputy speaker of the Wolesi Jirga, the lower house of parliament. *New York Times* correspondent Carlotta Gall named several staunch Karzai allies, including Akhunzada and Nurzai, as widely believed to profit from the drug trade, and she quoted unnamed diplomatic sources as saying "there are even reports" that Ahmed Wali Karzai was also linked to the drug trade.[20] Wali Karzai denied the charges, but the president was furious and ordered an investigation into Gall's sources, which turned out to be a senior British diplomat whom the Afghan government briefly declared persona non grata.[21]

Reports about Wali Karzai intensified in June 2006 after the American television network ABC quoted U.S. Army files purloined from the Bagram base describing how Wali Karzai had received money from drug lords. "They want to give my brother a bad name," Wali Karzai retorted.[22] The U.S. military said the report was outdated but did not reject its authority. Wali Karzai lived in Kandahar, where he represented his brother in managing the southern Pashtun tribes. He was criticized by many Pashtuns for allegedly favoring his own tribe and other tribes loyal to the Karzai family, while pushing away tribes who were not natural allies, forcing them to join the Taliban. In the 2005 parliamentary elections, Wali Karzai was elected head of the Kandahar provincial council, further enhancing his power in the south. Many of the former NA warlords—ministers and generals in the north—were also involved in drug trafficking.

The Interior Ministry did not just fail to take down the warlords; it became a major protector of drug traffickers, and Karzai refused to clean it out. As warlord militias were demobilized and disarmed by the UN, commanders found new positions in the Interior Ministry and continued to provide protection to drug traffickers. Positions such as police chief in poppy-producing districts were auctioned off to the highest bidder, with the going rate reported to be one hundred thousand dollars for a six-month appointment to a position with a salary of just sixty dollars a month. The massive corruption within the police that was ignored by Germany, which was supposed to be training the force, was a major cause for public dissatisfaction and gave the Taliban further reason to mobilize public support. In 2004 the fragmented production of opium by thousands of dealers was consolidated under a smaller number of large dealers. By 2007, UNODC estimated that there were just twenty-five to thirty senior traffickers, each one running two hundred or more junior drug dealers, who in turn ran some five hundred local purchasers. Over 70 percent of the major traffickers were based in the south but none had been jailed.[23]

Tribal loyalties, politics, and links to the Taliban or the government were closely mixed up and it was impossible to unravel one thread without unraveling the entire ball of string. There was also a blurring of lines by powerful figures who trafficked in drugs and those who protected traffickers. The determining factor was Karzai's weakness and unwillingness to target major drug traffickers. I tackled him about this regularly, but he vehemently denied that anybody in his administration was involved in drugs, and if asked about particular individuals, he said they were needed for the time being or that there was no concrete evidence against them— which was often true. He repeated these arguments to Western donors, who found it more difficult to justify troops and aid to Afghanistan when the president was appointing drug dealers to top political posts. It was clear that improving the justice system, training police, or eradicating crops was meaningless unless the top traffickers were caught.

In 2005, after several U.S. congressmen shamed the Pentagon for its inaction, the Pentagon and the CIA finally came around to publicly accepting that drug money was fueling terrorism. The United States, Britain, and the G8 group of nations approved a major counter-narcotics plan at a summit meeting in London in June 2005. Rumsfeld reluctantly agreed to provide airlift and planning for five Afghan commando teams trained by U.S. and British Special Forces. However, he continued to drag his feet when it came to implementation. The Pentagon promised to embed DEA officials with U.S. troops and provide them helicopters to raid heroin labs, but the DEA officials in Afghanistan were ignored by the U.S. military.

Under pressure, Rumsfeld had accepted that there was a problem but then made sure that the U.S. military was not involved in doing anything to solve it.

The arrival of NATO forces in the south in 2006 made little difference. No NATO country mandated its troops to interdict drug convoys or catch traffickers. Despite the G8 plan, no practical help was offered by any country. "Afghanistan is teetering on becoming a narco-state," admitted Gen. James Jones, the overall commander of NATO in Europe in May 2006. But in the same breath he added, "You will not see NATO soldiers burning poppy fields. This is not our mandate."[24] Only Antonio Costa, head of the UNODC, had the courage to call a spade a spade. "Unfortunately Afghanistan is addicted to its own opium," said Costa. "Members of the local administration, police officials . . . and even politicians and members of parliament benefit from the trafficking."[25]

Opium production rose to a staggering 6,100 tons in 2006, the highest ever recorded, and to 8,200 tons the following year, when Afghanistan produced 93 percent of the world's heroin. In 2006 cultivation rose in Helmand by 162 percent, and there was an increase of 77 percent in the northeastern province of Badakhshan. In 2006 the opium sector contributed nearly half, or 46 percent, of Afghanistan's gross domestic product, which was now estimated at $6.7 billion. There was no doubt that the Taliban's major offensive in the summer of 2006 was due largely to the enormous income it now accrued from opium. "We are seeing a very strong connection between the increase in the insurgency on the one hand and the increase in cultivation on the other hand," warned Costa.[26]

In 2007 Helmand alone was responsible for 50 percent of the crop, or the equivalent of the total crop in 2005. Nevertheless, in 2007 thirteen provinces were declared drug-free, as the United States and UNODC had initiated a reward scheme in the shape of increased development funds for those governors and provinces that reduced production. The United States and European countries were now spending on average one billion dollars a year on counter-narcotics, but the effect in the south was still negligible.

Drug money was everywhere. It played a major role in the 2005 parliamentary elections. In a study, Andrew Wilder, a prominent American researcher based in Kabul, concluded that at least seventeen elected members of parliament were drug traffickers, while twenty-four were connected to drug gangs.[27] In Kabul, multistory glass and concrete shopping malls with the city's first lifts and escalators went up, as traffickers laundered their money through the construction industry. Huge, gaudy multicolored homes—some designed to look like the White House, others straight out of Disneyland—sprang up in Kabul's suburbs, looking uncomfortably incongruent next to the hovels of the poor, where plastic sheets kept out the rain and snow. New four-by-four vehicles and diamond-studded guns and watches became de rigueur for traffickers. There was another unseen cost: more than 170,000 Afghans, including 30,000 women, were hooked on heroin, consuming 90 tons of opium a year by 2005, and there were only a handful of clinics dealing with addiction.[28]

Drug money permeated the local government in every province, making it impossible to carry out the simplest development projects unless the drug lords cleared them first. Drug money paralyzed the building of a legal economy, as no industry, agriculture, or trade could compete with drug profits. People could not be persuaded to take ordinary jobs because the drug industry provided better salaries. Most significantly, drug money allowed the Taliban to pay and arm its troops, compensate the families of suicide bombers, and import new and better weapons while al Qaeda was able to reestablish training camps for international terrorists. In 2006 the State Department belatedly conceded that "Afghanistan's huge drug trade severely impacts efforts to rebuild the economy, develop a strong democratic government based on the rule of law, and threatens regional stability."[29]

U.S. and NATO forces still failed to develop either a coherent interdiction or an eradication strategy. "Even now, the Bush administration is disproportionately concentrating on the most visible, but least effective approach, forcible crop eradication, which merely moves the problem around and enriches traffickers by raising the price of their opium holdings," said *The New York Times*.[30] In any effective counter-narcotics strategy, eradication had to follow rather than precede development and the creation of alternative livelihoods. A revival of agriculture had to take place across the board. This is what experts such as Barnett Rubin and I had argued to Andrew Natsios and USAID right after 9/11, and continued to argue to U.S. and NATO officials six years later—but to little avail.

The Afghan drug trade is sucking in all its neighbors as well. Traffickers in Afghanistan's six neighboring states are all involved in exporting opium, with the accompanying ills of local addiction and corruption. After 9/11, UNODC and the U.S. DEA put in place Operation Containment, a project involving twenty countries in the region, designed to prevent precursor chemicals from entering Afghanistan and drugs from leaving, but its success has been very limited. The five Central Asian republics provide a major gateway for Afghan opium to Russia and Europe. All five states are weak, undermined by dictatorship and underdevelopment, and heroin has become an important means for the small, corrupt ruling elites there to enrich themselves. Meanwhile, intravenous drug use in the region is fueling some of the fastest-growing HIV/AIDS rates in the world.

Afghan opium has helped destabilize Tajikistan, which shares a 750-mile border with Afghanistan and is still recovering from its bloody civil war in the early 1990s. It is one of the poorest countries in the world and provides an easy target for both traffickers and drug abuse. The twenty-thousand-strong force of Russian border guards who once guarded the Afghan frontier is gone, replaced by poorly trained Tajik conscripts who are easily corrupted by the traffickers. There are now more than seventy thousand addicts in a country of just six million people. In August 2004, Ghaffor Mirzoyev, who headed the country's Drug Control Agency, was arrested with a stockpile of three thousand weapons, including antiaircraft missiles. He was later charged with tax evasion, abuse of power, murder, and trafficking.[31]

Interpol investigators told me a year before 9/11 that they suspected leading politicians in Turkmenistan, including some in the office of President Saparmurat Niyazov, of being deeply involved in the drug trade. Turkmen dissidents in exile have made similar charges.[32] In the late 1990s, I saw heroin being openly sold outside five-star hotels in the Turkmen capital, Ashgabat. Turkmenistan's easily accessible border with western Afghanistan, along stretches of flat open desert, allow drug convoys to enter that country. The Taliban had a close relationship with the Turkmen regime in the 1990s, and Taliban leaders continued to frequent Ashgabat even after 9/11. Opium was also transiting through Uzbekistan, enriching many in the government, while Kyrgyzstan provided an outlet for drug shipments to Xinjiang province in China, where there was a huge increase in heroin addiction. Heroin addiction in Central Asia was estimated to have increased tenfold since the breakup of the Soviet Union in 1991.[33]

The drug surfeit was most apparent in Iran and Pakistan. Iran has the highest proportion of opium addicts in the world, with nearly 3 percent of the population over the age of fifteen addicted to heroin, according to the UN. Only Kyrgyzstan and Mauritius pass the 2 percent addiction mark. Nearly half of Iran's 170,000 prisoners are held on drug-related charges.

Yet Iran has rigorous antidrug surveillance on its border with Afghanistan, having spent more than $1 billion on fences, ditches, and minefields patrolled by thousands of Iranian troops. Since 1990, some 3,000 Iranian security officials have been killed in battles against smugglers.[34]

The drug crisis in Pakistan is not much better. Pakistan was heroin free in 1979, but by 1986 there were 650,000 addicts, 3 million by 1992, and 5 million by 2000. Drug money has fueled criminals and smugglers and has allowed ethnic, Islamic, and sectarian extremist groups to arm and fund themselves. The country became a major route for heroin exports from Taliban-controlled Afghanistan in the 1990s, a role that increased after 9/11, when the Taliban were based in Pakistan. "Pakistan is part of the massive Afghan opium producing/refining system," the State Department said in 2006. Pakistani traffickers financed Afghan poppy farmers as well as al Qaeda and the Pakistani and Afghan Taliban while they, the traffickers, supplied opiates to Turkey, Iran, and Europe.[35]

After 9/11, in 2002, opium growing started again in Pakistan, despite the country's having been declared free of poppy cultivation in 2000. In 2002 poppy was being grown on sixteen thousand acres across the North-West Frontier Province. Afghanistan's drug problem has now become a regionwide problem, fueling extremism and undermining governments.

♦ ♦ ♦

Drug money was to play a major role in Afghanistan's parliamentary elections. Just as there had been serious doubts about holding the presidential elections too soon, there were even greater doubts about holding the parliamentary elections so early in the regime's life. The Taliban were resurgent, reconstruction had barely started, and there were insufficient foreign troops on the ground. Karzai was adamant that he wanted the elections held on time. Yet Karzai himself was to create major problems by delaying the resolution of vital issues—e.g., determining provincial and district boundaries, creating constituencies, and promulgating an electoral law—and by refusing to form a political party.

The UN asked for $148 million to conduct the elections, but the money was delayed by the donors, making preparation time far too short for what was already a risky operation. When Peter Erben, the UN chief electoral officer, arrived in Kabul in March 2005, he found his headquarters "a ghost town" and the Afghan-UN Joint Election Management Board (JEMB) was overwhelmed with responsibilities it could not fulfill.[36] Civic education of the voters—so essential because most Afghans had no idea what they were voting for—started only ten weeks before the elections. Up to 50 percent of the population did not even know there was an election going on. Those who did had little idea what a parliament was.

There were to be two elections, one for the lower house of parliament—the Wolesi Jirga, or the House of People, with 249 elected members—and the other for provincial councils in all 34 provinces. A 102-seat upper house of parliament, or Meshrano Jirga, would have two thirds of its candidates elected by the provincial councils and one third nominated by the president. The lower house would also have two women elected from every province—68 in all. The distribution of seats according to population estimates created major tensions, as there was no agreement on population figures. The Hazaras were incensed when Kabul received 33 seats in the lower house, while the two Hazara provinces of Bamiyan and Dai Kundi received only 4 each. Moreover, the voting system was incomprehensible to most Afghans and allowed far too many candidates to stand. In Kabul there were 390 candidates, and the ballot paper was seven pages long.[37] Karzai had rejected the idea of the elections being based on political parties. Instead, the single non-transferable vote system was adopted—a complicated and wasteful method whereby each voter indicated only one favored candidate. The new parliament would consist of individuals with no party or group loyalty or manifesto.

The UN, the EU, and NGOs lobbied Karzai furiously to accept a party-list system, but he remained opposed. Every time we met, I raised the issue, but he would insist that parties were evil and reminiscent of the Communist Party system. Only the U.S. ambassador, Zalmay Khalilzad, supported Karzai's decision—and it was Khalilzad's most disastrous mistake, as it undermined the very process the United States supported. Democracy without political parties was meaningless, as politics would continue to revolve around warlords. The lack of any viable party organization in the south would over time cost Karzai dearly as the Taliban insurgency spread.

There was little campaigning and few rallies. As name recognition and literacy were low, each ballot slip would show photographs of the 5,800 candidates. Drug money was more potent in wooing voters than manifestos. Almost all the former Mujahedin warlords stood for election, as did several former communists and Taliban and a dozen former members of

Hikmetyar's Hizb-e-Islami, who had all made their peace with the government.[38] The Tajik Panjsheris under Younus Qanuni's leadership forged an alliance of non-Pashtuns called Jabahai Tafahim Millie, or National Understanding Front, made up of fourteen political groups. The Front put up 500 candidates in opposition to pro-Karzai candidates.

The Taliban tried (and failed) to disrupt the election campaign, killing eight candidates, but everyone expected the worst on election day. On September 18, six thousand polling stations opened to receive voters. It was clear that there was nothing like the euphoria or public participation generated by the 2004 presidential elections. The public turnout was just 53 percent, compared with 73 percent in the presidential elections and 90 percent in the indirect polls for the first Loya Jirga.[39] The turnout in Kabul was a poor 36 percent, while in troubled Zabul province it was just 13 percent. The final results were not declared until November 13, nearly two months later, due to disputes over the stuffing of ballot boxes.[40]

The low turnout was a reflection of growing public disillusionment with the government. Voters had seen the warlords win seats and realized that despite their promises of reform, Karzai and the United States just wanted to maintain the status quo. Even after General Fahim's removal, Karzai had merely continued to shuffle warlords around in an endless game of musical chairs as they held on to posts in the cabinet or the provinces. Not a single senior official was removed or retired for drug trafficking, corruption, or maintaining an illegal militia. One of the key reformers in the cabinet, interior minister Ali Ahmad Jalali, resigned in a mood of "anger and frustration." Jalali said Karzai was unwilling to take on drug traffickers, while Karzai alluded to corruption on Jalali's part—whatever the reason, the two men fell out badly.[41] Karzai's other promise—to start taking responsibility for the human rights violations over the past three decades—was delayed indefinitely. Even to his close supporters, Karzai appeared to be weak and indecisive, refusing to take the bold steps that were needed to counter Taliban propaganda and retain public support.

Afghan skepticism about U.S. intentions redoubled after Rumsfeld made a remarkably insensitive statement just five days before the elections. The U.S. secretary of defense told a NATO meeting in Berlin that the United States would withdraw three thousand to four thousand American troops in early 2006.[42] The new CENTCOM chief, Gen. John Abizaid, confirmed this on a visit to Kabul and asked NATO to deploy more forces to offset the U.S. withdrawal. President Bush, battered by the growing in-

surgency in Iraq, Hurricane Katrina in Louisiana, and the lowest poll rat-
ings ever seen for a U.S. president in his second term, was desperate to show
the American people that the war on terrorism in Afghanistan was such
a success that he could now afford to bring troops home.

Rumsfeld's comment, coming in the midst of a Taliban insurgency and
elections, stunned Afghans and the government, who read it as a signal
that the United States was preparing to abandon Afghanistan. Pakistan's
military leaders appeared to be vindicated for their long-standing predic-
tion that the Americans would not stay long in Afghanistan. Afghans were
convinced that leaving their country in the hands of a much weaker NATO
would increase ISI support to the Taliban before the Taliban's spring 2006
offensive. Yet again Rumsfeld was completely out of touch with the politics
and mood in Afghanistan and the region. In dismissing the Taliban, he
seemed to be ignoring the worsening reality on the ground.

The elections resulted in a fragmented parliament. The supporters of
the three defeated presidential candidates, Gen. Rashid Dostum, Younus
Qanuni, and Mohammed Mohaqiq, won between twenty and twenty-five
seats each. Karzai's supporters won more than eighty seats, while around
one hundred winning candidates were nonaligned or, rather, they would
switch sides according to whoever offered the best deal. Drug traffickers,
militia commanders, and twelve former members of the Taliban or Hizb-
e-Islami had won their seats.[43] Remarkably six women won seats by actually fighting the elections.

Karzai continued his efforts to woo the Taliban, despite opposition by
the United States and the Northern Alliance. He had appointed the former
president Sibghatullah Mujaddedi to head the Peace and Reconciliation
Commission charged with trying to persuade Taliban members to return
home under amnesty.[44] However, the non-Pashtuns led by Qanuni opposed
any such reconciliation, leading to severe tensions in and out of parliament.
These were made worse by the CIA and MI6, who were in touch with the
Taliban but who hyped up their negotiations, saying a breakthrough with
top Taliban leaders was imminent—although one never happened. This
unfounded optimism percolated into the U.S. military, which insisted that
the Taliban were now incapable of an offensive. Lt.-Gen. David Barno, the
commander of U.S. forces, declared that the Taliban were "collapsing and
rejoining the Afghan political and economic process."[45] However, the Taliban's opening salvo in their 2005 campaign demonstrated new tactics and
greater firepower than ever before.

May was a terrible month, in which each deadly incident increased the widening of the insurgency. In early May the Taliban ambushed a U.S. patrol in Zabul province, blowing off the legs of two American soldiers and wounding four others in a six-hour battle. When aircraft bombed the Taliban and killed forty-four fighters, among the dead were Pakistanis, Arabs, Chechens, and Uzbeks—a dramatic indication of the unity among all the jihadi groups operating out of Pakistan.[46] Two days later nine Afghan soldiers were killed in another ambush. In the most devastating attack, which took place on June 1 in Kandahar's main mosque, a suicide bomber killed the Kabul police chief, Mohammed Akram Khakrezwal, and eighteen other Afghan worshippers. An implacably honest cop in a sea of corruption, Khakrezwal had been widely respected by all Afghans.[47]

As the insurgency escalated, Karzai urged Bush to sign a strategic partnership agreement with Afghanistan. Washington had little need for one, as it already controlled Afghanistan's air and land space and conducted the war as it wanted. However, an insecure Karzai insisted that such an argument would boost his standing at home and convince Pakistan that he enjoyed complete U.S. support. On a visit to Washington in late May, Karzai met with Bush to sign the agreement, prompting a severely negative reaction both in Afghanistan and among its neighbors.[48] The agreement infuriated Pakistan, Iran, and Russia, as it signaled the possibility of permanent U.S. bases in Afghanistan; Afghans accused Karzai of surrendering Afghan sovereignty. Instead, they argued, the United States should have agreed to sign "a status of forces agreement," which would have reaffirmed Afghan sovereignty. Moreover, the two men signed the agreement just as two Afghans died under torture at the hands of U.S. interrogators at Bagram. Furthermore, Bush humiliated Karzai by turning down his request for Afghan control over suspected Afghan terrorist prisoners.[49] All these instances not only provided the Taliban with propaganda to claim that Karzai was an American stooge, but also lowered his prestige among his own supporters.

Over the summer the Taliban deployed an array of tactics to win back control of their former heartland of Kandahar, Helmand, Zabul, and Uruzgan provinces. In stand-up battles, suicide attacks, ambushes, roadside explosions, and the assassination of aid workers, the Taliban demonstrated that they could create insecurity and mayhem in the south. In the first half of 2005, fifty-four U.S. soldiers were killed, compared with fifty-two for the whole of 2004.[50] Al Qaeda had helped the Taliban reorganize even as the ISI was separately allowing Taliban commanders to rearm and recruit fighters in Pakistan. Mullah Dadullah declared that he was receiving help from al Qaeda in Iraq.[51] The Taliban insurgency had now become an international conflict.

CHAPTER SIXTEEN

Who Lost Uzbekistan?

Tyranny in Central Asia

The turmoil in Afghanistan dramatically affected Central Asia, which witnessed its first regime change through a popular movement since 1991, when Kyrgyz president Askar Akayev was overthrown. A former university professor, Akayev was elected as the only noncommunist president of a Central Asian state in 1991. I met him several times in the 1990s, when he was still affable, engaging, and trying to move his country toward greater democracy and the West. However, Kyrgyzstan was desperately poor and economically unsustainable, with a deeply polarized population. There were divisions between the rich new elite and the mass of poor, a north-south divide as a result of greater development in the north, clan rivalries that went back to the time of Genghis Khan, and ethnic divisions. In the south the dominant Kyrgyz were challenged by a powerful eight-hundred-thousand-strong Uzbek minority, which made up 16 percent of the country's five million people. The country's single gold mine accounted for 40 percent of exports, and in 2002 the government was forced to ask Western donors to reschedule repayments on its $1.5 billion foreign debt.

After a decade in power, Akayev, like other Central Asian leaders, stood accused of being enormously corrupt, power hungry, and dictatorial. His political troubles began in March 2002, when five people were killed and more than sixty injured in antigovernment demonstrations in the south by protestors demanding the release of a popular opposition leader, Azimbek Beknazarov. Instead of yielding some of his presidential powers, as the opposition demanded, Akayev held a rigged referendum in

February 2003 on new constitutional provisions, which concentrated even greater power in his hands. In June, following the example of Uzbekistan and Kazakhstan, the pliant Kyrgyz parliament granted Akayev lifelong immunity from criminal prosecution.

Even before 9/11, Kyrgyzstan was the only Central Asian state that had tilted toward the West as it tried to escape the stranglehold of Russia, China, and Uzbekistan. Facing repeated incursions and threats from the Islamic Movement of Uzbekistan (IMU) in the 1990s, Kyrgyzstan had joined NATO's Partnership for Peace program in 1994, and after 9/11 its fledgling army of twelve thousand men held military exercises with U.S. forces. Akayev had allowed U.S. and NATO forces to operate out of Manas Air Base outside Bishkek, which became a major hub for Western forces operating in Afghanistan. However, in October 2003, after enormous pressure from Moscow, he allowed the Russians to establish another air base near Bishkek as he tried to satisfy both powers.

As lawlessness, political assassinations, and nepotism increased, Akayev defended himself by criticizing Western influences and NGOs, which he accused of undermining stability. He expressed extreme wariness of the popular Rose Revolution in Georgia in November 2003 and of Ukraine's Orange Revolution in late 2004. A wave of opposition protests dubbed the Tulip Revolution erupted in January 2005 in Bishkek as the parliamentary elections neared. Akayev's family was accused of benefiting from the contracts given out by the U.S. military at Manas, pilfering international aid and loans, and buying up businesses in the country. The opposition's main targets were Akayev's daughter Bermet, thirty-four, and son Aidar, twenty-eight, who had briefly been married to Aliya Nazarbayev, the daughter of the Kazakh president. While the family denied the accusations, there was no doubt that they had suddenly become fabulously wealthy.

On February 27, 2005, after the first round of parliamentary elections, the opposition cried foul and coalesced around Kurmanbek Bakiyev, the silver-haired former prime minister and now head of the People's Movement. Protests intensified after the opposition won only a handful of seats in the second round, held on March 14. In cities in the south, mobs took over government offices and police stations, emptied jails, occupied airports, and set fire to government installations. The opposition mounted its first show of strength in Bishkek on March 23. The next day, when twenty thousand people surrounded the presidential palace, Akayev's guards quickly abandoned him, and rather than resisting, he fled to Moscow. Akayev was widely condemned by other autocratic Central Asian leaders for his apparent cowardice.

Two businesses linked to the Akayev family received lucrative contracts to supply fuel for the U.S. airbase in Kyrgyzstan in 2001. According to an article in *The New York Times,* both Kyrgyz prosecutors and FBI agents were investigating whether Akayev family members "pocketed millions of dollars" before his ouster. "An internal FBI report given to Kyrgyz prosecutors in September [2005] found that the two businesses might have been involved in money-laundering" via bank accounts in New York and Holland. "The companies also had transactions with 'a myriad of suspicious U.S. shell companies' associated with Mr. Akayev, his family and arms traffickers, the report said." [1] The fall of Akayev and the continuing instability in Kyrgyzstan unnerved all the Central Asian leaders and led to a fierce clampdown on Western media and NGOs. The events in Bishkek were a reminder that changes in leadership in Central Asia were more likely to reflect a change in faces rather than one toward greater democracy.

In Bishkek, Kurmanbek Bakiyev was declared interim president and formed a new government, but he failed to check lawlessness and looting. Akayev, in Moscow, threatened to return. While some political groups accepted the newly elected parliament, others insisted that the old one was still legitimate. Unlike Ukraine and Georgia, Kyrgyzstan had seen no prolonged popular movement, nor was there a credible political figure to lead such a movement. The opposition looked more like a coup by a section of the out-of-power former communist elite. The old guard quickly established itself in power and assumed Akayev's contracts, businesses, and benefits.

In early July fresh presidential elections were held, which Bakiyev won. To gain greater popularity he demanded that the United States renegotiate its base rights. "We can therefore review the usefulness of the presence of American forces in Kyrgyzstan," Bakiyev announced in his first post-election speech. [2] U.S. forces had to quit their base in Uzbekistan after the Andijan riots, and on July 5, Russia and China had demanded at a summit meeting of the Shanghai Cooperation Organization that all U.S. forces quit Central Asia. Rumsfeld arrived in Bishkek, where he promised to increase the $50 million a year the United States paid for use of the base and also pledged a $200 million interest-free loan. Gen. Richard Myers was blunter, rebuking China and Russia for pressuring Kyrgyzstan. "It looks to me like two very large countries were trying to bully some smaller countries," he said.[3]

In Turkmenistan there was a similar change of faces when the autocratic and bizarre president Saparmurat Niyazov died of a heart attack on December 21, 2006, at the age of sixty-six. After twenty-one years in power, he left the country impoverished, although he, too, had amassed enormous wealth abroad—reportedly over $1 billion. His successor was Gurbanguly Berdymukhamedow, forty-nine, a former dentist and health minister who came to power after another rigged election. The opposition, largely living in exile abroad, was refused entry into the country for the election.[4] Niyazov had taken Turkmenistan back into the Middle Ages, closing theaters, libraries, and newspapers and reducing public access to health care, education, and travel abroad while drastically cutting wages and pensions. Berdymukhamedow promised some changes, but a year after taking office he had barely implemented any reforms. Once again a change of faces did not mean significant change.

The major crisis in Central Asia, however, was in Uzbekistan, where President Islam Karimov had refused to open up his country after the end of the war in Afghanistan and despite the presence of a large U.S. base and massive American aid. The Bush administration hoped that the combination of aid and greater security in the shape of military training and weapons for the Uzbek army would allow Karimov to be more forward-looking with regard to carrying out long-neglected economic and political reforms. Instead, everything got worse. The regime became more oppressive and restrictive, while the lack of reforms and economic policies, which helped only the cronies around the president get rich, fueled an economic crisis after 9/11. The government's restrictions on traders buying goods from neighboring countries had crippled the economy, which produced very little in terms of consumer goods. Tashkent slashed salaries of teachers and increased rates for public transport and utilities while raising salaries for the repressive police and armed forces. A decent monthly wage was now no more than twenty-five to forty dollars, far less than a family could live on. According to the IMF, the Uzbek economy grew only 0.3 percent in 2003.[5]

Once again a president's family was profiting. Karimov's daughter Gulnora Karimova was reputed to be a major shareholder in many of the largest state-owned and private companies in the country.[6] "The degree to which Karimova appears to have embedded herself and her allies in

Uzbekistan's economy far exceeds that of her regional counterparts," said a recent report.[7] The Karimov family learned little from the events in Kyrgyzstan, where Akayev's family's alleged corruption was to lead to his downfall. "Poverty, corruption, repressive security agencies, price controls on cotton sales, steep taxes on small businesses and restrictions on small traders have created a disgruntlement that has nothing to do with religion. Karimov's cronies have monopolized industries for their own advantage," wrote the Central Asia scholar Martha Brill Olcott.[8]

As with other autocrats in the region, Karimov thought that as long as he stayed with the United States on the big regional issues, Washington would not bother with how he ruled. Thus Uzbekistan and Georgia were the only countries in the former Soviet Union that backed the U.S. invasion of Iraq. Karimov exploited his new leverage to persuade the Bush administration to add Hizb ut-Tahrir (HT) to its list of terrorist groups, a list that included the Islamic Movement of Uzbekistan. In January 2003, Germany banned HT, accusing it of spreading anti-Semitic propaganda. However, Karimov's key leverage over Washington was the assistance his security services provided the CIA in its rendition program.[9]

In April 2003 at a meeting of the United States–Uzbekistan Joint Security Cooperation Council in Washington, D.C., both countries pledged long-term cooperation, and Uzbekistan promised again to pursue democratic reforms. Yet its crackdown on political dissent had already reached new heights. Human rights groups said that eleven prisoners had died as a result of torture in Uzbek jails that year, even as the State Department claimed that the country was making progress in human rights. No longer were just the accused tortured, but also their families if they dared ask where relatives were imprisoned. In May the Uzbek parliament granted the president perpetual immunity from prosecution.

The signs of increased crackdowns were inescapable in January 2004, when the Uzbek government issued new laws restricting the one hundred Western media and foreign NGO offices operating in the country. All NGOs were now ordered to register anew. The silence from Washington was deafening. The State Department, which was eager to take a public position against the measures, was once again overwhelmed by the Pentagon and the CIA when it came to policymaking for Uzbekistan. Rumsfeld continued to heap praise on Karimov. Visiting Tashkent in February 2004, as major U.S. NGOs were being thrown out of the country, he spoke of "the wonderful cooperation we've received from the government of Uzbekistan" and promised $57 million in aid for 2004.[10] As if on cue, just a few hours before his arrival, the government freed a sixty-two-year-old woman, Fatima Mukadyrova, who had been arrested after accusing the authorities of torturing her son to death.

When the cities of Tashkent, Bukhara, and Chorsu were hit by suicide bombers in the last days of March 2004, there was widespread suspicion among Western diplomats that the government's secret services had orchestrated the drama. Female suicide bombers tried to target the police but mostly managed to kill civilians. In four days of bombings, police raids, and shoot-outs, forty-seven people were killed, including ten policemen. The government immediately blamed HT, the IMU, and al Qaeda, closed its borders, and arrested more than four hundred people. Two weeks after the attacks, the Islamic Jihad Union, a previously unknown group whose members had broken away from the IMU and been trained by al Qaeda in Waziristan, claimed responsibility for the attacks.

The government then moved to completely shut down Western NGOs, starting with the Open Society Institute in April, even though George Soros's foundation had contributed $22 million in aid to Uzbekistan since 1996. The U.S. Democratic Party's National Democratic Institute and the International Republican Institute were also shut down. "NGOs have no future in Uzbekistan, they went far beyond their declared charters and aim at certain mercenary goals," Karimov thundered.[11] In fact, as in Kyrgyzstan, the popular revolutions in Tbilisi and Kiev had unnerved the Uzbek regime.

To counter possible U.S. pressure, Karimov now assiduously courted Russia, which made no demands about respecting human rights. In June 2004, President Putin visited Tashkent to sign a security pact with Karimov. Both sides pledged to "coordinate their efforts in order to create a reliable and effective defense system in Central Asia." Russia's oil and gas giants Gazprom and Lukoil signed deals to invest $1 billion each in developing Uzbekistan's energy resources and increasing its gas exports to Russia.[12] Uzbekistan was back to playing the great game among the big powers, using Russia to show the United States that it was not alone, that it had other friends.

The mass arrests and the closure of the NGOs forced the U.S. State Department to become more declaratory, and on July 13, 2004, it suspended $18 million worth of U.S. military and economic aid to Uzbekistan because of continued human rights violations. Rumsfeld was furious with Powell for taking such a measure, and the internal battle between Powell and the military continued. In the next few weeks, in separate visits to Tashkent, CENTCOM chief Gen. John Abizaid and Gen. Richard Myers pledged continued military support to Uzbekistan. Myers brazenly contradicted State by pledging $21 million in military aid to Uzbekistan. The U.S. military, which was heavily dependent on the K2 base, where now eighteen hundred U.S. troops and twenty C-130 transport aircraft were based for supplying U.S. bases in Afghanistan, also continued to train the fifty-three-thousand-strong Uzbek army. The CIA was equally determined to continue its secret relations on renditions with the Uzbek security services.

In his defense, Karimov continued to cite the threats he faced from Islamic extremists. Those threats again appeared to be justified when on July 30, 2004, simultaneous suicide attacks took place in Tashkent, on the U.S. and Israeli embassies and the state prosecutor's office—just four days after the start of the trial of fifteen suspects involved in the March bombings. Three policemen were killed and nine people injured as the government accused the Islamic Jihad Union of carrying out the attacks. There were also rising tensions in the Ferghana Valley due to growing poverty and the influence of underground Islamic movements. An explosion was waiting to happen and it took place in Andijan, an important town in the Ferghana Valley, where the population had been incensed by Karimov's earlier decision to turn the main mosque into an art gallery.

On May 13, 2005, armed men stormed a jail in the town to free twenty-three traders and businessmen on trial for belonging to the Islamic group Akramia—followers of Akram Yuldashev, a local trader and preacher who was also on trial. The next day thousands of demonstrators gathered in the central square to hear speeches by the freed men and to protest rising prices. Some of the speakers even asked Karimov to come to the square to hear their complaints. Instead, heavily armed security forces were flown in from Tashkent and in the evening opened fire on the crowd, killing at least 850 people, although as many as 1,500 may have died. "From the sky there was a storm of rain, from the streets a storm of bullets," said Mohammed Mavlanov, a shopkeeper in Andijan. "You could see blood all over the asphalt and women and children falling down all around like grass when you cut it with a scythe."[13]

Security forces quickly removed the bodies of the slain and covered up signs of the shootings. The government claimed that only 187 people were killed, mainly foreign terrorists, while 10 security personnel had died. Meanwhile, hundreds of survivors from the square fled to the Uzbek-Kyrgyz border, where an unknown number were mown down by Uzbek border guards as they tried to cross into Kyrgyzstan. The protests and violence spread to villages along the border until government forces regained control of them a week later. Around the world people were stunned, and there was enormous international condemnation of the massacre. Washington remained silent for two days until it finally condemned the government for firing on unarmed civilians.

Only China and Russia endorsed Karimov's actions and invited him to visit. Without offering any evidence, Russian defense minister Sergei Ivanov claimed that the rebels were led by Afghan Taliban. Karimov said the militants wanted "to unite the Muslims and establish a caliphate. Their aim is to overthrow the constitutional government."[14] He rejected calls by Europe, the United States, and the UN for an international investigation into the killings. Human Rights Watch said that "the killing of unarmed protestors . . . was so extensive and unjustified that it amounted to a massacre."[15] Along with Amnesty International, it urged tougher international action and sanctions on the regime.

In early June, Condoleezza Rice joined European countries in stepping up criticism of Uzbekistan. Rice was determined to take control of U.S. policy toward Uzbekistan away from Rumsfeld and the Pentagon. Rumsfeld snapped back that there had been no debate on the policy in the cabinet. The Pentagon blocked attempts by European members of NATO, who wanted a NATO condemnation of the massacre.[16] Rice's tough statements led to an immediate response from Tashkent, which suspended night flights for U.S. aircraft out of the K2 base.

Some 560 Uzbeks who had escaped into Kyrgyzstan sought political asylum under the auspices of the UN High Commissioner for Refugees (UNHCR). The Kyrgyz authorities came under severe pressure from Uzbek security services to return the refugees, and acute tensions between the two countries developed. Uzbek security agents penetrated the refugee camps in Kyrgyzstan and threatened people to get them to return home. Terrified, the Kyrgyz government began to return a few refugees, despite protestations from the UNHCR. The fate of the refugees hung in the balance until on July 27, 455 Uzbek refugees were flown out of Bishkek by UNHCR to several other countries, including the United States and Canada, which granted them asylum.

Two days later the Uzbeks formally evicted the United States from K2, giving U.S. forces 180 days to pack up and leave. The eviction did not include the German military base at Termez, although all NATO countries who had condemned Uzbekistan were barred from using it.[17] Karimov showed his pettiness and vindictiveness by going further, banning UNHCR from Uzbekistan and giving the army a 20 percent pay raise.[18] Russia and China gloated at the decisive setback the United States had received in Central Asia. Russia moved swiftly to reassert its influence in Uzbekistan, signing a military pact in November that for the first time allowed Russia to establish military bases in Uzbekistan. The same month, the EU imposed mild sanctions on Uzbekistan, which included an arms embargo and a ban on twelve senior Uzbek officials seeking to travel to Europe. It was too little too late, for Karimov had already weathered the storm of international protest and had shown that with support from Russia and China, he was not alone.

The Uzbek authorities stepped up prosecution of hundreds of dissidents from Andijan and the Ferghana Valley. In their trials, which were broadcast on television, many of the accused, who had been tortured and traumatized in jail, came up with fantastical stories as to how the uprising took place; the BBC and Voice of America, it was said, had been involved in trying to topple Karimov. Regional countries accused of helping the rebels included Afghanistan, Pakistan, Saudi Arabia, Kyrgyzstan, and Kazakhstan. The public was repeatedly told that the whole world envied Uzbekistan while the government had nothing to blame itself for. Some 250 people were eventually sentenced for participating in the uprising and were given jail terms of between fourteen and twenty years. The Andijan massacre placed Karimov beyond the pale of civilized behavior. No government in recent memory had carried out such a wanton and deliberate act of killing so many of its own people.

Karimov's seven-year presidential term expired in January 2007, but he remained in power unconcerned about legalizing his tenure. On December 23, 2007, Karimov ran for president for the third time. In another Soviet-style rigged election, he was elected virtually unopposed, winning 88 percent of the votes cast. International monitors condemned the poll as farcical. Now aged seventy and reported to be seriously ill, Karimov was still refusing to give up power as he took the presidential oath for another seven-year term. While Turkmenistan had managed a peaceful transition following the death of Niyazov, there is every reason to believe that Karimov's death or departure will lead to serious instability and violence, with potentially grave consequences for the region. The ruling elite is sharply divided, while some Karimov loyalists may try to put forward his daughter Gulnora Karimova as president.

Since 9/11 the IMU and other Islamic extremist groups, some of them linked to al Qaeda and the Taliban but others quite independent, have developed a strong underground base inside Uzbekistan. Since 9/11 hundreds of young Uzbek militants have traveled to Waziristan for training and have fought in Afghanistan, Pakistan, and Iraq. The IMU leader Tahir Yuldashev remains in Waziristan and has reestablished links with Uzbekistan. After 9/11 no more than five hundred to six hundred Uzbeks were taking refuge in Pakistan's tribal areas. By 2008 that number had grown to between three and four thousand Uzbek and Central Asian militants in the tribal areas under IMU command, indicating that new recruits were constantly arriving for training. Moreover, new splinter groups such as the Islamic Jihad Union, which worked directly under al Qaeda, had also appeared. In September 2007, German authorities arrested three German Muslims who had trained with the Islamic Jihad Union and al Qaeda in Pakistan's tribal areas and had returned to Germany to try to bomb the U.S. air force base at Ramstein, from which U.S. troops are flown to Iraq and Afghanistan. Another half a dozen extremists who had also trained with the Union were still being sought by the authorities. These included a Siberian Russian who had converted to Islam and had come from Siberia for training in the tribal areas.

U.S. policy toward Uzbekistan and Central Asia was one-directional, ham-fisted, and without an ounce of nuance. The Bush administration had claimed to be advancing human rights and democracy in Central Asia, even as the CIA was becoming dependent on Uzbekistan's security services for handling rendered prisoners and the Pentagon directed 80 percent of U.S. aid to the Uzbek military rather than to economic development. Once the Uzbeks had handed over the K2 base to the Americans, it would have been difficult but not impossible for the United States to use its aid, training programs, and personnel as leverage to push for reform and encourage a cadre of reformers to emerge from within the Uzbek elite. Instead, the Bush administration treated the country as a mere dumping ground for rendered prisoners and a logistics base for Afghanistan. Uzbekistan and its people—their hopes and aspirations—did not exist for anyone in Washington.

After the United States was evicted, nobody in Washington got up to ask, "Who lost Uzbekistan?" The question is important in the geostrategic context, given the massive gains made by China and Russia, the enormous setback to democracy, the continued sufferings of the Uzbek people, and the spread of Islamic extremism. U.S. aid for Central Asia declined by 24 percent in 2008 as the Bush administration yielded influence in the region to China and Russia. Uzbekistan's trade with Russia ballooned from $2 billion in 2005 to $3 billion in 2007. Russian oil and gas companies began to make serious investments in the Uzbek oil industry and to buy increasing quantities of gas from Uzbekistan.

When I introduce Central Asia in this book I describe how the Central Asian regimes and their peoples wanted different things from the American presence in the region. The Bush administration's lack of a strategy ensured that the regimes won and that public sympathy turned against the United States as Washington failed to support democracy or economic reforms. The United States lost a major opportunity to influence Central Asia for decades to come while gaining greater access to its energy resources. In 2001 the United States held a pivotal position in Central Asia, yet five years later it was forced to yield that position to Russia and China. Ultimately President Bush was responsible for losing Uzbekistan and Central Asia, as the U.S. administration pursued one-track policies that put torturing prisoners above the need for nation building.

CHAPTER SEVENTEEN

The Taliban Offensive

Battling for Control of Afghanistan, 2006–2007

On the eve of the U.S. invasion of Iraq, as divisions between Washington and some European capitals grew, the twenty-six countries that make up NATO began discussions at headquarters in Brussels about how NATO could take over command of the International Security Assistance Force outside Kabul on a permanent basis and expand a peacekeeping presence beyond Kabul.

French president Jacques Chirac, German chancellor Gerhard Schröder, and his intellectually charged and charismatic foreign minister, Joschka Fischer, had led European opposition to the U.S. invasion of Iraq. Fischer now took the lead in trying to persuade NATO to help the United States out in Afghanistan. Fischer, a former radical leftist from the late 1960s, had trimmed his politics sufficiently to become leader of the Green Party and to persuade it to ally with Schröder's Social Democrats. When the Red-Green Coalition won the 1998 German general elections, Schröder appointed Fischer as foreign minister—a post he was to hold until November 2005. Underlying the discussions at NATO were how the relationship between the United States and Europe could be salvaged despite Iraq and whether Afghanistan could bring the two together.

Fischer desperately wanted to find a way to continue Germany's close ties with the United States. He proposed sending additional German troops to Afghanistan, who would carry out peacekeeping outside Kabul. However, Fischer refused to do so until the current UN Security Council mandate for ISAF was extended beyond the capital. He wanted a UN resolution that would mandate German troops to operate as part of a formal NATO presence in Afghanistan. The German army mapped out a deployment in one of the safest parts of Afghanistan—the northeast, where there was no fighting—making it easier for Fischer to sell the idea to the German parliament and the Greens. Hamid Karzai and the UN's Lakhdar Brahimi had long been advocating just such an ISAF deployment outside Kabul. By now Rumsfeld, who had so vehemently opposed any deployment outside Kabul, was now also in favor. The Europeans had smarted at the contemptuous manner in which Rumsfeld dispensed with NATO's offer of help after 9/11 to topple the Taliban.

Fischer was using German troops as bait for a new NATO role with a new UN mandate in order to hook many reluctant European nations that were not at all keen on expanding their commitment to Afghanistan. NATO itself was ill prepared for its first deployment outside the European continent. However, Fischer's timing was perfect and made good sense. The smaller European countries did not want to lose U.S. support because of their opposition to the Iraq war. And in Kabul, the crisis within ISAF was becoming hugely detrimental. Every six months ISAF-contributing countries struggled to find a nation willing to take over command of ISAF headquarters. In late 2002 Britain had handed over command of ISAF to Turkey, which was followed by a joint German-Dutch command and later a Canadian command. Each handover was marred by haggling, compromises, and interminable delays. "The unseemly scramble to find a country to command [the force] in Kabul gives neither the Afghans, their neighbors nor the remnants of the Taliban and al Qaeda the sense we are there for the long haul," said a sarcastic George Robertson, NATO secretary-general, in February 2003.[1]

Germany was taken seriously in Afghanistan. In the late 1990s, Berlin had tried to end the civil war in Afghanistan by hosting a series of unofficial dialogues between the UN, the Taliban, and the Northern Alliance. It hosted the Bonn talks in December 2001 and had taken on the task of rebuilding the Afghan police force while contributing a thousand troops to ISAF in Kabul. Germany's limitation was that under its constitution it could not deploy troops in an offensive role, but it had already helped out with peacekeeping in the former Yugoslavia.

Six months after the first discussions, on August 8, 2003, NATO took command of ISAF, while a UN Security Council resolution authorized ISAF to expand beyond the capital. Two hundred German troops and forty civilian advisers set up a Provincial Reconstruction Team (PRT) in

Kunduz, in the northeast. There were now two separate command structures for foreign forces in Afghanistan—the NATO-ISAF command was responsible for peacekeeping in Kabul and the provinces; while the hunt for terrorists would continue to be carried out by the U.S.-led Coalition under Operation Enduring Freedom. "Afghanistan will be . . . tough but it has to be a success . . ." Robertson warned. "Nations will have to waken up to what they have taken on."[2]

In September, I, along with other experts, was invited to brief NATO ambassadors in Brussels. We stressed how important it was to expand NATO forces into the provinces to help stabilize the country, improve governance, and send a forceful message to the Taliban. A halfhearted NATO response would only give the Taliban a propaganda coup. Some of the NATO ambassadors were clearly disinterested in or nervous about an increased deployment or they did not take the Taliban resurgence seriously. Privately some criticized Fischer, whom they blamed for steamrolling NATO into Afghanistan when NATO was unprepared to go there.

NATO had no standing army or ready-to-go equipment and aircraft. It had no central budget; deployments were paid for by individual countries. Troops, aircraft, helicopters, and artillery had to be extracted from each country after endless meetings and then matched up with other donations. All this had been difficult enough to carry out in the former Yugoslavia. NATO urgently needed heavy airlift, special training, large numbers of helicopters, and culturally sensitized troops—a tough checklist for European governments that had chronically underspent on their militaries since the end of the cold war. In 2005 the total military budget of the twenty-six NATO member states was just $265 million, compared with the U.S. defense budget of $472 billion. NATO countries were expected to spend at least 2 percent of their GDP on defense, but only six out of the twenty-six members met that goal.

Yet it was still difficult to understand why with two million soldiers, NATO countries could not find the troops for Afghanistan. European governments won support from their parliaments and people by promising that their troops would be carrying out risk-free peacekeeping and reconstruction—a military mission that would build hospitals and schools and promote democracy, rule of law, and development, in the best traditions of European liberalism. No European leaders dared mention the possibility of war, combat deaths, or having to fight a counterinsurgency against the Taliban. To further reassure their publics at home, every

European country set down its own caveats—restrictions on what its troops could and could not do. These caveats would soon come to paralyze the entire NATO effort.

Despite these problems, NATO set itself ambitious targets. It promised to undertake a four-phase expansion across Afghanistan, starting with the deployment of German troops across the entire north by June 2004 with headquarters in Mazar-e-Sharif. Phase two, to be completed three months later, would see NATO deploy to Herat and western Afghanistan after setting up new Provincial Reconstruction Teams. In Phases three and four NATO would deploy to the turbulent south and east, for which no timetable was set. When NATO defense ministers met in Munich in February 2004, they pledged to install a PRT in every one of Afghanistan's thirty-four provinces.

NATO missed its very first deadline, failing to man the five PRTs in the north on time, which then delayed completion of phase two. Countries did not come up with enough troops and equipment on time. For the first six months of 2004, Jaap de Hoop Scheffer, the new NATO secretary-general and its supreme commander, Gen. James Jones, could not find three helicopters to send to Kabul, prompting a frustrated Jones to tell the U.S. Senate that "the alliance has agreed, the donor countries have been identified, and yet we find ourselves mired in the administrative details of who's going to pay for it, who's going to transport it, how it's going to be maintained."[3] There was further cynicism in the Pentagon, where Paul Wolfowitz told me in February 2004, "We needed some helicopter support, and NATO did not come through. There's a tendency to talk very boldly about the European security structure and then not make available any of the funding necessary to make them happen."[4]

NATO's inability to complete phase one on time deeply frustrated Karzai, who had asked for even more troops to be temporarily deployed for the upcoming 2004 presidential elections. NATO promised an "over the horizon" deployment—troops who would not leave their base in Italy but who in theory would be ready to go to Afghanistan. It was an absurd arrangement that angered Karzai and buoyed the Taliban. "I don't mind taking out my begging bowl once in a while. But as standard operating procedure, this is simply intolerable," Scheffer said.[5]

By now the United States was bogged down in Iraq and desperately needed NATO to take up more responsibility in Afghanistan so that it could withdraw some of its own troops. In February 2005, at a meeting in

Nice, France, NATO defense ministers discussed the idea of creating a single unified command by merging the NATO-ISAF command with Operation Enduring Freedom. Predictably, France, Germany, and others objected because it would mean getting involved in fighting the Taliban. "NATO is not equipped to do counter-terrorism missions," said the French defense minister Michèle Alliot-Marie.[6] Those at the Nice meeting did agree on Italy's heading the deployment to Herat, and phase two was finally completed eight months late.

Rumsfeld's intentions in speeding up a merger became clearer after he dropped the bombshell that Washington would cut its nineteen-thousand-strong troop level in Afghanistan by 20 percent by the spring of 2006.

I interviewed a senior official at the White House just after Rumsfeld's statement and asked what had prompted him to say such a thing at such a sensitive time. The official looked at the ceiling, as if to say that Rumsfeld's decisions were his own and could not be questioned even by the White House. Yet at the same time Rumsfeld was arguing just the opposite for Iraq, saying the United States could defend the homeland only if its forces stayed in the Middle East. "If we left Iraq prematurely, the enemy would tell us to leave Afghanistan and then withdraw from the Middle East. And if we left the Middle East, they'd order us . . . to leave what they call the occupied Muslim lands from Spain to the Philippines."[7]

On December 19, 2005, Rumsfeld signed orders pulling out three thousand U.S. troops from the south, reducing the total number to sixteen thousand. It was the worst possible moment, as the largest Taliban offensive was about to unfold, but Rumsfeld refused to accept that the Taliban insurgency was expanding. To demonstrate that it would maintain its presence, Washington announced the building of a new $83 million runway at Bagram air base and the improvement of fourteen military airfields across the country. The American pullout speeded up agreement on creating a joint command. All NATO forces and half the U.S. force in Afghanistan would come under NATO-ISAF command, while the remaining eight thousand American troops would continue to carry out counterterrorism operations under a separate U.S. command.

Meanwhile, British and Canadian forces were preparing to deploy to Helmand and Kandahar provinces, respectively, as part of phase three. They were desperately trying to persuade the Dutch to take command of neighboring Uruzgan province. The Dutch government was keen, but there was a strong left-wing opposition in the Dutch parliament, which blocked any deployment to Afghanistan. Britain told NATO that it would lead the deployment in the south as long as it could raise sufficient numbers of troops to take on the Taliban and received adequate backing from NATO allies, the Dutch deployed in Uruzgan, and funds were available for development and reconstruction. It was already clear to the British that unlike the NATO deployments in the north and west, phase three in the south would involve heavy fighting with the Taliban.

Yet even as phase three got under way, the list of caveats about what countries would and would not do grew to the size of a telephone directory. General Jones called the seventy-one listed caveats in 2006 "NATO's operational cancer . . . a sign of weakness and an impediment to success."[8] Some troops could not attack the Taliban; they were unauthorized to help in poppy eradication or interdiction of drug convoys; they could not engage with Afghan warlords or separate them if they fought each other, and they could not protect NGOs, schools, government buildings, or major infrastructure projects. Neither could they help with UN voter registration or UN disarmament programs.

The Germans had the most bizarre list of caveats. Their troops could not operate after dark; Afghan soldiers could not travel on German helicopters; and an ambulance had to accompany every patrol, thereby making it impossible to conduct foot patrols in the mountains. The first camp the Germans set up in Kunduz was in a poppy field, but their officers pretended not to see it. Self-protection reached extraordinary proportions. When they built their headquarters at Mazar-e-Sharif airport to house fifteen hundred troops at a cost of $70 million, German engineers erected a military city that used seventy-five thousand tons of steel and three hundred thousand tons of concrete.

To Western and Afghan aid workers on the ground, these NATO troops acted like scared rabbits rather than professional soldiers. Aid workers cynically commented that the first ones into a dangerous region were the aid agencies, followed by the UN and other international organizations, while the last ones in were the heavily armed NATO soldiers, who were then disallowed from protecting any of the above. Even after forty thousand NATO troops were deployed around the country and a full-scale Taliban offensive had erupted, the NATO mandate continued to be the "maintenance of security" in the interests of "reconstruction and humanitarian efforts."[9]

As Taliban leaders in Quetta spent the winter preparing for their spring 2006 offensive, the international community spent the winter negotiating a new Afghanistan Compact with the Afghan government. The Compact would commit international development funding for the next five years and would become the successor to the 2001 Bonn Agreement. Its most significant feature was setting mutually agreed deadlines and targets that would force Kabul and the international community to complete projects on time. While Karzai was deeply frustrated at the lack of aid going through government ministries, Western donors were equally frustrated at the corruption and nepotism within his government. The Compact took five months to negotiate between the government, the UN, the World Bank, and a large number of donor countries and agencies.

On January 31, 2006, seventy foreign ministers and heads of international aid agencies met in the palatial rooms of Lancaster House in London at a sumptuous event put on by the British government. The Afghan government launched its Interim National Development Strategy, which required $4.0 billion in funding every year for the next five years. At the meeting, donors pledged $10.5 billion in aid to Afghanistan over the next five years. The United States was the largest single donor, giving $1.1 billion, followed by Britain with $800 million. The donors and the Afghan government made a series of pledges to one another. While the international community promised to recognize "Afghan ownership" and "build lasting Afghan capacity," Kabul promised to "combat corruption and ensure public transparency and accountability." The donors promised to create an Afghan army, border security, and a police force by 2010, as well as to provide electricity to 65 percent of all households in urban areas.

To many Afghans, the Compact was just a list of more unfulfilled promises and more grandstanding by foreign dignitaries talking about basic Afghan needs that should have been provided for already. Kabul still had insufficient electricity or clean water. Yet such thoughts were far from the minds of the well-heeled diplomats who crowded into Lancaster House that day. Even further from their minds was the prospect of a Taliban offensive, which was to relegate the Compact to the history books. The Taliban and al Qaeda, after all, were flush with cash from the drug trade.

NATO troops began to deploy in the south, but the task was immediately fraught with difficulties. The south had been a war zone since 2003, yet NATO failed to articulate a counterinsurgency strategy. All three countries deploying in the south—Canada, Britain and the Netherlands, which had agreed to deploy to Uruzgan—knew they would have to fight but did not declare so, as they all faced continued political opposition at home. Much rested on Britain, which would command NATO forces in the south, deploy the largest number of troops (more than 5,700), and had pledged to curb opium production.

However, compared with its influential role in 2002—when Gen. John McColl had stood up the first ISAF force and when Tony Blair's advice to Bush on Afghanistan was critical—Britain now found its political credibility hitting rock bottom. Blair had been the first foreign leader to visit Afghanistan in January 2002, but he did not visit again for another four years, and the issue seemed to have disappeared from his agenda. Instead, he followed the Americans so unquestioningly and blindly into Iraq that he lost his influence in the White House. The neocons now saw Blair as their poodle, someone who could easily be bullied and told what to do. Blair lost his ability to change Bush's mind on anything, including policies for Afghanistan and Pakistan.

Attempts by Foreign Secretary Jack Straw to prop up Colin Powell to take on the neocons were constantly undermined by Blair. "Not only did we fail ourselves to exert any recognizable influence over the conduct of US policy, we also reduced the influence of those we might have regarded as like-minded internationalists in Washington," said the conservative politician Chris Patten. Former president Jimmy Carter bemoaned how Blair was too "compliant and subservient" to Bush, adding that he was "extremely disappointed by Tony Blair's behavior."[10] The British were at a loss as to why Bush had ceded so much power to Cheney, who had a huge staff to deal with foreign policy and often overruled the State Department.[11]

In late 2005 in London, I was invited to brief British officers to give them a taste of what Helmand would be like. Although they were enthusiastic about their deployment, the officers were disturbed by Blair's failure so far to give them a clear and concise mandate. They asked many questions. Why had Britain chosen the most volatile and drug-infested province in Afghanistan to send underresourced British troops? Why was the government still unclear as to what British troops would do there? What should be done about Pakistan's support to the Taliban? And was their mandate to be reconstruction or counterinsurgency? Could they do both? Meanwhile, the British army was vastly overstretched and received only

2.5 percent of British GDP in 2006—the smallest proportion of GDP since 1930.[12]

None of these questions was answered by the government, even after the deployment had taken place. British officials admitted that Blair's office was increasingly cut off from reality. There was infighting between the Ministry of Defense and the Foreign Office over the terms of the deployment. Like the Pentagon, Defense refused to allow its soldiers to get their hands dirty by doing drug control. It demanded heavy air support to protect the troops, while the Foreign Office and the Treasury wanted the operation done on the cheap. Blair just wanted the troops to do anything he asked and to stop asking questions. As London dithered on deciding the mandate, the troops' deployment was delayed. Soldiers were trained, and then sat on their haunches in a state of limbo. British container ships packed with military equipment idled off Karachi port, waiting to know if they should dock or not. The start of the deployment was already proving to be massively demoralizing for the army.

Britain had urged Karzai to sack Sher Mohammed Akhunzada and Jan Mohammed Khan, the corrupt governors of Helmand and Uruzgan, as the price for its deployment. British intelligence officers were trying to put together a profile of Helmand province, where intelligence was virtually nonexistent, as U.S. satellite intelligence had never covered Helmand. The Americans promised the British that they would "handle" Musharraf and persuade him to stop the flood of Taliban recruits coming from Pakistan, but Cheney was to block any U.S. criticism of Musharraf.

When Britain's defense secretary, John Reid, finally announced the details of the deployment on the eve of the London conference, there was no mention of possible fighting. Fifty-seven hundred British troops would be deployed in Helmand, at a cost of $1 billion over five years. Tanks, artillery, Harrier jets, and Apache helicopters would provide backup. The British would establish a PRT in Lashkargah, while their main base would be Camp Bastion, in the desert. Reid described the mission as obtusely as possible—denying terrorists "an ungoverned space."[13] After heavy criticism from the Conservative opposition, Reid described the mission more fully several weeks later: "Our aim is to extend the authority of President Karzai's government, to protect those civilian agencies assisting them to build a democratic government and to enable security, stability and economic development throughout the country."[14]

There was still no mention of fighting the Taliban or the drug mafias.

In April 2006, Reid uttered words that would come to haunt the Blair government: "We would be perfectly happy to leave in three years and without firing one shot," he said. Such statements only increased British public cynicism and opposition to the deployment, as the media rightly commented that the government was lying through its teeth.[15]

In Canada the newly elected conservative prime minister Stephen Harper took a different tack. He tried to reassure the public that Afghanistan could not become another Iraq, but he did not diminish the dangers of the mission: "Unless we control the security situation in countries like Afghanistan we will see our own security diminished," he said while visiting Canadian troops in Kandahar.[16] The Canadians had received an early setback when Glyn Berry, a senior Canadian diplomat who headed the Kandahar PRT, was killed by a suicide bomber on January 15, 2006. By March, Canada had suffered the heaviest casualties in the south, with ten soldiers killed and thirty-three wounded. In May, when the Canadian parliament voted to extend its Afghan mission by another two years, Harper only narrowly won the vote, by 149 to 145. On the same day, the first Canadian female soldier to die in combat was killed near Kandahar. By May, over half of all Canadians opposed the deployment of Canadian troops.[17]

The Dutch were committed to sending twelve hundred troops to Uruzgan—a place whose name most Dutch could neither spell nor pronounce. Dutch generals were extremely wary of any foreign deployment, as in 1995 some four hundred lightly armed Dutch troops deployed in the Bosnian enclave of Srebrenica were forced to stand by helplessly as the Serbs massacred eight thousand Muslim men and boys. Dutch prime minister Peter Balkenende governed with a coalition that held only a slim majority in parliament. He decided to have an open parliamentary debate on the deployment, so those opposing it could air their views—something that Blair had refused to allow. In the meantime, Balkenende put the Dutch deployment on hold, angering the British and Canadians. In the end, 131 out of 150 members of the Dutch parliament backed the deployment, showing that transparency was a better political strategy than obscuring the truth. Within a few weeks the first Dutch troops arrived in Uruzgan.

The drama in European capitals was fully reported on the Pushtu and Dari language services of the BBC and Voice of America and played up by the Taliban, who told their fighters that NATO was weak, poorly armed, and demoralized as compared with the Americans. With advice from their supporters in the Pakistani military, the Taliban would exploit the time gap and power vacuum—as U.S. forces withdrew from Kandahar and Canadian and British forces arrived—to attack NATO forces. The Taliban's strategic aim was to further weaken the resolve of European countries in sending troops to Afghanistan. Copying tactics being used by Iraqi insurgents, the Taliban stepped up suicide attacks and used larger mines and roadside bombs against NATO and Afghan security forces while hiding behind the civilian population.

NATO officers described to me their intelligence about the Taliban in the south as "appalling." The British discovered that between 2002 and 2005 the United States had not bothered to monitor Taliban activity in four provinces in the south or across the border in Quetta. One U.S. general in Kabul admitted to me that NATO would pay the price for the U.S. military's lack of a "lookdown satellite capability" in the south because the Iraq war had taken up so many resources and because the Pentagon had ignored the south, believing there to be no al Qaeda leaders there.

In the winter of 2005/2006 NATO intelligence estimated that Mullah Dadullah, the overall Taliban commander in the south, had just three hundred men under him and that the Taliban's total manpower was no more than two thousand. The first realization as to how wrong these estimates were occurred in the first week of February, when Dadullah threw three hundred Taliban into a bid to capture Sangin, a district headquarters in Helmand with important supply lines to Pakistan. The Taliban lost forty men but battled for three days before NATO air strikes forced them to retreat. Fearing a Taliban offensive just before British troops arrived, U.S. forces launched a counteroffensive called Operation Mountain Thrust. The British had planned to secure Lashkargah, acclimatize their troops, build up intelligence, and initiate development projects. Instead they were immediately sucked into battle.

The Taliban countered by launching their own offensive. Over several days, starting on May 18, the Taliban launched attacks in four provinces, involving up to one thousand fighters, storming towns just a twenty-minute drive from Kandahar city. Dadullah claimed he had control of twenty districts in the south and twelve thousand Taliban under arms. It was the worst violence since 2001, and more than three hundred Afghans were killed. British soldiers occupied small towns in Helmand and were forced to hold them to prevent their falling back into the hands of the Taliban, even though they were undermanned, their logistics chain was not yet set up, and helicopters had not arrived. In the summer desert heat of

50° Celsius (122° Fahrenheit) British troops were stuck inside fortified "platoon houses," or "hellholes," for up to forty days at a stretch, holding off the Taliban.

Relief convoys could not get through to the British garrison in Musa Qala for a month, and soldiers were forced to drink water from a rancid well. In Sangin, one hundred paratroopers fought back forty-four Taliban attacks in twenty-five days. Instead of these British garrisons becoming a security anchor for NATO to win over the population, they became a magnet for hundreds of Taliban, who poured in from Pakistan to do battle and were ready to take heavy losses. Officials from Britain's Department for International Development (DFID), who were supposed to spearhead development with a budget of $50 million, never showed up.

Lt.-Gen. David Richards took over command of all NATO troops on May 4. Like other British generals of his generation, Richards was known for both his military acumen and intellectualism. He had served in failing states in Africa and in East Timor and the former Yugoslavia. He arrived in Kabul with a plan to implement an ink spot strategy—occupy key locations, secure and develop them, and then spread out control like an ink stain on paper. However, with British troops surrounded by Taliban the moment they arrived in towns, the ink could not flow.

Richards suffered under too many masters. NATO states wanted him to preserve their caveats, while Blair insisted that he go softly on Pakistan because of the ISI's cooperation with MI5 in catching Britain's domestic terrorists—even though British officers under fire in Helmand were seething with anger at the ISI's support to the Taliban. The Americans and the Afghans said Richards was too soft with the Pakistanis. Open conflict erupted between Richards and the most senior U.S. officials—the new U.S. ambassador to Afghanistan, Ron Neuman, and Lt.-Gen. Karl Eikenberry, who was the commander of U.S. forces in Afghanistan and was doing his second stint of duty after having launched the creation of the Afghan National Army in 2002, when he was a major general—over a cease-fire at Musa Qala in Helmand, which British commanders negotiated with Afghan tribal elders in September and which led to the withdrawal of all armed groups, including the British. The Americans were convinced that the cease-fire was a surrender to the Taliban. Richards defended the action, suggesting that it was the way of the future.

The battles in Helmand provided NATO with incontrovertible proof of Pakistan's involvement in backing the Taliban. NATO intelligence officers now estimated that there were half a dozen Taliban "commanders' *shuras,*" or councils, operating in neighboring Balochistan province. More than one hundred small and medium Taliban commanders—leading between fifteen and three hundred men—were loyal to these *shuras,* which provided them with recruits, arms, ammunition, money, and food. The Taliban began to operate in battalion-size units of up to four hundred men, with separate units providing logistics. In June the Taliban had sent to Helmand more than one hundred Toyota Land Cruisers from Quetta packed with soldiers and supplies.[18]

With the help of al Qaeda and Pakistani extremists, the Taliban had also set up a lethal cottage industry along the Afghanistan-Pakistan border—the manufacture of improvised explosive devices (IEDs). The components of the IEDs—electronic panels, triggers, explosives materials, and casings—were manufactured by tribal households on the Pakistani side and then collected by the Taliban, who sent them into Afghanistan, where they were assembled. Soon the Pakistani Taliban would be using the same IEDs against Pakistani forces.

NATO's unwillingness to take casualties forced it to depend more heavily on air power than the Americans had ever done, but in doing so it lost any hope of winning over the population. In May alone an estimated 400 Taliban fighters and Afghan civilians were killed in 750 air strikes in the south, more than Afghanistan had ever seen. Capt. Leo Docherty, a British officer in Helmand, later described the campaign as "a textbook case of how to screw up a counterinsurgency." After quitting the army, he wrote, "We've been grotesquely clumsy—we've said we'll be different to the Americans who were bombing and strafing villages, then behaved exactly like them."[19]

The heavy fighting in the south, the widespread publicized deaths of civilians, and a new refugee crisis as families fled the war zone caused a pall of gloom to envelop Kabul, which soon exploded into fury. On May 29 a U.S. Army truck, part of a convoy, had brake failure on a steep hill on the outskirts of Kabul and careened down, hitting a dozen vehicles and killing five people. As crowds gathered, nervous American soldiers in the other trucks opened fire. The killings sparked riots across the city. Police deserted their posts and threw away their uniforms as small groups of rioters rampaged through residential areas, stoning, burning, and ransacking offices of Westerners and NGOs. One mob tried to march on the U.S. embassy, another on the presidential palace, shouting, "Down with Karzai" and "Death to America." Karzai made no public appearance until the evening. Finally, the ANA restored order, a curfew was imposed, and Karzai appeared on TV to appeal for calm. However, 17 Afghans were dead, scores were injured, and 250 were detained. Karzai promptly accused the NA warlords of instigating the riots, an accusation that led to further political tension.

Karzai insisted to me that his government was not paralyzed, but that is what it felt like in Kabul as Afghans and Western diplomats openly asked how long the regime could survive with firefights with the Taliban taking place just forty miles away. The riots should have been a wake-up call for the Afghan government about how swiftly it was losing public support. Ministers had stayed at home rather than dealing with the crisis, while NATO and U.S. forces had refused to move out of their barracks. The performance of the police had been downright treacherous. As the Taliban insurgency spread, the police were on the front line, losing more men than the ANA and Western forces combined. In 2005 at least six policemen were killed for every Afghan soldier.[20] During the 2006 offensive the Taliban targeted police. Over a year (May 2006 to May 2007), 406 policemen were killed, compared with 170 ANA soldiers. In June 2007, one of the worst months, 67 policemen were killed.

In April 2005 the U.S. Defense Department took over police training from the Germans, embedding four hundred American advisers with the local police and providing $1.1 billion for training.[21] Karzai was expected to carry out police reforms, but in what was now becoming the norm with difficult decisions, he procrastinated indefinitely. After the riots, he finally appointed 69 new police chiefs from a list of 270 officers trained and vetted by the Germans. However, he also appointed 14 other officers who had failed their tests and were known to be crooks.[22] In appointing them, Karzai ignored a merit-based system that had been set up with great difficulty. In 2007, as the police crisis remained fraught, the European Union agreed to become a major partner alongside the United States in training the police. In June a European Union Police Mission, or EUPOL, was created to standardize police training, but the Europeans were slow to send trainers into the field.

On several counts the Taliban began to provide the Pashtuns in the south the semblance of an alternative government. The absence of justice had become one of the primary recruiting tools for the Taliban, who carried out a primitive "justice on the spot" system, according to their interpretation of Sharia law. Their system was brutally harsh but effective, compared with that of the existing courts, which were riddled with corruption and long delays. People did not necessarily prefer Sharia law, but they were comparing it with the absence of any other kind of law. Crime dropped dramatically in areas where the Taliban provided such services. The public also took note when Mullah Omar issued a thirty-point rule book for Taliban fighters to improve their performance in governance and behavior.[23] Yet the old bad ways were still there, as the Taliban could not tolerate education, especially for girls. In 2006 the Taliban killed 85 teachers and students and burned down 187 schools, while another 350 more schools were shut down in the south because of Taliban threats.

At the end of the summer of 2006 the Taliban aimed to rout the Canadians and capture Kandahar city. Over the summer the Taliban collected hundreds of men in Panjwai, a district near Kandahar, and one at a time began to infiltrate them into Kandahar. NATO retaliated belatedly on September 2, when some 10,000 troops, including 2,300 Americans, 2,200 Canadians, and 3,300 British, launched Operation Medusa to clear Panjwai. They discovered thousands of well-entrenched Taliban. Panjwai's dense orchards, vineyards, mud walls, alleys, and tunnels provided ideal cover for the Taliban as they fought house to house, often using civilians as shields. The Canadians surrounded some 700 Taliban in a cluster of villages called Pashmul, but the Taliban called in heavy reinforcements from Pakistan. Heavy fighting ensued until September 17, when Pashmul, spread across just four square miles, was finally cleared by Afghan troops, who fought the Taliban in hand-to-hand combat.

NATO chalked up 512 Taliban killed and 160 captured, but then significantly hiked its figures to more than 1,000 killed. Hundreds of Taliban reinforcements coming from Pakistan had been killed in air strikes. While NATO troops were still counting the dead, a suicide bomber killed four Canadian soldiers in Pashmul on September 18.[24] Once again the Taliban had taken advantage of a rotation of Canadian troops to mount their offensive. Lt.-Gen. Michael Gauthier, head of the Canadian forces in Afghanistan, later described how "at the point of transition we had insurgents who chose to make a stand and go conventional on us . . . as the next rotation arrived there was a clear and present danger to Kandahar city."[25]

After the battle a report compiled by U.S., NATO, and Afghan forces described the preparations the Taliban had made to capture Kandahar. In the battle, the Taliban had fired an estimated four hundred thousand rounds of ammunition, two thousand rocket-propelled grenades, and one thousand mortar shells, all of which had been stockpiled in Panjwai over many months. More than a million rounds of unused ammunition were unearthed. The Taliban had established training facilities to carry out suicide bombings. A full surgical field hospital was uncovered. NATO intelligence was now better able to map out the Taliban support structure in Balochistan, from ISI-run training camps near Quetta to ammunition dumps to arrival points for the Taliban's new weapons and meeting places for Taliban commanders in Quetta. "Madrassas run by the Jamiat-e-Ulema Islam Party continue to provide the main source of recruitment while Taliban decision making and its logistics are all inside Pakistan," the Afghan defense minister, Gen. Rahim Wardak, told me.

NATO had only just been able to prevent a massive Taliban assault on Kandahar city. There was growing anger within NATO at Pakistan. "It is time for an 'either you are with us or against us' ultimatum delivered bluntly to Musharraf," one NATO commander told me in Kabul. "Our soldiers in the south are hurting because of what is coming out of Quetta, where the Pakistanis are providing the Taliban with a logistics chain and operating cushion."[26] General Richards delivered a blunt message to Musharraf in the first week of October, warning the Pakistani leader that if Kandahar fell, so might his government in Islamabad, because the West would not have tolerated such a setback and would lay the blame squarely on Pakistan.

The first six months of 2006 witnessed the greatest number of conflict-related deaths since the fall of the Taliban—more than one thousand dead, compared with sixteen hundred killed in the whole of 2005. Twenty-four aid workers had been killed in the same period, compared with thirty-one for the whole of 2005, and forty-seven American and seventeen European soldiers had died in the same period.[27] Although they had failed to penetrate Kandahar, the Taliban had put so many men in the field that they were able to continue suicide bombings, ambushes, and attacks in the western and eastern provinces for several weeks. On October 31 they launched simultaneous attacks in five provinces in which 150 people were killed, including four NATO soldiers. It was impossible to improve governance or carry out reconstruction in such a state of insecurity. "The violence is hollowing out government institutions, cowering the population, and testing even enlarged NATO force levels," said Chris Alexander, the deputy chief of UNAMA.[28]

Yet according to a UN survey, some of the violence was also due to tribal, factional, and drug-related rivalries.[29] Putting a stop to such localized violence and corruption was Karzai's responsibility, but he seemed to be rejecting the fledgling institutions of government the UN and others were trying to build. Instead, he resorted to traditional tribal methods of governance that were retrograde and ultimately contributed to more violence and fear. Karzai saw good governance as a projection of powerful tribal personalities rather than as the building of institutions. His own office was still disorganized, even though millions of dollars had been spent on it by British and American consultants. The presidential staff were just as dysfunctional as they had been in 2002, with no teamwork or accountability and nobody accepting responsibility when things went wrong. The chronic disconnect between the government, NATO, the UN, and the major donors continued.

The cabinet and its decisions barely registered in the public consciousness. Ministers did not travel in the provinces unless they were taken there by U.S. or NATO commanders. Pashtun elders described the cabinet as *waraktun,* or Karzai's kindergarten. At the same time, Karzai still refused to build a political party, while he blamed Pakistan for everything that was going wrong. The Afghanistan Compact had ensured better funding for development than ever before, but that did not resolve the problem of how the money could be put to better use when the government itself appeared to be paralyzed. Karzai's own concept of nation building was fatally flawed.

On July 30 General Richards took over command of the merged NATO and U.S. forces. It was the first time that a non-American officer had commanded American troops in battle since the Korean War. All year, NATO had insisted that it would conduct the war differently from the Americans. There would be less "kicking down of doors," fewer civilian casualties, and captured Taliban would be treated as prisoners of war under the Geneva Conventions. However, NATO's intentions remained at odds with its primary aim of protecting its own forces, which entailed substituting manpower for firepower. Without adequate armor, artillery, or helicopters, NATO forces continued to depend on air strikes to support ground troops in combat.

In the last six months of 2006—from June to December—there were a staggering 2,100 air strikes, compared with just 88 air strikes in Iraq over the same period, and more than were expended in the first four years of the war in Afghanistan.[30] In addition, U.S. Special Forces operating under the Coalition also used excessive air power, and their secret maneuvers were largely unaccountable to NATO or the Kabul regime. Afghan civilian casualties rose dramatically and became a major embarrassment for Karzai.

The Taliban became expert at claiming civilian casualties after every battle. They also began to use more suicide bombers to sow insecurity and fear. This was something completely new for the Afghan people. There had not been a single suicide attack during the Afghan war against the Soviets. The first known suicide attack was in 1992, when a Saudi-backed warlord, Maulvi Jamil-ur Rehman, was killed in Kunar province. In 2001, Ahmad Shah Masud was killed by two al Qaeda suicide bombers. The Taliban mounted only six suicide attacks in 2004, and twenty-one in 2005. Then, in 2006, there were a staggering 141 suicide attacks, causing 1,166 casualties, and the following year 137 attacks took place, raising casualty numbers by 50 percent, to 1,730.

Many of the initial suicide bombers were orphans and mentally unstable teenagers from the asylums and orphanages in Pakistan. Mullah Dadullah correctly predicted that their sacrifice would create a wave that would enable him to recruit more capable bombers from the madrassas and Afghan refugee camps in Pakistan. The Taliban glorified suicide bombers, calling them "Mullah Omar's missiles" and "our atomic bombs."[31] Dadullah warned that "an increase in the number of foreign troops in Afghanistan will make it easier to inflict losses on them."[32] By the spring of 2006, suicide bombers were blowing themselves up outside the gates of the British PRT in Lashkargah and targeting Canadian convoys in the middle of Kandahar city.

Even Kabul was not immune. In one brazen attack on September 8, 2006, a suicide bomber hit a U.S. convoy just outside the American embassy in Kabul, killing sixteen Afghans and two U.S. guards. The resulting crackdown led to the arrests of a suicide bomber network in the city, which revealed to interrogators how extremist groups in Pakistan supplied the group with explosives. Several captured Afghan and Pakistani suicide bombers recounted how they were recruited in Pakistani madrassas, then moved to safe houses in Quetta and Chaman, where they were trained. Taliban couriers then took them into Afghanistan, where they were lodged at safe houses and provided with explosives and cars.

The links to Pakistan were unmistakable. "Every single bomber we arrest is linked to Pakistan in some way. The training, provisions, explosives, technical equipment, are all being manufactured in Pakistan, and the CIA knows this," said Amrullah Saleh, the head of Afghan intelligence. During the summer of 2006 seventeen would-be suicide bombers who had been arrested in Kabul were interrogated by the CIA and NATO about their recruitment and training in Pakistan.[33] There was also a huge increase in the Taliban's use of IEDs, which rose from 530 in 2005 to 1,297 in 2006, a strategy that took NATO totally by surprise.

Many of these new tactics were a result of a new wave of foreign fighters who were flowing back to Pakistan and Afghanistan for the first time since 2002. Fighters from Central Asia, western China, and Turkey and Arabs from a multitude of countries came as a result of al Qaeda's call to help the Taliban. They worked in Pakistan's FATA region, helping train a new generation of Taliban and Pakistani extremists in the arts of bomb making and fund-raising and also as sub-commanders in Afghanistan, honing the Taliban on new tactics. The Arabs in the camps used their international contacts to encourage more Muslim militants living in Europe to travel to Pakistan and Afghanistan for training. These included Muslims from Britain, France, Germany, and Scandinavia. In 2007, many of these militants were to fight alongside the Pakistani Taliban as they extended their writ across the North-West Frontier Province. Al Qaeda was reconstituting itself in ways that were unimaginable after its initial rout in Afghanistan.

In June, U.S., NATO, and Afghan intelligence compiled their information in a secret report that detailed how the Taliban movement was constituted. The report was discussed at a meeting of Western countries and the Afghan government on July 9, with Karzai in the chair.[34] It surmised that the Taliban comprised four distinct elements: hard-core extremist leaders linked to al Qaeda, fighters recruited in Pakistan, unemployed youth, and disaffected tribes. The hard-core leaders had to be isolated, and no compromise could be shown to them. At least four of the top ten Taliban leaders were based in Pakistan. Fighters recruited primarily from the Afghan refugee camps in Pakistan were "heavily indoctrinated" and "trained within Pakistan in combat, communications, IEDs and suicide operations." The report described how the "elder fighters with experience are producing a steady throughput of fighters for the insurgency." The last two categories of Taliban could be won over with jobs, education, and development projects, as they were not heavily indoctrinated but were "a result of the insurgency, not the cause of the insurgency." The report described Pakistan's role in the most unflattering light of any intelligence report so far:

> ISI operatives reportedly pay a significant number of Taliban living/operating in both Pakistan and Afghanistan to fight.... A large number of those fighting are doing so under duress as a result of pressure from ISI. The insurgency cannot survive without its sanctuary in Pakistan, which provides freedom of movement, safe havens, logistic and training facilities, a base for recruitment, communications for command and control, and a secure environment for collaboration with foreign extremist groups. The sanctuary of Pakistan provides a seemingly endless supply of potential new recruits for the insurgency.

As the report circulated to NATO capitals it became impossible for European governments to ignore Pakistan's duplicity. Cabinet ministers of two NATO member governments told me that their ignorance about the ISI was compounded by Washington, particularly the State Department, which had assured them that the United States would deal with the Pakistanis. The Bush administration had not only failed to do so but had continued to heap praise on Musharraf. The ISI's refusal to disrupt the Taliban's command and control in Quetta now posed a major threat to NATO's entire effort in southern Afghanistan. The UN presented an equally tough report to the Security Council in September. Tom Koenigs, a seasoned German diplomat and now head of UNAMA in Kabul, painted a grim picture of the worsening insurgency.[35] He described how five Taliban command centers were operating "with widespread use of safe havens outside the country." The five were the Taliban northern command, active in Afghanistan's northeastern provinces, a Taliban eastern and southern command, and separate fronts established by two Taliban allies, Gulbuddin Hikmetyar and Jalaluddin Haqqani.[36]

A stream of foreign and defense ministers from NATO member states visited Washington to complain to Rice and Rumsfeld about ISI's role and then traveled to Islamabad to privately admonish Musharraf, who remained in total denial. In ever-frequent displays of pique, Pakistani foreign minister Khurshid Kasuri lost his temper when the criticism became too strident. Pakistani officials complained that because the United States and NATO were losing the war in Afghanistan they were making Pakistan the scapegoat, just as the United States was doing with Iran in relation to its failures in Iraq. There was certainly truth to this, but it did not excuse the ISI's failure to rein in the Taliban.

Musharraf's schizophrenic behavior toward Karzai only heightened international concern about Pakistan's president. On July 20, after denying there were any Taliban in Pakistan and accusing Karzai of being controlled by India, Musharraf suddenly admitted in a TV speech that there were Taliban in Pakistan, although their center was in Afghanistan and not Pakistan. Then, on September 6, just before he visited Washington and three days after signing the agreement with the Pakistani Taliban in North Waziristan, Musharraf unexpectedly visited Kabul, where he again admitted that "there are al Qaeda and Taliban in both Afghanistan and in Pakistan." He told Afghan parliamentarians that "the best way to fight this common enemy is to join hands, trust each other and form a common strategy."[37] The Afghan leadership hoped this was a genuine change of heart, but Musharraf's aim was merely to deflect any American criticism before he arrived in Washington. A few days later, in Brussels, he contradicted himself again by glorifying the Taliban, saying they were Pashtuns with roots in the people who had always resisted foreign forces, and in Washington he again attacked Karzai for his ignorance and kowtowing to the Indians.

The White House did not want to understand how the Taliban were destabilizing Afghanistan and Pakistan. U.S. leaders remained unwilling to rattle Musharraf, fearing a backlash from the Pakistan military. Senior U.S. diplomats later told me that Bush refused to push Musharraf on the Taliban issue when Bush had visited Islamabad in March, on his way back from a trip to India. "Nobody gave the Taliban much importance then," said a senior U.S. official. "To hunt the Taliban we would have to take away focus on al Qaeda, and that was not possible because al Qaeda posed the main threat to the U.S."[38] In June, Condi Rice had briefly raised the issue of the Taliban for the first time when she visited Islamabad, but Musharraf denied any Taliban presence in Pakistan.

Bush declined to raise the issue of the Taliban sanctuary in Quetta when he hosted a tense tripartite dinner for Musharraf and Karzai at the White House on September 28. Karzai told me he had posed the issue, much to the chagrin of Musharraf, but that Bush had remained silent. "I raised in a very clear way the question of terrorist sanctuaries and that no country should rely on extremism as an instrument of policy," Karzai said.

However, senior U.S. military officers had become enormously frustrated with the cover-up that Bush and Cheney were providing Musharraf, and they now took the initiative in becoming more outspoken. At a Senate Foreign Relations Committee hearing on September 21, Gen. James Jones, who was due to retire as NATO supreme commander, testified for the first time that the Taliban headquarters were based in Quetta.[39] After the Democrats won congressional elections in November 2006, the new Speaker, Nancy Pelosi, accused Pakistan of failing to deal with the Taliban. Congress passed a resolution saying it would stop all military aid to Pakistan if it did not contain the Taliban. For the first time, the legislation mentioned Quetta by name, calling on Bush to certify that "the Government of Pakistan is making all possible efforts to prevent the Taliban from operating in areas under its sovereign control, including in the cities of Quetta and Chaman and in the North-West Frontier Province and Federally Administered Tribal Areas."[40]

After Bush replaced Rumsfeld, the new defense secretary, Robert Gates, encouraged his generals to be frank in their public assessments about the ISI's role. The new openness by Gates forced the State Department—whose dour assistant secretary of state for South and Central Asian affairs, Richard Boucher, had long resisted any criticism of Musharraf—finally to admit that the Taliban were using regions of Pakistan "for sanctuary and for command and control and for regrouping and supply."[41] Several NATO countries added their voices, publicly calling on Pakistan to shut down Taliban operations on its soil.[42]

The unmistakable international pressure on Pakistan led to some changes in the winter of 2006/2007. The Pakistanis now appeared to be providing better intelligence about the movement of at least some Taliban leaders. On December 19, a U.S. drone fired a missile on a car in Helmand, killing Mullah Akhtar Mohammed Usmani, the number two to Mullah Omar in the Taliban *shura*. Two other Taliban commanders were killed along with him. His car had been tracked from Quetta by a British RAF plane working alongside the U.S. Delta Force. The ISI had helped track him down in Quetta, forcing him to flee into Helmand.

The military regime also feared a cutback in U.S. aid from the new and very hostile Democratic-controlled Congress. Between 2002 and 2006 Pakistan had received $10.0 billion in U.S. aid, of which more than half—$5.5 billion—the Pakistan army received directly as Coalition Support Funds, or compensation for helping U.S. military operations in Afghanistan. That came to an average of $80 to $100 million a month for services rendered.

Congress now determined that the army had been overbilling the United States, for which "there is no formal auditing mechanism to verify costs apart from local U.S. embassies and military officials vouching for the accuracy of the submitted bills."[43] Moreover, the army did not want to endanger its global shopping spree, in which it was buying new weapons systems at a cost of $8.4 billion. However, as we see in the next chapter, the main shift in the military's thinking came as a result of the emergence of the Pakistan Taliban in the tribal areas and the growing spate of terrorist violence, with suicide attacks launched against the army, police, and politicians.

As pressure on Pakistan increased from the U.S. Congress, John Negroponte, the director of national intelligence, gave a startling assessment in January 2007 to the Senate, stating that al Qaeda "are cultivating stronger operational connections and relationships that radiate outward from their leaders' secure hideout in Pakistan, to affiliates in the Middle East, North Africa and Europe."[44] Whereas previously U.S. intelligence officials spoke of al Qaeda as being based on the Pakistan-Afghanistan border, now the United States was admitting—six years after 9/11—that the group was based solely in Pakistan.

* * *

The Taliban's summer offensive created major problems within the NATO alliance. Thirty-seven countries now contributed troops to the NATO force in Afghanistan, and criticism mounted from those countries doing the fighting against those who refused to fight. In 2006, NATO forces in Afghanistan had grown from thirty-two thousand to forty-five thousand troops, but only one third were available for fighting. The issue blew up on November 28, 2006, at NATO's annual summit at Riga. Bush, Tony Blair, and Canadian prime minister Stephen Harper demanded that all NATO countries give up their caveats and provide fighting troops. They demanded that Germany, Spain, and Italy, who jointly had seven thousand troops in Afghanistan, send troops to the front line in the south. German chancellor Angela Merkel took the lead in declining, but she offered to send Tornado reconnaissance aircraft to the south. A poor compromise was reached in which all countries promised to help each other "in extremis"—that is, if help was needed on a battlefront. Only Poland offered a much-needed strategic reserve of one thousand troops, but there were still insufficient soldiers and helicopters for the NATO force.

As al Qaeda opened new fronts in North Africa and threatened to carry out suicide attacks on mainland Europe, there were fears of an even larger Taliban offensive in 2007, and European governments anticipated greater opposition from their publics toward their troop deployments in Afghanistan. In Italy, Prime Minister Romano Prodi's government fell on February 21, 2007, on account of the left's opposition to Italy's deployment in Afghanistan. Prodi was reinstated a week later but with a wafer-thin parliamentary majority of five. In Germany and Britain there were demands for a parliamentary debate on Afghanistan, and in Canada in April, the ruling Conservative Party narrowly defeated an opposition motion to pull out Canadian troops, by 150 votes to 134. Fifty-four Canadians had been killed in Afghanistan—the third-highest casualty rate, after American and British losses. Nine Canadians were killed in the ten days preceding the vote.

NATO had bet a great deal on its mission in Afghanistan: that it would find meaning for its continued existence and re-create the unity that Western Europe showed during the cold war. Yet NATO had arrived with little understanding of the Afghan conflict, a lack of realism regarding public opposition at home, a complete lack of transparency in dealing with the public, and an overreliance on U.S. leadership and analysis of the conflict. General Richards was later to admit that "probably we all underestimated the potential for a [Taliban] resurgence."[45] Increasingly NATO officers blamed the Bush administration for refusing to get tough with Pakistan. Above all, NATO had addressed Afghanistan as though it were a classic post-conflict peacekeeping operation confined to the country's borders, whereas it was actually an insurgency that was a cross-border phenomenon, as the Taliban were also present in the neighboring countries.

Moreover, NATO's counterinsurgency effort required the close integration of civil and military objectives, but NATO was unable to get it right, as it failed to provide adequate reconstruction efforts in the war zone. By 2007, NATO had established PRTs in almost every province, but they were too small to be effective, too cut off from the people because of the PRTs' own security concerns, while their quick-impact projects made no dent in the rebuilding of infrastructure that was desperately needed to get the economy moving and to provide jobs for people.

All the PRTs operated under different mandates and caveats, decided upon by the home government rather than by the needs on the ground. In 2006 a large proportion of international aid was being delivered to just four opium-growing and insurgency-hit provinces in the south, leaving the rest of the country bereft and angry. USAID, the largest donor, directed half of its aid for 2006—some $119 million—to these four provinces but had little to show because the lack of security there prevented aid workers from venturing out. Britain's development agency DFID and the Canadian International Development Agency (CIDA) had enormous funds at their disposal but were unable to deploy in Helmand or Kandahar.

Karzai's indecisiveness and his apparent unwillingness to improve the performance of his government angered NATO countries. The ease with which some Afghan officials continued to benefit themselves contrasted sharply with the self-sacrifice espoused by the Taliban. The European governments wanted the Americans to put more pressure on Karzai. NATO's Scheffer warned Karzai that " 'parliamentary and public support' in NATO countries for their troops in Afghanistan depends on the respect for universal values demonstrated by the Karzai government."[46] In Kabul, deep disillusionment set in, which resulted in the best and brightest of the Western-trained Afghans, who had come to work for the government, beginning to leave.

The divisions in NATO, its recourse to intensified aerial bombing, which only increased civilian casualties, and the continued refusal of many European countries to fight the Taliban left Afghans asking how committed the international community really was to Afghanistan. Before the world's eyes in the summer of 2006, East Timor, a once-failed state that had received the most aid money per capita in the world and had been administered by the UN, fell apart through riots and mayhem. There was no guarantee that the same thing could not happen in Afghanistan. There was a lesson here, said Kofi Annan.[47] International aid, money, and troops did not guarantee a quick fix or a solution to failing states unless the entire package was welded together with a coherent nation-building strategy that everyone agreed upon. NATO had bet its future role on bringing peace to Afghanistan, but every day the risks of failure and the fear of a geostrategic meltdown seemed to increase. "In committing the alliance to sustained ground combat operations in Afghanistan . . . NATO has bet its future," said Gen. James Jones, the former NATO chief. "If NATO were to fail, alliance cohesion will be at grave risk. A moribund or unraveled NATO would have a profoundly negative geostrategic impact."[48]

CHAPTER EIGHTEEN

◆ ◆ ◆

Conclusion

The Death of an Icon and a Fragile Future

Anyone who has ever studied the history of American diplomacy, especially military diplomacy, knows that you might start in a war with certain things on your mind as a purpose of what you are doing, but in the end, you found yourself fighting for entirely different things that you had never thought of before. In other words, war has a momentum of its own and it carries you away from all thoughtful intentions when you get into it.

—American diplomat George Kennan, October 2002[1]

In the last few moments of her life, Benazir Bhutto, a youthful and still beautiful fifty-four, stood up on the backseat of her bulletproof Toyota Land Cruiser and popped her head through the sunroof. She waved to the crowd surrounding the vehicle as it slowly edged out of the rally ground in Rawalpindi, where she had just finished delivering a stirring election speech in the late afternoon of December 27, 2007. Elections were due on January 8, 2008. Hundreds of police patrolled the ground, but only one was anywhere near Bhutto's vehicle. A young, thin man wearing a black waistcoat and sunglasses standing to the vehicle's left suddenly pulled out a Chinese-made pistol and fired at Bhutto at close range. We will never know the exact cause of death, as no autopsy was carried out, but Bhutto dropped down through the sunroof as the vehicle picked up speed. She may have been shot by the assassin or hit her head on the latch of the sunroof as she ducked. Seconds later a suicide bomber, probably the shooter or another man standing just behind him, detonated explosives strapped to his body.

The massive explosion tore through the crowd, killing the bomber and twenty-one others—many of them Bhutto's young bodyguards. The blast shook Bhutto's vehicle and blew out its tires but injured no one inside. Naheed Khan, Bhutto's devoted friend and secretary, who was sitting next to the former prime minister, thought Bhutto had just slumped in her seat, until Khan noticed blood forming a thick pool on the plastic floor mat. The explosion, the blood flowing from Bhutto's wounds, the bumpy ride, numb eardrums, and the shock of the blast had affected all the vehicle's occupants, but the driver had the wherewithal to stop and transfer Bhutto into another vehicle, which rushed her to a hospital. Doctors there tried to revive her for nearly forty minutes, but it was too late. She was already dead. She'd loved her country and in the end gave her life for it.

A few moments earlier she had been onstage in Liaquat Gardens—the site of the assassination in 1951 of Pakistan's first prime minister, Liaquat Ali Khan—giving the speech of her life. "Wake up, my brothers!" she shouted. "This country faces great dangers. This is your country! My country! We have to save it," she implored.² Ultimately she was unable to save herself from the very extremists whom she cursed in her final speech.

After eight years of self-imposed political exile in London and Dubai, Bhutto had returned home only two months earlier, on October 18, to a large bomb blast—one that tore through her convoy as she traveled from Karachi airport to her home. She barely escaped with her life, but 179 of her supporters and bodyguards were killed and more than 600 injured. It was the single largest terrorist attack in Pakistan's history, and Bhutto was distraught at the staggering loss of life. Afghan intelligence had privately warned her that there was a plot by extremists to assassinate her. It was clear that somebody was out to get her, but she refused to falter in her campaign or to stop appearing in public. The security promised by Pakistan's government never materialized, and it was certainly not there on that terrible December day.

Benazir Bhutto's Pakistan Peoples Party (PPP), whose green, black, and red flags could be seen from the Karakorum Mountains to the Arabian Sea, came the closest of any party in the Islamic Republic of Pakistan to espousing a secular, democratic, antimilitary political culture. Election results proved that the PPP, the country's only national party, consistently commanded the loyalty of about one-third of the electorate, a faction mostly against military rule and Islamic extremism. Bhutto's longest-running battle was with the army, whose generals never trusted her. Gen. Zia ul-Haq had hanged her father, former prime minister Zulfiqar Ali Bhutto, and placed Benazir in jail for nearly five years while she was still in her twenties. She was forced into exile by Musharraf as the government launched one corruption case after another against her.

Under Musharraf, Pakistan's democratic politics had regressed and Islamic extremism became ever stronger. Bhutto's promise to restore civilian rule and democracy while combating extremism was a breath of fresh air for millions of Pakistanis, and vital if Pakistan was to avoid becoming a failed state. Her past mistakes, her inability to deliver on her promises to the people even though she had been prime minister twice, the allegations of corruption against her and her husband, Asif Ali Zardari, were all forgotten as Pakistanis now pinned their hopes on Bhutto's ending military rule.

The Bhutto family had lived through many tragedies. After Benazir's father was hanged, her two brothers were hounded into exile. Her youngest brother, Shahnawaz, died from poisoning under mysterious circumstances in Cannes in 1985. In 1996 her other brother, Murtaza, was killed by police in Karachi, an incident that appeared to be an assassination. What made his death doubly troubling for Benazir was that she was prime minister at the time. That year she was deposed from power, losing the elections to Nawaz Sharif, and went into exile.

For eight years the U.S. State Department studiously ignored Bhutto, with even junior U.S. officials declining to meet with her lest their doing so anger Musharraf. Yet, over the twelve months preceding her death, the State Department and London's Foreign Office had quietly tried to tie up an agreement between Musharraf and Bhutto, one that would allow her to return home after all corruption charges against her had been withdrawn, to contest free and fair elections, and, if she was elected prime minister, to share power with President Musharraf. The aim was to use Bhutto to revive Musharraf's flagging fortunes, cover him with a varnish of legitimacy, bolster Pakistan's dwindling fight against extremism, and mobilize the masses. The Taliban's expansion into Pakistan demanded a new political dispensation.

The "deal," as it was dubbed by the Pakistani media, proved to be immensely unpopular in the PPP and among the opposition leaders, including Nawaz Sharif, who were banking on Bhutto to lead a movement in the streets to topple Musharraf rather than to bail him out. To fulfill her side of the bargain, Bhutto was to overrule her party, courting major criticism and leaving many wondering if she was a front for the Americans or just hungry for power. Bhutto had calculated that this was the only chance for her to make a comeback, enjoy the full support of the international community, and cleanse her reputation. She knew that in the army, only Musharraf, who was an Urdu-speaking Muhajir, now irrevocably weakened, could be persuaded to accept her. The next army chief and the majority of generals were Punjabis, who would prefer to deal with fellow Punjabi Nawaz Sharif, who satisfied their political preferences: he was sufficiently right-wing, anti-American, and close to the Islamic parties. Moreover, Bhutto knew that no matter how weak he was, Musharraf was solidly backed by the army and the Americans; confrontation would not remove him, but a slow, steady inching into the spaces he provided just might.

For Musharraf, the deal was an opportunity to extend his tenure as president safely into a second term, to transition the country to a more genuine democracy, and to complete the political transformation he had promised back in 1999. All that was needed was that he shed his uniform as army chief, hold free and fair elections, show a little modesty, agree to share power with an elected prime minister and parliament, and keep the army from hogging the limelight of political and economic power.

However, Musharraf would double-cross both the Americans and Bhutto, implementing none of the benchmarks he had earlier agreed to in two face-to-face meetings with Bhutto in Dubai and London, in which the Americans had acted as guarantors. These benchmarks included appointing a neutral interim government and an independent election commission to supervise the elections, and disbanding local government officials, the nazims who could influence the vote on the side of the ruling party. As Musharraf refused to fulfill his side of the bargain, and the Americans refused to pressure him, Bhutto was left struggling against the odds.

Two weeks before her death, Bhutto told me she was facing enormous pressure from the White House—particularly Vice President Cheney's office—to conform, while there was no similar pressure placed on Musharraf to carry out his side of the bargain. U.S. officials refused to accept that the deal was dead or that Musharraf was double-crossing them, even though the U.S. embassy in Islamabad reported extensively on plans being drawn up by the ISI to rig the elections. Still, U.S. deputy secretary of state

John Negroponte traveled to Islamabad in late November and urged Bhutto to continue collaboration with Musharraf, as did Richard Boucher, head of the State Department's Bureau of South Asia Affairs.

With the elections just days away, Bhutto's main message the day she died was that Musharraf was preparing to rig the elections in favor of the ruling Pakistan Muslim League–Q (PML-Q) or the Qaid-e-Azam faction. On the previous evening, she was scheduled to meet with two U.S. lawmakers— Senator Arlen Specter and Congressman Patrick J. Kennedy—to hand them a dossier of evidence describing the preelection rigging being carried out by the ISI. She spoke of this rigging both to the crowd who assembled to hear her final speech and to Afghan president Hamid Karzai, who met with her that morning. "She was very frank to me about the ISI and the role they were playing in undermining her," Karzai later told me. "She was a brave, brave unafraid woman who wanted the best for her country. The sad thing about her death is that she predicted it, and she was proved right."[3] There is little doubt that Bhutto and Karzai, working together, would have formed a team committed to combat extremism.

The Bhutto-Karzai meeting reminded me of another day of hope in 1989, when the young Bhutto—only thirty-six when she first became prime minister—hosted in Islamabad Rajiv Gandhi, the equally young prime minister of India. Both had promised to usher in a new era of peace and cooperation between their two countries—a promise soon thwarted by the insurgency in Indian Kashmir.

As her body was carried in an air force plane to her hometown of Larkana, in Sindh province, public grief and suspicions about possible government involvement turned into anger. The government managed to act guilty even as it claimed not to be so. The fire brigade hosed down the site of the bombing within a few hours, destroying all evidence, and doctors at the hospital where Bhutto was treated changed their statements after being pressured by unknown intelligence officials. No autopsy was held— although Bhutto's husband did not insist upon one. Musharraf refused PPP calls for an international investigation led by the United Nations, but he eventually agreed to Scotland Yard detectives being brought in—although they were mandated to discover only how Bhutto died, not who killed her.

For the next three days the country experienced mayhem as banks, railway stations, government offices, and container trucks in Sindh province and Karachi were attacked and burned. Nearly forty people were killed in the ensuing riots and disturbances. In panic, the government delayed the general elections until February 18, and quickly claimed to have identified the perpetrators of the assassination plot. It blamed Baitullah Mahsud, the leader of the Pakistani Taliban in the tribal agencies, for organizing the assassination and released a telephone transcript of him asking a colleague about the plot.

In 2007 there had been 56 suicide bombings in Pakistan, which killed 419 security officials and 217 civilians, compared to just 6 such attacks the previous year. Despite this tenfold increase in suicide bombings, the regime had failed to track down a single culprit.[4] Now the public was expected to believe that the military had resolved the Bhutto murder in a couple of days, blaming the very man with whom the ISI had struck a peace deal earlier in the year. Reinforcing this sense of disbelief and anger at the government was Musharraf's failure to show any remorse over Bhutto's death. Instead, he blamed her for sticking her head out of the sunroof and said that the army had never liked her anyway.[5]

"The United States thought Benazir was the right person to fight terrorists," Musharraf said after her death. "Who is the best person to fight? You need three qualities today if you want to fight the extremists and the terrorists. Number one, you must have the military with you. Well, she was very unpopular with the military. Very unpopular. Number two, you shouldn't be seen by the entire religious lobby to be alien—a nonreligious person. The third element: don't be seen as an extension of the United States. Now I am branded as an extension, but not to the extent she was."[6]

A few weeks later, in January 2008, the police in Dera Ismail Khan, close to the Afghan border, arrested Aitezaz Shah, a fifteen-year-old boy alleged to be a member of the group responsible for killing Bhutto. Shah told police that Baitullah Mahsud had planned the murder, that the shooter was a man named Ikram, and that the suicide bomber standing behind Ikram was Bilal—the latter two both Pashtun tribesmen from South Waziristan.[7] Two more tribesmen from South Waziristan were arrested in Rawalpindi in early February. A report by Scotland Yard on the cause of Bhutto's death agreed with the government that she had died not from a gunshot but from hitting her head on the latch of the sunroof. However, the Pakistan Peoples Party continued to insist upon a full inquiry by the United Nations.[8]

◆ ◆ ◆

Bhutto's death was the latest in the past ten months of crises as Musharraf came under intense domestic and international pressure to share power, doff his uniform, and allow free and fair elections. Instead, he was to manipulate the political scene in order to ensure his political survival and a second term as president. Now, as a result, the country hovered on the edge of political meltdown.

In the spring of 2007, Musharraf was confident that he faced no real political threats to his reelection as president. The opposition parties were subdued, divided, and unable to mobilize mass agitation against the regime; the Bush administration fully supported his reelection and described him as indispensable in the war against terrorism; and the Pakistani economy was doing relatively well, posting annual growth rates of 7 percent.

The only unpredictable danger Musharraf faced was from the country's Supreme Court. In June 2005, Musharraf had appointed Iftikhar Chaudhry as chief justice of the Court. The senior judiciary had traditionally been compliant and accepting of military rule. However, as the date for Musharraf's reelection approached, Chaudhry moved Supreme Court judges to become proactive in the defense of civil rights and the rule of law. The Court began to issue rulings against police abuse and torture, forced marriages, discrimination against women, and unjust rape laws, and it even blocked high-rise land-development schemes—some sponsored by army officers—because they endangered the environment.

However, the most controversial issue the Supreme Court tackled was the case of hundreds of disappeared prisoners. Arrested secretly by the ISI in a manner already described in chapter 14, these prisoners were never brought to trial. None of the intelligence agencies even admitted holding them. When the courts started demanding their release or at least their appearance in court, some two hundred missing people were mysteriously set free during the winter of 2006/2007. Musharraf told the Americans that Chaudhry had become dangerous because he was releasing al Qaeda militants. In fact, most of those released were the regime's political opponents from Sindh and Balochistan.

The army found such judicial activism quite intolerable, while Musharraf feared that the Supreme Court would rule against his seeking a second term as president on at least two counts—a serving military officer could not be elected president, and a government servant needed to be retired for two years before seeking public office. Poorly advised by hawkish generals and in a hurry to secure his position, on March 9 Musharraf suspended Chaudhry on charges of corruption and misuse of authority and placed him under house arrest.

The next day, demonstrations led by lawyers took place in every bar association in the country. Days of strikes followed, paralyzing law courts in even the smallest towns. The striking lawyers were soon joined by journalists, urban professionals, women activists, and members of nongovernmental organizations, all demanding the release of Chaudhry, the resignation of Musharraf, and the holding of free and fair elections. Musharraf had unwittingly galvanized Pakistan's small but highly vocal middle-class civil society, who were tired of military rule. His advisers told him that the protests would peter out in a few days. Instead, they escalated, becoming larger and more abusive of Musharraf. When Chaudhry attended a hearing of the Supreme Judicial Council—the court that was to determine if he should be permanently suspended—tens of thousands of lawyers accompanied him to the courthouse, precipitating a daylong battle with police.

Over the next few months, Chaudhry toured the country to speak to bar associations, where he insisted that the rule of law, democracy, and the constitution be upheld. His speeches, although never overtly political, were a direct challenge to the army. On May 5 he took twenty-seven hours to travel the usually four-hour journey from Islamabad to Lahore as hundreds of thousands of people turned out to cheer his motorcade. A few days later, in Karachi, fifty people were killed as government-sponsored opponents to Chaudhry ran riot just before he was due to arrive in the city. On every occasion the police used excessive brutality to beat up lawyers, women, and journalists; thousands of peaceful protestors were arrested. The government imposed press censorship and forbade live TV broadcasts. Musharraf lost the battle and his credibility when on July 20 the Supreme Court bench hearing his case reinstated Chaudhry as chief justice. There was euphoria in the country and widespread celebrations.

While the security forces were focused on beating up lawyers, a more ominous threat was emerging from Islamic extremists, who now directly challenged the army. In January 2007 the government had tolerated madrassa students and armed extremists from the Red Mosque in the center of Islamabad who threatened citizens. The mosque and its complex of madrassas housed thousands of male and female students. The ISI had used the mosque as a sleepover station for militants traveling to Afghanistan and Kashmir as early as 1984, when foreign Muslims first arrived to fight the Soviets in Afghanistan. More recently, the mosque housed the orphans and female relatives of suicide bombers who had died in Kashmir. The mosque was run by two brothers, Maulana Abdul Rashid Ghazi and Maulana Abdul Aziz Ghazi, who had long-standing links to the ISI and the military. Over time, the brothers had used their army contacts to seize more land around the mosque to enlarge their empire.

Although the mosque is located just two miles from the president's residence and half a mile from ISI headquarters and the diplomatic quarter, the regime saw the unruliness of its militants as a convenient message to Western embassies—that the threat of Islamic militancy in the heart of the capital made the Musharraf regime even more indispensable. In one cabinet meeting, Prime Minister Shaukat Aziz was said to have voiced the opinion that the militancy was a convenient distraction from the negative media coverage the government was receiving on the Chaudhry case.

Militants from the mosque sallied out to threaten women not wearing the veil and shopkeepers selling Western movies, while an all-female veiled vice squad armed with batons kidnapped alleged prostitutes from private homes and took them in for reeducation. In April, as militant Pashtuns from Waziristan and Swat took up residence in the mosque and more arms were brought in, the Ghazi brothers threatened civil war if the government did not accept Sharia law. It was clear that the movement was out of control, the Ghazi brothers had overstepped their limits and gotten carried away, and the militants were no longer listening to their ISI handlers.

The crisis was to continue for six months, until the army was forced to take action, turning Islamabad into a war zone. Whereas in January 2007 a small police party could have arrested the few culprits, by July an army brigade was needed to clear out the estimated ten thousand students and militants who now had barricaded themselves in the Red Mosque and pledged to become martyrs. The first clashes between the militants and the army began on July 3, after which several thousand students either escaped the mosque or surrendered. On July 8 Musharraf ordered a full-scale assault on those remaining inside, but it took another three days of heavy fighting before the complex was cleared. Abdul Aziz was arrested while trying to flee dressed as a woman, while his brother, Abdul Rashid, was killed in the final shootout. The government said 102 students and militants were killed, against a loss of 10 soldiers. However, the militants insisted that hundreds of their number had been killed, and those who escaped vowed to become suicide bombers.

Following the fall of the Red Mosque, a wave of retaliatory attacks and suicide bombings swept across the North-West Frontier Province. In the three weeks following the July assault, 167 people, including 120 soldiers and policemen, were killed in 21 attacks by militants, which included 12 suicide bombings. The government, the army, and the public were shocked. The country had never faced such a devastating bout of terrorism by its own citizens. Hundreds of militants now gathered in the Swat Valley, some one hundred miles north of Islamabad, in a bid to turn it into a new redoubt for Islam.

The government's inept handling of the crisis was a turning point for al Qaeda, Pakistani Taliban, and other extremist groups, who now joined together and vowed to topple the government and create an Islamic state. Hundreds of suicide bombers born out of the rubble of the Red Mosque traveled to FATA, where they were trained and armed with explosives belts by the Pakistani Taliban. Others set up cells in urban areas or joined existing terrorist groups, such as Jaish-e-Mohammed and Lashkar-e-Jhangvi. Al Qaeda's focus also shifted from Afghanistan to Pakistan, where it saw a demoralized army, a terrified citizenry, and an opportunity to destabilize the state. For the first time, senior Pakistani officials told me, the army's corps commanders accepted that the situation had radically changed and the state was under threat from Islamic extremism. In fact, the Pakistan army was now fighting a civil war.

◆　◆　◆

The deteriorating situation in Pakistan distracted Washington, but it did not hide the fact of the equally deteriorating situation in Afghanistan. Lt.-Gen. Karl Eikenberry, who commanded ISAF-NATO and U.S. forces in Afghanistan, warned the U.S. Congress in February 2007 about "the reconstituted enemy" and "growing narcotics trafficking," which could lead to "the loss of legitimacy of the government of Afghanistan." Eikenberry became the first U.S. general to state publicly that NATO could not win in Afghanistan without addressing the sanctuaries the Taliban enjoyed in Pakistan.[9] Bush took his cue from Eikenberry when, on February 15, 2007, speaking of the coming spring offensive by extremists in Pakistan and Afghanistan, he described the FATA region of Pakistan as "wilder than the Wild West."[10]

To persuade Pakistan to do more in FATA, U.S. defense secretary Robert Gates, Vice President Dick Cheney, and several U.S. military commanders traveled to Islamabad separately in the spring to meet with Musharraf. However, the Pakistanis were reluctant to break the September 2006 cease-fire they had agreed to with the new Pakistani Taliban leader, Baitullah Mahsud. Some Pakistani officials still gave the Taliban a kind of legitimacy that appalled the Americans. The governor of the NWFP, Ali Jan Orakzai, claimed that the Taliban movement was becoming "a national liberation movement"—a far cry from the epithet of "terrorists" given to them by the United States.[11]

The peace agreement in FATA was only torn apart after the assault on the Red Mosque in July 2007, as the Pakistani Taliban again began to attack the army in FATA. As Musharraf debated with his generals whether to relaunch an offensive in FATA, the Americans weighed in with unprecedented public statements, saying that Pakistan's counterterrorism strategy had failed. In July 2007, a U.S. National Intelligence Estimate, a summary of sixteen American intelligence agencies, said that al Qaeda had reestablished its central organization, training infrastructure, and lines of global communication primarily due to its safe havens in FATA. Mike McConnell, the director of national intelligence, said that al Qaeda was "working as hard as they can in positioning trained operatives here in the United States."

For the first time in six years, Bush officials admitted that the peace deals in FATA had been a failure. "It hasn't worked for Pakistan. It hasn't worked for the United States," said Frances Fragos Townsend, White House homeland security adviser, on July 17, 2007.[12] All options were on the table, Townsend added, including a possible U.S. military strike against al Qaeda in Pakistan.[13] These new assessments were a huge embarrassment for the U.S. intelligence community, which had been claiming since 2003 that al Qaeda's leadership had been decisively depleted.[14] The change in U.S. public opinion toward Pakistan had come as a result of growing frustration with Musharraf and strong indications that al Qaeda was planning terrorist attacks in the United States.

FATA was now perceived as a global threat, as many plans for terrorist attacks discovered in Europe were traced back to training or contacts in the tribal region. In June 2007, Islamists had attempted to bomb a London nightclub and Glasgow airport. In July, a suicide bomber killed seven Spanish tourists in Yemen. That same month, three people in Germany—two converts to Islam and a Turk—were found in possession of fifteen hundred pounds of chemicals that were to be used to blow up the U.S. air base in Ramstein. The accused ringleader, Fritz Gelowicz, and two others reportedly trained at an al Qaeda camp near Mir Ali, in Waziristan, in March 2006, where they worked with a German-speaking trainer. Seven more German Muslims are believed to have later trained at the same camp, after having entered Pakistan through Iran.

All these men belonged to the Islamic Jihad Union, the Central Asian terrorist group allied to al Qaeda that had carried out several bombings in Tashkent and that had a base in Waziristan. Germany's deputy interior minister, August Hanning, warned that his country was now a major target for al Qaeda and that "there is a new quality in the threat to Germany."[15] In September 2007, eight men, including several Pakistanis, were arrested in Denmark after having received training in FATA. In January 2008, twelve Pakistanis and two Indians were arrested in Barcelona for planning a wave of suicide attacks in several European cities, starting with Barcelona. All had received training in Waziristan. "In my opinion the jihadi threat from Pakistan is the biggest emerging threat we are facing in Europe," said Baltasar Garzón, Spain's leading antiterrorism judge. "Pakistan is an ideological and training hotbed for jihadists, and they are being exported here."[16]

U.S. pressure and public disclosures about the Pakistan army's lack of performance in the war on terror sparked outrage in Islamabad but helped yield the results Washington sought. Moreover, the army high command was itself feeling threatened by the monster it had helped create. Musharraf abandoned the truce with the Pakistani Taliban, sacked Governor Orakzai in Peshawar, and, on July 19, 2007, formally launched a military offensive in FATA. There were pitched battles between the army and the militants, who retaliated by carrying their suicide bombing campaign into Punjab province. To overstretch the army, they also successfully occupied the Swat Valley, assaulting police stations, driving out the local administration, and forcing thousands of people to flee. Mullah Fazlullah, the local extremist leader in Swat, had the support of hundreds of fighters from FATA, including Arabs, Chechens, and Uzbeks.

In early September two suicide bombers targeted a military bus just outside the army's general headquarters in Rawalpindi, killing twenty-six officers and soldiers and wounding another sixty-six. A few days later the army faced its biggest humiliation when Baitullah Mahsud's men surrounded a convoy carrying 270 Frontier Corps soldiers and forced them to surrender. In the following days, dozens more soldiers were kidnapped, surrendered, or even deserted to the militants. This reflected the low morale among the troops, which caused enormous concern in the army and in the West. The army dubbed Baitullah Mahsud, forty-two, the principal leader of the militants, and every terrorist attack was now laid at his door. Shy and unwilling to be photographed—like his mentor Mullah Omar, the leader of the Afghan Taliban—Mahsud is a short man, just a little over five feet, with thick locks of hair that fall halfway down his back and invariably cover his face. He had fought for the Taliban in the 1990s and helped al Qaeda and the Taliban escape from Afghanistan after December 2001.

Now Mahsud was in regular contact with al Qaeda, which increasingly seemed to be giving strategic direction to the Pakistani Taliban movement. Although uneducated, Mahsud resorted to rhetoric laden with references to the global jihad ideas of al Qaeda, as he threatened the United States and Europe with destruction. He said, "The main objective of this coalition is 'defensive' jihad."[17] In mid-December 2007, forty extremist militia commanders in FATA and the North-West Frontier Province met to set up an umbrella organization, the Tehreek-e-Taliban, or Movement of the Taliban, in Pakistan, appointing Mahsud as their amir, or leader.

The ISI had no inkling of the meeting until it was well over. Other key commanders who took part in the meeting included Mullah Fazlullah, thirty-two, who had become an important figure after the insurrection he led in the Swat Valley; Faqir Mohammed, based in the Bajour tribal agency, who worked closely with al Qaeda; and Sadiq Noor, another young and powerful leader from North Waziristan, who is closely allied to the veteran Afghan fighter Jalaluddin Haqqani. Together these commanders now led some forty thousand heavily armed tribesmen and militants, who had joined them from the cities.

As the battles in the north intensified and mass arrests continued in Pakistani cities, Musharraf came under much greater American pressure to open up the political system in order to salvage his crumbling reputation. On October 4, after secret talks with Bhutto in London and Dubai, Musharraf finally issued a National Reconciliation Ordinance that provided amnesty from prosecution and dropped corruption charges against Bhutto and all politicians who had served in government between 1988 and 1999. In return, Bhutto agreed that the members of parliament belonging to her Pakistan Peoples Party would abstain from voting when Musharraf ran for a second term as president. (To be elected president, one needs a simple majority from the 1,170 members of the national and four provincial assemblies.) On October 6, 2007, Musharraf won his election with just 57 percent of the total number of MPs voting for him, as several hundred MPs had resigned from parliament rather than taking part in the sham election. On October 18, 2007, Bhutto returned home to Karachi to a tumultuous public reception—and the assassins who awaited her.

The Supreme Court could still challenge Musharraf's second term in office, however, which would endanger him just before the scheduled elections. So on November 3, 2007, he mounted a second coup by declaring a state of emergency—virtually martial law. He suspended the constitution and basic rights and sacked all Supreme Court judges, including Chaudhry. Thousands of activists, ranging from politicians to human rights workers and lawyers, were arrested overnight. All private TV satellite news channels were taken off the air, which left only the state-controlled Pakistan television network to relay news. Strict censorship was imposed over the print media. It was a throwback to a 1950s coup.

On November 3, 2007, Musharraf issued a new provincial court order, or PCO, which forced all judges to take a new oath of office that would validate his actions. Thirteen of the seventeen judges of the Supreme Court refused to take the oath and were placed under house arrest. Sixty out of ninety-seven judges in the four provincial high courts also refused to take the oath. This did not deter Musharraf, who appointed Abdul Hamid Dogar, a close friend, as chief justice. In addition, the Army Act disciplining army officers was amended so that civilians, too, could be tried for treason in military courts.[18] Parliamentary elections were scheduled for January 8, 2008. Prime Minister Shaukat Aziz, who vehemently defended the Emergency, threatened that if protests continued the elections could be delayed for a year.

Musharraf met with foreign ambassadors in Islamabad to admit that his intervention was a matter of self-preservation but also that it would better enable the army to fight the extremists in the Swat Valley. However, the day the Emergency was declared, the army, which had been holding secret talks with Baitullah Mahsud, released twenty-eight terrorists from jail, including eight self-confessed suicide bombers. In exchange, Mahsud released the hundreds of soldiers he was holding. One such released bomber was Sohail Zia, twenty-two, who had been sentenced to twenty-four years in jail just a month earlier for being caught carrying two suicide belts. The army agreed to withdraw some troops from FATA and to mount patrols only in conjunction with Mahsud's commanders. The Emergency was thus an excuse not to confront but rather to appease the extremists in the mountains.

It was not until two weeks after the declaration of Emergency that the army was fully deployed in Swat and went after the militants. The valley was cleared by December, after heavy fighting and the extensive use of helicopter gunships and artillery. Some 290 militants were killed, but the entire leadership, including Mullah Fazlullah, was able to escape into the mountains. There were no large-scale arrests of militants in the cities and not a single madrassa known to be supporting terrorism was closed down. Instead, Pakistan's middle-class and civil society bore the brunt of the police and ISI crackdown. Bhutto was placed under house arrest in Lahore for several days. On seeing the thousands of police surrounding her house, she sarcastically asked "when we have this huge deployment, [why] police of this kind can't be used to hunt down Osama bin Laden."[19]

Following Bhutto's arrest, a wave of revulsion against Musharraf and the army swept the country. Lawyers and civil-society activists continued to protest outside courthouses, but they were mercilessly clubbed by the police, and up to ten thousand people were jailed for the duration of the Emergency. Washington defended Musharraf, although it demanded that he quickly lift the Emergency, and President Bush said he still trusted Musharraf to hold elections. "I take a person for his word until other-wise. . . . And he made a clear decision to be with us and he's acted on that advice," Bush said at Crawford on November 10, 2007.[20] However, Pakistan became a hot debating item for the Democratic Party candidates. Both Hillary Clinton and Barack Obama accused Bush of supporting a dicta-torship in Pakistan. "The failed policies of the Bush administration are part of the reason we are in this difficult and dangerous position," Clinton said on November 6, 2007.[21]

Before lifting the Emergency on December 15, Musharraf passed six more amendments to the constitution that made it impossible for the courts or a future parliament to question his past actions. Only then were thou-sands of innocent people freed from jail. On November 28, Musharraf had finally taken off his uniform and handed over command of the army to the American-trained general Ashfaq Kayani, who had previously headed the ISI. Kayani's appointment was welcomed by Washington, who had worked well with him over the past few years. However, it was on Kayani's watch that the growth of extremism and the debacles in Swat, in FATA, and at the Red Mosque had occurred.

The forty-two-day-long Emergency had blighted Pakistan, undermined its economy, destroyed what little trust the political parties and the public had in Musharraf, and turned the increasingly influential middle-class and civil society against both the army and the president. After Bhutto's death, the elections were postponed to February 18. Musharraf became more arrogant and was in total denial about the crisis he had himself created. As with other absolute rulers on the verge of losing control, he insisted that everyone—judges, lawyers, politicians—was conspiring against him.

The political vacuum Musharraf had helped to create only encouraged the Pakistani Taliban to intensify their suicide attacks in the weeks before the elections. Lahore faced its first major suicide bombing on January 9, when nineteen policemen were killed on the city's busiest road. In North Waziristan, groups of militants, sometimes as many as six hundred, overran army posts and again started capturing soldiers. In late January 2008 the militants audaciously seized the Kohat Tunnel, a key communications link south of Peshawar city. Peshawar, the capital of the North-West Frontier Province, received rocket fire on almost a nightly basis from militants parked on the outskirts. Between Bhutto's death on December 27, 2007, and the election on February 18, 2008, another four hundred people were killed.

Pakistan was now a major cause of concern for Washington. CENT-COM chief Admiral William Fallon said that during November and December 2007 the level of violence in Afghanistan's eastern provinces was down by 40 percent because the Taliban were concentrating all their efforts on destabilizing Pakistan. Al Qaeda also had turned its face toward Pakistan, Fallon said. On January 9, 2008, Mike McConnell, director of national intelligence, and Gen. Michael Hayden, director of the CIA, visited Islamabad, where they discussed with Musharraf and Ashfaq Kayani a plan to make operational in FATA a secret CIA base that could mount attacks on militants by Predator drones armed with missiles. Musharraf agreed and also accepted help from U.S. Special Forces to train and mentor Pakistani counterterrorism units. "The plan to counter insurgents is to work with the Pakistanis to share intelligence, increase cross-border cooperation between ourselves, the Afghans and the Pakistanis" and to increase the Pakistani army's capability, said Fallon.[22] Hundreds of millions of additional U.S. dollars would now pour in for the military.

There was one quick success with the death on February 1, 2008, of the number three man in the al Qaeda hierarchy, Abu Laith al-Libi, who was killed in a missile strike on a tribesman's house near Mir Ali, in North Waziristan. At least seven other Arabs died with him. Libi, who had been a leader of the Libyan Islamic Fighting Group, was a key organizer and trainer of several militant groups in Afghanistan, Pakistan, and Europe.

However, there was still a lack of trust between the CIA and the ISI as long as the ISI refused to deliver hard intelligence about the Afghan Taliban leaders who had safe sanctuary in Quetta. According to U.S. officials, surrendering Mullah Omar would be the ultimate test of the Musharraf regime's sincerity. Dell Dailey, the State Department's counterterrorism chief, said the U.S. administration was displeased with "the gaps in intelligence" it was receiving from Pakistan. "We don't have enough information about what's going on there. Not on al Qaeda. Not on foreign fighters. Not on the Taliban," Dailey said in January 2008.[23]

The elections were held in a state of widespread national despair. The wave of violence, the death of Bhutto, the refusal of the government to establish norms of transparency, and fears of large-scale rigging by the ruling Pakistan Muslim League–Q led to expectations of low voter turnout as people stayed away from the polls. Nobody believed that Musharraf would actually share power with the winners, especially if they were the PPP, as was widely expected. A huge sympathy vote was anticipated for the PPP, of which Bhutto's husband, Asif Ali Zardari, was now co-chairman. In fact, the results turned out to be much better than expected, defying all the pundits.

The election commission had failed to stop the PML-Q from carrying out extensive pre-poll rigging before the elections. However, army chief General Kayani had signaled to the administration and the intelligence agencies two days before the elections that there was to be no interference or rigging. More than 46 percent of the population came out to vote, and it did so in favor of the opposition. The final results for the National Assembly announced by the election commission on March 6 showed that the PPP had won 120 seats; the PML-N, the party of Nawaz Sharif, had won 90 seats; and the formerly ruling PML-Q had won only 51 seats.

More significant, the Islamic parties were wiped out. The combined Islamic parties' alliance, the Muttahida Majlis-e-Amal—including the pro-

Taliban Jamiat Ulema-e-Islam, which had swept the Pashtun areas in 2002—had now won only 6 seats. Instead, the secular and moderate Pashtun-based Awami National Party had won the most seats in the North-West Frontier Province provincial elections and 13 seats in the National Assembly, making it certain that it would form the new provincial government in Peshawar.

No party held a majority, however, so a coalition government would have to be formed. Despite pressure from George Bush, Condi Rice, and Musharraf that Zardari join up with the remnants of the PML-Q, the PPP refused and immediately announced an alliance with Nawaz Sharif. Zardari wisely said he wanted to form a national unity government at the center and similar alliances in the provinces, where he embraced all moderate parties. For the first time in nearly a decade there was widespread hope that a popular coalition government would come to power and the democratic system would be allowed to take root.

The election results led to renewed calls for Musharraf to step down. After 9/11 his popularity had soared to 80 percent; now it was barely 20 percent. With his desire for continued power and his belief that he was indispensable to Pakistan, the army, and the world, he had undermined his own achievements. In fact, Musharraf had stayed in office for so long by concentrating all power in the presidency and being fully supported by the army and the intelligence services. He had co-opted a small section of the political elite by offering them office and patronage, but gave them no share in power or decision making. In return, they were expected to mobilize civilian support as Musharraf needed it. He had also co-opted the major Islamic parties, who maintained a fiction that they were opposed to military rule while, in fact, they helped sustain it.[24]

However, it is to the army that Musharraf owed everything, and in turn he had pampered it like no other army chief before him. Since his rule, the army had developed even greater stakes in the economy, and so exercised ever greater social and political control of the country. Author Ayesha Siddiqa estimates that Pakistan's military-industrial complex was worth around $20 billion in 2007.[25] The three armed services were running hotels, shopping malls, insurance companies, banks, farms, and industries. Army-owned factories made cornflakes, bread, cement, textiles, and sugar. Two army-run conglomerates, Fauji Foundation and the Army Welfare Trust, controlled one third of the entire heavy manufacturing in the country.

The army's most important asset and reward for loyalty is the land parceled out to officers during their careers and again when they retire. The army owns an estimated twelve million acres, equivalent to 12 percent of total state-owned land. In 1900 the British began the tradition of granting agricultural land to loyal native officers. After 1947 more lucrative urban plots were given out to officers at nominal prices. Officers sold these plots at market rates, reaping profits of fifty to one hundred times. Under Musharraf, bureaucrats quipped that army officers at general headquarters were too busy trading plots of land on their mobile phones to protect the country. Musharraf fiercely defended the new greed he had perpetrated. "So, what is the problem if [the armed forces] are contributing to town development," he said when quizzed about the issue. "The defence societies everywhere are the top societies of Pakistan. . . . Now, why are we jealous of this? What is the problem? . . . There's no problem."[26]

Musharraf had also inducted more than twelve hundred retired and serving military officers into all-civilian institutions and government departments. In 2000, he had more than one hundred generals working under contract in the government. As a result, the civilian bureaucracy and civilian institutions were ruthlessly undermined.[27] At one point the vice chancellor of every university in the country was an army officer. Every general who retired from the army was promised a civilian job, and in this way Musharraf silenced any criticism from his corps commanders. He promoted this policy as "national development," which could not be trusted to civilians. Yet corruption and incompetence were no less prevalent under the military than under civilian rule.

Musharraf had become increasingly callous and totally disregarding of public opinion. The only time I met him one-on-one was when he summoned me to his office to warn me directly to stop writing articles about the ISI's support of the Afghan Taliban. The meeting, scheduled for half an hour, carried on for nearly two and a half hours. Musharraf gave me an hour-long lecture on how, since 1979, Pakistan had never interfered in Afghanistan.[28] Many of the facts, dates, and names he mentioned were incorrect, but he was never contradicted by the two generals sitting in the room with us. Clearly he had not read his history, or the ISI had poorly briefed him. After his lecture, I bluntly told him that nobody believed Pakistan's denials about supporting the Taliban. The discussion went in circles, but I had to be grateful that instead of arresting me, Musharraf had tried to engage me and change my mind. However, the encounter convinced me that he considered himself a master of spin and tragically believed that his spin was the absolute truth.

✦ ✦ ✦

In Afghanistan the expanding Taliban offensive and the burgeoning failure of the Karzai government to deliver services and sustain its popularity among the Afghan people coincided with an even larger crisis in NATO. For much of 2007 the entire international community seemed to be at odds, unable or unwilling to agree on how to meet the growing threat of instability in Afghanistan, the expanding war against the Taliban now engulfing northern Pakistan, and the largely unspoken fear that al Qaeda was planning another major terrorist strike in Europe or the United States. The United States and the handful of European nations fighting the Taliban in southern Afghanistan bitterly resented the continued refusal of other NATO countries to get their hands dirty and support the war effort. The list of caveats these latter nations imposed on their troops in order to prevent them from seeing combat became even longer.

There was no overarching NATO strategy to deal with the problems of Afghanistan and Pakistan or the cross-border nature of the Taliban, or to coordinate nation building between the Afghan government and all the various agencies and NGOs. There was no coordinator with the clout of a Lakhdar Brahimi to knock Afghan and Western heads together so as to produce a common plan. One year the Americans decided that the Afghan National Army had to be built up, and all funding was poured into it. The next year it was the police who were to be funded. Trying to get sustained money for any service-sector project for any length of time was next to impossible. When the West earmarked a powerful coordinator—the British politician Lord Paddy Ashdown—as UN special envoy to Afghanistan, his imperial manner and a few of his interviews alienated Karzai from him.

U.S. secretary of defense Robert Gates was later to raise the specter of NATO's becoming a two-tier organization, with one group of countries prepared to fulfill all the obligations of the alliance and fight and the other group refusing to do so. However, the Europeans had their own criticism. They continued to resent the Bush administration and were now palpably awaiting the U.S. elections and a new president. They still doubted the extent of U.S. commitment to nation building in Afghanistan, and they resented not being consulted when the United States took unilateral decisions about Afghanistan. Yet no European nation had significantly raised its level of defense spending since 9/11. NATO had two million men under arms, but only 25 percent were deployable overseas—a figure that had not changed since 9/11. Even though European governments spoke existentially of terrorist threats emanating from Afghanistan, they refused to explain to their publics how helping Afghanistan was directly related to ensuring the security of Europe.

The divisions within NATO, and between governments and their opposition, generated acute political crises. In 2007 two governments fell as a result of internal domestic opposition to the war in Afghanistan. The first to fall, in February 2007, was the fragile government of Italy's Romano Prodi, which lost a vote of confidence in parliament on the issue of maintaining two thousand Italian troops in Herat. Prodi was reinstated by the Italian president ten days later, but his government remained fragile until elections were called in 2008. The second government to fall, in September 2007, was that of Japan. Prime Minister Shinzo Abe and his Liberal Democratic Party had struggled to maintain Japan's commitment to refueling the Western-led warships in the Arabian Gulf that monitored sea-lanes used by al Qaeda. The Japanese opposition demanded that Tokyo cease all such cooperation with NATO and on September 12 Abe was forced to resign, ending Japan's help to the allies. Japan resumed refueling the warships only in January 2008, after Yasuo Fukuda, the new prime minister, rammed legislation through parliament making it obligatory for Japan to support Afghanistan.

The entirety of 2007 was spent with the United States demanding more troops and equipment from NATO countries, and NATO stalling. In January 2007, at a meeting in Brussels, the United States asked for more troops from NATO countries, especially troops that could be used on the front against the Taliban. Once again, European nations refused to oblige. The Germans and the French, with the largest armies in Europe, were the worst offenders. Both had large troop contingents in safe areas in Afghanistan—the Germans in the north, and the French around Kabul. After much browbeating, Germany finally agreed to allow six Tornado aircraft to carry out reconnaissance surveys in the south.

When NATO members met again, in Quebec in April, just as the Taliban summer offensive started, Robert Gates was even blunter about demanding more troops and helicopters. He reminded his European counterparts that at a time when the U.S. military was overstretched because of Iraq, it still had fifteen thousand troops as part of the ISAF-NATO force, plus another eleven thousand troops deployed as part of Operation Enduring Freedom hunting down terrorists. On the other hand, twenty-six NATO countries and eleven other allies were contributing a total of thirty-five thousand troops.

The lack of an overall NATO response to helping out in Afghanistan led those countries fighting in the south to react as they saw fit. In the space of one week, in April 2007, Canada's twenty-five-hundred-strong forces in Kandahar province lost nine soldiers. The opposition Liberal Party leader Stéphane Dion demanded that Prime Minister Stephen Harper and his minority Conservative government commit to withdrawing all Canadian troops by the scheduled February 2009. The Canadians had lost fifty-four soldiers, a quarter of all foreign troops killed in Afghanistan and third only to the United States and Britain in number of casualties. Public anger in Canada against the deployment was rising daily. An independent team commissioned by the Ottawa government recommended in January 2008 that if no NATO forces were prepared to join Canada in Kandahar, then all Canadian troops should be withdrawn and redeployed to a more peaceful zone by February 2009. By then, Canada had lost seventy-eight soldiers. For several weeks Harper tried to persuade European nations to help Canada, but failing to raise any attention, he declared on February 21, 2008, that Canada would withdraw its troops from Kandahar by 2011.

Similarly, the sixteen hundred Dutch troops based in the southern province of Uruzgan were prepared to fight, but their mission was defined by the Dutch government as limited to peacekeeping and reconstruction. In mid-June 2007, after three days of intense fighting in Uruzgan between the Taliban and Dutch troops in which fifty Taliban and nearly one hundred Afghan civilians were killed, the Dutch public began to take serious umbrage at the deployment. By August 2007, only 45 percent of the Dutch supported the Afghan mission, and by December 3 the government had announced that it would pull back its troops by 2010. The public and media debates in Canada and the Netherlands were also about the huge cost of such military missions for these small countries. The Dutch deployment to Uruzgan for two years cost $1.4 billion. From 2001 to late 2007, Canada had spent a total of $6.3 billion on its deployments in Afghanistan. Both governments were also spending large sums on aid projects for the Afghan people.[29]

There were also tensions within NATO's fighting forces. As a result of the heavy fighting in Helmand, borne largely by the 7,800 British troops deployed there, tensions arose between the British and the Americans on strategy and tactics. The U.S. military resented Britain's secret dealings with and attempts to divide the Taliban, as well as the British refusal to accept U.S. requests to carry out aerial spraying of the opium crop. U.S. military officers began privately to disparage their British counterparts, while British officers blamed the Americans for their shoot-from-the-hip philosophy. The biggest bone of contention was why the British had allowed the Taliban to keep control of Musa Qala, a key terrorist training center and drug-producing city. Musa Qala was held by the Taliban for a year and then finally retaken by British and U.S. forces in December 2007.

In fact, the real problem was that Helmand province was critical to the war effort and affected all other NATO forces. It was the center of Taliban activity, a major Taliban gateway into southern Afghanistan for manpower, food, and ammunition from their bases in Pakistan and for the all-important flowering drug trade that provided growing income for the Taliban and al Qaeda war chest. In 2007 there was a 45 percent increase in production of opium in Helmand—the total opium harvest increased from 6,100 tons in 2006 to 8,200 tons in 2007, while the cultivated land area for opium increased by 17 percent across the country. The British were responsible for drug control across Afghanistan, so the lack of progress in Helmand was acutely embarrassing, especially when thirteen provinces in the north were declared drug-free by the UN, compared to only six in 2006.

By December 2007, Robert Gates became more belligerent, telling the U.S. Senate Armed Services Committee that NATO had failed to deliver three battalions of troops, twenty helicopters, and thirty-five hundred trainers for the ANA, as it had promised to do. He called for overhauling NATO's Afghan strategy over the next three years, shifting NATO's focus from one primarily of rebuilding to one of waging "a classic counterinsurgency" against a resurgent Taliban. "I am not ready to let NATO off the hook in Afghanistan at this point," Gates told the committee.[30]

He could not have been more serious. Taliban attacks were up 27 percent from 2006, and there had been a 60 percent increase in attacks in Helmand despite the large British presence, which seemed to attract rather than deter Taliban strikes. However, the U.S. commitment to Afghanistan remained far less than that to Iraq. Adm. Michael Mullen, chairman of the Joint Chiefs of Staff, admitted in the same hearing that "in Afghanistan, we do what we can. In Iraq, we do what we must. There is a limit to what we can apply to Afghanistan." This message was pounced on by Afghans and Europeans to show that as far as the United States was concerned, Afghanistan came a distant second to Iraq. Nevertheless, Poland promised to send four hundred troops in addition to the twelve hundred soldiers already in Paktika province, while the United States said it would make up the shortfall by sending three thousand U.S. Marines for a short duration, including one thousand trainers for the ANA. There were now fifty-six thousand U.S. troops in Afghanistan. Nobody, however, offered to help out the Canadians or the Dutch.

NATO was not the only problem. The international community was failing to coordinate its military and security strategy with its development architecture, and there had been a breakdown in relations with the Afghan government and Karzai. Nobody seemed to know what the other was doing, even though several bodies had been set up ostensibly to coordinate strategy between all the players. In July 2006 the Policy Action Group, composed of leading donors and generals in Kabul and chaired by Karzai, had been established to meet every month and decide upon policy priorities, but it became increasingly ineffective. London's Afghanistan Compact had set up the Joint Coordination and Monitoring Board, or JCMB, which was tasked with overseeing that the Compact's targets, both from the Kabul government and the international community, were met. However, the JCMB failed to hold anyone accountable for shortcomings or for targets not met.

The problems in Kabul were compounded by the sheer number of actors there. Thirty-nine countries were now involved in contributing troops to ISAF in Kabul. More than sixty large donor institutions and dozens of small NGOs were supposed to be coordinating with the Afghan government, but frequently were not. Three heavyweight civilian ambassadors, representing the UN, NATO, and the European Union, were supposed to coordinate their assistance and strategy with the government. Instead, coordination was noticeable only by its absence.[31] Things were getting worse, not better, and nobody seemed to be able to find a way out of the morass.

In 2007 the Taliban had mounted fewer human wave assaults on secure NATO positions than they had in 2006. Instead, they had stepped up suicide attacks—in 2007, 137 suicide attacks led to 1,730 casualties, compared to 141 such attacks and 1,100 casualties in 2006. In 2007, there were 42 suicide attacks in Kandahar province alone. Some of the deadliest attacks took place in Kabul; in one such incident, a suicide bomber boarded an Afghan army bus in late September 2007 and killed 31 ANA recruits. One of the worst bombings took place in Baghlan, on November 6, when a suicide bomber killed 72 people, including 5 members of parliament and Syed Mustafa Kazemi, the brilliant former commerce minister who had opened trade links through Iran. Fifty-nine of the victims were the children who had been waiting to receive him.

The Taliban brought the war into the heart of the Western policymaking process when a group of suicide attackers stormed into the Serena Hotel in Kabul on January 14, 2008, and killed six people, including a Norwegian journalist; the Norwegian foreign minister, Jonas Garh Soere, escaped the massacre by hiding in the basement. Such tactical successes emboldened the insurgency, further cowered the population, who were in awe of the Taliban, and forced NATO and Afghan security forces to deploy more static guards rather than go after the insurgents.

The Taliban also targeted the police in 2007, killing some nine hundred. Nearly forty aid workers were killed that year, while another seventy-six were abducted. Such attacks began to have a major impact on education, as nearly six hundred schools in the south were closed down, sending three hundred thousand children home on account of the lack of security.

The Taliban also seemed to be winning the propaganda war. Tens of thousands of tapes and DVDs produced by the Taliban media outlets Omat [Nation] Productions and Manbaul-Jihad (Source of Jihad) were sold for a few pennies in the bazaars of Pakistan and Afghanistan. Al Qaeda's own production company, al-Sahab, issued eighty-nine messages in 2007, one every three days, or double the rate it had issued them in 2006.

In the short term there seemed to be some improvement in intelligence sharing among Pakistan's ISI and NATO and U.S. intelligence. Several key Taliban commanders based in Balochistan were killed. Mullah Akhtar Mohammed Usmani, the former commander of the Taliban's Second Corps, was killed in a targeted British air strike in Helmand on December 23, 2006, as he traveled from Pakistan. In March 2007, Mullah Obaidullah Akhund, one of the two senior deputies of Mullah Omar, was arrested in Quetta. It was later reported that the ISI had freed him in a hostage exchange for Pakistani soldiers being held by Baitullah Mahsud.

Mullah Dadullah, the much-reviled commander of southern Afghanistan who had kicked off the insurgency in 2003 by killing a Red Cross worker and who had committed multiple atrocities since then, was finally killed on May 13, 2007, in a firefight in Garmser, in Helmand province. He had been tracked by Britain's Special Boat Service in Quetta and killed after he left the city. On August 30, 2007, Mullah Barader Akhund, the former Taliban deputy defense minister, was killed in Sangin, in Helmand province. Some of these commanders had fallen out with Mullah Omar and the ISI, and it was rumored in Taliban circles in Quetta that in fact they had been "delivered up," or betrayed, by the ISI so that they could be killed by NATO, allowing Pakistan to show its sincerity about catching Taliban commanders. The truth is not known, because privately and publicly, the Americans praised the ISI for being more cooperative.

NATO kept boasting that it won every battle its soldiers fought. This was true because of the overwhelming firepower NATO forces could bring to bear in a single theater. However, NATO had no overarching strategy for winning or for transforming military victories into development, re-construction, good governance, and political strategies. Nobody had yet come up with a solution to the major problem of how to reconstruct a na-tion in the midst of an insurgency—something that was most evident in the south. Admiral Mullen described the NATO-ISAF command as "plagued by shortfalls in capability and capacity, and constrained by a host of caveats that limit its ability."[32] It was this lack of strategy that Gates was trying to get NATO to address, but it was not certain if the Europeans were refusing to listen or were just plain tired of another lecture by the now lame-duck and much-disliked Bush administration.

The Taliban were seeking to outlast NATO, and they were succeeding; for as in Iraq, as long as the Afghan government failed to create effective governance and provide services to the people, the Taliban were winning by default. The outcome of the fighting was becoming less relevant be-cause, even when faced with a string of tactical defeats, the Taliban were expanding their influence and base areas and cowing more of the popula-tion. Corruption alone was creating enormous misgivings among the peo-ple and making Karzai hugely unpopular. "If nothing is done about corruption, Afghanistan's development prospects will be severely threat-ened and undermined," warned William Byrd of the World Bank. "Cor-ruption is profoundly inimical to state building."[33] Moreover, even in 2008 the World Bank estimated that up to 30 percent of all aid was being wasted by the donors.[34]

However, the economy was not entirely moribund. The U.S. Geological

Survey showed that Afghans were sitting on a gold mine of natural resources, with huge deposits of copper, iron, gold, coal, gemstones, gas, and oil. Undiscovered petroleum resources in northern Afghanistan range from 3.6 to 36.5 trillion cubic feet of natural gas, while estimates of oil range from 0.4 to 3.6 billion barrels.[35] In November 2007 the government finalized the first mineral deal, with a Chinese company, to exploit the Aynak copper reserves outside Kabul, which could yield some $400 million in revenue per year—equivalent to the total government revenues in 2007—and provide more than five thousand jobs. However, if corruption continued to prevail at every level of the government, then it would be impossible for such projects to raise living standards.

What the country still needed was an effective security apparatus and a functioning judicial and policing system that could face up to the Taliban and deal with local issues such as land disputes and criminality. The Americans were speeding up the building of the ANA and also focusing on revamping the police. In 2007 the United States furnished $10.1 billion for the ANA and the police, providing them with much-needed equipment and increasing their salaries. This was more than double what had been spent in any previous single year since 2001, and it reflected a recognition that past NATO and U.S. priorities had been misplaced.

Yet for ordinary Afghans, how much had life really changed? Seven years on, Afghanistan was still listed fifth from last on the UNDP's Human Development Index in terms of education, longevity, and economic performance. Its position of 174 out of 178 placed it only above the poorest countries in Africa.[36] One third of Afghans did not have enough to eat, and only 12 percent of women were literate, compared to 32 percent of men. Life expectancy was just a miserable forty-three years, half of that in the United States.

However, the Taliban are now expanding in Pakistan much faster than anyone could have imagined. It has not been their successful strategy as much as the failed policies of the army and Musharraf that have created this crisis. The world's terrorist leaders were already living on the Pakistan side of the border, but with the creation of the Pakistani Taliban, they are now able to expand their influence, base areas, and training camps at will across northern Pakistan. The 2008 election offers a panacea, but it will bring relief only if the army, the politicians, and the international community come together to help the new Pakistan government tackle its myriad problems. Success depends on the army and the ISI being pressured or persuaded to give up their twisted logic of insecurity, national pride, and expansion in the region, to help sort out the country's problems, and to be good friends to Pakistan's neighbors, instead of constantly trying to undermine them. The army's insecurity, which since 1947 has essentially bred a covert policy of undermining neighbors, has now come full circle, for Pakistan's very future is at stake as extremists threaten to undermine Pakistan itself.

The past three periods of prolonged military rule in Pakistan coincided with large U.S. aid flows to the country, but never in such quantities as the Bush administration undertook to provide Musharraf. Between 1954 and 2002, the United States provided a total of $12.6 billion in economic and military aid to Pakistan, of which $9.19 billion was given during twenty-four years of military rule, while only $3.4 billion was provided to civilian governments over a nineteen-year period. Between 2001 and 2007, the United States gave more than $10.0 billion to the Musharraf regime. Yet what has been the gross profit of this aid?

Today, seven years after 9/11, Mullah Omar and the original Afghan Taliban Shura still live in Balochistan province. Afghan and Pakistani Taliban leaders live on farther north, in FATA, as do the militias of Jalaluddin Haqqani and Gulbuddin Hikmetyar. Al Qaeda has a safe haven in FATA, and along with them reside a plethora of Asian and Arab terrorist groups who are now expanding their reach into Europe and the United States. The United States and NATO have failed to understand that the Taliban belong to neither Afghanistan nor Pakistan, but are a lumpen population, the product of refugee camps, militarized madrassas, and the lack of opportunities in the borderland of Pakistan and Afghanistan. They have neither been true citizens of either country nor experienced traditional Pashtun tribal society. The longer the war goes on, the more deeply rooted and widespread the Taliban and their transnational milieu will become.

The Bush doctrine has been overburdened with lies, omissions, and spin—all of which has done little to increase global confidence in the United States. It is going to take a generation before the world begins to see America in a different light, and the next U.S. president is going to have a very hard time cultivating a new image of America—quite apart from the immediate problem of what to do about Iraq and Afghanistan.

The enormous cost of these wars has crippled the United States and world economies, the military deployments have shattered the U.S. and British armies, and the death and destruction have bled civilian populations and worsened the humanitarian crisis for neighboring countries.

According to one estimate, the cost of the wars in Iraq and Afghanistan will eventually reach $3.0 trillion.[37] In 2008 Iraq cost $12.5 billion a month and Afghanistan $3.5 billion a month. That is already double the cost of the Korean War and costlier than the twelve-year-long Vietnam War. Today's wars have been financed almost entirely by borrowing, with no new taxes being raised. As a consequence, Americans for generations will be paying off these debts. Meanwhile, al Qaeda continues to expand and there is the danger that one day it will wreak more havoc in the West.

The West's failure to follow through on nation building has disillusioned millions of people and made too many Muslims ready recruits for al Qaeda. It is ironic that finally, in 2008, the new U.S. Army doctrine stipulates that stabilizing war-torn countries is just as important as defeating the enemy.[38] If only that had been considered important in 2001. For those in organizations such as the UN, who try to do the best they can even under worsening circumstances and with smaller funds, the business of peacekeeping, peacemaking, and nation building is becoming harder. "The problem is that our expectations and agendas are not becoming any more realistic," says Lakhdar Brahimi, the wise old Afghan peacemaker. "Instead, they have become more ambitious and multifaceted, seeking to promote justice, national reconciliation, human rights, gender equality, the rule of law, sustainable economic development, and democracy, all at the same time, from day one, now, immediately, even including in the midst of conflict."[39]

◆ ◆ ◆

Bush promised a great transformation in 2001, and he has certainly transformed the world, but not in the way that any of us could ever have imagined. We now all have to live with the consequences, pick up the pieces, and help improve the world we are left with by tilting the earth's axis back to where it should be.

The region of South and Central Asia will not see stability unless there is a new global compact among the leading players—the United States, the European Union, NATO, and the UN—to help this region resolve its problems, which range from settling the Kashmir dispute between India and Pakistan to funding a massive education and job-creation program in the borderlands between Afghanistan and Pakistan and along their borders with Central Asia. The international community has to approach this region holistically rather than in a piecemeal fashion, and it has to persuade its own populations to agree to a long-term commitment of troops and money. Much will depend on how the new U.S. president sees this region and what importance he or she gives it. Only belatedly has the Bush administration admitted its failures. "I would have to admit that it is really important to be able to help others build their nations," U.S. secretary of state Condoleezza Rice acknowledged to Congress in March 2008.[40] For the first time, in the 2008–2009 budget, the administration designated nearly $250 million to create 350 diplomatic posts devoted to "nation building."

The Pakistan army has to put to rest its notion of a centralized state based solely on defense against India and an expansionist, Islamist strategic military doctrine carried out at the expense of democracy. Musharraf deliberately raised the profile of jihadi groups to make himself more useful to the United States and to enhance his country's strategic importance in Western eyes. No Pakistani leader can afford to take such a deadly gamble again, to play with the destiny of the nation, betray the people's trust, and foster Islamic extremism that bites the hand that feeds it. Pakistan needs national reconciliation that brings an end to the demonization of politicians by the army; a new military culture that is taught to respect civilians, institutions, and neighbors; and reformed intelligence agencies that cease to interfere politically.[41]

Members of the Afghan elite need to appreciate the opportunity to be born again as a nation, a chance they were given by foreign intervention in 2001 and international aid since then—even though the results and commitment of both have been at best halfhearted. The Afghans need to evolve a system of governance capable of delivering services to the people and relatively free of tribalism, sectarianism, and corruption. They need to tackle the drug problem themselves and show the world, first, that they are worthy of help and aid, and second, that they will assume responsibility for their nation in the quickest possible time. So far, President Karzai has taken his people only partially down that road. He has compromised too much with warlords, thieves, and brigands rather than collaborating with the mainstream Afghans who want to rebuild their nation. However, the international community has to do far better than it has done to defeat the Taliban and provide better coordination among the competing tasks of fighting, good governance, and reconstruction.

Central Asia needs a political transformation before it can move forward. A generation of leaders will have to die or step down before real change can be expected. In the meantime, Central Asia, but especially Uzbekistan, is a powder keg, and the West will have to make itself more aware of the region so that it can contain the fallout from any explosion there. We have seen in this book that Islamic extremism will flourish in a political vacuum, in the most backward, deprived, and neglected places but also among people who are educated and politically conscious. Central Asia is the new frontier for al Qaeda, and at present there is nobody there effective enough to resist them. As long as Central Asian extremist groups continue to find sanctuary on the Afghanistan-Pakistan border, they will remain a major threat to states in the region.

Solutions do not come easily in such a world or in a region that was traumatized well before 9/11. But the peoples and regimes of this region have to understand that unless they themselves move their nations toward greater democracy, the chaos that presently surrounds them will, in time, overwhelm them. Pakistan has shown a new beginning in 2008, and Afghanistan still has the potential to do so. If we can better understand what has happened before, what has gone wrong, and what needs to go right, as this book attempts to do, then we can better face up to our collective future.

ACKNOWLEDGMENTS

I owe an enormous debt of gratitude to Abu Bakr Siddique, who helped me research this book. Born into a Pashtun tribal family, he is now an outstanding scholar, journalist, and expert on the history and sociology of the Pashtun tribes on both sides of the Pakistan-Afghanistan border. He has acted as my researcher, travel companion, interpreter, interviewer, and guide in some of the most difficult terrain imaginable. This book would not have been written without his invaluable assistance, support, and friendship.

For nearly three decades all my work has owed a great deal to the ideas, inspiration, friendship, and humor shown by Barnett Rubin. We have become so close that I am not able to decipher whether some of the ideas in this book first originated with him or with me. This volume owes him an enormous debt of gratitude.

I also have to thank the hundreds of fellow journalists, aid workers, UN officials, politicians, military and intelligence officers, diplomats, commanders, warlords, and scholars in Pakistan, Afghanistan, Central Asia, Iran, the United States, Britain, Germany, Spain, Scandinavia, and the Netherlands who have contributed to this book. I hope they will understand that they are too numerous to mention by name. However, I must pay tribute to Lakhdar Brahimi and Francesc Vendrell, the architects of the 2001 Bonn Agreement, to whom I owe a great deal. I could not have written this book without the support of other heads of the UN mission in Kabul—Jean Arnault, Chris Alexander, and Tom Koenigs.

To Flip Brophy, my agent; Wendy Wolf, my editor; and to Liz Parker, Bruce Giffords, Noirin Lucas, Carla Bolte, and all the others at Viking Penguin who have worked so hard to bring this book out so quickly, after having waited so patiently for it to be completed, I owe enormous thanks and gratitude.

Finally, this book could not have been written without the love and support of my wife, who nursed me back to health through two major illnesses so I could finish the manuscript.

NOTES

Introduction. Imperial Overreach and Nation Building

1. Interview with Kofi Annan, former secretary-general of the UN, by the author, Oslo, June 27, 2007.

2. Karen DeYoung, "World Bank Lists Failing States," *The Washington Post,* September 15, 2006.

3. I wrote extensively about the dangers that the presence posed by al Qaeda in Afghanistan early on. A seminal article was published in *Foreign Affairs* magazine in 1999. Ahmed Rashid, "The Taliban: Exporting Extremism," *Foreign Affairs,* December 1999.

4. Niall Ferguson, "The Monarchy of George II," *Vanity Fair,* September 2004.

5. BBC, "Bush Triggers Row over Pakistan Coup," November 5, 1999. Bush said, "The new Pakistani general, he's just been elected—not elected, this guy took over office . . ." Bush gave an interview to *Glamour* magazine in which he confused the Taliban with a female pop group. The quote was recounted by the *National Journal,* May 4, 2002.

6. Richard Haass, "Defining US Foreign Policy in a Post–Cold War World," Speech to Foreign Policy Association, Washington, April 22, 2002.

7. Chalmers Johnson, *The Sorrows of Empire: Militarism, Secrecy, and the End of the Republic,* New York: Metropolitan Books, 2004. Irving Kristol, considered the neocon godfather, graciously defined a neocon as "a liberal mugged by reality."

8. "Given a choice between following the rules or carving out some unprecedented executive power the White House always shrugged off the legal constraints," wrote *The New York Times.* The administration has determined "never to consult, never to ask and always to fight against any constraint on the executive branch." Editorial, "The Real Agenda," *New York Times,* July 16, 2006.

9. Zbigniew Brzezinski, *The Choice: Global Domination or Global Leadership,* New York: Basic Books, 2004.

10. I have taken the liberty to draw from an article by Gabor Rona, legal adviser to the International Committee of the Red Cross. Gabor Rona, "When Is a War Not a War?" *The Financial Times,* March 16, 2004.

11. Bob Woodward and Vernon Loeb, "CIA's Covert War with Bin Laden," *The Washington Post,* September 14, 2001.

12. In July 2005, the global war on terrorism was officially changed to "the struggle against violent extremism," as the administration finally put the emphasis on longer-term initiatives. Chairman of the Joint Chiefs of Staff General Richard Myers admitted that the struggle is "more diplomatic, more economic, more political than it is military." See Alec Russell, "Don't Mention War on Terror," *The Daily Telegraph,* July 27, 2005.

13. Ron Suskind, "Without a Doubt," *The New York Times,* October 17, 2004.

14. Condoleezza Rice, then national security advisor, was to say, "we have solid evidence of the presence in Iraq of al Qaeda members." See Karen DeYoung, "US Evidence Still Unclear on Iraq Link to AQ," *International Herald Tribune,* September 28, 2002.

15. Paul Pillar, "Intelligence, Policy and the War in Iraq," *Foreign Affairs,* March 2006.

16. Dana Priest, *The Mission: Waging War and Keeping Peace with America's Military,* New York: W. W. Norton, 2003. This is one of the best books on the U.S. military's expanding powers.

17. Michael Abramowitz, "Bush to Request Billions for War," *The Washington Post,* February 3, 2007.

18. Richard Lugar, "Beating Terror," *The Washington Post,* January 27, 2003.

19. Walter Pincus, "Taking Defense's Hand out of the State's Pocket," *The Washington Post,* July 9, 2007.

20. Clyde Prestowitz, *Rogue Nation: American Unilateralism and the Failure of Good Intentions,* New York: Basic Books, 2003. SOF included army rangers, army special forces, Navy SEALS, Delta Force commandos, special mission units, special operations aviation units, and psychological operations units.

21. Maureen Dowd, "Rummy Runs Rampant," *The New York Times,* October 30, 2002.

22. Musharraf told Zinni, "I want democracy in substance and not just labels . . . I don't want you to think I did something that wasn't motivated by the best intentions for Pakistan." Dana Priest, *The Mission.*

23. Interview with Kofi Annan, former secretary-general of the UN, Oslo, June 27, 2007. See also Council on Foreign Relations, "In the Wake of War: Improving U.S. Post-Conflict Capabilities," Report of an Independent Task Force, July 2005.

24. U.S. State Department, President Bush press conference, White House, October 11, 2001.

25. Madeleine Albright, "Bridges, Bombs or Bluster," *Foreign Affairs,* September–October 2003.

26. Elisabeth Bumiller, "Freedom and Fear Are at War," *The New York Times,* September 20, 2001.

27. Reuters, "'US made some decisions,' says Rice," reprinted in *Dawn,* Karachi, Pakistan, January 19, 2005, Rice answering questions at her confirmation hearings before becoming secretary of state.

28. "The unwillingness to recognize a historical connection between the rise of anti-American terrorism and America's involvement in the Middle East makes the formulation of an effective strategic response to terrorism that much more difficult," wrote former national security advisor Zbigniew Brzezinski. See Zbigniew Brzezinski, *The Choice.*

29. Associated Press, "Secret Board Says Muslims Don't Hate US Freedoms," *Dawn,* November 25, 2004. See also Report of the Defense Science Board Task Force on Strategic Communication, Department of Defense, Washington, D.C., September 2004.

30. The sums are from the Congressional Budget Office, August 2007.

Chapter One. A Man with a Mission: The Unending Conflict in Afghanistan

1. I was told by an impeccable source in the office of President Hamid Karzai, on March 31, 2003, that a former Taliban deputy intelligence minister, Asadollah Sadozai, who had recently been caught in Ghazni, admitted to helping kill the elder Karzai and said the murder had been planned in Karachi by a pro-Taliban Pakistani group that was advised by the ISI. Hamid Karzai never really forgave the Pakistanis for killing his father.

2. I gave the speech upon receipt of the Nisar Osmani Award for Courage in Journalism, awarded by the Human Rights Commission of Pakistan on March 25, 2001. The entire speech was broadcast by the BBC and the Voice of America.

3. Save for a brief interlude in 1929, when the capital, Kabul, was seized by the Tajik brigand Bacha Saqao.

4. To verify many of these facts, I've carried out many interviews with Hamid Karzai since he became president of Afghanistan in 2001. I have also been greatly helped by Jon

Lee Anderson, "The Man in the Palace," *The New Yorker,* June 6, 2005, and Tolo TV, Kabul, interview with Karzai, August 12, 2005. See also Ahmed Rashid, "Profile of Hamid Karzai," *The Daily Telegraph,* December 8, 2001.

5. Ahmed Rashid, *Taliban: Islam, Oil and the New Great Game in Central Asia,* New Haven, Conn.: Yale University Press, 2000. I have used my earlier book to give a brief history of Afghanistan and the Taliban movement.

6. Ibid.

7. Ahmed Rashid, "The Taliban: Exporting Extremism," *Foreign Affairs,* December 1999.

8. These estimates are drawn from interviews with Western intelligence officials, UN diplomats, and Afghans in the field. I and others wrote about the extensive deployment of foreigners under Pakistani officers. Anthony Davis of *Jane's Intelligence Review* estimated in August that "foreign contingents now spearhead offensives and make up one fifth of a [total] Taliban force of 40,000." Anthony Davis, "Foreign Fighters Step Up Activity in Afghan Civil War," *Jane's Intelligence Review,* August 1, 2001.

9. See Ahmed Rashid, "US Weighs Up Options on bin Laden," *The Daily Telegraph,* November 22, 2000.

10. My last meeting with Masud was in Dushanbe on September 26, 2000. The most detailed book on the subject of the CIA's relationship with Masud is Steve Coll, *Ghost Wars: The Secret History of the CIA, Afghanistan, and bin Laden, from the Soviet Invasion to September 10, 2001,* New York: Penguin Press, 2004.

11. Several books confirm meetings between Masud and the CIA. Gary Schroen was one of the CIA agents who went to see Masud and then led a team into the Panjsher Valley after 9/11. Gary Schroen, *First In: An Insider's Account of How the CIA Spearheaded the War on Terror in Afghanistan,* New York: Ballantine Books, 2005. See also Steve Coll, *Ghost Wars.*

12. There are many emotional accounts of Masud's death, but the best by far is by Nasrine Gross, "Masud: An Afghan Life," personal message received by e-mail.

13. He had married Zeenat in Quetta in 1999. The daughter of an Afghan civil servant, she had trained as a gynecologist in Quetta, where she worked in a clinic and had been a doctor to the family when Karzai's mother suggested to him that he marry her.

Chapter Two. "The U.S. Will Act Like a Wounded Bear": Pakistan's Long Search for Its Soul

1. Mehmood had visited Washington in April 2000, where he had been bluntly told by Undersecretary of State Thomas Pickering that "you are in bed with those who threaten us."

2. Interviews with U.S. and Pakistani participants in the meeting, Washington, D.C., July 2004.

3. In March, Musharraf had written a four-page letter in Pushtu to Mullah Omar, asking him not to blow up the statues. Mehmood had secretly visited Kandahar and personally read the letter to the illiterate Mullah Omar, but to no avail.

4. The quotes are taken from interviews in 2001 and 2004 with Pakistani officials, who either were present at the meeting or had read the transcript. See also Bob Woodward, *Bush at War,* New York: Simon & Schuster, 2002.

5. Interview with Abdul Sattar in Islamabad, August 2004. He later wrote that Pakistan's cooperation with the United States "should indicate a generally positive disposition and negotiate details later. Such a 'Yes-but' approach would allow Pakistan tactical flexibility. It could then also seek modification of US policy and its expectations of Pakistan." See

Abdul Sattar, *Pakistan's Foreign Policy, 1947–2005: A Concise History,* Karachi: Oxford University Press, 2007.

6. Woodward, *Bush at War.* Woodward provides the list of demands, as does *The 9/11 Commission Report: Final Report of the National Commission on Terrorist Attacks upon the United States,* New York: W. W. Norton, 2004.

7. *The 9/11 Commission Report.*

8. Interviews with senior military officers and civilian advisers to Musharraf, December 2001 and November 2004. See also Hassan Abbas, *Pakistan's Drift into Extremism: Allah, the Army, and America's War on Terror,* New York: M. E. Sharpe, 2004, which also gives details about the corps commanders' meeting.

9. Interview with Pakistan Television, "Win-win Situation for Pakistan, says Musharraf," *The Nation,* Lahore, Pakistan, November 27, 2001.

10. *The 9/11 Commission Report.* See also Ahmed Rashid. "Hitting Kabul," *Far Eastern Economic Review,* September 20, 2001.

11. Ali Iftikar, "Powell defends US support to Pakistan," *The Nation,* September 9, 2004. Powell was addressing students of Georgetown University, in Washington, D.C.

12. Woodward, *Bush at War.*

13. These particular allegations first appeared on al-Manar, the TV channel of the Lebanese Islamic party Hezbollah. They quickly spread around the Muslim world on Web sites and were then headlined in the Urdu press in Pakistan, which tends to promote surreal and sensational news about Israel, India, and the United States.

14. The three layers of U.S. sanctions on Pakistan were as follows: In 1990 the U.S. president could not certify that Pakistan did not have a nuclear device in adherence with the Pressler Amendment, which stopped all military and economic aid. In May 1998, Pakistan's nuclear tests triggered further sanctions under the Arms Export Control Act. The 1999 coup triggered sanctions under Section 508 of the same act, which forbade aid to a military regime.

15. "Wrong Step Can Spell Disaster: Musharraf," *Dawn,* September 19, 2004.

16. "Text of President George W. Bush speech to the US Congress," *The Nation,* September 21, 2001.

17. Ian Talbot, *Pakistan: A Modern History,* London: Hurst and Co., 1998. Talbot offers the best discussion of the colonial era and the genesis of Pakistan's territorial makeup.

18. Pakistani sociologists Hamza Alvi and Eqbal Ahmad have termed the military and administrative institutions that Pakistan inherited and built on as "overdeveloped," in comparison to civil society. Historian Khalid bin Sayeed has described the military's ascendance as a continuation of the British "viceregal" tradition. Pakistan's most prominent historian, Ayesha Jalal, describes in his book *The State of Martial Law* how as early as 1951 the growth of the military-bureaucratic apparatus stunted the development of democracy. Hamza Alavi, "Class and State," in Hassan Gardezi and Jamil Rashid (editors), *Pakistan: The Roots of Dictatorship,* London: Zed Books, 1983. Also Eqbal Ahmad, *Between Past and Future: Selected Essays on South Asia,* edited by Dohra Ahmad, Karachi: Oxford University Press, 2004. Khalid bin Sayeed, *Pakistan: The Formative Phase,* Karachi: Oxford University Press, 1983. Ayesha Jalal, *The State of Martial Law: The Origins of Pakistan's Political Economy of Defense,* Lahore: Vanguard Books, 1991.

19. In 2002 there were 138 million Muslims in India, or 12 percent of the total population of 1 billion people. The Muslim population is expected to rise to 150 million by 2005. India has the third largest Muslim population, after Indonesia and Pakistan. Syed Shahabuddin, "Muslim Indians in Census 2001," *Mainstream,* New Delhi, October 23, 2004.

20. Shahabuddin, "Muslim Indians." Presidential Address to the Constituent Assembly

of Pakistan at Karachi, August 11, 1947. Jinnah went on to say, "Hindus would cease to be Hindus and Muslims would cease to be Muslims, not in the religious sense because that is the personal faith of each individual, but in the political sense as citizens of the State."

21. Attempts to get Jinnah's words back into the national agenda and school curricula have failed, even under Musharraf. On October 19, 2004, Minoo Bhandara, a Parsee member of the National Assembly, persuaded the assembly to adopt a resolution to include Jinnah's words in the academic curricula, but the state media and the Education Ministry blacked out the resolution in case it annoyed the fundamentalists.

22. Interview with Qazi Hussain Ahmed, www.newsline.com, April 2005.

23. Just after Partition, West Pakistan's population was 34 million, compared with 42 million in East Pakistan, or 56 percent of the total. In 1971 West Pakistan's population had climbed to 65 million, while East Pakistan's stood at over 70 million. East Pakistan's population consisted of a majority of Bengalis, and was thus more homogenous than that of the western wing; it always constituted an overall majority. However, that did not prevent a denial of Bengali rights by rulers in the west, which led to secession. Today Pakistan is the seventh largest state in the world, with a population of 151 million.

24. When U.S. secretary of state John Foster Dulles became the first high-level American official to visit Pakistan, in May 1953, the army's commander in chief, General Ayub Khan, gave him a paper outlining a cold war version of the Great Game—that the Soviets were seeking access to the warm waters in the Persian Gulf and that the Pakistani army needed to be modernized by the United States in order to stop them. In fact, Ayub was seeking arms for the army to stand up to India. Dennis Kux, *The United States and Pakistan, 1947–2000: Disenchanted Allies,* Washington, D.C.: Woodrow Wilson Press, 2001.

25. BBC World Service, interview with Zia ul-Haq, April 15, 1978. Quoted in Omar Noman, *The Political Economy of Pakistan, 1947–85,* London: Kegal Paul International, 1988.

26. Zia maintained that "we have no intention of leaving power till the accomplishment of our objectives of Islamization of the national polity . . . until then neither I will step down nor will let any one rise." Hasan-Askari Rizvi, "Military, State and Society in Pakistan," press conference by Zia ul-Haq, Islamabad, March 22, 1982.

27. I have outlined in much greater detail in my earlier book on the Taliban the ISI's ability to enrich itself. Ahmed Rashid, *Taliban: Islam, Oil and Fundamentalism in Central Asia,* London: I. B. Tauris, 2000. Published in the United States by Yale University Press.

28. Ibid. See chapter 10 for a detailed description of this process.

29. President George W. Bush was to do exactly the same in 2003, when he accepted without question the military's pardon of nuclear scientist Dr. A. Q. Khan, who had sold nuclear technology to several countries.

30. For a more detailed description of Zia's aims and desire for strategic depth see my book *Taliban.* Also Diego Cordovez, and Selig Harrison, *Out of Afghanistan: The Inside Story of the Soviet Withdrawal,* New York: Oxford University Press, 1995.

31. See Rizvi, "Military, State, and Society." In a case that went to the Supreme Court in 1997, it was charged that the ISI chief Lt.-Gen. Assad Durrani obtained 145 million rupees ($6.5 million) from a banker to fund IDA candidates, some journalists, and other IDA activities. The case is still undecided.

32. The PPP won 93 seats, compared to the IDA's 43 seats, out of a total of 207 elected seats in the National Assembly.

33. Benazir Bhutto's first term of government was from December 1988 to August 1990. Her second term was from October 1993 to November 1996. Nawaz Sharif's first term

was from December 1990 to May 1993, when he was dismissed as prime minister but reinstated by the Supreme Court (May 1993–July 1993), only to be dismissed again. His second term was from February 1997 to October 1999.

34. Sharif's Muslim League won 134 out of the 204 seats contested for the National Assembly, giving him a two-thirds majority, sufficient to amend the constitution at will. Since 1970, when voter turnout was 60 percent, it has steadily fallen. In the 1988 elections there was a 43 percent turnout; in 1990, 45 percent; in 1993, only 40 percent; and 1997, 32 percent.

35. Several former army chiefs told me that they had always rejected an incursion into Kargil in the past because they knew full well that crossing the LOC would invite swift Indian reaction and an international outcry. "In the ten of years of insurgency we never allowed our troops to operate with the militants but now that taboo has been broken," said one former army chief.

36. The generals who knew about the plan were the chief of general staff Lt.-Gen. Mohammed Aziz; the corps commander of Rawalpindi Lt.-Gen. Mahmood Ahmad; the force commander northern areas Maj.-Gen. Javed Hassan; and the director, general operations, Maj.-Gen. Tauqir Zia. The head of the ISI, Lt.-Gen. Ziuddin Ahmad, was not fully informed of the operation because he was considered too close to Sharif.

37. Alan Sipress and Thomas Ricks, "India, Pakistan Were Near Nuclear War in 1999," *The Washington Post,* May 15, 2002.

38. Ayaz Amir, "Core Issue," *Dawn,* July 28, 2000.

39. The commander of the Northern Light Infantry, Maj.-Gen. Javed Hasan, who had carried out the operation and considered himself a great intellectual, was promoted and appointed to head the National Defense College and later the Civil Service Staff College in Lahore. India set up a Kargil Review Committee, which issued a 2,200-page classified report to the government in February 2000. As a result, India ordered a complete review of its intelligence and security systems and admitted that Kargil had been a huge intelligence failure.

40. "Kargil was a military success . . . diplomatically it highlighted Kashmir. It's been in focus ever since. That was something the jihadis achieved," said Musharraf. Isabel Hilton, "The General in his Labyrinth," *The New Yorker,* August 12, 2002.

41. Council of Foreign Relations, "Engaging India," Speech by Strobe Talbott, New York, November 10, 2004.

42. Clinton had no doubt about the ISI's proximity to al Qaeda. "Pakistan supported the Taliban, and by extension, al Qaeda. The Pakistani intelligence service used some of the same camps that bin Laden and al Qaeda did to train the Taliban and insurgents who fought in Kashmir," said Clinton. Bill Clinton, *My Life,* New York: Alfred Knopf, 2004.

43. Ahmed Rashid, "Pakistan's Coup: Planting the Seeds of Democracy?" *Current History,* December 1999. Much of the following is based on my investigation of the Musharraf coup in 1999 for this article. An excellent blow-by-blow account of the coup is in Owen Bennett Jones's *Pakistan: Eye of the Storm,* New Haven, Conn.: Yale University Press, 2002.

44. Pervez Musharraf, speech to the nation, October 13, 1999.

Chapter Three. The Chief Executive's Schizophrenia:
Pakistan, the United Nations, and the United States Before 9/11

1. ABC television, Australia, documentary on Pakistan, interview by Mark Corcoran, February 2000.

2. Pervez Musharraf, *In the Line of Fire: A Memoir,* New York Simon & Schuster, 2006.

3. Ayeda Naqvi, "Hum dekhein gay," interview with Musharraf, *The Friday Times,* Lahore, Pakistan, December 12, 1999.

4. Ron Moreau and Zahid Hussain, "Pakistan's striving son," *Newsweek,* January 22, 2002.

5. My notes from Musharraf's first press conference, Islamabad, November 1, 1999.

6. George Polk, "Power Breakfast with Musharraf," *The Financial Times,* January 25, 2006.

7. After 9/11, I had the opportunity to meet many European prime ministers and foreign ministers, who all said they liked Musharraf at a personal level but had great qualms about his ability to deliver on policies and his inability to listen. "He should talk less and listen more," one foreign minister said.

8. Interview with Maulana Fazlur Rehman, Khushab, September 3, 2000.

9. Interview with Amir ul-Azim, Lahore, July 13, 2000.

10. Jeffrey Goldberg, "Inside Jihad," *The New York Times Magazine,* June 25, 2000.

11. Pervez Musharraf, speech to the nation, October 17, 1999. The aims and objectives of the military regime were to: (1) rebuild national confidence and morale; (2) strengthen the federation, remove interprovincial disharmony, and restore national cohesion; (3) revive the economy and restore investor confidence; (4) ensure law and order and dispense speedy justice; (5) carry out the depoliticization of state institutions; (6) devolve power to the grassroots level; (7) and ensure swift and across-the-board accountability of all corrupt people.

12. With a foreign debt of $32 billion, Pakistan was spending 90 percent of its revenue servicing interest repayments on its foreign debt and military expenditure. There was little left over for the social sector. Pakistan's traditional growth rate of 6.0 percent in earlier decades had come down to under 4.0 percent in the 1990s. With a population growth rate at 2.8 percent a year, real growth was just over 1.0 percent—barely sufficient to provide jobs for a population of 160 million people. One third of the country's industry was shut down and exports were collapsing.

13. I attended several hearings of the case in Karachi. Sharif's statement, personal record, Karachi, March 12, 2000.

14. There was a constant reshuffling of judges hearing the case, and Sharif's lawyer Iqbal Raad was shot dead in Karachi in March 2002 by unidentified gunmen. Sharif's wife, Kulsoom, was charged with treason after making provocative speeches against the army. "His lawyer was assassinated, judges were changed, reports of witness tampering arose repeatedly, the bench complained about the indirect influence of intelligence agents who packed the courtroom, and basic rights protection were missing," said Paula Newberg, an American legal expert.

15. Ahmed Rashid, "Nearing High Noon," *Far Eastern Economic Review,* January 27, 2000.

16. Inderfurth said, "Pakistan's support to the Taliban, who harbor and protect Osama bin Laden, is of concern to us. We hope that Pakistan will take steps against such extremist groups, which carry out acts of violence inside Pakistan as well as in the region, including the Harkat ul-Ansar and Hizb ul-Mujahedin." Transcript of press conference by Inderfurth, U.S. embassy, Islamabad, January 21, 2000.

17. Interview with Ambassador William Milam, Washington, D.C., November 19, 2005.

18. Independent commission investigating the September 11 attacks, public hearings, testimony of National Security Advisor Samuel Berger, Washington, D.C., March 24, 2004.

19. Bill Clinton, speech issued by U.S. embassy, Islamabad, March 25, 2004.

20. Ahmed Rashid and Nayan Chanda, "Deadly Games in South Asia," *Far Eastern Economic Review,* April 6, 2000.

21. Voice of America transcript, www.fas.org/news/pakistan/2000/000502=pak1 .htm.

22. Quoted in Ahmed Rashid, "Pakistan's Pashtun Policy in Afghanistan," *The Nation,* July 13, 2000. Musharraf made the comment on May 25 in a press conference in Islamabad.

23. Interview with Maj.-Gen. Ghulam Ahmad, May 15, 2000.

24. On May 17, 2000, Musharraf went back on his promise to reform the blasphemy law, which allowed anyone to bring blasphemy charges against another person without proof. The law carried the death sentence. Musharraf's promised reform was relatively mild—merely a procedural change—but General Aziz advised Musharraf to back down because it would annoy the fundamentalists.

25. In April several leading clerics, including Maulana Fazlur Rehman, said that ministers such as Javed Jabbar were dangerous for Pakistan. Such comments were repeated by other clerics through the summer, and Musharraf failed to support his ministers. The governor of Sindh province, Azim Daudpota, resigned on May 24, citing differences with the corps commander of Karachi, Lt.-Gen. Muzaffar Usmani, whom he blamed for dominating decision making in the province. Mohammed Shafiq, the governor of the North-West Frontier Province, resigned on August 13. Derek Cyprian, the minister for minorities affairs, resigned on August 16. In October, Shafqat Jamote, the minister for food and agriculture, resigned, as did Shafqat Mehmood, a key minister in Punjab province.

26. Pakistan television, Musharraf's speech to the nation, December 20, 2000.

27. Ahmed Rashid, "The General's New Power Play," *Far Eastern Economic Review,* May 3, 2001.

28. Ahmed Rashid, "Musharraf Appoints Deputy," *The Daily Telegraph,* May 3, 2001. See also "Politicians Played Useless Innings: CE," *The News,* Lahore, Pakistan, April 30, 2001.

29. "CE Rules Out Army Role in Future Set Up," *The Nation,* May 17, 2001.

30. Musharraf said, "I personally think with all sincerity and honesty that I have a role to play in this nation. I have a job to do here and therefore I cannot and will not let the nation down." Ahmed Rashid, "Coup Chief Makes Himself President," *The Daily Telegraph,* June 21, 2001. Ihtashamul Haq, "Takeover in National Interest," *Dawn,* June 20, 2001.

31. Editorial, *Dawn,* June 21, 2001.

32. Shaheen was replaced by Lt.-Gen. Ehsan ul-Haq, the former head of military intelligence, who after 9/11 became head of the ISI and a key Musharraf adviser and ally.

33. Interview with Musharraf's adviser, who asked to remain unnamed, as he still holds a key post, Lahore, November 30, 2004.

34. On March 1, 2001, the British issued a list banning twenty-one terrorist groups, including al Qaeda and Pakistan's Lashkar-e-Tayyaba, Harkat ul-Mujahedin, and Jaish-e-Mohammed.

35. Private correspondence between Lakhdar Brahimi and the author, July 8, 1999.

36. William Maley, *Fundamentalism Reborn?: Afghanistan and the Taliban,* London: Hurst and Co., 1998.

37. Vendrell headed UNSMA, or the UN Special Mission to Afghanistan, while UNOCHA, or the UN Office for Coordination of Humanitarian Affairs, was the economic and aid arm of the UN and run separately.

38. In track two, each country was represented by three officials. Pakistan sent three retired generals, the United States three former State Department officials, including Karl Inderfurth, the former assistant secretary of state for South Asia. Russia sent Yuli Vo-

rontsov, the former ambassador to the UN who had played a key role negotiating the Geneva Accords in 1998; while Iran's team was headed by its former ambassador to the UN, Saeed Rajai Khorassani.

39. Interview with Francesc Vendrell, Islamabad, March 1, 2006.

40. Some of the points from the concept paper were: "Neither the Taliban nor the NA can bring peace and stability and are thus not the solution for Afghanistan. At the same time, neither can be wished away. At present, neither is in a position to achieve a military victory, nor would they be allowed to by others. The Taliban as currently constituted are highly unlikely to be capable of real reform." Concept paper, United Nations, 2001.

41. Barnett Rubin, Ahmed Rashid, William Maley, Olivier Roy, and Ashraf Ghani, "Afghanistan: Reconstruction and Peacemaking in a Regional Framework," paper originally prepared for the Swiss government but widely circulated among European governments, spring 2001.

42. "The Situation in Afghanistan," Report of the UN Secretary-General's Special Representative to Afghanistan to the UN Security Council, New York, August 17, 2001. "The Security Council might wish to consider adopting a comprehensive approach to the settlement of Afghanistan, in its political, military, humanitarian, and human rights dimensions, setting forth the basic requirements for a settlement of the conflict and the principles on which it should be based, together with a coherent strategy to resolve the conflict . . . no military solution to the Afghan conflict is possible, desirable or indeed acceptable, that the pursuance of the conflict is futile since territorial gains achieved on the battlefield do not constitute the basis for the legitimization of power and that a piecemeal, as distinct from a step-by-step approach is unlikely to succeed."

43. Bill Clinton, *My Life,* New York: Knopf, 2004. The others were the Middle East, North Korea, and Iraq.

44. Scott Shane, "2001 Memo to Rice Warned of al Qaeda and Offered Plan," *The New York Times,* February 11, 2005. In 1998, Richard Clarke was elevated to become the national coordinator for counterterrorism with cabinet rank and a seat on the Principals Committee—an unusual position for a bureaucrat.

45. George Tenet, *At the Center of the Storm: My Years at the CIA,* London: HarperPress, 2007.

46. Rocca had last dealt with Afghanistan in the early 1990s, when she had helped run a covert $70 million program to buy back Stinger missiles from the former Afghan Mujahedin.

47. Bush went on to say, "The continued presence of Osama bin Laden and his al Qaeda organization is a direct threat to the United States and its interests that must be addressed. I believe al Qaeda also threatens Pakistan's long-term interests." Independent commission investigating the September 11 attacks, public hearings, testimony of Secretary of State Colin Powell, Washington, D.C., March 23, 2004.

48. Interview with Abdul Sattar, Islamabad, September 20, 2004.

49. Independent commission investigating the September 11 attacks, public hearings, testimony of National Security Advisor Condoleezza Rice, Washington, D.C., April 8, 2004.

50. "Interview with Richard Armitage," *The Nation,* June 18, 2001. The interview, which was lifted from an unnamed Indian newspaper, was conducted by Indian journalist Malini Parthasarathy.

51. "Pakistan Not Sponsoring Terrorism Says US," *Dawn,* August 18, 2001.

52. Independent commission investigating the September 11 attacks, public hearings,

testimony of National Security Advisor Condoleezza Rice, Washington, D.C., April 8, 2004.

53. Steve Coll, *Ghost Wars: The Secret History of the CIA, Afghanistan, and bin Laden, from the Soviet Invasion to September 10, 2001,* New York: Penguin Press, 2004.

54. *The 9/11 Commission Report: Final Report of the National Commission on Terrorist Attacks upon the United States,* New York: W. W. Norton, 2004.

55. Coll, *Ghost Wars.*

56. The deputies developed formal policy papers, which they discussed in three subsequent meetings in June and July. Independent commission investigating the September 11 attacks, staff text of events, Washington, D.C., March 2004.

57. I talked to several State Department and National Security Council officials about the April 30 meeting when I visited Washington, D.C., in July 2001. I met with Zalmay Khalilzad, the National Security Council director for Afghanistan and South Asia, on July 5, 2001.

58. Interview with Khalilzad, July 5, 2001.

59. "Musharraf Condemns UN Sanctions," *Dawn,* August 20, 2001, report from Moscow on Musharraf's interview to Russian newspaper *Kommersant.*

60. *The 9/11 Commission Report.* See also Bob Woodward, *Bush at War,* New York: Simon & Schuster, 2002.

Chapter Four. Attack! Retaliation and Invasion

1. Gen. Tommy Franks, with Malcolm McConnell, *American Soldier,* New York: Regan Books, 2004.

2. See Ron Suskind, *The One Percent Doctrine: Deep Inside America's Pursuit of Its Enemies Since 9/11,* New York: Simon & Schuster, 2006.

3. George Tenet, *At the Center of the Storm: My Years at the CIA,* London: HarperPress, 2007.

4. Bob Woodward, *Bush at War,* New York: Simon & Schuster, 2002.

5. One e-mail read, "US citizenship required for SECRET level security clearances, positions are also available for non-US citizens. . . . Positions available for language instructors, interpreters, translators, analysts, human intelligence, area experts, liaison elements, transcription technicians and interceptors. Current or previous security clearance highly desirable."

6. Gary Schroen, *First In: An Insider's Account of How the CIA Spearheaded the War on Terror in Afghanistan,* New York: Ballantine Books, 2005. Abdul Rasul Sayyaf, a former lecturer at Kabul University, was jailed after the communist coup in 1978, then released. He fled to Saudi Arabia. When he returned to Peshawar he set up the Ittehad-e-Islami party with Saudi funding. He set up a jihad university and hospital in Peshawar and was a close friend of Osama bin Laden. Sayyaf was the leading Wahhabi warlord in Afghanistan but rejected the Taliban and joined with the NA. After the defeat of the Taliban he remained at his base in Paghman, outside Kabul, from where he terrorized the local population. He was cultivated and funded by the CIA.

7. Franks, *American Soldier.*

8. Julian Borger, "Blogger Bares Rumsfeld's Post 9/11 Orders," *The Guardian,* February 24, 2006.

9. Richard A. Clarke, *Against All Enemies: Inside America's War on Terror,* New York: Free Press, 2004.

10. Wolfowitz raised the idea of attacking Iraq at the first full cabinet meeting after

9/11, at Camp David. See Woodward, *Bush at War.* Also Daniel Benjamin and Steven Simon, *The Next Attack: The Failure of the War on Terror and a Strategy for Getting It Right,* New York: Times Books, 2005.

11. Woodward, *Bush at War.*

12. Quoted in Franks, *American Soldier.*

13. George Packer, *The Assassins' Gate: America in Iraq,* New York: Farrar, Straus & Giroux, 2005.

14. John Kampfner, *Blair's Wars,* London: The Free Press, 2003.

15. The United States continued to play a little-noticed role in monitoring the huge Soviet-era nuclear industry in Central Asia, which included active research reactors, uranium mines, and nuclear waste dumps. Kazakhstan and Uzbekistan also hosted major chemical and biological warfare facilities.

16. Ahmed Rashid, *Jihad: The Rise of Militant Islam in Central Asia,* New Haven, Conn.: Yale University Press, 2002.

17. Ahmed Rashid, "US Builds Alliances in Central Asia," *Far Eastern Economic Review,* May 1, 2000.

18. Agence France-Presse, "Uzbekistan Not to Allow Use of Land Bases," Tashkent, October 5, 2001.

19. Agence France-Presse, "US, Uzbekistan Reach Agreement on Bases," Washington, D.C., October 12, 2001.

20. The figures come from Alexander Cooley, "Base Politics," *Foreign Affairs,* Winter 2005. See also Robert Rand, *Tamerlane's Children: Dispatches from Contemporary Uzbekistan,* Oxford: Oneworld, 2006.

21. In his more lucid moments, Zahir Shah would regale visiting American diplomats with stories of the last U.S. presidential visit to Kabul, on December 9, 1959, when Dwight Eisenhower arrived in Kabul on a daylong visit. The king's memory was perfect about the past, but details related to recent events were not so forthcoming.

22. In the weeks before the war started, deliberate ISI leaks encouraged the U.S. media to write about Taliban foreign minister Wakil Ahmed Muttawakil as being a leader of the moderates one day, while the next day it would be Jalaluddin Haqqani, one of bin Laden's closest associates, who had been on the ISI payroll since the early 1980s.

23. Agence France-Presse, "Who Are Moderate Taliban," *The Nation,* October 19, 2001.

24. Reuters, "Musharraf Keen to End Campaign Soon," *The Nation,* October 30, 2001.

25. See Franks, *American Soldier.* Phase one: Set conditions and build forces to provide the National Command Authority with credible military options. This involved laying the groundwork for the operation and arranging basing rights. Phase two: Conduct initial combat operations and continue to set conditions for follow-on operations. This involved the bombing campaign and infiltrating in Special Forces units. Phase three: Conduct decisive combat operations in Afghanistan, continue to build coalition and conduct operations across the area of operations. This involved defeating the enemy and bringing in American troops to eliminate pockets of resistance. Phase four: Establish capability of coalition partners to prevent the reemergence of terrorism and provide support for humanitarian assistance projects. This would stretch for a three- to five-year period and would involve limited reconstruction.

26. Ahmed Rashid, "A Path Paved with Pitfalls," *Far Eastern Economic Review,* October 4, 2001.

27. Ahmed Rashid, "The War Starts Here," *Far Eastern Economic Review,* September 27, 2001.

28. James Traub, *The Best Intentions: Kofi Annan and the UN in the Era of American World Power,* New York: Farrar, Straus & Giroux, 2006.

29. Agence France-Presse, "Powell Weighs Afghan Peacekeeping Option," Washington, D.C., October 22, 2001.

30. Interview with Lakhdar Brahimi, Paris, April 26, 2006. A year later Powell apologized and said he had been wrong, telling Brahimi that now he had another message for him: "Well done, well done, well done."

31. Gary Berntsen, *Jawbreaker: The Attack on Bin Laden and al Qaeda,* New York: Crown, 2005.

32. Ahmed Rashid, "Intelligence Team Defied Musharraf to Help Taliban," *The Daily Telegraph,* October 10, 2001.

33. Indian intelligence had leaked information that Omar Sheik, a Pakistani extremist who was later found guilty of murdering Daniel Pearl, had wired one hundred thousand dollars to Mohammed Atta, the ringleader of the nineteen 9/11 hijackers, at the instigation of General Ahmad. This so-called larger conspiracy was never investigated by the 9/11 Commission, indicating that it was nothing more than an Indian petard. The story first appeared in *The Times* of India in an article by Manok Joshi, "Shocking ISI leak," October 10, 2001. It was then picked up by the rest of the Indian press.

34. Ashraf Ghani, "The Folly of Quick Action in Afghanistan," *The Financial Times,* September 27, 2001.

35. Lt.-General Aziz became chairman of the Joint Chiefs of Staff Committee, with the rank of full general. Although his new job was largely ceremonial, as he had no troops to command, he had the job of helping the Americans set up their bases in Pakistan.

36. Ahmed Rashid, "Easy to Start, Hard to Finish," *Far Eastern Economic Review,* October 18, 2001.

37. The Taliban and al Qaeda had used Chechen heroin smuggling networks, which extended to Russia and Eastern Europe, to expand their control of the drug trade. High-ranking Chechen rebel leaders had sent their families to Afghanistan to escape the Russian crackdown in their homeland. In 2000, as the Taliban attempted to improve relations with China through the intercession of Pakistan, the Taliban moved the Uighur fighters from front lines outside Kabul to the north, to join up with the IMU. The Taliban then denied to the Chinese that they were enlisting Uighur militants.

Chapter Five. The Search for a Settlement:
Afghanistan and Pakistan at Odds

1. Interview with Hamid Karzai over satellite telephone, November 11, 2001. See Ahmed Rashid, "Hamid Karzai Escapes Taliban Encirclement," *The Daily Telegraph,* November 12, 2001. I spoke to him several times in the weeks ahead.

2. Interview with senior U.S. intelligence official, Washington, D.C., February 2005.

3. Interviews with senior aides to Musharraf and Pakistani diplomats present at the meeting, January 2002. See also James Carney, "Inside the War Room," *Time,* January 7, 2002.

4. Kamran Khan, "Kabul Fall Is Pak's Strategic Debacle," *The News,* January 14, 2001.

5. These militias belonged to Maulvi Younis Khalis, a former Mujahedin commander from the Soviet war era, Hazrat Ali, an NA commander, and Commander Mohammed Zaman, who had arrived from Peshawar.

6. His relatives included Hedayat Amin Arsala, who was in the king's camp while his elder brother Haji Abdul Qadir was one of the few Pashtun leaders in the Northern Alliance. Arsala would become vice president, and Qadir the governor of Nangarhar province before he was assassinated in 2003.

7. Rumsfeld had told NBC television on September 30 that "there is no question but that there are any number of people in Afghanistan, tribes in the south, the Northern Alliance in the north, that oppose the Taliban. We need to recognize the value they bring to this anti-terrorist, anti-Taliban effort and, where appropriate, find ways to assist them."

8. Gary Schroen, the CIA agent who led the CIA team into the Panjsher Valley, says that he was constantly resisting the complacent attitude of the CIA office in Islamabad. Gary Schroen, *First In: An Insider's Account of How the CIA Spearheaded the War on Terror in Afghanistan,* New York: Ballantine Books, 2005. The CIA station chief in Islamabad was Robert Grenier, the man who went to Quetta to meet with Mullah Usmani. He had remained undercover most of his life, until his cover was blown in February 2006, when it was reported that Grenier was removed as head of the Counterterrorism Center at the CIA. Greg Miller, "Top CIA Spy Removed," *Los Angeles Times,* February 7, 2006.

9. The Ritchie brothers were motivated by their love for Afghanistan, where they grew up and where their father had taught civil engineering before he died in a car crash in 1978. Their mother continued to work for Afghan charities. The Ritchies were joined by former national security advisor Robert C. McFarlane, a key figure in the Iran-Contra scandal and now an energy consultant. The Ritchie brothers lobbied hard to provide Haq with U.S. funds and support. They had personally donated funds to the office of Zahir Shah in Rome. The Ritchies' presence in Peshawar made the ISI even more suspicious of Haq's agenda.

10. Ahmed Rashid, "Abdul Haq Buried," *The Daily Telegraph,* October 29, 2001. See also Ahmed Rashid, "A Difficult War," *Far Eastern Economic Review,* November 8, 2001.

11. Franks, *American Soldier.*

12. The extent of Pakistan's support to Operation Enduring Freedom was inadvertently advertised by the CENTCOM Web site in May 2003, information that was swiftly taken down when the Pakistan government protested at the revelation of what were secret agreements with the United States. Some 330 vehicles, 1,350 tons of equipment, and 8,000 marines were off-loaded by the Americans on Pasni beach and flown directly to Kandahar in November.

13. TNSM was founded in 1989 to introduce Sharia law in Pakistan's far northwest corner. The TNSM had led protests in 1990 and had provided manpower to the Taliban since 1994. In Dir, Swat, and Chitral the mullahs were supported by the timber- and car-smuggling mafia, which had profited hugely from the lack of government controls. There were protests against and shootouts with the army in 1994, and again in April 2001. I am grateful to Khalid Ahmad for his articles in *The Friday Times* on the origins of the TNSM. For a brief history of the movement, see Muhammad Amir Rana, *A to Z of Jihadi Organizations in Pakistan,* Lahore: Mashal Books, 2004.

14. The ICRC sent démarches to the United States and its Coalition partners demanding that humanitarian principles be observed for prisoners who surrendered at Kunduz. A public ICRC statement on November 23, 2001, expressed concern about the rights of captured foreign fighters because of reports "in some parts of the country that no prisoners would be taken." The ICRC urges that "a fighter who clearly indicates his intention to surrender to an enemy is no longer a legitimate target according to rules of war."

15. "We are not interested in having a large, long-term presence of any kind or managing POWs, but clearly we would be interested in interrogating the prisoners," said an

American official. "We are looking for as limited a role as possible, with as much access to the prisoners as we can," he added. Dexter Filkins and Carlotta Gall, "Pakistanis Again Said to Evacuate Allies of Taliban," *The New York Times,* November 23, 2001.

16. Ibid.

17. "Efforts on for Pak Evacuation from Kunduz," *The News,* November 24, 2001.

18. Ibid.

19. Masood Haider, "No Pakistani Jets Flew into Afghanistan Says US," *Dawn,* December 2, 2001.

20. Seymour Hersh, "The Getaway," *The New Yorker,* January 28, 2002.

21. My conversation with the first U.S. official took place in February 2005 in Washington; I spoke with the other through e-mails, in 2006.

22. "U.S. forces were in the area at the time. What did the U.S. know, and when and where and what did they do about it?" asked Jennifer Leaning, from Physicians for Human Rights. John Barry, Ron Gutman, and Babak Dehghanipisheh, "The Death of a Convoy," *Newsweek,* August 26, 2002.

23. For the *Newsweek* cover story, see ibid. I am extremely grateful to John Heffernan, who investigated the grave sites, for his help on this issue.

24. Press conference by Lakhdar Brahimi, Kabul, August 27, 2002.

25. Interview with Lakhdar Brahimi, Paris, April 26, 2006.

26. Karl Vick, "Rout Near a Desert Stronghold Took the Heart out of the Taliban," *The New York Times,* January 2, 2002.

27. Mullah Naqibulla had first resisted the Soviets in the 1980s, then threw in his lot with the government of President Rabbani after 1992 and finally helped the Taliban come to power in 1994. He was considered the grand old man of Kandahar.

28. The breakdown was $1.9 billion for the deployment of sixty thousand troops, $400 million for munitions, $500 million for the replacement of damaged equipment, and $1 billion for fuel and operating costs.

29. Interview with Ryan Crocker, Islamabad, February 7, 2006.

30. Richard Clarke, *Against All Enemies: Inside America's War on Terror,* New York: Free Press, 2004.

31. Jonathan Steele, "Forgotten Victims," *The Guardian,* May 20, 2002. Statement by Human Rights Watch, "The Use of Cluster bombs," December 18, 2001.

32. Steele, "Forgotten Victims."

33. Mary Anne Weaver, "Lost at Tora Bora," *The New Yorker,* September 11, 2005. This is one of the best accounts of the battle.

34. Gary Berntsen and Ralph Pezzullo, *Jawbreaker: The Attack on bin Laden and al Qaeda—A Personal Account by the CIA's Key Field Commander,* New York: Crown, 2005.

35. "Osama Resurfaces on TV Screens," *Dawn,* quoting Agence France-Presse, Doha, December 27, 2001.

36. Peter Spiegel, "Ex-CIA Agent Says US Missed bin Laden in Afghanistan," *The Financial Times,* January 3, 2006. Franks wrote the *New York Times* piece on October 19, 2004.

37. Abdallah Tabarak, a Moroccan bodyguard of bin Laden's who spent twenty days guarding him in Tora Bora and was later captured in Pakistan and shifted to Guantánamo, provided details of bin Laden's presence. See Craig Whitlock, "Al Qaeda Detainee's Mysterious Release," *The Washington Post,* January 30, 2006. So did Ayman Saeed Abdullah Batarfi, a doctor from Yemen who was carrying out amputations on al Qaeda fighters in Tora Bora with a knife and scissors and who met with bin Laden. Associated Press, "Doctor Says bin Laden was at Tora Bora," September 7, 2007.

38. Associated Press, "US to Hunt AQ Fighters in Pakistan—General Franks," January 7, 2002.

39. Sean Naylor, *Not a Good Day to Die: The Untold Story of Operation Anaconda,* New York: Berkley, 2005. Shahi Kot is twenty-five kilometers south of Gardez. The valley is in the Sulaiman mountain range that forms the southern end of the Hindu Kush mountain system in Afghanistan. The Sulaiman range is also an extension of the Spin Ghar range, in southeastern Afghanistan.

40. Interview with Abdullah Abdullah, Kabul, November 23, 2001.

41. Ahmed Rashid, "I Would Step Down to Help My Country," *The Daily Telegraph,* November 24, 2001. Interviews with Vendrell in Kabul, November 22 and 24, 2001.

42. Rashid, "I Would Step Down."

43. The Northern Alliance had eleven delegates plus seven alternatives and two women. The Rome group had eight members plus three alternatives, seven advisers, and two women. The Peshawar and the Cyprus groups had three delegates each, two alternates each, and one woman each. Three women attended as full members of the conference, Amina Afzali and Siddique Balkhi from the Northern Alliance, and Sima Wali from the Rome delegation.

44. Reuters, "Bonn Conference opens," Bonn, November 27, 2001.

45. Communication with Fatemeh Zia, August 10, 2007.

46. James Dobbins, "How to Talk to Iran," *The Washington Post,* July 22, 2007.

47. Interview with Lakhdar Brahimi, Paris, April 26, 2006.

48. Interview with Kofi Annan, former secretary-general of the UN, Oslo, June 27, 2007.

49. Eighteen members of the Special Independent Commission for the Convening of the Loya Jirga would be appointed by Karzai and the UN. The chairman was Ismael Qasimyar, a lawyer and expert in constitutional law from the Qizalbash community in Herat who had lived in exile in Iran. The vice chairperson was Mahbooba Hoquqmal, a Tajik and a professor of law at Kabul University who had taught in exile at the Afghan University in Peshawar. Another vice chairperson was Abdul Aziz, a Pashtun and the dean of the Sharia faculty of Kabul University.

Chapter Six. A Nuclear State of Mind: India, Pakistan, and the War of Permanent Instability

1. Shirin Tahir-Kheli, *India, Pakistan and the United States: Breaking with the Past,* Lahore: Vanguard Books, 1998.

2. Jammu is predominantly Hindu, but one third are Muslims. Ladakh is dominated by Buddhists, but its Kargil region has a large number of Shia Muslims. The most popular Kashmiri Muslim leader, Sheikh Mohammed Abdullah, the head of the All Jammu and Kashmir National Conference, was closer to India than to Pakistan and favored independence. See Sumit Ganguly, *Conflict Unending: India-Pakistan Tensions Since 1947,* New York: Columbia University Press, 2001.

3. The three UN resolutions were passed on January 20, 1948; April 21, 1948; and August 13, 1948.

4. The APHC emphasized the nationalist ideology of Kashmiriyat, or Kashmiri identity, which was an amalgam of Muslim, Hindu, and Buddhist cultures. Its Islamic component included Sufism, which had a mass following in Kashmir and Shia Islam, as many Kashmiris were Shias. Kashmiris believed in a tolerant view of Islam, and over time resentment against the outsider jihadis increased.

5. Even though the State Department documented these abuses, it put little pressure on India to rectify them. Harsher documentation of these abuses came from Amnesty International and Human Rights Watch—even though they and the International

Committee of the Red Cross were all barred from visiting Kashmir for more than a decade.

6. On December 5 Jordan had arrested thirteen Arab extremists suspected of trying to organize a terrorist bombing campaign of Jewish and Christian holy sites. The terrorists had received training in Afghanistan and had arrived in Jordan from Pakistan.

7. Ahmed Rashid and Sadanand Dhume, "Price of Surrender," *Far Eastern Economic Review,* January 13, 2000.

8. Pakistani journalists who visited the destroyed camps after the missile attacks said that between five and ten ISI officers were killed in the raid. Later U.S. diplomats confirmed this to me. See Richard Clarke, *Against All Enemies: Inside America's War on Terror,* New York: Free Press, 2004. See also Strobe Talbott, *Engaging India: Diplomacy, Democracy and the Bomb—A Memoir,* Washington, D.C.: Brookings Institution Press, 2004. Both books make the same claim.

9. Azhar's diary, written in prison in India, described his experiences in Somalia in 1993 and the deaths of American soldiers. The sixteen-hour battle in Mogadishu on September 25, 1993, resulted in the deaths of eighteen Americans and some five hundred Somalis. Three Black Hawk helicopters were shot down. The FBI interviewed Azhar in his Indian jail in 1995, 1996, and again in 1998. Paul Watson, "Somalian Link Seen to al Qaeda," *Los Angeles Times,* February 25, 2000.

10. Bin Laden's bodyguard Abu Jandal later admitted that al Qaeda had carried out the hijacking because bin Laden admired Azhar and needed his help. Bin Laden threw a lavish party for Azhar when he was freed in Kandahar. Agence France-Presse, "Osama Guard Says Indian Plane Hijacked for Azhar's Release," Islamabad, September 17, 2006. Abu Jandal had given an interview to Al Jazeera TV.

11. On January 7, India issued a list of the five hijackers, naming them as Ibrahim Azhar (from Bahawalpur), Shahid Akthar Sayed (Karachi), Sunni Ahmed Qazi (Karachi), Mistri Zahoor Ibrahim (Karachi), and Shaqir (Sukkur). "India Names Hijackers," *Dawn,* January, 7, 2000.

12. Reuters, "US Issues Stern Warning to Pakistan," *The Nation,* January 6, 2000.

13. Tahir Mirza, "Kashmir May Provoke War," *Dawn,* February 8, 2001.

14. "Pakistan Does Not Want War," *The News,* December 30, 2002.

15. Associated Press, "President Asks Blair for Help in Defusing Crisis," Washington, D.C., December 30, 2001. White House spokesman Scott McClellan gave an account of Bush's conversation with Musharraf.

16. "Terrorism has always been Pakistan's state policy. The face of Afghanistan has been changed and that of Pakistan will change too," Vajpayee told reporters in Lucknow. Agence France-Presse, "Vajpayee Accuses Pakistan," *Dawn,* January 3, 2002.

17. Ahmed Rashid, "Give Peace a Chance," *Far Eastern Economic Review,* January 17, 2002. I carried out several interviews with U.S. diplomats and Pakistani generals.

18. Agence France-Presse, "Situation not defused says Bush," *The News,* January 6, 2002.

19. Ayaz Amir, "Excelling at the Aim of the Strategic U Turn," *Dawn,* January 17, 2002. The quote from Musharraf's speech comes from the text published in all the newspapers, January 12, 2002.

20. The ruling BJP was routed in four state elections in late February, demonstrating that the talk of war had also not gone down well with the Indian public. Hundreds of Muslims were slaughtered by Hindu right-wing extremists in Gujarat state. The massacres were to turn Muslims decisively against the BJP at the next general election.

21. Gen. Tommy Franks, with Malcolm McConnell, *American Soldier,* New York: Regan Books, 2004.

22. Reuters, "US Urges Restraint on Pakistan," St. Petersburg, Russia, May 25, 2002.

23. Interview with senior U.S. diplomat in Islamabad visiting from Washington, June 2001.

24. "President Musharraf wants to do this keeping intact the honor and dignity of the nation and the armed forces, I think we got a very good basis on which we can proceed," Armitage said in Islamabad. Agence France-Presse, "Armitage Satisfied with Pakistan Assurances," *The Nation,* June 7, 2002.

25. Agence France-Presse, "Powell for all Parties' Participation in Elections," *The Nation,* July 29, 2002.

26. In answer to Musharraf's charge that the elections had been rigged, Vajpayee replied, "If the elections are a mere fraud, why are terrorists being trained and infiltrated into India under the command of the ISI to kill election candidates and to intimidate voters. How can it [Pakistan] continue to use terrorism as an instrument of state policy against India." See Afzal Khan, "Vajpayee Says India Will Use All Means to End Terrorism," *Dawn,* September 13, 2002.

27. I am grateful to Graham Allison's excellent summary of bin Laden's intentions in her article "The Ongoing Failure of Imagination," *Bulletin of Atomic Scientists,* October 2006.

28. Interviews with senior U.S. officials, Washington, D.C., January 2006.

29. Ibid.

30. Amjad Siddiq, "Pak Scientist Regrets Meeting Osama, Omar," *The News,* March 19, 2002.

31. Douglas Frantz, "CIA Chief Urges Pakistan to Take Harder Line on Muslim Militants," *The New York Times,* December 3, 2001.

32. The best study of what happened after 9/11 is Gordon Corera, *Shopping for Bombs: Nuclear Proliferation, Global Insecurity and the Rise and Fall of the AQ Khan Network,* Oxford: Oxford University Press, 2006.

33. Jawed Naqvi, "India Must Hold Talks with Pakistan," *Dawn,* January 7, 2003.

34. Ahmed Rashid and Rahul Bedi, "Peace Hopes Rise as India Joins Pakistan Summit," *The Daily Telegraph,* January 3, 2004.

35. To Pakistan's satisfaction, the statement also read, "The two leaders are confident that the resumption of the composite dialogue will lead to a peaceful settlement of all bilateral issues, including Jammu and Kashmir, to the satisfaction of both sides." Ahmed Rashid, "Planned Kashmir Talks as 'Big Leap Forward,' " *The Daily Telegraph,* January 7, 2004.

36. "Let's agree to greater autonomy to both sides of Kashmir so the Kashmiris can better manage their affairs, but let's avoid formal agreements which involve new political arrangements," a senior Indian official told me in New Delhi. Interviews in New Delhi with J. N. Dixit, national security adviser to the prime minister; Shyam Saran, foreign secretary; and Salman Khorsheed, general secretary of the Congress Party, October 31 and November 1, 2004.

37. Shirin Tahir-Kheli, India, *Pakistan and the United States: Breaking with the Past,* Lahore: Vanguard Books, 1998.

Chapter Seven. The One-Billion-Dollar Warlords:
The War Within Afghanistan

1. See my articles: "Iran and US Vie for Influence on the Front Line," *The Daily Telegraph,* May 2, 2002, and "Warlord, Profiteer, Ideologue, Chief," *Far Eastern Economic Review,* May 23, 2002. In May 2002, I was told by several Afghan officials in Ghaurian, on

the Iranian border, that Arabs, Pakistanis, and Central Asians would come through Ghaurian at night, heading for the Iranian border. Two Iranian intelligence generals met with Khan regularly in Herat. He had now become a jihadi. "More urgently than reconstruction we need the spirit of jihad. *Jihad* is just one word to describe freedom; it's a holy word meaning independence, and we must keep the memory of the war against the Soviets and Taliban alive," he said.

2. Donald Rumsfeld visited Herat on April 29, 2002.

3. The Shura had ten separate associations under its umbrella, including those for lawyers, economists, teachers, engineers, painters, calligraphers, poets, sportsmen, and even a group that promoted "Agriculture, Livestock and Veterinary Medicine." Its charter said that "the Shura provides authorities and international aid agencies with professional consultations through its associations."

4. Ahmed Rashid, "Setback as Warlords Return to Old Ways," *The Daily Telegraph,* January 12, 2002.

5. Gary Berntsen, *Jawbreaker: The Attack on bin Laden and al Qaeda,* New York: Crown, 2005. He describes how he hired a Pashai commander from eastern Afghanistan, codenamed Barkat, to track down bin Laden without even meeting him. It is clear that Barkat is Hazarat Ali.

6. Sarah Chayes explains the situation in the south in great detail in Sarah Chayes, *The Punishment of Virtue: Inside Afghanistan After the Taliban,* New York: Penguin Books, 2006.

7. Afghanistan National Human Development Report, Kabul, 2004.

8. Interview with Ryan Crocker, Islamabad, February 7, 2006.

9. This term was popularized by Human Rights Watch. See their "Afghanistan's Bonn Agreement, One Year Later, a Catalog of Missed Opportunities," December 1, 2002.

10. Barton Gellman and Dafna Linzer, "Afghanistan, Iraq: Two Wars Collide," *The Washington Post,* October 22, 2004.

11. The war cost $17 billion between October 7, 2001, and May 1, 2002, according to congressional documents; $1.37 billion was spent on classified surveillance and intelligence, $1.76 billion for munitions, and $4.7 billion for deploying troops that were never used.

12. Interview with Ryan Crocker, Islamabad, February 7, 2006.

13. The full text of Joseph Biden's speech reported in "Biden Promises $130 Million for Security in Afghanistan," *Los Angeles Times,* May 17, 2002.

14. Ibid.

15. Jan Goodwin, "An Uneasy Peace," *The Nation,* April 29, 2002.

16. Editorial, "Warlords and Allies," *The Washington Post,* February 25, 2002.

17. *The New York Times* said in its editorial on March 27, 2002, "Rescuing Afghanistan will take more than defeating Taliban holdouts. . . . It will also require establishing the authority of the central government and the rule of law throughout the country. That can only be done with expanded international help and more effective American leadership." Editorial, "Afghanistan at Risk," *The New York Times,* March 27, 2002. The International Crisis Group urged that the "the immediate priority in Afghanistan has to be an expanded ISAF from 4500 to 25,000 troops." ICG, "Securing Afghanistan," March 15, 2002.

18. Ahmed Rashid, "Keeping the Peace in Afghanistan," *The Wall Street Journal,* February 15, 2002.

19. William Durch, "A Realistic Plan to Save Afghanistan," *International Herald Tribune,* July 31, 2002. Durch was the director of peace operations at the Stimson Center.

20. John Kampfner, *Blair's Wars,* London: The Free Press, 2003.

21. Chayes, *The Punishment of Virtue.*

22. Interview with Paul Wolfowitz, deputy secretary of defense, Department of Defense, Washington, D.C., August 21, 2002.

23. The president's spokesman Ari Fleischer had repeated the mantra on February 25, saying that "the president continues to believe that the purpose of the U.S. military is to be used to fight and win wars, and not to engage in peacekeeping." International Crisis Group, "Securing Afghanistan."

24. James Dao, "Bush Sets Role for US in Afghan Rebuilding," *The New York Times,* April 18, 2002. The United States had spent a total of $13 billion, or $90 billion in today's money, on the Marshall Plan for Europe.

25. David Rohde and David Sanger, "How the Good War in Afghanistan Went Bad," *The New York Times,* August 12, 2007.

26. The Rumsfeld quote is from ibid. The Wolfowitz quote is from Fred Hiatt, "Underachieving Afghanistan," *The Washington Post,* May 20, 2002. "Just think of the history of the British in Afghanistan in the nineteenth century or even the Soviets in the last century. It is a place that is notoriously hostile to foreigners, notoriously difficult to govern. And it is huge," said Wolfowitz. Such an argument was never applied to Iraq.

27. See my articles "Iran and US Vie for Influence" and "Warlord, Profiteer, Ideologue, Chief."

28. In the first stage, towns and villages representing 380 districts in the country were to choose 16,000 delegates. In the second stage, these delegates would hold further elections, whittling down their number to 1,050 delegates representing the 32 provinces.

29. Wali Masud told me that "if there is any such move for the king to become president, we would counter it by putting up our own candidate for the president, and there could even be a walkout from the LJ." The NA leaders had conveyed this threat to Khalilzad and Brahimi.

30. I reported extensively on the Loya Jirga in Kabul for *The Wall Street Journal* and *The Daily Telegraph* in day-to-day articles from which these quotes have been taken.

31. Interview with a senior European diplomat at the Loya Jirga.

32. A Hazara, Simar Samar was the popular minister for women's affairs who had stood up for women's rights and was despised by the fundamentalist warlords. She was later removed from her post by Karzai.

33. Interview with Lakhdar Brahimi, Paris, April 26, 2007.

34. Dexter Filkins, "Flaws in US Air War Left Hundreds of Civilians Dead," *The New York Times,* July 21, 2002.

35. Interview with Robert Finn, Princeton University, Princeton, N.J., November 22, 2005.

36. Interview with Hamid Karzai, Kabul, December 23, 2002.

37. The conference in Cordoba was attended by major donor countries and held June 28–30, 2002. I attended the conference and came away with the distinct impression that there was growing frustration among the Europeans as to how the United States was handling Afghanistan.

Chapter Eight. Musharraf's Lost Moment: Political Expediency and Authoritarian Rule

1. Text of President Pervez Musharraf's speech, *The Nation,* January 13, 2002. Five extremist organizations were banned, including Lashkar-e-Tayyaba and Jaish-e-Mohammed—two of the largest groups fighting in Kashmir and closely linked to al

Qaeda. The Sunni group Sipah-e-Sehaba and the Shia party Tehreek-e-Jafria were also banned, as was the Tehreek-e-Nafaz-e-Shariat-e-Mohammadi, led by Maulana Sufi Mohammed. Another Sunni extremist group, Sunni Tehreek, was put on a watch list.

2. Powell said, "The US applauds the banning of Jaish-e-Mohammed and Lashkar-e-Tayyaba and welcomes President Musharraf's explicit statements against terrorism and particularly notes his pledge that Pakistan will not tolerate terrorism under any pretext, including Kashmir." Text of Powell's statement, *Dawn,* January 13, 2002.

3. Poll carried out by the Office of Research, U.S. State Department, February 19, 2002.

4. "Religious forces have always aligned themselves with the military's views with regard to the defense budget and the Kashmir and Afghan policies," boasted former ISI chief Gen. Hameed Gul. Interview with Gen. Hameed Gul, *Herald,* December 2001.

5. "Bush Promises to Facilitate Pakistan India Talks," *The Nation,* February 14, 2002.

6. Ahmed Rashid, "Musharraf Announces Referendum," *The Daily Telegraph,* April 6, 2002.

7. The European Union had signed the agreement with Pakistan in November 2001 to help Pakistani exports, but the agreement needed to be ratified by the European parliament. The referendum was "wholly inappropriate and in conflict with the Pakistan constitution," stated the EU parliament. "EU delays Cooperation with Pakistan," *Dawn,* April 26, 2002.

8. These comments were made to me after the referendum.

9. Musharraf's interview with the editors of *The Washington Post,* February 9, 2002. See also Mariane Pearl, with Sarah Crichton, *A Mighty Heart: The Brave Life and Death of My Husband, Danny Pearl,* London: Virago Press, 2003.

10. This accusation was made by several ministers and police officials, including Syed Kamal Shah, the inspector general of police in Sindh province. "Daniel Was Overintrusive, Says IG," *The Nation,* March 13, 2002.

11. *The New York Times* reported that an ISI officer, Brigadier Abdullah, the head of the Kashmir cell, who had helped create Jaish-e-Mohammed in 2000, had also helped Sheikh in his frequent travels between Pakistan and Afghanistan. Abdullah had been replaced in the shake-up of the ISI after the removal of Gen. Mehmood Ahmad. Douglas Jehl, "Death of Reporter Puts Focus on Pakistan's Intelligence Unit," *The New York Times,* February 25, 2002.

12. Pearl, *A Mighty Heart.*

13. Azim Mian, "No ISI Role in Pearl Case," *The News,* March 3, 2002.

14. Threats and arrests were used repeatedly by the ISI to keep journalists away from sensitive areas. In December 2003 two French journalists, Marc Epstein and Jean-Paul Guilloteau, working for *L'Express* magazine and investigating the Taliban's regrouping inside Pakistan, were arrested in Quetta and put on trial for visa violations. Their Pakistani fixer, Khawar Mehdi Rizvi, was held by the ISI (which never admitted to holding him) until January 26, when he was charged with sedition and conspiracy. The arrests were seen as a blunt warning to Western journalists to deter them from visiting Quetta, where Taliban leaders were living openly. In May 2004, Afghan journalist Sami Yousafzai, a stringer for *Newsweek,* was held for several weeks by the ISI in North Waziristan. American journalist Eliza Griswold of *The New Yorker,* whom Yousufzai was accompanying, was also arrested but was extradited to the United States.

15. "If I am extradited, America will return me in the same way as Indian authorities had returned me and America will suffer if I am killed in a fake encounter," Sheikh

told Sindh high court judge Shabir Ahmad during his trial. He was referring to his being freed from an Indian jail after the Kandahar hijacking and to the fact that Pakistani police were prone to killing terrorist suspects in faked encounters after they had been arrested. "Omar Threatens US of Dire Consequences If Extradited," *The Nation,* March 13, 2002.

16. Massoud Ansari, "Daniel Pearl Refused to Be Sedated Before His Throat Was Cut," *Sunday Telegraph,* May 8, 2004. Three suspects believed to be guards who had watched over Pearl were arrested in the spring of 2004, but charges were never brought against them.

17. Steve Levine, "US Believes bin Laden Aide Murdered Pearl," *The Wall Street Journal,* October 21, 2003. See also Khalid Sheikh Mohammed's time with CIA in Jane Mayer, "The Black Sites," *The New Yorker,* August 13, 2007.

18. "We purchased the vehicle a few days before the Musharraf rally in Karachi, and set up the remote-control system to the light switch of the vehicle to assassinate him en route from the Army House, but the remote control developed some fault," said Mohammed Imran, one of the perpetrators at a police-held press conference. "Lady Luck Foiled Plot to Assassinate Musharraf," *Daily Times,* July 8, 2002.

19. Zulfiqar Shah, *Sectarian Violence in Karachi (1994–2002): A Study,* Lahore: Human Rights Commission of Pakistan, 2004. The United States gave $73 million to revive the police services in 2002.

20. Ahmed Rashid, "Can Musharraf Survive?" *The Daily Telegraph,* June 14, 2002.

21. "Musharraf's Ambitions Eroding State's Writ," *Daily Times,* June 27, 2002.

22. Interview with Aitezaz Ahsan, Lahore, September 2002.

23. I read the private European Union report.

24. In July, visitors included Colin Powell, British foreign secretary Jack Straw, the French foreign minister Dominique de Villepin, and the European Union's foreign policy chief Javier Solana.

25. Rocca was addressing Congress's foreign policy subcommittee. Agence France-Presse, "Washington Nudges Musharraf on Polls," *The News,* July 18, 2002.

26. David Rohde, "Musharraf Redraws Constitution," *The New York Times,* August 21, 2002.

27. Reuters, "'US, Musharraf Still Tight,' Says Bush," Washington, D.C., August 22, 2002.

28. The MMA evolved from the Pakistan-Afghanistan Defense Committee established in October 2001 by twenty-six Islamic parties and extremist groups to support the Taliban after the U.S. attack on Afghanistan began. Comprising six Islamic parties, the MMA was formed in January 2002 with direct encouragement from the ISI to revive the Islamic parties after the Taliban's rout, according to Jamiat-e-Islami leaders. The MMA includes the Jamiat-e-Islami, the largest nationwide Islamic party; the Jamiat-e-Ulema, the largest Islamic party in Balochistan; and the NWFP, the pro-Wahhabi Jamiat Ahle Hadith; the Shia party Millat-e-Jafri; and Jamiat Ulema-e-Pakistan, headed by Shah Ahmad Noorani, who became head of the MMA.

29. Andrew Wilder, "Elections 2002: Legitimizing the Status Quo," in *Pakistan on the Brink: Politics, Economics and Society,* edited by Craig Baxter, Lanham, Md.: Lexington Books, 2004. Wilder, an expert on Pakistani elections and the author of several books, wrote the best essay on voting trends in the elections.

30. The MMA won 48 of the 99 seats in the NWFP provincial assembly. In the 1993 elections, the Islamic parties won only 9 of 217 seats to the National Assembly. In the 1997 elections they won only 2 seats.

31. Ahmed Rashid, "Polls and Promises, Pakistan Election," *Far Eastern Economic Review,* October 17, 2002. Other monitoring groups included the U.S.-based National Democratic Institute, the European Union, Human Rights Watch, and the Human Rights Commission of Pakistan. See also Ahmed Rashid, "Elections 'Rigged' in Pakistan by Military Regime," *The Daily Telegraph,* October 10, 2002.

32. Khalid Hassan, "US Should Help Pakistan Become a Modern Islamic State—Milam," *Daily Times,* December 11, 2003. Milam was addressing the Middle East Institute in Washington. Other comments were made to me by U.S. diplomats when they visited Pakistan after the elections.

33. Personal communication with Professor Vali Nasir, October 2003.

34. Illyas Khan, "What Is al Qaeda? Interview with Akram Durrani," *Herald,* February 2003.

35. Ahmed Rashid, "Americans Under Threat as Islamists Take Frontier," *The Daily Telegraph,* November 30, 2002.

36. Zamir Haider, "Opposition Accuses ISI of Manipulating Senate Polls," *Daily Times,* March 13, 2003.

37. Masood Haider, "US Offers US $3 Billion Aid Package," *Dawn,* June 24, 2003.

38. Bob Woodward, *State of Denial: Bush at War, Part III,* New York: Simon & Schuster, 2006.

39. Reuters, "Franks Says No Permanent US Military Bases in Central Asia," Tashkent, January 24, 2002.

40. The meeting took place at an Italian air base near Rome. The Rome Declaration of May 28, 2002, appeared to signal the end of the cold war as both presidents Bush and Putin were present, along with NATO secretary-general George Robertson. Reuters, "US Doubts Russia Will Be a Future Threat," Pratica di Mare, Italy, May 29, 2002.

41. Ibid.

42. Joshua Machleder, "Wolfenshohn Puts Faith in Uzbek Government," EurasiaNet .org, April 18, 2002.

43. President Karimov told the media in May and June 2002 that Namangani was alive. Newspapers in Moscow and Almaty repeatedly reported that he was alive. The Kazakh newspaper *Megapolis* reported that "reports of his death are misinformation Namangani invented himself." See Artie MacConnell, "Islamic Radicals Regroup in Central Asia," EurasiaNet.org, May 15, 2002.

44. Ahmed Rashid, *Jihad: The Rise of Militant Islam in Central Asia,* New Haven, Conn.: Yale University Press, 2002.

45. Reuters, "Germany Bans Hizb ut-Tahrir," Berlin, January 15, 2003.

46. Edmund Andrews, "A Bustling U.S. Air Base Materializes in the Mud," *The New York Times,* April 27, 2002.

Chapter Nine. Afghanistan I: Economic Reconstruction

1. James Dobbins et al., *America's Role in Nation Building: From Germany to Iraq,* Washington, D.C., RAND, 2003.

2. These figures were quoted by James Dobbins in *The Washington Post.* Colum Lynch, "Peacekeping Grows, Strains UN," *The Washington Post,* September 17, 2006.

3. Kofi Annan, "The Secretary General's Message on the International Day of UN Peacekeepers," United Nations, New York, May 29, 2006.

4. These thoughts were helped greatly by Madeleine Albright, "Bridges, Bombs or Bluster," *Foreign Affairs,* September–October 2003.

5. Council on Foreign Relations, "In the Wake of War: Improving US Post-Conflict Capabilities," report of an independent task force, July 2005.

6. "Report of the Defense Science Board Task Force on Strategic Communication," Department of Defense, Washington, D.C., September 2004.

7. David Rohde and Carlotta Gall, "Delays Hurting US Rebuilding in Afghanistan," *The New York Times,* November 2, 2005.

8. Statement by Alonzo Fulgham, see Agence France-Presse, "Afghan Unrest Kills 100 USAID Staff in Three Years," Kabul, July 3, 2006.

9. Interview with Robert Finn, former U.S. ambassador to Afghanistan, Yale University, New Haven, Conn., November 22, 2005.

10. Notes taken in meeting with USAID officials in Washington, D.C., January 24, 2002.

11. Personal communication by USAID staffer, March 2002.

12. Susan Milligan, "Together but Worlds Apart," *The Boston Globe,* October 10, 2006.

13. Stephen Kinzer, *Overthrow: America's Century of Regime Change from Hawaii to Iraq,* New York: Times Books, 2006.

14. Francis Fukuyama, *State Building, Governance and World Order in the Twenty-first Century,* London: Profile Books, 2004.

15. Karzai said, "We have one fear that without a full partnership with the international community, Afghanistan may falter again. In an environment of inadequate security, fragmented governance, the nonintegration of Afghan returnees, Afghanistan could remain a source of instability to the world and the region. . . . It is an almost unprecedented situation where an administration has no immediate source of revenue." Text of speech by Hamid Karzai at Tokyo, January 22, 2002.

16. The pledges made at Tokyo were varied. The United States gave only a measly $296 million for 2002; the World Bank and the Asian Development Bank each gave $500 million for 2.5 years, as did Japan; the EU gave $177 million for 2002; Iran, $580 million over 5 years; China, $100 million for 2002; Saudi Arabia, $220 million for 3 years; Britain, $288 million for 5 years; and India and Pakistan, $100 million each for 5 years. Reuters, "Afghan Aid Pledges Made," Tokyo, January 22, 2002.

17. The name was changed to the Afghanistan Reconstruction Trust Fund on July 22, 2002, at another donors conference in Geneva. It was managed jointly by the Asian Development Bank, the World Bank, the UN Development Programme, the Afghan government, and the Islamic Development Bank.

18. The UN Development Programme set up the Law and Order Trust Fund in order to encourage donors to contribute to helping rebuild the police.

19. Arthur Hilton, "Strategies for Afghanistan's Immediate Recovery," Council on Foreign Relations, July 2002. Hilton was later killed in Baghdad. Interview with Finn, Yale University, November 22, 2005.

20. Ahmed Rashid, "Afghan Finance Minister Is in a Hurry," *The Wall Street Journal,* March 17, 2002.

21. Toby Proston, "The Battle to Rebuild Afghanistan," BBC, April 10, 2006.

22. See Barnett Rubin, Humayun Hamidzada, and Abby Stoddard, "Through the Fog of Peace Building: Evaluating the Reconstruction of Afghanistan," Center on International Cooperation, New York University, March 2003. The speech at the UN was delivered by Dr. Mukesh Kapila, who worked for the UN Assistance Mission for Afghanistan and Britain's Department for International Development.

23. Carl Robichaud, "Remember Afghanistan: A Glass Half Full on the Titanic," *World Policy Journal,* spring 2006.

24. Elizabeth Rubin, "Taking the Fight to the Taliban," *The New York Times Magazine,* October 29, 2006.

25. See Ahmed Rashid, "Massive Literacy Campaign Starts in Afghanistan," *The Nation,* March 17, 2002.

26. Interview with Robert Finn, Princeton University, Princeton, N.J., November 22, 2005.

27. Hearing by Peter Tomsen, former U.S. special envoy and ambassador to Afghanistan, 1989–1992, House Committee on International Relations, June 19, 2003.

28. David Rohde, "Afghan Symbol for Change Becomes a Symbol of Failure," *The New York Times,* September 5, 2006.

29. The Asian Development Bank had first offered to provide a loan of $150 million to the government to build the road, but Ghani had refused and demanded a grant.

30. Ahmed Rashid, "Karzai Threatens to Resign," *The Daily Telegraph,* May 22, 2003.

31. "With both his command of details and American largesse, the Afghan-born envoy has created an alternative seat of power since his arrival," wrote Amy Waldman in "In Afghanistan, US Envoy Sits in Seat of Power," *The New York Times,* April 17, 2004.

32. See Jon Lee Anderson, "American Viceroy," *The New Yorker,* December 19, 2005. Khalilzad's mother died in November 2005 while he was ambassador in Baghdad. She had joined him in the United States during the 1980s but had returned to Kabul in 2004. Khalilzad is married to Cheryl Benard, an Austrian-born writer and scholar. They have two adult sons.

33. Just before 9/11, on April 14, 2000, Khalilzad and I spoke at a conference at Meridian House in Washington, D.C., where he advocated the need for an alternative emerging in Afghanistan that would replace the Taliban.

34. The paper, called "US Policy in Afghanistan: Challenges and Solutions," published by the Afghanistan Foundation in July 1999, was cowritten by Zalmay Khalilzad, Daniel Byman, Elie Krakowski, and Don Ritter. Khalilzad suggested that "the US should offer to recognize and work with the Taliban if it agrees to a ceasefire [with the Northern Alliance] and meets a set of conditions regarding human rights, . . . terrorism and narcotics and the formation of a more genuinely representative government." His suggestion that Washington could make the Taliban "more responsible" by working with them was misread by many, who saw it as pro-Taliban. In fact, he concluded that the Taliban would never agree to U.S. conditions, so the U.S. had no choice but to try to weaken them.

35. In September 2003, Congress was asked to provide an additional $1.2 billion for Afghanistan. The breakdown was $37.0 million for voter registration, $20.0 million to fund technical experts, $105.0 million for the Kabul-Kandahar highway, $40.0 million to build 275 schools and train 10,000 teachers, $28.0 million to build 150 clinics, and $45.0 million to complete land registry and build market centers. The remaining money was for training the ANA and the police. There was still no money allocated for agriculture.

36. See Ahmed Rashid, "US Policy, Afghanistan Is Waiting for This," *Far Eastern Economic Review,* July 31, 2003. See also Elaine Grossman, "Bush Administration Readies New Security, Aid Package for Afghanistan," *Inside the Pentagon* 3 (July 2003).

37. Carlotta Gall and David Rohde, "Delays Hurting US Rebuilding in Afghanistan," *The New York Times,* November 7, 2005. Louis Berger said that progress had been slowed by various requirements. The number of buildings it was asked to renovate or construct eventually rose to one thousand, and Berger did not have the staff, engineers, or monitoring experience to complete all this work. Another company, Brown and Root, monopolized the servicing of the major U.S. military camps in the country. In June 2002, Brown and Root won a $22.0 million contract to run support services at the K2 base in Uzbekistan.

In November 2002, it won another $42.5 million contract to support the military bases at Bagram and Kandahar.

38. Joe Stephens and David Ottaway, "A Rebuilding Plan Full of Cracks," *The Washington Post,* November 20, 2005. A former head of USAID's Afghan operation was reported in a memo as saying that the numbers of schools and clinics to be built "were not determined through careful analysis . . . instead, they were based on back of the envelope calculations outside USAID."

39. Margaret Cooker, "US Aid to Afghanistan Falls Short," Cox News Service, November 19, 2005. Natsios was to leave USAID in January 2006 after five years as its head, calling his former agency "constipated." However, he still refused to criticize the neocons, whose policies had by now failed USAID in both Afghanistan and Iraq. Celia Dugger, "Planning to Fight Poverty Outside the System," *The New York Times,* January 14, 2006.

40. David Rohde and Carlotta Gall, "Delays Hurting US Rebuilding in Afghanistan," *The New York Times,* November 2, 2005.

41. Ahmed Rashid, "The Great Trade Game," *Far Eastern Economic Review,* January 23, 2003.

42. The shortest routes from Central Asia to the Gulf via Pakistan were Dushanbe-Kabul-Karachi, 1,270 miles; Tashkent-Kabul-Karachi, 1,706 miles; and Ashgabat-Kabul-Karachi, 1,761 miles. The shortest routes via Iran were slightly longer, with Dushanbe-Herat–Bandar Abbas, 1,769 miles; Tashkent-Herat–Bandar Abbas, 1,984 miles; and Ashgabat-Herat Bandar Abbas, 1,463 miles. Gawadar would shorten the route via Pakistan considerably.

43. Letter from U.S. Government Accountability Office report to Congress, "Afghan Reconstruction, Deteriorating Security and Limited Resources Impeding Progress," June 2004.

44. Anne Carlin, "Rush to Engagement in Afghanistan: The IFI's Post-conflict Agenda," World Bank, December 2003.

45. "US Made Some Decisions, Says Rice," Reuters, *Dawn,* January 19, 2005.

46. In fiscal year 2001–2002 (from October 1, 2001, to September 30, 2002), the United States spent a total of $928.0 million in Afghanistan; in fiscal year 2002–2003, a total of $926.0 million; and in fiscal year 2003–2004, a total of $1.6 billion. In 2006, the United States spent $3.2 billion, of which more than half went toward building up the army and police. The United States planned to spend $10.0 billion in 2007, of which 80 percent would go to the Afghan National Army, and $4.7 billion in 2008.

47. In 2004–2005, U.S. aid to developing countries was just $15.6 billion—with nearly one third going to Israel and Egypt. In comparison, the defense budget was $450.0 billion. The United States contributes just 0.14 percent of its total income as aid; Britain gives 0.34 percent and Norway, 0.92 percent.

Chapter Ten. Afghanistan II: Rebuilding Security

1. In Britain, fifty-six parliamentarians presented a petition to the government demanding an expansion of ISAF.

2. The quotes come from Ahmed Rashid, "US Embarks on New Afghan Strategy," *The Daily Telegraph,* December 23, 2002, and "America's New Strategy," *Far Eastern Economic Review,* December 12, 2002. I spoke with General McNeill several times, but the longest discussion about PRTs was at Bagram, on December 13, 2002. The team of outside experts, including Barnett Rubin and myself, discussed the idea of regional teams intensively with UN envoy Lakhdar Brahimi, U.S. commander Gen. Dan McNeill, and

Francesc Vendrell, the European Union envoy. There were also several concept papers put out by the UN.

3. The document was called "Principles Guiding PRT Working Relations with UNAMA, NGOs and Local Government," March 2003.

4. Reuters, "Afghanistan Being Stabilized, Says Rumsfeld," Kabul, May 1, 2003. See also David Rohde and David Sanger, "How the Good War in Afghanistan Went Bad," *The New York Times,* August 12, 2007.

5. Richard Clarke, *Against All Enemies: Inside America's War on Terror,* New York: Free Press, 2004.

6. In 2005 General Eikenberry was to return to Kabul as the commander of all U.S. forces in Afghanistan.

7. Interview with Gen. John McColl, Kabul, March 7, 2002.

8. I saw several reports and letters exchanged between the UN, the U.S. Department of Defense, and the U.S. embassy in Kabul.

9. United Nations document, "Creating the New Afghan National Armed Forces," June 2002.

10. Brahimi spoke to me in Kabul. He made these same points in his address to the UN Security Council on July 19, 2002, in New York.

11. William Maley, *Rescuing Afghanistan,* London: Hurst and Co., 2006.

12. See Michael Bhatia, Kevin Lanigan, and Philip Wilkinson, "Minimal Investments, Minimal Results: The Failure of Security Policy in Afghanistan," Afghanistan Research and Evaluation Unit, Kabul, June 2004.

13. Judy Dempsey, "Germany Assailed for Training Afghan Police Poorly," *International Herald Tribune,* November 15, 2006.

14. For the best discussion on U.S. policy related to the police, see Vance Serchuk, "Cop Out: Why Afghanistan Has No Police," American Enterprise Institute, July 25, 2006.

15. International Crisis Group, "Reforming Afghan Police," Brussels, August 30, 2007.

16. Interview with Chris Alexander, Kabul, November 2006.

17. Associated Press, "Unpopularity of Karzai Government Threatens Afghanistan War Effort, Holbrooke Warns," Brussels, April 28, 2007.

18. Confidential UN report to the UN secretary-general, Kabul, March 6, 2002.

19. The British Foreign Office–organized conference was held at Wilton Park, England, in October 2002.

20. In September the State Department's diplomatic security service took over Karzai's protection, and a few weeks later they arranged for the task to be taken over by DynCorp.

21. Interview with Gen. Mohammed Fahim, Kabul, December 14, 2002. See Ahmed Rashid, "Karzai Risks All to Confront the Militia Generals," *The Daily Telegraph,* December 24, 2002.

22. I was told these details by UN and U.S. officials. See also *Daily Times,* "NA Printed Themselves a Fortune," reprinted from *The New York Times,* May 3, 2002.

23. United Nations document, Report by Lakhdar Brahimi to the UN Security Council, January 15, 2003.

24. Report of the high-level panel set up by UN secretary-general, "Threats, Challenges and Change," December 2004.

25. Barnett Rubin and Ahmed Rashid, "S.O.S. from Afghanistan," *The Wall Street Journal,* May 29, 2003.

26. David Rohde, "Afghan Symbol for Change Becomes a Symbol of Failure," *The New York Times,* September 5, 2006.

27. Ahmed Rashid, "Warlord Adds to Woes of Coalition," *The Daily Telegraph,* July 4, 2003.

28. "Non-Paper: Centrist, Ethnic and Fundamentalist Politics in Afghanistan," paper circulated to senior U.S. officials in Washington and received by me on May 12, 2003.

29. Members of the Constitutional Commission of Afghanistan, appointed April 24, 2003, and their ethnic origins: Chair and deputy, Neyamatullah Shahrani (head of commission), Uzbek; Abdul Salam Azimi (deputy), Pashtun. Members: Mohammad Musa Maroofi, Pashtun; Mohammad Musa Ashari, Tajik; Dr. Rahim Shirzoi, Pashtun; Mohammad Sarwar Danish, Hazara; Dr. Abdulhai Elahi, Tajik; Mohammad Ashraf Rasooli, Tajik; Abdul Haq Wala, Tajik; Abdul Aziz, Pashtun; Dr. Mohammad Tahir Borgai, Pashtun; Dr. Mohammad Yaqub Wahidi, Uzbek; Shamsuddin Khan, Tajik; Dr Mohammad Alam Eshaqzai, Pashtun; Judge Mohammad Amin Wiqad, Pashtun; Eng. Mohammad Akram, Tajik; Nadir Shah Nekiyar, Pashtun; Likraj, Hindu; Mrs. Parwin Momand, Pashtun; Mohammad Amin Ahmadi, Hazara; Mrs. Fatima Gilani, Arab; Sulaiman Baloch, Baloch; Mrs. Shukria Barikzai, Pashtun; Mrs. Sidiqa Balkhi, Hazara; Mrs. Amina Afzali, Tajik; Mohammad Sidiq Patman, Pashtun; Abdulhai Khoorasani, Tajik; Mrs. Parwin Ali Majrooh. The following were of unknown ethnic origin: Mir Mohammad Afzal, Prof. Mohammad Hashim Kamali, Eng. Merajuddin, Mrs. Fatima Mashaal, Eng. Dawoud Musa, Nadir Ali Mahdawi, Prof. Tahir Hashimi. Three additional members' names are not available.

30. Ahmed Rashid, "A Strong Constitution," *Far Eastern Economic Review,* August 14, 2003.

31. The others were the 1931 Constitution issued by King Nadir Shah, the 1964 Constitution by King Zahir Shah, the 1977 republican constitution by President Daud, and a subsequent communist constitution, in 1987. Zahir Shah had set up a seven-member commission that spent a year deliberating the draft constitution, which was ratified on September 9, 1964, after just nine days of discussion by a 455-person Loya Jirga. See International Crisis Group, "Afghanistan's Flawed Constitutional Process," June 12, 2003.

32. Kofi Annan address to the UN Security Council, e-mail of speech received from the UN, December 8, 2003.

33. The four candidates were Dr. Ranjbar from Kabul, a former communist, who got 29 votes; Azizullah Wasifi, a monarchist, who received 43 votes; Hafiz Mansur, a firebrand from the Jamiat-e-Islami and close to Burhanuddin Rabbani; and General Fahim, who had headed Afghan state TV after the liberation of Kabul in December 2001 and received 154 votes; and Sibghatullah Mujaddedi, who received 252 votes.

34. I was present for much of the CLJ, both inside the main tent for several days listening to the debate and outside meeting foreign diplomats and soldiers. Ahmed Rashid, "Let's Make a Democracy," *Far Eastern Economic Review,* December 25, 2003.

35. Human Rights Watch, "Blood-Stained Hands: Past Atrocities in Kabul and Afghanistan's Legacy of Impunity," New York, July 7, 2005. Karzai refused to question Sayyaf about the brutal allegations made about him in this document.

36. Human Rights Watch, "Killing You Is a Very Easy Thing for Us: Human Rights Abuses in Southeast Afghanistan," July 2003. See also Ahmed Rashid, "The Mess in Afghanistan," *New York Review of Books,* February 12, 2004: "In Paghman district, the district's governor and the local police are under Sayyaf's command. One of the most powerful commanders in the Kabul region, Shir Alam, is also one of Sayyaf's subordinates and controls most military checkpoints in Paghman. Zalmay Tofan, a commander of the Kabul Liwa, a large military base in Kabul province, is loyal to Sayyaf and close to Defense

Minister Fahim. Mullah Taj Mohammad, the governor of Kabul province, is also a subordinate of Sayyaf."

37. Gary Schroen, *First In: An Insider's Account of How the CIA Spearheaded the War on Terror in Afghanistan,* New York: Ballantine Books, 2005.

38. President Hamid Karzai's closing speech to the CLJ, Kabul, January 4, 2004. Karzai also spoke out against ethnicity: "Our vision for Afghanistan is of a country where people relate to each other through reason and shared ideas, convictions and behavior, not through ethnic bonds, because this is not the way of building nations. I never want—neither do you—I am sure that a person who belongs to the majority ethnic group necessarily becomes the president, and another belonging to the second largest ethnic group becomes the vice president, leaving the leftovers to the smaller ethnic groups. I do not want such an Afghanistan."

39. Speech by Lakhdar Brahimi at the closing of the CLJ, Kabul, January 4, 2004. Karzai tried to prevent Brahimi from leaving: "I had told Mr. Brahimi that I would not let him leave Afghanistan, and that the Loya Jirga will not allow him to leave. We are not happy about his departure. He has been a real friend of Afghanistan. He has shown real feelings and shed tears for this country. We pray for him." Brahimi answered, "The president and many of you are telling me that I shouldn't leave. But I have a boss, a kind of central government in New York, and he has given me orders to leave. If I don't, then I will be called a warlord for refusing the instructions of the central government. I am sure that you don't want me to be called a warlord . . . I will leave, but my heart will stay here and my prayers will be with you and my support is yours as long as I live."

40. I am grateful for the use of several internal UN documents for this analysis. Barnett Rubin, private note for the UN, "A Brief Look at the Final Negotiations on the Constitution of Afghanistan," Kabul, January 4, 2004. Also "Political Analysis of CLJ Drafted on Behalf of Lakhdar Brahimi," an internal UN document, Kabul, January 4, 2004. I also saw daily UN reports on the progress of the various CLJ committees. The European Union also shared their reports with me. However, the best publicly available analysis of the CLJ is Barnett Rubin, "Crafting a Constitution for Afghanistan," *Journal of Democracy,* July 2004.

Chapter Eleven. Double-Dealing with Islamic Extremism: Al Qaeda and the Taliban in Pakistan

1. Al Qaeda had a close relationship with Harkat ul-Ansar in the early 1990s, until it was banned by Prime Minister Nawaz Sharif. It then divided into two groups, Harkat ul-Mujahedin and Harkat ul-Jihad-i-Islami. Both groups were active in Kashmir and Afghanistan. Jaish-e-Mohammed emerged as the third group after the hijacking of the Indian Airlines plane to Kandahar in 1999.

2. After 2002, I carried out numerous interviews with senior U.S., British, other European, and UN diplomats, military and intelligence officials in Islamabad and Kabul, and U.S. and British officials in Washington and London. I interviewed President Karzai frequently and Afghan ministers and officials from all the key ministries dealing with the insurgency. I also interviewed senior retired Pakistani army and ISI officers who were opposed to the policy of backing the Taliban. It was interesting to note that although mid-level Western officials in their respective embassies would admit to a clandestine ISI operation in support of the Taliban, their ambassadors refrained from doing so, because any such admission would have led to the inevitable question about whether Musharraf was directly giving the orders.

3. Yosri Fouda and Nick Fielding, *Masterminds of Terror,* London: Mainstream Publishing, 2003.

4. Abu Ressam, an Algerian militant who had been caught on the U.S.-Canadian border in December 1999 while planning to bomb Los Angeles airport during the millennium celebrations, had told U.S. interrogators that he had been recruited by Zubaydah in Peshawar.

5. Dan Eggen and Dafna Linzer, "Secret World of Detainees Grows More Public," *The Washington Post,* September 7, 2006.

6. Bin al-Shibh, a Yemeni living in Germany, had desperately wanted to join the 9/11 hijackers, but his four requests for a U.S. visa were turned down. He fled Germany six days before 9/11 and arrived in Afghanistan via Pakistan.

7. Fouda and Fielding, *Masterminds of Terror.* The authors give a fascinating account of the interview and of subsequent events.

8. See Ron Suskind, *The One Percent Doctrine: Deep Inside America's Pursuit of Its Enemies Since 9/11,* New York: Simon & Schuster, 2006.

9. That claim is made by Jane Mayer, "The Black Sites," *The New Yorker,* August 13, 2007. The quote comes from Ahmed Rashid, "The Net Tightens on al Qaeda Cells," *Far Eastern Economic Review,* March 13, 2003.

10. He had evaded capture in Karachi in September 2002, when his wife and two children were arrested along with Ramzi bin al-Shibh. In February 2003 he had again escaped capture in Quetta when police arrested Mohammed Abdel Rahman, the son of the blind Egyptian cleric Sheik Omar Abdel Rahman, who was convicted in New York in 1995 for conspiring to blow up the UN building. KSM had stayed with Rahman before traveling to Rawalpindi.

11. Jonathan Randal, *Osama: The Making of a Terrorist,* New York: Knopf, 2004. Randal gives the most insight into KSM's life and travels. Both Randal's and Fouda's books demonstrate how KSM had been thinking of such a plot since 1993, when he had failed to carry out the simultaneous hijacking of eleven commercial aircraft over the Philippines. Ramzi Yousuf, the perpetrator of the 1993 World Trade Center bombing, was one of KSM's nephews, while another nephew, Musaad Aruchi, organized attacks in Pakistan after 9/11. Aruchi was arrested in June 2004 in Karachi.

12. Pervez Musharraf, *In the Line of Fire: A Memoir,* New York: Simon & Schuster, 2006.

13. In 2002—the year of the worst tensions with India—Lashkar-e-Tayyaba claimed that 292 of its militants, including 23 suicide bombers, were killed in 118 clashes with Indian troops.

14. For a more detailed analysis of both parties, see Muhammad Amir Rana, *A to Z of Jihadi Organizations in Pakistan,* Lahore: Mashal Books, 2004. Also Mariam Abou Zahab and Oliver Roy, *Islamist Networks: The Afghan-Pakistan Connection,* London: Hurst and Co., 2004.

15. Hazaras living in Quetta migrated from the Hazarajat in Afghanistan in the nineteenth century after working as porters for the British army in the Anglo-Afghan wars. Subsequently they have monopolized trade and shops in Quetta. Ashura is the Shias' most revered day, when they mourn the death of Imam Hussain, the grandson of the Prophet Mohammed, who was killed in battle.

16. Shamzai, a close friend of Osama bin Laden, had also helped set up Jaish-e-Mohammed and had provided hundreds of cadres to Sipah-e-Sahaba, whose leader, Azam Tariq, has studied at Binori.

17. How the Pakistani military has used the sectarian conflict to its advantage is best described in Vali Nasr, "Military Rule, Islam and Democracy in Pakistan," *Middle East Journal,* Spring 2004. See also Vali Nasr, *The Shia Revival,* New York: W. W. Norton, 2006.

18. Mohammed Shehzad, "Suicide Bombing Is the Best Form of Jihad," *The Friday Times,* April 17, 2003.

19. UN expert group report on continued activities of al Qaeda, December 17, 2003.

20. Dexter Filkins, "US Might Pursue Qaeda and Taliban to Pakistan Lairs," *The New York Times,* March 21, 2003.

21. Musharraf interview with *The Washington Post,* Islamabad, June 25, 2003.

22. Khalid Hassan, "Pakistani Security Setup Not Fully Cooperative: Armitage," *Daily Times,* October 2, 2003. Pakistan's foreign office answered by saying, "All security agencies are answerable to the president and they follow his direction faithfully."

23. "Armitage Says Army Fully Backs Musharraf," *Dawn,* October 7, 2003.

24. Farhan Bohkari, "Pakistan Bans Three Hard Line Islamic Groups," *Financial Times,* November 15, 2003. The three banned groups were: Khuddam ul-Islam, formerly Jaish-e-Mohammed; Millat-e-Islamia Pakistan, formerly Sipah-e-Sahaba; and Islami Tehreek Pakistan, formerly Tehreek-e-Jafria, a Shia party. A few days later, on November 20, the government banned three more groups. These were Jamaat ul-Furqan, a splinter group from Jaish-e-Mohammed; Jamiat ul-Ansar, the renamed former Harkat ul-Mujahedin; and Hizbul Tehrir, a previously legal group.

25. Reuters, "Osama Calls on Pakistanis to Depose Musharraf," Islamabad, October 9, 2002.

26. BBC, text of broadcast of speech by Ayman al-Zawahiri on Al Jazeera, September 28, 2003.

27. The five officers under arrest and facing court-martial were Lt.-Col. Abdul Ghaffar Khan, Col. Khalid Abbas, Maj. Attaullah Khan, Maj. Rohail Faraz, and Capt. Usman Zafar. A sixth officer, Maj. Adil Qadoos Khan, had been caught in the aftermath of KSM's arrest in Rawalpindi. The army refused to allow their families to bring their cases to the civil courts.

28. Jaish-e-Mohammed had first attempted to kill him at a Pakistan Day parade in March 2002. When the parade was canceled, suicide bombers next tried to enter a mosque in Islamabad, on December 6, 2002, while Musharraf was saying his prayers, but the security cordon was too tight. They again planned to kill him in March, and then in April 2003, using car bombs. "Trial in Attack of Those Who Tried to Kill Musharraf," *Herald,* June 2005.

29. Farooqi had first joined Lashkar-e-Jhangvi and was held responsible for multiple murders of Shias in the early 1990s. He later joined Harkat ul-Jihad al-Islami, a splinter group of the main Harakat ul-Islam. The new group was formally allied to al Qaeda, and its chief, Qari Saifullah Akthar, was close to both Mullah Omar and bin Laden. Farooqi planned the murder of eleven French engineers in Karachi in 2002 and had a hand in the kidnapping of Daniel Pearl. See Alexis Debat, "Why Al Qaeda Is at Home in Pakistan," ABC News, March 3, 2004.

30. Interview with Deputy Secretary of Defense Paul Wolfowitz, Washington, D.C., February 19, 2004.

31. Teresita Schaffer and Pramit Mitra, "Aid as an Agent of Change: The Experience of Pakistan," Center for Strategic and International Studies, Washington, D.C., November 2004. The authors quote from the UN Development Programme reports on human development in Pakistan.

32. State Bank of Pakistan report, December 2004. In 1951, when the population of West and East Pakistan was 32 million, there were 22 million illiterates. By 2001, the population had reached 150 million.

33. Pervez Hoodbhoy, "Reforming Our Universities," *Dawn,* January 3, 2005.

34. Yvette Rosser, "Pakistani Studies Textbooks Can Cause Cognitive Dissonance in Students," paper read at Sustainable Development Policy Institute conference, December 8, 2004.

35. Stephen Cohen, *The Idea of Pakistan,* Washington, D.C., Brookings Institution, 2004.

36. The best history of the madrassa system in Pakistan is International Crisis Group, "Madrassas: Extremism and the Military," July 20, 2002.

37. Aga Khan Development Network, "Philanthropy in Pakistan: A Report of the Initiative on Indigenous Philanthropy," Karachi, Pakistan, 2001.

38. The Madrassa Registration Ordinance was issued by the government on June 19, 2001.

39. State Department, "Press conference of President George W. Bush and President Pervez Musharraf," Washington, D.C., June 24, 2003.

40. Irfan Raza, "Almost One Madrassa Opened Every Week," *Dawn,* December 31, 2006.

41. Khalid Hassan, "Americans Safer with Pakistan as Ally: Bush," *Daily Times,* July 12, 2004.

42. Some U.S. think tanks did question whether Pakistan was a reliable ally. "The Musharraf regime is unlikely to evolve into a long-term ally in the war on terrorism," said the Cato Institute. Pakistan's decision to abandon the Taliban in 2001 was "not a strategic choice but a tactical decision to avoid US retribution and prevent Indian advantage." Cato Institute Briefing Paper, reported by Khalid Hassan, "Musharraf Not a Long-Term Ally of the US," *Daily Times,* January 31, 2005.

43. Associated Press, "Karachi Militants Funding Terror with Heists," Karachi, September 21, 2004.

44. In August 2007 he was suddenly freed without a trial and without being charged by the ISI, which had held him in a secret prison in Pakistan. U.S. officials were angry that he had been freed. There were also strong suspicions that he was released as part of a deal with the ISI and may have been working for them at some stage. See Craig Whitlock and Griff Witte, "Al Qaeda Suspect Released by Pakistan," *The Washington Post,* August 22, 2007.

45. The Islambouli Brigades of al Qaeda claimed to have carried out the attack. The group had been responsible for the assassination of Egyptian president Anwar Sadat in 1981 and the bombing of the Egyptian embassy in Islamabad in 1995. However, subsequent arrests proved that Pakistani militants working with a faction of Jaish-e-Mohammed and under Amjad Farooqi's leadership were involved.

46. According to Western diplomats who spoke to Marcus Mabry, Aziz claimed to be able to conquer any woman in two minutes with his "Savile Row suited gigolo kind of charm." Mabry wrote that when Rice sat down with Aziz, "Aziz puffed himself up and held forth in what he obviously thought was his seductive baritone." See Marcus Mabry, *Twice as Good: Condoleezza Rice and Her Path to Power,* New York: Modern Times, 2007.

47. Interview with Sherry Rehman, Islamabad, October 15, 2004.

48. After the second suicide attack on Musharraf, General Kayani suggested that soldiers search the roofs of shops near the attack site for possible evidence. It was there that soldiers found the all-important chip from a cell phone that led to the disclosures about the identities of the suicide bombers. There are usually 115 major-generals in the Pakistani army.

Chapter Twelve. Taliban Resurgent: The Taliban Return Home

1. The former foreign minister Mullah Wakil Ahmed Muttawakil surrendered to U.S. forces in Kandahar on February 8, 2002. Mullah Abdul Salam Zaeef, the former Taliban ambassador to Islamabad, was handed over by Pakistan at the same time; while Mullah Fazel Mazloom, the former army chief of staff, was captured by U.S. forces.

2. Gul Agha met with Mullah Obaidullah Ahmed, the former defense minister, and Mullah Noorudin Turabi, the former justice minister. Bradley Graham, "Two al Qaeda Fighters Caught," *The Washington Post,* January 9, 2002.

3. Agence France-Presse, "Osama May Be Alive: Afghan FM," Washington, D.C., January 25, 2002.

4. Reuters, "Islamabad, Kabul Vow to Curb Terror," Kabul, April 4, 2002.

5. BBC, "Interview with Mullah Omar," May 17, 2002.

6. My earlier book gives a full history of the origins of the Taliban and their links with the JUI and the Deobandi tradition. See Ahmed Rashid, *Taliban: Islam, Oil, and Fundamentalism in Central Asia,* New Haven, Conn.: Yale University Press, 2001.

7. Ahmed Rashid, "Taliban Mounted Militia Prepares for Border Strike," *The Daily Telegraph,* October 8, 2003. See also Ahmed Rashid, "Safe Haven for the Taliban," *Far Eastern Economic Review,* October 16, 2003.

8. James Dao, "Afghans Raise Concern That Taliban Forces Are Reorganizing in Pakistan," *The New York Times,* November 3, 2002.

9. Elizabeth Rubin, "In the Land of the Taliban," *The New York Times Magazine,* October 22, 2006.

10. Ahmed Rashid, "US Bombers and Fighters Attack Afghan Rebels," *The Daily Telegraph,* January 29, 2003.

11. Text of Osama bin Laden's message "Fight the Invaders," *International Herald Tribune,* February 15, 2003.

12. Associated Press, "Afghan Rebels Urge Attack," Islamabad, February 23, 2003. "I ask the Muslims of the world to wage a guerrilla war by using suicide attacks—now is not the time for large-scale group assaults but rather for individual attacks," said Hikmetyar.

13. Sarah Chayes explains the situation in the south in great detail in her *The Punishment of Virtue: Inside Afghanistan After the Taliban,* New York: Penguin Books, 2006.

14. Ahmed Rashid, "Afghans Urge Pakistan to Help Rein in Taliban," *The Daily Telegraph,* April 23, 2003.

15. Ahmed Rashid, "Taliban Are Back, Says US General," *The Daily Telegraph,* July 21, 2002.

16. The ten were former corps commanders Dadullah, Barader, Razzaq; the former chief of the Kandahar air base Akhtar Mansoor; former army chief Akhtar Usmani; former defense minister Obaidullah; former Nimroz governor Mohammed Rasul; and Kandahar's ex–security chief Hafiz Abdul Majeed. The only two Pashtuns who did not belong to the south were Jalaluddin Haqqani and Saifur Rehman Mansur. Of these, Razzaq was killed in a NATO air strike in Zabul province in 2006, Usmani was killed in a NATO air strike in Helmand province in January 2007, and Obaidullah was captured in Quetta in March 2007. See Asif Farooqi, "Taliban's New Hierarchy," IslamOnline.net, June 25, 2003.

17. In a major speech on April 30, 2003, Karzai announced that "those who did not oppose the peace process and who were committed to non-violent means must be provided with the political space and equal opportunities . . . to help the peace process." John Heller, "Political Space Is Opening for Taliban Moderates," Radio Free Liberty, July 4, 2003.

18. Lakhdar Brahimi, "Address to the UN Security Council," New York, UN briefing paper, December 8, 2003.

19. Reuters, "Iraq Won't Weaken US Effort," Bagram, July 30, 2003.

20. The scene was reminiscent of the burning down of the Pakistani embassy in Kabul in 1995 by a crowd led by NA leaders after the Taliban had captured Herat.

21. Ahmed Rashid, "Karzai Pledges Good Relations but Demands Pakistan Stop Extremists," *The Nation,* July 22, 2003.

22. "I have spent 3 million rupees [$50,000] on tickets sending back Mujahedin to their homes—if I am a terrorist, the court should hang me," said Piracha. "If I Am a Terrorist, the Court Should Hang Me—Piracha," *Herald,* September 2004.

23. Ahmed Rashid, "The Betrayal of the Afghans," *New York Review of Books,* January 29, 2004.

24. My story was for the *Far Eastern Economic Review:* "Afghanistan and Pakistan: Safe Haven for the Taliban," October 9, 2003. The editorial was "Haven for the Taliban," *The Washington Post,* November 2, 2003.

25. Al Qaeda leaders made constant references to the Muslim kingdoms in the province of Andalusia in southern Spain in the Middle Ages as a period of greatness in the Muslim world that should be emulated. Lawrence Wright, "The Terror Web," *The New Yorker,* August 2, 2004.

26. A total of twenty-three U.S. soldiers were killed in 2003, and twelve were killed in the first six months of 2004.

27. Ahmed Rashid, "Karzai Expects to Discuss Critical Issues with Musharraf," *The Nation,* July 25, 2004.

28. Interview with Paul Wolfowitz, deputy defense secretary, Washington, D.C., February 19, 2004.

29. Interview with John McLaughlin, Washington, D.C., November 19, 2005.

30. See Robin Wright, "Untested Islamic Militants Emerging, US Official Says," *The Washington Post,* April 2, 2004.

31. Associated Press, "US Wants to Build Network of Friendly Militias to Combat Terrorism," Washington, D.C., August 11, 2004.

32. Afghanistan Research and Evaluation Unit, "Afghan Elections: The Great Gamble," Kabul, November 2003. Of the warlords, the report said, "It will be a cruel irony for Afghans if their first experience of voting is being to vote for those who have been responsible for so much of the misery of the last two decades."

33. Ahmed Rashid, "Afghan Elections to Be Delayed," *The Wall Street Journal,* January 8, 2004.

34. Ibid.

35. I saw several private cables sent by the UN and European embassies that outlined the deal, even though Karzai publicly continued to deny it. Karzai had agreed to give the warlords 50 percent of the ministries in return for their support to his candidacy. He promised that Fahim and Karim Khalili, the Hazara leader, would be on his slate as vice presidents, and Rabbani would become the speaker of the future parliament.

36. Carlotta Gall, "Karzai Casts Lot with Warlords," *The New York Times,* June 8, 2004.

37. A confidential UN discussion paper circulated among Western embassies stated: "The reformers have looked up to the transitional government and the international community to spearhead the transition. The jihadis have relied on their position in the security apparatus—and their military/political control over large parts of the territory—to achieve their own agenda." UNAMA discussion paper, "Debate on the 2004 Electoral Process," Kabul, March 2004.

38. Rashid, "Afghan Elections to Be Delayed."

39. Interview with Karzai, Kabul, July 20, 2004. See Ahmed Rashid, "A Vote Is Cast Against Warlords," *Far Eastern Economic Review,* July 28, 2004.

40. Ahmed Rashid, "No Going Back," *Far Eastern Economic Review,* September 24, 2004.

41. Due to the security situation, the UN felt that it could not protect hundreds of foreign election monitors, so thirteen Afghan and Western NGOs pooled their resources to set up the Free and Fair Elections Foundation of Afghanistan, which trained Afghan men and women as election monitors.

42. Private document, letter from Munir Akram to UN Secretary-General Kofi Annan, New York, October 4, 2004.

43. Private document, letter from UN Secretary-General Kofi Annan to President Pervez Musharraf, August 18, 2004. I was shown various UN letters and Pakistani replies to them by diplomatic sources in Islamabad and Kabul in September 2004.

44. All the quotes above were made to me personally. See Ahmed Rashid, "Afghanistan Hopes for Neighborly Goodwill," *Far Eastern Economic Review,* October 14, 2004.

45. Musharraf also appointed a new ISI chief, Lt.-Gen. Ashfaq Kiyani, the general who had uncovered the plot to blow up Musharraf a year earlier. The Afghans knew him because for the past year he had led the Pakistani delegation in regular meetings with the United States and Afghan militaries. In June 2003 a tripartite commission had been established among senior military commanders from the United States, Afghanistan, and Pakistan to discuss border violations.

46. Ahmed Rashid, "Karzai Looks to Rebuild a Nation," *Far Eastern Economic Review,* October 14, 2004.

47. There were other Panjsheri Tajiks and NA leaders in the hierarchy. Apart from Abdullah Abdullah, Ismael Khan remained minister of power and water, Amrullah Saleh headed the intelligence service, Gen. Bismallah Khan was army chief of staff, and the head of Counter-Narcotics was Gen. Mohammed Daud.

Chapter Thirteen. Al Qaeda's Bolt-Hole: Pakistan's Tribal Areas

1. For more information on FATA and the Durand Line issue, see Barnett Rubin and Abubakar Siddique, "Resolving the Afghanistan-Pakistan Stalemate," United States Institute of Peace, October 2006; International Crisis Group, "Pakistan's Tribal Areas: Appeasing the Militants," Islamabad, December 11, 2006; Hassan Abbas, "Profiles of Pakistan's Seven Tribal Agencies," Jamestown Foundation, *Jamestown Terrorism Monitor* 20 (October 2006).

2. Interview with Afrasiab Khattak, February 12, 2007.

3. The United States abandoned the Lawara firebase in December 2002, after phosphorous rockets fired on the base burned several U.S. SOF vehicles. The Taliban claimed the U.S. retreat as a major victory.

4. Reuters, "Pakistan Could Do More, Says US General," Bagram, December 27, 2002. Agence France-Presse, "US Says Attackers May Be Pursued in Pakistan," Bagram, January 3, 2003.

5. Marc Kaufman, "On Afghan Border, War Drags On," *The Washington Post,* January 25, 2003.

6. On October 2, 2003, Pakistani security forces, aided by gunship helicopters, attacked an al Qaeda camp in Baghar village, in South Waziristan, killing eight and arresting eighteen suspects. Ahmed Said Khadr, alias Abu Abdur Rehman Khadr al-Canadi, an Egyptian-born Canadian and a key al Qaeda financer, was believed to be among the dead.

7. Zulfiqar Ali, "Musharraf Warns Against Failure of Wana Operation," *Dawn,* March 16, 2004.

8. Major Qudoos, an officer of the Signal Battalion, who was arrested on March 1, 2003, for allegedly helping al Qaeda's Khalid Sheikh Mohammed, was sentenced to ten years in jail. Col. Khalid Abbasi, also a Signal officer, was arrested on May 30, 2003, and sentenced to six months in jail. Col. Abdul Ghaffar, serving at the Army Aviation Headquarters, was arrested on March 4, 2004, and sentenced to three years in jail. The cases of two majors and a captain were dismissed.

9. For more economic details, see International Crisis Group, "Pakistan's Tribal Areas." An interesting book on education in FATA by a Mahsud female school inspector is Zaiba Mahsud, *Touchstone,* Islamabad: self-published, 2006.

10. "FATA Sustainable Development Plan, 2006-15," Peshawar: Government of Pakistan, June 2006.

11. Interview (in July 2007) with Christine Fair, formerly of the United States Institute of Peace in Washington, D.C., and presently working with UNAMA in Kabul.

12. See Sohail Nasir, "Baitullah Mahsud," Jamestown Foundation, *Terrorism Focus,* July 5, 2006.

13. Owais Tohid, "Cash Weans Tribes from al Qaeda," *Christian Science Monitor,* February 16, 2005.

14. Carlotta Gall and Mohammed Khan, "Pakistan's Push in Border Areas Is Said to Falter," *The New York Times,* January 22, 2006. Those killed in the strike included Egyptians Midhat Mursi al-Sayid Umar, alias Abu Khahab al-Masri alias Abu Ubayda alias Mustafa Osman; the Moroccan Abdel Rehman al-Maghrebi; and Khalid Habib. Al-Maghrebi was believed to be the son-in-law of al-Zawahiri. Carlotta Gall and Douglas Jehl, "U.S. Raid Killed Qaida Leaders, Pakistanis Say," *The New York Times,* January 19, 2006.

15. The madrassa was run by Tehreek-e-Nafaz-e-Shariat-e-Mohammadi, or the Movement for the Enforcement of Islamic Law, the same extremist group that had persuaded thousands of tribesmen to cross into Afghanistan to fight U.S. forces during the war in 2001. The organization was banned in 2002 and its leader, Sufi Mohammed, jailed, but the ISI allowed it to reestablish its influence in FATA. Sufi Mohammad's son-in-law, Maulana Fazlullah, revived the movement. Nicknamed "Maulana Radio" due to his expertise in launching illegal FM radio stations, he had close ties with al Qaeda and the Taliban.

16. General Orakzai had been corps commander in Peshawar from October 9, 2001, to March 12, 2004.

17. Reuters, "Bush Says US Watching Pakistan Deal with Militants," Washington, D.C., September 7, 2006.

18. Ahmed Rashid, "Nato's Top Brass Accuse Pakistan over Taliban Aid," *The Daily Telegraph,* October 6, 2006.

19. Anwar Iqbal, "Taliban Command Structure in FATA Alarms US," *Dawn,* December 28, 2006. Boucher made the comments while on a visit to Canada.

20. The first agreement was the Shakai deal in South Waziristan in 2004; the second and third took place in North Waziristan, in 2005 and 2006.

21. Zahid Hussain, "Terror in Miramshah," *Newsline,* April 2006. "In Tank, the Taliban have ordered barbers not to shave beards, people are prohibited to play music, even at weddings, and the traditional fairs, which provided some form of entertainment to the public, have been banned. In Dera Ismail Khan, the Taliban have forcibly stopped people from organizing their spring fair and instead asked them to hold a religious conference. In Swat district, some pro-Taliban clerics set television sets on fire. In Peshawar, clerics have threatened to take action against those cable operators who show western television channels."

22. Letter from Ayman al-Zawahiri to Abu Musab al-Zarqawi, *The New York Times,* October 20, 2005.

23. Peter Bergen, "The Return of al Qaeda: Where You Bin?" *The New Republic,* January 29, 2007.

24. Nasir Jamal, "Musharraf Rules Out Pakistan Link to Blasts Abroad," *Dawn,* July 25, 2005.

25. The ringleader, Omar Khyam, testified in his trial that "they taught me everything I needed for guerrilla warfare in Kashmir, AK47s, pistols, RPGs, sniper rifles, climbing and crawling techniques, reconnaissance and light machine guns." See ibid.

26. Text of speech delivered by Eliza Manningham-Buller, director-general of MI5. "The Internationalist Terrorist Threat to the UK," *The Daily Telegraph,* November 9, 2006.

27. Jim Hoagland, "Message to Musharraf," *The Washington Post,* January 22, 2006.

28. Khalid Hasan, "US Paid Pakistan Billions of Dollars to Counter Terror," *Daily Times,* October 29, 2006. The figures are based on a report by the U.S. Congressional Research Service. In 2002 Pakistan charged the U.S. Defense Department $420 million for logistical facilities given to U.S. forces as they waged the war in Afghanistan. The charges were for the rental of air bases and the supply of fuel, water, and ammunition transported from Karachi port to U.S. forces in Pakistan and Afghanistan.

29. Tim Burger, "Ten Questions for Porter Goss," *Time,* June 27, 2005.

30. "Report on the Congressional Research Service of the US Congress," *Dawn,* February 25, 2005.

31. Haitham al-Yamani and Abu Hamza Rabia were killed in a missile strike in North Waziristan in 2005. In 2006, Muhsin Matwalli Atwah, an Egyptian bomb maker, was killed in an air attack in Miran Shah, while Abu Marwan al-Suri, a Saudi national, was killed at a checkpoint in Bajaur.

32. Dana Priest and Ann Scott Tyson, "Bin Laden Trail Stone Cold," *The Washington Post,* September 10, 2006. U.S. intelligence still referred to bin Laden and al-Zawahiri as High-Value Targets, or HVT 1 and HVT 2.

33. Agence France-Presse, "Al Qaeda Funding the Taliban, Says Top US Commander," Kabul, March 29, 2005.

34. Ron Moreau and Sami Yousfzai, "Unholy Allies," *Newsweek,* September 22, 2005.

35. Dafna Linzer and Walter Pincus, "Taliban, al Qaeda Resurge in Afghanistan, CIA Says," *The Washington Post,* November 16, 2005. Hayden and Gen. Michael Maples, director of the Defense Intelligence Agency, both spoke to the Congressional Intelligence Committee.

36. Sebastian Rotella, "War on West Shifts Back to Afghanistan," *Los Angeles Times,* October 26, 2006.

37. Text of John Negroponte speech to the Senate Intelligence Committee, Washington, D.C., January 11, 2007.

38. The initial cost of the port, which was opened in 2006, was $250 million, out of which China contributed $198 million.

39. Ahmed Rashid, "Explosive Mix in Pakistan's Gas Province," BBC News Online, January 24, 2005.

40. Carlotta Gall, "In Remote Pakistan Province, a Civil War Festers," *The New York Times,* April 2, 2006.

41. Hussain Haqqani, "Talking Without Thinking," *The Nation,* December 13, 2006.

42. They asked the Court for a judgment on whether the accession of Balochistan to

the Pakistan state in 1947 was legitimate—thereby questioning the very creation of Pakistan.

43. Two weeks before his death, Bugti had privately asked Karzai for political asylum in Afghanistan, which Karzai was sorely tempted to grant but declined, fearing greater tensions with Pakistan. The army said Bugti's killing had sent a strong message to India and Afghanistan that "Indian proxies" would not be in Balochistan.

44. Research carried out by the Center for Nonproliferation Studies, at Monterey Institute of International Studies. See Humayun Akhtar, "China Fully Supports Pakistan Nuclear Plans," September 7, 2000.

45. Dennis Kux, *The United States and Pakistan, 1947–2000: Disenchanted Allies,* Washington, D.C.: Woodrow Wilson Center Press, 2001.

46. General Beg apparently "thought in terms of 'democratizing' the global nuclear non-proliferation order and moving to a multipolar world." See Gordon Corera, *Shopping for Bombs: Nuclear Proliferation, Global Insecurity, and the Rise and Fall of the A. Q. Khan Network,* Oxford: Oxford University Press, 2006.

47. See note 14 of chapter 2.

48. Khan once explained succinctly how he made the bomb and put together his network: "Being an engineer has its own advantages. You do not have to do much. You just have to put a few parts of a machine together and you have done your job. This is how the nuclear program was done. We just picked up a few pieces, joined them together and it became a centrifuge producing enriched uranium and there you have an atom bomb." "Government Assures Dr Khan of Support, Islamabad," *Dawn,* December 24, 2002.

49. Much of this information comes from the most comprehensive book on Pakistan's nuclear program: See Corera, *Shopping for Bombs.*

50. David Sanger, "In North Korea and Pakistan, Deep Roots of Nuclear Barter," *The New York Times,* November 21, 2002.

51. Powell assured a skeptical world that Musharraf "gave me 400 percent assurances that Pakistan has not supplied any nuclear know-how to North Korea," but he added, "I cannot talk about the past." Masud Haider, "Nuclear Material Not Supplied to North Korea," *Dawn,* October 21, 2002.

52. Reuters, "Pakistan Nuclear Scientist Seeks Clemency for Leaks," *Dawn,* February 4, 2004. Text of Dr. Khan's statement, *Dawn,* February 4, 2004.

53. Josh Meyer, "Officials Say Pakistan Has Secretly Bought High-Tech Components for Its Weapons Program from U.S. Companies," *Los Angeles Times,* March 26, 2005.

54. Interview with Paul Wolfowitz, deputy secretary of defense, Washington, D.C., February 19, 2004.

55. Just before North Korea's nuclear test, the Americans publicly demanded that they be allowed to speak to Khan directly. Ryan Crocker, the U.S. ambassador to Pakistan, said, "I do not think any of us have the whole story. That is important for Pakistan to know, that is important for us to know and it is important for the international community to know, as we face the ongoing proliferation of Iran and North Korea." See "Let's Have the Whole Story: US Envoy," *The News,* October 3, 2006.

56. Carlotta Gall and Elisabeth Bumiller, "Bush Rules Out a Nuclear Deal with Pakistanis," *The New York Times,* March 5, 2006.

57. Pervez Musharraf, *In the Line of Fire,* New York: Simon & Schuster, 2006. *The Wall Street Journal* described the book "as a highly selective auto-hagiography, by turns self-congratulatory, narcissistic and mendacious." Quoted in Hussain Haqqani, "Talking Without Thinking," *The Nation,* December 13, 2006.

58. Fouad Ajami, "With Us or Against Us," *The New York Times,* January 7, 2007. Ajami was reviewing Musharraf's book.

59. Stephen Cohen, *The Idea of Pakistan,* Washington, D.C., Brookings Institution, 2004.

Chapter Fourteen. America Shows the Way:
The Disappeared and the Rendered

1. Gabor Rona, "Interesting Times for International Humanitarian Law: Challenges from the War on Terror," *The Fletcher Forum of World Affairs,* Summer/Fall 2003.

2. Bob Woodward, *Bush at War,* New York: Simon & Schuster, 2002.

3. Madeleine Albright, "Confidence in America: The Best Change the Next President Can Make," *The Washington Post,* January 7, 2008.

4. David Rose, *Guantánamo: America's War on Human Rights,* London: The New Press, 2004.

5. For the full text of the memos, see Michael Ratner and Ellen Ray, *Guantánamo: What the World Should Know,* Moreton, Eng.: Arris Books, 2004.

6. See Rose, *Guantánamo.*

7. This chapter is a result of interviews with many figures, including U.S., European, and NATO military officers and diplomats, officials from the United Nations, the International Committee of the Red Cross, Human Rights Watch, Amnesty International, and other humanitarian and aid agencies. Many of them had visited jails in Guantánamo, Kandahar, and Bagram. Due to the highly sensitive nature of their information, I cannot quote them by name or organization. As a result, I have usually defined their information as coming from "a Western official," unless I can give readers a more specific identity.

8. Interview by my researcher Abu Bakr with Noor Habibullah on June 2, 2004, in Sholana village, twenty-five kilometers south of Jalalabad, in eastern Afghanistan.

9. See Chris Mackey, with Greg Miller, *The Interrogators: Inside the Secret War Against Al Qaeda,* London: John Murray, 2004. For the abilities of the U.S. SOF, see Robin Moore, *The Hunt for Bin Laden: Task Force Dagger,* New York: Random House, 2003.

10. Robert Baer, *See No Evil: The True Story of a Ground Soldier in the CIA's War on Terrorism,* New York: Crown, 2002.

11. Mackey, with Miller, *The Interrogators.*

12. Human Rights Watch, "US Systematic Abuse of Afghan Prisoners," New York, May 13, 2004.

13. This list has been compiled from documents from Human Rights Watch, Amnesty International, the International Committee of the Red Cross, and the U.S. Defense Department.

14. Tim Golden, "In US Report, Brutal Details of 2 Afghan Inmates' Deaths," *The New York Times,* May 20, 2005. Golden published long extracts from the two-hundred-page military file.

15. Douglas Jehl and Eric Schmitt, "US Military Says 26 Inmate Deaths May Be Homicide," *The New York Times,* March 16, 2005. Also Douglas Jehl, "Some Abu Ghraib Abuses Are Traced to Afghanistan," *The New York Times,* August 25, 2004.

16. Douglas Jehl, "Army Details Abuse in Afghanistan and Iraq," *The New York Times,* March 12, 2005.

17. Elise Ackerman, "Blows That Led to Detainees' Death Were Common Practice," Knight Ridder newspapers, March 25, 2005. See also Carlotta Gall and David Rohde, "New Charges Raise Questions on Abuse at Afghan Prisons," *The New York Times,* September 17, 2004.

18. The autopsy was performed by Lt.-Col. Elizabeth Rouse, who testified in the trial. Associated Press, "Medical Examiner Testifies Beaten Afghan Falling Apart," Washington, D.C., August 16, 2005.

19. Tim Golden, "Years After Two Afghans Died, Abuse Case Falters," *The New York Times,* February 13, 2006.

20. Conversation with Nader Nadery, August 24, 2005. The minor punishments received by the fourteen men on trial were documented by the Associated Press, "A Look at the Afghanistan Prisons Abuse Scandal," September 28, 2005.

21. His case was well documented by the Afghan Independent Human Rights Commission in Kabul and by *The New York Times.* See Carlotta Gall, "An Afghan Gives His Own Account of US Abuse," *The New York Times,* May 12, 2004. Also Hamida Ghafour, "Afghan Held by US Troops Recounts Agony of Interrogation," *Globe and Mail,* May 15, 2004.

22. Craig Pyes and Kevin Sack, "Two Deaths Were a 'Clue That Something's Wrong,' " *Los Angeles Times,* September 24, 2006.

23. Dana Priest, "Salt Pit Case—What Went Wrong in Afghanistan?" reprinted in *Daily Times,* March 4, 2005.

24. Scott Shane, "CIA Contractor Guilty in Beating Afghan," *The New York Times,* August 18, 2006.

25. The other two men were Brent Bennett, also a former soldier, and a New York journalist Edward Carabella, who appeared to be recording Idema's activities. Idema and Bennett were each sentenced to ten years in jail, a term later cut to five years. Carabella's original sentence of eight years was reduced to two years in 2005. They were both freed in 2007.

26. Cabinet Office, "The Handling of Detainees by UK Intelligence Personnel in Afghanistan, Guantánamo Bay and Iraq," London, March 10, 2005.

27. "Rendition" is the capture or abduction of alleged terrorists. The prisoners are then sent to third countries, where they can be interrogated by foreign intelligence agencies who are known to use torture.

28. ICRC statement, Geneva, January 16, 2004.

29. Jane Mayer, "Outsourcing Torture," *The New Yorker,* February 14, 2005.

30. Ibid.

31. Rose, *Guantánamo.* Black was speaking to the House and Senate intelligence committees, September 26, 2002.

32. Human Rights Watch, "All Our Hopes Are Crushed: Violence and Repression in Western Afghanistan," New York, November 2002. One young Afghan in Herat described the torture of a friend: "Then they gave my friend electricity shocks. They used a crank generator. They had to crank it very fast to produce the shock. They tied two electrical lines to each of his big toes. Three or four times they shocked him. . . . Each time, my friend's body would be thrown by the shock. After that, my friend signed the confession paper. Then I signed it also so that I would not be beaten."

33. Some months earlier I had met with Ismael Khan, whom I had known for fifteen years, and asked him to grant freedom of the press in Herat so that an NGO I had set up could fund new magazines and newspapers there. Shahir's NGO received the first grant to publish a magazine, but he was arrested and beaten up.

34. Peter Beaumont, "UK Aid Funds Iraqi Torture Units," *The Observer,* July 3, 2005.

35. Human Rights Watch, "Ghost Prisoner: Two Years in Secret CIA Detention," New York, February 27, 2007. See also Dafna Linzer and Julie Tate, "New Light Shed on CIA's Black Site Prisons," *The Washington Post,* February 28, 2007.

36. Salman Masood, "Kin and Rights Groups Search for Pakistan's Missing," *The New York Times,* January 14, 2007.

37. Craig Murray, Speech at Freedom House, British embassy, Tashkent, October 18, 2003.

38. Center for Security Studies, ETH Zurich, "Diplomat: US, UK Used Torture Information," April 23, 2006.

39. Craig Murray, "Her Majesty's Man in Tashkent," *The Washington Post,* September 3, 2006.

40. Reuters, "US Adds Eleven Islamic Groups to Blacklist," Washington, D.C., April 30, 2003.

41. Josh White, "Lawyers Demand Release of Chinese Muslims," *The New York Times,* December 5, 2006.

42. Rose, *Guantánamo.*

43. ICRC press conference by Pierre Kraehenbuehl, director of operations, Geneva, May 8, 2004.

44. Isabel Hilton, "Held in Contempt," *Financial Times,* August 29, 2004. Hilton's account of the lawyers' attempts to obtain justice is the most comprehensive published thus far.

45. Evan Thomas and Michael Hirsh, "The Debate over Torture," *Newsweek,* November 21, 2005.

46. U.S. Senate, "Are American Interests Being Disserved by the ICRC?" June 2005. Kellenberger responded on June 17 in Geneva.

47. Ibid.

48. Human Rights Watch put together a list of thirty-eight prisoners whose whereabouts were unknown, but said there were certainly more. See Human Rights Watch, "Ghost Prisoner: Two Years in Secret CIA Detention," New York, February 27, 2007.

49. Associated Press, "27 Iraqis, Afghans Killed in US Custody," March 25, 2005.

50. Karen DeYoung and Peter Baker, "Bush Detainees Plan to Add to World Doubts of US, Says Powell," *The Washington Post,* September 19, 2006.

51. David Johnston, "Rice Ordered Release of German Sent to Afghan Prison in Error," *The New York Times,* April 22, 2005.

52. The fourteen countries involved in unlawful interstate transfers were Bosnia-Herzegovina, Britain, Cyprus, Germany, Greece, Ireland, Italy, Macedonia, Poland, Portugal, Romania, Spain, Sweden, and Turkey. David Rennie, "Britain Helped CIA Kidnappers," *The Guardian,* June 8, 2006.

Chapter Fifteen. Drugs and Thugs: Opium Fuels the Insurgency

1. Ahmed Rashid, *Taliban: Islam, Oil, and the New Great Game in Central Asia,* London: I. B. Tauris, 2000.

2. We interviewed Khan and several poppy farmers. Abubaker Saddique, "In Afghan Province, Poppy Planting Has Strong Appeal," EurasiaNet.org, October 11, 2003.

3. I give considerable detail about the involvement of the ISI in drug trafficking in my book on the Taliban. Also in Tom Carew, *Jihad: The SAS Secret War in Afghanistan,* London: Mainstream, 2000, the author describes how in the 1980s he saw Hikmetyar's Hizb-e-Islami bring opium out of Afghanistan and then deliver the opium to ISI offices on the border.

4. Rashid, *Taliban.*

5. Graham Farrell and John Thorne, "Where Have All the Flowers Gone? Evolution of the Taliban Crackdown Against Opium Poppy Cultivation in Afghanistan," *International Journal of Drug Policy,* March 2005.

6. Under *salam* contracts the farmer agreed to provide the drug dealer or moneylender with opium after the harvest and in return got paid half the value of his future harvest in cash at the market prices prevalent at the time of loan.

7. Ahmed Rashid, "Flood of Afghan Heroin Expected," *The Daily Telegraph,* September 26, 2001. I was told by UNODC officials that the Americans knew far more about drug labs than they claimed to know, and the failure to bomb them was a major setback to the counter-narcotics effort. See also James Risen, *State of War: The Secret History of the CIA and the Bush Administration,* New York: Free Press, 2006.

8. Barnett Rubin, *Road to Ruin: Afghanistan's Booming Opium Industry,* Washington, D.C., and New York: Center for American Progress and Center on International Cooperation, New York University, 2004. See also Michael Von der Schulenburg, "Briefing Paper on Revenues Generated by Illicit Drug Trafficking in Afghanistan," internal paper written for UNODC, 2000.

9. Quoted in David Rohde, "Afghan Symbol for Change Becomes a Symbol of Failure," *The New York Times,* September 15, 2006.

10. See ibid. Rohde quotes a 2006 statement by the UNODC chief Antonio Costa that names Sher Mohammed as being allegedly involved in drugs. Also Paul Watson writes that Sher Mohammed was caught with ten thousand kilograms of opium in his office in 2005. See Paul Watson, "US Military Secrets for Sale at Afghan Bazaar," *Los Angeles Times,* November 3, 2006.

11. Steve Shaulis headed the Central Asia Development Group (CADG), a for-profit aid agency carrying out agricultural reconstruction.

12. Ahmed Rashid, "Drugs Are Good for War," *Far Eastern Economic Review,* October 16, 2003. See also Ahmed Rashid, "Unequal Forces Line Up in Struggle over Afghan Heroin Trade," *The Daily Telegraph,* October 16, 2003.

13. United Nations Office on Drugs and Crime, "Afghanistan's Drug Industry, Structure, Functioning Dynamics and Implications for Counter-Narcotics Policy," edited by Doris Buddenberg and William Byrd, 2006.

14. Ashraf Ghani, "Where Democracy's Greatest Enemy Is a Flower," *The New York Times,* December 11, 2004. For the World Bank, see William Byrd and Christopher Ward, "Drugs and Development in Afghanistan," Washington, The World Bank, Social Development Papers, Conflict Prevention and Reconstruction Paper no. 18, Washington, D.C., December 2004.

15. Donald Rumsfeld visited Kabul on September 7, 2003.

16. James Risen, *State of War: The Secret History of the CIA and the Bush Administration,* New York: Free Press, 2006.

17. Barnett Rubin et al., "Too Early to Declare Success: Counter-Narcotics Policy in Afghanistan," Afghanistan policy brief by CARE International and the Center on International Cooperation, March 24, 2004.

18. In 2003, the United States had committed only $130 million for counter-narcotics. Risen, *State of War.* See also Sonni Efron, "Afghan Quandary for US," *Los Angeles Times,* February 1, 2005.

19. UNODC, "Afghanistan's Drug Industry."

20. Carlotta Gall, "Afghan Poppy Growing Reaches Record Level," *The New York Times,* November 19, 2004.

21. Personal communications with Western diplomats in Kabul.

22. Associated Press, "US Military Denies Report on Karzai's Brother's Drug Ties," Kabul, June 23, 2006. See also Ron Moreau and Sami Yousufzai, "A Harvest of Treachery," *Newsweek*, January 9, 2006.

23. See Mark Shaw, "Drug Trafficking and the Development of Organized Crime in Post-Taliban Afghanistan," in UNODC, "Afghanistan's Drug Industry."

24. Judy Dempsey, "General Calls Drugs Biggest Test for Afghans," *International Herald Tribune*, May 22, 2006.

25. Reuters, "UN Says Afghanistan Addicted to Own Opium," New Delhi, May 24, 2006.

26. Carlotta Gall, "Opium Harvest at Record Level in Afghanistan," *The New York Times*, September 3, 2006.

27. Quoted in Moreau and Yousufzai, "A Harvest of Treachery." Wilder did the study for the Kabul-based Afghanistan Research and Evaluation Unit.

28. UNODC Afghanistan Opium Survey, 2006, Vienna.

29. U.S. State Department's International Narcotics Control Strategy Report, 2006, Washington, D.C., March 1, 2006.

30. Editorial, "The Poppies of Afghanistan," *The New York Times*, May 27, 2005.

31. Eurasia Insight, "Arrest of Tajikistan's Drug Czar Stirs Political Tension in Dushanbe," EurasiaNet.org, August 9, 2004.

32. Rustem Safranov, "Turkmenistan's Niyazov Implicated in Drug Smuggling," EurasiaNet, March 29, 2002.

33. Robert Ponce, "Rising Heroin Abuse in Central Asia Raises Threat of Public Health Crisis," EurasiaNet, March 29, 2002.

34. IRIN (news service), "Bitter-Sweet Harvest: Afghanistan's New War," July 2004. See also Byrd and Ward, "Drugs and Development in Afghanistan."

35. State Department, International Narcotics Control Strategy Report 2006, Washington, D.C., March 1, 2006.

36. Three outstanding reports on the parliamentary elections are International Crisis Group, "Afghanistan Elections: Endgame or New Beginning?" Kabul, July 2005; Afghanistan Research and Evaluation Unit, "A Guide to Parliamentary Elections in Afghanistan," Kabul, August 2005; and Human Rights Watch, "Afghanistan on the Eve of Parliamentary Elections," Kabul, September 2005.

37. In September, Emma Bonino, a European Union commissioner and prominent human rights activist, led a large EU observer mission to monitor the elections and rounded on Karzai, saying that his marginalization of political parties had allowed warlords to stand and would not produce a democratic culture.

38. Those Taliban standing for the elections included Abdul Samad Khaksar, the former deputy interior minister, and three Taliban commanders: Rais al-Baghrani, Abdul Salam, alias Rocketi, and Abdul Hakim Mounib.

39. Just over half the electorate, or 6.6 million, voted. Some 41 percent of the voters were women and 59 percent were men.

40. Three hundred polling stations were excluded from the initial count on suspicion of fraud—sixty-two of them in the district of Paghman, outside Kabul, where the fundamentalist Abdul Rasul Sayyaf was contesting the polls, although he won his seat.

41. Ahmed Rashid, "It Takes Two Hands to Clap," *YaleGlobal Online*, October 6, 2005.

42. At the NATO meeting in Berlin on September 13, Rumsfeld had also urged NATO countries to drop their caveats or restrictions on their troops deployed in Kabul.

43. UN and European Union assessments of the makeup of parliament, private cables, Kabul, October 2005.

44. Four senior Taliban figures had accepted the amnesty in February: Abdul Hakim Mujahid, the former Taliban envoy to the UN; Arsallah Rahmani, the former deputy minister of higher education; Rahmatullah Wahidyar, the deputy minister for refugees; and Mullah Fawzi, the chargé d'affaires in Saudi Arabia. All four were from Paktika province.

45. Associated Press, "Commander Predicts Collapse of Taliban," Kabul, April 17, 2005.

46. Nick Meo, "The Taliban Rises Again for Fighting Season," *The Independent,* May 15, 2005.

47. Sarah Chayes explains his murder in great detail. See her *The Punishment of Virtue: Inside Afghanistan After the Taliban,* New York: Penguin Books, 2006. Khakrezwal was attending the funeral prayers for Maulvi Abdullah Fayaz, who had been killed by the Taliban on May 29 for organizing a meeting of one thousand mullahs that had stripped Mullah Omar of any religious authority.

48. The Joint Declaration of Strategic Partnership was signed on May 17, 2005, White House, Washington, D.C.

49. Michael Fletcher, "Bush Rebuffs Karzai Request on Troops," *The Washington Post,* May 24, 2005.

50. Fifty-twoAmerican soldiers were killed in 2004, forty-seven in 2003, and forty-three in 2002.

51. Al Jazeera, "Taliban Military Official Reveals Contacts with Iraq," Doha, July 13, 2005.

Chapter Sixteen. Who Lost Uzbekistan? Tyranny in Central Asia

1. David Cloud, "Pentagon's Fuel Deal Is Lesson in Risks of Graft-Prone Regions," *The New York Times,* November 14, 2005.

2. Agence France-Presse, "New Kyrgyz Leader Calls for Review of US Military Presence," Bishkek, July 12, 2005.

3. Eric Schmitt, "Rumsfeld Stop in Kyrgyzstan Aims to Keep Access to Base," *The New York Times,* July 26, 2005.

4. The Turkmen government passed a new law in December 2006 banning exiles from returning home to contest the presidential elections held in February 2007, which Berdymukhamedow won by a landslide, taking 89 percent of the votes cast.

5. In contrast, the average monthly wage was $55 in Kyrgyzstan and $120 in Kazakhstan.

6. For greater details on her holdings, see International Crisis Group, "Uzbekistan: Stagnation and Uncertainty," Brussels, August 22, 2007. See also Peter Baker, "Battle Royal," *The Washington Post,* April 13, 2004. Baker is one of the few journalists to have interviewed Gulnora Karimova. Also "Uzbekistan Offers Rich Pickings for Leader's Daughter," *Financial Times,* August 19, 2003.

7. International Crisis Group, "Uzbekistan."

8. Martha Brill Olcott, "In Uzbekistan, the Revolution Won't Be Pretty," *The Washington Post,* May 22, 2005.

9. "Karimov is thought to rely most heavily on the security services—the Ministry of Internal Affairs (MIA) and the National Security Service (usually known by its Russian initials, SNB)—to retain power. An uneasy balance existed between the two, but in the wake of Andijan massacre, the SNB emerged as the dominant force." International Crisis Group, "Uzbekistan."

10. Text of Secretary of Defense Donald Rumsfeld's remarks in Tashkent, U.S. em-

bassy, Islamabad, February 25, 2004. The United States had provided $220 million in 2002 as aid to Uzbekistan and $86 million in 2003.

11. "Uzbek Leader Seeks to Block Influx of Alien Ideologies," EurasiaNet.org, March 2, 2005. Karimov was addressing the Uzbek parliament.

12. Uzbekistan's gas output in 2004 was 60 billon cubic meters (bcm). However, it had no sizeable exports, and Russian companies wanted to buy Uzbek gas cheaply to feed it into the pool of gas that Russia sold to the European Union at a much higher price. Russia exported a total of 107 bcm to Europe in 2004, a 13 percent increase from 2003. Both Gazprom and Lukoil pledged to develop new gas fields in Uzbekistan and to increase production at old ones.

13. N. C. Aizenman, "In Uzbekistan Families Caught in a Nightmare," *The Washington Post,* May 18, 2005.

14. Steven Myers, "As Hundreds Flee, Violence Flares Anew at Uzbek Border," *The New York Times,* May 15, 2005.

15. Human Rights Watch, "Bullets Were Falling Like Rain," Moscow, June 7, 2005.

16. Jeffrey Smith, "US Opposes Calls at NATO for Probe of Uzbek Killings," *The Washington Post,* June 14, 2005. At a meeting of NATO defense ministers in Brussels, European countries pushed for NATO's support for the EU proposal of an independent investigation into the killings, but the U.S. delegates said they could not afford to lose the K2 base.

17. Germany refused to take a tough line against Uzbekistan after the Andijan massacre. After 9/11, Germany trained Uzbek officers, provided a munitions factory, and delivered arms and night-vision equipment to Uzbekistan. Germany was the third-largest contributor of aid to Uzbekistan, providing $300 million worth of assistance between 1992 and 2005. In December, Uzbek survivors of Andijan filed suit against the Uzbek interior minister, Zokirjon Almatov, who was in Germany seeking medical treatment. At the time of the massacre, he oversaw the special security forces that carried out the shootings. Berlin came under intense criticism for allowing Almatov to travel to Germany despite the EU ban on his entering Europe.

18. Basic pay for soldiers stood at $135 to $180 a month, compared with $40 a month for a bureaucrat.

Chapter Seventeen. The Taliban Offensive: Battling for Control of Afghanistan, 2006–2007

1. Victoria Burnett, "NATO May Take Prominent Role in Afghan Force," *Financial Times,* February 11, 2003.

2. Agence France-Presse, "NATO Chief in Parting Shot," Brussels, December 17, 2003.

3. Chris Marquis, "General Urges NATO to Send More Troops," *The New York Times,* January 27, 2004.

4. Interview with Paul Wolfowitz, deputy secretary of defense, Washington, D.C., February 19, 2004.

5. Reuters, "NATO Head Says Alliance Credibility on Brink," London, June 18, 2004.

6. Judy Dempsey, "Two Afghan Missions to Merge," *International Herald Tribune,* February 11, 2005.

7. Editorial, "The Sound of One Domino Falling," *The New York Times,* August 4, 2006.

8. Speech by Gen. James Jones heard by author at a NATO conference, Madrid, May

17, 2006. I met with Jones while his staff was decidedly nervous about his outspokenness on the caveats issue.

9. Roger Cohen, "Time for the Bundesmacht," *The New York Times,* October 25, 2007.

10. "Blair Has One Last Chance to Defy Bush: Chris Patten," *The Guardian,* January 9, 2007. For Carter's comments, see John Preston and Kate Melissa, "Compliant and Subservient: Carter's Explosive Critique of Tony Blair," *Sunday Telegraph,* August 27, 2006. Zbigniew Brzezinski, the national security advisor to President Carter, was equally scathing: "Too often Mr. Blair would emerge from meetings with Mr. Bush and give an eloquent rationale to the crude unilateralism that Bush had expressed in the meeting. In that sense Tony Blair did us all a great disservice." See Edward Luce, "Smooth-Talking Premier Gave Tongue-Tied President an Easy Ride," *The Financial Times,* May 11, 2007.

11. I was not surprised when Geoff Hoon, the former British defense secretary, echoed these same words, saying that Cheney exercised more power than the British had anticipated in comparison with Rumsfeld and Powell. "Sometimes Blair had made his point with the President [Bush], and I'd made my point with Don [Rumsfeld] and then Foreign Secretary Jack Straw had made his point with Colin [Powell], and the decision came out of a completely different place," Hoon said. Agence France-Presse, "Geoff Hoon Admits Poor Planning for Iraq Aftermath," London, May 2, 2007.

12. Speech by shadow defense secretary Liam Fox, Conservative Party Conference, October 4, 2006. He said the navy was now smaller than the French navy and the entire ninety-thousand-strong army could be seated in the new Wembley football stadium.

13. Thomas Harding, "5000 Troops Are to Be Sent to Afghanistan," *The Daily Telegraph,* January 27, 2006.

14. Agence France-Presse, "Reid Fears Taliban Comeback," Copenhagen, April 1, 2006.

15. A report drawn up by officers from the Sixteenth Air Assault Brigade gave a withering assessment of how insufficient troops and equipment were sent out, how the deployment was conducted too slowly, and how the entire operation suffered from "a lack of early political direction." Quoted in Daniel Dombey and Rachel Morajee, "UK to Send More Troops," *Financial Times,* July 10, 2006.

16. Reuters, "Canada's Help for Afghans Boosts Security," Kabul, March 14, 2006.

17. "Support Plummets for Afghan Mission," *Globe and Mail,* May 6, 2006.

18. Ahmed Rashid, "Intelligence Officers Widen the Net in Hunt for Taliban," *The Daily Telegraph,* June 29, 2006.

19. Christina Lamb, "Soldier Quits as Blundering Campaign Turns into Pointless War," *The Sunday Times,* September 10, 2006.

20. "Had the police been better trained, equipped and armed, they would have suffered less," said Ali Jalali. Ali Jalali, "The Future of Afghanistan," *Parameters,* Spring 2006. For figures of police dead, see International Crisis Group, "Reforming Afghan Police," Brussels, August 30, 2007.

21. James Glanz and David Rohde, "US Reports Fault in Training of Afghan Police," *The New York Times,* March 12, 2006.

22. The UN reported the status of these fourteen officers; see Tom Koenigs, "Briefing to the UN Security Council on Afghanistan," UN document, New York, July 26, 2006.

23. Henry Schuster, "The Taliban's Rules," CNN, June 12, 2006.

24. Dave Markland, "Operation Medusa: Fog of War, NATO's Failure and Afghanistan's Future," *ZNet,* February 5, 2007.

25. Matthew Fisher, "Top General Says Afghanistan Mission Unaffected by Political Furor," CanWest News Service, October 15, 2007.

26. Ahmed Rashid, "NATO's Top Brass Accuse Pakistan over Taliban Aid," *The Daily Telegraph,* October 6, 2006.

27. The figures are derived from UN Assistance Mission for Afghanistan statistics, Kabul, June 2006

28. Interview with Chris Alexander, Kabul, June 19, 2006.

29. United Nations, "Southern Region, Recommended Actions to Address Governance Issues," Kabul, September 2006.

30. David Cloud, "US Air Strikes Climb Sharply in Afghanistan," *The New York Times,* November 17, 2006.

31. Sami Yousufzai and Ron Moreau, "Suicide Offensive," *Newsweek,* April 16, 2007.

32. Reuters, "Taliban Say Hundreds of Suicide Attackers Ready," Spin Baldak, January 18, 2007.

33. I interviewed Saleh several times during the summer of 2006 and corroborated what he told me with NATO officers.

34. "Special Security Initiative of the Policy Action Group," papers presented to President Karzai at the meeting of the Policy Action Group, Kabul, July 9, 2006. The paper on the Taliban is called "Insurgency and Terrorism in Afghanistan. Who Is Fighting and Why?" and was prepared in June 2006.

35. Tom Koenigs, sixty-two, replaced Jean Arnault as head of UNAMA in Kabul in February 2006. Arnault had held the post from February 2004 to February 2005. Koenigs had headed UN peacekeeping operations in Kosovo and Guatemala and had worked at the German foreign office. He came from an illustrious Cologne banking family, but in 1973 he had given up his inheritance to Chilean resistance fighters and the Vietcong. He has been a member of the Green Party since 1983.

36. United Nations, "Report of the UN Secretary-General on the Situation in Afghanistan and Its Implications for Peace and Security," New York, September 2006.

37. All the quotes come from IWPR, "Afghans Bemused by Mixed Messages from Musharraf," Kabul, September 22, 2006. See also Reuters, "Pakistan Vows to Help Kabul Crush Taliban," Kabul, September 6, 2006.

38. Interview with senior U.S. diplomat, Islamabad, March 5, 2007.

39. Ahmed Rashid, "How to Turn the Tide in Afghanistan," *International Herald Tribune,* October 12, 2006.

40. David Montero, "Pakistan Faces a Less-Friendly US Congress," *The Christian Science Monitor,* January 29, 2007.

41. Anwar Iqbal, "Taliban Command Structure in FATA Alarms US," *Dawn,* December 27, 2006.

42. On November 4 the Dutch foreign minister Bernard Bot called for Pakistan to stop the Taliban from crossing into Uruzgan province, where 40 percent of them were coming in from Pakistan to attack Dutch troops. Two weeks later the Canadian foreign minister Peter MacKay called for Pakistan to arrest Taliban leaders based on its soil.

43. Center for Public Integrity, "Pakistan's Blank Check for US Military Aid after 9/11," Washington, D.C., March 27, 2007. See also RAND Corporation, "Securing Tyrant or Fostering Reform? U.S. Internal Security Assistance to Repressive and Transitioning Regimes," Washington, D.C., 2006.

44. Statement of John Negroponte to the Senate Select Committee on Intelligence, Washington, D.C., January 11, 2007.

45. Reuters, "World Underestimated the Potential for a Resurgent Taliban," Kabul, June 30, 2006.

46. Radio Free Liberty, "Kabul's Record Criticized at Brussels Forum," Brussels, April 28, 2007.

47. Colum Lynch, "UN Plans to Send Troops to East Timor," *The Washington Post,* June 14, 2006.

48. James Jones and Harlan Ullman, "What Is at Stake in Afghanistan," letter to *The Washington Post,* April 10, 2007.

Chapter Eighteen. Conclusion: The Death of an Icon and a Fragile Future

1. Quoted in Mark Danner, "Iraq: The War on the Imagination," *The New York Review of Books,* December 21, 2006.

2. Griff Witte and Emily Wax, "Bhutto's Last Day," *The Washington Post,* January 16, 2007.

3. Interview with President Hamid Karzai by the author at Davos, Switzerland, January 24, 2008.

4. Aziz Syed, "10 Fold Increase in Suicide Attacks," Islamabad, *Daily Times,* January 13, 2008.

5. Interior Ministry spokesman Brigadier Javed Iqbal Cheema told a press conference on the evening of December 28 that Bhutto had fatally cracked her head on the lever of the sunroof. He then released a telephone intercept of Baitullah Mahsud congratulating the leader of a suicide squad for carrying out the bombing. See Ahmed Rashid, "After Bhutto Death, Pakistan on Edge," *Yale Global,* January 1, 2008.

6. Fareed Zakaria, "Pakistanis Know I Can Be Tough," *Newsweek,* January 12, 2008.

7. Bureau report, "Suicide Bomber Identified," Islamabad, *The Post,* January 29, 2008.

8. British High Commission, Islamabad, "Scotland Yard Report into Assassination of Benazir Bhutto," press release, February 8, 2008.

9. Lt.-Gen. Karl Eikenberry's testimony was given at a hearing of the Senate Armed Services Committee, Washington, D.C., February 13, 2007. Text provided by U.S. Embassy, Islamabad.

10. Sheryl Gay Stolberg, "Pressing Allies, President Warns of Afghan Battle," Washington, D.C., *The New York Times,* February 16, 2007.

11. "West Must Match Pakistan's Efforts: Aurakzai," Peshawar, *Dawn,* February 16, 2007.

12. Mark Mazzetti and David Sanger, "Bush Aides See Failure in Fight with al Qaeda in Pakistan," *The New York Times,* July 17, 2007.

13. Townsend's interview with Chris Wallace, *Fox News Sunday,* Washington, D.C., July 22, 2007.

14. George Tenet, the CIA director, claimed in February 2003 that more than one third of al Qaeda had been killed or captured. In May 2003, President Bush increased that number to "about half." Karen De Young and Walter Pincus, "Safe Haven in Pakistan Is Seen as Challenging Counterterrorism Efforts," *The Washington Post,* July 18, 2007.

15. Reuters, "Al Qaeda Is Targeting Germany for Attacks," Berlin, July 21, 2007.

16. Elaine Sciolino, "Terror Threat from Pakistan Said to Expand," *The New York Times,* February 10, 2008.

17. Al Jazeera, Baitullah Mahsud's first TV interview in Pushtu, translation provided

by Gretchen Peters of ABC News, "Slaves to US, We Will Destroy White House, New York and London," January 27, 2008.

18. The Pakistan Army Act of 1952 was amended by ordinance on November 10, 2007.

19. James Naughtie, interview with Benazir Bhutto, BBC Radio 4, November 13, 2007.

20. AP, "Bush Sees Positive Signs in Pakistan," Crawford, Texas, November 10, 2007.

21. Khalid Hasan, "Clinton and Obama Oppose Emergency Rule in Pakistan," *The Daily Times,* November 7, 2007.

22. Ann Scott Tyson, "US to Step Up Training of Pakistanis," *The Washington Post,* January 24, 2008.

23. AP, "Musharraf: Pakistan Is Not Hunting Osama," Paris, January 23, 2008.

24. See Hasan-Askari Rizvi, "Towards a Solution of the Present Crisis," Lahore, *Daily Times,* June 17, 2007.

25. Ayesha Siddiqa, *Military Inc.: Inside Pakistan's Military Economy,* London: Pluto Press, 2007,

26. Ayesha Siddiqa, "The New Land Barons," *Newsline* magazine, July 2006.

27. Military officers worked in every sector, including communications, education, diplomacy, water and electricity management, information, post office, jails, local bodies, think tanks, industrial production, shipping, minority affairs, population welfare, health care, agriculture, railways, highways, housing, labor and manpower, social and women's development, law and justice, and subsectors of sports ranging from cricket to hockey. Nasir Iqbal, "1,027 Civilian Posts Occupied by Servicemen," *Dawn,* October 3, 2003.

28. The meeting with President Musharraf took place in Islamabad on August 11, 2005.

29. Murray Brewsyer, "Dutch Tally Cost of Afghanistan," Amsterdam, *Globe and Mail,* October 28, 2007.

30. Ann Scott Tyson, "Pentagon Critical of NATO Allies," *The Washington Post,* December 12, 2007.

31. See International Crisis Group, "Afghanistan: The Need for International Resolve," Brussels, February 6, 2008.

32. Tyson, "Pentagon Critical of NATO Allies."

33. William Byrd, "Responding to Afghanistan's Development Challenge," World Bank, Washington, D.C., October 2007.

34. See also Anthony Cordesman, "The Missing Metrics of Progress in Afghanistan and Pakistan," Center for Strategic and International Studies, paper presented at a conference on Afghanistan in Ottawa attended by the author, December 10, 2007. William Byrd of the World Bank was also at the conference.

35. Stephen Blank, "Afghanistan's Energy Future," EurasiaNet.org, August 3, 2006.

36. Agence France-Presse, "Afghanistan Trailing Badly on Development," Kabul, November 18, 2007. The report for Afghanistan was drawn up by the Centre for Policy and Human Development at Kabul University, supported by the United Nations Development Programme.

37. Joseph Stiglitz and Linda Bilmes, "The Three Trillion Dollar War," London, *The Times,* February 23, 2008.

38. Michael Gordon, "New Weight in Army Manual on Stabilization," *The New York Times,* February 8, 2008.

39. Lakhdar Brahimi, speech to the German Association of the UN, Munich, July 8, 2004. Text provided by the author.

40. "Rice Admits Mistakes in Iraqi Reconstruction," Reuters, March 13, 2008.

41. For the elaboration of some of these ideas, see Hussain Haqqani, "Democracy in Pakistan," *Yale Global,* February 22, 2008.

SUGGESTED READING

Books

Abrams, Dennis. *Hamid Karzai*. Modern World Leaders. New York: Chelsea House, 2007.

Ahmad, Ishtiaq. *Gulbuddin Hekmatyar: An Afghan Trail from Jihad to Terrorism*. Lahore: Society for Tolerance and Education, 2004.

Allen, Charles. *God's Terrorists: The Wahhabi Cult and the Hidden Roots of Modern Jihad*. London: Abacus, 2006.

Atwan, Abdel Bari. *The Secret History of al Qaeda*. London: Saqi Books, 2006.

Baer, Robert. *See No Evil: The True Story of a Ground Soldier in the CIA's War on Terrorism*. New York: Crown, 2002.

Banerjee, Indranil, ed. *India and Central Asia*. London: Brunel Academic Publishers, 2004.

Bengelsdorf, Carollee, Margaret Cerullo, and Yogesh Chandrani. *The Selected Writings of Eqbal Ahmad*. Pakistan: Oxford University Press, 2006.

Benjamin, Daniel, and Steven Simon. *The Age of Sacred Terror*. New York: Random House, 2002.

———. *The Next Attack: The Failure of the War on Terror and a Strategy for Getting It Right*. New York: Times Books, 2005.

Berntsen, Gary, and Ralph Pezzullo. *Jawbreaker: The Attack on Bin Laden and al Qaeda—A Personal Account by the CIA's Key Field Commander*. New York: Crown, 2005.

Blumenthal, Sidney. *How Bush Rules: Chronicles of a Radical Regime*. Princeton, N.J.: Princeton University Press, 2006.

Brzezinski, Zbigniew. *The Choice: Global Domination or Global Leadership*. New York: Basic Books, 2004.

Burke, Jason. *On the Road to Kandahar: Travels Through Conflict in the Islamic World*. London: Allen Lane Books, 2006.

Chayes, Sarah. *The Punishment of Virtue: Inside Afghanistan After the Taliban*. New York: The Penguin Press, 2006.

Chomsky, Noam. *Failed States: The Abuse of Power and the Assault on Democracy*. New York: Metropolitan Books, 2006.

Clarke, Richard A. *Against All Enemies: Inside America's War on Terror*. New York: Free Press, 2004.

Cohen, Stephen Philip. *The Idea of Pakistan*. Washington, D.C.: Brookings Institution, 2004.

Coll, Steve. *Ghost Wars: The Secret History of the CIA, Afghanistan, and Bin Laden from the Soviet Invasion to September 10, 2001*. New York: Penguin Press, 2004.

Corera, Gordon. *Shopping for Bombs: Nuclear Proliferation, Global Insecurity, and the Rise and Fall of the A. Q. Khan Network*. Oxford: Oxford University Press, 2006.

Darwin, John. *After Tamerlane: The Global History of Empire Since 1405*. London: Allen Lane, 2007.

DeYoung, Karen. *Soldier: The Life of Colin Powell*. New York: Knopf, 2006.

Dobbins, James, et al. *America's Role in Nation Building: From Germany to Iraq*. Washington, D.C.: RAND, 2003.

Dorronsoro, Gilles. *Revolution Unending: Afghanistan, 1979 to the Present.* London: Hurst and Company, 2005.

Einfeld, Jann. *The History of Nations: Pakistan.* Chicago: Greenhaven Press, 2004.

Forsyth, Frederick. *The Afghan.* London: Corgi Books, 2006.

Fouda, Yosri, and Nick Fielding. *Masterminds of Terror: The Truth Behind the Most Devastating Terrorist Attack the World Has Ever Seen.* London: Mainstream Publishing, 2003.

Franks, Gen. Tommy, with Malcolm McConnell. *American Soldier.* New York: Regan Books, 2004.

Friedman, George. *America's Secret War: Inside the Hidden Worldwide Struggle Between America and Its Enemies.* New York: Little, Brown, 2004.

Fukuyama, Francis. *After the Neocons: America at the Crossroads.* London: Profile Books, 2006.

————. *State-Building: Governance and World Order in the 21st Century.* London: Profile Books, 2004.

Gannon, Kathy. *I is for Infidel: From Holy War to Holy Terror—Eighteen Years Inside Afghanistan.* New York: Public Affairs, 2005.

Haqqani, Hussain. *Pakistan: Between Mosque and Military.* Washington, D.C.: Carnegie Endowment for International Peace, 2005.

Hersh, Seymour. *Chain of Command: The Road from 9/11 to Abu Ghraib.* New York: HarperCollins, 2004.

Hussain, Zahid. *Frontline Pakistan: The Struggle with Militant Islam.* London: I. B. Tauris, 2007.

Jaffrelot, Christophe, ed. *Pakistan: Nationalism Without a Nation?* London: Zed Books, 2002.

Johnson, Chalmers. *The Sorrows of Empire: Militarism, Secrecy, and the End of the Republic.* New York: Metropolitan Books, 2004.

Jones, Ann. *Kabul in Winter: Life Without Peace in Afghanistan.* New York: Metropolitan Books, 2006.

Kampfner, John. *Blair's Wars.* London: The Free Press, 2003.

Kaplan, Robert D. *Imperial Grunts: On the Ground with the American Military, from Mongolia to the Philippines to Iraq and Beyond.* New York: Random House, 2005.

Kassir, Samir. *Being Arab.* London: Verso, 2006.

Kepel, Gilles. *The War for Muslim Minds: Islam and the West.* Cambridge, Mass.: Belknap Press of Harvard University, 2004.

Khattak, Mohammed Aslam Khan. *A Pathan Odyssey.* Karachi: Oxford University Press, 2004.

Khosrokhavar, Farhad. *Suicide Bombers: Allah's New Martyrs.* London: Pluto Press, 2005.

Kinzer, Stephen. *Overthrow: America's Century of Regime Change from Hawaii to Iraq.* New York: Times Books, 2006.

Kolhatkar, Sonali, and James Ingalls. *Bleeding Afghanistan: Washington, Warlords, and the Propaganda of Silence.* New York: Seven Stories Press, 2006.

Kumar, Radha. *Making Peace with Partition.* New Delhi: Penguin, 2005.

Leach, Hugh, with Susan Maria Farrington. *Strolling About on the Roof of the World: The First Hundred Years of the Royal Society for Asian Affairs.* London: Routledge Curzon, 2003.

Mabry, Marcus. *Twice as Good: Condoleezza Rice and Her Path to Power.* New York: Modern Times, 2007.

MacDonald, David. *Drugs in Afghanistan: Opium, Outlaws, and Scorpion Tales.* London: Pluto Press, 2007.

Mackey, Chris, and Greg Miller. *The Interrogators: Inside the Secret War Against Al Qaeda.* London: John Murray, 2004.

Maley, William. *Rescuing Afghanistan.* London: Hurst and Co., 2006.

Meyer, Christopher. *DC Confidential: The Controversial Memoirs of Britain's Ambassador to the U.S. at the Time of 9/11 and the Run-up to the Iraq War.* London: Weidenfeld & Nicolson, 2005.

Moore, Robin. *The Hunt for Bin Laden: Task Force Dagger.* New York: Random House, 2003.

Musharraf, Pervez. *In the Line of Fire: A Memoir.* New York: Simon & Schuster, 2006.

Naylor, Sean. *Not a Good Day to Die: The Untold Story of Operation Anaconda.* London: Penguin/Michael Joseph, 2005.

Noman, Omar. *The Political Economy of Pakistan, 1947–85.* London: Kegan Paul International, 1988.

Odom, William E., and Robert Dujarric. *America's Inadvertent Empire.* New Haven, Conn.: Yale University Press, 2004.

Olcott, Martha Brill. *Central Asia's Second Chance.* Washington, D.C.: Carnegie Endowment for International Peace, 2005.

Packer, George. *The Assassins' Gate: America in Iraq.* New York: Farrar, Straus and Giroux, 2005.

Pearl, Mariane, with Sarah Crichton. *A Mighty Heart: The Brave Life and Death of My Husband, Danny Pearl.* London: Virago Press, 2003.

Pressfield, Steven. *The Afghan Campaign: A Novel.* New York: Doubleday, 2006.

Prestowitz, Clyde. *Rogue Nation: American Unilateralism and the Failure of Good Intentions.* New York: Basic Books, 2003.

Priest, Dana. *The Mission: Waging War and Keeping Peace with America's Military.* New York: W. W. Norton, 2003.

Rana, Muhammad Amir. *A to Z of Jehadi Organizations in Pakistan.* Lahore: Mashal Books, 2004.

Rand, Robert. *Tamerlane's Children: Dispatches from Contemporary Uzbekistan.* Oxford: Oneworld, 2006.

Randal, Jonathan. *Osama: The Making of a Terrorist.* New York: Knopf, 2004.

Rashid, Ahmed. *Jihad: The Rise of Militant Islam in Central Asia.* New Haven, Conn.: Yale University Press, 2002.

———. *The Resurgence of Central Asia: Islam or Nationalism?* London: Zed Books, 1994.

———. *Taliban: Militant Islam, Oil and Fundamentalism in Central Asia.* New Haven, Conn.: Yale University Press, 2000.

Ratner, Michael, and Ellen Ray. *Guantánamo: What the World Should Know.* Moreton, Eng.: Arris Books, 2004.

Rehman, Shahid ur. *Pakistan: Sovereignty Lost.* Islamabad: Mr. Books, 2006.

Ricks, Thomas E. *Fiasco: The American Military Adventure in Iraq.* New York: Penguin Press, 2006.

Risen, James. *State of War: The Secret History of the CIA and the Bush Administration.* New York: Free Press, 2006.

Robinson, Linda. *Masters of Chaos: The Secret History of the Special Forces.* New York: Public Affairs, 2004.

Rose, David. *Guantánamo: America's War on Human Rights.* London: The New Press, 2004.

Rubin, Barnett R. *Afghanistan's Uncertain Transition from Turmoil to Normalcy.* New York: Council on Foreign Relations, March 2006.

Saikal, Amin. *Modern Afghanistan: A History of Struggle and Survival.* London: I. B. Tauris, 2004.

Sattar, Abdul. *Pakistan's Foreign Policy, 1947–2005: A Concise History.* Karachi: Oxford University Press, 2007.

Scheuer, Michael. *Imperial Hubris: Why the West Is Losing the War on Terror.* Washington, D.C.: Brassey's Inc., 2004.

Schroen, Gary C. *First In: An Insider's Account of How the CIA Spearheaded the War on Terror in Afghanistan.* New York: Ballantine Books, 2005.

Shah, Zulfiqar. *Sectarian Violence in Karachi (1994–2002).* Lahore, Pakistan: Human Rights Commission of Pakistan, 2004.

Siddiqa, Ayesha. *Military, Inc.: Inside Pakistan's Military Economy.* London: Pluto Press, 2007.

Simons, Thomas W., Jr. *Islam in a Globalizing World.* Palo Alto, Calif.: Stanford University Press, 2003.

Simpson, William. *The Prince: The Secret Story of the World's Most Intriguing Royal, Prince Bandar bin Sultan.* New York: Regan Books, 2006.

Singh, Jaswant. *A Call to Honour: In Service of Emergent India.* New Delhi: Rupa and Co., 2006.

Smith, Gen. Sir Rupert. *The Utility of Force: The Art of War in the Modern World.* London: Allen Lane, 2005.

Suskind, Ron. *The One Percent Doctrine: Deep Inside America's Pursuit of Its Enemies Since 9/11.* New York: Simon & Schuster, 2006.

Tenet, George. *At the Center of the Storm: My Years at the CIA.* London: HarperPress, 2007.

Thompson, Paul. *The Terror Timeline: Year by Year, Day by Day, Minute by Minute.* New York: Regan Books, 2004.

Traub, James. *The Best Intentions: Kofi Annan and the UN in the Era of American World Power.* New York: Farrar, Straus & Giroux, 2006.

Unger, Craig. *House of Bush, House of Saud: The Secret Relationship Between the World's Two Most Powerful Dynasties.* London: Gibson Square Books, 2004.

Warde, Ibrahim. *The Price of Fear: The Truth Behind the Financial War on Terror.* London: I. B. Tauris, 2007.

Whitlock, Monica. *Land Beyond the River: The Untold Story of Central Asia.* New York: St. Martin's Press, 2002.

Williams, Paul L. *Osama's Revenge: The Next 9/11.* New Delhi: Viva Books, 2005.

Woodward, Bob. *Bush at War.* New York: Simon & Schuster, 2002.

———. *Plan of Attack.* New York: Simon & Schuster, 2004.

———. *State of Denial: Bush at War, Part III.* New York: Simon & Schuster, 2006.

Wright, Lawrence. *The Looming Tower: Al-Qaeda and the Road to 9/11.* New York: Knopf, 2006.

Zahab, Mariam Abou, and Olivier Roy. *Islamist Networks: The Afghan-Pakistan Connection.* London: Hurst and Co., 2004.

Reports

The 9/11 Commission Report: Final Report of the National Commission on Terrorist Attacks upon the United States. New York: W. W. Norton, 2004.

Report of the Defense Science Board Task Force on Strategic Communication. Department of Defense. Washington, D.C., September 2004.

Reports from the International Crisis Group, the United Nations, the UN Office on Drugs and Crime, the United States Institute of Peace, the Brookings Institution, the Council on Foreign Relations.

Securing Tyrants or Fostering Reform? U.S. Internal Security Assistance to Repressive and Transitioning Regimes. RAND Corporation. Washington, D.C., 2006.

Media

Pakistani newspapers: *Daily Times, Dawn, The Nation, The News, The Post*
Pakistani magazines: *Friday Times, Herald, Newsline*
International publications: *The Daily Telegraph, Der Spiegel* (English edition), *Financial Times, The Guardian, International Herald Tribune, Le Monde, Los Angeles Times, The New York Times, The Times* (London), *The Wall Street Journal, The Washington Post.*
Press agencies: Agence France-Presse, Associated Press, Reuters.
Radio and television: BBC, Radio Free Liberty, Voice of America.

Map Sources

Maps are by Jeffrey L. Ward, drawing on the following sources:

"Countries and Cities of Central Asia" (pp. xvi–xvii), after John Manley et al., report of the Independent Panel on Canada's Future Role in Afghanistan, Canada: Minister of Public Works and Government Services, 2008, p. 44; Ann Peters, ed., *Peters Atlas of the World,* New York: Harper & Row, 1990.

"Ethnic Distribution Within Pakistan and Afghanistan" (p. xviii), after Anthony H. Cordesman, "The Afghan-Pakistan War: A Status Report," Washington, D.C.: Center for Strategic and International Studies, 2007; "An Ethnic Patchwork," *The Washington Post,* 2008, based on CIA, www.achrweb.org; Manley, report of the Independent Panel on Canada's Future Role in Afghanistan, p. 41.

"Afghan Provinces and Federally Administered Tribal Areas" (p. xix), after Kamran Bokhari, "The Jihadist Insurgency in Pakistan," Stratfor Strategic Forecasting, 2008; Manley, report of the Independent Panel on Canada's Future Role in Afghanistan, p. 42.

"NATO Deployment and Provincial Reconstruction Team Locations in Afghanistan, 2007" (p. xx) after International Institute for Strategic Studies, "Strategic Survey 2007: The Annual Review of World Affairs," Routledge, p. xiv; Manley, report of the Independent Panel on Canada's Future Role in Afghanistan, p. 43.

"Opium Poppy Cultivation in Afghanistan, 2007" (p. xxi), after International Institute for Strategic Studies, "Strategic Survey 2007: The Annual Review of World Affairs," Routledge, p. xv.

"Military Offensives Launched by the Taliban in Pakistan and Afghanistan, 2007–2008" (p. xxii), after Seth E. Jones, "Pakistan's Dangerous Game," *Survival* 49:1 (2007), p. 20; Ashley J. Tellis, *Pakistan and the War on Terror,* Carnegie Endowment, 2008, p. 8.

INDEX

Abdali, Ahmad Shah, 7, 129

Abdullah, Abdullah, 22, 101–2, 139, 241, 261

Abdul Rehman, king of Afghanistan, 8

Abe, Shinzo, 394

Abizaid, John, 334, 344

Abu Ghraib prison, lvii, 299–300, 301, 302, 303, 307, 312–13

"accelerated success," 187–91, 193, 195, 202–3

Afghan Assistance Coordination Authority (AACA), 178, 180

Afghanistan, 3–23, 125–44, 171–218, 240–61, 317–37, 349–73, 383, 393–400, 403

  agriculture of, liv, 6, 76, 82, 126, 172, 174–75, 178, 183–84, 192, 317–22, 323, 325

  army of, 129, 143, 178–79, 190, 197, 201–3, 204, 205–8, 209, 210, 213, 248, 258–59, 303, 355, 362

  banking system of, 177–78, 184, 203, 208

  borders, 8, 9, 18, 28, 32, 34, 61, 66, 68, 70, 76, 77–78, 90, 98–100, 116–17, 125–26, 127, 131, 147–48, 166, 192–93, 202, 221–23, 228–29, 240–43, 248, 249–52, 259, 265–87, 355, 371, 372

  British relations with, xi, 4–5, 8, 20, 23, 61, 63, 132, 135, 136, 142, 179, 196, 197, 199, 304–5, 321, 323, 324, 326–27, 350, 353, 354, 355, 356–60, 365, 366, 371, 372, 373

  budget of, 186–87

  George W. Bush's policies on, xlii, xliv–lviii, 27–31, 56–60, 132–38, 172, 173, 176, 182, 183, 185–91, 193, 194, 195, 277–78, 334–35, 336, 356, 371–72

  business sector in, 192–93, 249, 258

  census of (1979), 256

  civil war in, 12–13, 14, 15, 17, 39, 53–54, 100–101, 127, 143, 171, 192, 214, 244, 319, 350

  communist regime of, 9–10, 126, 138, 206–7, 213, 333

  Constitutional Commission for, 211–12

  Constitutional Loya Jirga (CLJ) of, 212–18, 247, 251, 255

  constitution of (1923), 212

  constitution of (1964), 104, 138, 211, 212

  constitution of (2002), 211–18, 261

  corruption in, 63–64, 93, 161–68, 175–76, 180–81, 191, 204, 215–16, 320–21, 323, 324, 325–30, 333, 334, 336, 355, 362–63, 365, 399

  crime rate in, 101, 128, 197, 204, 215, 323, 362–63, 365

  currency of, 64, 178, 179, 184, 208

  customs revenue for, 127, 131, 186–87, 193, 210

  Defense Ministry of, 201–3, 206–8, 209, 251–16

  democracy in, 7, 63–64, 67, 69, 75, 104, 138–42, 141, 161–68, 188, 203–4, 211–18, 253–61, 332–35, 351

  drought in, 172, 192, 325

  economy of, 11, 18–19, 55–56, 82, 129–30, 131, 133, 171–95, 196, 202–3, 208, 249, 258, 319–20, 325, 326, 329–30, 399–400

  education in, 130, 140, 172, 177, 182–83, 190–91, 199, 203, 363, 367–68

  electricity supplies of, 178, 186, 191, 193, 355

  European relations of, 134, 137–38, 140, 143, 177, 179, 181, 186, 189–90, 197, 200–201, 202, 210, 254, 255, 257, 327, 329, 330, 334, 349–73

  as "failed state," xlii, xliv, 8–9, 177, 181, 194–97, 203–4, 296, 373

  famine in, 76, 172, 174, 178

  Finance Ministry of, 179–81, 186–87, 191, 324

  foreign aid to, xliv, liv–lv, 8–10, 11, 18–19, 33, 76, 80, 82, 95, 98, 128, 135–36, 137, 171–95, 199, 213, 245–46, 247, 251, 252, 317–18, 319, 323, 328, 329, 336, 354, 364, 372–73

  foreign investment in, 181–82

  foreign trade of, 192–93, 249, 258

  geography of, 6–7, 192

Afghanistan (*cont.*)
  government of, liii–liv, 8, 9–10, 11, 22,
    73–76, 78, 80, 81, 83, 94, 95–96, 101–
    2, 127, 129–30, 134–35, 137, 138–44,
    176–81, 182, 183, 184, 185–87, 190,
    194, 197, 198, 203–4, 207–8, 219,
    244, 248, 251, 253–61, 268, 306,
    316, 325, 326–30, 332–35, 355,
    357, 361–62, 364, 365, 366, 369,
    372–73
  gross domestic product (GNP) of, 203,
    329
  health care in, 172, 185, 190–91, 245–46,
    325
  heroin production in, xxxviii, xlii, liv,
    19, 20, 64, 127, 129, 131, 167, 175,
    179, 184, 193–94, 197, 200, 204,
    205, 209, 218, 282, 317–32, 333,
    334, 335, 354, 355, 356, 357, 365,
    372, 383, 396
  history of, 6–23, 129, 212, 267
  human rights abuses in, 12–13, 15, 18–
    19, 93–95, 132, 133, 140, 164–65,
    212–13, 214–15, 293–316, 334, 336
  income levels in, 131, 191, 258
  India's relations with, 20, 25, 110, 124,
    192, 206, 221, 229, 248–49, 283, 286,
    369
  infrastructure of, 133, 135–36, 136, 171,
    175, 176–77, 178, 182, 183, 184–86,
    189–91, 192, 193, 247, 248, 321–22,
    351, 354, 372–73
  intelligence services of, 12, 134, 206, 223,
    306–7, 324, 327 359, 360–61, 364,
    366–71
  interim government of, 95–96, 129–30,
    134–35, 137, 138–44
  Interior Ministry of, 204, 324, 327–28
  international involvement in, xxxix, xl,
    lvi, 4–5, 11, 18–21, 22, 53–56, 65–66,
    101–6, 132–33, 139, 140, 144, 176–78,
    189–90, 196, 202, 203–5, 212, 213,
    247–48, 251, 253–61, 306, 317–18,
    320, 322, 324, 328, 329, 355, 371–73
  International Security Assistance Force
    (ISAF) in, 132–33, 134, 140, 183,
    197–98, 199, 200–202, 206, 210, 213,
    215, 257, 258–59, 260, 306, 349–53,
    356
  Iranian relations of, 25, 55, 125–26, 127,
    187, 192, 193, 206
  Iraq compared with, xlix, lv, lvi–lvii,
    190, 197, 200, 358
  irrigation in, 174, 321, 323

  Islamic fundamentalism in, 9, 11, 13–23,
    25, 67, 68, 69, 126, 138, 211, 212–16,
    217, 255–58, 268, 333–34, 336
  as Islamic Republic of Afghanistan, 11,
    212–13
  jihadism in, 213, 214, 216, 255–58,
    336
  justice system of, 74, 179, 184, 197, 204,
    215, 216, 258, 293, 306–7, 324, 351
  languages of, 5, 6, 215, 216, 217, 300
  leadership of, 4–6, 7, 13–14, 19–22, 71–
    74, 81, 87–88, 101–2; *see also specific
    leaders*
  literacy rate in, 183, 203
  living standards in, 129–30, 131, 191–92,
    195, 258, 330
  Loya Jirga (LJ) of, 7, 13, 14, 20, 72, 104,
    127, 138–42, 179, 187, 201, 212–18,
    221, 247, 251, 255, 307, 334
  media coverage of, xlii–xliii, liv, 10–11,
    15, 126–27, 128, 135, 139, 140, 184,
    190, 217, 270, 327, 330
  Meshrano Jirga (House of Elders) of,
    212, 333
  militias disarmed in, 179, 201, 202, 203,
    209–11, 215, 247, 254, 255, 257, 327–
    28, 334, 354
  monarchy of, 4, 7, 8, 20, 21, 50, 55, 71–72,
    74, 75, 76–77, 81, 83, 87–88, 104,
    126, 138, 139–41, 142, 211, 212, 213,
    267
  Mujahedin fighters in, 5, 6, 9–12, 13, 38–
    39, 40, 78, 98, 132, 188, 226, 244, 267,
    283, 319, 333
  Musharraf's policies on, 22–23, 47,
    52–53, 57, 110, 248–49, 277–78,
    369
  nation building in, li, liii–liv, 8, 55–56,
    58, 63–64, 74–75, 129–31, 133, 137,
    146, 172–74, 178, 182, 194–97, 203,
    209–11, 317–18, 336, 365, 373
  NATO deployment in, 327, 329, 330,
    334, 349–73, 393–400
  natural resources of, 187, 188–89, 190
  Northern Alliance (NA) in, xlv, 14, 17,
    19, 20–22, 29, 30, 53–54, 55, 56, 57–
    58, 60, 110, 139, 192, 206, 208, 209,
    212, 214, 215, 216, 221, 251, 258, 261,
    306, 320–21, 327, 335, 350, 362
  Pakistan's relations with, 3, 9, 10, 11, 21,
    22–23, 38–39, 41, 46, 47, 52–53, 54,
    105, 110, 182, 192–93, 206, 219, 228–
    29, 244, 248–49, 259, 265–87, 335,
    369

parliamentary elections of (2005), 104, 141, 188, 193, 254–55, 327, 329, 332–35

parliament of, 104, 141, 188, 193, 212–18, 254, 255, 327, 329, 332–35

Pashtun tribes of, 4–6, 7, 8, 11, 12, 14, 16–17, 20, 21, 25, 34, 50, 55, 256, 265–67, 322, 326, 362–63, 365

peacekeeping efforts in, liii–liv, 132–33, 134, 135, 139, 172–73, 198–201, 209–11, 349–73

per capita income of, 191, 258

police force of, 135, 142, 179, 197, 202, 203–8, 248, 258, 322, 324, 328, 329, 355, 361

political factions in, 9, 12, 18, 71–72, 81, 95–96, 101–6, 127–28, 138–42, 207–8, 212–18, 254–61, 332–35

population of, 256, 333

poverty in, 129–30, 191–92, 195, 330

presidential elections of (2004), 104, 141, 188, 190, 193, 210, 247, 253–61, 332, 334, 352

prime minister of, 212, 216–17

private contractors in, 175–76, 177, 180–81, 184–86, 190–91, 248, 304

reconstruction of, 11, 18–19, 55–56, 63–64, 74–75, 127, 132–38, 141, 143–44, 171–97, 198, 200, 202–3, 217–18, 248–49, 251, 255–56, 258, 261, 321–23, 325, 329–30, 332, 334, 351, 354, 355, 356, 359, 364, 365, 367–68, 372–73

refugees from, 5, 6, 10, 11, 12–15, 19–20, 71–72, 76, 80, 125, 129, 130, 146, 172, 175, 176, 178, 183–84, 191, 193, 215, 221–22, 242, 243, 283, 361, 366, 367

road network of, 175, 176, 178, 182, 185–86, 190, 192, 193, 247, 248

Russian relations of, 8, 20, 25, 53–54, 128, 206–7, 208, 331

security situation in, 133, 194–218, 243–61, 349–73

Sharia (Islamic law) in, 13, 14, 212–13, 214, 216, 217, 362–63

Soviet invasion of, 5, 6, 8–11, 12, 13, 15, 25, 33, 38–39, 53, 61, 69, 71, 72, 78, 87, 95, 98, 126, 146–47, 162, 171, 179, 196, 207, 214, 226, 267, 319, 366

Supreme Council of, 74, 184, 215, 216

Taliban government of, *see* Taliban

taxation in, 179, 181, 319–20

tribes of, 3–8, 12, 34, 62, 68, 73–74, 81, 87, 94–95, 105, 128–29, 136, 138–42, 201–2, 214–17, 326, 332–35, 365; *see also specific tribes*

UN postwar presence in, 171–72, 176, 177, 179, 181–83, 200, 202, 203, 208, 209, 213, 229, 247–48, 253, 255, 256, 259, 260, 261, 303, 324, 325, 326, 332–33, 350, 354, 355, 364–65, 393–94

U.S. embassy in, 127, 129–30, 135, 185, 194, 209, 361, 366

U.S. foreign aid to, xliv, liv–lv, 8–10, 33, 135–36, 137, 171–95

U.S. postwar military forces in, xli, xlviii, lvii, 38–39, 125, 127, 173, 229, 245, 246, 248, 252–53, 269–70, 271, 276, 277, 279–80, 323, 324–26, 334–35, 336, 349, 351, 352–53, 358–59, 360, 365

U.S. relations with, xliv, liv–lv, 4–5, 8–10, 11, 15, 16, 17, 20, 21, 24–31, 33, 53–54, 55, 56–60, 125–44, 171–218, 219, 277–78, 322–26, 334–35, 336, 356, 361–62, 365, 366–72

vice president of, 257–58, 261

voter registration in, 247, 253–61, 332–35, 354

warlords in, xli, liv, 12–13, 14, 106, 125–44, 175, 177, 186–87, 189, 196–97, 199, 201, 202, 204, 205, 207–11, 213–16, 218, 247, 251, 254–58, 261, 307, 320–21, 327–28, 333, 334, 335, 354, 362, *see also specific warlords*

water supplies for, 126, 172, 174, 191, 192, 318, 321, 323, 325

Wolesi Jirga (House of People) of, 212, 327, 333

women in, 94, 100–101, 102, 126, 130, 135, 138, 140, 141, 172, 182–83, 212, 215, 217, 240, 256–57, 258, 260, 261, 323, 330, 333, 335, 363

see also specific provinces and towns

Afghanistan Compact (2006), 355, 365, 397

Afghanistan Liaison Team ("Jawbreaker" team), 63, 74

Afghan National Army (ANA), 129, 143, 178, 190, 197, 201–3, 204, 205–8, 209, 210, 213, 248, 258–59, 303, 355, 362, 396

Afghan National Police (ANP), 135, 142, 179, 197, 202, 203–8, 248, 258, 322, 324, 328, 329, 355, 361

Afghan-UN Joint Election Management
    Board (JEMB), 332–33
Afghan war, 61–106
    air support in, 32, 70–71, 73, 76, 78–82,
        84, 89, 91, 96, 98, 142, 361, 365–66
    al Qaeda forces in, xliii, xlv, 56, 61, 63–
        64, 65, 72, 73, 77, 80, 90–92, 98–100,
        125–26
    bombing campaigns in, 32, 73, 76, 78–82,
        84, 91, 98, 361, 365–66
    Bonn Agreement on, 95–96, 101–6, 125,
        132, 138, 139, 143, 196, 210, 211, 247,
        254, 350, 355
    British forces in, xi, 4–5, 8, 20, 23, 61, 63,
        65–66, 74, 79, 80, 97, 99, 297–98
    George W. Bush's policies on, 61–65, 70,
        74, 75, 78, 80, 83, 86, 87, 88, 91, 92,
        93, 99
    cavalry charges in, 81–82, 94
    Central Asian participation in, 66–71,
        81, 82, 83, 90, 161–68
    Cheney's role in, 63, 64, 91, 92, 93, 97, 99
    CIA operations in, 61–64, 69, 70, 71, 72,
        73, 74, 77, 78, 79–80, 81, 85–99, 162,
        215, 241
    civilian casualties in, 94–95, 97–98, 106,
        142, 361, 365–66, 373
    Coalition forces in, 65–66, 71, 81,
        89–90, 91, 172, 198, 351, 366,
        371–72
    European participation in, 65–66, 70–71,
        75, 79, 89, 101–6, 297–98
    foreign aid in, 76, 80, 82, 95, 98,
        172
    foreign militants in, 77, 80–81, 85, 90–94,
        95, 98–100
    funding for, 62, 63–64, 70, 71, 97, 98, 134,
        203, 215, 319–20, 402
    human rights record in, 93–95, 164–65,
        295, 297, 298–300
    intelligence operations in, 61–62, 72–73,
        77–78, 84–86, 106, 142
    Iran's participation in, 61, 62, 66, 73, 76,
        81, 103, 105, 110
    Iraq war compared with, 64–65, 97, 129,
        133–34, 144, 196, 209, 245, 246, 248,
        352–53
    ISI's role in, 62–63, 72–73, 77–78, 79, 84–
        96, 110, 146–47, 164
    in Kabul, 63, 78, 80, 81, 86–87, 100–101
    in Kandahar, 64, 77, 80, 87, 90, 91, 95, 96,
        240–41
    Hamid Karzai's role in, 74, 76–77, 84–
        86, 88, 89, 90, 92, 105–6

Kazakhstan's participation in, 66–68, 71
in Kunduz, 64, 82, 83, 90–93, 110, 242–
    43
Kyrgyzstan's participation in, 66–69, 71,
    165–66
in Mazar-e-Sharif, 71, 81–82, 83, 85, 86,
    90
media coverage of, 73, 75, 80, 87, 91, 94,
    96–97, 146–47
military casualties in, 90–94, 95, 96, 336–
    37, 363, 364
Musharraf's role in, 73, 77–79, 80, 86, 87,
    88, 89–92, 93, 106, 241
neoconservative support for, 64–65, 75,
    97, 172
Northern Alliance (NA) in, 62, 64, 66,
    68, 69, 70, 72, 73–74, 78, 79–83, 86,
    87, 90–91, 93–95, 96, 97, 98, 100,
    101, 102, 103, 105–6, 146, 147, 189,
    215, 241, 297, 299
as Operation Enduring Freedom, 74–75,
    351, 353, 395
Pakistan's participation in, 61, 62–63, 66,
    72–73, 76, 77–79, 80, 81, 84, 86, 87–
    93, 95, 99, 109, 110, 118, 145, 146,
    219, 235, 240–43, 298
Pashtun tribes in, 62–63, 71–72, 79,
    81, 83, 84–86, 89, 90, 94–95, 97,
    98, 105
Powell's role in, 66, 73, 74, 75, 76, 82, 88,
    89, 90–91, 92, 97, 118
POWs in, 71, 90–94, 95, 100, 146
Qala Jangi uprising in, 93–94
Rumsfeld's role in, 62, 64–65, 71, 74, 83,
    89, 92, 97, 118, 241
Russia's participation in, 61, 62, 65, 66–
    70, 71, 73, 81, 82, 83, 103, 110
Soviet invasion compared with, 61, 69,
    71, 72, 78, 87, 95, 98, 146–47, 196
Special Operations Forces in, 62–63, 69,
    74, 85–86, 89, 92–98, 162, 297, 298,
    300
Tajikistan's participation in, 66–68, 70–
    71, 83
Taliban defeated in, 64, 66, 68, 71, 74–77,
    78, 79–101, 102, 104, 106, 110, 126,
    146–47, 240–43
Taliban evacuation in, 90–93
Tora Bora battle in, 91, 93, 98–100, 106,
    128, 241, 268, 271
tribal conflicts in, 68, 73–74, 81, 87, 94–
    95, 105, 136
Turkmenistan's participation in, 66–68,
    71

UN participation in, xxxviii, xxxix, xliii, liii–liv, 11, 13, 18, 21, 26, 53–56, 60, 66, 75–76, 77, 81, 82, 83, 86, 90, 92, 94–95, 102, 103, 104, 127, 128, 129, 132, 136, 138, 139, 140, 142, 171, 181, 196

U.S. bases for, 64, 69–71, 82, 83, 89, 136, 161–68

U.S. invasion in, xxxviii, xlii–xliii, lvi, lviii, 22, 27–31, 61–79, 80, 81–82

U.S. military strategy in, 64–65, 71, 74–75, 81–82, 88, 96–97, 133–34

U.S. troops in, 62, 71, 74, 89, 90–91, 93, 95, 97, 99, 100, 133–34, 142, 241

Uzbekistan's participation in, 62, 66–70, 71, 81, 82, 91, 161–62, 163, 164

warlords in, 62, 63, 73–74, 81, 83, 87, 94, 95, 96, 101, 105–6, 125–26, 128, 189, 215, 298, 317, 325

African embassy bombings (1998), xlv, 16, 113, 224, 237

agriculture, liv, 6, 76, 82, 126, 172, 174–75, 178, 183–84, 192, 317–22, 323, 325

Ahady, Anwar-ul-Haq, 184, 191

Ahmad, Mehmood, 24, 25–29, 30, 50, 53, 72, 73, 77, 78

Ahmed, Qazi Hussain, 35, 226

Ahsan, Aitezaz, 156

Ajami, Fouad, 291

Akayev, Aidar, 339

Akayev, Askar, 166, 168, 338–41, 342

Akayeva, Bermet, 339

Akbari, Syed, 129

Akhund, Mullah Barader, 242, 399

Akhund, Mullah Obaidullah, 398

Akhunzada, Sher Mohammed, 322, 326–27, 357

Akram, Munir, 259

Akram, Zamir, 26–27

Albright, David, 289

Albright, Madeleine, lv, 295

Alexander, Chris, 205, 364

Ali, Hazrat, 98, 128

Alimov, Khusniddin, 165, 310

Al Jazeera, 80, 225, 270, 281

Alliance for Restoration of Democracy (ARD), 52, 233

Alliot-Marie, Michèle, 353

All Parties Hurriyat Conference (APHC), 111–12

al Qaeda, 219–39, 265–92, 380, 383, 384–85, 393

in Afghan war, xliii, xlv, 56, 61, 63–64, 65, 72, 73, 77, 80, 90–92, 98–100, 125–26

arrests of, 149, 155, 223–27, 249

bin Laden as leader of, xlviii, 4, 5, 14, 18, 53, 61, 69, 80, 99, 113, 115–17, 214, 231–32, 245, 270, 278, 281–82

bombing campaigns by, xxxvii, xxxix, xlv, xlvii–xlviii, xlix, lvi, 16, 17–18, 66, 113, 224, 225, 226, 237, 251, 252, 265, 270, 278–79, 281, 282, 295, 297, 366

cells of, 153–54, 225

foreign militants in, 17, 25, 77, 80–81, 148, 155, 221–28, 241, 243–44, 249, 265, 347

intelligence information on, 48, 56, 59–62, 110, 129, 131, 148, 149, 198, 222–24, 230–33, 252, 271, 279–81, 298–301

Iraq forces of, 281–82, 337, 347

jihad waged by, 14, 15, 110, 219–39, 242, 245, 248, 252

in Kashmir, 48, 110, 111, 112, 113, 115–16, 124, 224

leadership of, 6, 61, 90–92, 131, 136, 146–48, 149, 153, 219–39, 224–27, 230, 237–38, 241, 246, 249, 253–54, 276, 278–82, 299, *see also specific leaders*

messages from, 53, 80, 99, 245, 278, 281

nuclear weapons sought by, 120–21, 295, 296–97

organization of, xli, 15, 153–54, 221–22, 225, 230–33, 237–39

Pakistan's support for, lii, 6, 17, 22, 24–33, 39, 48, 58–60, 145, 146–48, 149, 154–55, 157, 219–39, 253–54, 259, 265–90, 307–10, 347

resurgence of, 16, 59–60, 66, 195, 251, 349–73, 401–2

September 11 attacks planned by, xxxviii, liv, 16, 22–23, 26–27, 30–31, 32, 33, 64

Taliban's alliance with, xliii, xlv, 4, 5, 14, 15, 20, 41, 56, 155, 224–25, 244, 278–79, 282, 308, 336–37

at Tora Bora, 91, 93, 98–100, 106, 128, 241, 268, 271

training camps of, xlv, 16, 18, 25, 41, 56, 110, 111, 113, 224–25, 244, 278–79, 282, 308

U.S. interrogations of, 91, 93, 100, 293–316, 336

al Qaeda (*cont.*)
   U.S. operations against, xxxviii, 56, 58,
      60, 91, 93, 100, 115–16, 124, 125, 131,
      133, 136, 149, 187, 236, 241, 253–54,
      259, 276, 279–81, 289–90, 293–316,
      336
   in Uzbekistan, xliii–xliv, lvii, 56, 345,
      347
   see also bin Laden, Osama
Amanullah, king of Afghanistan, 212
Amerine, Jason, 85–86, 95, 96
Amin, Hafizullah, 9
Amir, Ayaz, 42, 118
Amnesty International, 51, 345
Anaconda, Operation, 100, 243, 245
Andijan massacre (2005), 311, 340, 344–46
Angur Adda, 268–69
Annan, Kofi, xli, liii, 53, 55–56, 75, 104,
      135, 173, 178, 213, 259, 373
anti-Americanism, lv–lvi, lvii, 79, 140, 145,
      157, 161, 303, 313–14, 361–62
Arar, Maher, 305
Arif, Mohammed, 12, 206, 208, 245
Armitage, Richard, 27, 30, 58, 59, 89, 117,
      118, 119, 229–30, 270
Arnault, Jean, 216, 253, 257, 261
Ashdown, Paddy, 393
assassinations, 3–4, 16–17, 19, 21–22, 122,
      143–44, 161, 207, 213, 220, 227, 228,
      230–33, 236–37, 238, 239, 243–44,
      270, 275, 308, 336, 358, 366, 370
Atatürk, Mustafa Kemal, 44, 46
Atef, Mohammed, 224
Atmar, Hanif, 184, 194, 205
Atta, Mohammed, 74, 81, 83, 90, 128, 142,
      143, 187, 199, 206, 215
Attash, Khalid al-, 225
Austin, Reginald, 256–57
Avalanche, Operation, 213
Avazov, Muzafar, 165, 310, 311
Azhar, Maulana Masud, 112–14, 159
Aziz, Mohammed, 28–29, 50, 53, 79
Aziz, Shaukat, 47, 148–49, 238–39, 382, 387
Aziz, Sultan, 210
Aziz, Tariq, 122

Babar, Naseerullah, 9
Baer, Robert, 301
Bagram, 99, 100, 121, 134, 190, 198, 223,
      229, 269, 294, 298, 299, 301, 302, 316,
      327, 336, 353
Bakiyev, Kurmanbek, 339, 340
Bali bombings (2005), xxxvii, 226, 265

Balkenende, Peter, 358
Balochistan, xl, 3, 34, 35, 36, 77–78, 84, 110,
      124, 148, 158, 159, 160, 223, 234, 235,
      240, 242, 243, 247, 249, 250–51, 259,
      266, 267, 283–87, 309, 361, 401
Balochistan Liberation Army (BLA), 283–
      87
Bamiyan, 18, 26, 82–83, 199, 242, 299, 323,
      333
Bamiyan Buddhas, 18, 26, 82–83, 242
Bandar, Prince, 79, 161
Bangladesh, 33, 35, 36, 37, 111, 285
Barno, David, 252, 281, 335
Barot, Dhiren, 237–38
Bashardost, Ramazan, 191
Basra, Riaz, 227
Bassiouni, Cherif, 313
BearingPoint, 180, 191
Beg, Mirza Aslam, 39, 40, 288
Beknazarov, Azimbek, 338
Berdymukhamedow, Gurbanguly, 341
Berger, Samuel, 49
Berntsen, Gary, 78, 99
Berry, Glyn, 358
Bhandara, M. P., 78
Bhutto, Benazir, xxxix, 9, 39–40, 47, 52,
      150, 155–56, 158, 226, 238, 266, 287,
      374–79, 386–87, 388, 389
Bhutto, Mutaza, 376
Bhutto, Shahnawaz, 376
Bhutto, Zulfiqar Ali, 37, 39, 376
Biden, Joseph, 134
bin Laden, Osama:
   as al Qaeda leader, xlviii, 4, 5, 14, 18, 53,
      61, 69, 80, 99, 113, 115–17, 214, 231–
      32, 245, 270, 278, 281–82
   escape of, xxxviii, xli, 14, 61, 98–100, 110,
      115–17, 128, 148, 175, 265, 270, 282
   messages from, 53, 80, 99, 245, 270, 278,
      281
   nuclear weapons sought by, 120–21, 295,
      296–97
   Pakistan's support for, 15–16, 22, 24–33,
      53, 56, 58
   Taliban support for, 4, 5, 15, 18, 19, 20,
      56, 72, 73, 77, 172, 240–41
   in Tora Bora, 98–100, 128
   U.S. hunt for, 16, 20, 24, 28, 32, 43, 50,
      56, 58, 61, 63–64, 65, 72, 73, 77, 80,
      98–100, 115–17, 175, 198, 252, 253–
      54, 279–81, 282, 299
Binori Town, 228, 242
Bishkek Declaration (2002), 166
Black, Cofer, 305–6

"black sites," 224, 225–26, 294, 308–9, 314
Blackwell, Robert, 190
Blair, Tony, 65–66, 74, 79, 80, 89, 136, 165, 257, 279–80, 297–98, 326–27, 356–58, 360, 371
Bonn Agreement, 95–96, 101–6, 125, 132, 138, 139, 143, 196, 210, 211, 247, 254, 350, 355
Bonn group, 55, 139
Bosnia, 182, 189, 358
Boucher, Richard, 278, 370, 378
Brahimi, Lakhdar, xxxviii, 53, 54, 55, 75–76, 83, 94, 102, 103, 104, 135, 140, 141, 179, 180, 197, 202, 207, 209, 212, 214, 216, 217, 247–48, 253, 255, 257, 350, 402
Brand, Willie, 302–3
Bremer, J. Paul, 190
Brigade 555, 17, 61
British Empire, xlviii–xlix, 8, 33–34, 63, 110, 266, 267, 273
Brownback, Sam, 57
Brzezinski, Zbigniew, xlvii
Bugti, Baramdagh, 285
Bugti, Sardar Akbar, 284–86
Bush, George H. W., 11, 20, 65
Bush, George W., 402
    Afghanistan policy of, *see* Afghanistan; Afghan war
    "axis of evil" speech of, 125
    Central Asian policy of, 162–68, 347–48
    human rights record of, 293–97, 298, 305–6, 314–15
    India policy of, 110, 114–19, 290
    Karzai's relations with, 253, 259, 277–78, 336, 369
    Musharraf's relationship with, 57–60, 91, 118–19, 145–49, 157, 160–61, 219, 222, 232, 236–37, 253, 259, 276, 277–78, 368–71, 380, 388
    Pakistan policy of, xxxix–xl, xlv, 24–26, 39, 56–60, 86, 89, 110, 115–19, 124, 145–46, 160–61, 219–39, 273–74, 276, 277–78, 368–71, 380
    war on terrorism of, xxxviii, xli, xlii, xlvii–xlviii, xlix, li, liii, lvii, 27, 30–31, 32, 78, 93, 96, 109, 156, 225, 226, 236–37, 248, 293–316, 324, 335
Byrd, William, 177, 399

Cambodia, liii, 172
Cambone, Stephen, 64
Campbell, Charles, 201

Canada, 305, 315, 346, 353, 356, 358, 359, 363–64, 366, 371, 372, 373, 395
Carcassonne, Guy, 212
Carnahan, Michael, 180
Carter, Jimmy, 38, 356
Central Asia, xxxviii, xxxix, xl–xli, xliii, xlv, li, liv, lvii, lviii, 6, 8, 33, 38, 61, 66–71, 81, 82, 83, 90, 113, 130, 161–68, 187, 192, 193, 209, 258, 265, 268, 287, 293, 316, 331, 338–48, 403–4
    see also specific countries
Central Command, U.S. (CENTCOM), l–li, lii, 61–62, 88, 91, 93, 94, 133, 162, 201, 300, 334, 344
Central Intelligence Agency (CIA), xxxix, xlv, xlix, l, liv, 10, 11, 15, 21–32, 37, 38–39, 43, 56–64, 69–81, 85–99, 110, 115, 120–22, 125, 128–29, 131–36, 147–48, 149, 152, 153, 155, 162, 174, 175, 176, 185, 186, 189, 201, 209, 215, 221–25, 226, 241, 243, 245, 250, 253–54, 267, 280–81, 288–321, 328, 335, 342, 344, 347–48, 367, 389–90
Chaman, 77–78, 240, 242, 250, 251–52, 366, 370
Chamberlain, Wendy, 30, 146
Champagne, David, 74
Charles, Robert, 325–26
Chaudhry, Iftikhar, 310, 380–81, 382
Chayes, Sarah, 323
Chechnya, 17, 70, 113, 265
Cheney, Dick, xlvi, 63, 64, 91, 92, 93, 97, 99, 121, 149, 188, 195, 222, 232, 261, 296, 356, 357, 369–70, 377, 384
China, l, 17, 39, 67–68, 115, 123, 167, 193, 201, 265, 284, 287, 300, 311–12, 331, 339, 340–41, 345, 346, 348, 367
Chirac, Jacques, 349
Christians, 18–19, 145, 154, 159, 176, 237
Clarke, Richard, 56, 59, 64, 97
Clinton, Bill, xliv, xlv–xlvi, 15, 16, 18, 20, 25, 26, 41, 42, 49–50, 56, 57, 58, 61, 67, 72, 110, 113, 173, 188, 189, 224, 296
Clinton, Hillary, 388
CNN, 110, 152, 271
Coalition Support Funds, 370–71
Cohen, Stephen, 235
cold war, liii, 8, 11, 33, 36–37, 109–10, 167, 172–73, 174, 204, 351
Cole, USS, 17–18, 225
Combat Search and Rescue Units, 89
communism, 9–10, 126, 138, 206–7, 213, 333

Constitution, U.S., xli, 293, 295, 312, 314
Constitutional Loya Jirga (CLJ), 212–18, 247, 251, 255
Containment, Operation, 330–31
Costa, Antonio, 329
cotton, 164, 323
Crocker, Ryan, 97, 130, 134
cruise missiles, xlv, 16, 18, 61, 80, 88, 113
currency, 64, 178, 179, 184, 208
Curzon, George Nathaniel, Lord, xi
customs revenue, 127, 131, 186–87, 193, 210
Cyprus group, 55, 102, 105

Dadullah, Mullah, 90, 242–43, 245, 246, 247, 250, 251, 253, 272, 337, 359, 366, 398–99
Daud, Mir Suleiman, 286
Daud, Mohammed, 6, 8, 9, 128, 193, 206, 267
Defense Department, U.S., xlii, xlix–lii, liv, lvi, lvii, 24, 48, 59, 90–92, 118, 136, 137–38, 149, 173, 175, 176, 185, 201–3, 205–6, 207, 280, 328–29, 362
Delawari, Noorullah, 184
Denmark, 265, 279, 385
Deobandi, 53, 77, 111, 154–55, 228, 235, 242
dictatorships, xxxix, li–lii, 66–68, 293–94, 316
Dilawar, 301, 302–3
Dion, Stéphane, 395
Disarmament, Demobilization and Reintegration (DDR), 209–11, 225, 247, 254, 255, 257
Dobbins, James, 75, 103, 104, 182
Docherty, Leo, 361
Dogar, Abdul Hamid, 387
Dostum, Rashid, 12, 15, 20, 62, 63, 66, 68, 74, 81–82, 83, 90, 93–94, 103, 128, 132, 142, 143, 187, 193, 199, 206, 213, 215, 261, 297, 309, 335
Doucet, Lyse, 85, 96, 260
Drug Enforcement Agency (DEA), 319, 328–31
drug trafficking, xxxviii, xlii, liv, 19, 20, 38, 39, 64, 127, 129, 131, 167, 175, 179, 184, 193–94, 197, 200, 204, 205, 209, 218, 282, 317–32, 333, 334, 335, 354, 355, 356, 357, 365, 372
Dubai, 208, 283, 286, 287
Durand, Mortimer, 8, 267
Durand Line, 8, 267–68, 270
Durch, William, 135

Durrani, Akram, 159
Dushanbe, 19, 63, 70–71, 81, 83, 166
DynCorp International, 205, 304

Eastham, Alan, 57
East Timor, liii, 55, 172, 182, 194, 360, 373
East Turkistan Islamic Movement (ETIM), 311–12
Ecevit, Bülent, 66
Eikenberry, Karl W., 201, 202, 278, 360, 383
Enduring Freedom, Operation, *see* Afghan war
Erben, Peter, 332
Europe, Western, xxxvii, xxxviii, xlvi, xlvii, lvi, 20–21, 65–66, 70–71, 75, 79, 89, 101–6, 134, 137–38, 140, 143, 150–51, 156, 158, 177, 178, 179, 181, 186, 189–90, 194, 197, 200–201, 202, 210, 254, 255, 257, 297–98, 311, 315, 327, 329, 330, 333, 334, 346, 349–73
see also specific countries
European Convention on Human Rights, 297–98
European Parliament, 20–21, 150–51, 311, 315
European Union (EU), xxxix, 89, 156, 158, 178, 181, 186, 194, 333, 346, 362, 402
Evil Airlift, Operation, 90–93

Fahim, Mohammed, 12, 22, 62, 63, 73–74, 81, 87, 105–6, 128, 129, 131, 132–33, 141, 142, 143, 201–2, 206–8, 209, 210, 215–16, 255, 257–58, 261, 298, 334
"failed states," xlii, xliv, 8–9, 58, 75, 177, 181, 194–97, 203–4, 296, 360, 373
Fair, Christine, 273
Faisal, Prince Saud al-, 79
Faizullah, Maulana, 243
Fallon, William, 389–90
Farooqi, Amjad Hussain, 231–32, 238
FATA Sustainable Development Plan (2006–15), 273
Fazlullah, Mullah, 385, 386, 388
Federal Bureau of Investigation (FBI), 59, 152, 153, 225, 230, 231, 232–33, 296, 307, 340
Federally Administered Tribal Areas (FATA), 99, 147–48, 228–29, 243, 244, 249, 265–83, 307–8, 367, 370, 383–85, 389, 401

Ferghana Valley, 68, 165, 344, 346
Finance Ministry, Afghan, 179–81, 186–87, 191, 324
Finn, Robert, 130–31, 143, 174, 180, 185, 186, 187
Fischer, Joschka, 103, 349–50, 351
Fisher, Nigel, 181–82
Fleischer, Ari, 226
Florian, Pierre de Bousquet de, 282
Fouda, Yosri, 225
Frahi, Bernard, 320
France, 70–71, 75, 154, 166, 282, 349, 353, 394
Franks, Tommy, 61, 63, 74, 91, 94, 98, 99–100, 106, 118, 133–34, 154, 162, 201, 245
Fraser, Edwin, 183
Frontier Corps (FC), 9, 17, 78, 91, 221–22, 269, 270–72, 274
Fukuda, Yasuo, 394
Fukuyama, Francis, 177

G8 group, 197, 328, 329
Gailani, Ahmed Khalfan, 237
Gailani, Pir Sayed Ahmad, 72, 103
Gall, Carlotta, 301, 327
Ganci (Manas) Air Base, 71, 165–66, 167, 339, 340–41
Gandamak, Treaty of (1879), 267
Gardez, 106, 198, 258, 303
Garzón, Baltasar, 385
Gates, Robert, 370, 384, 393, 394–95, 396, 399
Gauthier, Michael, 363
Gawadar, 284, 287
Geneva Accords (1988), 53
Geneva Conventions (GC), 293–98, 365
Geneva Initiative, 55
Georgia, 339, 340, 342
Germany, 70, 101–6, 119, 140, 165, 172, 179, 190, 200, 202, 204, 265, 279, 282, 287, 315, 328, 342, 346, 347, 349–50, 351, 352, 353, 354, 362, 371, 372, 385, 394
Ghai, Yash Pal, 212
Ghani, Ashraf, 54, 75, 76, 78, 103, 142, 176, 179–81, 182, 186, 187, 191, 192, 205, 210, 216, 255, 261, 324
Ghani, Tarek, 179
Ghaus, Mullah Mohammed, 13
Ghazi, Mahmood, 72
Ghazi, Maulana Abdul Aziz, 382

Ghazi, Maulana Abdul Rashid, 382
"ghost detainees," 303–4, 305
Gonzales, Alberto R., 295–96
Goss, Porter, 24, 280, 301
Gouttierre, Tom, 74
Great Britain, xi, xxxvii, xlvii–xlix, lvi, 4–5, 8, 20, 23, 33–34, 48, 53, 61–66, 74, 79, 80, 97, 99, 110, 119, 122, 132, 135, 136, 142, 165, 179, 196, 197, 199, 222, 223, 226, 228, 237, 243, 265, 266, 267, 273, 278–80, 281, 282, 287, 297–98, 304–5, 310, 321–27, 350, 353–60, 365, 366, 371, 372, 373, 395, 396
"green-on-green" conflicts, 199–200, 209
Grenier, Robert, 77
gross domestic product (GDP), 167, 203, 229, 233, 234, 329, 340 (nat), 351, 356–57
Guantánamo Bay (Camp X-Ray), lvii, 100, 152, 153, 167, 274, 294, 297, 298, 299, 305, 311–16
Gul, Hameed, 222
Gulf War, 65, 97, 188
Gulzar, Habib, 192
Guthrie, Charles, 48

Haass, Richard, 72, 74, 75, 76, 122, 137, 185
Habeel, Mohammed, 91
Habibullah, Mullah Noor, 301, 302
Habibullah, Noor, 298–99
Hagenbeck, Franklin "Buster," 229, 246–47
Haider, Moenuddin, 50
Haiti, liii, 75, 172
Hakim, Abdul, 260
Hanning, August, 385
Haq, Abdul, 19, 20, 87–88, 98, 128, 207
Haq, Din Mohammed, 88
Haq, Ehsan ul-, 79, 103, 245
Haq, Izzatullah, 88
Haq, Muhammed Zia ul-, 10, 33, 37–39, 46, 52, 220, 235, 268, 375–76
Haqqani, Jalaluddin, 99, 221, 243–44, 268, 269, 276, 368, 386, 401
Haqqani, Sirajuddin, 243
Harkat ul-Ansar, 48, 112–13
Harper, Stephen, 358, 371, 395
Hawsawi, Mustafa Ahmed al-, 225–26
Hayat, Ahsan Saleem, 237, 239
Hayden, Michael, 282, 389
Hazarajat, 74, 82–83, 129, 242

Hazaras, 6, 8, 12, 14–15, 16, 18, 20, 21, 55, 62, 82–83, 103, 105, 129, 199, 202, 214, 216, 227–28, 242, 257–58, 261, 300, 333
Hellfire missiles, 59, 97
Helmand, 200, 223, 245, 247, 279, 318, 321–27, 329, 336, 353, 356, 357, 359–60, 370, 373, 396
Helton, Arthur, 180
Herat, 12, 14, 80, 82, 103, 125–27, 134, 142, 187, 193, 210, 229, 307, 352, 353
Herold, Marc, 97–98
Hersh, Seymour, 92
Hikmetyar, Gulbuddin, 9, 10, 11, 12, 19, 39, 111, 221, 244, 245, 246, 259, 333–34, 368, 401
Hizb-e-Islami, 10, 221, 333–34, 335
Hizb ut-Tahir (HT), 164–65, 342, 343
Hoagland, Jim, 280
Holbrooke, Richard, 205
Horton, Scott, 305
Human Development Index, 129–30
human rights, lii, lvi, lvii, 38, 51, 93–95, 118, 151–54, 164–65, 266, 293–316, 342–48
Human Rights Commission of Pakistan (HRCP), 51, 151, 309
Human Rights Watch, 94, 97, 214, 306, 308, 315, 345
"human security," 196–97
Hussain, Altaf, 47
Hussain, Chaudry Shujjat, 238
Hussain, Munawar, 118
Hussein, Saddam, xlvii, xlviii, xlix, 64, 65, 230, 252

Idema, Jonathan, 304
"illegal enemy combatants," 294–95, 296
improvised explosive devices (IEDs), 361, 367
Inderfurth, Karl, 48, 49
India, 109–24
    borders of, 41, 42, 116–20, 123, 274
    British rule of, 8, 33–34, 110
    consulates of, 248–49, 286
    economy of, 119, 291
    Hindu population of, 34, 35
    Musharraf's policy on, 115, 116–17, 122–24, 145, 152, 219, 220, 232, 248–49
    nuclear weapons of, 41, 56, 110, 124, 288, 290

Pakistan's relations with, xxxviii, xliii, xliv, xlv, 3, 15, 25, 29–30, 33, 37, 38, 40–43, 45, 46, 47, 48, 49, 50, 54, 73, 78, 87, 89, 109–24, 145, 147, 148, 149, 152, 219, 220, 228, 229, 232, 234, 235, 244, 248–49, 267, 268, 274, 283, 286, 291, 369, 402
    Pakistan's war with (1965), 37, 45
    Pakistan's war with (1971), 45, 111
    Partition of (1947), 34–35, 36, 44, 110–11, 266, 267
    U.S. relations with, 29, 30, 290
Indian Airlines hijacking (1999), 48, 112, 113, 114, 151
Indian Independence Act (1947), 266
Interim National Development Strategy, 355
Interior Ministry, Afghan, 204, 324, 327–28
International Committee of the Red Cross (ICRC), 90, 92, 93, 165, 171–72, 199, 245–46, 294, 297, 301, 303, 305, 306, 308–9, 312, 313, 316
International Criminal Court (ICC), xlvi, 286
International Deoband Conference (2001), 53
International Monetary Fund (IMF), 49, 163, 164, 184, 208, 237, 341
International Organization for Migration (IOM), 175–76
International Security Assistance Force (ISAF), 132–33, 134, 140, 183, 197–98, 199, 200–202, 206, 210, 213, 215, 257, 258–59, 260, 306, 349–53, 356
Inter-Services Intelligence Directorate (ISI), 3–4, 9–16, 22–33, 38, 40–53, 57, 60, 62–63, 68, 72–73, 77–78, 79, 84–96, 110–24, 129, 146–47, 150, 152, 155, 160, 164, 220–25, 227, 230–33, 237–51, 259, 267, 268, 269, 271, 275, 279, 280, 284, 289, 291, 307–10, 319, 335, 337, 360, 364, 366–71, 377–78, 380, 381–82, 390, 398, 399, 400–401
In the Line of Fire (Musharraf), 44, 291
Iran:
    Afghan refugees in, 6, 14–15, 19, 20, 76, 125, 130, 172, 183–84
    Afghan relations with, 25, 55, 125–26, 127, 187, 192, 193, 206
    in Afghan war, 61, 62, 66, 73, 76, 81, 103, 105, 110
    borders of, 125–26, 127
    drug trafficking in, 323–24, 331–32

nuclear weapons of, 122, 188, 236, 287–
89, 290
as terrorist state, xxxvii, xlvii, xlix, lv,
125–26, 244
U.S. relations with, 61, 125, 368–69
Iraq:
Afghanistan compared with, xlix, lv,
lvi–lvii, 190, 197, 200, 358
al Qaeda forces in, 281–82, 337, 347
Hussein's regime in, xlvii, xlviii, xlix, 64,
65, 230, 252
international involvement in, lvi, 349
nuclear weapons in, xlix, 121
oil resources of, xlvii, 65
reconstruction of, 190, 194–95, 197
as terrorist state, xli, xlvii, lv, 125
Iraq war, 402
Afghan reconstruction and, 182, 185,
194–95, 196, 200
Afghan war compared with, 64–65, 97,
129, 133–34, 144, 196, 209, 245, 246,
248, 352–53
Bush's strategy for, 182, 185, 200, 334–35
failure of, xlii, lvi, lvii, 121, 144, 356,
368–69
human rights record in, 295, 298, 299–
300, 301, 302, 303, 304, 305, 307,
312–13
insurgency in, 228, 236, 281–82, 334–
35
neoconservative rationale for, 64–65
public support for, xlix, lviii, 334–35
U.S. military forces in, xli, xlviii, 129,
133–34, 197, 352–53
Islam, xxxvii, xxxix, xlii–xliv, xlvii–xlviii,
4, 9, 11, 13–23, 24, 25, 29–49, 51, 53,
67, 68–69, 71, 77, 79, 80–81, 82, 92,
100–101, 103, 110, 111–18, 126, 133,
138, 140, 145, 154–55, 160–67, 183,
211, 212–39, 242, 245, 248, 249, 252,
255–58, 268–71, 275, 291–94, 299,
300, 307, 310, 314, 317, 333–34, 336,
339, 342–47, 362–63
Islamic Democratic Alliance (IDA), 39–
40
Islamic Jihad Union, 343, 344, 347, 385
Islamic Movement of Uzbekistan (IMU),
17, 68–69, 71, 80–81, 82, 92, 164,
166, 167, 221, 269, 270–71, 339, 342,
343, 347
Islamic Republic of Afghanistan, 11, 212–
13
Israel, xlvii, 30, 31, 59, 65, 152, 226, 228,
308, 344

Italy, 179, 204, 315, 352, 371, 372, 394
Ivanov, Sergei, 345

Jabbar, Javed, 51
Jabour, Marwan, 308
Jaish-e-Mohammed, 114, 159, 220, 224,
230–31, 270, 281, 383
Jalal, Masuda, 141, 255, 258, 261
Jalalabad, 12, 98, 229, 248, 286
Jalali, Ali Ahmad, 205, 216, 322, 334
Jamali, Zafarullah Khan, 158–59, 238,
239
Jamiat-e-Islami, 9, 35, 46, 118, 226–27
Jamiat-e-Khudamul Koran, 242
Jamiat Ulema-e-Islam, 46, 53, 158, 159,
240, 242, 243, 249, 250, 276, 283–84,
391
Jamil, Mohammed, 230–31
Janjalani, Abdurajak, 214
Janjua, Amina, 309
Japan, xxxvii, 89, 138, 172, 176, 177, 179,
181, 186, 210, 394
Jehangir, Asma, 309
Jews, 153, 226, 293, 342
Jilani, Faiz, 57
Jinnah, Mohammed Ali, 34, 35, 37, 234–35
Jones, James, 329, 352, 354, 370, 373
Joya, Malalai, 215
Justice Department, U.S., 295–96
"justice on the spot" system, 362–63

Kabul, liv, 7, 8, 10, 11, 12, 14, 15, 61, 63, 73,
78, 80, 81, 84, 86–87, 100–101, 105,
110, 129, 130–31, 132, 135, 139, 140,
171, 179, 183, 186, 191, 193, 194, 197,
199, 214, 244, 248, 258, 301, 303, 304,
307, 308, 322, 329–30, 351, 355, 361,
398
Kabulov, Zamir, 207
Kalosha, 270–71, 272
Kandahar, 3, 4, 5, 7, 10, 13, 16, 17, 48, 50,
61, 64, 77, 80, 87, 90, 91, 95, 96, 112,
128, 134, 136, 142, 143–44, 148, 167,
187, 215, 223, 229, 240–41, 245, 247,
249, 250–51, 256, 259, 286, 294, 297–
301, 307, 320, 325, 336, 353, 363–64,
366, 373
Karachi, 31, 36, 37, 43, 89, 90, 151, 152, 154,
155, 192, 193, 222, 225, 228, 233, 242,
283, 357
Kargil attack (1999), 41–43, 45, 112, 115,
116, 117, 124

Karimov, Islam, lii, 68, 69, 70, 71, 82, 162–
    65, 310–11, 341–48
Karimova, Gulnora, 341–42, 347
Karmal, Babrak, 9
Karshi-Khanabad (K2) air base, 70, 71,
    344, 345, 346, 347
Karzai, Abdul Ahad, 3–6, 16–17, 96
Karzai, Ahmed Wali, 5, 22–23, 251,
    327
Karzai, Hamid, 253–61, 378, 393, 397, 403
    in Afghan war, 74, 76–77, 84–86, 88, 89,
        90, 92, 105–6
    assassination attempt against, 143–44,
        205, 207, 244, 304
    background of, 3–6, 10, 12, 13–14, 16–17,
        19
    George W. Bush's relations with, 253,
        259, 277–78, 336, 369
    cabinet of, 129, 139–40, 180, 210–11,
        217–18, 221, 261, 326–27, 334, 365
    corruption and, 325–30, 334, 355, 365,
        399
    economic policies of, 133, 186–87, 191,
        192
    international support for, 352, 355, 357,
        362
    in Loya Jirga, 138, 141, 142
    Musharraf's relations with, 22–23, 106,
        110, 124, 221, 229, 241, 246, 248–49,
        253, 259, 277–78, 286, 369
    Pakistan policy of, 5–6, 13–14, 22–23,
        106, 110, 124, 221, 229, 241, 246,
        248–49, 253, 259, 267, 277–78, 283,
        286, 365, 369
    political affiliation of, 258, 332, 333, 365
    Popalzai tribe of, 3–4, 12, 16–17, 129, 327
    popular support for, 246, 253–61, 332–
        35, 361–62, 365, 372–73
    as president, xxxix, 7, 63, 84, 94, 95–96,
        103, 105–6, 110, 124, 126, 127, 129–
        30, 132, 135, 137, 139, 140, 141, 142,
        143, 176, 178, 181, 185–86, 187, 197,
        198–99, 206, 207, 209, 210–18, 221,
        243, 246, 247, 251, 253–61, 306, 323,
        325–30, 332–35, 350, 352, 365
    in presidential elections (2004), 188, 190,
        253–61, 352
    reconstruction efforts of, 176, 178, 185–
        87, 191, 198, 217–18, 255–56, 258,
        261, 334, 355, 372–73
    speeches of, 132, 140, 216–17
    Taliban opposition to, 84–85, 88, 229–30,
        243, 246, 247, 269–70, 286, 335, 357,
        366–71

U.S. support for, 96, 132, 133, 137, 185–
    86, 209, 210–11, 229–30, 253, 259,
    277–78, 336, 369
    warlords and, 19, 105–6, 126, 128, 132,
        135, 142, 143, 206, 210–11, 251, 334
Karzai, Zeenat, 23
Kashmir, 109–24, 378, 402
    al Qaeda forces in, 48, 110, 111, 112, 113,
        115–16, 124, 244
    elections for, 110–11, 119
    Indian-Pakistani conflict in, xxxviii,
        xliii, xliv, 3, 15, 25, 29–30, 41–43, 45,
        46, 48, 50, 78, 109–24, 145, 219, 232,
        244, 291
    ISI forces in, 15, 32–33, 38, 40–41, 111,
        112, 114, 115, 116, 117, 119, 122, 124,
        155, 231, 232, 291, 308
    Islamic militants in, 110, 111–20, 122,
        123–24, 145, 147, 155, 219, 225, 226,
        227, 231, 232, 235, 244, 265, 279, 286,
        291
    Kargil attack in (1999), 41–43, 45, 112,
        115, 116, 117, 124
    Musharraf's policies on, 29–30, 41–43,
        45, 48, 50, 53, 112, 114, 115, 116, 117,
        123–24, 145, 232, 291
    suicide bombings in, 114, 116, 227
    U.S. mediation in, 114–19
Kasuri, Khurshid, 368
Kayani, Ashfaq, 239, 388–89, 390
Kazakhstan, xxxix, 66–68, 71, 167,
    339
Kazemi, Syed Mustafa, 192, 398
Kellenberger, Jakob, 90–91, 305
Kennan, George, 374
Kennedy, Patrick J., 378
Kerry, John, 99, 237
KGB, 207, 306
Khakrezwal, Mohammed Akram, 336
Khalili, Karim, 62, 74, 128, 129, 257–58
Khalili, Masud, 21
Khalilzad, Zalmay, 60, 103, 139, 140, 142,
    179, 185, 187–90, 202–3, 207, 209,
    214, 215, 216, 246, 255, 259, 261, 333
Khamenei, Ayatollah, 125
Khan, Abdul Qadeer, 120–21, 122, 236,
    253, 287–90
Khan, Amanullah, 142
Khan, Amir Yaqub, king of Afghanistan,
    267
Khan, Ayub, 52
Khan, Ghulam Ahmad, 51
Khan, Ghulam Ishaq, 40
Khan, Hayatullah, 275

Khan, Ismael, 12, 14, 20, 62, 74, 82, 103, 125–27, 128, 129, 132, 142, 143, 187, 206, 210, 257, 261, 307
Khan, Jalaluddin, 318
Khan, Jamal, 129
Khan, Jan Mohammed, 357
Khan, Liaquat Ali, 375
Khan, Mohammed Siddique, 278–79
Khan, Muzaffar, 183
Khan, Naeem Noor, 237
Khan, Naheed, 375
Khan, Sahibzada Yakub, 268
Khan, Sher Mohammed, 302
Khan, Yahya, 52
Khandan, Malik, 275
Khan Research Laboratories, 122, 287–90
Khatami, Mohammad, 66, 125
Khost, 99, 243
Khyber, 98, 99, 265, 268
Khyber Pass, 77–78
Kinzer, Stephen, 177
Koenigs, Tom, 368
Kohat, 226, 279, 307
Koran, xlii–xliii, 164, 165, 217, 299, 310, 314, 317
Kosovo, 182, 189
Kunduz, 64, 82, 83, 90–93, 110, 193, 200, 210, 242–43, 350–51, 354
Kurram, 98, 99, 147, 265, 268
Kyrgyzstan, xxxix, 66–69, 71, 164, 165–66, 167, 168, 331, 338–41, 342, 345–46

Lahore, 3, 4, 53, 193, 224, 389
Laroche, Eric, 183
Lashkar-e-Jhangvi, 224, 227, 228, 383
Lashkar-e-Tayyaba, 53, 227, 228, 281
Lashkargah, 321–22, 357, 359, 366
law, international, xlvii, 266–67, 268, 269, 293–316
Legal Framework Order, 157
Libi, Abu Laith al-, 390
Libi, Ibn al-Sheikh al-, 224
Libya, 122, 236, 287, 288–89
Lindh, John Walker, 93
Line of Control (LOC), 41, 119
Lockhart, Clare, 180
Lodhi, Maleeha, 26–27
London bombings (2005), xxxvii, lvi, 265, 278–79
Louis Berger Co., 186, 190–91

Loya Jirga (LJ), 7, 13, 14, 20, 72, 104, 127, 138–42, 179, 187, 201, 212–18, 221, 247, 251, 255, 307, 334
Lugar, Richard, l

McCain, John, 313
McColl, John, 132, 201, 356
McConnell, Mike, 384, 389
McNeill, Dan K., 143, 197–98, 200, 269, 303
madrassas, 13, 25, 38–39, 46, 115, 147, 156, 157, 235–36, 240, 243, 249–50, 272–73, 274, 281, 364, 366
Madrid bombings (2004), xxxvii, lvi, 252, 265, 297
Mahmood, Sultan Bashiruddin, 120–22
Mahsud, Abdullah, 274
Mahsud, Baitullah, 274, 379, 384, 385–86, 398
Majid, Abdul, 120–22
Malaysia, 287, 288
Maley, William, 54
Malizai, Qadir, 250
Manas (Ganci) Air Base, 71, 165–66, 167, 339, 340–41
Manningham-Buller, Eliza, 279
Mansur, Abdul Hafiz, 213
Mansur, Khaled, 76
Mansur, Saif ur-Rahman, 100, 243
Maoism, 67, 124
Marine Corps, U.S., 89, 95
Marri, Balach, 285
Marri, Khair Bux, 284, 286
Marshall, George, 137
Marshall Plan, xliv, 75, 137, 172
Masri, Khaled al-, 315
Masud, Ahmad Shah, xlv, 4, 9, 11, 12, 14, 16, 17, 19, 20–22, 60, 62, 68, 72, 73, 101, 127–28, 208, 244, 257, 266, 306
Masud, Ahmad Wali, 101, 208, 257
Masud, Ahmad Zia, 101, 208, 257
Mavlanov, Mohammed, 344
Mazar-e-Sharif, 14, 16, 71, 81–82, 83, 85, 86, 90, 134, 193, 199, 229, 352, 354
Medusa, Operation, 363–64
Mehmood, Shafqat, 151
Mengal, Ataullah, 284, 285
Merkel, Angela, 371
Meshrano Jirga (House of Elders), 212, 333
MI5, 279, 360
MI6, 20, 63, 97, 120, 121, 222, 223, 279, 304–5, 306, 310, 321, 335

Middle East, xlii, xlvii, 37, 54, 61, 133, 148,
    223, 224, 235, 250, 353; see also
    specific countries
Milam, William, 48, 58–59, 158
Miller, Geoffrey, 312–13
Mirzoyev, Ghaffor, 331
Mishra, Brajesh, 122
Mohammed, Faqir, 386
Mohammed, Fida, 250
Mohammed, Khalid Sheikh, 153, 225–26,
    314
Mohammed, Maulana Nur, 243
Mohammed, Maulana Sufi, 90
Mohammed, Nazar, 250
Mohammed, Nek, 271–72
Mohammed, Wakil, 301, 303
Mohaqiq, Mohammed, 81, 129, 178, 261,
    335
Mountain Thrust, Operation, 359
Mountain Viper, Operation, 247
Mujaddedi, Sibghatullah, 10, 12, 213, 216,
    335
Mujahedin, 5, 6, 9–12, 13, 38–39, 40, 78,
    98, 132, 188, 226, 244, 267, 283, 319,
    333
Mujahid, Mullah Sakhi Dad, 253
Mukadyrova, Fatima, 343
"Mullah Omar's missiles," 366
Mullen, Michael, 396–97, 399
Munguia, Ricardo, 245
Murray, Craig, 310–11
Musa Qala, 360, 396
Musharraf, Pervez, 44–60, 145–68, 386–87,
    403
    Afghan policies of, 22–23, 47, 52–53, 57,
        110, 248–49, 277–78, 369
    in Afghan war, 73, 77–79, 80, 86, 87, 88,
        89–92, 93, 106, 241
    assassination attempts against, 122, 154,
        161, 220, 230–33, 236–37, 239, 270,
        308
    author's meeting with, 392–93
    autobiography of, 44, 291
    background of, 44–45, 220
    Benazir Bhutto's relations with, 376–79
    George W. Bush's relations with, 57–60,
        91, 118–19, 145–49, 157, 160–61,
        219, 222, 232, 236–37, 253, 259, 276,
        277–78, 368–71, 388
    Bill Clinton's relations with, 49–50, 57,
        58
    economic policies of, 31, 47, 233, 273–74,
        291
    elections rigged by, 378

    India policies of, 115, 116–17, 122–24,
        145, 152, 219, 220, 232, 248–49
    Islamic fundamentalism supported by,
        46, 51, 79, 145–54, 155, 219–39, 270,
        307, 376
    January 12 speech of (2002), 146–47,
        155
    Kargil attack organized by (1999), 41–
        43, 45, 112, 115, 116, 117, 124
    Karzai's relations with, 22–23, 106, 110,
        124, 221, 229, 241, 246, 248–49, 253,
        259, 277–78, 286, 369
    Kashmir policy of, 29–30, 41–43, 45, 48,
        50, 53, 112, 114, 115, 116, 117, 123–
        24, 145, 232, 291
    martial law imposed by, 45–47
    media coverage of, 44, 45–46, 52, 271,
        369
    military coup by (1999), lii, 24, 26, 28, 43,
        44, 45, 79, 112, 156, 238
    military dictatorship of, xxxviii–xxxix,
        xliii, lii, 21, 23, 24, 26, 28, 43, 44, 45–
        53, 79, 86, 112, 118, 123, 145–61,
        219–39, 289–92, 307–10
    military support for, 24, 27–30, 37, 40–
        47, 79, 145, 233, 292, 391–92
    nuclear policies of, 287–90, 291
    Pearl kidnapping and, 151–54
    popular support for, 46–47, 51–52, 146–
        51, 153, 155–60, 161, 290–93
    power-sharing agreement of, 376–77
    as president, 52, 123, 149–51, 156–60,
        233, 239, 290–91, 292
    Red Mosque and, 382–83
    "reform program" of, 46–47, 51–52,
        146–50, 161
    speeches of, 146–47, 150, 155,
        369
    state of emergency declared by, 387–89
    Supreme Court and, 380–81, 387
    Taliban policies of, 27–30, 43, 46, 49–53,
        57, 60, 77–79, 91, 92, 240, 246, 268,
        269, 271, 277–80, 289–90, 291, 307,
        357, 364
    tribal policies of, 268, 269, 270, 273–74,
        275, 284–87
    U.S. support for, xxxix–xl, xlv, lii, lvii,
        26, 27–30, 35, 39, 46, 49–51, 57–60,
        79, 118–19, 145–49, 160–61, 229–30,
        234, 280, 289–90, 357, 366–71
Muslim Brotherhood, 9, 111
Muslim League, 34–35, 37, 39–40, 51
Muslim League Party, 150, 156, 158–59
Muttawakil, Mullah Wakil Ahmad, 73

Muttehida Majlis-e-Amal (MMA), 157, 158, 159, 160, 161, 220, 227, 390–91
Myers, Richard, 91–92, 248, 340–41, 344

Nadai, Mir Mohammed Mahfooz, 141
Nadery, Ahmad Nader, 303
Najibullah, Mohammed, 11
Namangani, Juma, 68, 69, 70, 82, 164
Nangarhar, 87, 98, 128, 325
Naqibullah, Mullah, 96
Naseer, Jamal, 301
Nasir, Vali, 158
Nasr, Hassan Mustafa Osama, 315
Nasser, Jamal, 303
National Directorate for Security, 12, 223
National Intelligence Estimate (NIE), 282, 384
National Logistics Cell, 77–78
National Movement for the Restoration of Pakistani Sovereignty, 151–54
National Security Council (NSC), 137, 142, 149, 189
National Solidarity Program, 184–86, 194
nation building, xxxviii, xli, xliv–xlv, li, lii–liv, 8, 55–56, 58, 63–64, 74–75, 129–31, 133, 137, 146, 172–74, 178, 182, 194–97, 203, 209–11, 293–94, 317–18, 336, 348, 365, 373
Natsios, Andrew, liv, 174–75, 185, 330
Nazarbayev, Aliya, 339
Negroponte, John, 75, 282, 371, 378
neoconservatives, xli, xlvi–lii, liv, 56–57, 64–65, 75, 97, 114–15, 130–31, 172, 188, 295–96, 356
Netherlands, 353–54, 356, 358, 395
Neuman, Ron, 360
New Beginnings Programme, 210–11
Niyazov, Saparmurat, 331, 341, 347
No-Dong missiles, 287
nongovernmental organizations (NGOs), 126–27, 171–72, 176–78, 179, 180, 181, 185, 189–91, 198, 199, 221–22, 245–46, 247, 254, 266, 292, 322, 323, 333, 340, 342–43, 354, 361
Noor, Sadiq, 386
North Atlantic Treaty Organization (NATO), xxxix, liii, 65, 67, 71, 79, 162, 163, 166, 200–201, 203, 222–23, 258–59, 277, 279–80, 292, 327, 329, 330, 334, 339, 346, 349–73, 393–400, 402

Northern Alliance (NA), xlv, 14, 17, 19, 20–22, 29, 30, 53–74, 78–83, 86, 87, 90–106, 110, 139, 146, 147, 189, 192, 206–16, 221, 241, 251, 258, 261, 297, 299, 306, 320–21, 327, 335, 350, 362
North Korea, lv, 122, 125, 174, 236, 287, 288–89, 290
North-West Frontier Province (NWFP), 34, 35, 36, 147–48, 158, 160, 221, 223, 235, 243, 249, 265, 272, 276, 278, 286, 307, 332, 370, 383, 386, 389, 391
nuclear proliferation, xxxix, xl, xlii, lvii, 29, 32, 37, 38, 39, 40, 41–42, 43, 44, 56, 58, 67, 116, 120–23, 124, 219, 236, 253, 287–90, 291, 295, 296–97
Nurzai, Arif, 327
Nutsch, Mark, 94

Obama, Barack, 388
oil resources, xlvii, 15, 37, 65, 66–67, 188–89, 233, 343, 348
Olcott, Martha Brill, 342
Omar, Mullah Mohammed, 3, 4, 13, 15, 16, 17, 18, 19, 26, 32, 53, 69, 72, 73, 77, 78, 84, 85, 90, 95, 121, 138, 223, 228, 231–32, 240–42, 243, 246, 247, 252, 253, 259, 265, 274, 301, 363, 386, 398, 399, 401
Open Media Fund for Afghanistan, 126–27
Orakzai, Ali Jan, 269, 270–71, 276–77, 385
"over the horizon" deployment, 352
Owens, Joseph, 302

Pakistan, 24–60, 109–24, 145–68, 219–39, 265–92
    Afghan refugees in, 5, 6, 10, 76, 130, 146, 172, 183–84, 221–22, 243, 283, 366, 367
    Afghan relations with, 3, 9, 10, 11, 21, 22–23, 38–39, 41, 46, 47, 52–53, 54, 57, 105, 110, 182, 192–93, 206, 219, 228–29, 244, 248–49, 259, 265–87, 335, 369
    in Afghan war, 61, 62–63, 66, 72–73, 76, 77–79, 80, 81, 84, 86, 87–93, 95, 99, 109, 110, 118, 145, 146, 219, 235, 240–43, 298
    air force of, 86, 231–32, 280, 288, 319

Pakistan (*cont.*)

al Qaeda supported by, lii, 6, 17, 22, 24–33, 39, 48, 58–60, 145, 146–48, 149, 154–55, 157, 219–39, 253–54, 259, 265–90, 307–10, 347

army of, 9, 17, 78, 91, 221–22, 266–67, 269, 270–71, 274–77, 280, 282–83, 291–92, 319, 370–71, 375–76, 391–92, 400–401, 403

borders of, 8, 9, 28, 32, 34, 41, 42, 66, 76, 77–78, 98–100, 116–20, 123, 131, 147–48, 192–93, 221–23, 228–29, 240–43, 248, 249–52, 259, 265–87, 371, 372

British relations with, 33–34, 48, 53, 63, 122, 222, 223, 228, 243, 266, 267, 273, 278–80, 281, 282, 287, 356, 360

British rule of, 33–34, 63, 266, 267, 273

Christian minority in, 145, 154, 159, 237

CIA influence in, 147–48, 149, 152, 155, 221–25, 245, 250, 253–54, 267, 280–81, 288–89, 290, 367

civil war of, 33, 285

Bill Clinton's visit to (2000), 49–50

constitution of (1973), 36, 37, 43, 46, 150, 156, 157

corruption in, 38, 39–40, 51–52, 155, 156, 319

creation of, 33–35, 36, 44, 110–11, 266, 267

democracy in, 36, 39–40, 47, 49–50, 52, 58, 86, 145–46, 149–51, 156–60, 219, 220, 233, 235, 238, 266, 277

disappeared prisoners in, 380

drug trafficking in, 38, 39, 319–20, 323–24, 332

earthquake in (2005), 291–92

East, 33, 35, 36, 37, 111

economy of, 30, 31, 37, 41, 47, 49, 145, 146, 148–49, 156, 193, 233, 235, 238, 249, 272–73, 283, 284, 291

education in, 35, 46, 156, 157, 234–36, 272–73

elections in, 36, 37, 39–40, 124, 149–51, 156–60, 220, 283–84, 290–91

foreign debt of, 31, 49, 89, 146, 148, 233, 238, 280

foreign policy of, 13–14, 25, 28–30, 32, 40–41, 267–68

government of, 24, 36, 38, 39–40, 43, 44, 46–47, 51–52, 99, 150, 155, 156, 238–39, 272–74, 283–86, 290–92, 309–10, 316, 319

gross domestic product (GDP) of, 233, 234

history of, 33–43, 44, 110–11, 234–35, 266, 267

human rights record of, 38, 51, 118, 151–54, 266, 298, 305, 306, 307–10

India's relations with, xxxviii, xliii, xliv, xlv, 3, 15, 25, 29–30, 33, 37, 38, 40–43, 45, 46, 47, 48, 49, 50, 54, 73, 78, 87, 89, 109–24, 145, 147, 148, 149, 152, 219, 220, 228, 229, 232, 234, 235, 244, 248–49, 267, 268, 274, 283, 286, 291, 369, 402

international relations of, 25, 26, 31, 42, 44, 47, 53–54, 115, 123–24, 146, 149–51, 155–56, 220, 235–36, 266–67, 268, 269, 288, 289–92, 369, 370

Islamic fundamentalism in, xxxix, xliii, 13, 24, 25, 29–40, 44, 46, 51, 53, 79, 140, 145–60, 161, 219–39, 270, 291–92, 307, 376, 381–83

jihadism in, 145–46, 151–54, 219–39

Karzai's policy on, 5–6, 13–14, 22–23, 106, 110, 124, 221, 229, 241, 246, 248–49, 253, 259, 267, 277–78, 283, 286, 365, 369

in Kashmir conflict, *see* Kashmir

lawyer's demonstrations in, 381

legal system of, 38, 266–67, 293, 309–10

literacy rate in, 156, 234, 272

Loya Jirgas held in, 266, 267, 286

mass media in, 38, 44, 45–46, 47, 51, 52, 54, 87, 146–47, 150, 151–54, 161, 249, 250, 266, 270, 271, 286, 287, 289, 369

military coup in (1977), 37–38

military coup in (1999), lii, 24, 26, 28, 43, 44, 45, 79, 112, 156, 238

military rule of, xxxviii–xxxix, xl, xliii, lii, 3, 10, 21, 23, 24–33, 36–43, 44, 45–53, 79, 86, 112, 118, 123, 145–61, 219–39, 289–92, 293, 307–10

National Assembly of, 156–60, 161, 239

national identity of, lii–liii, 33–35, 36, 37–38, 146, 276

natural resources of, 188–89, 233, 284–85 (gas)

nuclear weapons of, xxxix, xl, lvii, 29, 32, 37, 38, 39, 40, 41–42, 43, 44, 56, 58, 116, 120–23, 124, 219, 236, 253, 287–90, 291, 295

Pashtun tribes of, 8, 9, 25, 36, 193, 235, 242, 250, 251, 265–67, 271, 277, 283, 379

police of, 4, 152, 154, 155, 228, 249, 280, 309

political parties in, 37, 39–40, 51–52, 156–60, 238, 239, 266

Sharia (Islamic law) in, 38, 160

state of emergency declared in, 387–89

suicide bombings in, xxxix, 145, 154, 159, 379, 383

Supreme Court of, 46, 309–10, 380–81, 387

Taliban in, 376, 379, 383, 389, 400–401

Taliban supported by, xli, lii, lvii, 13–14, 15, 16, 22, 24–33, 41, 43, 46, 49–54, 57, 58–60, 77–79, 91, 92, 147–49, 206, 219–61, 259, 265–87, 289–90, 291, 307–10, 332, 347, 356, 357, 358–71, 376

taxation in, 52, 156, 235

terrorism sponsored by, 27–33, 41, 47, 48–51, 53, 60, 145, 150–54, 265–87

tribes of, xl, 3, 36, 80, 98–100, 146, 265–87, 347; *see also specific tribes*

as UN member, liii, 267, 292

U.S. embassy in, 230, 243, 246

U.S. foreign aid to, xl, xliv, 10, 31, 33, 38–39, 49, 86, 148–49, 157, 160–61, 234, 273–74, 280, 289, 292, 370–71

U.S. military forces in, li, 36–37, 147, 292

U.S. relations with, xxxix–xl, xl, xliv, xlv, li, lii, lviii, 10, 24–33, 36–39, 41–43, 48–51, 56–60, 61, 86, 89–90, 109, 115–22, 124, 145–49, 157, 160–61, 219–39, 240, 243, 246, 259, 273–74, 280, 287, 289, 292, 356, 366–71

U.S. sanctions against, 26, 30, 31, 39, 48–49, 89, 287

West, 35

women in, 38, 51, 157, 160, 234, 272, 309

see also specific provinces and towns

Pakistan Muslim League–Q (Quaid-e-Azam) (PML-Q), 238–39, 286, 290–91, 378, 390

Pakistan People's Party (PPP), 37, 39–40, 150, 158, 239, 375–76, 379, 387, 390

Pakistan Resolution (1940), 34–35

Panjsher Valley, 14, 22, 62, 63, 64, 73–74, 81, 101, 129, 139–40, 142, 206, 207, 208, 209, 215–16, 261, 306, 334, 363–64

Partnership for Peace, 67, 166, 339

Pashtun, Yousuf, 251, 323

Pashtun tribes, 4–6, 7, 8, 9, 11, 12, 14, 16–17, 20, 21, 25, 34, 36, 50, 55, 62–63, 71–72, 79, 81, 83, 84–86, 89, 90, 94–95, 97, 98, 105, 128, 131, 139–40, 142, 146, 171, 183, 193, 199–200, 202, 205, 214, 215–16, 221, 235, 242, 250, 251, 256, 257, 258–59, 260, 261, 265–67, 271, 277, 283, 322, 326, 334, 362–63, 365, 379

Passaro, David, 304

Patten, Chris, 356

Pearl, Daniel, 113, 151–54, 308

Pearl, Mariane, 151, 152

Pelosi, Nancy, 370

People's Movement, 339–40

Perle, Richard, li

peroneal strikes, 302

Persons Under Control (PUC), 305

Peshawar, 10, 37, 48, 52, 72, 87–88, 242, 244, 267, 276–77, 282, 389

Peshawar Group, 72, 102, 103, 105

Piracha, Javed Ibrahim, 249

"platoon houses," 360

Poland, 226, 305, 315, 371, 397

Polk, George, 46

Popalzai tribe, 3–4, 12, 16–17, 129, 327

poppy cultivation, xxxviii, xlii, liv, 19, 20, 64, 127, 129, 131, 167, 175, 179, 184, 193–94, 197, 200, 204, 205, 209, 218, 282, 317–32, 333, 334, 335, 354, 355, 356, 357, 365, 372

poverty, 129–30, 191–92, 195, 272–73, 283, 330

Powell, Colin, l, 28, 30, 56, 57, 59–60, 66, 73, 74, 75, 76, 82, 88, 90–91, 92, 97, 116, 118, 119–20, 137, 146, 152, 163, 165, 270, 288, 314, 324–25, 344, 356

Powell, Nancy, 160, 230

Predator drone, 59, 60, 88, 97, 134, 223, 272, 370

"preemption" policy, lv, 116, 188

Pressler Amendment, 39

Priest, Dana, l

prison ships, 297

private contractors, 175–76, 177, 180–81, 184–86, 190–91, 248, 304

Prodi, Romano, 372, 394

Provincial Reconstruction Teams (PRTs), 198–201, 325, 350–51, 352, 357, 358, 366, 372

Punjab, 34, 35, 36, 90, 117, 159, 224, 385
Putin, Vladimir, 66, 67, 70, 81, 83, 162, 166, 343

Qadir, Haji Abdul, 98, 128, 207
Qadir, Maulana Abdul, 243
Qadoos, Ahmed Abdul, 226
Qala Jangi (Fort of War), 93–94
Qanuni, Younus, 101, 103, 140, 258, 261, 334, 335
Qasimyar, Ismael, 138
Quetta, 3, 10, 16–17, 22–23, 76, 85, 95, 187, 222, 223, 227–28, 229, 242, 246–47, 249–50, 259, 265, 267, 284, 285, 300, 355, 359, 364, 366, 368, 369, 370
Qureshi, Rashid, 91

Rabbani, Burhanuddin, 9, 11, 12, 53, 73–74, 83, 101, 102, 103, 104, 208, 214, 255, 257
Rakhmonov, Emomali, 70, 83, 166–67
Ramadan, 98, 102, 310
RAND Corp., 182, 188
Rashid, Abdul, 317
Rasul, Zalmay, 142, 159
Rawalpindi, 226, 230
Razzaq, Abdul, 312
Razzaq, Mullah Abdul, 242
Reagan, Ronald, 9, 38–39, 287, 289
"reconstruction opportunity zone," 273–74
Red Horse squadrons, 89
Red Mosque, 381–83, 384, 389
refugees, 5, 6, 10, 11, 12–15, 19–20, 71–72, 76, 80, 125, 129, 130, 146, 172, 175, 176, 178, 183–84, 191, 193, 215, 221–22, 242, 243, 283, 361, 366, 367
Rehman, Abdur, 131–32
Rehman, Attaur, 237
Rehman, Matiur, 231–32
Rehman, Maulana Fazlur, 46, 53, 276
Rehman, Maulvi Jamil-ur, 366
Rehman, Sherry, 239
Reid, Richard, 151, 357–58
"rendered prisoners," 298–300, 315, 342, 347–48
Republican Party, xliv, 114–15, 176, 188, 313, 314–15
Reza, Iqbal, 75
Riasat Amniat-e-Meli (National

Directorate of Security) (NDS), 306–7
Rice, Condoleezza, xliv, lvi, 56, 57, 58, 59–60, 90–91, 137, 187, 189, 194–95, 238, 326, 345, 368, 369
Richards, David, 360, 364, 365, 372
Riedel, Bruce, 42
Ritchie, James, 88
Ritchie, Joseph J., 88
Robertson, George, 65, 350, 351
Rocca, Christina, 56–57, 154, 156–57
Roed-Larsen, Terje, 54
Rome group, 55, 71–72, 75, 81, 102, 103, 105, 139
Rona, Gabor, 294
Rove, Karl, 187–88, 236
Roy, Oliver, 54
Rubin, Barnett, 54, 55, 75, 76, 103, 176, 179, 212, 217, 330
Rubin, Elizabeth, 244
Ruhani, Ghulam, 315
Rumsfeld, Donald, xi, xlvi, l–lii, 62, 64–65, 71, 74, 83, 89, 92, 97, 118, 126, 132–37, 143, 166, 173, 175, 197, 200, 201, 210, 241, 246, 252, 274, 296–97, 324, 325, 328–29, 334–35, 340, 342–43, 344, 345, 350, 353, 368, 370
Russia, 34
  Afghan relations with, 8, 20, 25, 53–54, 128, 206–7, 208, 331
  in Afghan war, 61, 62, 65, 66–70, 71, 73, 81, 82, 83, 103, 110
  Central Asian influence of, 161, 162, 163, 166, 287, 339, 340–41, 343, 345, 346, 348
  oil industry of, 343, 348
  see also Soviet Union
Ruzicka, Marla, 142

Saeed, Hafiz, 228
Saleem, Sheikh Ahmed, 223–24
Saleh, Amrullah, 306–7, 367
Salt Pit, 301, 303–4
Samar, Simar, 141
Saqlain, Raja, 226
Sassi, Nizar, 312
satellite surveillance, lvii, 134, 223, 324, 357, 359
Sattar, Abdul, 28, 57, 116
Saudi Arabia, 11, 14, 15, 16, 38, 47, 68, 78, 79, 111, 161, 186, 233, 305, 306, 316
Sayari, Mohammed, 301

Sayyaf, Abdul Rasul, 63, 214–15, 216, 226, 255, 307
Scheffer, Jaap de Hoop, 352, 373
Scheuer, Michael, 254
Schifferdecker, Arnold, 74
Schröder, Gerhard, 104, 349
Schroen, Gary, 63, 215
Scotland Yard, 378, 379
Secret Service, U.S., 49, 154
Senate Foreign Relations Committee, U.S., 370
September 11 attacks (2001), xi, xxxvii–xxxviii, xl, xli, xlii, xlv, xlvi, xlvii, xlviii, liv, lvi, 16, 22–23, 26, 27, 30–31, 32, 33, 60, 61–62, 64, 78, 109, 110, 115, 145, 147, 149, 153, 196, 224, 225, 226, 270, 295, 300, 305–6
Sethi, Najam, 151
Shah, Aitezaz, 379
Shah, Ejaz, 152
Shaheen, Imtiaz, 52
Shahir, Mohammed Rafiq, 127, 307
Shahrani, Nematullah, 211–12
Shamshatoo Camp, 221, 244
Shamzai, Maulana Nizamuddin, 77, 228
Shanghai Cooperation Organization, 67, 167, 340–41
Sharia (Islamic law), 13, 14, 38, 160, 212–13, 214, 216, 217, 362–63
Sharif, Nawaz, 24, 40, 41, 42–43, 45, 47, 52, 112, 156, 238, 376 77, 390
Sharodi, Hafiz Hussain, 243
Shaulis, Steve, 323
Sheehan, Michael, 48–49
Sheikh, Ahmed Omar, 112, 113, 151, 152, 153–54, 308
Sherzai, Gul Agha, 95, 96, 128–29, 136, 142, 167, 187, 241
Shia Muslims, 18, 31, 103, 133, 145, 154–55, 214, 216, 217, 224, 227–28, 235, 242, 257–58, 300
Shibh, Ramzi bin al-, 149, 225
Shinwari, Fazl Hadi, 216
Siddiqa, Ayesha, 391
Siddiqi, Syed Nabi, 303
Siddique, Abu Bakr, 272
"Silk Road Strategy," 67
Sindh, xl, 34, 35, 36, 45, 110, 283, 286
Singh, Jaswant, 113
Singh, Maharaja Hari, 110–11
Singh, Manmohan, 123, 290
"six-plus-two" group, 53–54
Smeal, Eleanor, 135

Smith, Clive Stafford, 313
Soere, Jonas Garh, 398
Somalia, liii, 113, 172, 197, 254
Soros, George, 343
Soviet Union:
    Afghan invasion of, 5, 6, 8–11, 12, 13, 15, 25, 33, 38–39, 53, 61, 69, 71, 72, 78, 87, 95, 98, 126, 146–47, 162, 171, 179, 196, 207, 214, 226, 267, 319, 366
    collapse of, xliii, xlix–l, 11, 161, 207
    U.S. relations with, liii, 8, 11, 33, 36–37, 109–10, 167, 172–73, 174, 204, 351
    see also Russia
Spain, xxxvii, lvi, 143, 252, 265, 297, 371
Spann, Johnny "Mike," 93
Special Investigation Group, 232–33
Special Operations Forces (SOF), li, lvii, 45, 56, 62–63, 69, 74, 85–86, 89, 92–98, 125, 131, 133–34, 136, 137, 162, 176, 189, 207, 243–44, 253, 297, 298, 300, 301–3, 307, 322, 324, 325, 328, 366
Specter, Arlen, 378
State Department, U.S., xlii, xlv, xlix–l, lii, 15, 20, 24, 26, 43, 48 49, 56–60, 64, 72, 74, 92, 116, 118, 134, 136, 137, 146, 149, 154, 162, 173, 176, 185, 186, 188, 189, 190, 194, 195, 198, 204–6, 207, 233, 236, 273–74, 278, 296, 304, 305–6, 330, 332, 342, 343–44, 356, 368, 370, 376
Straw, Jack, 66, 76, 356
Sufism, 10, 72
Suhail, Asim, 21
suicide bombings, xxxvii, xxxix, xlv, xlvii–xlviii, xlix, lvi, 16, 17–18, 21–22, 61–62, 66, 113, 114, 116, 144, 145, 154, 159, 224, 225, 226, 227, 228, 230–33, 237, 238, 245, 251, 252, 265, 270, 278–79, 281, 282, 295, 297, 300, 307, 336, 343, 344, 358, 359, 363, 364, 366, 367, 379, 383, 384–86
Sui gas fields, 284–85
Sultan, Hazir, 231
Sunni Muslims, 31, 53, 111, 154–55, 216, 217, 227, 228, 300
Supreme Court, U.S., 313, 314
Suskind, Ron, xlviii, 121
Swat Valley, 383, 385, 388, 389
Sweden, 138, 315

Tahir-Kheli, Shirin, 109, 124
Taj, Nadeem, 231

Tajikistan, xxxix, 20, 66–68, 70–71, 83, 164,
   165, 166–67, 193, 331
Tajiks, 6, 8, 11, 12, 14, 16, 68, 73, 81, 83, 90,
   94, 101, 103, 129, 132, 201–2, 206,
   207, 208, 209, 214, 215–16, 258, 334
Talbott, Strobe, 42, 49, 67
Taliban, 13–23, 240–61, 349–73, 393
   Afghan elections opposed by (2004),
      253–61
   al Qaeda's alliance with, xliii, xlv, 4, 5,
      14, 15, 20, 41, 56, 155, 224–25, 244,
      278–79, 282, 308, 336–37
   amnesty proposed for, 247, 272, 335
   defeat of, 64, 66, 68, 71, 74–77, 78, 79–
      101, 102, 104, 106, 110, 126, 146–47,
      240–43
   drug trafficking by, 317–21, 322, 325–29,
      330, 331, 332, 355
   escape of, 90–93, 98–100, 106, 128, 146–
      48, 241, 268, 271
   foreign fighters in, 17, 25, 77, 80–81, 148,
      155, 221–28, 240–44, 249, 265, 267,
      268–69, 336, 347
   government of, xxxviii, xl, xli, xliii, xlv,
      liii–liv, lvii, 3–5, 8, 13–23, 59–63,
      71–72, 100–101, 133, 160, 171–72,
      183, 249, 274, 275, 296, 362–63
   intelligence information on, 32–33, 271,
      357, 366–71
   international relations of, 13–14, 53–56,
      102, 104, 171–72
   Islamic fundamentalism of, 100–101,
      160, 183, 249, 275, 362–63
   Karzai opposed by, 84–85, 88, 229–30,
      243, 246, 247, 269–70, 286, 335, 357,
      366–71
   leadership of, 13–14, 17, 90–92, 128,
      146–48, 227–31, 240–43, 246, 247,
      249, 253, 259, 268, 269, 286, 301,
      358–61, 367, 370, *see also specific
      leaders*
   "moderates" in, 72–73, 76–77, 81, 87–88,
      89, 221, 243
   Musharraf's policies on, 27–30, 43, 46,
      49–53, 57, 60, 77–79, 91, 92, 240,
      246, 268, 269, 271, 277–80, 289–90,
      291, 307, 357, 364
   NATO operations against, 349–73
   overthrow of, 59–60, 133
   in Pakistan, 376, 379, 383, 389
   Pakistan's support for, xli, lii, lvii, 13–14,
      15, 16, 22, 24–33, 41, 43, 46, 49–54,
      57, 58–60, 77–79, 91, 92, 147–49,
      206, 219–61, 259, 265–87, 289–90,
   291, 307–10, 332, 347, 356, 357, 358–
      71, 376
   political influence of, 13–14, 102, 104,
      138, 253–61, 328, 333, 334, 335
   popular opposition to, 14–23, 59–63, 71–
      72, 133, 274, 275
   prisoners from, 293–316, 365
   propaganda of, 398
   recruitment by, xlv, 16, 18, 41, 56, 110,
      111, 113, 221–25, 249–50, 298–99,
      364, 366–71
   resurgence of, 95, 106, 125–29, 135, 142,
      143–44, 148, 186, 193, 194, 195, 196,
      199, 200, 203, 205, 211, 213, 221–23,
      239, 240–61, 317, 323, 325–27, 329,
      332, 333–34, 335–37, 345, 347, 349–
      73, 397–98
   training camps of, xlv, 16, 18, 25, 41, 56,
      110, 111, 113, 221–25, 228–29, 244,
      251, 259, 267, 269, 270, 271–72, 278–
      79, 282, 308, 317, 364, 365–71
   UN sanctions against, 25, 53, 54, 56, 60
   U.S. operations against, 24–26, 49–51,
      54–60, 125–29, 142, 253–54, 259,
      276
   weapons of, 131, 222–23, 244, 271–72,
      330, 359, 361, 363–64, 367
Taliban (Rashid), xliii, liv, 4, 65, 100, 126
Taraki, Nur Mohammed, 9, 10
tariffs, 127, 131, 186–87, 193, 210
Tarin Kot, 84–85, 95–96
Tariq, Maulana Azam, 227, 228
Tashkent, 54, 63, 68, 70, 82, 163, 164, 310,
   341, 342–43, 344, 345
Taylor, John, 143
Taylor, William, 185
Tenet, George, 24, 30, 56, 61–62, 79, 86,
   121–22, 175, 221
Termez air base, 70, 82, 346
terrorism, xxxviii, xli, xlii, xlvii–xlviii, xlix,
   li, liii, lv–lvi, lvii, 27–33, 78, 93, 96,
   109, 125–26, 156, 225, 226, 236–37,
   244, 248, 293–316, 324, 335, 383
Thailand, 224, 305, 319
Thomas, Harry, 58
Tomsen, Peter, 185
Tora Bora, 91, 93, 98–100, 106, 128, 241,
   268, 271
torture, xli–xlii, 38, 51, 69, 71, 88, 126, 127,
   153, 165, 225, 293–316, 336, 342, 343,
   348
Townsend, Frances Fragos, 384
Toynbee, Arnold, 321
Tulip Revolution, 339–40

Turkey, 15, 44, 46, 62, 66, 75, 128, 332, 350, 367
Turkmenistan, xxxix, 15, 66–68, 71, 127, 187, 188–89, 282, 331, 341, 347
"two-nation theory," 34

Uighur Muslims, 17, 67, 167, 300, 311–12
Ukraine, 339, 340
ummah, 34, 228
UN Assistance Mission in Afghanistan (UNAMA), 181 82, 202, 205, 247–48, 253, 255, 256, 259, 364, 368
UN Convention against Torture (1951), 294
UN High Commissioner for Refugees (UNHCR), 345–46
UN Human Development Commission, 129–30, 178, 210
UNICEF, 182–83
United Nations (UN), xxxviii, xxxix, xliii, liii–liv, 11, 13, 18, 21, 25, 26, 44, 48, 53–56, 60, 66, 75–82, 83, 86, 90–95, 102, 103, 104, 127, 128–32, 136–42, 167, 171–72, 176–83, 194, 196, 200–210, 213, 229, 247–48, 253, 255, 256, 259, 260, 261, 267, 292, 294, 303, 313, 324–33, 345–46, 350, 354, 355, 364–65, 368, 402
United States, 402
    Afghan relations with, xliv, liv–lv, 4 5, 8–10, 11, 15, 16, 17, 20, 21, 24–31, 33, 53–54, 55, 56–60, 125–44, 171–218, 219, 277–78, 322 26, 334–35, 336, 356, 361–62, 365, 366–72
    elections in, xliv–xlv, lviii, 99, 114–15, 187–88, 189, 193, 194, 236–37, 252, 254, 261, 314, 370
    foreign policy of, xl, xli–lviii, 56–60, 62, 66–67, 109–10, 119, 173, 195, 351
    human rights record of, 293–316
    Pakistan's relations with, xxxix–xl, xl, xliv, xlv, li, lii, lviii, 10, 24–33, 36–39, 41–43, 48–51, 56–60, 61, 86, 89–90, 109, 115–22, 124, 145–49, 157, 160–61, 219–39, 240, 243, 246, 259, 273–74, 280, 287, 289, 292, 356, 366–71
    Soviet relations with, liii, 8, 11, 33, 36–37, 109–10, 167, 172–73, 174, 204, 351
Unocal, 15, 188–89
UN Office on Drugs and Crime, 325, 328, 329, 330–31
UN Security Council Resolution 1267, 18

UN Security Council Resolution 1333, 18
UN Security Council Resolution 1363, 18
UN Security Council Resolution 1373, 66
UN Security Council Resolution 1378, 83
UN Strategy Group for Afghanistan, 75–76
UN World Food Programme, 76, 174
Uruzghan, 84–85, 142, 223, 245, 260, 323, 336, 353–54, 356, 357, 358
U.S. Agency for International Development (USAID), liv, 64, 136, 174–76, 181, 182–83, 185, 186, 190, 191, 195, 204, 236, 304, 321, 323, 330, 372–73
Usmani, Mullah Akhtar Mohammed, 77, 242, 246, 259, 370, 398
Usmani, Muzaffar, 29, 79
Uzbekistan, 338–48, 404
    Afghan relations with, 193, 206
    in Afghan war, 62, 66–70, 71, 81, 82, 91, 161–62, 163, 164
    al Qaeda presence in, xliii–xliv, lvii, 56, 345, 347
    authoritarian regime of, lii, 161–65, 310–11, 341–48
    as Central Asian state, xxxix, 187, 331, 338–39, 347–48
    human rights record of, 305, 306, 310–11, 342–48
    Islamic fundamentalism in, xliii–xliv, 17, 68–69, 71, 80–81, 82, 92, 164, 166, 167, 221, 269, 270–71, 339, 342, 343, 344, 345, 347
    oil industry of, 343, 348
    U.S. relations with, xlv, lii, 161–65, 310–11, 341–48
Uzbeks, 6, 8, 12, 14, 16, 21, 68, 81–82, 83, 90, 93, 94, 103, 105, 164, 202, 214, 216, 338, 347

Vajpayee, Atal Bihari, 114, 115, 118, 122–23, 232
Vendrell, Francesc, 55, 75, 102
Vietnam War, xxxvii, 171, 174, 258, 402
Vines, John, 200
Voice of America, 205, 346, 358

Wahhabism, 111, 154–55, 164–65, 214, 226, 235
Wali, Abdul, 72, 301–2, 304
Wall Street Journal, 151–54

Wardak, Rahim, 20, 261, 364
Wardak, Taj Mohammed, 142
Waziristan, North and South, 93, 99, 147–
    48, 164, 221, 223, 229, 231, 237, 243,
    265, 268–78, 282, 308–9, 347, 369, 389
wheat, 174, 319
Wilder, Andrew, 329
Williams, Robin, 198
Wolesi Jirga (House of People), 212, 327,
    333
Wolfensohn, James, 163
Wolfowitz, Paul, xlvi, xlviii, li, 64, 65, 89,
    97, 133, 136, 137, 188, 210, 233, 253,
    254, 289–90, 352
Wood, Carolyn, 302
Woodward, Bob, 62–63, 295
World Bank, xlii, 31, 160, 163, 177, 178,
    179, 180, 181, 184, 186, 193, 237, 324,
    355, 399
World War II, 137, 172, 252

Xinjiang Province, China, 17, 67, 167, 311–
    12, 331

Yakub, Daud, 75
Yemen, 254, 316

Yugoslavia, xlv, liii, 75, 98, 172, 173, 175,
    194, 350, 351, 360
Yuldashev, Akram, 344
Yuldashev, Tahir, 68, 164, 270, 272, 347

Zabul, 245, 247, 253, 334, 336
Zahir, Haji, 98
Zahir Shah, king of Afghanistan, 4, 5,
    6, 8, 20, 21, 50, 55, 71–72, 74, 75,
    76–77, 81, 83, 87–88, 104,
    126, 139–41, 142, 212,
    213
Zakheim, Dov, 137–38, 143
Zaman, Haji, 98
Zamir, Ihtesham, 156
Zardari, Asif Ali, 40, 376, 390
Zarqawi, Abu Musab al-, 281–82
Zawahiri, Ayman al-, 120–21, 230, 270,
    271, 276, 278
Zia, Fatemeh, 75–76, 103, 104
Zia, Nasir, 139
Zia, Sohail, 387–88
Ziauddin, Mohammed, 43
Zia ul-Haq, Muhammed, *see* Haq,
    Muhammed Zia ul-
Zinni, Anthony, lii
Zubaydah, Abu, 48, 149, 224–25